AIA GUIDE TO CHICAGO

SECOND EDITION

AMERICAN INSTITUTE OF ARCHITECTS
CHICAGO

CHICAGO ARCHITECTURE FOUNDATION

LANDMARKS PRESERVATION COUNCIL
OF ILLINOIS

with special assistance from the
COMMISSION ON
CHICAGO LANDMARKS

INTRODUCTION BY
PERRY R. DUIS

PREFACE BY
JOHN F. HARTRAY, JR., FAIA

ALICE SINKEVITCH, EDITOR

LAURIE McGOVERN PETERSEN,
ASSOCIATE EDITOR

A HARVEST ORIGINAL
HARCOURT, INC.
ORLANDO | AUSTIN
NEW YORK | SAN DIEGO
TORONTO | LONDON

ISBN 0-15-602908-1

The Library of Congress Catalog has
cataloged the paperback edition as follows:
Card Number: 93-078330
ISBN 0-15-222900-0 (Harvest:pbk)

Text set in Ocean Sans Book
Designed by Kaelin Chappell

Printed in the United States of America
Second edition
K J I H G F E D C B A

CONTENTS

GUIDE TO THE GUIDE

The *AIA Guide to Chicago* is the largest portable source of information on the city's built environment. The book will serve as both an introduction to Chicago's architecture for neophytes and as a sourcebook for those seeking to expand their knowledge beyond the well-documented buildings. The city's "greatest hits" are included and many are discussed in essay form; numerous neighborhood buildings are documented in print for the first time. Much information available in other books—biographical, theoretical, statistical, and critical—is deliberately minimized, while details concerning functional requirements, client tastes, and materials are often included. The purpose of the *Guide* is to encourage the reader to discover, look at, and appreciate man-made Chicago.

Genesis of the book: The *Guide* was originally created for, and is intended as, a legacy of the 1993 American Institute of Architects/International Union of Architects World Congress, the first national convention of the AIA held in Chicago since 1969. The three sponsoring organizations—the AIA Chicago, the Chicago Architecture Foundation, and the Landmarks Preservation Council of Illinois—provided the core of the Editorial Committee, which was expanded to include experts from the Chicago Park District, the Commission on Chicago Landmarks, and other groups. The Editorial Committee chose the featured tour areas and selected the bylined essayists. Each tour area had a "chapter captain" in charge of research and recommending entries. One important source of new information was the citywide Historic Resources Survey of pre-1940 buildings, conducted from 1984 to 1992 by the Commission on Chicago Landmarks. Many other new facts were uncovered by the authors and by the dedicated group of volunteer researchers.

Many photographs came from architectural firms and their clients, libraries, and other archives. Others were taken by architectural photographers, who, working as volunteers, traveled throughout the city to document neighborhood buildings.

Criteria for inclusion: Even at its present length, the *Guide* is illustrative rather than encyclopedic, presenting a representative selection of buildings in addition to the essential landmarks. The neighborhoods chosen display a range of types, styles, and eras.

The criteria for selecting buildings, landscape and park features, bridges, public art, and cemetery monuments included not only the quality of their design but also the degree to which they either exemplified a style, trend, or functional type or stood out as unusual. Other important factors included visibility, historical significance, and the "what the heck is that" curiosity factor. Practical considerations included the geographical "fit" with the tour itineraries, which were laid out to connect major points of interest. Good examples of common types—the CTA station, the modernized storefront, the public school—on a route connecting featured structures were chosen over those in remote locations.

The availability of information also played a part. If dedicated research failed to produce specific data for a post-1870s building, it was likely to be omitted in favor of another, better-documented example.

Building types were weighted, with criteria varying from one area to another. Houses get more attention than churches in Oak Park, for example, because of the important evolution of residential styles to be seen there.

The authors' likes and dislikes were significant factors, and no pretense is made of objectivity. Due to limited space, many of the city's prominent but dull buildings are omitted or only briefly noted in order to include a greater range and number of structures. Few buildings of historic rather than architectural interest are included.

Organization: The *Guide* is organized by neighborhood chapters, beginning with the central city and radiating outward. Each chapter has its own map that displays wherever possible each building's name next to its entry number. A small inset map locates the area within Chicago. All maps have north at the top.

Because of the large areas covered in each chapter, all but the Loop have their entries ordered to facilitate driving tours. Quirks in the numerical ordering are usually the result of accommodating one-way and dead-end streets, railway embankments, and other automotive impediments. Separate maps are provided for groups of entries, such as campuses and cemeteries, that lack street addresses.

Chapter introductions outline each area's historical development and describe its neighborhoods and prominent demarcations. All neighborhoods are within the city of Chicago except for suburban Oak Park, whose concentration of Frank Lloyd Wright designs compelled its inclusion.

Information on the entries: The heading for each nonresidential entry begins with the building's current name or address, followed by a parenthetical listing of the original name and, occasionally, well-known subsequent appellations. The use of current rather than historical names is intended to make it easier to locate buildings. In the case of a house, the name of the original owner is used.

Dashes between house numbers indicate a row of contiguous structures (such as row houses); an ampersand or the word "through" is used for a group of freestanding buildings unless they are commonly known as something else—as, for example, 860–880 N. Lake Shore Dr. Dates generally indicate the year of completion (except for prolonged construction) and are followed by the contemporaneous name of the responsible architecture firm. An ampersand joins the names of a single firm; "and" links the names of two or more separate firms.

The design architect's firm is listed first, except in the case of buildings commissioned by the City of Chicago. Subsequent work that is visually apparent is included with its year of completion and architect. Most major buildings more than ten years old have had many alterations; only major renovations and additions are cited. "Restoration" means the building was returned to its original appearance, but "renovation" or "adaptive reuse" entries may look substantially different as a result of the work.

Interiors are generally described only if they are open to the public or are especially noteworthy. Churches are usually open only during services and welcome visitors at those times.

A final word: The opinions expressed in the *Guide* are those of its many authors and in no way represent views or opinions of any sponsoring organization. Information is current as of May 2003; in a city as dynamic as Chicago many changes will already have occurred before publication. Most buildings are privately owned and not open to the public;

investigation of anything not visible from the street or from a public space constitutes trespassing. Neighborhoods that are off the usual traveler's itinerary do not always treat every tourist well. Italicized commentary flags a few—but by no means all—of these areas. Readers are urged to travel by car and in groups when exploring unfamiliar territory; visitors are encouraged to consult with a Chicago resident before planning a tour.

Ideally, this book will serve as a net in which much new information will be captured. Become a contributor to the next edition of the *AIA Guide to Chicago* by submitting corrections, additions, or information on alterations and demolitions to AIA Chicago, 222 Merchandise Mart Plaza, Suite 1049, Chicago, Illinois 60654.

—ALICE SINKEVITCH AND LAURIE McGOVERN PETERSEN

ACKNOWLEDGMENTS

The cover of this book isn't big enough to acknowledge all of the people who contributed to it, so we will do it here. First of all, we must thank the architects, contractors, craftspeople, tradespeople, and clients who created these structures. If they had been ordinary, this would be a very small book.

The contributors to the first edition must again be acknowledged.

Donors for the First Edition

The commitment of Chicago's business community, grants from many foundations, and the generosity of individuals passionately committed to the built environment made this book possible.

BENEFACTORS

The Chicago Community Trust; Graham Foundation for Advanced Studies in the Fine Arts; National Endowment for the Arts; AIA Chicago; John D. and Catherine T. MacArthur Foundation

PATRONS

American Architectural Foundation; Chicago Architecture Foundation; The Joyce Foundation; Landmarks Preservation Council of Illinois

SPONSORS

William B. Hinchliff; John A. Holabird, Jr., FAIA; Illinois Arts Council; Henry H. Kuehn; Lohan Associates; Petersen Aluminum Corporation

CONTRIBUTORS

Baird Foundation; Chicago Dock & Canal Trust; D & K Foundation; Ernst & Young; Greater North Michigan Avenue Association; Holabird & Root; Richard J. Hoskins; Knight Architects Planners, Inc.; Lucia Woods Lindley; Pamela Lohan; McClier, Inc.; Hope McCormick; Murphy/Jahn; O'Donnell Wicklund Pigozzi & Peterson Architects; The Pepper Companies; Perkins & Will; Seymour H. Persky; Schal Associates, Inc.; The Law Firm of Schiff Hardin & Waite; John I. Schlossman, FAIA; Jacqueline & Gene Summers, FAIA; U.S. Equities Realty, Inc.; Harry Weese Associates; Weese Langley Weese Architects; Doreen & Steven Weiss, FAIA

FRIENDS

Anonymous; Susan M. Baldwin; Beer Gorski & Graff, Ltd.; Anthony Belluschi, FAIA; The John Buck Company; Chicago Architecture Foundation Docents; Continental Bank Foundation; Employees of Loebl, Schlossman & Hackl; John Engman; Gerhardt Meyne Company; Gilbane Building Company; Ernest A. Grunsfeld III, FAIA; John F. Hartray, Jr., FAIA; Hinshaw & Culbertson; Edward C. Hirschland; Harold S. Jensen; Joseph D. La Rue; The Linpro Company; Jane Lucas; Robert G. Lyon Associates, Inc.; Lynn & Eva Maddox, Assoc. AIA; Matthei & Colin; Mekus Johnson Inc.; The Monadnock Building; Power Contracting & Engineering; Linda Searl, FAIA; Sears Tower; Bruce A. Simons; Stein & Company; Stein, Ray & Conway; Michael Tobin; Turner Construction Company; Carol Wyant

Volunteers

MANAGEMENT COMMITTEE

Steven F. Weiss, FAIA, Chair; Susan Baldwin; John Engman; Richard Hoskins; Henry H. Kuehn; Jane Lucas; Thomas R. Samuels, FAIA; Linda Searl, FAIA; Emese Wood; Carol Wyant

EDITORIAL COMMITTEE

Wim de Wit; John F. Hartray, Jr., FAIA; Robert F. Irving; Joseph D. La Rue; Vincent Michael; Joan Pomaranc; Deborah Slaton; Julia Sniderman; Cynthia Weese, FAIA

FUND-RAISING COMMITTEE

Pamela Lohan, Chair; Susan Baldwin; Kathryn Godfrey Benish; Joan Goldstein; John A. Holabird, Jr., FAIA; Henry H. Kuehn; John I. Schlossman, FAIA; Steven F. Weiss, FAIA

PROJECT TEAM

Alice Sinkevitch, Editor; Laurie McGovern Petersen, Associate Editor; Joan Pomaranc, Assistant Editor; Mary Alice Molloy, Special Projects Editor; Emese Wood, Photo Coordinator; Dennis McClendon, Map Designer

This book benefited from the involvement of many people. The following individuals contributed to the effort: Rolf Achilles; Deborah Allen; Margaret Babcock; Marguerite Bailey; Margaret Balanoff; Susan Baldwin; Barry Bebart, AIA; Kathryn Godfrey Benish; Susan Benjamin; Ellen S. Berkelhamer; Alice Blum; Robert W. Blythe; Elizabeth Borden; Michael Bordenaro; Robert Bruegmann; Adam Burck; Joan Campbell; Cathy Capriglione; Constance K. Casey; Sally A. Kitt Chappell; Jane H. Clarke; Earl Clendenon; Patricia Lee Cody; Carole Cosimano; Kathleen Cummings; Barbara Cunningham; Eric Emmett Davis, AIA; Mary Dawson; Wim de Wit; Yvonne DeMuyt; Karen Dimond; Thomas Drebenstedt; David DuPre; Perry R. Duis; Joan Eggers; Janice M. Elliot; Roy Forrey; Ferne Winifred Gerulat; Ann Erickson Gifford; Blair Gifford; Paul Glassman; Patricia Goldfein; Norma Green; Mary Griffin; Florence Gurke; Louise B. Haack; T. Gunny Harboe, AIA; Elaine Harrington; Kevin Harrington; Neil Harris; John F. Hartray, Jr., FAIA; Frances B. Hedlund; John Hern; Mary Beth Herr; William B. Hinchliff; Mark Hinchman; Richard Hoskins; William Jerousek; Robert F. Irving; Leo Jung; Nancy Kayman; Donald G. Kalec; Blair Kamin; Paul Kendall; Donald Kepler; Paul Kruty; Henry H. Kuehn; Joseph D. La Rue; Heather M. Lange; Bill Latoza; Beth LeGros; Margaret Lehto; Aldarcy C. Lewis; Jane Lucas; William Q. Lucas; Patricia Marks Lurie; John M. MacDonald; Laurel McCain; Harriet McShane; Suzanne Carter Meldman; Thomas Michael II; Vincent Michael; Frank P. Michalski, AIA; Mary Alice Molloy; Aurelia Moody; Harold Moody; Charlotte Myhrum; Kathleen Nagle; Kathryn Neary; Anders Nereim; Pat O'Brien; Dan O'Dair; Penny Obenshain; Lawrence Okrent; Maria Olson; Mary Lou Oswalt; Laurie McGovern Petersen; Charles Pipal; Joan Pomaranc; Helen Poot; Stephen W. Radke; Michael Ramirez; Judith Randall; John Ravitch; Diane Richard; Katherine Ross; Anne Royston; Bart H. Ryckbosch; Pauline Saliga; Thomas R. Samuels, AIA; Timothy Samuelson; John I. Schlossman, FAIA; Franz Schulze; Linda Searl, FAIA; R. Stephen Sennott; Robert A. Sideman; Joseph Siry; Deborah Slaton; Alice Sinkevitch; Julia Sniderman; C. Richard Spurgin; Joan Stinton; Patricia Talbot; Terry Tatum; Meredith Taussig; Laurence Terp; William W. Tippens; John Tomassi, AIA; Theodore Turak; David Van Zanten; John Vinci, FAIA; Gloria Wallace; Dina Wayne; Ben Weese, FAIA; Catharine Weese; Cynthia Weese, FAIA; Michael Weiland; Lauren S. Weingarden; Timothy Wittman; Carol Wyant; Ethel Zitnik; and Atie Zuurdeeg.

The "chapter captains" who led the research teams for each chapter were Adam Burck (Beverly/Morgan Park); Wim de Wit and Robert F. Irving

(Lakeview/Uptown/Ravenswood); William B. Hinchliff (North Michigan Avenue/Streeterville and Edgewater/Rogers Park); Joseph D. La Rue (Near South Side and Oakland/Kenwood); Patricia Marks Lurie (Gold Coast/Old Town and Lincoln Park);Vincent Michael (Near West Side and Lower West Side); Mary Alice Molloy (Loop, River North, South Loop, and Pullman/Roseland); Kathleen Nagle(Bridgeport/Canaryville/McKinley Park/Back of the Yards); Anne Royston (Chicago–O'Hare International Airport); R. Stephen Sennott (Hyde Park/South Shore); Alice Sinkevitch (Garfield Park/Austin and Oak Park); and Julia Sniderman (Northwest Side).

The category of special supporters and advisers is large and includes attorneys Ross Altman and Mark Feldman of Rudnick and Wolfe; the Law Firm of Jenner & Block; and the Law Firm of Sidley & Austin; each helped to structure the sponsoring joint venture and our contracts. Also critically important were the librarians and photo specialists at the Art Institute of Chicago and the Chicago Historical Society; including Patrick Ashley, Emily Clark, Denise English, Lorraine Estreich, Eileen Flanagan, Charles McMorris, Janice McNeill, Susan Perry, Larry Viskochil, and Mary Woolever. Past AIA Chicago Presidents Frank Heitzman, AIA, Sherwin Braun, AIA, and Leonard Peterson, FAIA, were instrumental in supporting the project in its infancy. Key advice and assistance were also given by Timothy Barton; Daniel Bluestone; Eric Brightfield; Janice Curtis; Jan Dubin; Ann Dumas Swanson; Charles Fiori; Mary Jo Graf; T. Gunny Harboe, AIA; Jack Hedrich; Sally Hess; Michael Houlahan; Bob Johnson; Mary Sue Kranstover; Bonita Mall; William McLenahan; Lawrence Okrent; Kevin Putz; Pat Rosenzweig; Richard Solomon, FAIA; Ben Weese, FAIA; and John Zukowsky.

The Project Coordinators for the first edition were Aldarcy C. Lewis, Audrey Cusack, Eva Silverman, and Joyce de Vries; for the second edition, Phil Rahill coordinated our efforts.

Second Edition Team

Our donors for the second edition were once again our partners in this project, the American Institute of Architects Chicago Chapter, the Chicago Architecture Foundation, and the Landmarks Preservation Council of Illinois. AIA Chicago is a chapter of the American Institute of Architects, the nation's largest professional association for architects. Since its founding in 1869, the chapter has worked to advance the architect's professional development and to enrich the cultural, economic, and environmental vitality of the local community.

The Chicago Architecture Foundation, founded in 1966, is a nonprofit organization dedicated to advancing public interest and education in arhitecture and design. The foundation pursues this educational mission through a comprehensive program of tours, exhibitions, lectures, and special events, all designed to further the general public's awareness and appreciation of the architecture of metropolitan Chicago.

Landmarks Preservation Council of Illinois is a private, nonprofit membership organization dedicated to promoting the vitality of Illinois's historic architecture. LPCI is committed to community revitalization by preserving the economic and social strength of neighborhoods throughout Illinois.

For this edition we thank especially team members Kathy Nagle, Dennis McClendon, Mary Alice Molloy, Joan Pomaranc, and Harold Wolff. And we thank our chapter captains and our focus building essayists for reviewing and helping to update their essays.

We also want to thank helpers and sources Catherine Bruck, Kathy Cummings, Sally Draht, Thomas Drebenstedt, Mary Jo Graf, Elaine Harrington, William Hinchliff, Joseph LaRue, Ann Royston, Tim Samuelson, Julia Sniderman, and Emese Wood.

We also thank our editor at Harcourt, Jennifer Charat, our managing editor, Gayle Feallock, and our copy editor, Dan Janeck. And we thank the other members of the Harcourt team: Elizabeth Royles, Kaelin Chappell, and Lori Asbury.

And, again, a special thank you goes to the late Paul Gapp, the architecture critic for the *Chicago Tribune,* who gave us enthusiastic interest and support when we needed it the most.

—ALICE SINKEVITCH AND LAURIE PETERSEN

PREFACE TO THE FIRST EDITION

Chicago's eminent position in the history of architecture has been so firmly established that it borders on cliché. The modernist myth describes our past in terms of a succession of great episodes: the heroic Chicago School of the 1880s and 1890s, the Beaux Arts fall from grace, a sophisticated Art Deco interlude in the 1920s and 1930s, and the triumphal flowering of modernism after World War II. Louis H. Sullivan, John Wellborn Root, and Ludwig Mies van der Rohe are the central heroes. The steel frame, the high-speed elevator, and the curtain wall provided their technological expressions. But in the best biblical sense, each golden age has ended in disaster. Burnham tempts us to leave Sullivan's paradise, Root is toppled by Herbert Hoover's economic depression, and a postmodern plague descends upon us after Mies dies.

This legend is illustrated by photos of buildings that we have learned to admire, but the story is too simplistic to be of much use when we actually look at the city. Frank Lloyd Wright is too complex both as a person and as an artist to fit into any historic theory; and when we examine the work of Burnham, Sullivan, Root, and Mies, we find many plausible but contradictory interpretations. Bertrand Goldberg exemplifies the architect who has consistently followed a vision that does not fit neatly into a simple view of history, while the buildings of gifted experimenters like Harry Weese seem to fit into history in several places.

Some of our most productive architects never became aware of an overriding historic mission; they simply sought to design useful buildings. Firms like Hausner & Macsai, Gordon & Levin, and Solomon, Cordwell & Buenz invented a form of urban housing so well adapted to the economy and technology of our time that it has become almost invisible.

There is also a large body of work that those of us who were educated as architects were trained not to see. Rapp & Rapp, in their great movie palaces, adapted the formal vocabulary of the opera house to an unprecedented optical and acoustic technology, culminating in a seating geometry that enabled every spectator to have an undistorted view of a vast rectangle of space. But the quality and originality of their work, like that of the movies themselves, was not immediately apparent.

Some dedicated architects endured isolation and ridicule to do what they felt was right. Belli & Belli responded to the programs of scores of Catholic congregations, which wanted recognizable polychrome saints at a time when the professional elite was searching for salvation in the structural grid. Their work now seems to have been prematurely postmodern, but their practice displayed a tough-minded consistency and commitment that sets them worlds apart from more recent trend followers.

This guide should clarify our vision of Chicago. For the past two years Alice Sinkevitch has sent into our neighborhoods a dedicated troop of scouts who have trained themselves to see the city with open minds and keen eyes. There were a few practicing architects among them, but the majority were amateurs in the most loving sense of the word. Many are docents for the Chicago Architecture Foundation and have had a critical part in creating a political and educational environment in which preservation is possible. Others are dedicated preservationists who have worked within the city government and cultural institutions.

Their greatest accomplishment, however, was not only to have catalogued the city's famous buildings but also to have captured the rich diversity of the built environment. There is a gritty integrity to Chicago's neighborhoods. Their buildings remind us that, until quite recently, architecture was a craft handed down through the generations. Our city was built largely by people who could not legally be called architects today. This book amply demonstrates that the loss of this craft tradition has not improved the quality of our lives.

This guide is a monument to the breadth of our scouts' interests and to the clarity of their observations. It will help us to see Chicago as a whole and to recognize in it a much richer architectural culture than many of us might have expected.

Now that we have the book, let's go out and look at the city. It's all here—the vain efforts to scratch out a place in architectural history, the confident works of genius, and the spontaneous outpourings of decorative invention that sometimes result from the simple task of laying brick.

—JACK HARTRAY, FAIA, 1993

PREFACE TO THE SECOND EDITION

If we don't count the Potawatomi administration and its predecessors, Chicago's history covers only a little over two centuries, with less than 150 years after our great fire. This is a very short time in terms of architectural history, which may be why the changes to the city, since the previous edition of the *Guide,* can be best seen in our demographics rather than in individual buildings.

A generation of young suburbanites has returned to the city in search of sensory stimulation. Restaurants, boutiques, and oversized town houses have sprouted in old, established neighborhoods. These newcomers do not respond to precinct captains, and seem to believe that aldermen are there to represent them. They may not even be Democrats. The pressures growing out of this migration have led to an increased interest in neighborhood planning and the rewriting of the 1957 Zoning Ordinance.

A parallel development in high-rise condominium towers has occurred in what were areas of small-scale retail shops and professional offices. In the past, the spread of this building type was limited by neighborhood politics. After one or two towers were built, the local community, including the tower residents, would organize to prevent repetitions. Astor St. is a good example of the limits on high-rise development imposed by local politics.

The area west of the North Michigan Avenue retail strip, however, had few residents and no political defense mechanisms to resist large developments. Many projects were started simultaneously, and there was no overall plan. The result is an interesting geometric model of laissez-faire economics (another kind of "Chicago School").

Parking structures crowd the streets, while in the sky each new tower must be located and shaped to peek around those that were built a few months earlier. The natives of this fifty-story pueblo live in intimate spatial proximity behind large glass windows, balcony railings, elevator banks, and security guards. This unique environment will not be repeated due to the city's new energy code and revised zoning ordinance.

On the positive side, we are doing better at preserving landmark buildings, although our enthusiasm for history sometimes leads to fakery. In spite of great successes like Crate & Barrel on Michigan Ave., we have trouble mixing contemporary and historic buildings. This may grow out of bad experience with a zoning ordinance that never respected the scale of our existing streets and neighborhoods.

To our credit, we have not privatized everything, and the public sector has been greatly improved by Mayor Richard M. Daley, who has commissioned landscaped medians on streets and boulevards, planters on retail and business streets, and wrought-iron fences around almost everything. Our historic parks have been restored and new parks developed, in most cases with great sensitivity.

Larger scale public sector planning is less consistent. The rebuilding of Wacker Dr. has restored one of the key elements in the Burnham Plan, and the extension of the rail transit system has reinforced the urban structure, but the expansion of Soldier Field and continuing growth of the Convention Center are probably not compatible with the City's historic planning goals.

Little things mean the most. In the last decade we have built more places to sit, have a coffee, dine, or just loiter. Something always seems to be happening at Daley Plaza. There is a greater variety of boats in the river and the water looks almost clean. The city seems to be more alive.

When we sally forth with this new edition of the *Guide,* we will find more to enjoy than just the buildings.

Buon divertimento,
—JACK HARTRAY, FAIA, 2004

AIA GUIDE TO CHICAGO

SECOND EDITION

THE SHAPING OF CHICAGO

PERRY R. DUIS

CHICAGO HOLDS A SPECIAL PLACE IN THE HISTORY OF AMERICAN CITIES.
It frequently assumes the role of the great American exaggeration, the place where common characteristics are stretched to their limits. Other cities grew during the nineteenth century, but Chicago mushroomed. Every town had its boosters, but the Windy City's were obstreperously boastful. Crime and political corruption were everywhere, but in Chicago they seemed to be elevated to an art. More positively, Chicago became a synonym for "the new" and "the first," leading the way in architecture, literature, and social reform—in part because, as a brash upstart, it possessed few encumbering traditions.

As the archetypal American industrial city, Chicago's rise and metamorphoses not only illustrate the urbanization process at its most basic. They also demonstrate how the compelling forces of concentration, which allow efficiencies of space and time to outweigh all other considerations, both attract people and activities into cities and drive them outward toward the fringes.

The creative efforts of talented individuals are the substance of this book. But location, challenges, opportunities, and calamities also shaped Chicago and stimulated the city's problem-solvers to reach inventive solutions. Many conditions, events, and movements have shaped the city; the following are some that have had a special impact on the built environment.

The Power of Place

Chicago's location was both a curse and a blessing. The land at the banks of the Chicago River was swampy, and the stream itself flowed too slowly to turn a waterwheel or clear the mouth of silt. But it sat at the southwestern end of the massive Great Lakes navigation system. Via these waterways, prerailroad commerce penetrated the midsection of the continent and, interrupted only by a dry-weather portage, was linked to the Mississippi and Missouri rivers via the Illinois and Des Plaines rivers and the south branch of the Chicago River. Its advantages made Chicago's site a spot to control. When the first outsiders, Jacques Marquette and Louis Joliet, explored the region in 1673, the warlike Potawatomi had already displaced peaceful Indian tribes. Around 1779 Jean Baptiste Point Du Sable built a cabin roughly where the Equitable Building stands today and became Chicago's first permanent resident. A French-speaking black man, Du Sable was one of many Great Lakes traders who exchanged iron and cloth goods for furs.

In 1803, the year of the Louisiana Purchase, the United States established Fort Dearborn, the nation's westernmost military post, near what is now the south end of the Michigan Ave. Bridge. In 1812, in an incident known as the Fort Dearborn Massacre, the Potawatomi attempted to regain the valuable site. They burned the stockade, while three miles to the south, a raiding party killed most of the garrison and their families as they fled along the lakeshore.

ILLINOIS & MICHIGAN CANAL IN BRIDGEPORT

The fort was rebuilt in 1816, the same year that surveying began for the Illinois & Michigan Canal, which would provide a year-round link between the Chicago River and the Illinois-Mississippi river system some seventy-five miles away. A national financial panic in 1819 and fears of Indian unrest halted progress until the 1830s. On August 5, 1833, thirteen electors gathered to incorporate the Town of Chicago, and newcomers—many of whom were land speculators—began arriving in droves. By 1836, when work on the canal began in earnest, optimism about Chicago's future had boosted land prices to astronomical levels and attracted over 3,000 more residents. In March 1837 Chicagoans demanded and received a city charter from the state legislature.

The Golden Funnel and the Growth of Transportation

In the mid-1840s Chicago's merchants began to exploit the city's site by creating what might be called the golden funnel. The settlement of farmland throughout the West produced agricultural surpluses that could be shipped to eastern markets most efficiently via Chicago's water linkage. Wheat shipped through Chicago rose from a meager few bushels in 1840 to nearly two million bushels seven years later.

In 1848 several events improved the funnel's flow. The Illinois & Michigan Canal was finally opened; plank roads to the hinterlands made it easier for farmers to roll their grain wagons into town; and the telegraph linked national and international markets to the Chicago Board of Trade, newly formed to provide a standardized, self-policing market that farmers could trust. Most significant, on October 25, 1848, a tiny locomotive named the Pioneer made its inaugural run between Chicago and present-day Oak Park.

The promises of the 1840s became prosperous realities in the 1850s. Rail lines extending west to the Mississippi and east to Philadelphia and New York transformed Chicago into a national transportation hub. Grain elevators now towered over the city, while huge stacks of timber along the riverbanks proved that Chicago was the nation's leading lumber center.

The Civil War ushered in a new era for Chicago. The city's size and remoteness from military action made it an ideal site for producing war goods. The golden funnel now supplied the Union Army with horses and hay and fed its troops with carloads of bread, condensed milk, dried fruit, and cans of cooked meats from Chicago slaughterhouses. So great was the movement of livestock into the city that the need for efficiency forced packers and shippers to consolidate. On Christmas Day, 1865, they opened the Union Stock Yards four miles southwest of the city. The yards soon enabled Chicago to displace Cincinnati as the nation's pork-packing capital.

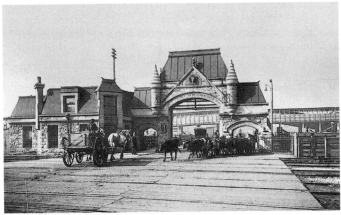

UNION STOCK YARDS ENTRANCE GATE

Dire Necessities and Creative Technologies

The new city offered few amenities. Depending on the season, the streets were graded dust or mud that regularly disappeared under ponds left by springtime rain. Visitors were uniformly unimpressed by the buildings. Shortages of structural wood and skilled labor led to lightweight "balloon frame" construction, invented in 1833, which gave the mushrooming population housing easily built by unskilled laborers.

Only gradually did more substantial masonry structures join the tiny buildings of logs or crudely cut boards. In 1837 William B. Ogden, the city's first mayor, enticed John M. Van Osdel, a carpenter and architect, from New York to Chicago to begin providing something more than an architecture of expediency.

City officials also turned to engineering experts to solve problems generated by exploding growth. To combat epidemics by improving drainage flow, the city's chief engineer, Ellis S. Chesbrough, designed a sewer system to be constructed on top of the existing streets, an expensive project that began in 1855 and continued for decades. The pavement grade was then raised a dozen feet, and building owners turned to

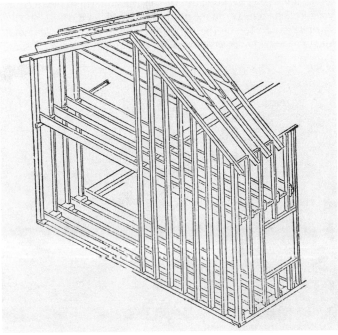

"BALLOON FRAME" CONSTRUCTION

youthful talents such as George Westinghouse and George M. Pullman to jack up old structures and insert new foundations. In older neighborhoods, such as Pilsen, these raised street grades are still visible.

Public health reformers began a long crusade against unsanitary burial places in 1858. Their efforts eventually closed the city cemetery, now the southern part of Lincoln Park, and increased the attractiveness of landscaped plots in rural areas. Cemeteries such as Graceland, Rosehill, and Oak Woods became accessible to city dwellers because of advances in public transportation. These improvements included steam railroad commuter service, a horse-drawn street railway system, and a pivoting span bridge over the river at Rush St. (1856), touted as the first iron bridge west of the Alleghenies. Architects such as W. W. Boyington, Edward Burling, and Otis L. Wheelock joined Van Osdel as designers of specialized structures for stores, public buildings, and homes.

With heavy maritime traffic keeping bridges open almost perpetually, tunnels were excavated under the river at Washington (1869) and La Salle (1871) Sts. When pollution from the sewage-laden river threatened the water supply, engineers designed a new water plant, the Chicago Water Tower & Pumping Station (1869), with an intake crib two miles from shore.

The Great Conflagration

To this day no one really knows how the fire of October 8–9, 1871, started. Whether it was lightning, raucous tenants, a drunken neighbor, or even a cantankerous cow kicking over a lantern, the blaze definitely began near the barn behind Patrick and Katherine O'Leary's DeKoven St. home. Incompetent dispatchers and lookouts allowed it to flare out of control, and an intense firestorm proceeded to consume block after block of a city that had had no rain since July. The conflagration raged for thirty-six hours, sweeping away a third of the city before burning itself out four miles away on the northern edge of town. Over 300 people perished, 17,450 structures were reduced to ashes, the downtown was devastated, and on the North Side only a few scattered houses and the Water Tower were spared. At least 90,000 people were left homeless, and the livelihoods of thousands more had disappeared with their workplaces.

Residential Chicago would never be the same. The Common Council soon banned any new nonmasonry construction within the city limits (roughly Fullerton Ave. on the north, Pulaski Rd. on the west, and Pershing Rd. on the south). Thousands of North Siders who could not afford to rebuild in brick were forced to sell their lots and move just over

AFTERMATH OF THE FIRE OF 1871

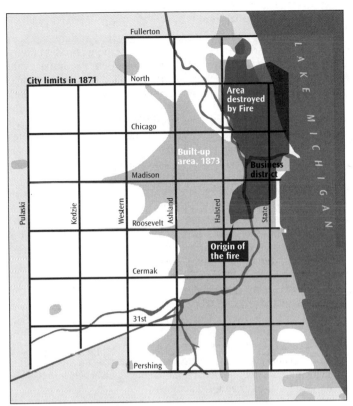

MAP OF THE FIRE'S DESTRUCTION

the border, where developers were only too happy to put them in inexpensive new wooden houses. The contrast between the masonry city and
the wooden suburbs on the old city borders can still be seen in spots
along Fullerton Ave. west of Halsted St. The undamaged South and West
sides were also dramatically transformed. Owners subdivided houses
near the "burnt district" and rented space at premium rates. Overcrowding quickly deteriorated thousands of these structures and hastened
inner-city decay.

In contrast to the neighborhoods, the problem downtown was the
seemingly impossible one of reestablishing as quickly as possible the
heart of Chicago's economic and cultural life. Rebuilding began even
before the rubble cooled, and Chicagoans turned to their architects and
engineers. John M. Van Osdel, Edward Burling, W. W. Boyington, Otis L.
Wheelock, Gurdon P. Randall, Augustus Bauer, Asher Carter, and Peter B.
Wight had as many commissions as they could handle, and for two years,
as crews worked around the clock and throughout the winters, they kept
track of their designs in terms of miles of building fronts constructed.
The new structures appeared to be much the same as pre-Fire ones, but
most were slightly taller and had more elevators. Innovations were limited to improved fireproofing techniques.

The Fire hastened the evolution of city-use patterns. Downtown residential use, which had been declining, was not reestablished, and most
of the manufacturers whose North Side factories were destroyed soon
relocated in outlying industrial districts along rail lines or the river's
branches. The McCormick Reaper Company, for example, replaced its
plant on the north bank of the river's mouth with what would eventually
be one of the nation's largest manufacturing facilities (now demolished)
at Western and Blue Island Aves. The new factories were generally much
larger than their predecessors and housed heavier, more complex equipment. This reduced the mobility of the enterprises, and land-use patterns were thereby fixed for decades to come.

The Logic of Centralization

By 1870 the city's population surged to 298,977, but wartime shortages of building materials and carpenters had hampered housebuilding, and many areas were overcrowded. This congestion, aggravated by the noise and smoke of postbellum factories, instilled thoughts of escape. The middle and upper classes could choose to move to quiet, orderly sections of the city serviced by expanded horsecar lines and commuter railways. Those seeking permanent residential refuge found homes in subdivisions and suburban towns that sprang up along railroad routes.

The population of Chicago exploded to 500,000 in 1880 and to more than a million in 1890. The city had become big, and in this largeness was an overwhelming logic of concentration, of which post-Fire factories were only one example. The savings of time and economies of scale that resulted from putting many departments under one roof—so that belts and pulleys from one huge stationary steam engine could drive the greatest number of machines—more than paid for the cost of building the structure. Downtowns were seen as also benefiting from economies of size and geographic convenience. In Chicago most of the public transit lines, which included the world's largest cable car system, were built to carry passengers into the central business district. This area acquired the nickname the Loop in the early 1880s because it was encircled by transit tracks. Electric trolleys went into service in 1890, and two years later an elevated "iron highway" was inaugurated—the first of five radial rapid transit lines that would be united in 1897 by the Union Loop built above the downtown's perimeter. Steam suburban lines brought an estimated 100,000 additional daily passengers into their six depots, which also ringed the downtown.

Nineteenth-century urban residents also exercised the logic of concentration in their division of city spaces. For them, domestic dwellings were clearly private spaces, and the wealthy were better able than others to use private areas for sheltering their affairs. They built their homes in exclusive districts, like Prairie Ave. on the South Side or Astor St. on the Near North, and their luxurious world of private clubs, schools, opera boxes, and carriages permitted selective contact with the rest of Chicago. Conversely, the streets, sidewalks, parks, river, and government facilities made up the public places. These were commonly owned, primarily utilitarian, and usually undistinguished in design—with one great exception, Chicago's well-landscaped parks and boulevards. In 1869 Illinois Health Board member Dr. John H. Rauch, along with real estate developers and civic boosters, persuaded voters and the Illinois General Assembly to create three tax districts to fund an ambitious ring of parks several miles beyond the built-up neighborhoods.

A third category of city space might be called semipublic places, privately owned areas to which the public had access. Some were noncommercial, such as churches, which by the 1890s were often grand buildings with Sunday school or meeting facilities at least partly available to all. Most semipublic spaces, however, were profit-making, and the degree to which they had become objects of civic pride reflected the progress of urbanization and centralization. The office building was an example. Although it featured private offices, it offered services ranging from barbershops to restaurants, and its elevator lobby had evolved into a showplace meant to make a good impression and attract tenants. In the (now demolished) Chicago Stock Exchange Building, for instance, the elevator cages were enclosed in delicate metalwork; the Marquette Building presents a Chicago history lesson in mosaic tiles; and the Rookery has an airy, naturally illuminated core.

The concentration of activities downtown encouraged the creation of districts within the Loop. The railway stations girding the central busi-

THE ROOKERY LOBBY BY BURNHAM & ROOT

ness district, for example, encouraged a similarly shaped placement of hotels for the convenience of passengers. The Chicago Board of Trade at the foot of La Salle St. drew not only brokers but also law firms, banks, and insurance companies to adjacent blocks. To the east, Marshall Field had moved his retail business from Lake St. to State St. just prior to the Fire. His competitors followed, so that within months a residential area had been transformed into the city's main mercantile district. Randolph St. emerged as Chicago's theater row, as well as the home of a thriving music publishing industry. Warehousing, printing, and clothing concerns located on the edges of downtown to be near suppliers and customers.

Department stores were examples of semipublic spaces designed for public use. Before the Fire, merchants had offered undifferentiated varieties of wholesale and retail goods. Eventually, merchandise and services were centralized under one roof, and the stores functioned as "factories of consumption" that saved consumers time and steps. The store that Marshall Field built after the Fire was one of America's most lavishly furnished. By the end of the century, Field had begun what would become a complex that would cover more than a square block on State St.; Schlesinger & Mayer had commissioned the Louis H. Sullivan building at State and Madison Sts. (later known as the Carson Pirie Scott store); and Siegel, Cooper & Co. had fifteen acres of floor space in the Second Leiter Building. Elsewhere on "That Great Street," new buildings for Maurice Rothschild, Mandel Brothers, and the Boston Store would soon create a retail district of enormous drawing power. Huge plate glass windows allowed each store to display its wares to lure passersby, while lighting counters deep within the buildings.

Hotels had matured from rude inns into spectacularly appointed rivals to the palaces of European nobility. They offered such specialized amenities as billiard parlors, sunrooms, and ballrooms, as well as several classes of guest rooms and dining facilities. The six major railway stations near which the hotels were concentrated had in turn evolved from homely barns into spectacular urban gateways featuring so many services that they were called "cities within cities." The Auditorium, the most remarkable structure of all, combined three types of grand semipublic places. It had an office block on its Wabash Ave. side, a luxurious 400-room hotel fronting on Michigan Ave., and an acoustically perfect theater, the world's largest when it opened in 1889.

In the 1890s the battle between centralization and dispersal continued, with new factors favoring decentralization. One of these was the replacement of the steam engine as the power source for an entire factory by small electrical motors for each machine. This spawned "electrical manufacturing suburbs," such as Harvey, Maywood, and Chicago Heights, which had room for both new factories and cheap workers' housing. Another element was the continuing migration to the urban fringe by those who could afford spacious homes.

Labor Unrest in the Industrial City

Raw materials flowed through the golden funnel to post-Fire industries, where many tasks carried on in the new plants created a dependence on repetitive jobs requiring few skills. Long hours and low wages fomented worker dissatisfaction, which led to an era of labor unrest and violence. The nation's attention focused on Chicago in 1886, when demands for an eight-hour workday produced a series of strikes at the McCormick works. On the night of May 4 police charged into a labor rally at Haymarket Sq., near the corner of Randolph and Desplaines Sts. A bomb exploded, and the police opened fire. This Haymarket Riot led to a conspiracy trial, executions, and international protests.

The self-sufficient model factory and town thirteen miles south of Chicago, begun in 1880 by George M. Pullman, was the epitome of the new industrial order. Architect Solon S. Beman designed an efficient factory, workers' housing, and amenities such as a shopping arcade, stables, a market, a park, a hotel, and a church. It was hardly utopia, however. Pullman sought a sober, dependable workforce that did not have to live in the city's slums, but workers chafed under planning that kept them isolated from executives and placed controls on how they lived and where they shopped. During a serious depression that began in 1893, the company slashed wages and laid off workers, but Pullman refused to lower his rents. The Pullman strike of 1894 and a nationwide boycott resulted in the firebombing of Pullman's cars and occupation of his town by federal militia. Although the company won the struggle, the courts eventually forced it to sell the houses and to hire nonresidents. The Haymarket and Pullman incidents produced front-page headlines worldwide, not only because they were startling events but also because Chicago's economic importance and position as the nation's fastest-growing city prompted widespread concern that battles between workers and police might eventually be repeated everywhere.

The Development of the Skyscraper

Downtown centralization required special buildings to draw together thousands of people simultaneously, and a rapid succession of technological developments made this possible. Advances in foundation engi-

FIRST INFANTRY ARMORY BY BURNHAM & ROOT (DEMOLISHED)

neering and in metal-frame construction, reliable lighting systems (first gas, then electric), improvements in steam heating and fireproofing, and faster, safer elevators made vertical expansion possible. Soaring land values demanded the intensive use of downtown lots, just as telephone and telegraph communications were enabling business leaders to move away from their manufacturing facilities and near their lawyers, bankers, and other downtown services.

It took more than demand, however, to create tall buildings. Chicago was blessed with a talented cadre of architects and engineers. John M. Van Osdel and Peter B. Wight were seasoned veterans among a group of varied talents. William Le Baron Jenney and William Sooy Smith concentrated on foundations and structure. Dankmar Adler, an expert in acoustics, teamed with Louis H. Sullivan, the master of detail. Daniel H. Burnham, who understood the business of architecture, formed a partnership with John Wellborn Root, who excelled in its artistry. William Holabird and Martin Roche were among the steadiest producers, with a stream of successful designs.

The architects and engineers had to find ways to secure tall buildings in Chicago's spongy soil. Initially, following suggestions from structural engineer Frederick Baumann, they designed raft foundations that spread a building's weight over as much of the subsurface soil as possible, and they set entrance levels high enough to compensate for expected settling. Particularly heavy or tall buildings required more substantial support. Adler & Sullivan, for instance, placed the structural walls of the Auditorium on continuous reinforced concrete foundations and carried the massive weight of the seventeen-story tower on a floating raft of crisscross layers of timbers, steel rails, and I-beams. In their seventeen-story Schiller Building, raft foundations were supported on wooden pilings driven to refusal; the same architects subsequently made an important breakthrough in settlement problems when they supported the

CONSTRUCTION OF THE MARQUETTE BUILDING

west party wall of the Chicago Stock Exchange with tubular concrete cais-sons (the first used in Chicago) that reached fifty-five feet down to hard-pan, an oxidized clay.

Framing problems also had to be resolved. The six-foot-thick walls and tiny windows of the lower floors of Burnham & Root's Monadnock Build-ing demonstrated that extending load-bearing construction to sixteen stories limited interior space and light so severely that taller masonry projects were pointless. But a feasible way to go higher had already been worked out gradually, so that in Jenney's Home Insurance Building (1885), metal framing had eliminated the need for exterior load-bearing walls. As the construction of tall buildings evolved into all-steel structures, "curtain walls" came to function only as skins and could be made of al-most any material, including glass or terra-cotta. Interiors were flooded with light through Chicago windows, which were bay-filling frames hold-ing movable sashes on either side of large fixed panes. Most impor-tant, there were now almost no theoretical limits to a building's height.

Chicago's skyline altered at a dizzying pace after 1880, and what was daringly tall in one decade became the norm of the next and small twenty years later. The distinction of being the city's tallest building passed quickly from the ten-story Montauk Building (1882), the first la-beled a skyscraper, to the thirteen-story Royal Insurance Building (1885). The Rookery, Austin, and Adams Express Co. buildings (all eleven stories) were exceptionally large when built in 1886—but of only average size once the Auditorium was under way. The Monadnock, with its load-bearing walls, and the Manhattan, with its metal frame, both reached a world's-record sixteen stories in 1890. Two years later they would be dwarfed by the twenty-one-story Masonic Temple.

Rampant Growth and Annexation

Few cities had less geographical constraint on dispersal than Chicago. The abundance of land kept down the cost of a lot or factory site, while the transportation networks that brought passengers downtown to work or shop also made it convenient for them to live great distances away. Developers aggressively marketed life on the urban fringe. They cut building costs by mass-producing limited varieties of designs, adver-tised their developments heavily in every language, and even gave away samples—weekend excursion rides to their subdivisions. Housing for every budget was available beyond Chicago's borders, while the conges-tion, crime, disease, and political corruption within them made daily headlines and provided the motivation to leave.

By the 1880s Chicago risked being rivaled by its adjacent areas, which were growing far faster than the city. Since its founding, the city had grown steadily by annexation. Now the municipal government proposed a massive annexation that would take in such communities as Hyde Park, Kenwood, and Pullman to the south and Lake View and Jefferson to the north. Many of those affected realized annexation would offer the benefits of Chicago's more advanced municipal infrastructure and better services, including schools. Others, feeling safer and morally supe-rior to their city counterparts, earnestly wanted the status quo. None-theless, on June 29, 1889, by a thin majority, suburbanites spread over 125 square miles—much of it farmland—voted to join with Chicago. The city's territory almost quadrupled in one day, and its population was recorded at one million in the following year's census. Among Ameri-can cities only New York was larger.

"A World of Unmixed Bliss"

The success of the annexation vote aided Chicago's efforts to become host to an international exposition being proposed to celebrate the 400th anniversary of the discovery of America. Not only did it help the negotiations for the host city to be as large as possible, but the best sites for the fairgrounds were now inside the city limits. The self-promotion

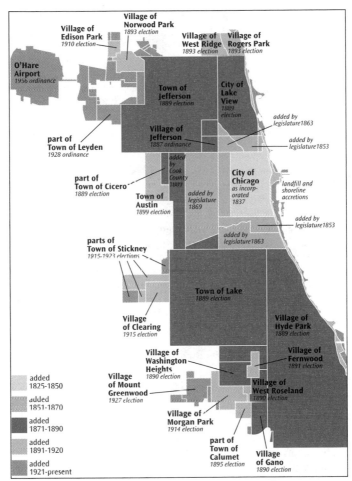

of the Chicago delegation seeking congressional approval was so aggressive that it earned for the city its "Windy City" nickname. A struggle at home over location ended with the commissioners' choice of Jackson Park on the South Side. An illustrious group of architects from the East Coast and Chicago, led by Daniel H. Burnham, designed an immense architectural wonderland. Workers constructed a neo-Classic "White City" from steel frames finished in lath and staff, a mixture of plaster, cement, and jute.

To help the city look its best for the fair, several cultural institutions opened new buildings, including the Chicago Historical Society, the

PALACE OF FINE ARTS BY CHARLES B. ATWOOD, WORLD'S COLUMBIAN EXPOSITION

Chicago Academy of Sciences, and the Newberry Library. The Art Institute rented its new home to the exposition congresses, a series of international scholarly meetings. The realization that visitors would also note what Chicago lacked motivated the founding of the Chicago Symphony Orchestra and a second University of Chicago (the first one had gone bankrupt in 1886). The World's Columbian Exposition opened amid a severe national depression, but when visitors passed through its gates in numbers that reached 750,000 a day, they found a plaster paradise in which the world's technical knowledge, mechanical skills, and manufacturing prowess had been collected, classified, subdivided, and displayed as never before. More than a million objects filled more than a hundred buildings. No exposition before or since ever aspired to such comprehensiveness.

The exposition left Chicago with two significant legacies. First, the fair drew hundreds of talented young people to the city, and despite a persistently depressed economy that hampered the arts in general, they created an innovative cultural milieu. Experimental theaters staged avant-garde productions. Small-scale publishers and little magazines, such as the *Chap-Book,* commissioned Art Nouveau illustrations and featured works by new authors, including Theodore Dreiser and George Ade. This creative community gathered in buildings especially designed for the arts, such as the low-rent artists' studios that Judge Lambert Tree erected in 1894 in the backyard of his N. Wabash Ave. house. The former Studebaker carriage works was remodeled by new owners in 1898 into the Fine Arts Building, housing a unique collection of studios, theaters, and music schools.

Second, Chicago's first elevated line was built to carry visitors between the downtown and the fairgrounds, and hundreds of small hotels and apartments were built along it and other South Side transit routes. Often hastily and poorly constructed by underfinanced opportunists whom the depression bankrupted, these buildings quickly fell into disrepair. From 1900 to 1930, African Americans arriving from the South could find few housing opportunities outside this broad band of exposition housing, and the so-called Black Belt emerged.

"Make Big Plans, Aim High in Hope"

By the 1890s Chicago seemed to be choking on its own success. Each new downtown skyscraper added to traffic woes. The clatter of hoofs and metal wheels, peddlers' shouts, and streetcar bells had reached an unbelievable din. Some health officials worried that the darkness of the skyscraper canyons would turn the ubiquitous layers of horse manure and refuse into germ incubators. Finding one's way around was complicated by a house-numbering system that used the meandering river as its baseline and allowed countless duplicate addresses.

Proposals to relieve the city's woes took several forms. To reduce street congestion the elevated system was extended, and a network of tunnels enabled miniature electric locomotives to haul freight, coal, and ashes to and from downtown buildings. (In 1992 a leak from the Chicago River flooded the long-abandoned system, creating an estimated $1 billion in damage.) By the beginning of the new century, the extensive use of automobiles was being proposed as a solution to several ills. Their maneuverability would help relieve traffic jams involving fixed-route vehicles, they would eliminate the health hazards connected with manure and animal carcasses, and they would reduce the dense smoke from commuter trains because fewer trains would be needed. There were also several governmental efforts to untangle Chicago's street chaos. The City Council voted in 1893 to limit building heights to 130 feet. (Lobbying interests successfully raised the ceiling in following years.) The aldermen also renamed hundreds of streets and in 1909 instituted a rational house-numbering system with State and Madison Sts. as baselines.

The most significant proposal combined careful restructuring of the street system with strict planning for future development. Calling upon his experience with the Columbian Exposition, Daniel H. Burnham and his assistant, Edward H. Bennett, backed by the Merchants' and Commercial clubs, began work in 1906 on a master plan for the city. When published three years later, the *Plan of Chicago* presented a grand blueprint of transportation for the entire region and a demonstration of how public spaces could be made as magnificent as semipublic ones. The plan reserved the lakefront for recreation and proposed a string of offshore islands. Monroe Harbor and Grant Park would become a formal "front door," while the seat of government would be relocated to an immense plaza at the junction of Congress and Halsted Sts. Burnham and Bennett took great pains to demonstrate how railroad facilities could be efficiently concentrated in outlying districts, how commercial and recreational use of the river's downtown banks could be compatible, and how attractive a city of uniform height might be. The most important feature, however, was the treatment of streets as the veins and arteries of a living organism. Impediment-free circulation required widening many streets, including Michigan Ave., designated as the new gateway to the North Side. Diagonal streets would improve crosstown travel. The plan was lavishly illustrated by artist Jules Guerin, who purposely depicted the streets as low-density mixtures of automobiles, horse-drawn vehicles, and pedestrians to demonstrate the benefits of proper urban planning.

To promote Burnham's grand scheme, the Commercial Club established the Chicago Plan Commission of civic and business leaders, chaired by brewer Charles H. Wacker and with Burnham as its chief architect. The commission not only lobbied for individual projects that would conform to the plan but also campaigned intensively to sell it to the citizenry. Pamphlets on the plan blanketed the city, nickelodeon audiences found promotional movies on it sandwiched between standard features, and eighth-grade children were required to pass examinations based on *Wacker's Manual of the Plan of Chicago*, a textbook version published in 1912.

Many people objected to the plan. The Army Corps of Engineers, which was responsible for harbor development along the Lake Michigan shore, thought Chicago would be foolish to relinquish miles of potential docking facilities for recreation. The city negotiated a compromise under which Municipal (later Navy) Pier was built to combine both uses. Property owners objected to street-widening plans that destroyed their front

JULES GUERIN RENDERING FROM PLAN OF CHICAGO

yards or buildings. Railroads resisted consolidation. And A. Montgomery Ward, the mail-order baron, opposed the idea of clustering public buildings in the downtown lakefront park. Ward's lawyers invoked an obscure clause in the original federal land grant that gave Michigan Ave. property owners, of which he was one, veto power over any construction there. Ward did not challenge building the Art Institute, but he pursued lawsuits to the Illinois Supreme Court to prevent the construction in the park of the John Crerar Library and the Field Columbian Museum.

The Burnham Plan shaped public-works construction for decades. Its success depended on a bold government to borrow and spend on a grand scale, and William Hale ("Big Bill") Thompson, who was elected mayor in 1915, was willing to do just that. During the next eight years, Thompson began a physical transformation of the city. He enhanced the southern bank of the river with a bilevel street named in honor of Wacker, and he built new bridges, including the double-decker at Michigan Ave., thereby making that street a major thoroughfare on both sides of the river. Thompson also extended Ogden Ave. and Roosevelt Rd. to speed traffic across the city, and he even straightened out an obtrusive bend in the Chicago River between 12th and 16th Sts.

The plan also inspired passage in 1923 of Chicago's first comprehensive zoning law, in an attempt to regulate both vertical and horizontal sprawl. The law replaced the rigid height limit with an elaborate formula that allowed towers above the twenty-second story—provided they did not occupy more than one-fourth of the area of the lot and that tower space was not more than one-sixth of the entire building. While this did not help traffic problems, it slightly reduced canyon effects. The zoning law proved quite compatible with the skyscraper developments of the 1920s, a decade that witnessed an enormous building boom and the first significant appearance of tall buildings outside the Loop. The Burnham Plan urged making the Chicago River a focal point, and by 1929 the Merchandise Mart—with more than four million square feet of floor space the world's largest building—was gracing the northern bank of the main branch, while the Chicago Daily News Building peered across the river at the forty-five-story Civic Opera Building, built by utilities magnate Samuel Insull. The opening of the Michigan Ave. Bridge in 1920 extended development north of the river, much as Burnham had envisioned. The dazzling white Wrigley Building was soon joined by hotels, a Northwestern University campus, and other office buildings, most notably the Tribune Tower, whose design was chosen in an international competition. A string of new apartment buildings stretched northward along Lake Shore Dr. In the Loop itself buildings of twenty and twenty-five stories became the norm, while the Chicago Board of Trade, at 605 feet, loomed over its neighbors.

Elsewhere the zoning law not only protected property values in built-up areas from incompatible or detrimental intrusions but also provided a general guideline for developing the remaining open lands. Throughout the 1920s developers lured workers into almost endless rows of sturdy, spacious, one-story brick bungalows. Shopping in the "bungalow belt" was usually nearby, because the zoning law fostered the development of outlying business districts centered on major transit intersections where heavy pedestrian traffic was generated. These shopping districts were also likely to include the "popcorn palace" movie theaters in which architects such as Rapp & Rapp had mastered sight lines and acoustics and created spectacular interiors based on escapist themes.

Poverty, Racism, and the Growth of Slums

In stark contrast to the Loop's nineteenth-century splendors were the slums adjacent to them. Owners had deferred maintenance on properties that they expected to raze as the downtown expanded outward. Tall-building construction had instead restricted development to the core of downtown, and decrepit transient housing soon ringed the Loop on all sides. On the South Side was the Levee, one of the nation's largest vice districts, controlled by colorful turn-of-the-century scoundrels, First Ward aldermen "Bathhouse John" Coughlin and Michael ("Hinky Dink") Kenna.

The residential slums began about a mile west and south of the Loop. The poor, many of them immigrants, lived in old wooden houses standing cheek by jowl with factories and bars or in once elegant apartments and mansions converted into rooming houses and then tenements. Some lots were filled front to back with ramshackle frame houses; others became refuse pits in front of houses that had not been elevated when the street grade was raised. Many of the tiny units had no bathroom or kitchen. While other neighborhoods were adopting electricity and steam heat, the slums had yet to see gas lighting or coal stoves in every room.

Among the few constant features of slum life were the buildings themselves, the high death rates, and political bosses who prevented reforms. By doling out city jobs, they got enough votes to remain on the City Council for decades. Efforts were largely ineffectual to end the hegemony of the gray wolves, as the press called such grafters as Coughlin, Kenna, "Foxy Ed" Cullerton, and "Johnny De Pow" Powers. Political reformers could count on support only from the middle-class residents of the neighborhoods adjacent to the slums, and the political parties could not supply sufficiently strong challengers.

The multiplicity of slum problems called for a multifunctional solution. Such a "department store" approach to social reform was pioneered by Jane Addams, who arrived on the West Side in 1889 with Ellen Gates Starr to establish Hull House. The traditional approach to charity had been to dole out food and money from a downtown office or to intrude on humble homes with prying questions about worthiness. Addams felt that the proper way to help the poor was to live among them and create a semipublic place, the settlement house, where those in need could find a variety of services. Hull House offered the arts, job training, health services, child care, physical education, domestic science, a library, and a savings bank. Hull House expanded to thirteen buildings covering a square block and inspired the creation of fifty similar facilities across the city, most notably the University of Chicago and Northwestern University settlements and Chicago Commons. Ironically, by teaching job skills and thrift, settlement houses—instead of instilling neighborhood loyalty and cohesiveness—contributed to the transience of the slum by showing its occupants how to move on to better lives elsewhere.

Burnham's vision of the City Beautiful made only vague comments about how deconcentration could solve slum problems, and it failed to

CHA—STATEWAY GARDENS UNDER CONSTRUCTION

recognize that racial discrimination and poverty are perversely central-
izing forces. So while preservation or dispersal were options elsewhere
in Chicago, the Madison St. skid row still sheltered the homeless, and
the dense ring of slums surrounding the downtown continued to house
those too poor to afford anything else. The 50,000 African Americans
who migrated to Chicago during World War I were trapped by racial
discrimination within overcrowded areas, regardless of their economic
circumstances. Their competition with returning veterans for jobs and
housing led to a bloody race riot in July 1919. Threats of violence, combined with racial covenants in sale and rental agreements, kept the
Black Belt a firmly walled enclave.

After World War II, although vast neighborhood-clearance lands lay
vacant, the Chicago Housing Authority began a policy of erecting high-
rise buildings on compact sites, claiming as its motives the high costs
of land and federal pressure to save money on construction. It was clear
to critics, however, that the policy ensured that the maximum number
of African Americans arriving from the South would be absorbed within
the existing Black Belt, thereby decreasing the possibility that middle-
class black families near its edges might move into adjacent white
neighborhoods. By the early 1960s Chicago officials had accepted the
widespread belief that it was easier and cheaper to demolish whole
neighborhoods of substandard old flats and bungalows than to renovate
structures on an individual basis. The result was massive land clearance in a swath that encircled the downtown and expanded several
miles into the South Side.

The Depression and Public Works

For most Chicagoans, prosperity disappeared as the 1920s ended. De-
clines in construction and other economic indicators had begun around
1927, and by the time Wall Street crashed in October 1929, welfare cases
were beyond the capabilities of private agencies. Ironically, the central
location that underlay much of Chicago's past prosperity made the city
a prime destination for the homeless traveling in boxcars. Unfinished
lower Wacker Dr. provided temporary shelter for both transients and
residents who found themselves evicted or foreclosed. The "Winded
City" seemed to be moving backward. Health and education services
were cut to nineteenth-century levels, streets were strewn with garbage,
and at least thirty downtown buildings were demolished to save paying
taxes. Among them were Henry Hobson Richardson's Marshall Field
Wholesale Building and Burnham & Root's Masonic Temple.

Chicago turned to dramatic solutions. Where Republican Mayor
Thompson had built with bonds, voters in 1931 backed a new Democratic machine under Anton Cermak and his successor, Edward J. Kelly,
who funneled federal New Deal money into massive public works projects. Not only was the Outer Drive Bridge opened in 1937 and Municipal
(now Midway) Airport upgraded into a major facility, but new viaducts,
sidewalks, school athletic fields, and other projects put paychecks in
thousands of hands. Mayor Kelly enthusiastically backed the wholesale
replacement of the slum belt with public housing projects. The first three
were built in 1935: the Jane Addams Homes, the Julia C. Lathrop Homes,
and Trumbull Park Homes. Chicago also began work on a long-delayed
subway system, the first section of which opened under State St. in 1943.

In the boldest of all moves, at the nadir of the Depression in 1933,
Chicago celebrated its centennial with the Century of Progress Exposition, sprawled along the lakefront and focused on what became
the site of Meigs Field. The fair offered an optimistic statement that
science, industry, and business would bring a return of prosperity. Its
futuristic buildings were made of such unconventional materials as
rolled steel, Masonite, and plywood; bright colors, accents of neon and
fluorescent lights, and a whimsical midway gave the fair an escapist
atmosphere.

CHRYSLER BUILDING BY HOLABIRD & ROOT, 1933 WORLD'S FAIR

The Depression ended with the military buildup of World War II, and Chicago's central location again shaped its role. Its diverse industrial base made the metropolis second only to Detroit as a producer of war materiel, but to fulfill 1,400 federal contracts, companies sought larger quarters outside the city. The gigantic Dodge-Chicago plant at 76th St. and Cicero Ave., in what is now Ford City Shopping Center, the Buick aircraft engine plants in Melrose Park, and the Amertorp torpedo plant in Forest Park led the industrial suburbanization, which also drew the latest influx of workers to suburban "defense housing."

The Loop Reborn versus the Logic of Decentralization

Urban patterns entrenched by the Great Depression and wartime controls crumbled with the arrival of postwar prosperity and mobility, and although few noticed at first, among the traditions in decline was centralization itself.

Many businesses remained eager to locate downtown. Beginning with the ground breaking in 1952 for the Prudential Building, the first Loop skyscraper since the Field Building of the 1930s, tower after tower appeared in rapid succession. "The tall boys are sprouting in bunches," proclaimed one journalist in 1967. The Loop seemed reborn: The Inland Steel, the Chicago Civic Center (now Richard J. Daley Center), the Brunswick, and the First National Bank buildings were just a few of the additions. Most buildings of the 1960s and 1970s were at least indirectly influenced by the careful, ordered style of Ludwig Mies van der Rohe, whose strong, black-framed glass towers became the ultimate statement of the curtain wall. Innovations gradually came into style, as in the graceful curves of Lake Point Tower and the bold bracing of the John Hancock Center. The greatest structural achievement of the era was the Sears Tower, at 1,454 feet the world's tallest building. Although pundits questioned its site west of the Loop, Sears chairman Arthur M. Wood defended it, using the logic of the centralization argument. The major factor in choosing the location was "our employees—how they would get to and from work," he explained. "The site we chose offers all the advantages we were looking for . . . close to the post office, financial district, government offices, and the major attractions."

For many others, the trend toward dispersal greatly accelerated in the postwar years. The first evidence was the suburban exodus of industry made possible by a superhighway system that had begun in 1954 with the Congress (later Eisenhower) Expressway. By 1960 work was either finished or under way on the Northwest (later Kennedy), Southwest (later Stevenson), Edens, and Kingery; the Dan Ryan would soon follow. Industrial developers, who had long complained that zoning in Chicago stunted expansion by preserving too much land for residential purposes, grabbed at the irresistible lure of lower taxes and cheaper land in suburbia. They were quick to take advantage of the independence from rail depots that was made possible by the increasing use of truck transportation. The opening of O'Hare International Airport in 1962, on a former Douglas Aircraft Co. plant site, provided a new form of transportation hub particularly suited for manufacturers of high-value, low-bulk goods such as electronics. Chicago reached its peak population of 3.6 million in 1950, as developers were filling in the open tracts on the Northwest and Southwest sides. But land in the suburbs was cheaper, and by the early 1960s virtually all new single-family construction was taking place beyond the city limits. In some suburbs, failed developments from the 1920s were completed near commuter lines; in others, the dominance of the automobile was recognized and developments were oriented toward highways.

Within the city, neighborhoods became less cohesive and no longer the focus of residents' lives. Many Chicagoans had traditionally met most of their needs with local churches, stores, saloons, newspapers, movie theaters, and schools. Outings to a major park or shopping expeditions to the Loop were special events. That world evaporated after World War II, especially in the wake of 1949 federal legislation that made it easier to obtain a GI Bill or FHA mortgage on a house in the suburbs than on one in the city. Two new phenomena, malls anchored by large chain stores and franchise food outlets, drew clientele from wide areas, forcing many neighborhood businesses to close, while television sealed the fate of the local movie house and local newspaper. Small manufacturing plants also closed, and more breadwinners had to travel longer distances to work, often by auto. As neighborhood populations aged, their schools and churches struggled to survive.

The disintegration of neighborhoods affected the fate of Chicago's Democratic machine, which had begun the postwar years in a swirl of scandals that ended the fourteen-year mayoralty of Edward J. Kelly. His successor, Martin H. Kennelly, a moving-and-storage company executive, presented enough of a good-government image to hold the organization together while planners were laying out the expressway and urban renewal programs, but in 1955 the aloof incumbent found himself ousted by the city clerk, Richard J. Daley. Promising greater emphasis on neighborhood and family concerns, the new mayor kept the machine alive for the next twenty-one years, in part because he functioned as a symbolic bulwark against change. His early years in office benefited

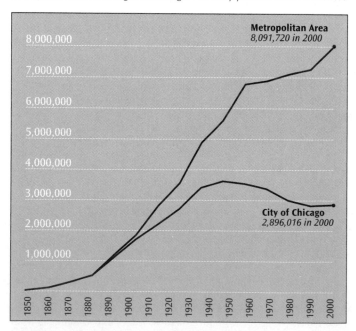

from the infusions of federal money that built O'Hare, the expressways, and a new water-filtration plant, and he adjusted the machine to reflect Chicago's changing ethnic and racial makeup—while critics charged that his moves were too slow and too limited. He even survived the charge of a "police riot" at the 1968 Democratic National Convention.

But Daley's ability to deliver the vote began to wane in the early 1970s, and the city's Democratic political organization was slowly unraveling when he died in office in 1976. Voters now paid more attention to the media than to their precinct captains, and middle-class African Americans felt alienated. A half century of political stability was replaced by a succession of five chief executives in just over twelve years. In 1979 a political maverick, Jane M. Byrne, upset Daley's machine successor, Michael A. Bilandic, but she, in turn, lost four years later to Chicago's first black mayor, Harold Washington, who proclaimed that the machine was dead. Washington's sudden death in November 1987 was followed by the interim mayoralty of Eugene Sawyer, who was defeated in a special election by Daley's son, Richard M. Daley. In 1989 Daley won a full term—but not as the head of the centralized, cohesive machine that had put his father in office.

The Birth of the Preservation Movement

The creation of the magnificent postwar skyline forced Chicagoans to deal with the constraints invariably imposed by each generation of urbanites on its successors. Should they destroy the institutional artifacts of earlier ages, modify them to conform to present needs, or preserve them as is? The earliest response was destruction. Federally funded urban renewal and land-clearance programs leveled entire neighborhoods, including churches, small businesses, and social institutions. Demolition occasionally had a specific intention, such as the clearance of the Hull

CHICAGO STOCK EXCHANGE BY ADLER & SULLIVAN (DEMOLISHED)

House area to build the Chicago campus of the University of Illinois (opened in 1965), but more often the land was left vacant for decades.

In the Loop the wrecker's ball was in the hands of private speculators who claimed many first-generation skyscrapers before Chicagoans began to realize that the demolished structures included some of the best examples of Chicago School architecture. In 1957 the City Council created a landmarks commission, but all it could do was issue plaques. Its inadequacy was underscored by the demolition of Adler & Sullivan's Schiller Building in 1960 and by its replacement with a parking structure whose facade parodied the lost classic. Nonetheless it took eight years before Chicago had a preservation law and a commission (now the Commission on Chicago Landmarks) empowered to administer it. The subsequent loss of Adler & Sullivan's Chicago Stock Exchange in 1972 and the McCarthy Building in 1990 demonstrated that the commission could do little more than delay demolition unless the City Council designated a building and enforced its decision. Meanwhile, the Landmarks Preservation Council of Illinois, the Chicago Architecture Foundation, the Chicago Chapter of the American Institute of Architects, neighborhood groups, and countless newspaper articles worked to foster a sense of pride in the city's physical heritage.

The Emergence of a Service Economy

A most significant postwar change was the gradual shift in employment from a preeminence of manufacturing to service-sector jobs. Although Chicago was still a leading industrial center, blue-collar jobs dropped by 77 percent between 1947 and 1982. By the early 1980s more employment dollars were earned in nonmanufacturing employment than in industry. Chicago's role as the nation's transportation hub, strengthened by O'Hare's steady growth, attracted corporate headquarters and research facilities, rekindling intense competition between the city center and periphery for buildings. The continued lure of lower taxes and quick access by expressway, combined with the available acreage on which to build horizontally oriented office parks, generated a new wave of exurban construction. One hub for this was the O'Hare area; another was the East-West Tollway between Oak Brook and Naperville. Even Sears, which had found the downtown so advantageous in 1974, moved in 1992 to a "campus" of low buildings in the northwestern suburbs.

The service-sector world, held together by silicon chips and fiber optics, is also potentially much more mobile than the industrial one. It is no easy task to move heavy equipment; outmoded factories, such as steel mills, are simply closed. But service businesses can be transferred

W. WACKER DR. IN 1964

quickly and constantly seek newer, more flexible spaces that can accommodate rapidly evolving office technology. This mobility has increased the competition for tenants in the downtown towers.

The most exciting result of Chicago's transition to a service economy has been the latest generation of downtown construction. Since the completion of the Sears Tower, well over 100 buildings have appeared in the central area. They represent a construction boom even greater than that of the Richard J. Daley years. On many of these buildings the Miesian frame box has yielded to shimmering glass and mirrors cast in curves and points. Michigan Ave.'s Magnificent Mile is the hub of a second downtown, an idea that had been promoted since the late 1940s by real estate mogul Arthur Rubloff.

Summary

Chicagoans have discovered the depth and variety of their architectural heritage. Not only has popular interest in downtown gems expanded, but the Tax Reform Act of 1981 sparked the interest of commercial developers who invested heavily in renovating historic buildings. Although these incentives were subsequently reduced, older neighborhoods have been rediscovered and rebuilt, and many old factories adjacent to downtown have been reborn as lofts and galleries.

There are negatives, of course, most notably in the loss of semipublic spaces in the Loop. Except for the waiting room at Union Station, the great railway depots are only memories. The vertical malls that draw crowds to the Magnificent Mile exemplify a new breed of semipublic space that seems to shield customers from the city rather than immerse them in it, as the Loop stores did. One of the most dramatic interior spaces of the type previously associated with department stores is a public one: the atrium of the James R. Thompson State of Illinois Center, which reinterprets the rotunda of a capitol building.

But cities change constantly, and in Chicago that is always cause for optimism. For if history proves anything about Chicago, the city will continue to find new ways to be a leader, both as a special place and as the quintessential American metropolis. Chicago is both a museum and a laboratory in which to observe how an agglomeration of peoples deploys the finite space within the city's borders and how architects respond to the challenge of designing for them. Chicago's story relates the triumphs and failures, the problems and prospects, of all American cities.

W. WACKER DR. IN 1992

Key to Maps

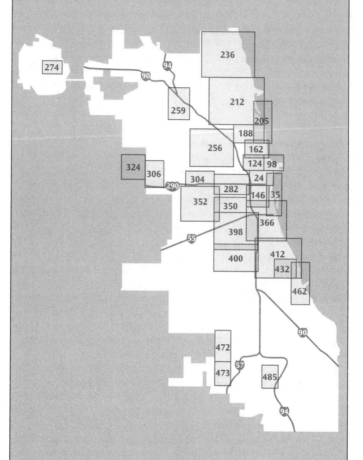

detailed feature maps are not shown on this key map

CENTRAL CITY

THE LOOP

NORTH MICHIGAN AVENUE | STREETERVILLE

RIVER NORTH

SOUTH LOOP

Loop West Area

158 One Financial Place
159 Chicago Board Options Exchange
160 LaSalle Atrium Bldg
161 Chicago Board of Trade Bldg
162 Federal Reserve Bank
163 Bank of America
164 The Rookery
165 208 S La Salle
166 190 S La Salle
167 135 S La Salle
168 120 S La Salle
169 Northern Trust Bldg
170 39 S La Salle
171 19 S La Salle
172 11 S La Salle
173 Chase Plaza
174 1 N La Salle
175 2 N La Salle
176 33 N La Salle
177 Savings of America Tower
178 Palace Theatre
179 State of Illinois Bldg
180 200 N La Salle
181 203 N La Salle
182 La Salle–Wacker Bldg
183 222 N La Salle
184 Reid-Murdoch Center
185 325 N Wells
186 Engineering Bldg
187 Century of Progress
188 CTA Lake/Wells entrance canopies
189 188 W Randolph
190 180 W Washington
191 "I Am" Temple
192 175 W Washington
193 Concord City Centre
194 212 W Washington
195 Washington Block
196 Hotel La Salle Garage
197 Madison Plaza
198 181 W Madison
199 205 W Monroe
200 CTA Quincy Station
201 Insurance Exchange Bldg
202 Dixon Bldg
203 Van Buren Bldg
204 Brooks Bldg
205 City Colleges Bldg
206 AT&T Corporate Center/USG Bldg

207 303 W Madison
208 1 N Franklin
209 225 W Washington
210 Bldg for White Estate
211 Bldg for Cole
212 Bldg for Rowney
213 Bldg for Kent
214 225 W Wacker
215 333 Wacker Drive
216 Merchandise Mart
217 Apparel Center
218 Riverbend
219 191 N Wacker
220 150 N Wacker
221 123 N Wacker
222 110 N Wacker
223 101 N Wacker
224 29 N Wacker
225 Civic Opera Bldg
226 UBS Tower
227 1 S Wacker
228 Chicago Mercantile Exchange Center
229 Hartford Plaza
230 200 S Wacker
231 Sears Tower
232 311 S Wacker
233 Exelon Plant
234 300 S Riverside
235 222 S Riverside
236 Union Station Multiplex
237 Union Station
238 10 S Riverside
239 120 S Riverside
240 525 W Monroe
241 Heller International Tower
242 2 N Riverside Plaza
243 Citicorp Center
244 River Center
245 165 N Canal
246 100 N Riverside
247 Ogilvie Transp Center
248 North Western Terminal Powerhouse
249 Clinton St Lofts
250 Burlington Bldg
251 550 W Jackson
252 IIT–Kent College of Law
253 Glessner Center
254 Presidential Towers
255 Washington Social Security Center
256 ABN–AMRO Plaza
257 St Patrick's

Hubbard

Kinzie

Fulton

Lake

Randolph

Washington

Madison

Monroe

Adams

Jackson

Van Buren

Harrison

Desplaines

Jefferson

249

256

255

254

253

257

252

Eisenhower Expwy   I-290

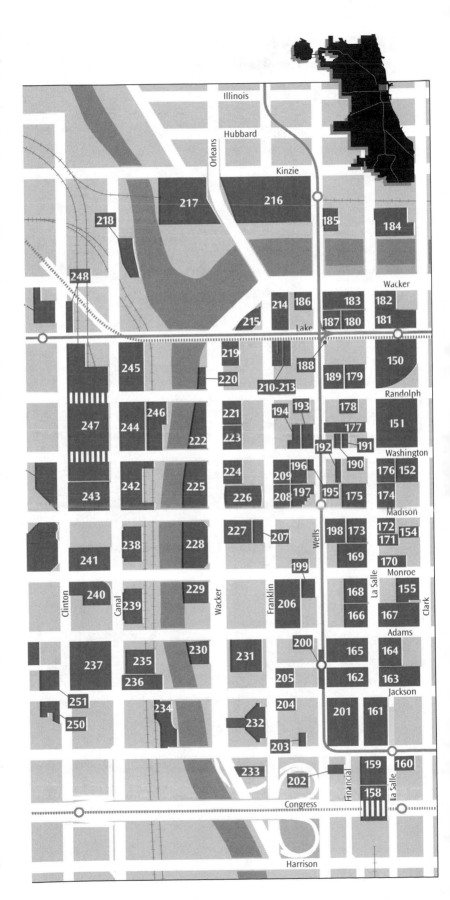

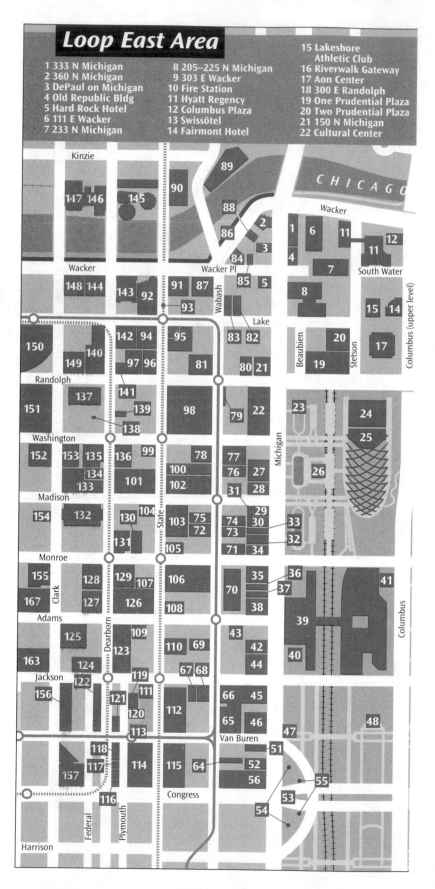

Loop East Area

1 333 N Michigan
2 360 N Michigan
3 DePaul on Michigan
4 Old Republic Bldg
5 Hard Rock Hotel
6 111 E Wacker
7 233 N Michigan

8 205–225 N Michigan
9 303 E Wacker
10 Fire Station
11 Hyatt Regency
12 Columbus Plaza
13 Swissôtel
14 Fairmont Hotel

15 Lakeshore
   Athletic Club
16 Riverwalk Gateway
17 Aon Center
18 300 E Randolph
19 One Prudential Plaza
20 Two Prudential Plaza
21 150 N Michigan
22 Cultural Center

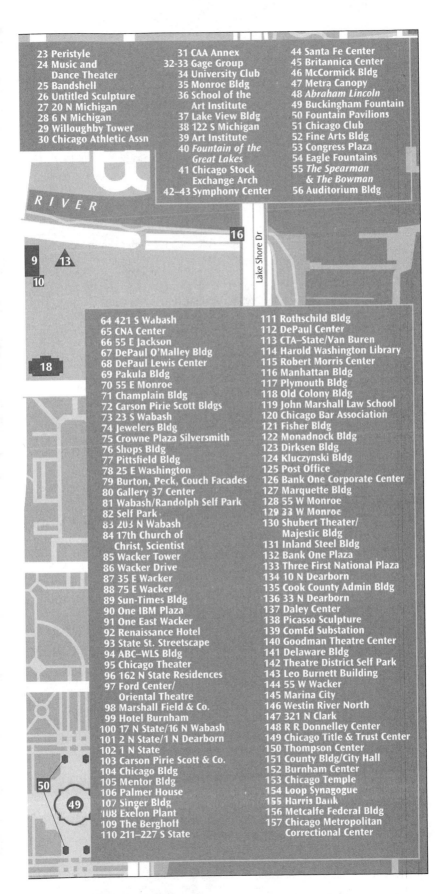

23 Peristyle
24 Music and Dance Theater
25 Bandshell
26 Untitled Sculpture
27 20 N Michigan
28 6 N Michigan
29 Willoughby Tower
30 Chicago Athletic Assn

31 CAA Annex
32-33 Gage Group
34 University Club
35 Monroe Bldg
36 School of the Art Institute
37 Lake View Bldg
38 122 S Michigan
39 Art Institute
40 *Fountain of the Great Lakes*
41 Chicago Stock Exchange Arch
42–43 Symphony Center

44 Santa Fe Center
45 Britannica Center
46 McCormick Bldg
47 Metra Canopy
48 *Abraham Lincoln*
49 Buckingham Fountain
50 Fountain Pavilions
51 Chicago Club
52 Fine Arts Bldg
53 Congress Plaza
54 Eagle Fountains
55 *The Spearman & The Bowman*
56 Auditorium Bldg

RIVER

16

Lake Shore Dr

9
13
10

18

64 421 S Wabash
65 CNA Center
66 55 E Jackson
67 DePaul O'Malley Bldg
68 DePaul Lewis Center
69 Pakula Bldg
70 55 E Monroe
71 Champlain Bldg
72 Carson Pirie Scott Bldgs
73 23 S Wabash
74 Jewelers Bldg
75 Crowne Plaza Silversmith
76 Shops Bldg
77 Pittsfield Bldg
78 25 E Washington
79 Burton, Peck, Couch Facades
80 Gallery 37 Center
81 Wabash/Randolph Self Park
82 Self Park
83 203 N Wabash
84 17th Church of Christ, Scientist
85 Wacker Tower
86 Wacker Drive
87 35 E Wacker
88 75 E Wacker
89 Sun-Times Bldg
90 One IBM Plaza
91 One East Wacker
92 Renaissance Hotel
93 State St. Streetscape
94 ABC–WLS Bldg
95 Chicago Theater
96 162 N State Residences
97 Ford Center/ Oriental Theatre
98 Marshall Field & Co.
99 Hotel Burnham
100 17 N State/16 N Wabash
101 2 N State/1 N Dearborn
102 1 N State
103 Carson Pirie Scott & Co.
104 Chicago Bldg
105 Mentor Bldg
106 Palmer House
107 Singer Bldg
108 Exelon Plant
109 The Berghoff
110 211–227 S State

111 Rothschild Bldg
112 DePaul Center
113 CTA–State/Van Buren
114 Harold Washington Library
115 Robert Morris Center
116 Manhattan Bldg
117 Plymouth Bldg
118 Old Colony Bldg
119 John Marshall Law School
120 Chicago Bar Association
121 Fisher Bldg
122 Monadnock Bldg
123 Dirksen Bldg
124 Kluczynski Bldg
125 Post Office
126 Bank One Corporate Center
127 Marquette Bldg
128 55 W Monroe
129 33 W Monroe
130 Shubert Theater/ Majestic Bldg
131 Inland Steel Bldg
132 Bank One Plaza
133 Three First National Plaza
134 10 N Dearborn
135 Cook County Admin Bldg
136 33 N Dearborn
137 Daley Center
138 Picasso Sculpture
139 ComEd Substation
140 Goodman Theatre Center
141 Delaware Bldg
142 Theatre District Self Park
143 Leo Burnett Building
144 55 W Wacker
145 Marina City
146 Westin River North
147 321 N Clark
148 R R Donnelley Center
149 Chicago Title & Trust Center
150 Thompson Center
151 County Bldg/City Hall
152 Burnham Center
153 Chicago Temple
154 Loop Synagogue
155 Harris Bank
156 Metcalfe Federal Bldg
157 Chicago Metropolitan Correctional Center

50
49

THE LOOP

THE LOOP IS QUINTESSENTIAL CHICAGO! HERE THE "CITY OF BIG SHOULDERS" flaunts its continuing vitality with an unequaled display of dazzling towers and crowded streets. Jammed with a medley of cars, trucks, buses, and darting pedestrians, the Loop is an urban canvas framed by its famous "El." It is home to banks, national and international corporate headquarters, stock and commodities trading centers, and a myriad of shops, restaurants, and other support services.

The small tongue of land on which the Loop is situated, bounded by Lake Michigan on the east and the Chicago River on the north and west, determined not only the shape but also the nature of Chicago's downtown, for it demanded the utmost in concentration. Land for efficient corporate enterprise was at such a premium here that almost all other competing uses—factories, residences, civic institutions, and cultural facilities—were soon priced out of the area. The dynamics of American business required that the successful businessman be on the scene, close to where "the action" was. Thus, the second half of the nineteenth century in the Loop witnessed an increasing concentration of fewer and fewer businesses and support functions crowded into congested streets. Even before the Great Fire of 1871, Chicago's downtown had become a business hub. Horse-drawn omnibuses, introduced on State St. in 1859, laid the groundwork for a network of transit lines to serve a commuter population.

The Fire of 1871 reinforced these tendencies. The gridded streets of pre-Fire downtown were re-created as the most efficient pattern for the rapid development of business and commerce. Chicago's "new" downtown would provide little space for parks, churches, or recreational facilities, and none at all for residences. The 1880s saw the introduction of cable car lines, which, circling part of the downtown area, gave that area the name "Loop." The term was firmly fixed when the Union Loop Elevated Railway was completed in 1897.

Technology stood ready in that same decade to generate a forest of office towers. The safety elevator, the telegraph and telephone, the flush toilet, the modern coal furnace—all already existed. Construction methods using iron and then steel developed rapidly, as well as revolutionary foundation techniques to anchor the new skyscraper city firmly to the ground.

So rapid, indeed, were these developments that some historians have posited a whole new architecture—the Chicago School—that they claim emerged in the Loop from the early 1880s to 1910. They suggest that this architecture, direct, pragmatic, and ahistorical, rests upon the pioneering efforts of designers like Burnham & Root, Holabird & Roche, William Le Baron Jenney, and, perhaps most notably, Louis H. Sullivan. The dictum attributed to Sullivan, "Form follows function," encapsulates the school's aesthetic and characterizes its importance as a forerunner of modernism.

More recently, some critics have challenged the concept of a "Chicago School," noting that many of its designs are neither functionalist nor ahistorical. Though Sullivan had suggested the elimination of architectural ornament to the young Viennese architect Adolf Loos when the latter visited Chicago in 1893, he himself certainly did not follow his own advice.

Perhaps the wisest way to resolve this controversy is by reverting to a term frequently used a century ago: Chicago construction. The great Chicago architects devised less a new architecture than a new means of creating it—efficient, cost-effective, and speedy. The Reliance Building, for example, whose glassy facade is often hailed as the prototype of the glass curtain-wall skyscraper, was praised in the 1890s for the rapidity with which its steel frame was erected, and for the practicality of its washable terra-cotta sheathing. The speed with which Chicago's architects adopted a new and changing technology can be demonstrated in the shift from almost full bearing-wall construction in the 1891 or northern portion of the Monadnock Building to the almost full skeletal construction of its 1893 or southern section.

Chicago designers maintained a sense of decorum or "keeping" in their works. Martin Roche could design a simple, straightforward loft building, the Great Lakes Building, in 1910, the verticals and horizontals of its skeletal frame neatly and modestly encased in brick and clearly expressed on its facades. That year he also designed the lavishly ornamented Monroe Building, whose gabled roof and facades sheathed in terra-cotta reflected the building's more prestigious location and "higher calling" as an office building.

Today's movement toward decentralization, ever more efficient transportation and communication, and the suburbanization of the white-collar class are again changing the future of the Loop. After decades of confinement within the "old" Loop, business has burst these bonds, and new "downtowns" are springing up to the north and west of the old central city. Some planners suggest that these movements spell the inevitable demise of the Loop as Chicago's hub. Others envision a new and more variegated life for the area, pointing out that, for the first time in well over a century, residential construction is once more under way in the Loop. Major State St. retail stores have spent millions to remodel and update their facilities, and new retail outlets have begun to appear. Cultural and educational institutions have expanded and remodeled, revivifying sections of the Loop. Despite the inevitable changes that will continue to confront Chicago's Loop, there is little doubt that it will remain an impressive urbanistic symbol. Those who have doubts about the Loop's vitality are invited to stand at the foot of La Salle St. on the morning of an active market day. They'll need no further convincing!

—ROBERT F. IRVING

1 | 333 N. Michigan Ave.

1928, HOLABIRD & ROOT

Its pronounced verticality, spare lines, and dramatic setbacks were inspired by Eliel Saarinen's second-prize entry in the 1922 Chicago Tribune Tower Competition. The polished marble base and stylized bands of ornament are the only embellishments on this elegant limestone tower. Low reliefs by Fred M. Torrey depict pioneers, traders, hunters, and Native Americans at Fort Dearborn, which occupied part of this site.

2 | 360 N. Michigan Ave. (London Guarantee & Accident Building)

1923, ALFRED S. ALSCHULER
2001, RENOVATION AND LOBBY RESTORATION, LOHAN ASSOCS.

The river's bend dictated the building's unusual shape, which provides a graceful forecourt. The neo-Classical ornament includes a triumphal-arch entry with colossal Corinthian columns, a second rank of columns in a three-story top, and a crowning belvedere. The lobby and grand entrance were meticulously re-created in 2001.

360 N. MICHIGAN AVE.

HARD ROCK HOTEL
(CARBIDE & CARBON BUILDING)

3| DePaul on Michigan
320 N. Michigan Ave.
1983, BOOTH HANSEN ASSOCIATES

This stylish infill building was designed for residences but was leased as offices before finding its niche as a dormitory. Concrete was shaped into moldings, curves, and capitals on the main facade and expresses the building's structural grid on the sides.

4| Old Republic Building
(*Bell Building*)
307 N. Michigan Ave.
1925, VITZTHUM & BURNS

Classicism is stressed throughout, from the beige granite base with its triumphal-arch entrance through the cream terra-cotta shaft and colonnaded top.

5| Hard Rock Hotel
(*Carbide & Carbon Building*)
230 N. Michigan Ave.
1929, BURNHAM BROS.
2003, CONVERSION TO HOTEL,
LUCIEN LAGRANGE ARCHITECTS

The most beautiful skyscraper on this stretch of N. Michigan Ave. is decidedly Art Deco in massing and detail. The polished granite base has a black marble and bronze entrance, ornamented with delicate grillework. The dark green and gold terra-cotta shaft rises without horizontal cornices or projections to a fifty-foot tower trimmed with gold leaf.

Illinois Center
Bounded by the Chicago River, N. Lake Shore Dr., N. Michigan Ave. (excluding 151, 333 & 307 N. Michigan Ave.), and E. Lake St.
MASTER PLAN BEGUN 1967,
LUDWIG MIES VAN DER ROHE

6| 111 E. Wacker Dr.
(*One Illinois Center*)
1970, OFFICE OF MIES VAN DER ROHE

7| 233 N. Michigan Ave.
(*Two Illinois Center*)
1973, OFFICE OF MIES VAN DER ROHE

8| 205–225 N. Michigan Ave.
1981, FUJIKAWA, CONTERATO, LOHAN & ASSOCS.; 1985, FUJIKAWA, JOHNSON & ASSOCS.

9| 303 E. Wacker Dr.
1980, FUJIKAWA, CONTERATO, LOHAN & ASSOCS.

10| Fire Station
259 N. Columbus Dr.
1982, FUJIKAWA, CONTERATO, LOHAN & ASSOCS.

11| Hyatt Regency Chicago
151 E. Wacker Dr.
1974, WEST TOWER; 1980, EAST TOWER AND ATRIUM LOBBY, A. EPSTEIN & SONS

12| Columbus Plaza
233 E. Wacker Dr.
1980, FUJIKAWA, CONTERATO, LOHAN & ASSOCS.

This mixed-use development, one of the nation's largest, is a densely packed mixed bag of colors, materials, and styles, built to a colossal scale around dark, cramped plazas. Development of the eighty-three-acre site, which uses air rights over former Illinois Central Gulf Railroad tracks, has followed the original plan for a self-contained city of offices, shops, apartments, and hotels. Master planning in this case seems to have been a euphemism for a means of squeezing the highest density onto the land. There is no hierarchy of buildings or spaces, just a thicket of structures competing for land, light, and—in the postmodern era—visual dominance. A trilevel street system segregates service vehicles, arterial traffic, and local traffic; dreary and confusing pedestrian concourses link most of the buildings.

The urbanistic amenities are nil; the project lacks even a meaningful relationship to the river. Architectural discord has been the rule from the early days of construction, when the Miesian steel-and-glass towers of One and Two Illinois Center were made to share their site with the clunky, brick-faced Hyatt Regency hotel. One of Mies's successor firms, Fujikawa, Conterato, Lohan & Assocs., has stayed remarkably faithful to the original design aesthetic—for better or worse—in its office buildings, while compounding the visual incoherence of Wacker Dr. with the concrete Columbus Plaza apartment building. They did, however, provide a small grace note of Miesian modernism in the fire station at the base of 303 E. Wacker Dr.

The last major piece of land, southeast of Columbus and Wacker Drs., was christened Lakeshore East and began to be developed in 2002. The award-winning master plan by Skidmore, Owings & Merrill groups town houses and high rises (residential as well as commercial) around a five-acre public park that had been promised decades earlier when Illinois Center was created.

**13| Swissôtel Chicago
(Swiss Grand Hotel)
323 E. Wacker Dr.**
1989, HARRY WEESE & ASSOCS.

Wrapped in alternating bands of opaque and reflective glass, the tower reiterates the triangular massing of Weese's Metropolitan Correctional Center.

**14| Fairmont Hotel
200 N. Columbus Dr.**
1987, HELLMUTH, OBATA & KASSABAUM; FUJIKAWA, JOHNSON & ASSOCS., ASSOC. ARCHS.

The towered top and pink granite walls offer a deliberate contrast to the surrounding austerity.

**15| Lakeshore Athletic Club
211 N. Stetson Ave.**
1990, KISHO KUROKAWA; FUJIKAWA, JOHNSON & ASSOCS., ASSOC. ARCHS.

This small building, the nation's first by Japanese architect Kurokawa, is the gem of the Illinois Center complex. The white-painted steel frame and window mullions are scaled to elements of traditional Japanese wooden buildings. The quartet of steel-frame rooftop towers pay homage to the towers of Louis H. Sullivan's People's Savings Bank (1911) in Cedar Rapids, Iowa. They also mark a dramatic interior space that extends an additional three stories below Stetson Ave.: a six-story skylit atrium with a curving staircase and a 100-foot rock-climbing wall.

**16| Riverwalk Gateway
S. bank of the Chicago River underneath N. Lake Shore Dr.**
2000, SKIDMORE, OWINGS & MERRILL

This previously menacing walkway is now a true urban amenity. The pleasant passageway under Lake Shore Dr., for pedestrians and cyclists only, features a series of tile murals by artist Ellen Lanyon illustrating highlights of Chicago history. Lantern-topped towers echo the Art Deco motifs of the 1930s bridge above.

17 | Aon Center
(Standard Oil Building)
200 E. Randolph St.
1973, EDWARD DURELL STONE; PERKINS & WILL, ASSOC. ARCHS.

1994, PLAZA RENOVATIONS, VOY MADEYSKI ARCHITECTS

Chicago's second-tallest building was originally the world's tallest marble-clad structure but is now most famous—or notorious—as a colossal failure of building technology. In order to sheathe the eighty-two-story skyscraper, the architect and the client depleted the Carrara marble quarry that had served Michelangelo. Perhaps in retribution for their hubris, the slabs began to buckle at the southeast corner. Cut as thin as permitted by then-new methods, the material was unable to withstand extremes of temperature. Total recladding was the only solution; from 1990 to 1992, the marble was replaced by thicker slabs of speckled North Carolina granite.

With a new skin that is matte rather than glossy, the building's banality is even more pronounced. Structurally, it is a long hollow tube. The V-shaped perimeter columns house pipes and utility lines and allow column-free interiors.

18 | 300 E. Randolph St.
1997, LOHAN ASSOCS.

The thirty-two-story building was designed to accommodate an unprecedented vertical expansion of twenty-two floors so that the client could grow without relocating. An interior atrium breaks up the large rectangular floor plates and will facilitate the addition of elevator banks.

19 | One Prudential Plaza
(Prudential Building)
130 E. Randolph St.
1955, NAESS & MURPHY

Although lacking their soaring verticality, this limestone and aluminum-clad skyscraper looks back to the towers of the 1920s rather than emulating the steel-and-glass curtain walls coming into favor after World War II. Construction ended a twenty-year hiatus in major downtown building and created what was then Chicago's tallest building, complete with observation deck. The first project to use the air rights of the Illinois Central Railroad yards, it established a pattern for developers. The enormous sculpted relief of Prudential's trademark Rock of Gibraltar is by Frank Lloyd Wright collaborator Alfonso Iannelli.

20 | Two Prudential Plaza
180 N. Stetson Ave.
1990, LOEBL, SCHLOSSMAN & HACKL

With its soaring spire and chevroned top, Two Pru seems determined to compensate for its earlier neighbor's modesty. Although the architects cite the Chrysler Building as design inspiration, a closer parallel can be found in the work of Helmut Jahn, especially his One Liberty Place in Philadelphia (1987) and his unbuilt 1982 design for the Bank of the Southwest Tower in Houston. The best feature is the landscaped plaza to the northwest, which leads to an atrium lobby serving both Prudential buildings.

21 | 150 N. Michigan Ave.
1984, A. EPSTEIN & SONS

Ten more floors would be needed for the height to balance the overwhelming slice cut through the top. The light color and aggressive orientation command attention, but the proportions and detailing are a disappointment. Yaacov Agam's colorful sculpture Communication X9 promises less and delivers more.

22 | Chicago Cultural Center
(*Chicago Public Library*)
78 E. Washington St.
1897, SHEPLEY, RUTAN & COOLIDGE
1977 AND 1993, RENOVATIONS, HOLABIRD & ROOT

This latter-day Renaissance palace belongs to an illustrious family of civic and social institutions that grace Michigan Ave. and Grant Park. The spur to the founding of a free public library for the city came, ironically, from the Fire of 1871. Responding to the devastation, British sympathizers sent over 8,000 books, many of them autographed by such noted donors as Disraeli, Carlyle, Tennyson, and even Queen Victoria. To circulate the "English book donation," the Chicago Public Library was established in 1872 and temporarily housed in an old water tank, while the board sought a permanent site in Dearborn Park, a remnant of the Fort Dearborn military outpost. Contending for the same parcel was a Civil War veterans' organization. A compromise reached in 1891 permitted the erection of a public library that contained a memorial hall dedicated to the Grand Army of the Republic.

The commission was awarded to the Boston-based successors to the practice of Henry Hobson Richardson, the firm of Shepley, Rutan &

CHICAGO CULTURAL CENTER—EXTERIOR

CHICAGO CULTURAL CENTER—INTERIOR

Coolidge, which was then completing the Art Institute. Responsibility for designing and testing the foundation went to engineer William Sooy Smith; to this day there has been no appreciable settlement. The library board stipulated that the new building should "convey to the beholder the idea that it is an enduring monument worthy of a great and public-spirited city." To fulfill this dictum the final design was an amalgam of Italian Renaissance, Greek, and neo-Grec elements executed in Bedford limestone and granite.

The interior decoration is of majestic splendor, realized in rare marble, fine hardwood, stained glass, and polished bronze. Most sumptuous of all is the jewel-like luster of the cosmati work: mosaics of Favrile glass, colored stone, mother-of-pearl, and gold leaf inlaid in white marble. The mosaics and marble were practical as well, durable against the onslaught of Chicago's sooty air. Among the more interesting motifs are Renaissance printers' marks and quotations in ten languages. Robert C. Spencer, Jr., later famed as a Prairie School architect, designed the mosaics, which were executed by Tiffany-trained J. L. Holzer.

In 1977 the building was renovated and modernized into a cultural center. It remains emblematic of Chicago in the 1890s when, eager to no longer be identified solely for meat-packing and merchandising, the city sought to secure its status as a sophisticated and culturally conscious metropolis.　　　　　　　　　　　—MEREDITH TAUSSIG

Grant Park and Burnham Park
Between Michigan Ave. and Lake Michigan,
from Randolph St. to Roosevelt Rd.
1909, D. H. BURNHAM
1915–1930, BENNETT, PARSONS, FROST & THOMAS AND PREDECESSORS

Though the land along the lakefront east of Michigan Ave. was among the first to be designated as public land, what is now Grant Park has been a work-in-progress for over a century and a half. Chicago's formal front garden was created from sandbars, landfill, and Chicago Fire debris and was shaped by the guiding visions of the 1893 World's Columbian Exposition and the 1909 Plan of Chicago. Its origins as a public space date from 1835 when federal land was given to the Illinois & Michigan Canal commissioners to be platted and sold to help fund the canal's construction. In response to concerned residents, space was set aside for a town common on the lakeshore. The commissioners wrote on their 1836 map, on the space defined by Michigan Ave. and the lake, Randolph St., and what is now 11th St., "Public Ground—A Common to Remain Forever Open, Clear and Free of any Buildings, or Other Obstruction whatever." The public ground was named Lake Park in 1847, but wave action caused continual erosion of the undeveloped site. In 1852 the Illinois Central Railroad offered to build a stone break-water in the lake, in exchange for an easement permitting the construction of an offshore trestle as far north as the mouth of the Chicago River. Sand, which accumulated in the lagoon created by the break-water, was augmented by the unofficial dumping of garbage and rubble from the Fire of 1871.

In 1861 the state legislature had passed a law confirming the establishment of Lake Park and requiring the consent of all adjacent property owners for any encroachments on the public ground. Nearly thirty years later, however, the park contained little more than squatters' shacks, two federal armories, and refuse awaiting removal by train. In 1890 Aaron Montgomery Ward, creator of the mail-order business with headquarters at Michigan Ave. near Madison St., brought a lawsuit to force the City to clean up and improve the site. At this time, planning for the World's Columbian Exposition was under way; so, too, were plans for

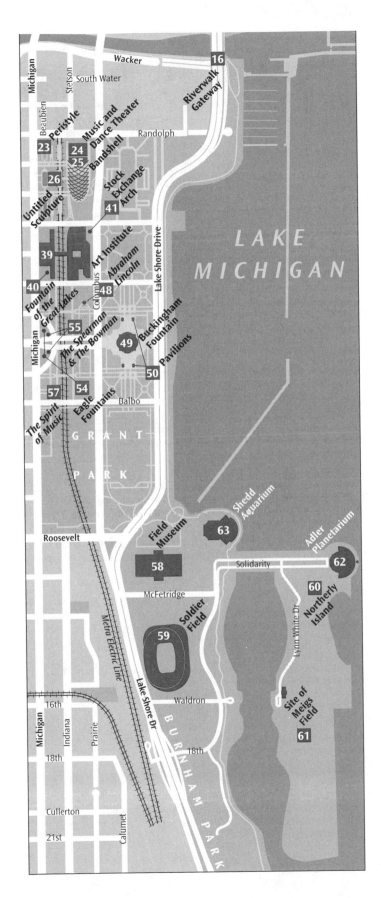

GRANT PARK BEFORE THE CREATION OF CONGRESS DR.

a new Art Institute, which had outgrown its home on the west side of Michigan Ave. at Van Buren St. A park site was proposed for the museum and approved by adjacent property owners. After the fair, Daniel Burnham began to develop his visions for the park, which included civic and cultural institutions, with the Field Museum at its center. These plans were included in the 1909 Plan of Chicago. The Olmsted Brothers were also involved in developing Burnham's vision, but ultimately their plans were not followed. At this point Ward initiated a series of lawsuits to prevent further construction in the park, which had been taken over by the South Park Commission and renamed Grant Park in 1901. In 1911 the Illinois Supreme Court ruled in Ward's favor. Frequently vilified as an impediment to progress by newspaper editorials and fellow businessmen, he never wavered in his fight to protect the park "for the poor people of Chicago, not for the millionaires."

Burnham's vision of a formal Beaux Arts plan was ultimately the guideline for future development of the park, though without the buildings. In an agreement with the Illinois Central Railroad in 1911, the South Park Commission was able to gain rights to an area south of the existing park. Landfill extended the park south, for the new Field Museum site. This extension was also the connection to Burnham's vision of a linear park, also built on landfill, which would extend south to Jackson Park. Due to additional legal issues, work on the future Burnham Park did not begin until the early 1920s. In further cooperation with the commission and the City, the Illinois Central also agreed to electrify its trains and depress its tracks below street level to minimize its presence.

In 1915 Edward H. Bennett, who had helped Burnham create the 1909 Plan, was retained by the South Park Commission to take charge of Grant Park. In 1924 the commission adopted a comprehensive plan for the park, and the following year philanthropist Kate Buckingham provided funds for a centerpiece in the form of Buckingham Fountain. Work on the park progressed through the 1920s, and significant improvements, including further landfill in Burnham Park, were also made in anticipation of the 1933–1934 World's Fair. In 1934 Grant Park came under the auspices of the newly consolidated Chicago Park District. Over the next few years, the Park District added major plantings, including the flowering crab apples and lilacs. With WPA funding, projects such as the Outer Dr. bridge over the river were designed in the Art Deco style.

As envisioned and developed, the park is a series of symmetrical spaces, or "rooms," defined by paths and plantings, with small enclosed spaces for passive recreation and large open areas for active pursuits. Allées of trees define promenades, and sculptures and fountains create focal points for vistas. The heart of the park is Buckingham Fountain, situated on the main east–west axis at Congress Dr.

Since the 1950s, changes to the park have, for the most part, reinforced the original plan. One glaring exception took place in 1955 when Congress Pkwy. was widened and extended through the park, destroying Congress Plaza and its grand stairway. Green space was incrementally increased with the construction of underground garages between the 1950s and 1970s and the 1986 realignment of Lake Shore Dr. at the northeast corner of the park. Daley Bicentennial Plaza (1976) added an ice rink and a bermed field house under Randolph St.

In the 1990s major improvements have greatly increased park space and moved toward Burnham's vision of a continuous green lakefront. In the early part of the decade, after some thirty years of planning, the City announced its intention to relocate the northbound lanes of Lake Shore Dr. to the west of the Field Museum, opening up a landscaped Museum Campus. Work associated with the Soldier Field addition has added green space by eliminating additional surface parking. These projects have strengthened the connection of Burnham Park and the Museum Campus to Grant Park. At the park's opposite end, one of the last unimproved areas, an open pit of railroad tracks and surface parking, has been covered and the park extended to Randolph St. through the creation of Millennium Park. The design of this latest extension began in the late 1990s and includes indoor and outdoor theaters. A Master Plan for Grant Park has been developed to properly locate a large venue performance area, recreational fields, and popular large outdoor festivals to best preserve the character of Chicago's lakefront garden. —JOAN POMARANC AND KATHLEEN NAGLE

Millennium Park
Between Michigan Ave.
and Columbus Dr., from
Randolph St. to Monroe St.
1999–2005, SKIDMORE, OWINGS &
MERRILL AND CHICAGO DEPT. OF
TRANS. LANDSCAPE: TERRY GUEN
DESIGN ASSOCS. AND CAROL J. H.
YETKEN, LANDSCAPE ARCHITECTS

The last major extension of Grant Park, Millennium Park extends the history of Grant Park development into the twenty-first century. One of the largest public projects in the city in years, the twenty-four-and-a-half-acre park reclaims an area that was until recently occupied by train tracks, right-of-ways, and surface parking, all on land leased by the City to the Illinois Central Railroad. It also involved removing and replacing the N. Grant Park garage and the park above it. Originally intended to be completed for the millennium, this complex undertaking, requiring construction over active commuter rail lines and a new parking garage, was pushed a few years into the new century.

The design of the park attempts to straddle the centuries as well. Along Michigan Ave., architectural elements are consistent with the nineteenth-century Beaux Arts vision of Grant Park. The Peristyle, McCormick Tribune Ice Rink (2001, OWP&P), railings, balustrades, and plantings are all a continuation, and in some cases replication, of existing park features. To the east, however, the theater, outdoor pavilion, Monroe Garden (Gustafson Partners, Ltd., Piet Oudolf, Robert Israel), and sculptures employ forms more consistent with the new millennium, within the framework of Beaux Arts planning.

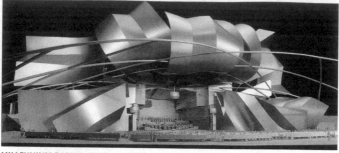

MILLENNIUM PARK BANDSHELL

**23| Millennium Monument
in Wrigley Square
(*Peristyle*)
Michigan Ave. and Randolph St.**
2002, OWP&P (ORIGINAL PERISTYLE
1917–1953, EDWARD H. BENNETT)

The semicircle of paired Doric
columns is a nearly full-scale
version of the original. The first
Peristyle occupied the site until
it was demolished to make way
for the N. Grant Park parking
garage. Details of the pool and
base have been altered for ac-
cessibility and donor inscriptions, and the new version
is in limestone rather than the
original concrete.

**24| Joan W. and Irving B. Harris
Theater for Music and Dance
205 E. Randolph St.**
2003, HAMMOND BEEBY RUPERT
AINGE, INC.

In keeping with the century-
old desire for Grant Park to be
"forever open, clear and free,"
this theater is primarily buried
under landscaped terraces,
except for a simple two-story
precast concrete and glass
entrance lobby on upper Randolph. The 1,500-seat theater
houses 12 midsize, local music
and dance companies. Backstage facilities are shared with
the outdoor music pavilion to
the south.

**25| Outdoor Music Pavilion,
Trellis, and Pedestrian Bridge
Columbus Dr. and Randolph St.,
immediately south of the Music
and Dance Theater**
2004, FRANK O. GEHRY & ASSOCS.,
INC.; SKIDMORE, OWINGS & MERRILL,
ASSOC. ARCHS. AND ENGINEERS

Stainless-steel ribbons soar
and twist thirty-five to forty feet
above the pavilion. In his signature style, Gehry has created
an urban scale sculpture that
almost lifts off from the theater
buried in the earth. The pavilion backs up to the Music and
Dance Theater, whose backstage
facilities it shares, and faces an
oval lawn south of the fixed
seating area. The painted steel-
pipe "trellis" over the lawn distributes the sound system over
a 320- × 700-foot column-free
space.

Gehry's sinuous stainless-
steel-clad pedestrian bridge over
Columbus Dr. connects Millennium Park to the lakefront.

**26| Untitled Sculpture
Madison St. and Michigan Ave.**
2004, ANISH KAPOOR

The structure below had to be
specially engineered to carry
the 110-ton load of this 32-foot-
tall, 65-foot-long stainless-steel
sculpture, dubbed the "jelly
bean" before its arrival. The
highly polished and reflective
elliptical form is the Indian-
born Kapoor's first public work
in the United States.

**27| Illinois State Medical Society
(*Ward Building*)
20 N. Michigan Ave.**
1885, BEERS, CLAY & DUTTON;
1892, ADDITION, 1985 RENOVATION,
NAGLE, HARTRAY & ASSOCS.

A red brick, timber-frame warehouse for Montgomery Ward's catalog operations was converted into a modern office building sympathetic to its past.

28| 6 N. Michigan Ave. (*Montgomery Ward & Co. "Tower Building"*)

1899, RICHARD E. SCHMIDT
1923, FOUR-STORY ADDITION, HOLABIRD & ROCHE
1955, REMODELING, LOEBL, SCHLOSSMAN & BENNETT
2004, CONVERSION TO RESIDENCES, DESTEFANO AND PARTNERS

The design is attributed to Schmidt's employee Hugh M. G. Garden, who later became his partner. The firm's first major commission was much grander when new, when it sported a ten-story tower topped by a three-story pyramidal roof, tempietto, and an eighteen-foot gilded statue of *Diana*. Although the addition of four floors and the demolition of the tower (1947) have drastically altered the massing, interesting details such as plants, birds, and fish are still dimly visible through the dirt on the terra-cotta spandrels. Images of the long-lost *Diana* are on the bronze elevator doors.

29| Willoughby Tower
8 S. Michigan Ave.

1929, SAMUEL N. CROWEN & ASSOCS.

The graceful profile is complemented by the foyers and lobbies, with their spectacular green marble walls, rich bronze ornament, and strapwork ceilings.

30| Chicago Athletic Association Building
12 S. Michigan Ave.

1893, HENRY IVES COBB

31| Annex Building
71 E. Madison St.

1907, RICHARD E. SCHMIDT, GARDEN & MARTIN
1926, SEVEN-STORY ADDITION, RICHARD E. SCHMIDT, GARDEN & MARTIN

Built to impress the crowds that flocked to the World's Columbian Exposition of 1893, the building is a lavish display of Venetian Gothic inside and out. The far simpler annex suggests Chicago's own Prairie School.

Gage Group

32| Edson Keith and Theodore Ascher Buildings
24 & 30 S. Michigan Ave.

1899, HOLABIRD & ROCHE
1971, ASCHER BUILDING ADDITION, ALTMAN-SAICHEK ASSOCS.

33| Gage Building
18 S. Michigan Ave.

1899, HOLABIRD & ROCHE; FACADE, LOUIS H. SULLIVAN
1902, ADDITION, HOLABIRD & ROCHE
1986, RENOVATION, BOVINE GROUP, FOR AUBREY GREENBERG ASSOCS.

These steel-frame loft buildings were built on Michigan Ave. because of the unobstructed daylight needed for the millinery businesses that they housed. Clad in the red brick common to Chicago lofts, the two southern facades clearly express their framing systems. At the request of the Gage Brothers, the third facade was designed by Sullivan because they felt it would benefit their business. It is

18 S. MICHIGAN AVE. (GAGE BUILDING)

finished in buff terra-cotta and displays his philosophy that a skyscraper's design should express its height. He did this by presenting the facade as a hung curtain. Because the base, originally framed in foliate cast iron, hid the first-floor columns, the piers would have appeared to exert insupportable weight on the first-floor spandrel without the pair of "clasps" on the cornice.

34| University Club of Chicago
76 E. Monroe St.
1909, HOLABIRD & ROCHE

35| Monroe Building
104 S. Michigan Ave.
1912, HOLABIRD & ROCHE

The University Club's details recall the University of Chicago's Gothic inspirations. Inside are two multistory rooms, one of which features medieval hunt murals by Frederic Clay Bartlett. The height of the gabled Monroe Building was chosen to complement its neighbor. Step inside to see the vaulted lobby with its glazed Rookwood tile.

36| School of the Art Institute of Chicago
(*Illinois Athletic Club*)
112 S. Michigan Ave.
1908, BARNETT, HAYNES & BARNETT
1985, ADDITION, SWANN & WEISKOPF

MONROE BUILDING

The six-story limestone and glass addition was intended to complement the original but doesn't. Leon Harmant's frieze depicts Zeus presiding over athletic contests.

37| Lake View Building
(*Municipal Court Building*)
116 S. Michigan Ave.
1906, 1912, JENNEY, MUNDIE & JENSEN

This white terra-cotta pencil of a building was commissioned by Jacob L. Kesner to lease as courtrooms while City Hall was being demolished and rebuilt. When the City moved out, Kesner added four stories and a vaulted ceiling in the lobby to attract other tenants.

THE ART INSTITUTE OF CHICAGO—STOCK EXCHANGE ROOM

38| 122 S. Michigan Ave.
(*People's Gas Co.*)
1910, D. H. BURNHAM & CO.
1987, RESTORATION, ECKENHOFF
SAUNDERS ARCHITECTS

To keep the weight of the upper stories off the ornamental granite columns, steel cantilevers at the third floor transfer the load to an interior steel frame.

39| Art Institute of Chicago
Michigan Ave. at Adams St.
1893–1916, SHEPLEY, RUTAN
& COOLIDGE
ADDITIONS INCLUDE:
1901, RYERSON AND BURNHAM
LIBRARIES, SHEPLEY, RUTAN &
COOLIDGE
1924, MCKINLOCK COURT, COOLIDGE
& HODGDON
1926, GOODMAN THEATER, HOWARD
VAN DOREN SHAW
1958, FERGUSON BUILDING,
HOLABIRD & ROOT & BURGEE
1962, MORTON WING, SHAW, METZ &
ASSOCS.
1977, COLUMBUS DR. ADDITION
AND SCHOOL OF THE ART INSTITUTE,
SKIDMORE, OWINGS & MERRILL
1988, DANIEL F. & ADA L. RICE
BUILDING, HAMMOND, BEEBY &
BABKA
2001, FULLERTON HALL
RESTORATION, WEESE LANGLEY
WEESE; GILMORE, FRANZEN
ARCHITECTS

Along with the art treasures guarded by Edward Kemeys's famous bronze lions flanking the entrance (1894) are several special architectural spaces; a map available in the main lobby will guide your exploration. The restored lobby (1987, Office of John Vinci) is the museum's oldest and grandest space; atop the staircase (1910) is an exhibit of fragments of Chicago's architectural past. The Trading Room, salvaged from Adler & Sullivan's demolished Chicago Stock Exchange Building, was restored and installed in the Columbus Dr. addition in 1977 by the Office of John Vinci. Its virtuoso stenciling is one of the most lyrical examples of Sullivan's decorative talent.

McKinlock Court is an unexpected oasis, open for dining in the summer months. The neo-Classical Rice Building galleries and Tadao Ando's Japanese screen gallery are newer favorites. In 2001 the museum revealed schematic plans by Renzo Piano for a new wing at the northeast corner of their property, to be completed in 2007.

40| *Fountain of the Great Lakes*
Art Institute South Garden,
S. Michigan Ave. south of main
entrance
1913, LORADO TAFT; BASIN SHEPLEY,
RUTAN & COOLIDGE

This sculpture symbolically represents the five Great Lakes as they flow into each other. The modern garden by the Office of Dan Kiley (1962) provides a serene setting for the composition.

41| Chicago Stock Exchange Arch
Monroe St. and Columbus Dr.
1893, ADLER & SULLIVAN

This building fragment from the Chicago Stock Exchange Building (1893–1972) is the Wailing Wall of Chicago's preservation movement.

42| Symphony Center
(*Orchestra Hall*)
220 S. Michigan Ave.
1905, D. H. BURNHAM & CO.
1908, TOP-FLOOR ADDITION,
HOWARD VAN DOREN SHAW
1967, REMODELING, HARRY WEESE &
ASSOCS.
1981, REHABILITATION, SKIDMORE,
OWINGS & MERRILL
1997, RENOVATION AND NEW
CONSTRUCTION, SKIDMORE, OWINGS
& MERRILL

A member of the orchestra's board, Burnham encouraged efforts to acquire a hall of its own and, as owner of this land, was the logical choice for architect. The 1997 expansion created a narrow addition on Michigan Ave., the Arcade, which leads to a skylit rotunda that links all of the buildings: Orchestra Hall, the Education and Administration Wing on Adams, a single-story restaurant, and the new Artistic Support Wing, whose blank concrete facade is visible on Wabash Ave.

43| Symphony Center Education and Administration Wing
(*Chapin & Gore Bldg.*)
67 E. Adams St.
1904, RICHARD E. SCHMIDT AND HUGH M. G. GARDEN

The facade's unusual composition reflects the special retail, storage, and office needs of the client's liquor business. Between the retail base and the office stories are two storage floors, which needed a sturdier structure and less window space. The second- and third-floor windows are joined by ornamental spandrels that show Garden's adaptation of Louis H. Sullivan's geometric forms. The windows' width matches that of the central panes in the Chicago windows of the office floors, while a decorative terra-cotta frame expands the composition to the larger overall width. The incongruously stark upper floors originally had foliate capitals crowning the piers and a projecting cornice. This building is now part of Symphony Center.

44| Santa Fe Center
(*Railway Exchange Building*)
80 E. Jackson Blvd./224 S. Michigan Ave.
1904, D. H. BURNHAM & CO.
1985, RENOVATION, METZ, TRAIN & YOUNGREN AND FRYE GILLAN & MOLINARO

A building around a light well, a form common to Daniel H. Burnham's work from the mid-1880s onward, received an undulating white-glazed terra-cotta skin, oriel bays, and a top floor of distinctive porthole windows. As in the Rookery, there is a two-story covered court at the base of the light well dominated by a grand staircase. In the renovation a new skylight

SANTA FE CENTER

was placed at the top, and the light well's inner walls were opened up. The building housed Daniel H. Burnham's offices, where the 1909 Plan of Chicago was worked out and a decade of buildings were planned.

45| Britannica Center
(*Straus Building*)
310 S. Michigan Ave.
1924, GRAHAM, ANDERSON, PROBST & WHITE

This was the first building to take advantage of Chicago's 1923 zoning ordinance, which permitted the erection of occupied towers above 260 feet if setback provisions were satisfied. In most other ways the main block is a variant of the firm's La Salle St. banking buildings, which featured second-story banking floors behind Classical facades. Behind the tall windows was the elegant banking floor of the investment firm of S. W. Straus & Co. The glass beehive atop the pyramidal roof symbolized industry and thrift and originally housed a directional beacon signifying the company's global reach.

46| 330–332 S. Michigan Ave.
(*McCormick Building*)
1910, 1912 (NORTHERN EXPANSION), HOLABIRD & ROCHE

Although dismissed by *Architectural Record* as "not calculated to attract remark," the

McCormick Building is one of the firm's more prominent and solidly designed office buildings. Its windows are punched out uniformly across a neutral facade, in a negation of the steel frame. The Michigan Ave. site, where legislation ensured that no building would ever block the light, allowed exceptionally deep offices.

47| Metra Entrance Canopy
Northeast corner of Van Buren St. and Michigan Ave.
2002

The entrance to this commuter station is a cast-iron replica of an Art Nouveau Parisian Métro station, cast from molds of an original designed by Hector Guimard in the early twentieth century. It is part of a gift exchange between Paris and Chicago, organized by the Union League Club of Chicago.

48| *Abraham Lincoln ("The Seated Lincoln") Court of the Presidents*
Between Columbus Dr. and Illinois Central tracks at Van Buren St.
1908, AUGUSTUS SAINT-GAUDENS; EXEDRA MCKIM, MEAD & WHITE

Installed in 1926, Saint-Gaudens's second Lincoln statue in Chicago was intended as the centerpiece of a collection of presidential statues, but it stands—or sits—alone.

49| Clarence Buckingham Memorial Fountain
East end of Congress Dr. at Columbus Dr.
1927, MARCEL FRANÇOIS LOYAU & JACQUES LAMBERT; BENNETT, PARSONS & FROST, ARCHS.
1995, RESTORATION, HARRY WEESE & ASSOCS.

The fountain is the focal point of the park, terminating the Congress Pkwy. axis as envisioned in the 1909 Plan of Chicago. Built of pink Georgia marble, it is based on the Bassin de Latone at Versailles, doubled in size. Four pairs of fanciful bronze sea creatures symbolize the states bordering Lake Michigan, which the fountain is intended to represent.

50| Buckingham Memorial Fountain Visitor Service Pavilions
East end of Congress Dr. at Columbus Dr.
1997, DAVID WOODHOUSE ARCHITECTS

Four low horizontal buildings sited at the corners of the plaza reinforce the park's Beaux Arts symmetry and views. While sited and sized to minimize their presence, the pavilions' details are worth noting. The fountain's exuberant ornament has been cleverly evoked in contemporary materials. Color and structure conjure the tree canopy

CLARENCE BUCKINGHAM MEMORIAL FOUNTAIN

BUCKINGHAM FOUNTAIN PAVILIONS

above while the glazed end canopies capture the sunlight like the nearby fountain's spray.

51| Chicago Club
81 E. Van Buren St.
1929, GRANGER & BOLLENBACHER

This building was designed in the spirit of an earlier structure by Burnham & Root that housed the Art Institute in the late 1880s. It collapsed in 1929 while being remodeled for this private club's use.

52| Fine Arts Building
(*Studebaker Building*)
410 S. Michigan Ave.
1885, SOLON S. BEMAN
1898, THREE-STORY ADDITION AND CONVERSION TO FINE ARTS BUILDING, SOLON S. BEMAN
1917, RENOVATION FOR STUDEBAKER THEATER, ANDREW N. REBORI

The Romanesque rough stone base and ranks of floors under arches established a prototypical rhythm for this stretch of S. Michigan Ave. The arches and the huge red granite columns that carry them were a means of opening the load-bearing east wall for the Studebaker carriage showrooms, which occupied the first five floors. A shift in function within was recorded in the upper stories; groupings of smaller windows mark where wagons and carriages were assembled.

When the building no longer suited Studebaker's needs, Beman altered it for music publisher and real estate developer Charles C. Curtiss into a proto-arts center with two theaters, offices, shops, and studios for musicians, artists, and writers. This included the replacement of the top story with three new ones, including skylit studios. The building was a locus of activity for women's suffrage efforts and, later, of the Chicago literary movement of the 1920s. Inside it has a rabbit warren of woody hallways, a light well with internal balconies appropriately called Venetian Court, and tenth-floor muraled walls as reminders of former tenants.

53| Congress Plaza
Congress Pkwy. and Michigan Ave.
1929, EDWARD H. BENNETT
1995, RESTORATION, DLK ARCHITECTURE

Completed for the 1933 World's Fair, Congress Plaza is the formal gateway to Grant Park along the central east–west axis envisioned in the 1909 Plan of Chicago. The bridges and ornamental concrete elements have been restored and lost features such as lampposts replaced. Two flights of stairs recall the 100-foot-wide grand stair that was lost when Congress was extended in the 1950s.

54 | Eagle Fountains
Michigan Ave. at Congress Dr.
1931, FREDERICK C. HIBBARD

These graceful eagles grasping fish in their talons made more sense years ago, when the pools were filled with water.

55 | *The Spearman and the Bowman*
Michigan Ave. at Congress Dr.
1928, IVAN MESTROVIC

The sculptor proposed a cowboy and an Indian, but two Native Americans were felt to be more suitable for so prominent a site, which originally featured a grand stair and plaza leading to Buckingham Fountain. Their weapons must be supplied by the viewer's imagination.

THE BOWMAN

56 | Auditorium Building
430 S. Michigan Ave.
1887–1889, ADLER & SULLIVAN
1967, AUDITORIUM THEATRE RESTORATION, HARRY WEESE & ASSOCS.
2001–03, AUDITORIUM THEATRE RESTORATION, DANIEL P. COFFEY & ASSOCS.
2003, GANZ HALL RESTORATION, BOOTH HANSEN ASSOCS.

The Auditorium Building commission was the single most important factor in establishing the internationally recognized role of Dankmar Adler and Louis H. Sullivan in the evolution of modern architectural thought. Adler's previous successes as a theater designer secured the coveted job, while the publicity generated by the project promulgated Sullivan's innovative architectural ideals.

Created to provide a permanent home for Chicago's operatic, symphonic, and other cultural events, the building was planned with large

AUDITORIUM BUILDING—EXTERIOR

AUDITORIUM BUILDING—INTERIOR

multiuse commercial components, a 400-room hotel, and rental offices in order to offset possible losses from the operation of the 4,300-seat theater. It was a civic achievement of enormous stature, made even more impressive by the modernist style of its design.

The composition of the street facades, suggesting the Romanesque character of H. H. Richardson's demolished Marshall Field Wholesale Store (1887), is a highly original expression of the building's bearing-wall construction: a rugged base of supporting rusticated granite contrasts with the smooth, machined Bedford limestone skin above. Except for the entrance, the theater was almost completely enclosed from the street by the hotel, which was located along the Michigan Ave. and Congress Pkwy. frontages, and by the office section along Wabash Ave. Rising above the ten-story block on Congress Pkwy. is an eight-story tower that originally housed additional offices, tanks for the hydraulic elevators and stage equipment, and a rooftop observatory, initially the highest point in the city. Adler & Sullivan's own offices were behind the stone colonnade at what is now the sixteenth floor.

In contrast to the heavy treatment of the masonry exterior, the interiors are reflections of the light, modular, post-and-beam metal frame, and of the fireproof tile partitions, articulated by the creative manipulation of interior finishes in plaster, wood, cast iron, art glass, mosaic, and other materials. The primary space is the theater itself, enclosed within a fireproof brick shell. Its excellent acoustics and sight lines are testament to Adler's theater expertise and were given creative form through Sullivan's integral collaboration.

Other significant interior spaces can be seen by touring the facilities of Roosevelt University, which has owned the building since 1946. With the expansion of Congress Pkwy., an exterior arcade was created, which destroyed several first-floor spaces. The former hotel lobby is entered on Michigan Ave., and its central grand staircase leads to the second-floor parlor. The finely restored Ladies' Parlor, now the Sullivan Room and usually closed, is partially visible through a door at the south end of the loggia. The barrel-vaulted tenth-floor hotel dining room is now the university's library. The restored southern alcove reflects its original appearance, while the main room's restoration awaits funding. One of Adler & Sullivan's finest interior spaces is the hotel's banquet hall/ballroom, built of lightweight plaster and birch paneling. Now the Rudolph Ganz Memorial Recital Hall (Room 745), it was an afterthought planned when the building was largely complete. The remarkable room spans forty feet over the theater's roof on twin bridge trusses bearing on the theater's perimeter masonry walls.   —JOHN VINCI

57| _The Spirit of Music_ Sculpture and Park
S. Michigan Ave. between Harrison St. and Balbo Dr.
1923, ALBIN POLASEK, SCULPTOR; HOWARD VAN DOREN SHAW, ARCH.

Dedicated to the first conductor of the Chicago Symphony Orchestra, the _Spirit_ has at long last been reunited with the granite relief carvings of the orchestra members. In storage since the sculpture's first relocation in 1940, the carvings were eventually found dumped along the lakefront. The entire work was restored in its present location in 1991.

Museum Campus
1994–1998, LAWRENCE HALPRIN, TENG & ASSOCS.

The long-awaited relocation of the northbound lanes of Lake Shore Dr. to the west of Soldier Field and the Field Museum has created a true unified museum campus. Acres of concrete are now green space connecting the three museums, Soldier Field, and the rest of Burnham Park to the south. In addition, a vast area of surface parking north of the stadium is now terraced gardens. Open pedestrian ways connect the campus to the south end of Grant Park and the rapidly developing Near South Side.

58| Field Museum of Natural History
Roosevelt Rd. and S. Lake Shore Dr.
1909–1912, D. H. BURNHAM & CO.; 1912–1917, GRAHAM, BURNHAM & CO.; 1917–1920, GRAHAM, ANDERSON, PROBST & WHITE
1977, RENOVATION, HARRY WEESE & ASSOCS.
2004, EAST ENTRANCE AND UNDERGROUND EXPANSION, SKIDMORE, OWINGS & MERRILL

Exhibits from the 1893 World's Columbian Exposition were the nucleus of the collections, housed for the first twenty-seven years in what was later reconstructed as the Museum of Science and Industry. The design was inspired by the Greek temple; the caryatids are especially reminiscent of the Erechtheion. The great central hall, ringed by Ionic columns, is one of Chicago's grandest neo-Classical spaces, monumental yet serene.

59| Soldier Field
425 E. McFetridge Dr.
1922 1926, COLONNADE, HOLABIRD & ROCHE
2003, STADIUM, WOOD & ZAPATA, LOHAN CAPRILE GOETTSCH, ASSOC. ARCHS.

This enormous colonnaded stadium has been used for sports events, religious gatherings, and concerts. It was named to honor soldiers of the first World War; at the same time, Municipal Pier was renamed Navy Pier to honor sailors. But that meaning was diluted when the enormous new stadium was built in the middle of Soldier Field. The new stadium isn't so much bad as it is wrong at this location. Beautiful materials, dramatic form, a complex geometry, and all of the new amenities the players need and the fans want—this stadium has all that. In the middle of a former megamall parking lot, it would look stunning. But it is on the lakefront, blocking a substantial amount of the lake view and causing tremendous congestion on event days.

60| Burnham Park & Northerly Island
From Solidarity Dr. south to 57th St., east of Illinois Central tracks
1917–1930

Northerly Island (1928–1930) was the only actualization of the chain of man-made islands proposed in the 1909 Plan of Chicago. It was intended to be a park, but its first role, and that of the parallel section of Burnham Park, was as the site for the 1933–1934 World's Fair, "A Century of Progress." After the

fair, one of the temporary connections between the mainland
and the island (Solidarity Dr.)
was made permanent.

61| Site of Merrill C. Meigs Field
**South portion of
Northerly Island**

The small airport that occupied
the island's southern portion
was demolished in 2003 on
orders from Mayor Daley, with
the intention of converting it
to a park.

62| Adler Planetarium &
**Astronomy Museum
1300 S. Lake Shore Dr.**

1930, ERNEST A. GRUNSFELD, JR.
1998, SKY PAVILION, 1999,
RENOVATION, LOHAN ASSOCS.

In a departure from the neo-
Classical details of the nearby
museums, Grunsfeld designed
a twelve-sided domed structure
with simple lines and Art Deco
details to house the nation's
first public planetarium. Each
corner of the variegated granite
mass is adorned with a zodiacal
sign. The central domed room is
still used for viewing projected
images of the sky. A panel in
the lobby has emblems for each
of the eight planets; the ninth,
Pluto, was discovered after the
panel had been installed. The
C-shaped sky pavilion addition
partially wraps the historic
structure with a dynamic steel-
and-glass structure, a clear
counterpoint to the original
form. A narrow skylight separates the new from old on the
inside, and highlights the original Alfonso Iannelli bronze
plaques and richly textured
walls. The new sweep of column-free exhibit space affords
splendid vistas of the lake and
skyline.

63| John G. Shedd Aquarium
1200 S. Lake Shore Dr.

1929, GRAHAM, ANDERSON, PROBST
& WHITE
1991, OCEANARIUM ADDITION,
LOHAN ASSOCS.
1999, ROTUNDA RESTORATION;
2000, AMAZON RISING EXHIBIT;
2003, WILD REEF ADDITION;
PERKINS & WILL AND EHDD

Designed to harmonize with
the Field Museum, the original
building is covered inside and
out with aquatic motifs. Recent
additions have strived to preserve the integrity of the 1929
building while updating exhibits. The lakeside Oceanarium
is a low modern extension of
the building. The marble of its
flanking walls was recycled from
the original east wall, and it
will eventually fade to match
the original. From the inside, the
sweep of curtain wall creates
the illusion of an unbroken line
of water from the interior pools
to Lake Michigan. The latest
addition to the south extends
the existing terrace level and
creates new plaza space over
underground exhibit space.

64| 421 S. Wabash Ave.
(*Fine Arts Building Annex*)

1924, REBORI, WENTWORTH, DEWEY
& MCCORMICK

This charming sliver was built to
house the Fine Arts Building's
heating plant and five floors of
studio space, connected by a
bridge to the main building. The
polychrome facade of verde
antique marble is accented with
pale yellow and green, matte-
glazed terra cotta and iron
balconettes.

ADLER PLANETARIUM & ASTRONOMY MUSEUM

65| CNA Center
333 S. Wabash Ave.
1972, GRAHAM, ANDERSON, PROBST
& WHITE

66| 55 E. Jackson Blvd.
(*Continental Center*)
1962, C. F. MURPHY ASSOCS.

The bays of 55 E. Jackson
Blvd., originally connected to
310 S. Michigan Ave., have forty-
two-foot spans; they were the
largest constructed to that time
but were soon surpassed by the
Richard J. Daley Center's gargantuan bays.

67| DePaul University—
O'Malley Building
(*Finchley Building*)
23 E. Jackson Blvd.
1928, ALFRED S. ALSCHULER

The Gothic style of the stone
base changes incongruously to
a Tudor half-timbered treatment at the top.

68| DePaul University—
Lewis Center
(*Kimball Building*)
25 E. Jackson Blvd.
1917, GRAHAM, ANDERSON, PROBST
& WHITE

Step inside to see the well-
preserved L-shaped lobby of
buff ceramic tile.

69| Pakula Building
(*formerly McClurg Building,
originally Ayer Building*)
218 S. Wabash Ave.
1899, HOLABIRD & ROCHE

This steel-frame loft building
is a small but resonant example
of the qualities for which the
Chicago School—especially the
work of Holabird & Roche—is
famous. The grid of the wall
clearly expresses the underlying
structure, with large Chicago
windows set between the thin-
nest possible piers and spandrels. As with Mies's I-beams of
a half century later, the deep
fluted piers and mullions give di-
mensionality and rhythm to the
skeletal facade. Unfortunately,
the cornice that once capped
the composition is missing.

70| 55 E. Monroe St.
(*Mid-Continental Plaza*)
1972, ALFRED SHAW & ASSOCS.

This International Style behemoth has closely spaced piers,
clad in stainless steel and ascending uninterrupted to the
flat roof. A 1991 renovation by
Swanke Hayden Connell gave
the building a presence on the
night skyline with three bands
of light that surround the
mechanical penthouse.

71| School of the Art Institute
of Chicago
(*Champlain Building*)
37 S. Wabash Ave.
1903, HOLABIRD & ROCHE

This archetypal Holabird &
Roche office building follows
the firm's successful formula
exploited between 1895 and
1910. Features include continuous piers, recessed spandrels,
wide Chicago windows, and a
tripartite organization of base,
shaft, and cornice. The simple
treatment maximized light and
air while expressing the structural steel frame.

72| Carson Pirie Scott Buildings
(*Haskell and Barker Buildings*)
18–24 S. Wabash Ave.
1875, WHEELOCK & THOMAS
1896, HASKELL BUILDING
REMODELING, LOUIS H. SULLIVAN
(*J. P. Atwater Building*)
26–28 S. Wabash Ave.
1877, JOHN M. VAN OSDEL

In the 1890s the Schlesinger &
Mayer store began acquiring
space on Wabash Ave. near the
planned Madison St. elevated
station. Sullivan was commissioned to open the first two
stories of the Haskell Building's
load-bearing facade by spanning it with ironwork finished
in his own decorative style and
painted white. It is the only
surviving exterior example of
Sullivan's alterations to the company's buildings before receiving the commission for their
State St. store.

73 | 23 S. Wabash Ave.
(*Rae Building*)
1872, FREDERICK BAUMANN
1928, REMODELING, GRAVEN &
MAYGER

This sober Italianate facade,
which follows the design of earlier cast-iron fronts, is the perfect foil for Sullivan's exuberant
Jewelers Building.

74 | Jewelers Building
19 S. Wabash Ave.
1882, ADLER & SULLIVAN

Disregard the ground-floor
alterations and look up, or view
this oldest surviving Adler &
Sullivan design from the El platform. The color and materials
are Ruskinian Gothic; the details
exhibit the emergence of Sullivan's distinctive ornament.
The chunky, rather stiff plant
forms are akin to the work of
Philadelphia architect Frank
Furness, or the designs of Owen
Jones as found in such publications as *The Grammar of
Ornament* (1854).

JEWELERS BUILDING

75 | Crowne Plaza Chicago—
The Silversmith
(*Silversmith Building*)
10 S. Wabash Ave.
1897, D. H. BURNHAM & CO.
1998, CONVERSION TO HOTEL,
FITZGERALD ASSOCIATES ARCHITECTS

On a richly colored facade composed of expressed structural
elements, brick mullions placed
on the spandrels and the column faces emphasize verticality.

76 | Shops Building
21 N. Wabash Ave.
1875, ARCHITECT UNKNOWN
1912, REMODELING, ALFRED S.
ALSCHULER

An old loft building became a
retail center with the addition
of a metal-frame facade covered
with polychrome terra-cotta.

77 | Pittsfield Building
55 E. Washington St.
1927, GRAHAM, ANDERSON, PROBST
& WHITE

This tower was briefly Chicago's
tallest building. Its emphasis on
verticality and use of setbacks
recall the era's Art Deco high
rises, but it uses the Gothic vocabulary of earlier skyscrapers.
The building accommodated
the special electrical and plumb-
ing needs of medical and dental
offices and the security requirements of jewelers. Beyond the
Washington St. lobby is a well-
preserved five-story shopping
arcade surrounded by balconies
and shop windows.

78 | 25 E. Washington St.
(*Marshall Field & Co. Annex*)
1914, GRAHAM, BURNHAM & CO.

Field's established a popular
practice of offering a separate
men's store. The six retail levels
of this mixed-use building are
surmounted by fourteen office
floors.

79 | Facades of the Burton Estate,
Peck, and Couch Estate
Buildings
129, 137 & 139 N. Wabash Ave.
1872, 1877 (BURTON ESTATE),
JOHN M. VAN OSDEL

This fragment of a post-Fire
commercial streetscape shows
the variations possible in
Italianate facades.

80 | Gallery 37 Center for the Arts
66 E. Randolph St.
1872, WILLIAM W. BOYINGTON
2000, ADAPTIVE REUSE, DANIEL P.
COFFEY & ASSOCS.

The City's Department of Cultural Affairs purchased two
decrepit buildings—a non-
descript 1920s structure and

a rare remnant of early post-Fire construction—and commissioned their reuse as an art center with studios, theater, art gallery, and café. A unified storefront and canopy joins the disparate structures at street level.

81 | Wabash/Randolph Center Self Park
20 E. Randolph St.
1990, LUCIEN LAGRANGE & ASSOCS.; DESMAN ASSOCS., ASSOC. ARCHS.

The facades pay homage to the Chicago School with their tripartite organization and vertical green pipes set against the concrete to suggest Chicago windows.

82 | Self Park
60 E. Lake St.
1986, STANLEY TIGERMAN & ASSOCS.

A classic touring car inspired the facade. The turquoise of the baked enamel panels was selected from the 1957 Chevrolet color schedule.

83 | 203 N. Wabash Ave.
(Old Dearborn Bank Building)
1928, C.W. AND GEORGE L. RAPP

Movie palace confectioners Rapp & Rapp also designed sober business buildings. This tower's only indulgence is the ornament of the spandrels.

84 | Seventeenth Church of Christ, Scientist
55 E. Wacker Dr.
1968, HARRY WEESE & ASSOCS.

A 200-foot travertine curve marks the auditorium and creates a commanding presence for this low building set among skyscrapers. Structural elements, including the lower columns and roof ribs, are clearly visible. A school is located under the auditorium level; offices are slipped in behind.

85 | Wacker Tower
(Chicago Motor Club)
68 E. Wacker Pl.
1928, HOLABIRD & ROOT

This modestly scaled tower equals the firm's more celebrated Art Deco skyscrapers in refinement and soaring verticality. The theme of travel was beautifully elaborated in a large lobby mural by John W. Norton.

86 | Wacker Dr. East–West segment
1926, EDWARD H. BENNETT
2001–2002, REBUILDING, CHICAGO DEPT. OF TRANS.

Along the south bank of the main branch of the Chicago River is a double-level street and embankment built of reinforced concrete with Bedford limestone details. Called Wacker Dr., it honors the first president of the Chicago Plan Commission. The initial conception was part of Daniel H. Burnham's 1909 Plan of Chicago; the design was elaborated with businessmen's needs in mind. The world's first two-level street replaced the congested, dilapidated South Water Street Market in little more than two years. Demolition and construction had to safeguard existing buildings and tunnels, contain the river, and mesh with streets, bridges, and ramps.

The upper level is a flat slab system, supported by octagonal columns that carry a roadway 110 to 115 feet wide plus sidewalks and a riverfront promenade. Images of the banks of the Seine are deliberately encouraged by such garniture as balustrades similar to those on the Pont de la Concorde, grand staircases from street to dock level, and obelisk lampposts modeled on a Parisian example. The lower level provides truck access to the area and carries four lanes of through traffic.

Wacker Dr. was extended southward to W. Congress Pkwy. along the former Market St. from 1949 to 1958 but this time without water contact. East of Michigan Ave. it was extended to Lake Michigan as Illinois Center developed.

87 | 35 E. Wacker Dr.
(*formerly Pure Oil Building, originally Jewelers Building*)
1926, GIAVER & DINKELBERG; THIELBAR & FUGARD, ASSOC. ARCHS.

The initials "JB" in the terra-cotta commemorate the original plan to attract tenants in the jewelry trade. When new, the building was noted for its internal garage. Tenants could drive in from lower Wacker Dr. and have their cars taken by elevator to assigned stalls on the lower twenty-two floors. In 1940 the system was abandoned due to mechanical failures and larger cars, and the garage space was converted to office use. The setbacks at Floors 24 and 26 created terraces punctuated by corner tempietti that artfully hid water towers. "The Belvedere" on top, whose dome hides mechanical equipment, provided an expansive view above a restaurant and lounge. More recently, it has served as a dramatic presentation room for Murphy/Jahn, which occupies space below.

35 E. WACKER DR.

88 | 75 E. Wacker Dr.
(*formerly Lincoln Tower, originally Mather Tower*)
1928, HERBERT HUGH RIDDLE
1983, RENOVATION, HARRY WEESE & ASSOCS.

The city's slenderest skyscraper, a twenty-four-story rectangle topped by a telescoping eighteen-

75 E. WACKER DR.

story octagon, is like a terra-cotta Gothic rocket poised for takeoff. Its crumbling crown was rebuilt in 2002–2003.

89 | Sun-Times Building
401 N. Wabash Ave.
1957, NAESS & MURPHY
1958, RUSH ST. RIVER PLAZA, ATKINSON & FITZGERALD, LANDSCAPE ARCHS.

An undistinguished building has elevations enlivened by views of the pressroom in action and by one of the city's earliest riverfront plazas.

90 | One IBM Plaza
330 N. Wabash Ave.
1971, OFFICE OF MIES VAN DER ROHE; C. F. MURPHY ASSOCS., ASSOC. ARCH.

Mies's last American building, and his largest, follows his familiar model. It is sited so as to avoid obstructing Marina City and to capture the lake views made possible by a jog in the river.

91 | One East Wacker
1962, SHAW, METZ & ASSOCS.
1989, RENOVATION, LUCIEN LAGRANGE & ASSOCS.

The *luxe* marble finish does little to disguise the absence of the pristine detailing and proportions of stronger modernist designs. The 1989 renovation interrupted the rhythm of the facades—which had never been better than dull—with new, elegantly detailed entries.

92 | Renaissance Hotel Chicago
(*Stouffer Riviere Hotel*)
1 W. Wacker Dr.

1991, WILLIAM B. TABLER ARCHITECTS; MANN, GIN, EBEL & FRAZIER LTD., ASSOC. ARCHS.

Pedestrian access to this automobile-oriented hotel is death-defying. Set back from the streetline, it claims to be upholding Chicago traditions in the large proportions of the windows in its base and in the bay windows in the setback tower.

93 | State St. Streetscape
State St. from Congress Pkwy. to Wacker Dr.

1996, SKIDMORE, OWINGS & MERRILL

The redesign and reconstruction successfully removed all vestiges of the disastrous 1979 "malling" that had widened sidewalks, narrowed the street, and restricted traffic to buses. The historic elements that look as though they have been there for decades in fact date from the 1996 renovation. Streetlights are reproductions of those that lined the sidewalks between 1926 and 1958, and the subway entrances feature festive new designs with abundant clear glass. Planters, tree grates, and signage all recall the era of "that great Street."

94 | ABC–WLS Building
(*State–Lake Theater*)
190 N. State St.

1917, C.W. AND GEORGE L. RAPP
1984, RENOVATION, SKIDMORE, OWINGS & MERRILL

This former movie palace and office building now serves the television industry.

95 | Chicago Theater Center
(*Chicago Theater; Page Brothers Building*)
175 N. State St. and
177–191 N. State St.

175 N. STATE ST.,
1921, C.W. AND GEORGE L. RAPP
177–191 N. STATE ST.,
1872, JOHN M. VAN OSDEL
1902, STATE ST. FACADE, HILL & WOLTERSDORF
1986, RENOVATION, DANIEL P. COFFEY & ASSOCS.

Though the architects went on to design larger movie palaces, the Chicago, along with the Tivoli Theater (1921, demolished) at Cottage Grove Ave. and 63rd St., set the standards for the type. Their success was so great that Rapp & Rapp became architects "in residence" for their client, Balaban & Katz, and later for the entire Paramount/Publix theater chain.

The theater has been restored to its condition in 1933,

PAGE BROTHERS BUILDING

when it was refurbished in preparation for the World's Fair. The triumphal-arch facade of off-white terra-cotta opens into a series of lavish, Versailles-inspired spaces. The 3,800-seat auditorium's excellent sight lines derive from the unusually shaped site.

The Page Brothers Building was built immediately after the Fire, and in the same style and materials as the destroyed buildings. This building has one of the Loop's two remaining cast-iron facades. Such facades became unpopular after the Fire because they had melted in the heat, bringing down masonry walls with them. The Page Brothers Building originally fronted on Lake St.; its brick side wall was given a fancy facade after State St. had become the city's premier mercantile address. In 1986 the building was rehabilitated to provide speculative office space that would support the Chicago Theater, which wraps around it in an L-shaped plan. The linkage could be accomplished only after upgrading the Page Brothers Building's wood-frame structure, which did not conform to building codes. In order to preserve the delicate Lake St. cast-iron facades, the original structure was used as formwork for the new concrete system and was then replaced in stages.

96| 162 N. State St. Residences
2000, BOOTH HANSEN ASSOCIATES

This dormitory commissioned by the School of the Art Institute of Chicago features a pale facade of undulating bays that emulates the Hotel Burnham one block south. Precast, glass-fiber-reinforced concrete mimics terra-cotta. Circular windows at cornice level illuminate a common room. The complex includes the renovated former Butler Building (1924, Christian A. Eckstorm) to the north and steps back to the west on Randolph behind the remnants of the Old Heidelberg restaurant

(1923, Holabird & Roche). The Noble Fool Theater moved into the space behind this fanciful facade in 2002 (Morris Architects/Planners) but it was not a success, and the City announced plans in 2003 to redevelop the theater site.

When plans were announced for the renovation of the Oriental and Palace theaters and the building of a new Goodman Theatre, the long-deferred dream of a theater district along Randolph St. finally became a reality. The 1998 streetscape, designed by Skidmore, Owings & Merrill, celebrates the area's vitality with historic streetlights hung with banners, sidewalk elements such as medallions and "doormats" beneath theater marquees, and kiosks. Although concentrated on Randolph St. from Michigan Ave. to Wacker Dr., the streetscape improvements were extended to the surroundings of nearby landmarks such as the City/County Building and Daley Plaza.

97| Ford Center for the Performing Arts
(*Oriental Theatre*)
24 W. Randolph St.
1925, C.W. AND GEORGE L. RAPP
1998, RESTORATION AND EXPANSION, DANIEL P. COFFEY & ASSOCS.

To be commercially viable in the modern theater world, this fanciful cinema palace needed a much deeper stage, but there was no room for expansion—except in the adjacent Oliver Building, which was gutted to accommodate a pair of twenty-ton trusses that transfer the load of a stage-obstructing column. The Oliver's preserved facade (1908, 1920, Holabird & Roche), with its cast-iron spandrels decorated with typewriters, is visible on Dearborn St.

98| Marshall Field & Co.
111 N. State St.
1892, ON N. WABASH AVE.: SOUTH SECTION, D. H. BURNHAM; 1906, MIDDLE SECTION, D. H. BURNHAM &

CO.; 1914, NORTH SECTION, GRAHAM, BURNHAM & CO.; ON N. STATE ST.: NORTH SECTION 1902 AND SOUTH SECTION 1907, D. H. BURNHAM & CO. 1992, RENOVATION, HTI/SPACE DESIGN INTERNATIONAL

The grande dame of State St. has an appropriately massive, stolid design that contrasts with the more skeletal facades of its competitors. The southeastern structure is the earliest, designed with load-bearing walls and heavy arched windows by Charles B. Atwood in complete contrast to his contemporaneous Reliance Building. The high ceilings are supported by forests of decorated columns; the two arcades are topped by a skylight and by shimmering Tiffany mosaics.

99| Hotel Burnham
(*Reliance Building*)
32 N. State St.
1891, FOUNDATIONS AND BASE, BURNHAM & ROOT
1895, ADDITIONAL STORIES, D. H. BURNHAM & CO.
1996, EXTERIOR RESTORATION (ABOVE STOREFRONT LEVEL), MCCLIER
1999, RECONSTRUCTION OF STOREFRONTS AND LOBBY; ADAPTIVE REUSE, ANTUNOVICH ASSOCS.; MCCLIER, RESTORATION ARCH.

HOTEL BURNHAM

Its chief virtue is as clear support for the Chicago School's claim to be a precursor of modern architecture: it is very glassy. Designer Charles B. Atwood used glass at every opportunity. He folded the bay windows out from the frame to completely hide the columns, and he balanced huge picture windows with narrow ones of double-hung sashes in the fullest early example of the Chicago window. His achievement is all the more remarkable because his work had to use the foundations and base executed four years earlier according to John Wellborn Root's plans. Root, Daniel H. Burnham's original design partner, died in 1891, and his plans for the elevations are lost.

On the terra-cotta facades Atwood stressed the overriding continuity of the horizontal spandrels. This was a clear break with the prevailing tradition of letting vertical load-bearing piers carry down to the ground. At the corner, where the structural columns could not be suppressed behind the glass, two bundled sets of colonnettes slide up the covering pier to dematerialize it, a technique used by Gothic stone masons for exactly the same purpose. This corner treatment makes an interesting comparison with those on tall buildings designed by Mies van der Rohe.

The Reliance Building is almost as weightless as it looks. The vertical loads are borne down to preexisting foundations by lightweight, open, trusswork columns. Constructing the frame out of factory-assembled two-story columns with staggered joints reduced the number of field connections and allowed the steel for the top ten stories to be erected in fifteen days. Structural engineer Edward C. Shankland relied for wind bracing on these tall, stiff columns rigidly coupled to extra-deep girders. This method of construction was a significant departure from the heavier portal bracing derived from railroad viaducts and used frequently for such tall buildings as Holabird & Roche's Old Colony Building (1894) and Cass Gilbert's Woolworth Building (1913) in New York. The Reliance's construction methods have much in common with more recent construction and wind-bracing techniques, such as those used in the Aon Center (1973).

Predominantly glassy facades could be found before 1895 on, for example, the Crystal Palace in London (Joseph Paxton, 1851) and on Oriel Chambers in Liverpool (Peter Ellis, Jr., 1864), but the promise of these early aesthetic speculations had to wait a generation for delivery. The perfection of the high-speed elevator made the Reliance Building's height possible; the explosive demand for modern office space in Chicago after the Fire of 1871 made it essential.

After decades of decay, the building was brought back to life in two phases. In 1994 the City of Chicago purchased it and commissioned a thorough restoration of the terra-cotta exterior, including reconstruction of the original cornice. A private developer then converted the building to a hotel, faithfully reconstructing the storefront level and historic elevator lobby. —ANDERS NEREIM

100| **17 N. State St./**
16 N. Wabash Ave.
(*Charles A. Stevens Store Building*)
1912, D. H. BURNHAM & CO.

Recognizing the need to accommodate small retailers on a street that had become filled with grand emporiums, the Stevens brothers topped the seven floors of their own department store with eleven levels of shops for others.

101| **2 N. State St./1 N. Dearborn St.**
(*Boston Store*)
1905, 1917, HOLABIRD & ROCHE
2001, RENOVATION, OWP&P
(1 N. DEARBORN), DANIEL P. COFFEY & ASSOCS. (SEARS ON STATE)

Sears' return to State St. capped the resurgence of retail here

that was spurred by the street's 1996 "de-malling."

102| **1 N. State St.**
(*formerly Wieboldt's Department Store, originally Mandel Brothers Store*)
1912, HOLABIRD & ROCHE

8–14 N. Wabash Ave.
(*Mandel Brothers Annex*)
1900, HOLABIRD & ROCHE
1905, TOP TWO FLOORS ADDITION, HOLABIRD & ROCHE

The restored State St. building has been subdivided to accommodate smaller retailers. The more distinguished Wabash Ave. structure has unusually wide bays, very narrow spandrels, and slim projecting courses, all of which stress horizontality.

103| **Carson Pirie Scott & Co.**
(*Schlesinger & Mayer Department Store*)
1 S. State St.
1899; 1903, LOUIS H. SULLIVAN
STATE ST. ADDITION (FIVE BAYS)
1906, D. H. BURNHAM & CO.
STATE ST. ADDITION (THREE BAYS)
1961, HOLABIRD & ROOT
1980, RESTORATION, OFFICE OF JOHN VINCI

One of the first large department stores to be erected entirely with fireproof steel-frame construction, Carson Pirie Scott served American and European architects as a model for this modern building type. Designers perceived it as a representation of its architect's axiom, "Form follows function," for in it Louis Henri Sullivan had ingeniously extended the technology of skyscraper construction to the department store. However, as he had in his office buildings, Sullivan took artistic license with the expression of practical forms and their functions.

On his skyscrapers, Sullivan modified the expression of the grid of steel construction by emphasizing the vertical dimension with unbroken lines of piers and recessed spandrels. The main portion of the Carson Pirie Scott Store comprises a corner entrance pavilion and tower, flanked by twelve-story elevations. In the tower Sullivan reproduced the skyscraper effect, but on the elevations he emphasized the horizontal dimension by using unbroken stringcourses to unite expanses of Chicago windows.

Sullivan's emphasis on horizontality was initially determined by the lighting and spatial requirements of modern merchandising practices. Steel framing required minimal internal support, allowed the maximum amount of daylight for merchandise display, and increased open space for easy movement around display cases and between floors. This post-and-lintel construction is exhibited on the exterior as a thin white-tiled grid that frames recessed windows and defines layered floors. Its clearest expression is in the plate-glass show windows, which are as wide as the vertical supports allow.

The ornamented display windows at the base were to attract customers. Equally important, they served Sullivan's artistic purpose: to show the originality of his style of ornament close up. Sullivan used ornament as an artistic finish or, in his words, as "a garment of poetic imagery." He wrote extensively about architecture as a kind of poetic representation of nature capable of offsetting the materialist culture of an industrialized modern city. The intertwining geometric forms and botanical motifs (and his initials, LHS, above the corner entrance) are cast in iron and painted green over a red undercoat, emulating both oxidized bronze and dappled sunlit foliage. Sullivan's metaphor of the natural landscape is made manifest by strolling along the base and

CARSON PIRIE SCOTT & CO.

CARSON PIRIE SCOTT & CO.—DETAIL

walking through the entrance. Together with the mahogany-paneled vestibule and foliate column capitals, the experience recalls a tree-lined forest walk.

Sullivan's store was built in two sections for the retail firm of Schlesinger & Mayer. The first section (1899), three bays wide on Madison St., has nine stories. The twelve-story corner section (1903) extended the frontage through the seven northernmost State St. bays. The building lease and business were sold to Carson Pirie Scott & Co. virtually upon completion. The building has twice been sympathetically extended southward and has been subjected to numerous external and internal alterations, including the unfortunate removal of original ornamentation in metal, wood, and mosaics. Major restoration work was done on the facades and the main entrance in 1978-1980.

—LAUREN S. WEINGARDEN

104 | Chicago Building
(*Chicago Savings Bank Building*)
7 W. Madison St.
1904, HOLABIRD & ROCHE
1997, ADAPTIVE REUSE,
BOOTH HANSEN ASSOCIATES

Highly visible on State St. from the north because of an eastern shift in the roadway is this Holabird & Roche archetype. Large Chicago windows—flat on State St., alternately projecting and flat on Madison St.—dominate the facades. The emphasized corners and the rare intact cornice are also noteworthy. Everything above the first floor is now dormitory space for the School of the Art Institute of Chicago.

CHICAGO BUILDING

105 | Mentor Building
39 S. State St.
1906, HOWARD VAN DOREN SHAW

Shaw's only skyscraper presents an unusual amalgam of styles, with windows grouped in horizontal bands between a four-level base of large showroom windows and a classically inspired top. The details are typically robust and idiosyncratic, retaining the character of their classical sources but used as large-scale, conspicuous motifs.

106 | Palmer House
17 E. Monroe St.
1927, HOLABIRD & ROCHE

Built by the same architects and at the same time as the Stevens (Hilton) Hotel and only slightly smaller, the Palmer House shares its massing of narrow towers grouped around light courts. Below the palatial second-floor lobby is an elegant commercial arcade.

107 | Singer on State Building
120 S. State St.
1926, MUNDIE & JENSEN
1997, ADAPTIVE REUSE, HASBROUCK PETERSON ZIMOCH SIRIRATTUMRONG

The Singer Sewing Machine Co. wanted a distinctive building but had only twenty-five feet of frontage. The white glazed terra-cotta molded into Gothic tracery and the polygonal top floor are arresting, and the exceptionally tall lower floors provide maximum street exposure and daylight.

108 | Exelon Thermal Technologies State/Adams Plant
137 S. State St.
1995, ECKENHOFF SAUNDERS ARCHITECTS

Above the ground-floor retail space, this is an industrial facility that supplies chilled water from ice melt to cool nearby buildings via a belowground distribution network. Behind the structurally expressive grid of glass block and concrete panels are huge ice tanks and chillers, while fiberglass walls on the upper stories conceal cooling towers. When ice making occurs at night, the glass block glows and small blue rooftop lights are illuminated.

109 | The Berghoff
17 W. Adams St.
1872, ARCHITECT UNKNOWN
27 W. Adams St.
1872, CHARLES M. PALMER

The Berghoff is housed in the Loop's only surviving public-hall building; the top-floor meeting room is indicated by the larger-scaled windows. One of two remaining cast-iron facades in the Loop is at 27 (the other is the Page Brothers Building).

110 | 211–227 S. State St.
1949, SHAW, METZ & DOLIO

The holdover Moderne facade has strong vertical strips of windows and dark spandrels to counteract the boxy horizontality.

111 | 300 S. State St.
(*Maurice L. Rothschild Building*)
1906, HOLABIRD & ROCHE
1910, THREE-BAY SOUTH ADDITION, HOLABIRD & ROCHE
1928, FOUR-STORY ADDITION, ALFRED S. ALSCHULER

The original, eight-story building had foundations and walls that would accommodate an additional four floors; but when they were added, the building lost its cornice to a simple parapet. The chamfered corner was designed to admit extra daylight to the selling floors.

112 | DePaul Center
(*formerly Goldblatt's, originally Rothschild & Co. Store*)
333 S. State St.
1912, HOLABIRD & ROCHE
1993, RENOVATION, DANIEL P. COFFEY & ASSOCS.

On the remarkably intact facade, the deep, bracketed cornice is especially noteworthy. Converted to a multiuse structure, it has shopping and food courts on the lower levels, rental offices in the middle, and academic floors on top.

113| Chicago Transit Authority— State/Van Buren Station

2001, DLK ARCHITECTURE

With the ticket functions placed under the track level, platform and street-level spaces are open and light. The new station, which replaced an aging facility at the same location, uses color, material, and traditional forms to relate to the adjacent library and the historic buildings nearby.

114| Harold Washington Library Center

400 S. State St.

1991, HAMMOND, BEEBY & BABKA; A. EPSTEIN & SONS INTERNATIONAL, ASSOC. ARCHS.

The winner of a highly publicized design competition in 1988, the library was the most overtly traditional of the diverse proposals designed to house the main library collection, which had been in temporary quarters for a decade. The building recalls neo-Classical institutions, but is not literal in all its details. Classical details such as the garlands and flamboyant acroteria adorn a massive red brick and granite block that anchors the south end of the Loop at State St. The building's sense of solidity and permanence is reinforced by small, deeply recessed openings in its rusticated base, and deep-set arches above. A completely different impression is created, however, when one views the facade along Plymouth Ct. Here it appears that the building has been sliced away to reveal a taut glass skin. The intention was to create a neutral mirror for the Manhattan and Old Colony buildings to the west. Its neutrality is a counterpoint to the way glass is a vehicle for reinterpreting Classicism elsewhere in the building, particularly in the pediments. The grand interior space that one would expect to enter in a building this scale is found not on the ground floor, but at the top of the building. The skylit Winter Garden is a restful space that recalls an exterior courtyard.

115| Robert Morris Center
(*long known as the Second Leiter Building, originally Siegel, Cooper & Co. Store*)
403 S. State St.

1891, WILLIAM LE BARON JENNEY

In the Second Leiter Building what seems to support *does* support. Cornices and colonnettes articulate the underlying skeleton, with piers and spandrels resolving themselves into magnificent ranks of glass-filled grids. The exterior reflects an interior extraordinarily spacious, especially for its time. Each of the eight stories is an open composition of broad avenues and slender iron columns sixteen feet high. Contemporaries saw the building as a manifestation of a new age.

The building constitutes the response of William Le Baron Jenney, who must be considered one of the century's most significant architects, to the demands of its developer, Levi Z. Leiter, Marshall Field's partner from 1867 to 1881. Leiter wanted a "complete and perfect" building to house a single major retail establishment, but not without the ability to subdivide if required. In the diminutive First Leiter Building (1879), which stood at Monroe and Wells Sts. until 1972, Jenney had given Leiter a predominantly glass envelope by supporting timber joists and girders on cast-iron columns. For Leiter's second commission all of the beams and girders were steel; supports remained cast iron. The steel's high tensile strength enabled Jenney to open the exterior walls to glass to an unprecedented extent. The system, introduced by Jenney with wrought-iron horizontals on the demolished Home Insurance Building (1884), obviated the need for supporting partitions, permitting Leiter

SECOND LEITER BUILDING

to arrange the interior as he saw fit. The extensive exterior glazing made space-consuming light courts unnecessary.

For most of its history the building functioned as a store for a single retailer, originally Siegel, Cooper & Co., and later Sears, Roebuck & Co. Until the building was subdivided in 1981, the open qualities of its steel framing were instantly obvious.

Striking in its formal excellence, the Second Leiter Building recalls Jenney's training in the early 1850s at the École Centrale des Arts et Manufactures in Paris: the school's architectural curriculum taught that purpose and structure determine form. Leiter was the rare client who made the fullest use of Jenney's training, permitting the most modern materials and their expression in the building's design. The forward-looking qualities of the building's functionalism have fascinated historians such as Sigfried Giedion, who described it as "the first high building to exhibit the trend toward pure forms." And so it does. With a little imagination, one can see the Second Leiter Building as a modern composition of the mid-twentieth century.   —THEODORE TURAK

116| Manhattan Building
431 S. Dearborn St.
1891, WILLIAM LE BARON JENNEY
1982, RENOVATION, HASBROUCK HUNDERMAN

Viewed with awe by visitors to the 1893 World's Columbian Exposition, who called it Hercules, the Manhattan earned a long line of firsts: the first tall building to use skeleton construction throughout; the first sixteen-story building in the United States and briefly the world's tallest building; and the first building with a structurally sophisticated wind-bracing

MANHATTAN BUILDING

system. The north and south bays are cantilevered to avoid overloading the footings of adjacent buildings.

117| Plymouth Building
417 S. Dearborn St.
1899, SIMEON B. EISENDRATH
1945, WEST FACADE REMODELING, W. SCOTT ARMSTRONG

The Gothic face-lift was intended to give a collegiate image to a correspondence school. Eisendrath's design remains visible on Plymouth Ct. with Sullivanesque ironwork executed by Winslow Bros. Inside is a newel post identical to those executed by Winslow for the Schlesinger & Mayer (Carson Pirie Scott & Co.) store—not surprising, since Eisendrath had worked for Adler & Sullivan.

118| Old Colony Building
407 S. Dearborn St.
1894, HOLABIRD & ROCHE

Here is the Loop's sole survivor of a group of Chicago School skyscrapers with gracefully rounded corner bays. To offset its narrowness, continuous piers and recessed spandrels visually contract the long sides, while enhanced spandrels on the narrow elevations attempt to emphasize the horizontal. This was the first American structure to use portal arches (fillets joining column and girder) for wind bracing. Phoenix columns are wrought iron, and the girders and floor beams are steel.

119| John Marshall Law School
(*The City Club*)
315 S. Plymouth Ct.
1910, POND & POND

The gently curving limestone arch that ties together windows on the second floor is repeated at the top of the building.

120| Chicago Bar Association Building
321 S. Plymouth Ct.
1990, TIGERMAN MCCURRY

Gothicism à la Eliel Saarinen imbues this small building with a vivid presence. Emphasis is on the decorative facade at street level and at the pinnacled top. The cast-aluminum figure above the entry is *Themis* by Mary Block.

121| Fisher Building
343 S. Dearborn St.
1896, D. H. BURNHAM & CO.
1907, NORTHERN ADDITION, PETER J. WEBER
2001, RESTORATION AND ADAPTIVE REUSE, PAPPAGEORGE/HAYMES, COORDINATING ARCH.; EIFLER & ASSOCS., LOBBY ARCH.; DESMAN ASSOCS., FACADE RESTORATION ARCH.

OLD COLONY BUILDING

FISHER BUILDING

The building's lavish facade—full of marine creatures in homage to the developer's name, Lucius G. Fisher—was painstakingly restored in a process that required replacement of more than 6,000 pieces of terra-cotta. The destroyed main entries on Dearborn St. and Plymouth Ct. were re-created, and 1,200 wood-frame windows were repaired or replaced. Mosaic flooring and Carrara marble walls on the interior were also restored. The main lobby is a mixture of restoration and new design.

122 | Monadnock Building
53 W. Jackson Blvd.
1889–1891, BURNHAM & ROOT
ADDITION
54 W. VAN BUREN ST.
1893, HOLABIRD & ROCHE

The Monadnock Building was erected in two parts along Dearborn St. for Peter C. and Shepherd Brooks, Boston developers who commissioned many prominent Chicago buildings. The northern section was designed with exterior masonry walls; the southern addition has a steel frame clad in terra-cotta. At sixteen stories it was briefly the world's tallest office building.

The northern half has always been the subject of attention and wonder. It was constructed as a thick-walled brick tower, 66 feet wide, 200 feet long, and 200 feet high. The *American Architect* in 1892 described it as a chimney. Two cross walls divide the interior space into three fluelike cavities, the centers of which are open from street to roof. A freestanding staircase spirals down from the brilliance of the skylit sixteenth floor to the dark lobby cut lengthwise through the ground floor. Around this open stairwell a light structural grid sustains stacks of rental floors. From these extend the modular alcoves pushing through the facade to become bay windows.

The thick, perforated exterior wall is an expansion of the series of thick wall slabs that Burnham & Root originally proposed to divide the building vertically, like bookends, into a series of steel-framed cells. This is a modification of the steel system first decisively demonstrated in Holabird & Roche's demolished Tacoma Building (1889), where two such thick walls were set at right angles to discipline the grid and achieve stability. In the Rookery (1888) Burnham & Root themselves used two perforated masonry facade walls and four elevator and stair stacks to stabilize the iron skeleton. There is a nice play of hard and soft, enclosure and exposure in each of these designs. Steel and masonry are in balance. The old material has not yet been abandoned; the new material has not yet supervened.

It was not the Monadnock's remarkable constructive organization that contemporaries particularly remarked but, rather, the lack of exterior ornament. Burnham & Root shaped it as a single massive unit: a plinthlike base below a curved brick plane moving inward and upward, transformed into a subtle batter for

MONADNOCK BUILDING

fourteen floors before returning outward to overhang in a cavetto cornice, giving the whole a shape suggestive of an Egyptian pylon. As the walls retreat, the window alcoves emerge as bays. Bevels at each corner expand and pace the rise of the facade.

The windows are not outlined with decoration but remain mere holes cut in this huge shape. Contemporary critics saw this as rational, honest, and exemplary of the starkness that a commercial building should accept; the Monadnock came to be cited as a model for steel-framed buildings of entirely different structure. But, as Sigfried Giedion observed in *Space, Time and Architecture* (1941), the nature of steel construction is a grid of panels, as in the Reliance Building (1895). The Monadnock was exceptional. Its sense of upward thrust and the contrast of thick masonry and fragile steel look back to the traditional craft of building brick by brick and are appropriate to its fiercely archaic Egyptoid form. —DAVID VAN ZANTEN

Chicago Federal Center
Dearborn St. between Adams St. & Jackson Blvd.
1959–1974, LUDWIG MIES VAN DER ROHE; SCHMIDT, GARDEN & ERIKSON;
C. F. MURPHY ASSOCS.; A. EPSTEIN & SONS, ASSOC. ARCHS.

123| Everett McKinley Dirksen Building
(1959–1964)
219 S. Dearborn St.

124| John C. Kluczynski Building
(1966–1974)
230 S. Dearborn St.

125| U.S. Post Office—Loop Station
(1966–1974)
219 S. Clark St.

By accident rather than design, the axial siting of three great plazas forms a rhythmic pattern that adds a discernibly urbanistic unity to the Loop. The outermost spaces, at the Richard J. Daley Center to the north and the Federal Center to the south, are oriented inward, as if addressing the intervening First National Bank (now Bank One) plaza. The symbolism of government bowing to finance, while fortuitous in this instance, is not without poetic appropriateness to Chicago's history.

CHICAGO FEDERAL CENTER

Such a metaphor, however, would have meant little to the chief architect of the Federal Center, Ludwig Mies van der Rohe, whose design is notable as much for its indifference to a traditional iconography of government as for the evidence it offers of his lifelong search for a universal order and grammar of the building art.

Outwardly, the Chicago Federal Center "reads" as many of Mies's residential and commercial works do: as abstract and nonallusive, rather than as representational, architecture. It has been criticized for this. Even so, Mies's uncompromising devotion to principle, together with his vaunted sensitivity to proportion and structural detail, and, in this case, the organizational scale, combine to give the complex a monumental urban presence.

Three buildings occupy a space divided by Dearborn St. The thirty-story Dirksen courtroom building takes up a half square block to the east. The forty-two-story Kluczynski office building and a one-story postal facility are sited on the full block to the west. This ensemble encloses a large space at the southwest corner of Adams and Dearborn Sts., where in 1974 Alexander Calder's vermilion-painted steel construction *Flamingo* was installed. Its color and organic contours serve as a counterfoil to the matte-black geometries of Mies's buildings.

Both towers are curtain-wall structures characteristic of the highrise designs of Mies's American period. Their steel frames, suppressed behind uniform walls of glass and steel, are marked off by projecting steel I-beam mullions. The Post Office, a unitary space with a central core, is similarly typical of Mies's reductivist concept of the single-story pavilion. Externally thin yet powerful structural columns of steel brace enormous panes of tinted glass.

Commissioned by the U.S. General Services Administration, the Federal Center was part of a 1950s plan to modernize the federal government's administrative and judiciary buildings. Begun in 1959, the center had been fully designed by 1964, the first of Mies's urban, mixed land-use projects. Budgetary problems delayed completion until 1974.

—FRANZ SCHULZE

126| **Bank One Corporate Center**
131 S. Dearborn St.
2003, RICARDO BOFILL
ARQUITECTURA, DESIGN
CONSULTANTS; DESTEFANO
AND PARTNERS, ARCH.
OF RECORD

The classically inspired limestone detailing that is so prominent on the skin of the architects' earlier R. R. Donnelley Center is here reduced to a thin wall just inside the lobby's glass exterior. The effect of the reflective glass skin is fearsome.

127| **Marquette Building**
140 S. Dearborn St.
1893–1895, HOLABIRD & ROCHE;
1906, WESTERNMOST ADAMS ST. BAY, HOLABIRD & ROCHE;
1980, RENOVATION AND RESTORATION, HOLABIRD & ROOT;
2003, CORNICE RE-CREATION, MCCLIER

The Marquette Building is an exemplar of the Chicago style: the rectangular grid of its structural steel skeleton is clearly articulated by its brick and terra-cotta cladding. The decorative treatment establishes the organization of the elevation, with its hierarchy of base, shaft, and capital, and gives it a sense of verticality that is expressed through the

MARQUETTE BUILDING

greater sculptural depth of the piers in comparison to the spandrels.
The arms of the E-shaped building embrace a large light well with the
elevator and service shafts in the central projection. All of the offices,
which line the arms of the plan, have a window either to the street or
the light well. This design, combined with the structural and aesthetic
treatment of the wall, guaranteed the maximum amount of natural
light for the interior spaces.

The architects, William Holabird and Martin Roche, would become
recognized as among the most prolific working in the Chicago commercial style. They had met as draftsmen in the office of pioneer
skyscraper designer William Le Baron Jenney and founded their own
firm in the early 1880s. The prominent structural engineer Corydon T.
Purdy collaborated on this design.

The building was named in honor of Jacques Marquette, a Jesuit
priest and explorer. His journal, in which he recorded his expedition
through the Illinois Country in 1674–1675, included the first description
by a European of the site of Chicago. Owen F. Aldis, a real estate developer, amateur historian, and one of the building's original owners,
had translated Marquette's journal in 1891, providing the inspiration
for the structure's name and decorative program. Relief sculptures over
the main portal by Hermon A. MacNeil depict events associated with
Marquette's expedition. The two-story lobby is sumptuously decorated
with marble trim and mosaic scenes of Marquette's trek designed by
J. A. Holzer and executed by the Tiffany Glass and Decorating Co. Bronze
reliefs above the elevator doors by Edward Kemeys depict French explorers and Native Americans.

Alterations include the removal of the original Ionic columns from
the main portal and the replacement of the cornice by the top floor
(1950). —TIMOTHY WITTMAN

128| 55 W. Monroe St.
1980, C. F. MURPHY ASSOCS.

Taut and streamlined, the curtain wall slides around the corner, while diagonals in the sidewalk and on the roof slice across it. To cut energy costs, the proportion of glass to aluminum paneling changes from 75 percent on the north elevation, which receives little direct sun, to 50 percent elsewhere.

129| 33 W. Monroe St.
1980, SKIDMORE, OWINGS & MERRILL

The three stacked atriums were a first in office design, but the colors, materials, and lighting are unusually dreary.

130| Shubert Theater & Majestic Building
16–22 W. Monroe St.
1905, EDMUND R. KRAUSE

Here is a celebration of the terra-cotta modeler's skills at imitating heavy stonework.

131| Inland Steel Building
30 W. Monroe St.
1954–1958, SKIDMORE, OWINGS & MERRILL

Chicago has always been a city where measurable superlatives like "largest," "tallest," and "busiest" have been the cornerstones of civic pride. It is indeed ironic that the Inland Steel Building, an office tower of modest scale and limited visual prominence, has achieved celebrity status, while its taller, larger, and significantly more conspicuous contemporary, the Prudential Building, is now virtually ignored.

Inland Steel's pioneering attributes are well known. Its unobstructed floor plate (177 × 58 feet) was unprecedented. This was accomplished by placing core services in the adjacent tower to the east. For the first time, steel pilings, driven eighty-five feet through mud and clay into bedrock, were used to support a high-rise structure. Inland Steel was Chicago's first fully air-conditioned building, the first with dual glazing, and the first to provide indoor below-grade parking. It pioneered the use of stainless steel as a cladding material. Critics and scholars have consistently praised its graceful proportions, the elegance of its detailing, and the sophistication of its public art.

But the Inland Steel Building has not been adequately cited for one of its most praiseworthy attributes, the civic benefit of its presence

INLAND STEEL BUILDING

on the streetscape. Avant-garde for its time, the building has become increasingly engaging, compatible, and understated as the character of the surrounding area has evolved. This is attributable in large measure to the excellence of its site plan and to the civility of its scale. The placement of its principal mass respects and reinforces the established building lines of the fronting streets. The longer dimension, along the line of Dearborn St., is interestingly maintained by seven projecting columns encased in stainless steel. The alignment of the shorter Monroe St. dimension not only enhances the sculptural quality of the services tower but also imparts a personal scale and orientation to the entrance, which is recessed at grade, glazed on three sides, and flooded by natural light. A substantial single-story annex houses loading docks, mail rooms, and the garage entrance. Its skillful placement on the site's northeastern corner makes it all but invisible to the public.

The economics of modern urban development and current code standards have secured the uniqueness of the Inland Steel Building and have qualified it to be a protected architectural landmark. It survives as an enduring reminder of an optimistic period when the future was a beacon and long-restrained architectural skill and creativity blossomed once again. While its designers could not possibly have anticipated the adjacent construction, especially of the plaza on the west side of Dearborn St., they could not have prepared for it more effectively.

—LAWRENCE OKRENT

132| Bank One Plaza
(*First National Bank of Chicago*)
Block bounded by S. Dearborn, W. Madison, S. Clark, & W. Monroe Sts.
1969, PERKINS & WILL; C. F. MURPHY ASSOCS., ASSOC. ARCHS.

When this building was first built, state laws prohibited branch banking in Illinois. The building had to accommodate tens of thousands of daily transactions on a single site. Departments with public access required large spaces at or near street level; tenants needed traditional office-building floors and access outside of banking hours. The graceful solution was this tapering shape and a pair of end cores that hold all services. The spread base and the cores combine to achieve stability and efficient load carrying; they also create the landmark profile. The multilevel, sunken plaza combines services with spaces around a fountain and Marc Chagall's mosaic mural *The Four Seasons* (roof structure, 1996, Skidmore, Owings & Merrill). The ancillary building at 20 S. Clark St. was known as the Two First National Building (1973, C. F. Murphy Assocs.).

133| Three First National Plaza
W. Madison St. at N. Dearborn St.
1981, SKIDMORE, OWINGS & MERRILL

SOM broke their own mold with this carnelian granite-clad companion to Bank One Plaza (formerly First National Bank). Two towers are connected by a nine-story atrium with exposed steel truss supports. The sawtooth, setback configuration provides many corner offices and greenhouses at the top, which is lower than Bank One Plaza in order to leave the views from the bank's boardroom unobscured.

134| 10 N. Dearborn St.
(*Covenant Club*)
1923, WALTER S. AHLSCHLAGER
1987, FACADE RESTORATION AND INTERIOR REMODELING, ECKENHOFF SAUNDERS ARCHITECTS

Designed for a Jewish men's social and service club, this Renaissance Revival structure was completely gutted and rebuilt for office and retail uses.

BANK ONE PLAZA

135| Cook County Administration Building
(*Brunswick Building*)
69 W. Washington St.
1965, SKIDMORE, OWINGS &
MERRILL
2001, CHILD DEVELOPMENT CENTER,
ROSS BARNEY + JANKOWSKI

The weight is carried by the innovative tube-in-a-tube system—a concrete elevator core at the center and concrete exterior walls—that allows flexible, column-free floors. To provide a visually open base, a massive ring girder (behind the thick windowless line at the second floor) transfers and distributes the weight of over five dozen vertical members to the perimeter first-floor columns. Above the girder, the walls curve gracefully inward, recalling the profile of the nearby Monadnock Building. In the plaza to the west is Joan Miró's *Miss Chicago* (1981). The outdoor play area for the building's day-care center is located directly behind the Miró sculpture and is enclosed by a fence whose bollards mimic the artwork.

136| 33 N. Dearborn St.
(*Connecticut Mutual Life Building*)
1967, SKIDMORE, OWINGS &
MERRILL

On this masonry-clad Miesian steel frame, visual enhancement is limited to subtle emphasis around the window openings. The first floor was originally arcaded, a configuration favored by Chicago's zoning ordinance, but later filled in to provide better retail spaces.

137| Richard J. Daley Center
(*Chicago Civic Center*)
Block bounded by W. Washington, W. Randolph, N. Dearborn & N. Clark Sts.
1965, C. F. MURPHY ASSOCS.; LOEBL, SCHLOSSMAN & BENNETT AND
SKIDMORE, OWINGS & MERRILL, ASSOC. ARCHS.

Sternly elegant in its skin of rusting steel, the Daley Center is an outstanding example of Chicago's love for Miesian architecture. The scale is remarkable: at 648 feet it is immensely tall for only 31 stories, and its structural bays are an unprecedented 87 feet wide and 47 feet 8 inches deep. Warren trusses frame each floor, stiffening the overall structure and allowing ample room between floors for service ducts and conduits. In its logic and execution, the resulting structure resembles a beautifully detailed bridge.

A framework of such scale and precision was deemed necessary to allow varied interior spaces. The structure was built to house more than 120 court and hearing rooms, a law library, and office space. Offices were accommodated by normal floor-to-ceiling heights of twelve feet, while twenty-six-foot-high courtrooms extended through two floors. Future space needs were taken into consideration; courtrooms can be converted into office space—and vice versa—with minimal structural rearrangement.

In its interior flexibility the Daley Center is truly Miesian in spirit. The ruggedly handsome exterior reflects the underlying structure in its refined detailing. Cruciform columns stand outside

RICHARD J. DALEY CENTER

the exterior wall plane, which is composed of six-foot-high spandrel panels and twelve-foot-high bronze-tinted windows. Both the spandrels and columns are clad in Cor-Ten, a self-weathering steel developed in the 1930s for use in railway hopper cars and not previously used in building construction. The building's bronzed coloring and hefty proportions give it a Promethean character, conjuring images of the foundry infernos of WPA murals.

The Daley Center brought a building of immense visual power to the Loop but at a heavy price—the destruction of an entire block of shops and restaurants that encouraged downtown pedestrian traffic day and night. Yet something wonderful was gained; the Daley Center plaza has become Chicago's Forum. With its large-scale sculpture by Pablo Picasso, the plaza is the location of activities as diverse as concerts, farmers' markets, and peace rallies, as well as memorial services. Through these and other activities, the Daley Center fulfills a civic purpose consistent with its architectural dignity.　　—TERRY TATUM

138| Untitled Sculpture
("The Picasso")
Daley Center Plaza,
W. Washington St. between
N. Dearborn and N. Clark Sts.
1967, PABLO PICASSO, ARTIST

Though many hated it at first, locals and visitors alike have come to love this enigmatic Cor-Ten head, which resembles the artist's drawings both of his wife and his Afghan hound, Kaboul. The frontal view looks more like the dog; walk around toward the rear to see how in profile it resembles a woman.

139| Commonwealth Edison Company—Dearborn St. Substation
115 N. Dearborn St.
1931, HOLABIRD & ROOT

Despite such changes as filled-in windows, elegance prevails in this Art Deco shell, which houses electrical equipment. In a canted panel above the window is a low-relief panel by Sylvia Shaw Judson.

140| The Goodman Theatre Center
170 N. Dearborn St.
2000, KUWABARA PAYNE MCKENNA BLUMBERG ARCHITECTS AND DLK ARCHITECTURE; SOUTH FACADE, LIGHTSWITCH

A round pavilion marks the corner and a kinetic display of colored lights enlivens the Randolph St. elevation, but the real action is on Dearborn St., where glass walls reveal the two-story lobby. Anchoring the north end are the preserved facades of the Harris and Selwyn theaters (1923, Crane & Franzheim), which, like the Oliver Building across the street, sacrificed their interiors to a larger new facility.

141| Delaware Building
(Bryant Building)
36 W. Randolph St.
1874, WHEELOCK & THOMAS
1888, TWO-STORY ADDITION, JULIUS H. HUBER
1982, RENOVATION, WILBERT R. HASBROUCK

A rare survivor from the early post-Fire years demonstrates High Victorian variety: bays of differing widths, rectangular and segmental arches, dissimilar stringcourses, and competing horizontal and vertical emphases. Added to the mix are a variety of materials: glass and cast iron on the first two floors, cast stone (an early form of precast concrete) on the next four levels, and pressed metal on the top two floors. Step into the lobby from Randolph St. to see the interior court. The beveled glass blocks, which allow light to filter down from the skylight, are also a product of Huber's addition.

142| Theatre District Self Park
181 N. Dearborn St.
1987, HAMMOND, BEEBY & BABKA

The precast concrete base of this early "theme" garage reflects the neo-Classical styling of nearby theaters. Music and posters from Broadway shows are assigned to each floor to help customers find their cars.

143 | Leo Burnett Building
35 W. Wacker Dr.
1989, KEVIN ROCHE–JOHN DINKELOO & ASSOCS.; SHAW & ASSOCS., ASSOC. ARCHS.

Roche's Chicago debut is an overly detailed and dreary interpretation of the columnar skyscraper; rows of columns and pilasters constitute the base and capital as well as a mid-point break for a mechanical floor. Stainless-steel bullnose mullions, which have been compared to pencils, add sparkle but do not make a brilliant design.

144 | 55 W. Wacker Dr.
(*Blue Cross–Blue Shield Building*)
1968, C. F. MURPHY ASSOCS.

Concrete is both the major structural material and the primary design element. Eight huge pylons act as structural members; duct enclosures are counter-balanced by concrete spandrels and cornices. Perpendicular surfaces have bush-hammered corrugations; horizontal ones are smooth, with exposed tie holes.

145 | Marina City
300 N. State St.
1959–1967, BERTRAND GOLDBERG ASSOCS.

Few Chicago buildings were as innovative in design or had as great an impact on their environment as Marina City. Marina City stood out immediately among Chicago's many architectural highlights and was for a long time one of the most photographed buildings in the city. The two round apartment towers with their semicircular balconies—for many people they resembled corncobs—were especially intriguing, as were the spiraling garages that occupy the lower half of each tower.

Marina City was designed for the yuppie *avant la lettre*. Goldberg and his client, the Building Service Employees International Union, decided that despite the exodus to the suburbs, many of those employed in the Loop were single or childless and wanted an apartment close to their work. They were right. The complex was a success from the start and a prototype for many others on the edge of the Loop.

In the absence of facilities that would glamorize living in an area previously devoted to railroading, Goldberg incorporated stores, a restaurant, a health center, a swimming pool, a skating rink, an exhibition space, a theater, a marina, a bowling alley, and an office tower. The complex was advertised as a "city within a city," a place for "24-hour urban living," both clearly commentaries on the suburbs, in which commuters spent only their nights.

Goldberg's masterful design imparts an open feeling to the small, packed complex, every part of which seems to defy gravity and move upward; the plaza, for example, is lifted above the water and dematerialized by the windows of the restaurant. Despite recent additions, it is experienced as

MARINA CITY—UNDER CONSTRUCTION

MARINA CITY

a thin slab, very different from the heavy box beneath its neighbor, Mies van der Rohe's One IBM Plaza. Because of the spiraling garage floors, the apartment towers seem to grow out of the plaza. Indeed, the towers appear virtually transparent, with the garage floors and balconies cantilevering from the perimeter columns. The office tower, now a hotel, is also lifted off the plaza, to stand on columns above a windowless slab containing the bowling alley. This structure, in turn, is separated from the plaza by a glass-enclosed floor housing the hotel lobby and retail space. The irregularly shaped theater is the only structure that seems to rest on the plaza instead of taking off from it.

The apartments themselves are also designed to create feelings of openness. Not only are they placed above the garages and the warehouses formerly in the vicinity, but also their pie shapes allow for ever-expanding views of the city. More than in any other high-rise apartments, in Marina City one has the feeling of having the whole city at one's feet.

Although modernistic in design, Marina City's round, cast-concrete forms were a clear reaction against the glass and steel towers of Mies van der Rohe, whose style was prevailing in Chicago at the time.

—WIM DE WIT

146| **Westin River North**
(*Hotel Nikko*)
320 N. Dearborn St.
1987, HELLMUTH, OBATA & KASSABAUM; TAKAYAMA & ASSOCS., ASSOC. ARCHS.

The Japan Air Lines hotel chain placed on the riverfront a simple design of light masonry and dark trapezoidal bays.

147| **321 N. Clark St.**
(*Quaker Tower*)
1987, SKIDMORE, OWINGS & MERRILL

This late example of flat-topped, rectangular modernism includes a transparent ground floor, designed to the departed client's taste. Semicircular stainless-steel mullions stress verticality.

148 | R. R. Donnelley Center
77 W. Wacker Dr.
1992, RICARDO BOFILL
ARQUITECTURA, DESIGN ARCH.;
DESTEFANO AND PARTNERS,
SUPERVISING ARCHS.

For his first American sky-scraper, the Spanish proponent of modern classicism supplied a square, silver-tinted glass column, under four pedimented roofs. At night, theatrical lighting downplays the inglorious mismatch between the glazing and the white granite exoskeleton.

149 | Chicago Title & Trust Center
161–171 N. Clark St.
1992, KOHN PEDERSEN FOX

Lacking the prominent unobstructed sites of their 225 and 333 W. Wacker Dr. buildings, the designers created an intriguing top to make the building leap out of the skyline. An identical tower is intended for the site's northern half.

150 | James R. Thompson Center
100 W. Randolph St.
1979–1985, MURPHY/JAHN; LESTER KNIGHT & ASSOCS., ASSOC. ARCHS.

It's either breathtaking or exhausting, depending on your threshold for retinal fatigue, but it draws crowds of tourists and ennobles such humble tasks as renewing a driver's license and picking up tax forms. A series of dazzling concepts traveled a rocky road in translation to actual buildable materials. Helmut Jahn's original design called for silicone glazing, which would have produced a mullionless skin, but it scared off contractors fearful of liability problems. Salmon, silver, and blue were already in Jahn's palette and fit the standard governmental red, white, and blue but as executed look tawdry and ill chosen. But the central "people place," the massive atrium that rises a full seventeen floors and is expressed by a sliced-off cylindrical crown, is a resounding success. The plaza placement of Jean Dubuffet's

JAMES R. THOMPSON CENTER

fiberglass sculpture, *Monument with Standing Beast,* was resented by the champions of Illinois artists and has been uncharitably compared to piles of dirty, melting snow.

151 | County Building/ Chicago City Hall
118 N. Clark St.
(*County Building*)
121 N. La Salle St.
(*City Hall*)
1911, HOLABIRD & ROCHE

This is in essence an office building—or, rather, two office buildings built around light wells—one of which has its offices interrupted for two stories to accommodate the City Council. The goal was to erect a building of eleven very high stories that would not look like a skyscraper. It was accomplished by doubling the scale of the exterior mask, minimizing fenestration, and introducing what were at construction Chicago's biggest columns, seventy-five feet high, hollow, and comprising fifteen arc-shaped granite segments. The Corinthian capitals are the height of an entire floor. To support these purely decorative elements required caissons ten feet in diameter

152 | Burnham Center
(*Conway Building*)
111 W. Washington St.
1913, D. H. BURNHAM & CO. AND GRAHAM, BURNHAM & CO.

1986, RENOVATION, JACK TRAIN ASSOCS.

Burnham's version of the Chicago skyscraper (this was the firm's last before his death in 1912) continued to use the open light well introduced in the Rookery. Designed by Frederick P. Dinkelberg, the Conway Building eschewed the expression of its skeleton frame in favor of the image (but not the low scale) of the Beaux Arts city that permeated the pages of the 1909 Plan of Chicago.

153| Chicago Temple
(*First Methodist Episcopal Church*)
77 W. Washington St.
1923, HOLABIRD & ROCHE

A twenty-one-story office tower is crowned by an eight-story spire, the Loop's only church spire, which tops the world's tallest church (568 feet), according to the *Guinness Book of Records*. The shaft uses the vertical styling, small windows, and Gothic detailing that characterize the Tribune Tower; the spire, however, is more accurately executed. Officially, this is the home of the First United Methodist Church of Chicago, which has a ground-floor sanctuary and a chapel in the spire.

154| Chicago Loop Synagogue
16 N. Clark St.
1957, LOEBL, SCHLOSSMAN & BENNETT

This congregation began in a hotel room where travelers and businessmen could assemble a daily minyan. The building now serves that function in a ground-level chapel and an upper sanctuary. Reached by a ramp, the sanctuary is dominated by an eastern wall of Abraham Rattner's stained glass, *Let There Be Light.*

155| Harris Trust & Savings Bank
111 W. Monroe St.
1911, SHEPLEY, RUTAN & COOLIDGE
1960, EAST TOWER, SKIDMORE, OWINGS & MERRILL
1974, WEST TOWER, 115 S. LA SALLE ST., SKIDMORE, OWINGS & MERRILL

Stainless-steel Miesian towers are fitted around a neo-Classical, red granite and brick "traditional" bank in a way that affords each its own identity. The centerpiece features a five-story base in which three stories are deeply recessed behind Ionic columns. The East Tower uses thin window mullions to obtain a lively vitality and to avoid the surface distortion characteristic of large flat surfaces. It also makes a virtue of a mid-height mechanical floor, recessing it to fully expose the columns. The West Tower's wide bays and huge spandrels add horizontality to the mix.

156| Ralph H. Metcalfe Federal Building
77 W. Jackson Blvd.
1991, FUJIKAWA, JOHNSON & ASSOCS.

Tall, rectangular, flat-topped (rare in 1991), and designed to blend with Mies's Federal Center buildings, this concrete structure is finished in granite (not painted steel).

157| Chicago Metropolitan Correctional Center
(*William J. Campbell U.S. Courthouse Annex*)
71 W. Van Buren St.
1975, HARRY WEESE & ASSOCS.

More people ask "What the hell is that?" about the Chicago Metropolitan Correctional Center than about any other building in the Loop. And well they should, for there are few buildings like this twenty-seven-story, triangular federal detention center. However, a simple analysis of the concrete, slit-windowed exterior reveals much about the prison's interior, which houses only those awaiting trial in nearby federal courts.

CHICAGO METROPOLITAN
CORRECTIONAL CENTER

The shape is a response to the U.S. Bureau of Prisons' then-new approach to incarceration. In an attempt to reform prisons, the Bureau had Weese's office experiment with placing cells around a loungelike common area supervised by an unarmed officer. Weese found that a triangular floor plan allowed the maximum number of cells to be most efficiently centered around the lounge. The triangular plan was not intended to symbolize the three branches of government, although some members of those branches have been guests at the facility.

The first nine floors contain administrative facilities. The windows in this section are ten inches wide, to provide ample light and views for the staff. Above the tenth-floor mechanical room, identifiable by its angled air intakes, are five-inch-wide windows for the inmates' rooms. The long, thin windows were meant to symbolize an opening that people could not pass through. Not caring much about symbolism, some architecturally disrespectful inmates discovered a way around this design feature and escaped. Lights now wash the exterior, and bars have been added to the interiors of the cells.

The eight two-level housing units have recreation and private meeting rooms. These secured areas are represented by the long strips of horizontal windows at the upper floors. A rooftop basketball and volleyball court, covered by wire mesh, tops the building. Attempted helicopter escapes necessitated the installation of struts, which support cables that deter unauthorized aerial exits.

Although the Metropolitan Correctional Center can be seen as a straightforward solution to a building program, it is not without its architectural precedents. It owes a great deal to Le Corbusier, whose mixed-use Unité d'Habitation in Marseilles (1952) includes two-level housing units, a rooftop garden, and smooth concrete finishes. Although Le Corbusier hoped to create designs that would inspire worldwide imitation, it is Weese's building that has been widely copied.

The direct-supervision method of running correctional facilities has been successful, and Weese's triangular plan has been the basis for many of the housing units. His provocative but graceful building form, however, has not been matched.   —MICHAEL BORDENARO

158| One Financial Place
440 S. La Salle St.
1985, SKIDMORE, OWINGS & MERRILL

Built on the site of the La Salle St. Station's shed and tracks are an unadorned, flat-roofed office tower with forty bay windows per floor—a recollection of a Chicago School characteristic— and the five-story Midwest Stock

Exchange straddling the Eisenhower Expressway approach. The Stock Exchange's two arched windows (lighting a fitness center, not the trading area) are meant to honor Adler & Sullivan's demolished Chicago Stock Exchange Building. Access to the present La Salle St. commuters' station is through these buildings. The plaza, a gentle element in an otherwise hard environment, contains a bronze horse created by Ludovico de Luigi in homage to the horses of St. Mark's, Venice.

159| Chicago Board Options Exchange
141 W. Van Buren St.
1985, SKIDMORE, OWINGS & MERRILL

This virtually windowless box occupies the site of the La Salle St. Station's headhouse and turns its back on Van Buren St. It features a 44,000-square-foot trading floor.

160| The LaSalle Atrium Building
(*Fort Dearborn Hotel*)
401 S. La Salle St.
1914, HOLABIRD & ROCHE

1985, RENOVATION, BOOTH HANSEN ASSOCIATES

Strategically positioned next to the La Salle St. Station, this relatively modest former hotel has a symmetrical Georgian facade, a luxurious lobby sheathed in Circassian walnut and Rookwood tile, and a mezzanine adorned with murals depicting early Chicago. These elements were refurbished, retained, or replicated when the hotel was converted into offices. This was accomplished by closing the south end of the original U-shape with an elevator bank and adding skylights at the second floor and roof.

161| Chicago Board of Trade Building
141 W. Jackson Blvd.
1930, HOLABIRD & ROOT
1980, ADDITION, MURPHY/JAHN; SHAW & ASSOCS. AND SWANKE, HAYDEN, CONNELL, ASSOC. ARCHS.
1997, SECOND ADDITION, FUJIKAWA, JOHNSON ARCHITECTS
1998, FOUNTAIN IN EAST PLAZA, DESTEFANO AND PARTNERS

CHICAGO BOARD OF TRADE BUILDING

The Chicago Board of Trade is that rare hybrid in American architecture that successfully combines designs from two periods. The main portion, which faces north from the foot of La Salle St., Chicago's main financial artery, is a striking forty-five-story tower whose facade features the jagged, sawtooth profile often associated with Art Deco skyscrapers. The twenty-four-story steel and glass postmodern addition to the south is entered on Van Buren St. Although its black and silver exterior contrasts sharply with the gray limestone cladding of the original, the new is visually linked to the old through a skillful updating of the Art Deco building's vocabulary of setbacks and symmetry and a recapitulation of its pyramidal roof.

Likewise, the lobbies throughout the building complement each other, with the abstracted sculptural forms of

CHICAGO BOARD OF TRADE ADDITION

the 1930 entry inspiring two equally intriguing spaces in the 1980 structure. The original building's three-story lobby features streamlined cascades of buff-colored marble that alternate with massive black marble piers. Its sculptural volumes are further articulated by dramatic lighting, particularly through a panel that cuts a wide swath across the ceiling and down the wall.

In the 1980 addition the first-floor lobby is a compact, two-story variation of its antecedent executed in shades of jade and turquoise. On the twelfth floor is a second lobby—actually a spectacular atrium—another twelve stories high, made up of cascading walls of gleaming steel and reflective glass. The north wall is the limestone exterior of the original building, a skillful combination of contemporary and historic structures.

Sculpture and painting were important in both building campaigns. The carved figures holding wheat and corn on the La Salle St. facade were designed by Illinois artist Alvin Meyer; the pyramidal roof is topped by an aluminum statue of Ceres, the Roman goddess of agriculture, by the renowned American sculptor John Storrs. The similarly shaped skylight on the addition features an ornamental abstraction of a trading pit. Finally, reinstalled in the addition's atrium is a monumental mural of Ceres by Chicago artist John Warner Norton, removed years before from the original trading room.

—PAULINE A. SALIGA

162| Federal Reserve Bank Building
230 S. La Salle St.
1922, GRAHAM, ANDERSON, PROBST & WHITE
1957, SOUTHWEST ADDITION, NAESS & MURPHY
1989, RENOVATION AND NORTHWEST ADDITION, HOLABIRD & ROOT

163| Bank of America
(Continental Illinois)
(Illinois Merchants Bank Building)
231 S. La Salle St./230 S. Clark St.
1924, GRAHAM, ANDERSON, PROBST & WHITE
1990, RENOVATION, SKIDMORE, OWINGS & MERRILL

The southern end of La Salle St. is flanked by a pair of virtually identical buildings with Classical columns and cornices neatly lined up. The Federal Reserve Building has Corinthian columns;

B of A's are Ionic. On the interiors, similarity ends. B of A's second-level banking floor is a richly appointed re-creation writ large of a Roman temple, lacking only the god's statue. It

BANK OF AMERICA (CONTINENTAL ILLINOIS)

prompted Louis H. Sullivan to suggest that bankers here wear togas and speak Latin. Jules Guerin's murals adorning the frieze are allegorical references to international commerce. The Federal Reserve's dictate to avoid extravagance left the corresponding space dressed in white limestone under a restrained coffered ceiling. B of A is largely unchanged except for the introduction of escalators; most of the Federal Reserve has been reworked.

164| The Rookery
209 S. La Salle St.
1885–1888, BURNHAM & ROOT
1907, LOBBIES AND LIGHT COURT RENOVATION, FRANK LLOYD WRIGHT
1931, LOBBIES RENOVATION, WILLIAM DRUMMOND
1992, RESTORATION AND REHABILITATION, MCCLIER

After the Fire of 1871 a temporary city hall stood at the southeast corner of La Salle and Adams Sts. The site and nearby stables attracted pigeons and these—together with roosting politicians—gave the building the name the Rookery. When a new city hall was completed in 1885 and a group of investors acquired the lot, the name stayed with the new structure to be designed by Daniel H. Burnham and John W. Root.

More than two dozen Burnham & Root designs for commercial buildings were under construction in downtown Chicago in the 1880s and 1890s. Of these only the Rookery remains. To support the building on Chicago's notorious clay soils, Root utilized a rail-grillage foundation. The street facades are entirely load-bearing masonry construction, while the lower floors on the alleys are supported by cast-iron columns and wrought-iron beams. The floor system and the walls of the light well are supported by iron framing, allowing large expanses of glazing. The design took advantage of other innovations: fireproof clay tile, plate glass, improved mechanical systems, and that remarkable invention, the hydraulic passenger elevator.

The nearly square Rookery is organized around a central court surmounted by a skylight above the second story. A cast-iron oriel stair extends the height of the light well above. A walkway encircles the court at the mezzanine level, with grand stairways leading to that preeminent rental floor from two light-filled lobbies.

The bold facades feature a red granite base, pressed brick facades, terra-cotta ornament, and turrets. The light court is faced with light-colored glazed brick and terra cotta. All public spaces are clad in incised and gilded marble and copper-plated and Bower-Barff ironwork. Contemporaries extolled the Rookery as "the most modern of office buildings" and "a thing of light."

In 1905 Frank Lloyd Wright was commissioned to redesign the lobbies and light court, and he replaced Root's iron railings and terra-cotta cladding with those of his own more geometric design. Wright's former student William Drummond later altered the lobbies into one-story spaces and replaced the open-grille elevator cages with solid doors ornamented

THE ROOKERY—EXTERIOR

THE ROOKERY—INTERIOR

with rook motifs designed by Annette Byrne. During the following decades the skylight was covered over, the mosaic floor was removed, and the interior surfaces grew dim.

A comprehensive program completed in 1992 revitalized the offices and public spaces and restored the Rookery's historic features. The exterior was returned to its original ruddy hues, the public lobbies were re-created to approximate the 1907 renovation, and Drummond's elevator lobbies were retained. The skylight over the light court was re-opened, with a second skylight added at the top of the light well. The court's 1905 marble and ironwork were restored. Because of this remarkable commitment to preservation, the Rookery offers a rare glimpse of downtown Chicago at the turn of the twentieth century.

—DEBORAH SLATON

165| 208 S. La Salle St.
(*formerly City National Bank, originally Continental & Commercial Bank Building*)
1914, GRAHAM, BURNHAM & CO.

The street-level colonnade establishes the "financial" look of La Salle St. in many minds. The granite Doric columns have steel cores to support the block-filling structure. The colonnade reappears atop the building, where loss of the cornice destroys the "temple" effect.

166| 190 S. La Salle St.
1987, JOHN BURGEE ARCHITECTS WITH PHILIP JOHNSON; SHAW ASSOCS., ASSOC. ARCHS.

Philip Johnson's only Chicago building is postmodernism at its most serious and successful, responding strongly to its context and proclaiming its deep roots in Chicago's architectural history. The granite base is topped by a many-gabled summit that echoes similar elements on neighboring buildings. Its arched windows and doors parallel those on the Rookery; its overall design is drawn from John W. Root's demolished Masonic Temple (1892); the upper elevations alternate the punched-window limestone facades of the 1920s with contemporary curtain walls. The overscaled, barrel-vaulted lobby features rich marble and a gold-leaf ceiling.

167| 135 S. La Salle St.
(*formerly La Salle Bank Building, originally Field Building*)
1934, GRAHAM, ANDERSON, PROBST & WHITE

Conceived as the Loop's largest office building, the Field Building was one of the city's last

135 S. LA SALLE ST.

sizable buildings under construction as the Depression deepened. It is an H-plan building with a central rectangular tower rising from a base with four lower corner towers. The limestone exterior creates strong verticals alternating with window tiers of similar size. Embellishment consists only of a dark granite base and incised lines at the summits of the five shafts. The marble lobby is lush by contrast, offsetting beige walls with white pilasters and metalwork of nickel silver bronze. Mirrored Art Deco bridges connect the north and south balconies.

168| 120 S. La Salle St.
(*State Bank of Chicago Building*)
1928, GRAHAM, ANDERSON, PROBST & WHITE
1994, BANKING HALL RESTORATION, VOA ASSOCS.
1998, RENOVATION, LOHAN ASSOCS.

The overall lines are slimmer and the colonnade is reduced to a four-column entrance, but the outline is similar to the firm's bank at 208. What's more, the second-floor banking space is intact.

169| **Northern Trust Company Building**
50 S. La Salle St.
1905, FROST & GRANGER
1928, TWO-STORY PENTHOUSE ADDITION, FROST & HENDERSON

This banking house *without* an office tower above it is singular on a street that is a virtual canyon.

170| 39 S. La Salle St.
(*formerly La Salle–Monroe Building, originally New York Life Building*)
1894, JENNEY & MUNDIE
1898, EASTERN HALF, JENNEY & MUNDIE
1903, ONE-STORY ADDITION, ARCHITECT UNKNOWN

This early steel-frame building is one of the first whose walls were built simultaneously at several stories instead of from the ground up.

171| 19 S. La Salle St.
(*Association Building, known as Central YMCA building*)
1893, JENNEY & MUNDIE

The heavy banding and the shifting design characterized much of Jenney's work at this time.

172| 11 S. La Salle St.
(*formerly Roanoke Building, originally Lumber Exchange Building*)
1915, HOLABIRD & ROCHE
1922, FIVE-STORY ADDITION, HOLABIRD & ROCHE
1926, TOWER, HOLABIRD & ROCHE; REBORI, WENTWORTH, DEWEY & MCCORMICK, ASSOC. ARCHS.
1984, RENOVATION, HAMMOND, BEEBY & BABKA

This building with an unusual number of changes and additions began as the Lumber Exchange, a sixteen-story late Chicago School commercial building with windows under arches at the fourth and top floors. The top rank of arches disappeared in 1922, when five floors were added under a re-creation of the original cornice. The vertical ranks of paired windows were later adapted to a tower addition at the eastern end of the Madison St. frontage. The tower, one of the first to incorporate setbacks, was primarily the design of Andrew N. Rebori. The 1984 renovation replaced a 1950s modernization with a postmodern evocation of the original, profusely ornamented features.

173 | Chase Plaza
10 S. La Salle St.
1989, MORIYAMA & TESHIMA;
HOLABIRD & ROOT, ASSOC. ARCHS.

The exterior walls of the base of the Otis Building (1912, Holabird & Roche) were reused in order to retain the scale of La Salle St., while building a sleek tower. No attempt was made to disguise either the old or the new: the stone base is contrasted by the facade, whose grid it sets. The new elevations are of matching blue-painted aluminum and glass with details picked out in bright green. The surface is interrupted for a seven-story semicircular entry and for a single strip of bay windows from the nineteenth floor to the roof.

174 | 1 N. La Salle St.
1930, VITZTHUM & BURNS

Slim strips of windows and limestone alternate to assert the tower's verticality. Virtually the only break is at the fifth floor, where sculptured panels commemorate the explorations of Robert Cavalier, Sieur de La Salle, who allegedly camped on this site in 1679.

175 | 2 N. La Salle St.
1979, PERKINS & WILL

Ribbons of windows, set flush in alternating bands with structural aluminum wall panels, stress the smoothness of this building's skin; rounded corners emphasize its continuity. The unglazed corners at the second level identify the mezzanine of transfer beams that allowed the building to reuse the foundations of the demolished La Salle Hotel.

176 | 33 N. La Salle St.
(Foreman State National Bank Building)
1930, GRAHAM, ANDERSON, PROBST & WHITE

The upward thrust is enhanced by facing the recessed spandrels on the central portion of each facade in a darker terra cotta than the piers. The gradual tapering of the peak and the sculpted relief on the rose granite base, which includes suggestions of pediments at the fourth floor, are forms of stripped eclecticism.

177 | Savings of America Tower
120 N. La Salle St.
1991, MURPHY/JAHN

Through carefully executed, elegant detail the building enriches the La Salle St. corridor with a vigorous three-dimensionality. East and west facades feature a gently curving, gray-tinted, butt-glazed window wall, bordered by a contrasting, deeply suppressed vertical bank of windows. Both facades are crowned by a glazed three-story half vault. A cantilevered trellis on the north wall extends the length of Court Pl. Curving over the entrance is artist Roger Brown's *Flight of Daedalus and Icarus,* executed in a colorful mosaic. Above the entrance loggia, all masonry is coursed in alternating bands of light and dark gray flame-cut granite. Dividing the facade into two unequal parts, a vertical granite-clad plane pulls the window wall out over the sidewalk and separates the office spaces from the service and mechanical areas. Polished

SAVINGS OF AMERICA TOWER

granite clads the horizontally banded, deeply rusticated lobby walls; at the height of the door lintels, a brass strip lines the horizontal joint in the granite.

178| **Cadillac Palace Theatre**
151 W. Randolph St.

Hotel Allegro Chicago
171 W. Randolph St.
1925, C.W. AND GEORGE L. RAPP
1999, RENOVATION, DANIEL P. COFFEY & ASSOCS.

This is the western anchor to the Randolph St. Theatre District. The theater's historic elements were restored or re-created and its stage and sup-port spaces greatly expanded. The Allegro's cultural image contrasts with the smoke-filled, backroom-political identity of the predecessor Bismarck Hotel.

179| **State of Illinois Building**
(*Burnham Building*)
160 N. La Salle St.
1924, BURNHAM BROS.
1992, RENOVATION AND ADDITION, HOLABIRD & ROOT

A U-shaped office building with a traditional tripartite facade was retrofitted to create court-rooms and offices for the State of Illinois. A mechanicals floor was added, sheathed in lime-stone and fitted with a cornice and belt courses that resemble the original summit. The walls of the light well were opened up behind a reflective glass curtain wall. The single arched entry was expanded into a new lobby resembling a walled Italian courtyard.

180| **200 N. La Salle St.**
1984, PERKINS & WILL

This "extruded ice cube" is clad in a curtain wall of green-tinted glass, half of which has been sprayed from behind to make it opaque. The perimeter is serrated to create ten corner offices per floor. The taller windows at these corners help to emphasize verticality.

181| **203 N. La Salle St.**
1985, SKIDMORE, OWINGS & MERRILL

The horizontal slits ventilate the parking levels and are repeated for unity above. The massive glass column on Clark St. houses the elevator; slanting skylights above it cover two interior atriums.

182| **La Salle–Wacker Building**
221 N. La Salle St.
1930, HOLABIRD & ROOT; REBORI, WENTWORTH, DEWEY & MCCORMICK, ASSOC. ARCHS.

Dramatically sited at the "gate-way to finance" on La Salle St., this building allows a clear reading of the H-shaped plan devised in response to the 1917 ordinance restricting buildings to floor areas one-quarter of their site above a certain height. Stripped-down Classicism and setbacks mark the changes. The three-story base shifts to an H configuration with north and south light courts. At the twenty-third-story cross of the H, the tower ascends uninterrupted for another eighteen floors.

183| **222 N. La Salle St.**
(*Builders Building*)
1927, GRAHAM, ANDERSON, PROBST & WHITE
1986, RENOVATION AND ADDITIONS, SKIDMORE, OWINGS & MERRILL

This is a late appearance of Daniel H. Burnham's tripartite, limestone-clad, flat-roofed office block around a light court. Don't miss the central atrium, which the building trades that devel-oped the structure used as an indoor fair.

184| **Reid-Murdoch Center**
(*Reid, Murdoch & Co. Building*)
325 N. La Salle St.
1914, GEORGE C. NIMMONS
2002, RENOVATION, DANIEL P. COFFEY & ASSOCS.

The most visible of Nimmons's warehouse designs, this is re-garded as perhaps his best work. The building lost its rigid sym-

REID-MURDOCH CENTER

metry with the removal of the westernmost bay in 1930, when La Salle St. was widened.

185 | 325 N. Wells St.
(*Helene Curtis Building*)
1912, L. GUSTAV HALLBERG
1984, RENOVATION, BOOTH HANSEN ASSOCIATES

An old riverfront warehouse was transformed into a distinctive office building by inserting green glass topped by a terraced crystalline addition housing the company boardroom.

186 | Engineering Building
205 W. Wacker Dr.
1928, BURNHAM BROS.
1982, RENOVATION, HIMMEL BONNER

This U-shaped building had its original entrance below an open court on Wells St. The windows are uniform except at the corners; ornament is restricted to the base and top, where it projects slightly in the manner of Art Deco skyscrapers. Traces of the original lobby were retained in a renovation that moved the entrance to the Wacker Dr. side.

187 | Skyline Century of Progress
(*Trustees System Service Building*)
182 W. Lake St.
1930, THIELBAR & FUGARD
2003, CONVERSION TO RESIDENTIAL, FITZGERALD ASSOCS. ARCHS.

This was Chicago's last skyscraper begun before the stock market crash of October 1929. It introduced to the city an Art Deco device used elsewhere: above the fourth floor the brick is purple, shading lighter to the top, which is buff to match the sunburst terra-cotta ornament. It is topped by a ziggurat and lantern. Around the original banking entrance on Lake St. are panels depicting finance through the ages by Eugene van Breeman Lux, who also designed the allegorical figures at the second-floor level. The lead panels of workingmen are by Edgar Miller.

SKYLINE CENTURY OF PROGRESS

CHICAGO TRANSIT AUTHORITY
—LAKE/WELLS ENTRANCE CANOPY

**188| Chicago Transit Authority—
Lake/Wells Entrance Canopies**
**Northeast and southeast corners
of W. Lake and N. Wells Sts.**
1997, TENG & ASSOCS.

Each sleekly modern entrance
canopy is a beautiful piece of
street furniture and brightens
the way out of this station.

189| 188 W. Randolph St.
(*Steuben Club Building*)
1929, VITZTHUM & BURNS
1993, RENOVATION, STENBRO LTD.

This is possibly the last of the
historicist limestone tower
buildings whose shapes were
conditioned by the 1923 zoning
ordinance. The silhouette of
telescoping "towers" also characterizes the firm's later design
for 1 N. La Salle St.

190| 180 W. Washington St.
(*Equitable Building*)
1929, HYLAND & CORSE

191| "I Am" Temple
(*Elks Club Building*)
176 W. Washington St.
1916, OTTENHEIMER, STERN &
REICHERT

Two narrow eccentric structures:
180 is a veritable terra-cotta
catalog, while the Temple's unusual character is ascribed to
the fact that the Viennese-born
Rudolph Schindler was working
for this firm. It was his first
American job, after his studies
with Otto Wagner and before
joining the office of Frank Lloyd
Wright.

192| 175 W. Washington St.
(*Chicago Federation
of Musicians*)
1933, N. MAX DUNNING
1949, ADDITION, ARCHITECT
UNKNOWN

The added third story of this
tiny Bedford limestone gem
carefully respects the original
facade.

193| Concord City Centre
208 W. Washington St.
1926, GRAHAM, ANDERSON,
PROBST & WHITE
2002, CONVERSION TO
CONDOMINIUMS, HARTSHORNE &
PLUNKARD

194| 212 W. Washington St.
1912, HOLABIRD & ROCHE
2002, CONVERSION TO
CONDOMINIUMS, FITZGERALD
ASSOCS. ARCHS.

The unusual sight of flower-
bedecked balconies on this block
heralds a pioneering residential
conversion in this previously
business-only district.

195| Washington Block
40 N. Wells St.
1874, FREDERICK & EDWARD
BAUMANN

This rare survivor from the
immediate post-Fire years has
remained virtually intact. It is
singularly well conceived, with
a facade of alternating wide
and narrow stone courses and
windows clearly outlined and
topped with a variety of Italianate crowns. Frederick Baumann advocated isolated-pier
foundations as more suitable
than continuous perimeter ones
to Chicago's compressible soil.
This building is assumed to have
them, since it was designed just
after he published a pamphlet
on the subject.

196| Hotel La Salle Public Garage
219 W. Washington St.
1919, HOLABIRD & ROCHE
1923, ADDITIONAL FIVE BAYS,
HOLABIRD & ROCHE

The aesthetics of the multilevel
parking structure were resolved
in this early uncelebrated gem

by mimicking a conventional office building. However, there is nothing conventional about the way the fifteen narrow bays with their sash windows alternate with the vigorous uninterrupted piers. The wonderful rhythm is enhanced by the use of black Roman brick as striping in the red facade and by crisply detailed spandrel panels. A stringcourse above the shops and a well-proportioned cornice contain the design. Unlike most later garages, this one has flat, not sloped, floors and a single elliptical ramp in the center of the rear wall, with an elevator to move cars in the low-traffic direction.

197| Madison Plaza
200 W. Madison St.
1982, SKIDMORE, OWINGS & MERRILL

The serrated front creates a distinctive plaza and a setting for Louise Nevelson's steel sculpture *Dawn Shadows;* the stepped-back top allows views to the east from the top floors. A partially prefabricated, steel framing system limited on-site welding, resulting in high-speed erection of the exterior tube.

198| 181 W. Madison St.
1990, CESAR PELLI & ASSOCS.

Frankly echoing Eliel Saarinen's second-prize design in the 1922 Chicago Tribune Tower Competition, this symmetrical tower has truncated setbacks to enhance the strongly expressed—even exaggerated—verticality. The cladding is white granite, reflective metal mullions are set forward from the windows, and the finials are nickel-plated. A five-story lobby with a vaulted, coffered ceiling is meant to echo an entrance of the Uffizi Gallery in Florence, Italy. Each end wall of the lobby displays a large sculpture by Frank Stella.

199| 205 W. Monroe St.
1898, HOLABIRD & ROCHE

This wholesale building clearly reveals its metal framing on its upper floors and its low cost in the sparse ornament around the doorways.

200| Chicago Transit Authority— Quincy Station
W. Quincy and S. Wells Sts.
1897, ALFRED M. HEDLEY
1988, RESTORATION, CITY OF CHICAGO, DEPT. OF PUBLIC WORKS, BUREAU OF ARCHITECTURE

Lightweight and inexpensive materials were used in elevated stations. This one had its wood framing and decorative, pressed sheet-metal cladding restored to the original design and what paint analysis indicated was the original color.

CHICAGO TRANSIT AUTHORITY— QUINCY STATION

201| Insurance Exchange Building
175 W. Jackson Blvd.
1912, D. H. BURNHAM & CO.
1928, SOUTH ADDITION, GRAHAM, ANDERSON, PROBST & WHITE
2001, RENOVATION, LUCIEN LAGRANGE ARCHITECTS

Finished in enameled brick and terra-cotta trim, it has the styling of the first-quality buildings by the Burnham firm and its successors. Architect Ernest R. Graham was part owner of this project; its success enabled him to endow the Graham Foundation for Advanced Studies in the Fine Arts

202| Dixon Building
411 S. Wells St.
1908, NIMMONS & FELLOWS

This loft design is easily identified by the firm's characteristic ahistorical capitals, the banding of the piers near the summit, and the portions blocked out in light limestone against the dark brick.

203| Van Buren Building
212 W. Van Buren St.
1893, FLANDERS & ZIMMERMAN

A second-floor Romanesque oriel adds a graceful touch to this midblock building.

204| Brooks Building
223 W. Jackson Blvd.
1910, HOLABIRD & ROCHE

Gothic shafts and moldings in beige terra-cotta articulate the columns, presaging the Gothic office towers of the coming decades. But the walls are as clear and precise an articulation of their skeleton frame as the Chicago School could produce. The clasplike ornament atop the piers recalls its use a decade earlier by Louis H. Sullivan on the Gage Building.

205| City Colleges Building
(*Chicago & North Western Railway Office*)
226 W. Jackson Blvd.
1904, FROST & GRANGER
1978, RENOVATION, ALTMAN-SAICHEK ASSOCS.

As sons-in-law of Marvin Hughitt, the railroad's president, Charles S. Frost and Alfred H. Granger received many commissions, including the demolished Chicago & North Western Railway Terminal; they were not known for their office buildings. This one, like their railway stations, stresses structural sufficiency: strong corners, larger-than-necessary piers, a heavy base tapering into the wall above, and an entrance marked by sturdy columns.

206| AT&T Corporate Center and USG Building
227 W. Monroe St. and 125 S. Franklin St.
1988, 1992, SKIDMORE, OWINGS & MERRILL

There is a lot to be said for quality materials and craftsmanship, and this building says it all. This block-long complex of two high rises with a connecting base represents a reinterpretation of the conventions of the late 1920s setback office tower. Pronounced vertical lines, granite cladding, spiky pinnacles at the roof and setbacks, and lavish lobbies characterize this Adrian Smith design. The materials and general approach are the same for both buildings, but the details vary. The centers of the main facades are set-in vertical curtain walls; elsewhere windows are punched into the granite sheathing. On the AT&T Building the granite shades from deep red at the base to a light rose-beige at the top. Sporting a hipped roof, the USG Building has a lower profile. The lobby is a sequence of spaces of varying ceiling heights and a symphony in stone.

207| 303 W. Madison St.
1988, SKIDMORE, OWINGS & MERRILL

Designer Joseph Gonzalez integrated references to the work of Frank Lloyd Wright, Otto Wagner, and the Chicago School in a design that emerges as distinctly his own. The debt to Wright is in the interlocking right-angle geometries; Wagner is quoted in the glass-block storefronts; and the facade's tripartite composition and Chicago windows evoke the Chicago School. The relatively small building is clad in granite and tinted glass in white-painted aluminum frames. The horizontal banding of contrasting-colored granite serves to broaden the narrow facades. The general scale, treatment of the Washington St. entrance, and arcading at the top are reminiscent of Wright's unbuilt 1912 Press Building project in San Francisco.

208| 1 N. Franklin St.
1991, SKIDMORE, OWINGS & MERRILL

Sheathed in cast stone, the primary facade has various window types arranged in vertical rows; in sharp contrast the south facade has uniform ranks of Chicago windows. Two cylindrical glass towers set within square railings suggest the Art Moderne of the 1930s. The notched corners at the base are filled with glassy bays cantilevered over the sidewalk.

1 N. FRANKLIN ST.

209| 225 W. Washington St.
1986, SKIDMORE, OWINGS & MERRILL

This slablike building makes several references to the Chicago School. Within its tripartite facade, the shaft is articulated with full-bay variations of the Chicago window, drawing attention to the underlying frame. The glassy corner bays are another reference to the first Chicago School. The top floors on Franklin St. have a three-bay-wide recessed arcade. Prominent arches signal the entrances on both streets, but the arch on Washington St. leads to a blank stone wall.

210| Building for the Alexander White Estate
227–229 W. Lake St./
177 N. Franklin St.
1872, BURLING & ADLER

211| Building for Samuel Cole
233 W. Lake St./
185 N. Franklin St.
1873, BURLING & ADLER

212| Building for William Rowney
235 W. Lake St.
1873, ARCHITECT UNKNOWN

213| Building for Albert E. Kent
175 N. Franklin St.
1875, GEORGE H. EDBROOKE
1983, RENOVATION, STUART COHEN & ANDERS NEREIM

Known informally as the Lake-Franklin Group, this quartet constitutes the Loop's largest concentration of 1870s commercial buildings. They are typical of construction before the general use of passenger elevators and steel framing. All have load-bearing walls and relatively narrow Italianate windows.

BUILDING FOR ALBERT E. KENT

214| 225 W. Wacker Dr.
1989, KOHN PEDERSEN FOX; PERKINS & WILL, ASSOC. ARCHS.

The skillfully combined glass-and-granite cladding lightens considerably near the top, crowned by corner lanterns that pierce the skyline without dominating it.

333 W. Wacker Dr.

1979–1983, KOHN PEDERSEN FOX; PERKINS & WILL, ASSOC. ARCHS.

Sited at the bend of the Chicago River, this green glass tower has been called Chicago's first postmodern skyscraper. But William E. Pedersen, the design partner of Kohn Pedersen Fox, would never use that term to describe his buildings. He does, however, use such phrases as "a strategy of assemblage or collage—pieces, each of which has references to its context."

Indeed a "collage" of contextual "references," 333 is a quintessentially Chicago building in its tripartite structure of base, shaft, and clearly defined top. But base and shaft are strikingly different: a modern tower rests on a classically inspired base. These disparate forms are united by their color, utilized uniformly for the curtain wall and as a strong accent in the base, where bands of dark green polished marble alternate with gray granite. The same verde antique marble, combined with black granite, sheathes octagonal entrance columns that take their shape from the towers on the Merchandise Mart, which dominates the opposite bank of the river.

Above all, 333 is site-specific, its form adapted to its triangular lot. The Wacker Dr. facade is a graceful arc that follows the river's curve. The taut skin of mirrored glass reflects water, sky, and buildings in a constantly changing montage and, in an unmodern fashion, conceals the cross-braced steel supporting skeleton. The entrance is flush with the street, elegantly detailed and exactly centered.

The opposite facade, facing the edge of the Loop at the junction of Franklin and Lake Sts., is sliced and notched. To defy the neighborhood's generally dilapidated state in the late 1970s, Pedersen gave this side a splendid center entrance that invites passersby to ascend its curving steps, symbolic of his belief that the tall urban office building should be brought into a "more social state of existence." Twenty-five years

333 W. WACKER DR.

later, this entrance faces an area undergoing rapid redevelopment, and the riverside entrance looks out upon one of the city's grandest boulevards, the totally reconstructed and beautifully landscaped Wacker Dr.

This thirty-six-story tower established the seven-year-old firm as award-winning skyscraper designers. Worldwide commissions followed, including 333's immediate neighbors at 225 W. Wacker Dr. and 191 N. Wacker Dr. An element of contextualism with 225 is porthole medallions that recall the ventilation covers for 333's third-story mechanicals. This circular motif has become almost a signature of Pedersen's designs. It appears, for example, on the firm's Procter & Gamble complex in Cincinnati and as blind medallions on 900 N. Michigan Ave.

—JANE H. CLARKE

216| Merchandise Mart
222 Merchandise Mart Plaza
1930, GRAHAM, ANDERSON, PROBST & WHITE
1992, RENOVATION, BEYER BLINDER BELLE; JACK TRAIN ASSOCS., ASSOC. ARCHS.

Impressive for its size, beautiful in its detail, the Merchandise Mart is still a major icon of Chicago. Built as a wholesale store by Marshall Field & Co., it now serves primarily as a display center for furniture and furnishings dealers, apparel and gift wholesalers, and major art and art furniture shows. With some 4.2 million square feet of rentable space, it was when new the world's largest building. It remains the world's largest commercial building.

The design is typical of the late 1920s: prominent piers, recessed spandrels of darker color, and geometric ornament. Jules Guerin murals glow in the lobby and depict worldwide trade and commerce. Juniper berries and foliage combine to enrich the metalwork around the windows and on the elevators. The pedestrian bridge (1991, Murphy/Jahn) that links the Mart with the Apparel Center echoes the Deco geometry.

217| Apparel Center and Holiday Inn Mart Plaza
350 N. Orleans St.
1977, SKIDMORE, OWINGS & MERRILL

One of the central city's dreariest high rises assaults the eye from one of Chicago's most prominent sites.

218| The Residences at Riverbend
333 N. Canal St.
2002, DESTEFANO AND PARTNERS

MERCHANDISE MART

The building's massing was determined by the curve in the river and a rail line to the west. Sleek upper floors top a concrete midsection for parking and town houses at ground level. A single corridor on the west side of the apartment floors gives all the units an eastern orientation, with western light coming through high transom windows.

219| 191 N. Wacker Dr.
2002, KOHN PEDERSEN FOX;
KENDALL/HEATON ASSOCS.,
ASSOC. ARCH.

Given a once-in-a-lifetime opportunity to design a riverfront triptych with their two earlier buildings, the architects created a simple glass box that complements but does not compete with their own 333 W. Wacker Dr. The transparent facade at lobby level reveals how the structure cantilevers to the west above the second floor, an accommodation to the 2002 widening of Wacker Dr.

220| 150 N. Wacker Dr.
1975, JOEL HILLMAN
2001, RENOVATION, VON WEISE
ASSOCS.

The renovation minimized a jarring contrast of concrete and glass with dark paint, and covered the unsightly parking levels with a dark metal screen.

221| 123 N. Wacker Dr.
1988, PERKINS & WILL

An arcade repeats the one on the Civic Opera Building; both the opera house and the Merchandise Mart are echoed in the pyramidal roof, the granite skin with punched windows, and the tripartite organization.

222| 110 N. Wacker Dr.
1961, GRAHAM, ANDERSON,
PROBST & WHITE

The Wacker Dr. elevation of this International Style building is balanced with a central lime-stone wall, flanked by matched, three-story curtain-wall segments with fluted stainless-steel panels above and below paired windows.

223| 101 N. Wacker Dr.
1980, PERKINS & WILL
1990, ARCADE ALTERATION,
KOBER/BELLUSCHI

A cool, comfortable effect pervades this modernist block, in which energy efficiency was a major aim. Monitors behind the white aluminum curtain wall adjust to shifting sunlight, and vision and spandrel glass reflect or absorb light and heat as needed.

224| 29 N. Wacker Dr.
2000, SKIDMORE, OWINGS &
MERRILL

An undistinguished 1950s remodeling received a dramatic face-lift with new glass and a suspended metal grid, making for a richly textured facade.

225| Civic Opera Building
20 N. Wacker Dr.
1929, GRAHAM, ANDERSON,
PROBST & WHITE
1996, RENOVATION, SKIDMORE,
OWINGS & MERRILL

The last big real estate venture of Chicago's traction and utilities mogul Samuel Insull is an office building wrapped around a 3,500-seat opera house. Art Deco and French Renaissance styling pervade the building, along with musical motifs. An arcade runs the entire length of the east facade, in which the entrances to the theaters are marked with pediments. The Grand Foyer of the opera theater is forty feet high, with colors chosen by Jules Guerin, the designer of the theater's fire curtain.

226| UBS Tower
1 N. Wacker Dr.
2001, LOHAN CAPRILE GOETTSCH
ARCHITECTS

UBS TOWER

This office tower makes its most dramatic moves at street level, where clear glass walls encase the lobby on three sides. Using technology pioneered in Europe, the cable net wall allows huge sheets of very transparent glass to be supported with minimal structure, advancing the integration of plaza and lobby first seen in Mies van der Rohe's buildings.

227| 1 S. Wacker Dr.
1982, C. F. MURPHY ASSOCS.

Designer Helmut Jahn speaks of such buildings as a synthesis of Sullivanian and Miesian Chicago architecture with 1980s technology. Here he faced a concrete stepped-back structure with a curtain wall of black, silver, and coral tones in which the dark glass defines grouped vertical bands of "windows." The "draped curtain" entrance leads to a streamlined, well-ordered lobby.

228| Chicago Mercantile
Exchange Center
10 & 30 S. Wacker Dr.
1983 (30 S. WACKER DR.), 1988
(10 S. WACKER DR.), FUJIKAWA,
JOHNSON & ASSOCS.

To get a pair of office buildings and two large trading floors onto the site required cantilevering substantial portions of the towers over the trading rooms in the intervening base pavilion. To do this—while keeping trading floors column-free—required diverting loads to the ground via a system of thickened walls, wide columns, and huge trusses. The serrations boost the number of corner offices to sixteen per floor.

Ground was broken in 2002 for the Hyatt Center office building at 71 S. Wacker Dr., designed by Henry Cobb of Pei Cobb Freed.

229| Hartford Plaza
(*Hartford Fire Insurance Building*)
100 S. Wacker Dr.
1961, SKIDMORE, OWINGS & MERRILL

"Simple technique uncelebrated" marks this column-and-slab concrete frame, later covered in polished gray granite.

230| 200 S. Wacker Dr.
1981, HARRY WEESE & ASSOCS.

Responding to an irregularly shaped riverfront site, Weese experimented with triangular geometries, as he had in the Metropolitan Correctional Center, designing a building composed of two triangles joined at the hypotenuse. One segment is seven stories taller than the other, making the scheme most apparent at the top of the building. The perimeter columns of the concrete frame are rotated 45 degrees to present a slim edge on a taut curtain wall of white-painted aluminum and tinted glass.

231| Sears Tower

233 S. Wacker Dr.

1968–1974, SKIDMORE, OWINGS & MERRILL

1985, GROUND-FLOOR RENOVATION AND WACKER DR. ATRIUM ADDITION, SKIDMORE, OWINGS & MERRILL

1994, RENOVATION AND LOWER-LEVEL REMODELING, DESTEFANO AND PARTNERS

Stand back . . . waaaaaay back . . . and look at the 110-story Sears Tower. Its modernist rendition of base, middle, and top clearly illustrates the goals of client Sears, Roebuck & Co. and architect Bruce Graham: housing 5,000 Sears employees in the base, leasing the middle to tenants, and using the top to establish the world's tallest building for the world's largest retailer.

By creating the massive, 50,000-square-foot floor plates in the first fifty floors, Sears was able to consolidate its merchandising group employees from seven Chicago locations. The large floors allowed the greatest amount of employee interaction without moving up and down elevators. By stepping the building back above the fiftieth floor, Graham created prestige leasable space that helped Sears pay for—and profit from—the $186 million project.

Of that amount, one-third was used for the superstructure. Structural engineer Fazlur R. Khan skillfully carried out his duties by designing a "bundled tube" consisting of nine squares, sixty-five feet each. These squares, formed by I-beams spaced fifteen feet apart, are anchored in a deep concrete slab below the three subbasements. The slab rests on 114 steel and concrete caissons embedded in bedrock sixty-five feet below.

SEARS TOWER

Two of the nine tubes stop at the 50th floor, two more end at the 66th floor, and the last three terminate at the 90th, leaving two tubes to rise the full 1,454 feet. The termination of the tubes was determined as much by the lateral stiffness required to resist wind loads as by spatial conditions or aesthetic needs.

The daily movement of 25,000 tenants and visitors in and around the building has been problematic. The windswept plaza was difficult to access and rarely used. A redesign of the entry and lower levels in 1985 improved the original circulation design, which was confusing. Following Sears's move to Hoffman Estates in 1992, another lower-level renovation sorted out circulation for the building's new post-Sears life.

Sears Tower has always been more of a structural engineering triumph than an architectural accomplishment. While Graham and Khan were like a well-oiled, twin-cam engine firing on all cylinders when they designed the elegant John Hancock Center, the architectural manifold was slightly backfiring when they were running the Sears 500.

—MICHAEL BORDENARO

232| **311 S. Wacker Dr.**
1990, KOHN PEDERSEN FOX;
HARWOOD K. SMITH & PARTNERS,
ASSOC. ARCHS.

The world's tallest concrete-framed building (a title it took away from Water Tower Place) was to have had two companions, presumably with their own back walls and tower projections; the winter garden, which serves as an open space, would have been blocked off from sunlight. The summit, a seventy-foot drum surrounded by four smaller ones, now looks overdone at any hour. At night, lit by nearly 2,000 fluorescent tubes, it is a visual poke in the eye. Three of them are unthinkable.

233| **Exelon Thermal Technologies Franklin/Van Buren Plant**
400 S. Franklin St.
1996, ECKENHOFF SAUNDERS
ARCHITECTS

A giant ice factory, like its predecessor at State and Adams, this chilled water plant houses

EXELON FRANKLIN/VAN BUREN PLANT

the world's largest reinforced cast-in-place concrete ice tank, measuring 110 × 100 × 40 feet high. The "prow" that is oriented toward the river features the main supply and return chilled water piping as a signature element. The curving green glass wall is a reference to 333 W. Wacker at the north end of the Drive. The rooftop metal screen, reminiscent of nearby freeway signage, masks evaporative condensers.

234| **300 S. Riverside Plaza**
1983, SKIDMORE, OWINGS &
MERRILL

This ungainly addition to the riverfront has an odd curve meant to echo the bend in the river.

235| **222 S. Riverside Plaza**

236| **Union Station Multiplex**
(*MidAmerica Commodity Exchange*)
444 W. Jackson Blvd.
1971, SKIDMORE, OWINGS & MERRILL
2001, REMODELING, PRISCO SERENA
STURM ARCHITECTS

The complex that replaced Union Station's vaulted concourse comprises a bland tower and a low building designed to accommodate a trading-exchange floor. Enormous black aluminum trusses make the latter look like a supine version of the John Hancock Center.

UNION STATION

237 | Union Station
210 S. Canal St.
1913–1925, GRAHAM, ANDERSON, PROBST & WHITE
1992, RENOVATION, LUCIEN LAGRANGE & ASSOCS.

One of the last of the grand American railroad stations, Union Station was intended as the major element in West Loop development under Burnham's 1909 Plan of Chicago. The austere facade encloses a huge travertine-clad waiting room. The eight-story office tower above, set well back from the base and virtually invisible from the sidewalk, was meant to be twenty stories high. The double "stub end" tracks are the only ones in the United States where northbound and southbound tracks for different railroads end at the same point.

238 | 10 S. Riverside Plaza
1965, SKIDMORE, OWINGS & MERRILL

239 | 120 S. Riverside Plaza
1968, SKIDMORE, OWINGS & MERRILL
1986, ESPLANADE RENOVATION, SKIDMORE, OWINGS & MERRILL

This pair of Miesian office buildings is carried over active rail yards by columns. "Riverside Plaza" is used by virtually all

of the new waterfront buildings east of Canal St.—although no such street exists.

240 | 525 W. Monroe St.
1983, SKIDMORE, OWINGS & MERRILL

This pedestrian office building was overshadowed soon after construction when developers expanded the West Loop glitz zone from Franklin St. and Wacker Dr., bringing taller, more dramatic "signature" buildings.

241 | Heller International Tower
500 W. Monroe St.
1992, SKIDMORE, OWINGS & MERRILL

This granite-clad skyscraper stands in contrast to the firm's glassy modernism as seen at its S. Riverside Plaza buildings. A tower marks the southeastern corner, where the structure is built to the street edge; the building steps down to the west.

242 | 2 N. Riverside Plaza
(*Daily News Building*)
1929, HOLABIRD & ROOT

For evidence of the continuing cheapening of the urban vista, just compare the grand civic enhancement of this former newspaper building with Freedom Center, the *Chicago Tribune*'s modern printing plant. The interlocking vertical masses of the office block rise

2 N. RIVERSIDE PLAZA

from the public plaza, Chicago's first to be planned as part of an office building.

243 | Citicorp Center
500 W. Madison St.
1987, MURPHY/JAHN

Designer Helmut Jahn's sinuous curtain wall reads like a waterfall that cascades in precise sheets down the southern facade. Enter through the receding arch at the base or via the walkway from 2 N. Riverside Plaza to a dazzling multilevel space where steel structure is articulated, exposed, and celebrated.

244 | River Center
111 N. Canal St.
1913, D. H. BURNHAM & CO.
1982–2002 RENOVATION, BALSAMO/OLSON GROUP

245 | 165 N. Canal St.
(*Butler Bros. Warehouses*)
1922, GRAHAM, ANDERSON, PROBST & WHITE
1992, RENOVATION, GRAHAM-THOMAS ARCHITECTS
1999, CONVERSION TO RESIDENTIAL, HARTSHORNE & PLUNKARD

Detailed like a nineteenth-century armory, complete with machicolations, the design of these warehouses was *retardataire* by 1913 but greatly admired by Andrew Rebori, who found remarkable the "very noble largeness and simplicity." The building at 111 stands in its original spot; its twin originally stood on its eastern side but was demolished and reincarnated at 165.

246 | 100 N. Riverside Plaza
1990, PERKINS & WILL

Located atop active train tracks, the building accommodates lower floors with large uninterrupted spaces for computer operations. With much smaller floor plates for offices, the tower rises from a long base, an entire corner

100 N. RIVERSIDE PLAZA

of which is suspended over the tracks from an exposed truss on the roof.

247 | Ogilvie Transportation Center
(*Chicago & North Western Station Yards*)
Bounded by N. Canal, W. Lake, and N. Clinton Sts. and Citicorp Center
1911, FROST & GRANGER
1996, RENOVATION AND REBUILDING, HARRY WEESE & ASSOCS.

The new lightweight canopy structure has only half the number of columns as the original and perforated beams that harmonize with the modern industrial vocabulary of the Citicorp Center.

248 | North Western Terminal Powerhouse
N. Clinton St. between Milwaukee Ave. & W. Lake St.
1911, FROST & GRANGER

A 226-foot chimney is the exclamation point of the complex, which began four blocks to the south. The powerhouse's nine arches along Clinton St. recall the Beaux Arts styling of the demolished station.

249 | Clinton St. Lofts
226 N. Clinton St. and 541–547 W. Fulton St.
1883–1889, FREDERICK WAESCHER; ADLER & SULLIVAN
1997, CONVERSION TO RESIDENTIAL, HARTSHORNE & PLUNKARD

The genealogy of this sequence of substantial brick buildings is confusing. We know for certain that E. W. Blatchford, trustee of the Newberry estate, used its architect, Waescher, to design one of these buildings for his own business, which manufactured lead pipe and linseed oil. After a fire Adler & Sullivan rebuilt the interiors; they may (or may not) have received the commission for another Blatchford building.

250| Burlington Building
547 W. Jackson Blvd.
1911, MARSHALL & FOX

Gleaming terra cotta celebrates steel construction in the former headquarters of the Chicago, Burlington & Quincy Railroad. The arched arcades of the base are repeated at the top.

251| 550 W. Jackson Blvd.
2001, BELLUSCHI/OWP/P

One of many high rises to spring up west of the commuter train stations, this one has an unusual history of being built atop an existing four-story building whose telephone switching station could not be disrupted. Exterior columns and inverted V-shaped trusses transfer the weight of the new floors around the old structure. The curving roof hides the mechanical system and adds interest to the profile.

252| Illinois Institute of Technology—Chicago–Kent College of Law
565 W. Adams St.
1992, HOLABIRD & ROOT

With security a paramount planning issue, public spaces such as classrooms and auditoriums were located on lower floors; more private areas such as faculty offices and the library are on higher ones. The reading room, atop the building, features a ceiling with an exposed lamella truss.

253| Glessner Center
(*Warder, Bushnell & Glessner Co. Office and Warehouse*)
130 S. Jefferson St.
1883, JAFFRAY & SCOTT; WILLIAM W. BOYINGTON
1985, CONVERSION TO OFFICES, BOOTH HANSEN ASSOCIATES

Comprising a southern office and a northern warehouse, the building was completed by Boyington after a series of construction disasters. The firm made farm machinery; partner John J. Glessner commissioned Glessner House, H. H. Richardson's masterpiece.

254| Presidential Towers
555, 575, 605 & 625 W. Madison St.
1986, SOLOMON CORDWELL BUENZ & ASSOCS.

These four enormous and mundane apartment towers are noteworthy for the neighborhood change they hastened— the eradication of several blocks of seamy, colorful, and "underdeveloped" Skid Row.

255| Harold Washington Social Security Administration— Great Lakes Program Service Center
600 W. Madison St.
1976, LESTER B. KNIGHT & ASSOCS.

The design of this dull office building has one saving grace— the reflective curtain wall that is a beautiful backdrop to Claes Oldenburg's strong and structural, yet totally whimsical *Bat Column*.

256| ABN AMRO Plaza
540 W. Madison St.
2003, DESTEFANO AND PARTNERS

Placement of the tower on its podium is designed to maximize views for its occupants as well as those of the planned second tower. Raised floors and multiple risers accommodate the extensive and changing technological needs of the client, a bank consolidating several Loop offices in this location.

BAT COLUMN

ST. PATRICK'S ROMAN CATHOLIC
CHURCH

**257 | St. Patrick's Roman
Catholic Church**
140 S. Desplaines St.
1852, 1856, CARTER & BAUER
1990–2000, RENOVATION, BOOTH
HANSEN ASSOCIATES

Chicago's oldest church has a
simple facade of Milwaukee
common brick above a Joliet
limestone base. The onion dome
symbolizes the Church in the
East; the spire, the Church in the
West. The renovation created a
Celtic wonderland of decoration
in the church interior. It is a
masterpiece of harnessing computer technology to fulfill a historic decorative program.

NORTH MICHIGAN AVENUE/ STREETERVILLE

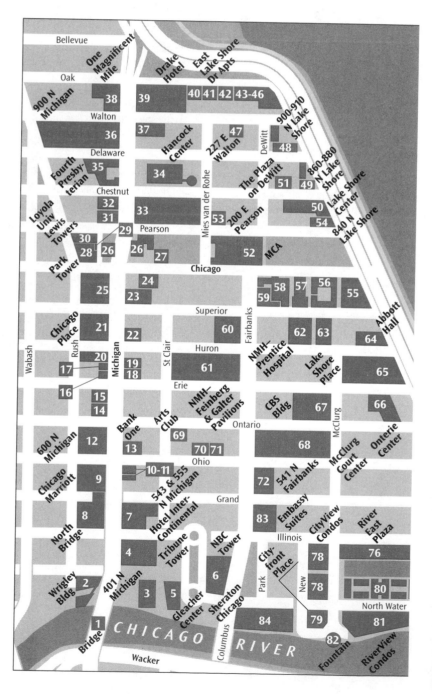

LAKE MICHIGAN

14 Woman's Athletic Club
15 Crate & Barrel
16 664 N Michigan
17 Terra Museum
18 663 N Michigan
19 669-675 N Michigan
20 City Place
21 Chicago Place
22 Allerton Crowne Plaza
23 Neiman Marcus
24 Olympia Centre
25 730-750 N Michigan
26 Water Tower and Pumping Station
27 Chicago Fire Dept
28 Park Tower
29 Perkins, Fellows & Hamilton Office
30 Loyola Lewis Towers
31 830 N Michigan
32 840 N Michigan
33 Water Tower Place
34 Hancock Center
35 Fourth Presbyterian
36 900 N Michigan
37 Palmolive Bldg

55 Rubloff Bldg
56 Mayer Hall
57 Wieboldt Hall
58 Ward Bldg
59 Tarry Bldg
60 NMH—Olson & McGaw Pavilions
61 NMH—Feinberg & Galter Pavilions
62 NMH—Prentice Hospital
63 Rehabilitation Institute

70 230 E Ohio
71 232 E Ohio
72 541 N Fairbanks

James Jardine Water Filtration Plant

73

OLIVE PARK

Lake Shore Dr

Peshtigo

North Pier Apts

77

East Water Place Town-houses

Lake Point Tower

75

Navy Pier

74

NORTH MICHIGAN AVENUE/ STREETERVILLE

IN A CITY NOTABLE FOR DRAMATIC TRANSFORMATIONS, THE STORY OF NORTH Michigan Avenue/Streeterville deserves a special place. It is amazing to contrast a picture of today's densely built-up neighborhood with an aerial photograph taken in 1926. Then, apart from a handful of scattered buildings, the roughly square-mile area was a gigantic vacant lot, awaiting development. More remarkably, forty years earlier there had been little land there at all. Lake Michigan then covered virtually all of Streeterville, from the east side of N. Michigan Ave. (then Pine St.) reaching from Chicago Ave. north to Oak St. The scruffy land south of Chicago Ave. was mostly uninhabited sand dunes.

Now one of Chicago's most valuable real estate parcels, the area was created almost by accident. A breakwater, constructed to the north of the mouth of the Chicago River in the early 1830s, was extended eastward during the following decades, creating sand dunes along the shoreline to the north. By the 1880s there was a considerable accumulation up to about Chicago Ave.

In July 1886 George Wellington ("Cap") Streeter arrived on the scene. A show and circus promoter, and surely one of Chicago's most memorable mavericks, the eponymous Streeter ran aground with his rickety ship on a sandbar near today's John Hancock Center. As the weeks went by and the water failed to rise and free his ship, the wily captain built a crude causeway to the land and encouraged builders who were developing the nearby Gold Coast residential area to dump their excavated materials around his ship. Since the land thus created stood outside the official boundaries of the State of Illinois as depicted in the 1821 shoreline survey, he declared it a free "federal district" answerable only to the national government—and set himself up as its governor. He was soon selling off the land to gullible investors.

The rapid development of the Near North Side increased the size of the "District of Lake Michigan," and Chicago's initial indifference to Streeter's claim turned to indignation. Repeated attempts to evict him met with no success until 1918, when the enormous clout arrayed against him proved overwhelming, and his claim was rejected by the courts. He was finally evicted for selling whiskey on Sundays.

The southern part of Streeterville, along with Ogden Slip and the Chicago River, burgeoned in the 1890s with warehouses and dock facilities. After 1900, additional factories, lofts, and offices appeared to the north and west; the Pugh warehouses (now River East Plaza) date from this period. The other area of early development lay to the north, when the elegant Gold Coast residential district spread south of Oak St., beginning with the construction of 999 N. Lake Shore Dr. in 1911–1912.

Between these industrial and residential areas lay an extensive tract of land that remained largely undeveloped until 1920, when Northwestern University purchased a large parcel along E. Chicago Ave. as a campus for its professional schools. The university soon expanded to the west and south, primarily to accommodate a large hospital complex.

Michigan Ave. experienced as rapid and dramatic a transformation as Streeterville itself. A new and Europeanized "grand" boulevard for Pine St., proposed in the 1909 Plan of Chicago, became a reality with the opening of the monumental Michigan Ave. Bridge in 1920. The great building boom of the Soaring Twenties left its distinctive mark on the new avenue in the modestly scaled, limestone-clad, neo-Classical and Art Deco buildings that made this street unique in Chicago.

Although comparative "skyscrapers" anchored its northern and southern ends, Michigan Ave. retained its human scale until the erection in 1969 of the 100-story John Hancock Center. This behemoth amply demonstrated the truth of the real estate adage that giants attract giants, for five more towers only slightly less titanic now cluster around it. What the astute real estate developer Arthur Rubloff dubbed the Magnificent Mile in 1947 has become, alas, the Manhattanized Mile.

The Gold Coast has gradually expanded southward east of Michigan Ave. to Pearson St. Postwar development has generally followed the pattern set by Mies van der Rohe's pathbreaking steel-and-glass towers at 860–880 N. Lake Shore Dr.

That old visionary scoundrel "Cap" Streeter must be saying *I told you so.* Only a stone's throw from where he ran aground a century ago, twenty million people come every year to shop, dine, see, and be seen at this shopping mall Mecca of the Middle West.

—WILLIAM B. HINCHLIFF

1| Michigan Ave. Bridge
Chicago River at E. Wacker Dr.
1920, EDWARD H. BENNETT;
THOMAS G. PIHLFELDT, CITY BRIDGE
ENG.; HUGH YOUNG, ENG. OF
BRIDGE DESIGN

Chicago has more movable bridges than any other city in the world, and most, like this one, are trunnion bascules. Ideal for this visible and busy location, it spans the river gracefully

MICHIGAN AVE. BRIDGE

and economically with no protruding superstructure, while leaving a wide, navigable channel. Construction of this bridge was a top priority in the 1909 Plan of Chicago, and it led the way to the rapid redevelopment of real estate on N. Michigan Ave. The exemplar for its design was Paris' Alexander III Bridge (1900), with four corner pylons, ornamental abutments, a graceful flat arch profile, and integrated embankments. The forty-foot pylons are functional operator houses. Each is embellished with sculptural reliefs depicting events in Chicago's history: *Defense* and *Regeneration* by Henry Hering grace the south pylons, while the north pylons feature *The Discoverers* and *The Pioneers* by James Earle Fraser.

2| William Wrigley, Jr., Building
400 & 410 N. Michigan Ave.
1919–1924, GRAHAM, ANDERSON, PROBST & WHITE
1957, PLAZA, L. R. SOLOMON,
J. D. CORDWELL & ASSOCS.

WILLIAM WRIGLEY, JR., BUILDING

London has Big Ben, Paris has the Eiffel Tower, and Chicago has the Wrigley Building. With its towering form, its lively white cladding, and its incomparable setting on the Chicago River, the Wrigley symbolizes the city in the hearts of its citizens. Because of the bend in Michigan Ave. at the river, the building is also the glittering climax of the Magnificent Mile's southern end. From the east and west its impact is doubled by its watery reflection.

But the Wrigley is not just a popular emblem: it embodies the essentials of the history of Chicago architecture up to the 1920s as transformed into a new synthesis by the gifted young architect Charles G. Beersman of Graham, Anderson, Probst & White, one of the city's most prolific firms. Beersman gave the building a tripartite division, borrowing from the European tradition, as Chicago commercial architects had done since the rebuilding after the Fire of 1871. The dazzling effects of the 1893 White City inspired the sparkling terra-cotta cladding, and Beersman further specified six shades of tiles, ranging from creamy white at the bottom to blue-white at the top, so that the brightness increases as the building rises. At night, banks of floodlights mounted on adjacent buildings illuminate the building in ever-increasing intensity upward. At noon or at midnight it stands out in a brilliant blaze against the sky.

The Wrigley Building is actually two structures conceived consecutively, but the parts stand side by side almost like fraternal twins. The taller, southern building with its tower seems stately; the shorter, northern building, constructed later, seems monumental. The seeming subservience of the "annex" is all the more noteworthy given the area of its site: 21,000 square feet, compared to 11,000 of the "original." The pleasantly proportioned offices have large windows and handsome moldings, but there are no great public rooms. The tower soars to 398 feet, where an observation room in the round, templed "Lysicrates" cupola once allowed visitors to view the city from its highest peak.

Ernest R. Graham and Beersman, the architects, and William Wrigley, Jr., their client, were keenly aware of the soaring verticality in the Manhattan skyline. They must have admired Cass Gilbert's Woolworth Building (1913), but it was more likely McKim, Mead & White's Municipal Building (1913), with its combination of Classicism and a tower, that inspired the Chicagoans. They hoped their new building would have the dignity of the traditional architecture of Daniel H. Burnham's day and the great heights of the modern age, the best of both worlds, a synthesis of aspiring monumentality. —SALLY A. KITT CHAPPELL

3 | 401 N. Michigan Ave.
(Equitable Building)
1965, SKIDMORE, OWINGS & MERRILL

The height and setback were dictated by the Tribune Company when they sold the land, to ensure the prominence of their own building. The Tribune also mandated the development of an intervening plaza, christened Pioneer Court. In 1992 it received a welcome face-lift designed by Cooper, Robertson & Partners to harmonize with the pedestrian spaces of Cityfront Center to the east. In a gracious urbanistic gesture that was twenty years ahead of its time (although it had been recommended in Burnham's 1909 plan), the plaza continues down to the riverfront

401 N. MICHIGAN AVE.

via a curving staircase. The building itself is a strong Miesian statement, with an articulated facade that emphasizes the underlying steel frame.

4 | Tribune Tower
435 N. Michigan Ave.
1923–1925, HOWELLS & HOOD

Addition
441–445 N. Michigan Ave.
1934, JOHN MEAD HOWELLS; HOOD & FOUILHOUX AND LEO J. WEISSENBORN, ASSOC. ARCHS.
1997, GROUND FLOOR RENOVATION, VINCI/HAMP ARCHITECTS

To observe its seventy-fifth anniversary, the *Chicago Tribune* in 1922 announced an international competition for the design of "the most beautiful office building in the world." Hyperbole notwithstanding, the competition was a major event: the 264 entries constituted a compendium of skyscraper design and sparked considerable debate about the proper form of the modern office building.

Approximately 90 percent of the entries relied on the historical precedents that had dominated American architecture at the beginning of the decade: Beaux Arts ideals inspired nearly 40 percent of them, and another 20 percent employed the neo-Gothic style popularized by Cass Gilbert's Woolworth Building (1913) in New York, then the tallest and one of the best-known American office buildings. Other entries reflected an emerging modernism: Walter Gropius submitted an exercise

TRIBUNE TOWER

TRIBUNE TOWER—ELIEL SAARINEN'S DESIGN

in the International Style, and Eliel Saarinen's second-prize entry, with its abstract and insistent verticality and graduated setbacks, pointed toward the skyscrapers of the late 1920s.

The first prize was awarded to the studied Gothic design of New York architects John Mead Howells & Raymond M. Hood. Rising thirty-six stories (460 feet), its structural steel frame is sheathed in Indiana limestone elaborately carved at the base and top in Gothic forms. At its base the structure covers a rectangle that extends 100 feet along Michigan Ave. and 326 feet eastward to adjoin the newspaper's former printing plant (1920, Jarvis Hunt). At the twenty-first floor the easternmost portion ends, and the tower becomes square in plan. Above the twenty-fourth floor the building steps back and rises as an octagonal tower. Two prominent piers from each of the four sides continue in the form of flying buttresses above the setback, creating a spidery crowning silhouette that recalls the thirteenth-century Butter Tower of the Rouen Cathedral.

The three-story arched entryway contains a richly detailed stone screen depicting characters from Aesop's fables. Note the howling dog and Robin Hood figures at the midpoint of the arch's curve, visual allusions to the architects' names. Embedded in the exterior walls are stones from well-known structures throughout the world. Some were gifts to Colonel Robert R. McCormick, the *Tribune*'s publisher; others were secured at his request by the paper's foreign correspondents.

The Tribune Tower, together with the Wrigley Building to the west and the 333 and 360 N. Michigan Ave. buildings across the Chicago River, frames the monumental Michigan Ave. Bridge (1920), a major gateway to the North Side. Each of these office towers represents a facet of 1920s architecture documented by the contest entries; as a group they define one of Chicago's most dramatic spaces. —ROY FORREY

5| **University of Chicago Graduate School of Business, Gleacher Center**
450 N. Cityfront Plaza Dr.
1994, LOHAN ASSOCS.

The windowless west side, where the classrooms are, has been criticized for its empty look at a vivid neighborhood. But it is a deliberate device to help the students focus. The public spaces make the most of the location, with windows facing east and south to the Chicago River.

NBC TOWER AT CITYFRONT CENTER

6| NBC Tower at Cityfront Center
454 N. Columbus Dr.
1989, SKIDMORE, OWINGS & MERRILL

Chicago's popular and arguably the most beautiful skyscraper of the past twenty years borrows from New York's Rockefeller Center in its streamlined verticality and from the Tribune Tower in its upper-floor buttresses. Good proportions and the high level of finish in the lobby and entries show what extra care and a little extra money can do. The west lobby has a special treat: a 1989 painting by Roger Brown entitled *City of the Big Shoulders*.

7| Hotel Inter-Continental Chicago
(*Medinah Athletic Club*)
505 N. Michigan Ave.
1929, WALTER W. AHLSCHLAGER
1989, RESTORATION, HARRY WEESE & ASSOCS.

The decorative program and the idiosyncratic gold-leafed dome hint at the feast of illusion and artifice within. Neo-Egyptian low reliefs designed by George Unger are carved into three sides of the facade, depicting masons on the south, builders on the north, and architects presenting a model of the building to the pharaoh on the west. The interior spaces are modest in scale but grandiose in spirit, infused throughout with a romantic historicism. The indoor swimming pool rivals that at Hearst Castle in San Simeon, California.

HOTEL INTER-CONTINENTAL CHICAGO

MCGRAW-HILL BUILDING

543–545 N. MICHIGAN AVE.

8| Le Meridien Hotel and The Shops at North Bridge
(*McGraw-Hill Building*)
520 N. Michigan Ave.
1929, THIELBAR & FUGARD
2000, ANTHONY BELLUSCHI ARCHITECTS; FARR ASSOCS., PRESERVATION CONSULTANTS

Chicago's largest "facadectomy" was performed here in response to public outrage at the proposed destruction of the McGraw-Hill Building. More than 6,000 pieces of the limestone skin were removed, cleaned, and rehung on a new steel frame structure. The Art Deco panels were designed by Eugene and Gwen Lux. Four panels that were not reattached are on display in the atrium. The glassy four-story shopping arcade that spans both Grand and Rush Sts. and slices through the lower floors of the building is designed to provide Michigan Ave. frontage for a new Nordstrom store one block west—the market driver of the whole development. The new building clad with the old limestone skin houses the hotel on its upper floors.

9| Chicago Marriott Downtown
540 N. Michigan Ave.
1978, HARRY WEESE & ASSOCS.
1998, FACADE REPLACEMENT, DESTEFANO AND PARTNERS

The original "faceless, graceless clunk" is now a shiny, dressy box on a still clunky hotel.

10| 543–545 N. Michigan Ave.
(*Jacques Building*)
1929, PHILIP B. MAHER

Maher had studied in France in 1925–1926, and his supremely elegant buildings lent credibility to the appellation "Boul Mich." Easily overlooked among its larger, more strident neighbors, this narrow retail building combines classical proportions and a mansard roof with the flattened ornamentation of Art Deco. The female figures in panels above the doors recall the building's origins as a luxury dress shop.

11| 555 N. Michigan Ave.
1999, TIGERMAN MCCURRY ARCHITECTS

Compatible in scale to its older neighbors, this limestone-clad retail building combines the open modern grid with subtle references to Classical and Gothic details.

12| 600 N. Michigan Ave.
1996, BEYER, BLINDER, BELLE

To preservationists' dismay, the entire block, including a building housing Mies van der Rohe's Arts Club interior, was razed to make room for yet another retail box on Michigan Ave. Adding insult to injury, materials such as terra-cotta and dark granite were employed to supposedly recall traditional storefronts, a poor replacement for the two 1920s facades that gave the boulevard its original character.

13 | Bank One
(*Lake Shore Trust Building*)
605 N. Michigan Ave.
1922, MARSHALL & FOX
1982, RENOVATION AND ADDITION,
PERKINS & WILL
1996, RENOVATION, LUCIEN
LAGRANGE & ASSOCIATES

The original windows were replaced with large, undivided panes of glass, drastically altering the bank's character and making the wall vanish between the colossal engaged Corinthian columns. The monumental, freestanding bank modeled on a temple, though common in many cities, is relatively rare in Chicago.

WOMAN'S ATHLETIC CLUB

14 | Woman's Athletic Club
626 N. Michigan Ave.
1928, PHILIP B. MAHER

This unusually well preserved reminder of the Avenue's gentility has a sober elegance typical of Maher's French-influenced

work. Tall windows at the second and seventh floors indicate the location of the important public spaces.

15 | Crate & Barrel
646 N. Michigan Ave.
1990, SOLOMON CORDWELL
BUENZ & ASSOCS.

Wearing summer whites to a black-tie affair, Crate & Barrel's flagship store issues a brazen challenge to the architectural conventions of Michigan Ave. Unlike its masonry-clad neighbors, the building is bright, shiny, and shamelessly transparent; a glass-enclosed, crisp corner cylinder nestles slightly inward from the outer walls. The smooth, white skin and continuous bands of windows pay homage to Le Corbusier, while the continuation of the specially finished sidewalk through to the building's interior flooring is a favorite Miesian device. Nothing constructed on the Avenue since the Hancock Center has made such a strong modernist statement.

16 | 664 N. Michigan Ave.
(*Farwell Building*)
1927, PHILIP B. MAHER

The success of this prominent commission led Maher to five more Michigan Ave. projects in rapid succession. Despite the round-arched entrances and mansard roof, the strong vertical lines of the piers and window-spandrel combination impart a strong Art Deco feeling. The

CRATE & BARREL

building was saved from destruction when it found a new function as gallery space for the Terra Museum.

17| Terra Museum of American Art
666 N. Michigan Ave.
1987, BOOTH HANSEN ASSOCIATES

The glassy central portion reveals that this small building is devoted primarily to circulation space for the galleries, which occupy renovated space next door at 664. The museum announced in 2003 that it would close its doors as of the following year, with key pieces of its collection going to the Art Institute of Chicago on extended loan.

18| 663 N. Michigan Ave.
1966, HOLABIRD & ROOT

19| 669–675 N. Michigan Ave.
**(*Blackstone Shops, later*
expanded for Saks Fifth Avenue)**
1925, PHILIP B. MAHER
1966, RENOVATION, HOLABIRD & ROOT

The verticality of the earliest two buildings was re-created surprisingly well in all of the subsequent work.

20| City Place
676 N. Michigan Ave.
1990, LOEBL, SCHLOSSMAN & HACKL

One of the trio of mixed-use behemoths that invaded Michigan Ave. in the late 1980s, this building presents its slimmest profile to the Avenue but commands attention from the side, with its garish pink-red palette and potpourri of window patterns. In an inversion of the typical formula, the hotel is located on the middle floors, giving offices the best views.

21| Chicago Place
700 N. Michigan Ave.
1990, RETAIL BASE, SKIDMORE, OWINGS & MERRILL; CONDOMINIUM TOWER, SOLOMON CORDWELL BUENZ & ASSOCS.

The Chicago theme crops up everywhere in this overdesigned temple to commerce. The exterior of the base is meant to recall the great emporiums of State St.—Marshall Field & Co. (Classical columns) and Carson Pirie Scott (curved corners)—but the result is ersatz. In a formula firmly established by Water Tower Place, the skyscraper tower is set well back from the mid-rise base. The eight-level atrium offers the acrophobe's usual nightmare of freestanding escalators and glass-enclosed elevators, but with a dizzying distraction of color and pattern.

22| Allerton-Crowne Plaza
(*Allerton House*)
140 E. Huron St.
1924, MURGATROYD & OGDEN; FUGARD & KNAPP, ASSOC. ARCHS.
1999, RENOVATION, ECKENHOFF SAUNDERS ARCHITECTS

CITY PLACE

ALLERTON-CROWNE PLAZA

Built as part of a New York City–based chain of residential "club hotels" for single men and women, the Allerton has a northern Italian Renaissance style that proved popular as a model for other hotels and apartments. The thronelike massing reflects Chicago's 1923 zoning ordinance, which required setbacks on large buildings that covered their entire lot. The 1999 rehabilitation revealed a good look at another age. The renovation architects convinced the new owners of the hotel to emphasize its historic character. The limestone base and the arched windows on the twenty-third-floor towers were restored. And although the former bar is now a ballroom, the TIP TOP TAP sign shines again.

23| Neiman Marcus
737 N. Michigan Ave.
1983, SKIDMORE, OWINGS & MERRILL

24| Olympia Centre
161 E. Chicago Ave.
1986, SKIDMORE, OWINGS & MERRILL

Postmodernism was slow to penetrate the citadels of Chicago orthodoxy; Neiman Marcus, in design since 1978, was one of the first examples. The large glass arch evokes the work of H. H. Richardson and Louis H. Sullivan, but with an obligatory wink: the glass slit in place of a keystone underscores the arch's structural irrelevance. The highrise Olympia Centre tapers on two sides as it rises. The changes in fenestration reflect reduced structural loads, with larger windows where the function shifts from office to residential.

25| 730–750 N. Michigan Ave.
1997–1998, ELKUS/MANFREDI ARCHITECTS

The block-long Michigan Ave. frontage is divided into four storefronts, each with a distinct style. The Peninsula Hotel entrance is on Superior St.

26| Chicago Water Tower & Pumping Station
806 & 811 N. Michigan Ave.
1866, PUMPING STATION, WILLIAM W. BOYINGTON
1869, TOWER, WILLIAM W. BOYINGTON
2003, PUMPING STATION ADAPTIVE REUSE FOR LOOKINGGLASS THEATRE, MORRIS ARCHITECTS/PLANNERS

One of only a few buildings to survive the Great Fire, the Water Tower is a potent symbol of Chicago's "I Will" spirit. In three days in October 1871, the city's commercial center and a third of its residences were leveled by fire. But the tower stood, holding out the promise that Chicago would rise from the ruins and ashes around it. Within months the city was rebuilding, resuming its role as the nineteenth century's fastest-growing city.

The famous 154-foot tower was actually a secondary structure. It was built to house a 138-foot standpipe that stabilized the pressure of the water distributed from the adjacent pumping station. Both buildings were built in the "castellated Gothic" style of locally quarried Joliet-Lemont limestone, widely used in Chicago before it was replaced by Indiana graystone in the 1890s. The stone is recognized by its distinctive yellow patina.

The Pumping Station and Tower are two of only a few surviving buildings by William W. Boyington, one of the city's most prominent early architects who gave shape to the Chicago that burned as well as to the phoenix that replaced it. Working in the popular revival styles, Boyington designed major hotels, commercial structures, churches, and other institutions from the 1850s to the 1890s.

The four facades of the Water Tower are identical and feature a massive arched door flanked by pointed-arch windows surmounted

CHICAGO WATER TOWER & PUMPING STATION

by drop moldings. Small towers with lancet windows, castellated crowns, and tourelles frame each level as the base rises to the tower itself, which is surmounted by a crown of eight tourelles and a copper cupola. The overall effect led Oscar Wilde to call it "a castellated monstrosity with salt and pepper boxes stuck over it." Boyington used the same styling not only on the pumping station but also on the first University of Chicago (demolished), the prison at Joliet, Illinois (1858), and the entrance to Rosehill Cemetery (1864).

A Chicago landmark of great visceral magnitude, the Water Tower has nonetheless battled three times for its life. In 1906 the standpipe became obsolete, and only a public outcry saved the tower from demolition. In 1918 the tower obstructed the northward progress of the new Michigan Ave., but preservationists prevailed over planners. A 1948 plan for an art center on the site was also defeated, and the first restoration of the tower began in 1962. Today the Water Tower is a focus of Michigan Ave., whose buildings have come to dwarf the structure that once stood tall amid smoldering ruins.

—VINCENT MICHAEL

27| **Chicago Fire Department**
202 E. Chicago Ave.
1902, CHARLES F. HERMANN, CHICAGO CITY ARCH.

This tiny fire station repeats in miniature the castellated Gothic of the Water Tower & Pumping Station.

28| **Park Tower**
800 N. Michigan Ave.
2000, LUCIEN LAGRANGE & ASSOCS.

The sixty-seven-story mixed-use building has forty-seven floors of luxury condominiums above a Park Hyatt hotel, five floors of parking, and a retail base. The reinforced concrete structure is clad in precast concrete except for the first two stories, which are of limestone. The east and west sides look quite different than the narrower north and south sides. Balconies are sculpturally woven into the facade.

29| **Facade of former Perkins, Fellows & Hamilton Studio & Office**
814 N. Michigan Ave.
1917, PERKINS, FELLOWS & HAMILTON

This is a rare example of an originally freestanding building designed by architects for their own offices. The brick facade, with Gothic details and extensive sculpture by Emil R. Zettler, is all that remains; behind it is the Park Hyatt that is part of the Park Tower.

30| Loyola University— Lewis Towers
(*Illinois Women's Athletic Club*)
820 N. Michigan Ave.
1927, RICHARD E. SCHMIDT, GARDEN & MARTIN

This Gothic skyscraper had shops on the first two floors, offices to the ninth floor, and club facilities above. A relief of Diana with her dog guards the entrance. Around the corner at 25 E. Pearson St. is a newer Loyola building by Holabird & Root, 1994.

31| 830 N. Michigan Ave.
(*Bonwit Teller*)
1949, SHAW, METZ & DOLIO
1994, RENOVATION, SOLOMON CORDWELL BUENZ & ASSOCS.

After I. Magnin's tenancy here in the 1970s and 1980s, the building was converted to a small multitenant mall and large bay windows were added.

32| 840 N. Michigan Ave.
1992, LUCIEN LAGRANGE & ASSOCS.

This dignified low-key addition to the Avenue extends the human scale that reigns on its western side between Superior St. and Delaware Pl. The corner tower and mansard roof evoke earlier retail establishments, and the six shades of limestone harmonize with the masonry of the streetscape.

33| Water Tower Place
845 N. Michigan Ave.
1976, LOEBL, SCHLOSSMAN & HACKL
2001, RENOVATION, WIMBERLY ALLISON TONG AND GOO

This marble-clad monument to mammon forever changed the Avenue's character—for better or worse. It moved the retail center of gravity north from State St. in the Loop and heralded the arrival of a more international and luxurious marketplace. Despite the setback of the building's tallest part, great violence was done to the streetscape with its blank walls and recessed storefronts, a mistake avoided by its imitators. The bland marble walls cover a reinforced-concrete frame that was the world's tallest until the construction of 311 S. Wacker Dr.

34| John Hancock Center
875 N. Michigan Ave.
1969, SKIDMORE, OWINGS & MERRILL
1994, LOWER-LEVEL REMODELING, INCLUDING PLAZA, HILTSCHER SHAPIRO

Of the three giants that dominate the early twenty-first-century Chicago skyline, Sears Tower and the Aon Center are taller, but the John Hancock Center best exemplifies the Chicago tradition of combining bold structural advances with brawny architectural form.

Despite its gigantism, the 1,127-foot, 100-story, 2.8-million-square-foot Hancock is a beloved urban icon. Nicknamed "Big John" soon after its completion, it features a distinctive tapering profile and exterior cross-bracing that have inspired countless schoolchildren to portray it as a cartoonlike series of stacked Xs. So deeply is the building ingrained in the Chicago psyche that in 1989 Mayor Richard M. Daley attacked the owner's plan to fill in the tower's sunken plaza and add a three-story retail atrium to its base. The scheme was replaced by one that reconfigured the rectangular plaza into an elliptical space that was more welcoming and less moatlike. The happy result is that the Hancock's striking silhouette remains intact, a high-water mark for Skidmore, Owings & Merrill and a triumph of modern architecture.

JOHN HANCOCK CENTER

Designed by SOM architect Bruce Graham and engineer Fazlur R. Khan, the Hancock exemplifies another Chicago tradition, the multi-purpose building. The first and second floors, as well as the underground concourse, are devoted to retail space; floors 3–12 to parking; 13–41 to offices; 42–43 to mechanical equipment; and 44–93 to residences. The 94th floor houses a public observatory; a bar and restaurant occupy floors 95 and 96, with television and communications equipment housed on 97 and mechanical equipment on 98–100. Supporting it all, as well as the television and radio antennas that bring the building's total height to 1,502 feet, are 46,000 tons of steel. Exterior columns, horizontal beams, and cross-braces form a highly efficient structural system comparable to a rigid box; the tower was erected for the cost of a conventional forty-five-story office building.

The tapering form provides large floor areas for retail and office use and smaller spaces for the condominiums. The form also evokes the permanence and monumentality associated with the obelisks of ancient Egypt or the Washington Monument.

Monumental presence is both a blessing and a curse. For all its swaggering presence on the skyline, the Hancock has a history of stumbling as it meets the street. The base of the black aluminum tower originally was covered in travertine marble, leading tour guides to compare the Hancock to a man in a tuxedo wearing white socks. The 1994 remodeling of the tower's base replaced the travertine with a gray granite cladding that is far more sympathetic to the dark colossus.

Still, the Hancock maintains an uneasy relationship with its ever-shifting environs. Before the tower was built, N. Michigan Ave. largely resembled a Parisian boulevard of elegant low- and mid-rise Classical buildings. After the Hancock shattered that fragile scale, the Avenue became an urban canyon of hulking blockbusters. That trend, which has since spread to the streets flanking N. Michigan, makes the open space of the Hancock's sunken plaza all the more valuable, even if it dims somewhat the tower's brilliant synthesis of engineering and architecture, pragmatism and poetry.　　　　　—BLAIR KAMIN

35| Fourth Presbyterian Church
866 N. Michigan Ave.
1914, RALPH ADAMS CRAM; HOWARD VAN DOREN SHAW, ASSOC. ARCH.
1914, CLOISTER, HOWARD VAN DOREN SHAW
1925, MANSE, PARISH HOUSE, BLAIR CHAPEL, HOWARD VAN DOREN SHAW

One of Chicago's wealthiest congregations turned to a nationally renowned practitioner of the Gothic Revival for their church. Parishioner Shaw collaborated with Cram on the interior and designed the less formal buildings that create a peaceful courtyard, or garth. The stained glass is by Charles J. Connick of Boston; local artist Frederic Clay Bartlett designed the illuminated ceiling and the wooden statuary.

36| 900 N. Michigan Ave.
1989, KOHN PEDERSEN FOX; PERKINS & WILL, ASSOC. ARCHS.

Known as the Bloomingdale's Building, this mixed-use structure by the developers of Water Tower Place builds on that project's commercial success and corrects some of its errors.

The eight-story shopping block extends to the lot line with a welcoming entrance and plenty of large display windows. The spacious, understated neo-Deco atrium has the anchor store at the back, so that shoppers pass the boutiques first. The hotel, office, and condominium floors have entrances on the side streets. Like Water Tower Place, the exterior is a stack of embellished boxes, but with a more ambitious decorative program. Though it does not all hang together, the four huge lanterns atop the building are a visual delight.

37| The Palmolive Building
159 E. Walton St.
1929, HOLABIRD & ROOT
1982, STOREFRONT RENOVATION, SKIDMORE, OWINGS & MERRILL
2004–2005, CONVERSION TO CONDOMINIUMS, BOOTH HANSEN ASSOCIATES

Like New York, Chicago enacted a zoning law for skyscrapers (in 1923) that set the stage for the Art Deco buildings soon in vogue. This building, like the

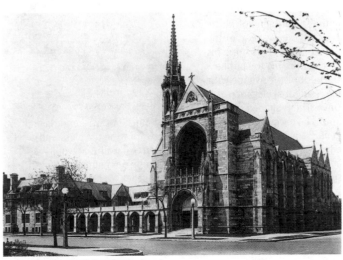

FOURTH PRESBYTERIAN CHURCH

THE PALMOLIVE BUILDING

Chicago Board of Trade by the same architects, is a shining example of the style, with setbacks making it a powerful sculptural object. Long an office building, it is now being converted to condominiums.

38| One Magnificent Mile
940–980 N. Michigan Ave.
1983, SKIDMORE, OWINGS & MERRILL

Although it uses the bundled tube structure of the Sears Tower, this pink granite triad is clad in 1980s garb. The window patterns express the familiar divisions of retail, office, and residential use.

39| Drake Hotel
140 E. Walton St.
1920, MARSHALL & FOX

This luxurious hotel anchors both the north end of Michigan Ave. and the west end of the E. Lake Shore Dr. Historic District, combining the public splendor of the Avenue with the residential elegance of the Drive. The H-shaped plan maximizes lake views. The Italian Renaissance–inspired facades effectively incorporate a *piano nobile* treatment for the public spaces on the lower floors.

E. Lake Shore Dr.
Historic District
From Michigan Ave. east
through 999 N. Lake Shore Dr.

40| Drake Tower Apartments
179 E. Lake Shore Dr.
1929, BENJAMIN H. MARSHALL

41| Mayfair Regent Hotel
(*Lake Shore Drive Hotel*)
181 E. Lake Shore Dr.
1924, FUGARD & KNAPP

42| 199 E. Lake Shore Dr.
(*The Breakers*)
1915, MARSHALL & FOX

43| 209 E. Lake Shore Dr.
1924, MARSHALL & FOX

44| 219 E. Lake Shore Dr.
1922, FUGARD & KNAPP

45| 229 E. Lake Shore Dr.
1919, FUGARD & KNAPP

46| 999 N. Lake Shore Dr.
1912, MARSHALL & FOX

This remarkable group creates a harmonious street wall that is one of the few lakefront stretches with no recent structures interrupting its cohesiveness. It also provides an intriguing glimpse of Benjamin H. Marshall's design evolution, from the Second Empire exuberance adorning the corner at 999 to the sober ahistoricism of the Drake Tower Apartments.

999 N. LAKE SHORE DR.

47| 227 E. Walton St.
1956, HARRY WEESE & ASSOCS.

While Mies was refining and simplifying the glass-and-steel curtain wall that would become de rigueur for high-rise facades, Weese was moving toward greater variety and plasticity. Inspired by the multibayed facades of the early Chicago School, he used a warm palette of red brick with concrete trim here.

48 | 900–910 N. Lake Shore Dr.
(*Esplanade Apartments*)

1953–1956, LUDWIG MIES VAN DER ROHE; PACE ASSOCS. AND HOLSMAN, HOLSMAN, KLEKAMP & TAYLOR, ASSOC. ARCHS.

The success of 860–880 N. Lake Shore Dr. led developer Herbert Greenwald to commission another pair. They have a sleeker version of the expressive curtain wall, with dark-tinted glass and without the contrasting aluminum window frames. The structural system is not a steel skeleton but a flat-slab concrete frame, resulting in complete independence of skin and structure.

49 | 860–880 N. Lake Shore Dr.

1949–1951, LUDWIG MIES VAN DER ROHE; PACE ASSOCS. AND HOLSMAN, HOLSMAN, KLEKAMP & TAYLOR, ASSOC. ARCHS.

These towers constitute the first and most forceful demonstration of Ludwig Mies van der Rohe's ideas for tall buildings. No other building by Mies had as immediate or strong an impact on his American contemporaries, and the influence of these structures was to pervade much of modern architecture.

860–880 N. LAKE SHORE DR.

Mies had come to Chicago from Germany in 1938 to become director of the school of architecture at what would later become the Illinois Institute of Technology. He also established an architecture practice and in 1948 designed the concrete-framed Promontory Apartments in Hyde Park, the first of many projects for developer Herbert Greenwald. Mies had prepared two versions of the Promontory. One was the form actually used; the other had a steel-and-glass exterior on the long elevations, his first use of the curtain wall that came to be his hallmark.

While the Promontory was under construction, Greenwald commissioned these apartments. The plan was developed from the alternative version for the Promontory and from sketches that Mies had drawn between 1919 and 1921 for two radically innovative glass towers, which had brought him to the forefront of the modern movement. The unexecuted designs reemerged here and in 1968, through the hands of Mies's former students, in Lake Point Tower.

The buildings acquire their strong verticality from the narrow I-beams welded to the columns and mullions, a feature necessitated in part by the building code's requirement that steel-framed buildings be fireproofed with concrete. Mies satisfied the code and achieved the appearance he desired by finishing the framing elements with steel plate, which served as formwork for poured concrete, and by welding I-beams onto the plate.

Questioned on his use of a structural material as applied ornament, Mies gave a good reason and then the real reason. He noted that the I-beams would function well as mullions. "But why weld them onto the column plates?" he was asked. "It strengthens the plates," Mies replied. "Do the plates need strengthening?" "Well, no," he confessed, "but if you leave out the I-beams there, it breaks the rhythm!"

The "Glass Houses" were startling not only in terms of form but also as habitation; critics wondered at the psychological impact of transparent homes. The apartments were a financial success, however. The buildings became the international prototype for steel-and-glass structures and engendered an architecture now so commonplace that it is almost impossible to appreciate their initial impact, when it was "as if steel and glass [were] seen for the first time."

—JOAN POMARANC

---

50 | Northwestern University—Lake Shore Center
(*Lake Shore Athletic Club*)
850 N. Lake Shore Dr.
1924, JARVIS HUNT

This student residence was built as a combination clubhouse and apartment building. The hulking mass consists of a large neo-Classical base topped by rather plain upper floors.

51 | The Plaza on DeWitt
(*DeWitt–Chestnut Apartments*)
260 E. Chestnut St.
1963, SKIDMORE, OWINGS & MERRILL

This was Chicago's first building with a tubular structural system, in which closely spaced exterior columns create a load-bearing screen wall. The reinforced-concrete frame is sheathed in marble. It was the first collaboration of SOM architect Bruce Graham and engineer Fazlur R. Khan, the team that created the Hancock Center and Sears Tower.

52 | Museum of Contemporary Art
220 E. Chicago Ave.
1996, JOSEF PAUL KLEIHUES;
A. EPSTEIN & SONS INTERNATIONAL, ARCH. OF RECORD

This boxy bunker landed on the streetscape with a dull thud rather than the anticipated splash. The steep front stairway is intimidating rather than inviting, and the cast aluminum facade panels lend the dreariness of concrete but at a much higher cost. Glittering stainless-steel screws fasten the panels to the building frame at precise intervals but offer little visual relief. Fortunately, the interior has more to recommend it. The four-story atrium has glass walls that offer spectacular views. Barrel-vaulted top-floor galleries are lit with indirect natural light. And tucked against the northern wall, a curving stairway wraps around an almond-shaped reflecting pool.

53 | 200 E. Pearson St.
1916, ROBERT S. DEGOLYER

This vintage palazzo was home to Ludwig Mies van der Rohe, who chose not to live at his free apartment at 860–880 N. Lake Shore Dr., the story goes, because he didn't want the tenants to treat him like the maintenance man.

54 | 840 N. Lake Shore Dr.
2003, LUCIEN LAGRANGE ARCHITECTS

Of the group of three buildings that comprise the Residences on Lake Shore Park, 840 N. Lake Shore Dr. is the most interesting. Chicago has not attempted Gallic grandeur on this scale since the Belden Hotel was completed in 1922.

Northwestern University—Chicago Campus

This campus houses law, business, medical, and dental schools and is concentrated between Chicago Ave. and Huron St., from the lake west to St. Clair St. James Gamble Rogers created a campus plan in 1924 and designed a row of buildings in his signature Collegiate Gothic style. The original

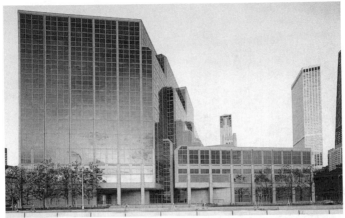

NORTHWESTERN UNIVERSITY SCHOOL OF LAW—ARTHUR RUBLOFF BUILDING

group marched west from the lake along Chicago Ave., with the buildings increasing in height. This pattern has been broken by subsequent construction, but Rogers's Gothic precedent has proved amazingly durable. Fallen from grace and superseded by bland modernist buildings, the style was strongly evoked in two major additions of the 1980s: the Law School's Rubloff Building and the Medical School's Tarry Building.

55| Northwestern University School of Law—Arthur Rubloff Building
375 E. Chicago Ave.

American Bar Association Center
750 N. Lake Shore Dr.
1984, HOLABIRD & ROOT

This handsome addition to the campus has a finely detailed curtain wall, the base of which gestures to its Gothic neighbors with abstracted buttresses. A glazed atrium links it with the Gary Law Library building.

56| Northwestern University School of Law—Levy Mayer Hall
357 E. Chicago Ave.
1927, JAMES GAMBLE ROGERS;
CHILDS & SMITH, ASSOC. ARCHS.

The Law School quadrangle surrounds a leafy courtyard and includes Rogers's Albert H. Gary Law Library (1927; note the owls perched atop the buttresses) on Chicago Ave. and Robert R. McCormick Hall (1960, Holabird & Root) at 350 E. Superior St., executed in a self-effacing and harmonious nonstyle.

57| Wieboldt Hall of Commerce
339 E. Chicago Ave.

58| Montgomery Ward Memorial Building
303–311 E. Chicago Ave.
1926, JAMES GAMBLE ROGERS;
CHILDS & SMITH, ASSOC. ARCHS.

An attractive arcade links these two buildings (a twin links Wieboldt to the Law School complex) and creates a peaceful courtyard, a hallmark of Rogers's campus designs. The Ward Building was the nation's first Collegiate Gothic skyscraper. Although stylistically dull in comparison with the architect's better-known buildings at Yale University, the planning makes the most of the cramped urban site.

59| Tarry Research & Education Building
300 E. Superior St.
1990, PERKINS & WILL

Collegiate Gothic returns in 1990s materials in this addition, which completes the block begun by the Montgomery Ward Building and continued in the Morton (1955) and Searle (1956)

NORTHWESTERN MEMORIAL HOSPITAL—PRENTICE WOMEN'S HOSPITAL AND MATERNITY CENTER

TARRY RESEARCH & EDUCATION BUILDING

Medical Research Buildings (310 & 320 E. Superior St.). Method Atrium (part of Tarry), an elegant glassy lobby, links all four buildings.

60| Northwestern Memorial Hospital—Northwestern University Health Sciences Building/Olson & McGaw Pavilions
710 N. Fairbanks Ct.
1979, HOLABIRD & ROOT

This unabashedly high-tech building lost some of its edge when its gleaming white metal panels were painted buff to blend in with the surrounding limestone and concrete. Pedestrian bridges with exposed trusses make connections to buildings across both streets.

61| Northwestern Memorial Hospital—Feinberg & Galter Pavilions
251 E. Huron St. &
675 N. St. Clair St.
1999, ELLERBE BECKET; HOK; VOA ASSOCS.

NMH conducted an aggressive building replacement campaign in the 1990s. Wesley and Passavant pavilions were demolished to make way for these facilities. Feinberg was designed for inpatient care; Galter houses outpatient care.

62| Northwestern Memorial Hospital—Prentice Women's Hospital and Maternity Center
333 E. Superior St.
1975, BERTRAND GOLDBERG & ASSOCS.

At street level, this is just another modern hospital building, but above the fifth story is a curving concrete shell that seems to have landed like a spaceship on the steel-and-glass podium. The split personality reflects split functions. The conventional base contains generic space adaptable to the constant remodelings that hospital treatment facilities undergo, while the curving portion is a "bed tower" with separate nursing stations for each of the four wings. The oval windows enhance energy efficiency and construction economy. Goldberg repeated this curving plan in many hospital designs. Prentice will be replaced by a new facility at 250 E. Superior St., scheduled to open in 2007.

63| Rehabilitation Institute of Chicago
345 E. Superior St.
1974, C. F. MURPHY & ASSOCS.

The campus's most purely Miesian hospital building has a bronze-tinted skin that clearly expresses the steel frame.

64| Abbott Hall
710 N. Lake Shore Dr.
1939, HOLABIRD & ROOT

Built as a student residence, this unadorned limestone structure has more bulk than style. The ornamental wrought-iron gate, designed for the original 1920s campus, sits uselessly on the site's southeast corner.

65| Lake Shore Place
(*American Furniture Mart*)
680 N. Lake Shore Dr.

1924, EAST END, HENRY RAEDER ASSOCS.; GEORGE C. NIMMONS & CO. AND N. MAX DUNNING, ASSOC. ARCHS.
1926, WEST END, GEORGE C. NIMMONS AND N. MAX DUNNING
1984, CONVERSION, LOHAN ASSOCS.

This lavishly ornamented monument to the wholesale furniture trade was built when Chicago was at the industry's center. Although the exterior seems all of a piece, a closer look reveals a difference between the sixteen-story east end, which has a reinforced-concrete structure, and the twenty-story western section, which is a steel-framed skyscraper. The Gothicism of the exterior reaches its apogee in the thirty-story tower, which was inspired by the Houses of Parliament. The interior carries out the theme in the lavish Whiting Hall lobby, which runs the length of the building. The Furniture Mart declined with the industry's decentralization

and the move of many showrooms to the Merchandise Mart. It is now a mixed-use building of apartments, offices, parking, and stores.

66| Onterie Center
446–448 E. Ontario St./
441 E. Erie St.

1979–1986, SKIDMORE, OWINGS & MERRILL

This building was the final collaboration between architect Bruce Graham and engineer Fazlur R. Khan, who died in 1982 after completing the structural design. A pair of reinforced-concrete tubes, their cross-bracing expressed by concrete infill panels, embrace a central core. This system combines the cross-bracing of the Hancock Center with the tubular structure of the Sears Tower, though it lacks their elegance. Retail and office space occupy the lower floors, with apartments in the tower.

67| CBS Building
(*Chicago Riding Club*)
630 N. McClurg Ct.
(William S. Paley Pl.)

1924, REBORI, WENTWORTH, DEWEY & MCCORMICK

The unusual roof, with sloped planes designed to provide light and ventilation, was more often found on industrial buildings.

68| McClurg Court Center
333 E. Ontario St.

1971, SOLOMON CORDWELL BUENZ & ASSOCS.

This apartment complex offers the kind of self-contained, multiuse environment popular since the 1970s. Although some shops face the street, it presents a forbidding presence. The curved corner towers are placed at right angles to each other in order to maximize views.

69| The Arts Club
201 E. Ontario St.

1997, VINCI/HAMP ARCHITECTS

This understated two-story building is a comfortable

LAKE SHORE PLACE

permanent home for the Club, which lost its Mies van der Rohe–designed interior to the wrecking ball. The focal point for the new building is the Mies stair (1951), which was salvaged from the old location two blocks west. Galleries on the first floor and salon and dining on the second are simple and restrained in their materials and detailing, as is the exterior with its Norman brick and large steel-framed windows.

70| 230 E. Ohio St.
(*Pelouze Building*)
1916, ALFRED S. ALSCHULER

71| 232 E. Ohio St.
(*Pelouze Scale & Manufacturing Co. Factory*)
1916, HILL & WOLTERSDORF

These are among the few remaining loft buildings in this former industrial area.

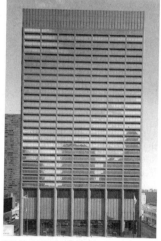

541 N. FAIRBANKS CT. BUILDING

72| 541 N. Fairbanks Ct. Building
(*Time and Life Building*)
1968, HARRY WEESE & ASSOCS.
1989, RENOVATION, PERKINS & WILL

This brawny building of Cor-Ten steel with bronze-tinted mirror glass is a foray by Weese into the Miesian realm. The reflective glass, unusual at the time, conserves energy. Double-deck elevators are programmed to stop at two floors at the same time during rush hours and to provide regular service at other times.

73| James Jardine Water Filtration Plant
(*Central District Filtration Plant*)
1000 E. Ohio St.
1952–1964, C. F. MURPHY ASSOCS.

On this long finger of landfill is a campus of buildings that filter and purify water for the metropolitan area. The low buildings are of steel-frame construction with metal-and-glass curtain walls.

74| Navy Pier
(*Municipal Pier No. 2*)
600 E. Grand Ave. at Lake Michigan
1916, CHARLES S. FROST
1976, RENOVATION, JEROME R. BUTLER, JR., CHICAGO CITY ARCH.
1995, RECONSTRUCTION, BENJAMIN THOMPSON & ASSOCS.; VOA ASSOCS., ASSOC. ARCHS.

Shakespeare Theater
1999, VOA ASSOCS.

A 1910 plan called for the construction of five municipal piers, of which only Navy Pier was built. Its 3,000-foot length, set on 20,000 wooden piles, made it then the world's largest pier. During its golden age (1918–1930) it was an important terminal for freight and passenger traffic, as well as a site of public entertainment. The rise of trucking combined with the Depression to curtail both uses; it became a naval training facility during World War II and served as the Chicago branch of the University of Illinois from 1946 until 1965. When the east buildings were restored in 1976, the Pier was again host to civic and cultural events.

But the reconstruction of the Pier infrastructure and the new construction of museums, shops, and entertainment and recreational facilities has made the Pier one of Chicago's greatest attractions. The Crystal Garden and the 230,000-square-foot Festival Hall convention facility join the Grand Ballroom in making the Pier a prime site for small conventions and large parties. A food court, stores, and museums offer something for everyone. The Shakespeare Theater is the newest element. Multilevel glass corridors wrap around the main theater, insulating it from noise and providing patrons with spectacular views of the Pier and the city. But the view and the sense of being over the water while still on firm ground remain the biggest attractions.

LAKE POINT TOWER

75| Lake Point Tower
505 N. Lake Shore Dr.
1968, SCHIPPOREIT-HEINRICH; GRAHAM, ANDERSON, PROBST & WHITE, ASSOC. ARCHS.

Inspired by a 1919–1921 visionary project of Mies van der Rohe, two of his former students and employees designed this undulating glass tower as their firm's first commission. The first skyscraper with curving glass walls, it still outshines its imitators. The Y-shaped plan (which differs from Mies's asymmetrical model) provides the optimal combination of density, views, and privacy. The tower sits on a large podium that contains parking and commercial space and is topped with a private park, designed by Alfred Caldwell.

Cityfront Center
Bounded by the Chicago River, N. Lake Shore Dr., E. Grand Ave., and N. Michigan Ave.
MASTER PLAN. 1985, COOPER, ECKSTUT ASSOCS.; SKIDMORE, OWINGS & MERRILL
PLANNING: LOHAN ASSOCS. (EAST OF COLUMBUS DR.); SKIDMORE, OWINGS & MERRILL (WEST OF COLUMBUS DR.)

Scaled to the pedestrian but convenient for traffic, it consciously repudiates the kind of urban planning that resulted in bleak landscapes of isolated towers. Its pleasant river orientation could be possible only in this postindustrial era, when waterways are more important as pleasure grounds than as transportation arteries. Development has been carried out separately, with land ownership divided between the Chicago Dock & Canal Trust (east of Columbus Dr.) and the Equitable Life Assurance Society (between Columbus Dr. and Michigan Ave.).

76| River East Plaza
(*formerly North Pier Chicago, originally Pugh Terminal*)
435 E. Illinois St.
1905–1920, CHRISTIAN A. ECKSTORM
1990, RENOVATION, BOOTH HANSEN ASSOCIATES; AUSTIN CO., ASSOC. ARCHS.

Constructed as an exhibition center for wholesale products, this sprawling building capitalized on Chicago's emerging role in American merchandising to locate numerous manufacturers and product lines under one roof. It was originally more than twice as long and stretched east across the path of Lake Shore Dr. The conversion to a three-story retail mall with four office floors was the first completed project at Cityfront Center.

Fan-shaped steel canopies punctuate the ground floor on Illinois St. between windows that were originally loading docks. This facade is of face brick and, although simple, presents a more finished appearance than the common-brick river and side walls, which are now more prominent. Inside, a three-story rotunda introduces the inventive combination of materials that evoke the area's nautical and industrial past in a 1990s vocabulary. The Ogden Slip facade has been extended with two neo-Miesian glass-and-steel gallerias.

77| North Pier Apartment Tower
474 N. Lake Shore Dr.
1991, DUBIN, DUBIN & MOUTOUSSAMY; FLORIAN-WIERZBOWSKI, DESIGN CONSULTANTS

This grim box is sorry evidence that the level of design quality will vary widely in the Cityfront development, despite guidelines. The sixty-one-story tower, Cityfront's first major residential project, is crudely detailed and faced with precast concrete panels in dissonant shades of rust and brown. Worst of all, it occupies one of the development's most prominent sites.

78| CityView Condominiums
440 & 480 N. McClurg Ct.

79| Cityfront Place
400 N. McClurg Ct.
1991, GELICK FORAN ASSOCS.

A mid-rise tower of thirty stories and a pair of linked twelve-story structures are Cityfront's second major residential development, and a welcome improvement on their predecessor. Although the tower-on-a-podium composition of the mid rise is a faux pas in this pedestrian-friendly context, the public plaza formed by the lower buildings more than compensates for it. A grand staircase leads to a terrace whose west section features a long, low fountain and glorious views of the skyline. To the east, a curving section like the prow of a boat provides a good perch for people watching at River East Plaza.

80| East Water Place Townhouses
430 E. North Water St.
1997, BOOTH HANSEN ASSOCIATES

Town house living close to Lake Michigan is an unusual kind of luxury. Fifty-six units are clustered in eight buildings laid out around private roads that create a mews effect.

81| RiverView Condominiums
445 E. North Water St.
2001, DESTEFANO AND PARTNERS

The steel cornice, well-articulated facade, and restrained yet lively palette of materials elevate this twenty-seven-story tower above its more mundane neighbors.

82| Nicholas J. Melas Centennial Fountain
McClurg Ct. at the Chicago River
1989, LOHAN ASSOCS.

This monument honors the centennial of the Metropolitan Water Reclamation District, the agency charged with ensuring a constant supply of healthy drinking water. The summit of the stepped granite pavilion represents the eastern continental divide (located just southwest of Chicago), with water flowing east to the Atlantic Ocean and west to the Gulf of Mexico. During the day, in season, a water cannon shoots an eighty-foot arc of water across the river every hour.

83| Embassy Suites Hotel
511 N. Columbus Dr.
2001, DESTEFANO AND PARTNERS

The transparent glass wall of the hotel's 190-foot-tall atrium is worth a look.

84| Sheraton Chicago Hotel & Towers
301 E. North Water St.
1992, SOLOMON CORDWELL BUENZ & ASSOCS.

This enormous but well-articulated convention hotel anchors the southwest corner of the Chicago Dock & Canal property. Automobile access is from the north; to the south the hotel opens onto a river esplanade linking it with the rest of Cityfront Center. The public spaces, which include the city's largest ballroom, are surprisingly warm and welcoming, with large windows taking advantage of the river views.

RIVER NORTH

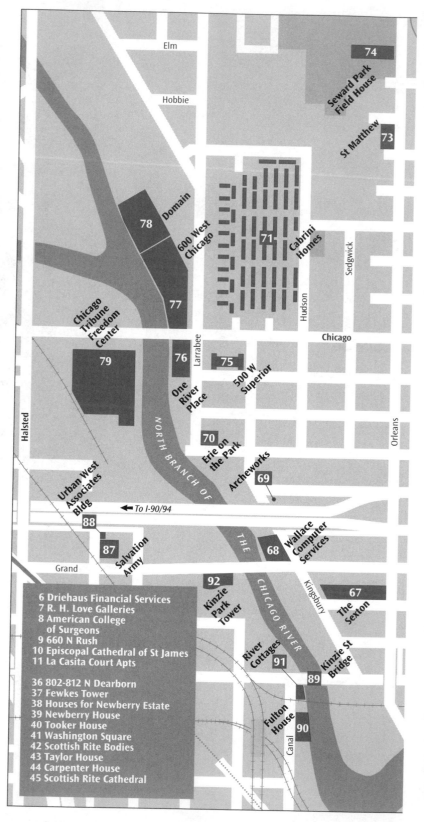

Elm

Hobbie

74

Seward Park Field House

St Matthew

73

Domain

78

600 West Chicago

71

Cabrini Homes

Sedgwick

Hudson

77

Chicago

Chicago Tribune Freedom Center

79

Larrabee

76

75

500 W Superior

One River Place

70

Erie on the Park

Archeworks

69

North Branch Of

Halsted

Urban West Associates Bldg

← To I-90/94

Wallace Computer Services

88

The

68

Orleans

87

Salvation Army

Grand

92

Kinzie Park Tower

Chicago River

Kingsbury

67

The Sexton

River Cottages

91

89

Kinzie St Bridge

Fulton House

90

Canal

6 Driehaus Financial Services
7 R. H. Love Galleries
8 American College
    of Surgeons
9 660 N Rush
10 Episcopal Cathedral of St James
11 La Casita Court Apts

36 802-812 N Dearborn
37 Fewkes Tower
38 Houses for Newberry Estate
39 Newberry House
40 Tooker House
41 Washington Square
42 Scottish Rite Bodies
43 Taylor House
44 Carpenter House
45 Scottish Rite Cathedral

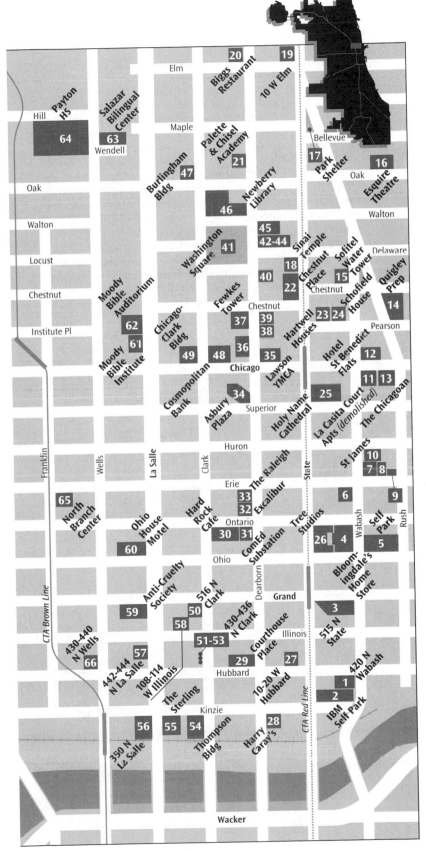

RIVER NORTH

RIVER NORTH IS THE NEWEST NAME FOR ONE OF CHICAGO'S OLDEST NEIGHBOR-
hoods. In the 1970s the long-forgotten area north and west of the towers that border the Chicago River and N. Michigan Ave. featured open
blocks of surface parking in its southeastern sector and, elsewhere,
ranks of mill-construction factory and warehouse buildings, many dating from the 1880s. Loft conversions to commercial and residential use
brought with them new life and a new name, and by 2000 new construction had filled the parking lots with high-rise apartments, multistory
garages, and retail complexes.

The poorest part of the city when incorporated in 1837, River North
was the site of Chicago's first industries; of the city's first railroad line,
which ran down Kinzie St.; and of its first slum, an Irish ghetto near the
fork of the north branch. In the late 1850s three bridges—at Rush St.,
Erie St., and Grand Ave.—established the first stable links between the
North Side and the rest of the city. From then on the area's role as the

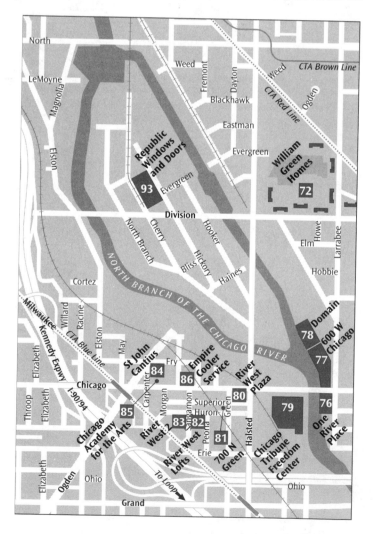

city's industrial district expanded, with the river and the rail lines attracting more factories, warehouses, and lumber- and brickyards. Miles of frame cottages soon appeared to house the neighborhood's laborers.

In an exception to this pattern of land use, an exclusive residential enclave emerged north of Grand Ave. along Rush and adjacent streets. Leading citizens established estates here on quarter-block parcels. The city's oldest park, Washington Square, was a developer's creation to stimulate upscale residential expansion north of Chicago Ave.; a legacy of this venture is the deviation of the city's grid in the surrounding blocks.

The 1871 Fire devastated the residential portions but left the lumberyards and industries untouched. Rebuilding followed the old patterns, with luxury neighborhoods east of La Salle St. and ethnic enclaves—first Irish and Swedish, later Italian—to the west. After 1900, however, factory construction spread northward and eastward from the river edges and gradually turned poor neighborhoods into slums.

The opening of the Michigan Ave. Bridge in 1920 was the coup de grace that sent everything west of the Magnificent Mile into a decline. As grand mansions were subdivided into rooming houses, the residential area near the Water Tower briefly became a Left Bank bohemia known as Tower Town. Washington Square, dubbed Bughouse Square, became a lively forum for free speech. The slums to the west were razed beginning in the 1940s for the enormous public housing complex that became known as Cabrini-Green. Industries in the southwest corner gradually closed or moved their operations elsewhere.

The transformation in the 1970s was begun by artists and gallery owners who converted warehouses into inexpensive, light-filled living and working spaces. As in other cities, the artists' alterations raised real estate values, and they ultimately found themselves edged out by boutiques, trendy restaurants, and luxury apartments. Offices, hotels, and major retail development followed, especially in the southeast corner, and in essence expanded the Loop northward and the Magnificent Mile westward. The area west of the north branch of the Chicago River, dubbed River West in the late 1980s, was touted as a less-expensive location for loft residences and small businesses.

The 1990s saw the rapid rise and swift demise of garish theme restaurants and entertainment venues, a few of which remain in toned-down incarnations. The twentieth century ended with the death of one of its great failed experiments, the high-rise public housing of Cabrini-Green, even as clusters of residential skyscrapers came to dominate the skyline in the rest of River North. —MARY ALICE MOLLOY

Buildings on the north bank of the river are included in the Loop chapter.

1| 420 N. Wabash Ave.
1983, CONVERSION, PAPPAGEORGE/HAYMES

One of the city's best-designed loft conversions creatively uses negative space by inserting a second skin of glass and metal behind the partially hollowed-out brick facade.

2| IBM Self Park
401 N. State St.
1974, GEORGE SCHIPPOREIT

A delicate screen of vertical, self-weathering Cor-Ten fins conceals intricate scissor ramps and space for 800 cars. The gentle curve of the Wabash Ave. elevation has a sculptural quality.

3| 515 N. State St.
1990, KENZO TANGE; SHAW & ASSOCS., COORDINATING ARCHS.

Modernism is alive and well in this strong opening statement in the redevelopment of almost twelve acres controlled by the American Medical Association. The sculptural glass-and-aluminum curtain-wall building

MEDINAH TEMPLE

creates a distinctive top with a four-story cutout near its summit. The leftover wedge of space houses mechanical equipment.

4| Bloomingdale's Home Store (*Medinah Temple*)
600 N. Wabash Ave.
1913, HUEHL & SCHMID
2002–2003, RENOVATIONS, DANIEL P. COFFEY & ASSOCS.

Built for the Shriners to host conventions, circuses, and concerts, it displays the Arabic motifs that lent exoticism to the organization's rituals. The textured brickwork is laid in an unusual variety of Flemish bond. Huehl & Schmid created scores of fanciful Shriners auditoriums; this is one of their largest and best preserved. It now has a new life as a retail store. Exterior changes were kept to a minimum.

5| Rush/Ohio/Wabash Self Park
50 E. Ohio St.
1999, SOLOMON CORDWELL BUENZ & ASSOCS., DESIGN ARCH.; DESMAN ASSOCS., ARCH. OF RECORD

As surface parking lots in this neighborhood disappeared in the 1990s, multilevel garages became increasingly prominent. This one is distinguished by metal grids, suspended from the concrete structure, installed on an angle to indicate the slopes of the parking ramps within.

6| Driehaus Financial Services (*Ransom R. Cable House*)
25 E. Erie St.
1886, COBB & FROST
1992, RENOVATION, JOHN VICTOR FREGA ASSOCS.

This house introduced to Chicago such Richardsonian design elements as rock-faced ashlar (here of Kasota stone), the slightly battered foundation, the low-sprung triple arches of the corner entry, and encrustations of neo-Byzantine carving. The medieval coach house is a superb complement.

7| R. H. Love Galleries (*Samuel M. Nickerson House*)
40 E. Erie St.
1883, BURLING & WHITEHOUSE

The sedate sandstone facade conceals an opulent palace with alabaster, onyx, and twenty-seven varieties of marble. The excessive weight required a perfectly level parquet base set into hardpan, or compacted clay, and four parallel brick walls, each about two feet thick.

8| American College of Surgeons—John B. Murphy Memorial Auditorium
50 E. Erie St.
1922–1926, MARSHALL & FOX

This auditorium-library was intended as the center of a complex devoted to postgraduate medical education. It is mod-

R. H. LOVE GALLERIES

eled remarkably closely on the Chapelle de Notre-Dame de Consolation in Paris (1900, Albert Guilbert), including the central street-level door and the curving stairs to the pillared and porticoed upper entrance, with its bronze doors by Tiffany Studios.

9 | 660 N. Rush St.
(*Double House for Leander McCormick and son Robert Hall McCormick*)
1875, FREDERICK AND EDWARD BAUMANN
1997, CONVERSION TO OFFICES, SEARL & ASSOCS.

Built as a double house for the brother of the reaper's inventor, Cyrus H. McCormick, it was converted into a single building after Leander's death in 1900.

10 | Episcopal Cathedral of St. James
65 E. Huron St.
1857, EDWARD J. BURLING
1875, REBUILDING, BURLING & ADLER
1913, CHAPEL OF ST. ANDREW, BERTRAM GROSVENOR GOODHUE
1928, MEMORIAL NARTHEX, GOODHUE ASSOCS.
1985, RESTORATION, HOLABIRD & ROOT

The stenciled nave, a chorus of color, is one of the nation's finest Victorian interiors. It was designed in 1888 by Edward

EPISCOPAL CATHEDRAL OF ST. JAMES

HOTEL ST. BENEDICT FLATS

Neville Stent, a student of William Morris. The church tower still bears the scars of the Great Fire.

11| La Casita Court Apartments
747 N. Wabash Ave.
1929, RICHARD E. SCHMIDT, GARDEN & ERICKSON

A rare reminder of the area's Left Bank atmosphere, this urbane limestone building with Art Deco–patterned spandrels features French doors opening onto balconettes. The entry on Wabash Ave. appears unaltered.

12| Hotel St. Benedict Flats
42–50 E. Chicago Ave./
801 N. Wabash Ave.
1882, JAMES J. EGAN

This is a rare and prominent example of the early years of the "flat craze" (1881–1893), when apartments were marketed to the upper middle class as "French flats." It uses Second Empire elements to resemble attached houses.

13| The Chicagoan
750 N. Rush St.
1990, SOLOMON CORDWELL BUENZ & ASSOCS.

This "lipstick building" is oval with octagonal bays at opposite corners, allowing six "corner" apartments per floor and living rooms with 180-degree views.

14| Archbishop Quigley Preparatory Seminary & Chapel of St. James
831 N. Rush St.
1919, ZACHARY T. DAVIS

The seminary building on Rush and Chestnut Sts. is Flamboyant Gothic, with energetic stonework throughout; the chapel on the southwest corner is modeled after the mid-thirteenth-century Sainte-Chapelle in Paris. Like that building, the chapel was conceived as an armature for a dazzling display of stained glass, executed in thousands of pieces of antique English glass by Robert T. Giles.

15| Sofitel Chicago Water Tower
20 E. Chestnut St.
2002, JEAN-PAUL VIGUIER; TENG & ASSOCS., ASSOC. ARCHS.

There is welcome drama and grace in this thirty-three-story hotel. The wedge and curve and thin vertical band of windows on the western facade make one stop, look, and go inside. The hotel lobby is atypical, with the bar to the side of the lobby and not even visible from the front door. This allows the bar to have sidewalk tables when the weather is right. The glass staircase carves the lobby into a relatively small space, but provides maximum effect.

ST. JAMES CHAPEL

SOFITEL CHICAGO WATER TOWER

16| Esquire Theatre
58 E. Oak St.
1938, PEREIRA & PEREIRA
1990, RENOVATION, GELICK FORAN
ASSOCS.

This streamlined and gracious cinema once served matinee tea and offered art exhibits. Now, chopped, diced, shopping-malled, and multiplexed, it shows six films at once and contains a bank and two-story commercial space.

17| Green Bay Triangle Shelter/Mariano Park
Rush St., State St., and Bellevue Pl.
1900, BIRCH BURDETTE LONG

In delicately colored polychrome terra-cotta the hardy, humble morning glory climbs the columns and blooms on the capitals of this simple Prairie School park shelter.

18| Chicago Sinai Temple
15 W. Delaware Pl.
1997, LOHAN ASSOCS.

The sanctuary is elevated above street level. A monumental exterior stair is placed sideways against the long elevation, providing a ceremonial approach on a tight urban site. An octagonal stained-glass window, designed by the architect, Dirk Lohan, marks the location of a small chapel.

CHICAGO SINAI TEMPLE

10 W. ELM ST.

19| 10 W. Elm St.

1928, B. LEO STEIF

With chevrons, zigzags, and fancifully imagined plant and animal forms, a group of French terra-cotta modelers brought a vivid new decorative vocabulary to Chicago. This high-rise apartment is clothed at top and bottom in the pastel decorative essays of Edouard Chassaing and his colleagues at the Northwestern Terra Cotta Company. He was one of six sculptors imported by the company in 1927 after the Exposition Internationale des Arts Décoratifs et Industriels Modernes (1925) in Paris. In contrast to the magisterial streamlining of Holabird & Root and Graham, Anderson, Probst & White, here is the brash side of the late 1920s.

20| Biggs Restaurant
(*John DeKoven House*)
1150 N. Dearborn St.
1874, EDWARD J. BURLING

This imposing Second Empire house has elaborate window surrounds and the original wrought-iron roof cresting and stoop railing.

21| Palette & Chisel Academy of Fine Art
(*William Waller House*)
1012 N. Dearborn St.
1874, ARCHITECT UNKNOWN

A relic of post-Fire residential grandeur, this Italianate mansion retains its principal features under the care of the academy, founded in 1895 under the sponsorship of sculptor Lorado Taft.

22| Chestnut Place Apartments
850 N. State St.
1982, WEESE, SEEGERS, HICKEY, WEESE

A vicarious trip to Florence awaits tenants in their private lobby, whose painted walls (by Richard Haas) evoke San Miniato al Monte. Bands of brick, dark at street level and lighter above, delineate each floor.

23| Edwin S. Hartwell Houses
14–16 E. Pearson St.
1885, JULIUS H. HUBER
1980, RENOVATION, BAUHS & DRING

This pair of town houses features terra-cotta portrait rondels of Hartwell's son and daughter, for whom these houses were built.

24| Frank Schofield House
18–20 E. Pearson St.
1934, FLORA SCHOFIELD; EUGENE B. REINER, SUPERVISING ARCH.

Designed by an artist, this simple but lively building has garages and an exhibition room on the ground floor, her studio and family's living quarters on the second floor, and a top-floor studio for her son. The facade has the handcrafted charm of Sol Kogen's work on W. Burton Pl., with mottled bricks, multicolored tiles, and a copper parapet.

25| Holy Name Cathedral
735 N. State St.
1875, PATRICK C. KEELEY
1890–1893, RENOVATION, WILLETT & PASHLEY
1914, ADDITION, HENRY J. SCHLACKS
1969, REMODELING, C. F. MURPHY ASSOCS.

LAMBERT TREE STUDIOS

Although not the archdiocese's most beautiful building, it is one of the hardiest and most embellished. Brooklyn architect Keeley was a very successful if unimaginative church specialist who usually relied on formula, which is Gothic here. Schlacks's ambitious changes moved the apse and inserted an additional fifteen feet of nave.

26| Lambert Tree Studios
601–623 N. State St.

1894, PARFITT BROS.; BAUER & HILL; AND HILL & WOLTERSDORF

1912, ADDITION, 12–16 E. OHIO ST., HILL & WOLTERSDORF

1913, ADDITION, 7 E. ONTARIO ST., HILL & WOLTERSDORF

2004, RESTORATION, DANIEL P. COFFEY & ASSOCS.

Built to entice out-of-town artists working at the Columbian Exposition to remain in Chicago, the Studios comprise ground-floor shops with large windowed studios above. Once slated for demotion along with Medinah Temple, the block was saved after a huge public outcry. The restoration entails creating an office entrance in the charming courtyard that had previously been closed to the public.

27| 10–20 W. Hubbard St.

1883, STEPHEN V. SHIPMAN

1975, CONVERSION HARRY WEESE & ASSOCS.

These quintessential examples of investor-built industrial lofts have interior brick walls twenty feet apart spanned by wood floors and plain, non-load-bearing facades. Weese, an early and strong Chicago preservationist, adapted the building for his own and other architects' offices.

28| Harry Caray's
(*Chicago Varnish Co.*)
33 W. Kinzie St.

1900, HENRY IVES COBB

This "quoin bank" is filled with Dutch Renaissance exuberance.

29| Courthouse Place
(*Cook County Criminal Courts Building*)
54 W. Hubbard St.

1892, OTTO H. MATZ

1986, RENOVATION, SOLOMON CORDWELL BUENZ & ASSOCS.

The Romanesque Revival mass, with more history than artistry, has a lavish if less than authentic lobby.

30| Hard Rock Café
63 W. Ontario St.

1985, TIGERMAN, FUGMAN, MCCURRY

31| Commonwealth Edison Substation
Southwest corner, Dearborn and Ontario Sts.

1989, TIGERMAN, FUGMAN, MCCURRY

It's the T-shirts and the decor that draw the tourists, not the Tuscan proportions and neo-Palladian windows. These elements were meant to identify the building with an adjacent Commonwealth Edison substation that proved to be scheduled for demolition. The replacement substation was then designed to respond to the Hard Rock Café, reusing the original's medallions, plaque, and wrought-iron fence.

32| Excalibur
(*Chicago Historical Society*)
632 N. Dearborn St.

1892, HENRY IVES COBB

Vigorous and picturesque, this fine Richardsonian Romanesque edifice housed the city's oldest

EXCALIBUR

cultural institution for more than thirty-five years before sheltering a Moose lodge, a school of design, a recording studio, and several nightclubs. Admiringly called a "pyramidal pile of brownstone" by an 1890s critic, this behemoth conveys a stability that belies its checkered past.

33| The Raleigh
650 N. Dearborn St.
1891, ARCHITECT UNKNOWN
1912, TOP-FLOOR REMODELING, ARCHITECT UNKNOWN
1990, RENOVATION, BERGER & ASSOCS.

With its serpentine stone skin, this was one of the more colorful hotels to open in anticipation of the World's Columbian Exposition.

34| Asbury Plaza
750 N. Dearborn St.
1981, GEORGE SCHIPPOREIT

The intriguing geometry, which gives this concrete high rise a different massing from every angle, also serves to reduce its bulk and maximize the lake views.

35| Victor F. Lawson YMCA House
30 W. Chicago Ave.
1930–1934, PERKINS, CHATTEN & HAMMOND

Intact if timeworn, this limestone and brick skyscraper emulates more lavish office buildings of the period. The Art Deco ornament includes spandrels with low-relief athletes above

the main entrance. A second-floor drawing room preserves its Deco fireplace, paneling, and etched-glass doors.

36| 802–812 N. Dearborn St.
EARLY 1870S, ARCHITECTS UNKNOWN

These well-preserved Italianate row houses have neo-Grec ornament on the low buildings to the south and lavish Second Empire trim on the four-story north buildings. At 810 is the fine Alliance Française de Chicago, remodeled by DeStefano and Partners in 1998 to include a building around the corner on Chicago Ave. At the rear of the property is a courtyard with a steel-and-glass addition that links the two buildings.

37| John Fewkes Tower
55 W. Chestnut St.
1967, HARRY WEESE & ASSOCS.

Fenestration is everything in this Ben Weese–designed tower. Eight-inch masonry walls alternate with thirty-story strips of trapezoidal bay windows and corners chamfered with slim windows. The windows even prompted a trapezoidal silhouette for interior partitions.

38| Houses for the Newberry Estate
827–833 N. Dearborn St.

39| Newberry House
(*Grant's Seminary for Young Ladies*)
839 N. Dearborn St.
1878, FREDERICK H. WAESCHER

NEWBERRY HOUSE

Although constructed as a set, the row houses have incised ornament that only hints at the Frank Furness–style detailing evident on the corner building's compressed columns and angled bay. The wall in front of 827–831 includes portrait roundels from Adler & Sullivan's demolished Schiller Building. Waescher was the Newberry estate's architect for over a decade, specializing in heavy structures such as warehouses and factories.

40 | Robert N. Tooker House
863 N. Dearborn St.
1886, JENNEY & OTIS

One of the few remnants of the two-year Jenney-Otis partnership has a two-tone rosy granite facade. Tooker Place, the adjacent alley, was the site of the Dill Pickle Club, a 1920s hangout for local bohemians and denizens of Bughouse Square.

41 | Washington Square

The land for this park was donated to the city in 1842 by Orsamus Bushnell as the centerpiece of his subdivision of the blocks bounded by State, Chicago, Division, and La Salle Sts. By the 1890s it was a genteel place of crossing walks, benches, and a central fountain. After 1900, as the buildings to the east were acquired by the Masonic Orien-

tal Consistory, and as other homes in the area were divided into rooming houses, the square became "the outdoor forum of garrulous hobohemia" known as Bughouse Square. The city now leases it to the Chicago Park District with the stipulation that the square remain usable as a public forum. Accordingly, in 1985 the dilapidated fountain was replaced by a raised concrete platform used for concerts and annual debates sponsored by the Newberry Library.

42 | Scottish Rite Bodies
(John Howland Thompson House)
915 N. Dearborn St.
1888, COBB & FROST

Superb masonry design, second only to that on H. H. Richardson's Glessner House, patterns the reddish brown Lake Superior sandstone, which provides rich texture but never overwhelms with massiveness. The balanced but asymmetrical bays on the Delaware Pl. elevation, the steeply pitched slate roof of gables and turrets exuberantly outlined in copper, and the tripartite entrance separated by bundled columns with rock-faced lintels below a handsome panel of foliate diaperwork all combine to demonstrate what can happen in an inspired partnership.

43 | George H. Taylor House
919 N. Dearborn St.
1895, TREAT & FOLTZ

44 | George B. Carpenter House
925 N. Dearborn St.
1891, TREAT & FOLTZ

These neighboring houses are a lesson in shifting tastes. The rough stonework on portions of the Carpenter House seems to be peeled away to reveal Georgian Revival forms like those of the Taylor House.

45 | Scottish Rite Cathedral
(*Unity Church*)
929 N. Dearborn St.
1867, THEODORE VIGO WADSKIER
1873, REBUILDING, BURLING & ADLER
1882, SOUTH TOWER, FREDERICK B. TOWNSEND

The original structure with a matched set of towers, touted as one of the grandest of the city's Joliet limestone churches, lost all of its wooden portions in the 1871 Fire. Rebuilding within the original walls gave Dankmar Adler his first experience with acoustical design by installing raked seating. The light color of the entry is a sprayed-on attempt to thwart deteriorating stone.

46 | Newberry Library
60 W. Walton St.
1890–1893, HENRY IVES COBB
1981, ADDITION, HARRY WEESE & ASSOCS.

The "uncommon collection of uncommon collections" provided for in the will of Walter Loomis Newberry (1804–1868) has an impressive housing whose original building is only half as deep as what Cobb intended. The jagged lines where the addition was to have picked up are visible on the side elevations. Cobb was asked to abandon his partnership with Charles S. Frost to devote full attention to this commission. The facade, which centers on a triple-arched entrance inspired by the twelfth-century church of Saint-Gilles-du-Gard, is attributed to Cobb's employee Louis C. Mullgardt. The interior plan was conceived by the Newberry's first librarian, William F. Poole.

In the addition, whose brickwork hints at the arches of the original, even the walls and their plenum spaces are part of the mechanical system, which provides climate-controlled storage for twenty-one miles of books, maps, and manuscripts. The replicated chandelier in the restored lobby has bulbs that point downward to prove that this was one of Chicago's first electrified buildings.

47 | Burlingham Building
1000 N. Clark St.
1883, ALFRED SMITH
1897, TWO-STORY ADDITION, ALFRED SMITH

NEWBERRY LIBRARY

A cast-iron corner turret, bays that feature cast-iron piers, slate spandrels, and colored window glass constitute an elaborate array of Queen Anne details. The bays have unusual proportions, with the central window narrower than those to the side.

48| Cosmopolitan Bank & Trust (*Cosmopolitan State Bank*)
801 N. Clark St.
1920, RICHARD E. SCHMIDT, GARDEN & MARTIN
1997, ADDITION, TILTON & LEWIS ASSOCS.

In 1921 *American Architect* called it "a fine example of unfashionable bank designing" in notable contrast to the Classical temples being erected everywhere else. Especially praiseworthy were the large, unbroken wall surfaces, simple and severe lines, and rich and neutral colors.

49| Chicago-Clark Building (*Bush Temple of Music*)
100 W. Chicago Ave.
1901, J. E. O. PRIDMORE

Unashamedly overblown and *retardataire,* it originally contained studios, practice rooms, rehearsal halls, and a large theater used by German performers.

50| 516 N. Clark St./101 W. Grand Ave.
1872, 1873, ARCHITECT UNKNOWN
1883, 1884, CYRUS P. THOMAS
1985, RENOVATION, SWANKE HAYDEN CONNELL

Beginning as a four-story grocery with lofts, it grew additions and extra stories until it became The Albany, an 1880s first-class apartment building with hardly a seam visible.

51| 430 N. Clark St.
1872, ARCHITECT UNKNOWN

52| 432 N. Clark St.
1900, FACADE, FLORIAN-WIERZBOWSKI

53| 436 N. Clark St.
1872, WILLIAM W. BOYINGTON

A clever copy filled in a gap between two of the city's oldest business buildings.

54| John R. Thompson Building
350 N. Clark St.
1912, ALFRED S. ALSCHULER
1983, RENOVATION, METZ, TRAIN & YOUNGREN

Known for years as the Commissary Building, it housed the general offices of the Thompson restaurant chain. Its creamy terra-cotta facade bespeaks good hygiene as well as Chicago School proportions.

55| The Sterling
345 N. La Salle Blvd.
2002, SOLOMON CORDWELL BUENZ & ASSOCS.

This actually is a sterling design, much better than most of the rows of high-rise apartments and condos filling River North. The painted concrete skin looks as good as many fancier materials because it is kept simple, as it curves around the building and peaks at the top, on the northwest corner.

N. La Salle Blvd. Renovations

From the river north to its terminus at Lincoln Park, La Salle was an Avenue in the post-Fire years, when it was lined with elms and some of the city's finest residences. In 1930—already a little seedy and with commercial structures encroaching on its southern end—it became a Street, as trees, lawns, porches, and often entire facades were sliced off to widen the roadway by fourteen feet on each side. The project had been proposed as part of the 1909 Plan of Chicago, to provide fast motor access to the Loop. Evidence of the widening can be seen along the length of the street, with the best examples of Art Deco facades on the east side between Chestnut and Delaware Sts. An estimated $13 million in private funds was spent in 1978–1979 to revitalize the street after decades

LA SALLE BLVD. BEFORE WIDENING

LA SALLE BLVD. AFTER WIDENING

of unbenign neglect. The move led to another name change to indicate its upscale image: La Salle Boulevard.

56 | 350 N. La Salle Blvd.
1990, LOEBL, SCHLOSSMAN & HACKL IN CONSULTATION WITH WOJCIECH LESNIKOWSKI

A conscious reuse of Chicago School elements articulates the skeleton frame with red brick and fills the bays with green glass. The curved and towered corners create internal variety in a very slim building.

57 | 442–444 N. La Salle Blvd.
1930, REMODELING, GEORGE F. LOVDALL

The street widening cost this old warehouse its front, but in the remodeling it gained a dazzling polychrome Art Deco terra-cotta facade.

58 | 108–114 W. Illinois St.
(*Grommes & Ullrich Warehouse*)
1901, RICHARD E. SCHMIDT

This former liquor distribution center, designed by Hugh M. G. Garden, expresses its structure boldly. Horizontality is emphasized by discontinuous recessed piers and unusually broad Chicago windows.

108–114 W. ILLINOIS ST.

59 | Anti-Cruelty Society
157 W. Grand Ave.
1935, LEON STANHOPE
1982, ADDITION ON LA SALLE BLVD., STANLEY TIGERMAN ASSOCS.

ANTI-CRUELTY SOCIETY

The original sleek Art Moderne building displays its purpose with low-relief carvings of pet owners on either side of the door. The cheeky addition has a "doggie in the window" storefront.

60| Ohio House Motel
600 N. La Salle Blvd.
1960, SHAYMAN & SALK

This may be the city's best-preserved expression of the colorful, angular, space-age design of the Sputnik era.

61| Moody Bible Institute
820 N. La Salle Blvd.
1937–1939, THIELBAR & FUGARD

62| Moody Bible Auditorium
840 N. La Salle Blvd.
1954, FUGARD, BURT, WILKINSON & ORTH

English Gothic styling gives a quasi-religious look to this high-rise school. The auditorium was completed after a fifteen-year hiatus.

63| Ruben Salazar Bilingual Center
(*James A. Sexton Public School*)
160 W. Wendell St.
1882, ARCHITECT UNKNOWN

This typical Italianate school is remarkable for its age and unusual cornice.

64| Walter Payton College
Preparatory High School
1034 N. Wells St.
2000, DESTEFANO AND PARTNERS, MANAGING ARCH.; MANN, GIN, DUBIN & FRAZIER, ARCH. OF RECORD

A glass circulation spine creates an internal "street" that links the academic and public wings of the building, the latter including after-hours activity centers such as the gymnasium and lecture/performance hall. The steel-framed building is clad in brick to harmonize with neighboring housing stock.

65| North Branch Center
223 W. Erie St.
CA. 1896, ARCHITECT UNKNOWN
1899, ADDITION, JOHN H. WAGNER
1980, RENOVATION, JEROME BROWN

This large industrial building uses exposed metal mullions to open up the facade, a technique unpopular after miles of cast-iron facades melted in the 1871 Fire.

66| 430–440 N. Wells St.
(*Liquid Carbonic Acid Manufacturing Co.*)
1903, HOLABIRD & ROCHE
1982, RENOVATION, HAMMOND, BEEBY & BABKA

This loft building has the large windows, high ceilings, and open-beam construction that made this type of structure so popular for office conversions in the 1980s. The facade is unusually well detailed, with terra-cotta ornament and recessed courses of brick.

67| The Sexton
(*John Sexton & Co.*)
500 N. Orleans St.
1916, 1919, ALFRED S. ALSCHULER
2001, CONVERSION, FITZGERALD ASSOCS. ARCHS.

JOHN SEXTON & CO.

Built by a grocery and food-processing company for use as its office, manufacturing plant, and warehouse, this building represents the final stage in Chicago loft construction. Unlike the previous generation of lofts, the elevations not only reflect the various uses of the interior space but also identify stairwells, light shafts, and elevators. Appearance and image were so important that the addition, which added the easternmost 150 feet, matched the original building's load-bearing walls, even though the structural system was now reinforced concrete.

During the 2000–2001 conversion to condominiums, balconies and additional stories were added.

68| Wallace Computer Services—Factory
(*Railway Terminal and Warehouse Co.*)
444 W. Grand Ave.
1909, NIMMONS & FELLOWS

The self-banding at the base and top, also reflected in the stone capitals, is tantamount to this firm's signature.

69| Archeworks
625 N. Kingsbury St.
1997, TIGERMAN MCCURRY ARCHITECTS, EVA MADDOX ASSOCS., ASSOC. ARCH.

This clever and unassuming building beneath the Ohio feeder ramp houses an innovative design school. Founded by Stanley Tigerman and Eva Maddox, Archeworks brings together interns in a variety of disciplines to develop creative solutions to problems relating to issues such as homelessness, disabilities, and gerontology. The DuroScreen-clad structure with wood trusses is capped by a continuous cupola that provides light from thirty-four clerestory windows.

70| Erie on the Park
510 W. Erie St.
2002, LUCIEN LAGRANGE ARCHITECTS

ERIE ON THE PARK

The narrow condominium tower, a parallelogram in plan, rises from a context of low brick warehouse and office buildings. The expressed steel structure with its distinctive cross-bracing and terrace setbacks is visible from all directions and is a welcome architectural expression in comparison to the more typical condominium construction.

This stretch of Orleans St. north to Division is best seen from the elevated train or a car.

71| Chicago Housing Authority— Frances Cabrini Homes
Chicago Ave., Larrabee St., Oak St., and Hudson Ave.
1942, HENRY HOLSMAN, GEORGE BURMEISTER, MAURICE B. RISSMAN, ERNEST A. GRUNSFELD, JR., LOUIS R. SOLOMON, GEORGE M. JONES, KARL M. VITZTHUM, I. S. LOEWENBERG, AND FRANK A. MCNALLY

72| Chicago Housing Authority— William Green Homes
Division and Larrabee Sts., Clybourn and Ogden Aves.
1962, PACE ASSOCS.

One of the nation's most notorious housing projects became one of its most closely watched models for the redevelopment of public housing. The 1990s brought demolition of most of Cabrini's red-brick high rises and the construction of numerous private developments that have 20 percent of their units set aside for Chicago Housing Authority (CHA) tenants. Public works projects include two new schools, a branch library, and a police station. The redevelopment pioneered here was continued and extended throughout the city under the auspices of the CHA's ten-year, $1.5 billion Plan for Transformation. Inaugurated in 2000, the plan calls for the demolition of all of the agency's high rises that house families (not seniors) and their replacement with units that are interspersed with market-rate and affordable housing. Cabrini's

prime location between River North and Old Town virtually assured the success of this mixed-income model. Whether it can be repeated in less-affluent communities on the south and west sides may not be apparent until much later.

73| St. Matthew United Methodist Church
1000 N. Orleans St.
1969, SKIDMORE, OWINGS & MERRILL

A pastor seeking to expand community programs in a very depressed area admired the University of Illinois at Chicago, and so engaged Walter Netsch, Jr., to apply his field theory to this church. A series of rotated squares constitutes the church, fellowship hall, classrooms, and two suites for day care. Sculptor Richard Hunt's Cor-Ten cross marks the church end of the site.

74| Seward Park Field House
375 W. Elm St.
1908, DWIGHT H. PERKINS
1999, CLOCK TOWER, JOHNSON JOHNSON & ROY

The Prairie School tradition is manifest in the clear, logical expression and use of materials. Sloping brick piers with metal capitals support the wood knee brackets, which in turn support the overhanging eaves with their exposed wooden rafters.

Return to Chicago Ave. via Wells St. rather than Larrabee St.

75| The Montgomery
(*Montgomery Ward & Co.— Corporate Offices*)
500 W. Superior St.
1974, MINORU YAMASAKI & ASSOCS.
2003–2004, CONVERSION TO RESIDENCES, PAPPAGEORGE/HAYMES

76| One River Place
(*Warehouse and Offices*)
619 W. Chicago Ave.
1930, WILLIS J. MCCAULEY
2002, CONVERSION TO RESIDENCES, FITZGERALD ASSOCS. ARCHS.

MONTGOMERY WARD WAREHOUSE

77| 600 W. Chicago
(*Montgomery Ward Warehouse*)
600 W. Chicago Ave./
800 N. Larrabee St.
1906–1908, RICHARD E. SCHMIDT,
GARDEN & MARTIN
2002, CONVERSION, GENSLER

78| Domain
(*Montgomery Ward Warehouse &*
Offices)
900 N. Kingsbury Ave.
2002, CONVERSION TO RESIDENCES,
PAPPAGEORGE/HAYMES

Richard E. Schmidt was a master
of concrete construction, and
this former warehouse is his
most impressive achievement.
It is best seen from the river,
whose contours it follows. The
facades are mostly the exposed
edges of the concrete frame
and are unmistakably horizontal, celebrating the building's
717-foot length. After Ward's
bankruptcy, the complex was
redeveloped for residential and
commercial use. But the figure
of *Commerce* remains atop the
tower of 619 W. Chicago Ave.

79| Chicago Tribune
Freedom Center
777 W. Chicago Ave. at
N. Branch of Chicago River
1982, SKIDMORE, OWINGS &
MERRILL

Built on a site that includes
railroad air rights, this sprawling

structure houses the nation's
largest newspaper printing and
distribution facility.

80| River West Plaza
(*Devoe & Raynolds Co.*)
770 N. Halsted St.
1902, HILL & WOLTERSDORF
1989, CONVERSION TO OFFICES,
BERGER & ASSOCS.

A four-building office complex
was made from former paint-
making business buildings. The
frontispiece, the two buildings
at the Halsted-Chicago corner,
acquired a glass link and an
atrium inserted around the old
elevator tower.

81| 700 N. Green St.
(*Koenig, Henning & Gaber Co.*)
1877, ARCHITECT UNKNOWN

Common brick walls set off with
small windows, tie rods, and
occasional touches of red brick
characterize this furniture
factory. John Koenig moved his
mechanized operations here
after having been burned out
in the 1871 Fire, in order to be
near riverfront lumberyards and
railroads.

700 N. GREEN ST.

82 | River West Loft Apartments
(*J. P. Smith Shoe Co.*)
915–925 W. Huron St.

1912, HORATIO R. WILSON & CO.
1919, HURON ST. ADDITION,
SHANKLAND & PINGREY
1987, CONVERSION, BERGER &
ASSOCS.

This factory was built within three years of Albert Kahn's demonstration of the advantages of metal sash windows in Ford's Highland Park, Michigan plant. The introduction of metal sash windows, covering fourteen-foot-wide areas in this case, changed the configuration of mullions and fenestration and the overall composition of factory facades. Vertical wall surfaces are merely thin piers rising from sidewalk to cornice; walls are embellished with very simple patterns of projecting and recessed brickwork. The building was dilapidated and underutilized when its conversion to apartment units sparked the revitalization of an area designated a slum.

83 | River West 2 Condominiums
939 W. Huron St.

1991, BERGER & ASSOCS.

This poured-in-place concrete building is a modern application of the old loft concept: concrete ceilings and columns, heating and air-conditioning ducts, and other industrial finishes are exposed. Stylistically the elevations call upon contemporary German and Japanese sources.

84 | St. John Cantius Roman Catholic Church
813–817 N. Carpenter St.

1893–1898, ADOLPHUS DRUIDING
1901, RECTORY, ARCHITECT
UNKNOWN

85 | Chicago Academy for the Arts
(*St. John Cantius Parish School*)
1010 W. Chicago Ave.

1903, THEODORE OSTROWSKI,
MASON

These three buildings exhibit very different styles. The church is described in parish publications as "Romanesque Ba-

ST. JOHN CANTIUS ROMAN
CATHOLIC CHURCH

roque"—perhaps meaning that the main elevation spans the history of round-arch styles. The Rectory's high mansard roof with gabled dormers shows the influence of S. S. Beman's Kimball House. The Parish School is a heavy-handed rendition of northern European Baroque.

86 | Empire Cooler Service
(*Paepcke-Leicht Lumber Co.*)
940 W. Chicago Ave.

1906, LOUIS GUENZEL

This small industrial building makes a bold statement with nontraditional stone ornament on a textured brick facade. Look above the roofline to see the tower of the Italianate house that it enveloped.

87 | Salvation Army Thrift Store
(*Braun & Fitts Butterine Factory*)
509 N. Union Ave.

1891, FURST & RUDOLPH
1917, ADDITION AND ALTERATIONS,
POSTLE & FISCHER
1947, ALTERATIONS AND
REMODELING, ALBERT C. FEHLOW

88 | Urban West Associates Building
685 W. Ohio St.

1992, REMODELING, KEITH TALBERT
& JAY KELLER, URBAN WEST ASSOCS.

These side-by-side examples of adaptive reuse were done forty-five years apart. The Salvation Army, as the client converting a margarine factory to institutional use, employed an Art Moderne seam of an elevator core and light well to wed the seven- and five-story pieces of the Braun & Fitts structure. Talbert & Keller, as owner-architects of a two-story heavy timber structure, slathered multicolored Dryvit on masonry bearing walls that had been wrecked by permanent imitation brick.

89| Kinzie St. Bridge
W. Kinzie St. at N. Branch of Chicago River
1908, JOHN E. ERICSON, CITY ENG.; THOMAS G. PIHLFELDT, CITY BRIDGE ENG.

This bridge was known locally as a mild irritant, because of its low clearance for navigation and its narrow roadway. But it gained international notoriety on April 13, 1992, when a piece of the abandoned freight tunnel system below its protective pilings sprang a major leak, flooding Loop basements.

90| Fulton House
(*North American Cold Storage Co.*)
345 N. Canal St.
1898, FRANK B. ABBOTT
1981, CONVERSION, HARRY WEESE & ASSOCS.

91| River Cottages
357–365 N. Canal St.
1988, HARRY WEESE & ASSOCS.

Sailor Weese's enthusiasm for riverfront living manifested itself in these very different projects. Fulton House's windows are carved out of the thick walls of an insulated warehouse. At the opposite end of the scale—and style—spectrum are River Cottages' futuristic facades adorned with porthole windows.

92| Kinzie Park Tower
501 N. Clinton St.
2001, NAGLE HARTRAY DANKER KAGAN MCKAY

This condominium tower achieves what many River North apartment and condo buildings miss. Instead of having balconies sticking out of the facade, on this building they are tucked neatly between each sculptural curve and angle. Those curves also provide unusually expansive views for a great number of the units.

REPUBLIC WINDOWS AND DOORS

93| Republic Windows and Doors
930 W. Evergreen St.
1998, BOOTH HANSEN ASSOCIATES

This sleek complex is the star of a new generation of industrial buildings on Goose Island, a protected manufacturing district. A three-story corporate headquarters fronts a large, single-floor factory whose twenty-seven-foot ceilings offer abundant light from huge roof monitors.

SOUTH LOOP

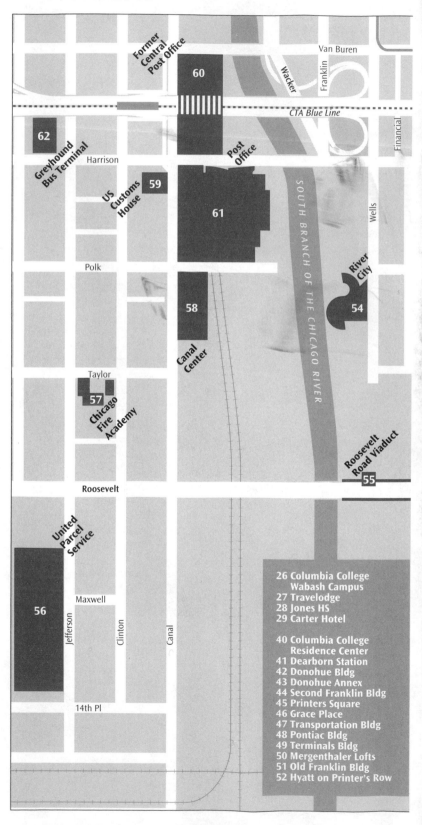

60

Former Central Post Office

Van Buren

Wacker

Franklin

Financial

CTA Blue Line

62

Greyhound Bus Terminal

Harrison

US Customs House

59

Post Office

61

SOUTH BRANCH OF THE CHICAGO RIVER

Wells

River City

54

Polk

58

Canal Center

Taylor

57

Chicago Fire Academy

Roosevelt Road Viaduct

55

Roosevelt

United Parcel Service

56

Jefferson

Maxwell

Clinton

Canal

14th Pl

26 Columbia College
   Wabash Campus
27 Travelodge
28 Jones HS
29 Carter Hotel

40 Columbia College
   Residence Center
41 Dearborn Station
42 Donohue Bldg
43 Donohue Annex
44 Second Franklin Bldg
45 Printers Square
46 Grace Place
47 Transportation Bldg
48 Pontiac Bldg
49 Terminals Bldg
50 Mergenthaler Lofts
51 Old Franklin Bldg
52 Hyatt on Printer's Row

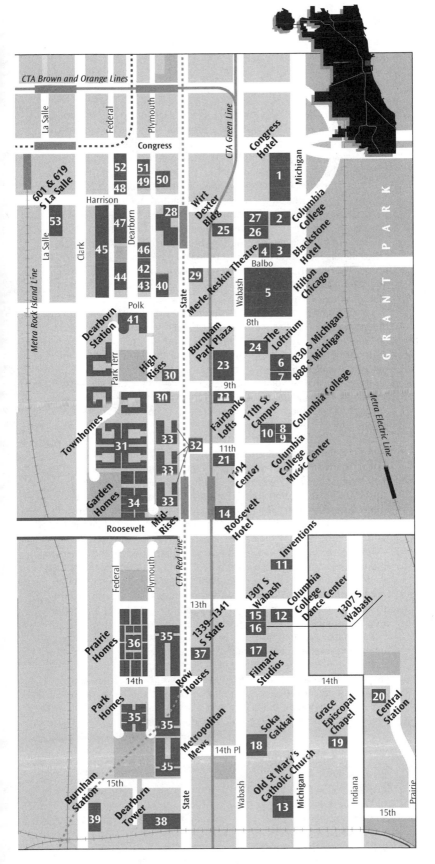

CTA Brown and Orange Lines

La Salle
Federal
Plymouth
Congress

Congress Hotel

Michigan

601 & 619 S La Salle

52
48
51
49
50

Harrison

53

Wirt Dexter Bldg

27
26
2

Columbia College

Blackstone Hotel

28

47

45

Dearborn

46
42
43
40

25

29

4
3

Balbo

Hilton Chicago

Wabash

5

Polk

Dearborn Station

41

High Rises

30

Burnham Park Plaza

8th

24

The Loftrium

830 S Michigan
888 S Michigan

6
7

Park Terr

30

23

9th

22

Fairbanks Lofts

11th St Campus

Columbia College

Townhomes

31

33

32

10

8
9

11th

21

11th Center

Columbia College Music Center

Garden Homes

34

33

33

14

Roosevelt Hotel

Roosevelt

Mid-Rises

CTA Red Line

Inventions

11

1301 S Wabash

Columbia College Dance Center

1307 S Wabash

13th

Federal
Plymouth

15
16

12

Prairie Homes

36

35

1339–1341 S State

37

17

Filmack Studios

14th

14th

Park Homes

35

35

Row Houses

Metropolitan Mews

18

Soka Gakkai

Grace Episcopal Chapel

19

20

Central Station

Indiana

35

14th Pl

Burnham Station

15th

39

Dearborn Tower

38

State

Wabash

Old St Mary's Catholic Church

13

Michigan

Prairie

15th

GRANT PARK

Metra Rock Island Line

Metra Electric Line

Merle Reskin Theatre

CTA Green Line

SOUTH LOOP

FASHIONABLE APARTMENTS FILL THE SHELLS OF FORMER INDUSTRIAL BUILDINGS, luxurious single-family houses cover abandoned railroad land, and a mixed-use complex with a marina hugs the banks of the Chicago River's south branch. College students live, learn, and perform in historic structures, and bank employees and postal workers toil in gargantuan new quarters. The South Loop offers wonderfully diverse examples of changing land-use patterns on the fringes of the central city.

For decades the area was dominated and divided by miles of railway trackage. Along the lakefront, the Illinois Central Gulf Railroad tracks stretched as far north as the mouth of the Chicago River at what is now called Illinois Center. Other tracks converged at the four depots clustered at the Loop's south edge. They carried freight as well as passengers, and printing industries sprang up just north of the Dearborn Station to take advantage of this proximity.

As trucks and planes superceded trains after World War II, vast tracts of land became available for development, but the question of by whom and for what purpose was subject to continuing debate. Municipal government skirted the issue by drawing up master plans for every area except the central city. Concerned about the Loop's economic and cultural decline, a group of business leaders formed the Chicago Central Area Committee and, in 1973, proposed that the abandoned South Loop railyards be used for mixed-use development that would include abundant middle-class housing.

Dearborn Park, developed on that land, has been a success as a residential neighborhood but never met expectations for other uses. To the north, restaurants and shops were filling the ground floors of the former printers' buildings, which were gradually being converted to apartments starting in the late 1970s. Dearborn Park and its successor to the immediate south offer urban models that contrast with that of Printers Row. The former are self-contained residential enclaves, while the latter is very much part of the urban fabric.

In the early 1990s another self-contained housing development began to take shape on abandoned railway land. Central Station extended the residential popularity of Dearborn Park farther east, linking the built-up city to the then-newly created Museum Campus. Like Dearborn Park, it was envisioned as a mixture of office, commercial. and residential uses, with only the latter proving easily marketable.

In the late 1990s Columbia College expanded its campus southward, purchasing several historic buildings that now anchor the area around Michigan and Wabash Aves. Just a decade earlier, these streets were the missing links in the South Loop's development, but with the conversion of old business buildings to residential lofts and construction of new infill town houses and apartments, the area has been transformed into a desirable, mixed-use neighborhood.

—LAURIE MCGOVERN PETERSEN

1| **Congress Plaza Hotel**
(*Auditorium Annex*)
520 S. Michigan Ave.
1893, CLINTON J. WARREN
1902, 1907, HOLABIRD & ROCHE

Built as an extension of the Auditorium Hotel, the "Annex" was designed to harmonize with it, even though its steel frame made the arcaded windows anachronisms more appropriate to the Auditorium's load-bearing walls. The additions respected the original section, including the generous bay windows overlooking the lake, but without the arcades.

2| Columbia College (*Harvester Building*) 600 S. Michigan Ave.
1907, CHRISTIAN A. ECKSTORM

Here is one of the most colossal cornices remaining on a Chicago high rise.

3| Blackstone Hotel 636 S. Michigan Ave.
1908, MARSHALL & FOX

4| Merle Reskin Theatre (*Blackstone Theatre*) 60 E. Balbo Dr.
1910, MARSHALL & FOX

The elegance of this opulently roofed palace is shared by the adjacent theater.

5| Hilton Chicago (*Stevens Hotel*) 720 S. Michigan Ave.
1922–1927, HOLABIRD & ROCHE
1986, RENOVATION, SOLOMON CORDWELL BUENZ & ASSOCS.

Built to be the world's "largest and most sumptuous" hotel and designed in a "modification of the style of Louis 16th," this twenty-five-story behemoth contained 3,000 rooms—all of them outside rooms with private baths—plus a convention hall seating 4,000, an exhibition hall "equal in dimensions to the Coliseum," and a rooftop golf course. Because the number and size of the public rooms on the lower floors required the frequent displacement of loads throughout the steel framing system, fewer than half of the 300 columns on a typical floor extended from the basement to the attic. In some cases trusses ran through several stories and required that corridors be threaded through them.

Purchased by the U.S. War Department for use as a barracks in 1942, the Stevens changed

hands several times until it was acquired in 1945 by Conrad Hilton, who renamed it in 1951. The renovated building now has 1,600 rooms as well as new parking and fitness facilities.

6| 830 S. Michigan Ave. (*YWCA Hotel*)
1894, JOHN M. VAN OSDEL II

Despite considerable abuse, poor paint choices, and "modernization," it still has a delicate air, especially in its top-floor bays.

7| 888 S. Michigan Ave. (*Crane Company Building*)
1912, HOLABIRD & ROCHE

This virtually intact Classical Revival version of the tripartite high-rise formula lacks the Chicago School's vertically emphasized central shaft.

8| Columbia College (*Lightner Building*) 1006 S. Michigan Ave.
1904, EDMUND R. KRAUSE

This highly refined office building features large amounts of glass set in Chicago windows as well as columns and beams that have been reduced to the minimum.

9| Columbia College Music Center 1014 S. Michigan Ave.
1912, CHRISTIAN A. ECKSTORM
1998, REMODELING, SAS ARCHITECTS

The mansard roof with pedimented pairs of windows is an unusual touch on what was constructed as a speculative commercial building.

10| Columbia College— 11th St. Campus (*Chicago Women's Club Building*) 72 E. 11th St.
1929, HOLABIRD & ROCHE
1985, REMODELING, MICHAEL ARENSON

The building for the city's premier women's service club included a recital room, various clubrooms, and three floors of hotel rooms. The Art Deco style was chosen to affirm the fifty-year-old club's youthful outlook.

COLUMBIA COLLEGE—
11TH ST. CAMPUS

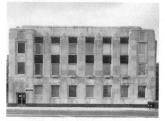

COLUMBIA COLLEGE DANCE CENTER

Film Row
Wabash and Michigan Aves.
from Roosevelt Rd.
to W. 16th St.

For almost fifty years exhibitors who ran Chicago's 1,100 movie theaters came here for everything they needed: feature films, cartoons, short subjects, and coming-attractions trailers; movie projectors and sound heads; lobby posters, billboards, and still photographs; numbered tickets, popcorn, and candy; seats, canopies, carpeting, lightbulbs for marquees—even dishes for premium nights. By the 1930s more than two dozen studios and independents were operating film exchanges here, mostly near 13th St. In the 1960s television changed the movie world, and neighborhood squalor began driving the exchanges elsewhere.

11| Inventions
(*Universal Pictures Film Exchange*)
1234 S. Michigan Ave.
1947, ARCHITECT UNKNOWN

This late film exchange replicates the Art Deco style of the earlier exchanges on Wabash Ave.

12| Columbia College Dance Center
(*Paramount Pictures Film Exchange*)
1306 S. Michigan Ave.
1930, ANKER S. GRAVEN
2000, ADAPTIVE REUSE, SAS ARCHITECTS

A calm, sedate limestone skin serves as a backdrop to Art Deco ornament highlighting flowers—with no suggestion of things cinematic.

13| Old St. Mary's Catholic Church
1500 S. Michigan Ave.
2002, PRISCO SERENA STURM ARCHITECTS

The light colors of the metallic roof and precast concrete walls were chosen for their ability to reflect light and heat. High-performance glass used throughout also reduces the amount of solar gain.

14| Roosevelt Hotel
1152 S. Wabash Ave.
1892, JULES DE HORVATH
2003, REHABILITATION FOR APARTMENTS, PAPPAGEORGE/ HAYMES

The abandoned and severely deteriorated hotel gained new life as moderate-income apartments. The gently undulating bays of the facade are reminiscent of some of Holabird & Roche's work of the 1880s.

15| 1301 S. Wabash Ave.
(*Universal Studios Film Exchange*)
1937, OLSEN & URBAIN

This yellow brick structure features an intact, curving glass-block corner.

16| 1307 S. Wabash Ave.
(*Warner Brothers Film Exchange*)
1929, ZIMMERMAN, SAXE & ZIMMERMAN

Integral zigzag brickwork rather than applied ornament lends interest to this Art Deco exchange.

17| Filmack Studios
(*Famous Players–Lasky Corporation Film Exchange*)
1327 S. Wabash Ave.
1923, C.W. AND GEORGE L. RAPP

Despite filled-in windows, the glistening terra-cotta triumphal doorway conveys some of the exuberance of Rapp & Rapp's cinema palaces. Paramount Pictures' logo remains in one corner of the cornice.

18| Soka Gakkai International USA Chicago Culture Center
1455 S. Wabash Ave.
1995, HARDING ASSOCS.

The Midwest headquarters for Soka Gakkai, Japan's largest religious organization, includes a Buddhist temple. A 150-seat chapel is located in the base of the masonry cylinder, with an office and conference room above. A Japanese garden atop the second floor is visible from the lobby, which is centered on the axis of 14th Pl.

19| Grace Episcopal Church Chapel
1448 S. Indiana Ave.
1928–1931, TALLMADGE & WATSON

The chapel for the old St. Luke's Hospital (whose buildings include 1435–1447 S. Michigan Ave., 1908, Frost & Granger; and 1440 S. Indiana Ave., 1925, Charles S. Frost) is a diminutive version of the Gothic churches that became a mainstay of this firm after the demise of the Prairie School.

20| Central Station
S. Michigan Ave./S. Indiana Ave. east to Lake Shore Dr., between E. Roosevelt Rd. and E. 21st St.
BEGUN 1992

Conceived as a mixed-use project with a significant office component, the development proved most popular for residential buildings. Everything is built on land and air rights over existing railroad tracks. The former Illinois Central station stood on Roosevelt Rd. at the north end of what is now this project.

21| Columbia College— 1104 Center
(*Ludington Building*)
1104 S. Wabash Ave.
1891, JENNEY & MUNDIE
2002, RESTORATION AND ADAPTIVE REUSE, SAS ARCHITECTS

This unusually well preserved high rise is one of the first all-steel structures, built at the same time as the Second Leiter Building (now Robert Morris Center), which has a steel-and-wrought-iron frame. In both, the exterior exactly reflects the form of the skeleton frame, and the demand for light is well satisfied.

COLUMBIA COLLEGE—1104 CENTER

22| Fairbanks Lofts
(*Fairbanks, Morse & Co.
Building*)
900 S. Wabash Ave.
1907, CHRISTIAN A. ECKSTORM

This completely intact loft
building has showrooms that
are outlined in ornamental
cast-iron trim and separated
from the rest of the facade
by a molded limestone sill.

23| Burnham Park Plaza
(*YMCA Hotel*)
828 S. Wabash Ave.
1916, ROBERT C. BERLIN; JAMES
GAMBLE ROGERS, CONSULTING ARCH.
1988, CONVERSION, SCHROEDER
MURCHIE LAYA

The hotel provided simple and
wholesome quarters at moderate cost. The small rooms,
placed around light wells, were
completely gutted in the conversion to apartments. A penthouse and roof deck and a new
building containing theaters,
commercial space, and a garage
were constructed.

BURNHAM PARK PLAZA

24| The Loftrium
(*Munn Building*)
819 S. Wabash Ave.
1909, CHRISTIAN A. ECKSTORM

The cast-iron storefront is
framed by handsome Sullivanesque ornament. Above, the
brick-sheathed frame is fully
expressed, and wide windows
light the interior.

25| Wirt Dexter Building
630 S. Wabash Ave.
1887, ADLER & SULLIVAN

Fire damage and two added
floors have somewhat obscured
the intent, but you can still see

how the firm was seeking to
open up a facade and light the
interiors. The central unit's cast-
iron frame makes large windows possible on the main
facade. Look to the rear, where
perforated cast-iron braces were
used for the same purpose.

**26| Columbia College—
Wabash Campus**
(*Second Studebaker Building*)
623 S. Wabash Ave.
1896, SOLON S. BEMAN

Look past the added story (1941)
and main-floor alterations to
the strikingly modern structural
expression and Gothic detailing.

27| Travelodge
65 E. Harrison St.
1930, ALFRED S. ALSCHULER

High-style Art Deco embellishments include voluptuous
figures and stylized foliage.

**28| William Jones College
Preparatory High School**
606 S. State St.
1965–1968, PERKINS & WILL

A skyscraper to house what
was originally a secretarial and
office training school was first
suggested in 1909 by Dwight H.
Perkins. The reinforced-concrete
tower is connected by covered
passageways with two-story
auditorium and gymnasium
buildings.

29| Carter Hotel
(*East 7th Street Hotel*)
1 E. Balbo Ave.
1930, MICHAELSEN & ROGNSTAD

Behind the fire escapes is an
Art Deco building with an intact
entry floor and window surrounds of terra cotta.

*Enter the Dearborn Park I com-
munity at 9th and State Sts. (the
only vehicular access point) to
tour the self-contained streets of
Plymouth Ct. and S. Park Terr./
Federal St.*

Dearborn Park I
State to Clark Sts., Polk St.
to Roosevelt Rd.
1974–1977, MASTER PLAN,
SKIDMORE, OWINGS & MERRILL
1979–1987, VARIOUS ARCHITECTS

Dearborn Park grew out of SOM's comprehensive blueprint for the central city, drafted in 1973 for the Chicago Central Area Committee and exploiting the abandoned railyards immediately south of downtown.

The site was split into two parcels, with the twenty acres north of Roosevelt Rd. to be developed first. The original scheme of high-density superblocks was scaled down to a mixture of town houses, mid rises, and high rises—a "suburb in the city"—with parks and heavily landscaped open space but no offices or entertainment complexes. Internal roads end in cul-de-sacs. In 1977 the design was parceled out to several architecture firms, with the first occupancies in 1979. Phase I was substantially complete by 1985, with just over 1,200 units, about half of them in mid-rise buildings.

Design guidelines specified white brick for the two-story town houses and red brick for all other buildings. Such cohesiveness as there may be relies on the abundant landscaping rather than a shared aesthetic. The tallest buildings, sited on the street perimeter, are centered on the landscaped spaces surrounding the town house clusters. The two **30| High Rises** (Ezra Gordon–Jack M. Levin & Assocs.) flank the 9th St. access road but fail to provide a significant gateway, serving only to create an inward-focused enclave. The **31| Two-Story Town Houses** (Hammond, Beeby & Babka) cluster around parking areas and are oriented toward private gardens that overlook shared green spaces. Recessed corner entrances and exterior corner columns are the main design elements. The **32| Three-Story Town Houses** in turn enclose the courtyards formed by the **33| Mid-Rise Buildings** (Booth Hansen Associates). The **34| Garden Homes of Dearborn Park** (Michael J. Realmuto), developed last, were intended as luxury housing, presaging the low-density, upmarket development of Phase II.

Dearborn Park II
State to Clark Sts., Roosevelt Rd.
to W. 15th St.
1988–1997

Phase II proceeded very differently from its predecessor. There is more parking, and buildings are no more than four stories high, with an abundance of luxury housing. The parcel lacks even minimal cohesiveness, with the variety of building types and architects making for something of a hodgepodge.

35| Row Houses, Metropolitan
Mews & Park Homes
1300 & 1400 blocks of S. State St.
1989–1992, BOOTH HANSEN
ASSOCIATES

The properties east of Plymouth Ct. are organized formally in long rows around central green spaces, while the freestanding Park Homes are far more suburban and seem out of place.

36| Prairie Homes
1300 to 1356 S. Plymouth Ct.,
1301 to 1357 S. Federal St.
1992, FITZGERALD ASSOCS. ARCHS.

Prairie School elements like brackets under hipped roofs and horizontal divisions of the facades make these the liveliest buildings, but the crowded siting and essentially vertical massing detract.

37| 1339–1341 S. State St.
(Arthur Dixon Transfer Co.
Truck Garage)
1921, HOLABIRD & ROCHE

Making an admirable virtue of spareness, this handsome, flat brick facade adorned only with stepped detailing conceals a single wood-framed space lit from rooftop monitor windows.

38| Dearborn Tower
1530 S. State St.
2000, ADDITION AND CONVERSION TO RESIDENTIAL, PAPPAGEORGE/ HAYMES

This cold-storage warehouse was converted to residential use by placing a recessed window wall behind the exposed concrete frame on the north side. The south facade has long balconies that provide shade from the summer sun. The seven-story addition is articulated with a smaller, lighter grid. A clock tower marks the building entry and unifies old and new construction.

39| Burnham Station
61 W. 15th St.
1997, TIGERMAN MCCURRY ARCHITECTS

Architect Tigerman describes the concrete and glass mid rise as his "Mies-building-as-a-wedding-cake."

Printing House District

The Dearborn St. Station was a source for paper and supplies and an easy route for outgoing publications, making Dearborn St. south from Jackson Blvd. a convenient center for the printing trades from the 1880s through the 1950s. Plymouth Ct. and Federal St. provided back doors for Dearborn St. buildings and were direct routes to the depot's loading docks. The widening of Congress St., called for in the 1909 Plan of Chicago, was finally accomplished (1945–1955) to create an expressway link. Construction destroyed twelve buildings on Dearborn St. and many others on adjacent streets, effectively separating everything south of Congress St. from the Loop. Rejuvenation began in the late 1970s, spurred by the development of the former railyards as Dearborn Park.

40| Columbia College Residence Center
(*Lakeside Press Building*)
731 S. Plymouth Ct.
1897, 1902 (FOUR NORTH BAYS), HOWARD VAN DOREN SHAW; SAMUEL A. TREAT, ASSOC. ARCH.
1986, RENOVATION, LISEC & BIEDERMAN

This exceptionally creative amalgam of traditional and non-traditional architectural detailing was Shaw's first nonresidential commission. It established his and owner R. R. Donnelley & Sons Co.'s reputations as creators of printing plants that are a joy to behold.

41| Dearborn Station
(*Polk St. Station, also known as Dearborn St. Station*)
47 W. Polk St.
1885, CYRUS L. W. EIDLITZ
1923, RECONSTRUCTION AFTER FIRE, ARCHITECT UNKNOWN
1985, CONVERSION, KAPLAN/ MCLAUGHLIN/DIAZ AND HASBROUCK HUNDERMAN

Chicago's oldest train station is a U-shaped Romanesque building whose Italian brick tower closes the Dearborn St. vista. The tower is a replacement of a Flemish one, destroyed in a 1922 fire, which also took the building's hipped roofs. The reworked station, comprising a cleaned-up but historic north facade and a modern galleria to the south, acts as a transition between the renovated printing district and the new Dearborn Park development.

42| Donohue Building
711 S. Dearborn St.
1883, JULIUS SPEYER

43| Donohue Annex
727 S. Dearborn St.
1913, ALFRED S. ALSCHULER

DEARBORN STATION

This was the first major printers' structure in the district. The main portion exhibits the basic masonry construction system with punched window openings, one window per opening. It utilizes both Romanesque rustication and incised designs, and its slightly enhanced round-arched sandstone and granite entrance bay was originally topped with a tower. The simple and functional annex harmonizes with the original.

44| Second Franklin Building
720 S. Dearborn St.
1912, GEORGE C. NIMMONS
1987, CONVERSION TO APARTMENTS, LISEC & BIEDERMAN

SECOND FRANKLIN BUILDING

Using the modified Prairie School style that characterized his factory and warehouse work, Nimmons incorporated colorful tilework designed by Oskar Gross depicting the history of printing. The sloped roofline, a frequent feature on factories of this era, permitted a very high top floor under an enormous skylight—helpful for hand binding.

45| Printers Square
(*Borland Manufacturing Buildings*)
700, 740 & 780 S. Federal St.
1909, 1912, AND 1928, FROST & GRANGER AND SUCCESSOR FIRMS
1983, CONVERSION TO APARTMENTS, LOUIS WEISS

This series of simply detailed loft buildings was constructed in sections from the designs of one architect. It now has 356 apartments and underground parking.

46| Grace Place
637 S. Dearborn St.
1915, ARCHITECT UNKNOWN
1985, RENOVATION, BOOTH HANSEN ASSOCIATES

The second floor of this renovated printers' building contains a worship space encircled by an internal wall with pointed-arch windows. A skylight floods the altar with natural light.

47| Transportation Building
600 S. Dearborn St.
1911, WILLIAM STRIPPELMAN
1980, REHABILITATION,
BOOTH HANSEN ASSOCIATES

Twenty bays wide but only four bays deep, this was designed to be built in sections and to have its great breadth broken regularly by vertical bands of roughened brickwork. The contrast is not enough to do the job. The rehabilitation of this building was crucial to the area's rejuvenation.

PONTIAC BUILDING

48| Pontiac Building
542 S. Dearborn St.
1891, HOLABIRD & ROCHE
1985, RENOVATION, BOOTH HANSEN
ASSOCIATES

An air of substance and repose emerges from this earliest extant Holabird & Roche skyscraper. The heavy corner piers rise from base to cornice, interrupted only by the shelf angles supporting each floor of brick sheathing; the windows are small and double-hung. The gently projecting oriels that span two bays are unique in the firm's work.

49| Terminals Building
(*Ellsworth Building*)
537 S. Dearborn St.
1892, JOHN M. VAN OSDEL & CO.
1986, RENOVATION, COMMUNITY
RESOURCES CORP.

A heavily rusticated rock-faced limestone base is balanced by the crisp modeling of the brick into vertical elements above.

50| Mergenthaler Loft Condominiums
(*Mergenthaler Linotype Building*)
531 S. Plymouth Ct.
1886, ARCHITECT UNKNOWN
1917, RENOVATION, RICHARD E. SCHMIDT, GARDEN & MARTIN
1980, REHABILITATION, KENNETH A. SCHROEDER & ASSOCS.

This early example of a loft building converted to stylish apartments is also one of the best. The new work included the introduction of windows in colorful framing on the south

MERGENTHALER LOFT CONDOMINIUMS

wall and the incorporation of the shell of Tom's Grill, a former adjacent eatery, as a sculptural *objet trouvé*.

51 | Old Franklin Building
525 S. Dearborn St.
1887, BAUMANN & LOTZ

This printers' building demonstrates how, in an effort to provide light for detail work, architects began to group windows by using iron spandrels between brick piers and supporting them with cast-iron mullions. The lobby shows the beamed ceilings found in the loft apartments.

52 | Hyatt on Printers Row
(*Morton Hotel*)
500 S. Dearborn St.
1987, RENOVATION AND ADDITION, BOOTH HANSEN ASSOCIATES

Duplicator Building
530 S. Dearborn St.
1886, EDWARD P. BAUMANN

Morton Building
538 S. Dearborn St.
1896, JENNEY & MUNDIE

This hotel combined new construction with two old buildings. The Duplicator is a traditional loft structure; the Morton shows how classical elements, in the form of atlantes supporting the projecting bay, were supplanting the vigorous expression of skeleton construction that had characterized that firm's earlier commercial work.

53 | 601 & 619 S. La Salle St.
(*Brock & Rankin Building*)
1901–1902, NORTH PORTION; 1903, TWO-STORY ADDITION; 1909, SOUTH ADDITION; HOLABIRD & ROCHE

What looks like two attached buildings is one loft built during two phases of Holabird & Roche's work. The northern part has colored tiles set on angle; the southern part relies on brickwork, especially the "zippered" window surrounds.

54 | River City
800 S. Wells St.
1986, BERTRAND GOLDBERG ASSOCS.
2003, CONVERSION TO CONDOMINIUMS, ROULA ASSOCS. ARCHITECTS

The curves for which Goldberg's buildings are famous result here in a complex form, a four-story base for a pair of S-shaped apartment buildings supported on concrete piers with penthouse towers above the rooflines. River Road, the combination corridor and atrium, has an array of monumental and undulating shapes softly lit from above.

55 | Roosevelt Rd. Viaduct
Roosevelt Rd. from Chicago River to State St.
1995, DLK ARCHITECTURE

The sculptural program included in the rebuilding of this elevated roadway recalls nearby bridges built in the twentieth century. The iconography of the sculptures emphasizes the link

RIVER CITY

between the University of Illinois at Chicago to the west and the museum campus to the east. The repetitive use of three sizes of obelisks along the 1,500-foot bridge weakens the potential power of that form, but the positive civic message is clear.

56| United Parcel Service— Distribution Center
1400 S. Jefferson St.
1965, EDWARD D. DART

By the mid-1960s highly automated package handling had helped the trucking industry to supersede the archaic operations of the Chicago tunnel system. This center uses two conveyor assemblies to sort parcels and has a mid-floor control center that employs a carousel with giant pigeonholes. Separate loading docks and marshaling areas, each with its own traffic control station, are sheltered under second-floor office space and steel sheds.

57| Chicago Fire Academy
558 W. DeKoven St.
1960, LOEBL, SCHLOSSMAN & BENNETT

Firefighters are trained on the site of the Patrick O'Leary barn, where a cow allegedly kicked over a lantern, setting off the holocaust of 1871. The tall build-

ing is the drill hall, where trainees learn to operate snorkels, maneuver on fire escapes, and open windows. The red glazed brick is a backdrop for the flame-shaped sculpture by Egon Weiner.

58| Canal Center
(*Northern Trust Company Operations Center*)
801 S. Canal St.
1990, ECKENHOFF SAUNDERS ARCHITECTS

The length of the precast concrete facade is mitigated by a recessed glass-walled entrance on Canal St. and by the terraces of a cafeteria and a day-care center on the eastern side.

59| United States Customs House
610 S. Canal St.
1932, JAMES A. WETMORE, ACTING SUPERVISING ARCH.; BURNHAM BROS. AND NIMMONS, CARR & WRIGHT, ASSOC. ARCHS.

Eagles hover in the parapets of this sleekly massed, pristine government facility.

60| Former Central Post Office
433 W. Van Buren St.
1921, 1932, GRAHAM, ANDERSON, PROBST & WHITE

It was designed to straddle the broad Congress St. projected in the 1909 Plan but not realized until decades after the build-

FORMER CENTRAL POST OFFICE

ing's completion. When opened this was the world's largest post office. With four large corner towers, the rectangular mass is further subdivided into base, shaft, and top; the verticality of uninterrupted piers and narrow windows somewhat mitigates the length. The Van Buren St. lobby is clad in cream marble with French glass and tile reliefs. Multistory postal operations require the heavy use of elevators and are regarded as inefficient, so a new post office to the south was completed in 1996. The building's mammoth size has stymied a series of redevelopment schemes.

61| U.S. Post Office Central Processing Center
433 W. Harrison St.
1996, KNIGHT ARCHITECTS ENGINEERS PLANNERS

Constructed just south of the outdated Central Post Office, the building spans thirteen commuter rail lines with 10-foot-deep, 100-foot-long steel I-beams, and encloses an elevated roadway that is nearly a mile long.

62| Greyhound Bus Terminal
630 W. Harrison St.
1991, NAGLE, HARTRAY & ASSOCS.

Drivers zooming past on the Eisenhower Expressway get an elevated view of this elegant essay in architectural engineering (structural design by Cohen-Barreto-Marchertas). The striking roof is suspended by steel supporting stays connected to ten slim vertical masts, whose upward sweep creates a taut, graceful contrast.

GREYHOUND BUS TERMINAL

NORTH SIDE

GOLD COAST | OLD TOWN

LINCOLN PARK

LAKEVIEW | RAVENSWOOD | UPTOWN

EDGEWATER | ROGERS PARK

GOLD COAST/OLD TOWN

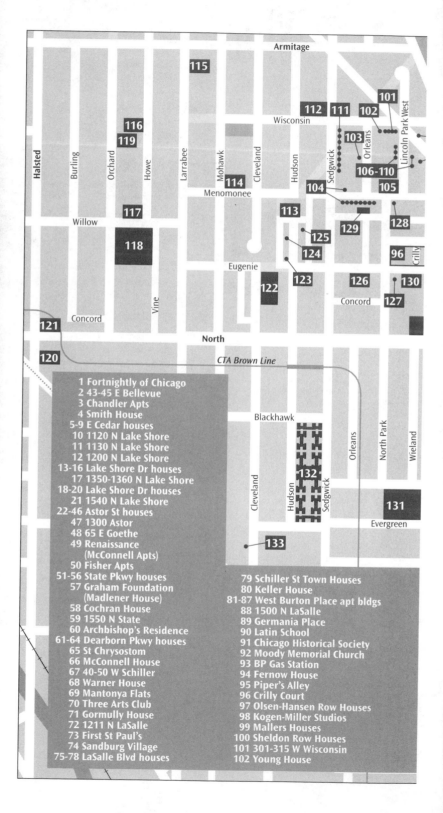

1 Fortnightly of Chicago
2 43-45 E Bellevue
3 Chandler Apts
4 Smith House
5-9 E Cedar houses
10 1120 N Lake Shore
11 1130 N Lake Shore
12 1200 N Lake Shore
13-16 Lake Shore Dr houses
17 1350-1360 N Lake Shore
18-20 Lake Shore Dr houses
21 1540 N Lake Shore
22-46 Astor St houses
47 1300 Astor
48 65 E Goethe
49 Renaissance
    (McConnell Apts)
50 Fisher Apts
51-56 State Pkwy houses
57 Graham Foundation
    (Madlener House)
58 Cochran House
59 1550 N State
60 Archbishop's Residence
61-64 Dearborn Pkwy houses
65 St Chrysostom
66 McConnell House
67 40-50 W Schiller
68 Warner House
69 Mantonya Flats
70 Three Arts Club
71 Gormully House
72 1211 N LaSalle
73 First St Paul's
74 Sandburg Village
75-78 LaSalle Blvd houses

79 Schiller St Town Houses
80 Keller House
81-87 West Burton Place apt bldgs
88 1500 N LaSalle
89 Germania Place
90 Latin School
91 Chicago Historical Society
92 Moody Memorial Church
93 BP Gas Station
94 Fernow House
95 Piper's Alley
96 Crilly Court
97 Olsen-Hansen Row Houses
98 Kogen-Miller Studios
99 Mallers Houses
100 Sheldon Row Houses
101 301-315 W Wisconsin
102 Young House

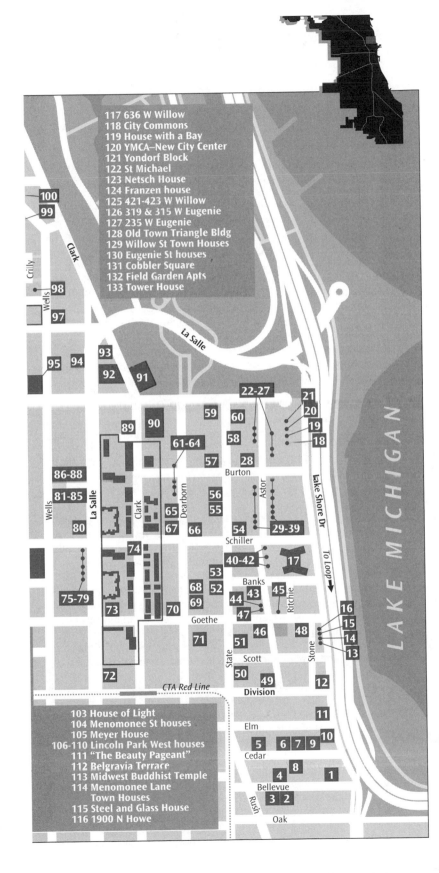

117 636 W Willow
118 City Commons
119 House with a Bay
120 YMCA–New City Center
121 Yondorf Block
122 St Michael
123 Netsch House
124 Franzen house
125 421-423 W Willow
126 319 & 315 W Eugenie
127 235 W Eugenie
128 Old Town Triangle Bldg
129 Willow St Town Houses
130 Eugenie St houses
131 Cobbler Square
132 Field Garden Apts
133 Tower House

103 House of Light
104 Menomonee St houses
105 Meyer House
106-110 Lincoln Park West houses
111 "The Beauty Pageant"
112 Belgravia Terrace
113 Midwest Buddhist Temple
114 Menomonee Lane
    Town Houses
115 Steel and Glass House
116 1900 N Howe

Crilly
Clark
Wells
La Salle
Burton
Dearborn
Clark
Wells
La Salle
Astor
Schiller
Banks
Ritchie
Goethe
State
Scott
Stone
Division
Lake Shore Dr
To Loop
LAKE MICHIGAN
CTA Red Line
Elm
Cedar
Bellevue
Rush
Oak

22-27
59
60
58
28
61-64
57
56
55
54
29-39
40-42
17
53
52
68
69
44
43
45
47
46
48
51
50
49
12
11
10
5
6 7 9
8
4
1
3 2
13
14
15
16
21
20
19
18
71
70
72
73
74
75-79
80
81-85
86-88
89
90
91
92
93
94
95
97
98
99
100
65
66
67

GOLD COAST/OLD TOWN

THROUGHOUT MOST OF THEIR HISTORY, THE NEIGHBORHOODS OF THE GOLD Coast and Old Town presented a sharp contrast between rich and poor, elegance and squalor. Today, however, their demographics are surprisingly similar. While many Gold Coast mansions have been replaced by high rises or subdivided into smaller but still desirable apartments, a tidal wave of money has swept over the workers' cottages and flats of Old Town, many of which have been converted into expensive single-family residences or sold as "tear-downs."

The streetscapes of the two communities are still worlds apart. Old Town is filled with charmingly restored cottages, row houses, and small flats as well as coach houses, many of which were built for Gold Coast residents. The Gold Coast, apart from its many modern high rises, has an abundance of mansions and large row houses. Along the Clark St./LaSalle Blvd. boundary between the two neighborhoods is that exemplar of 1960s redevelopment, Carl Sandburg Village, constructed as the Gold Coast's Maginot Line against the creeping disintegration of Old Town and points west.

Old Town, as one might guess, is the earlier community, although the entire area was not included in the city's 1837 charter. It was settled by German produce farmers, who were numerous enough to form St. Michael's parish in 1852. After the devastation of the Fire of 1871, wooden cottages sprang up to house the homeless. Most of the tiny, crudely built "relief shanties" are long gone, but many wooden cottages remain from the short period between the Fire and the northward extension of the city's strict building code in the 1874 fire ordinance. The area remained heavily Germanic throughout the following decades, and by 1900 North Ave. as far west as Halsted St. was known as German Broadway.

Industry, which located in the heart of the area as well as along the river, provided employment for many. Housing west of LaSalle Blvd., built for the working class and new immigrants, deteriorated in the twentieth century. By the 1940s most of the Germans had moved away, replaced by Italians, African Americans, Asians, and, later, Hispanics.

Artists took advantage of depressed real estate values. In the 1920s Sol Kogen and Edgar Miller turned decrepit housing on Burton Pl. into masterpieces of folk art, and in the 1960s artists began buying and rehabilitating many of Old Town's small houses. Wells St. became the center of Chicago's counterculture, with head shops selling drug paraphernalia and psychedelic posters and record stores catering to flower children and the inevitable gawking tourists.

The massive urban renewal that resulted in the 1960s construction of Sandburg Village, together with the pioneering efforts of artists and architects, bolstered the area's reputation and effectively extended the Gold Coast west of its traditional boundaries. Apart from the Sandburg complex and a few tall buildings near the lake, the area has retained its low scale. Scattered urban renewal and private projects in the 1960s and 1970s were confined mostly to town houses and three- to four-story apartment buildings.

Rising land values in the 1980s resulted in the replacement of many early cottages by postmodern multibathroom extravaganzas whose overblown character or scale —if not both—is frequently jarring. But the area also has much exemplary new construction: town houses that extend welcoming stairways to the sidewalk, freestanding houses that echo the materials and styles of their more modest neighbors, and renovations that return buildings to their original character after decades of concealment beneath ugly siding materials. Old Town's projects span the careers of such well-known residential architects as Stanley Tigerman, Ben and Harry Weese, Larry Booth and Jim Nagle, from early town houses and renovations to large new houses.

The Gold Coast was created almost single-handedly by State St. retail mogul Potter Palmer and his wife, Bertha, Chicago's reigning socialite. When they built their Henry Ives Cobb–designed castle (demolished) at 1350 N. Lake Shore Dr. in 1882, the locus of social power began an inexorable shift north from S. Prairie Ave. to this area. Palmer also bought land for speculative development in order to profit from his self-created gold rush, in which land values soared 400 percent within a decade.

Early development concentrated on the Drive itself and on adjacent streets from Bellevue Pl. north to Burton Pl. The north half was developed after the turn of the century, when the Catholic archbishop subdivided property on Dearborn, State, and Astor Sts. just south of his North Ave. mansion. Modest 1870s Italianate row houses farther west were joined in the 1880s by flashier Queen Anne and Romanesque residences. Commissions for houses from New York architects McKim, Mead & White in the 1890s started a trend toward neo-Classical and Georgian Revival styles; the latter was particularly well suited to the town house format and proliferated after 1900.

Apartment buildings had appeared in the Gold Coast as early as the 1890s, but their construction was concentrated in two great eras. The boom of the 1920s brought large revival-style towers, mostly on Lake Shore Dr. In the 1950s and 1960s many mansions were replaced by behemoths that changed the area's character forever. Even the narrow streets farther west have almost all had their scale disrupted by high-rise apartment buildings. Yet the Gold Coast remains a desirable address.

—PATRICIA MARKS LURIE WITH LAURIE MCGOVERN PETERSEN

1| **Fortnightly of Chicago**
(*Bryan Lathrop House*)
120 E. Bellevue Pl.
1891–1893, MCKIM, MEAD & WHITE
1972, RESTORATION, PERKINS & WILL

New Yorker Charles F. McKim, a leading architect of the 1893 World's Columbian Exposition, designed this elegant Georgian Revival trendsetter when Romanesque was still the dominant residential style. By 1900 Georgian was the favorite Gold Coast style. This exceptionally

FORTNIGHTLY OF CHICAGO

graceful essay has gently curving bays at each end of the unusually wide house. The symmetry is broken only by the off-center placement of the door. Occupied by a women's club since 1922, the building is in excellent condition, with a new fiberglass cornice that replicates the original.

2| 43–45 E. Bellevue Pl.
1892, CHARLES M. PALMER

This Romanesque double house, built by Potter Palmer as an investment, is on a much larger scale than many he built in the area. The rustication diminishes with each floor. Unfortunately, the cornice is gone.

3| Chandler Apartments
33 E. Bellevue Pl.
1911, RICHARD E. SCHMIDT, GARDEN & MARTIN

This Georgian Revival apartment building has lavish Classical detail. Some of it is treated rather originally, such as the keystone-and-lintel arrangement on the fifth-floor projecting bays.

4| Lot P. Smith House
32 E. Bellevue Pl.
1887, BURNHAM & ROOT

One of John Wellborn Root's few extant residential designs displays his flair for decorative detail in the unusual dormer with its knobby finials, and in the pattern of circles in the pediment and above the entry door.

5| 20 E. Cedar St.
1924, FUGARD & KNAPP

Splendid Gothic terra-cotta frames huge windows that illuminate two-story living spaces. The deep fourteenth-floor setback creates a large terrace and a "castle in the air" crown.

6| 42–48 E. Cedar St.
1896, CHARLES M. PALMER

7| 50–54 E. Cedar St.
1892, L. GUSTAV HALLBERG

Rusticated stone, roundheaded windows, and foliate capitals mark these Romanesque town houses. Each group was designed as a unit, with gabled ends flanking a flat-topped central section. The symmetry breaks down for the group at 42–48 (built by Potter Palmer), because 42 has a fourth floor with a ballroom.

8| 49 E. Cedar St.
1908, MARSHALL & FOX

The elegant semicircular bay of this small apartment building (built as an investment by the architects) recalls their larger buildings nearby, such as 1200 N. Lake Shore Dr. and 1550 N. State Pkwy. By contrast, this structure is Georgian, with its Flemish bond brickwork alternating red stretchers with dark brownish-black headers.

9| 60 E. Cedar St.
1890, CURD H. GOTTIG

Flamboyant even in this ritzy neighborhood, a gable and three turrets squeeze onto the roofline, while six squat columns support ground-floor arches. The facade is of rusticated Georgia marble, with abundant copper trim above the cornice line.

10| 1120 N. Lake Shore Dr.
1926, ROBERT S. DEGOLYER

The prosperous 1920s produced a variety of residential high rises in this neighborhood. This one offered smaller, customized apartments rather than the floor-throughs of nearby luxury buildings.

11| 1130 N. Lake Shore Dr.
(90 E. Elm St.)
1911, HOWARD VAN DOREN SHAW

One of the first tall apartment buildings to invade the line of mansions along the Drive was also a pioneer cooperative apartment, where occupants were shareholders in a corporation. Each apartment occupied an entire floor; Shaw was among the first owners. Tudor Revival, his favorite domestic style, gives the building the appeal and character of his country houses. The facade is dotted with medieval motifs and carved panels of fruit. Like many apartments with corner sites on the Drive, its entrance is on the side street, but the address has been changed to emphasize the lakefront location.

12| 1200 N. Lake Shore Dr.
(*Stewart Apartments*)
1913, MARSHALL & FOX

The architects' trademarks include the graceful Adamesque detailing, the rounded bays, and the spacious plan, which places living room and dining room on either side of a sun parlor with a generous bay.

13| Carl C. Heisen House
1250 N. Lake Shore Dr.
1890, FRANK B. ABBOTT

CARL C. HEISEN HOUSE

14| Mason Brayman Starring House
1254 N. Lake Shore Dr.
1889, L. GUSTAV HALLBERG
1990, RENOVATION, MARVIN HERMAN & ASSOCS.

This pair of single-family houses offers a fragmentary glimpse of the Drive's early appearance. The arched entries, squat towers, and deeply recessed porches are hallmarks of the Richardsonian Romanesque. The house at 1250 is rough and rugged, even down to the small columns and piers, while 1254 has smoothly polished columns with elaborately carved capitals, one of which includes a grinning face. In 1990 the buildings were joined and the interiors were gutted to create four new residences.

15| Arthur T. Aldis House
1258 N. Lake Shore Dr.
1896, HOLABIRD & ROCHE

Even no-nonsense architects had occasional flights of fancy. While designing this Venetian Gothic palazzo, they were also working for Aldis's brother Owen (agent for Boston developers Peter and Shepherd Brooks) on the Marquette Building.

16| Lawrence D. Rockwell House
1360 N. Lake Shore Dr.
1911, HOLABIRD & ROCHE

This is far more characteristic of the firm than the Aldis House. With its simple rectangular massing, minimal Classical details, restrained surfaces, and overall symmetry it is typical of houses built just after the turn of the century.

17| 1350–1360 N. Lake Shore Dr.
1949–1951, LOEBL, SCHLOSSMAN & BENNETT

Just as the construction of Potter Palmer's crenellated castle on this site in 1882 spurred a local boom in mansion building, its replacement by this pair of twenty-two-story towers led a new generation of high-rise development on the Drive. Richard M. Bennett's overriding concern was to give every unit a view of the lake. The brick walls, with their windows set flush, bend like paper around the irregular plan. The angled bay windows and the mid-building bends create a multitude of planes on the long facades.

1350–1360 N. LAKE SHORE DR.

**18| International College
of Surgeons**
(*Edward T. Blair House*)
1516 N. Lake Shore Dr.
1914, MCKIM, MEAD & WHITE

**19| International College
of Surgeons Museum**
(*Eleanor Robinson Countiss
House*)
1524 N. Lake Shore Dr.
1917, HOWARD VAN DOREN SHAW

20| Polish Consulate
(*Bernard A. Eckhart House*)
1530 N. Lake Shore Dr.
1916, BENJAMIN H. MARSHALL

This trio's austere neo-Classi-
cism belies their separate
authorship. The Blair House's
setback and restrained use
of Classical ornament on a
smoothly polished facade set
the standard for the others.
The Countiss House is a rare
Shaw essay in French architecture. His strong-minded clients
insisted on a copy of the Petit
Trianon at Versailles but with
four stories instead of three.
Go inside to see the many intact
interior features, including the
stone staircase with partially
gilded iron balustrade and a
lovely paneled library on the
second floor.

21| 1540 N. Lake Shore Dr.
1925, HUSZAGH & HILL

Mundane at ground level, it
has a top inspired by medieval
French châteaus. The expensive
upper floors are best seen from
the Drive.

22| 1524 N. Astor St.
1968, I. W. COLBURN & ASSOCS.

This 1960s essay in contextualism almost pulls a vanishing
act by continuing the brick wall
of its neighbors to the south.
Look at the north wall to see the
U-shaped plan that brings light
to the interior.

23| 1520 N. Astor St.
1911, JEREMIAH K. CADY

24| 1518 N. Astor St.
1911, JENNEY, MUNDIE & JENSEN

25| 1525 N. Astor St.
1916, ARCHITECT UNKNOWN

26| 1511 N. Astor St.
1911, ARTHUR HEUN

27| 1505 N. Astor St.
1911, JENNEY, MUNDIE & JENSEN

These variations on the popular
Georgian row house theme have
a ground floor of stone, usually
with banded rustication, and
upper floors of brick trimmed
with limestone. Each floor has
three window openings stacked
above those of the floor below,
usually decreasing in height
above the tall windows of the
second-floor *piano nobile*. The
parapet is frequently crowned
by a balustrade whose openings
align with those of the windows
below. The few details present
are usually classically inspired
(pediments above windows or
doors, etc.), as is the rigid system
of proportions.

28| 1500 Astor
(*Elinor Patterson–Cyrus H.
McCormick Mansion*)
20 E. Burton Pl.
1893, MCKIM, MEAD & WHITE
1927, ADDITION, DAVID ADLER
1978, CONVERSION TO
CONDOMINIUMS, NAGLE, HARTRAY
& ASSOCS.; WILBERT R. HASBROUCK,
CONSULTANT

Together with the Lathrop
House of a year earlier, this
Stanford White design is, for
Chicago, an early and influential
example of a neo-Classical
residence. Closer to an Italian
palazzo than its predecessor,
the materials here are orange

1500 ASTOR

Roman brick with terra-cotta trim. McCormick bought the house in 1914, and in 1927 David Adler doubled its size to the north.

29| Peter Fortune Houses
1451 N. Astor St. and 43 E. Burton St.
1910, HOWARD VAN DOREN SHAW

By 1910 Jacobethan was a close competitor of Georgian Revival, although better suited to expansive country properties than narrow city lots. The corner site makes this an only slightly scaled-down version of the country houses that Shaw was designing so prolifically at the time. His favored motif of carved fruit baskets tops the strapwork panels flanking the Astor St. entrance.

30| C. D. Peacock, Jr., House
1449 N. Astor St.
1898, E. R. KRAUSE

The massive château, made fashionable by Solon S. Beman's Kimball House, was even more difficult to adapt to narrow city lots than the Tudor Revival. The large bay and massive entry porch dominate the facade, which has an unusual frieze pattern of shells under the cornice and rather odd, twisted half-columns at each end.

31| Edward P. Russell House
1444 N. Astor St.
1929, HOLABIRD & ROOT

Sleek, urbane, sophisticated, and very French, this elegant Art Deco town house is timeless and unique. The poised and polished facade is of stone from Lens, France, with gleaming granite trim, a barely suggested three-story bay, and incised ornament.

32| C. Vallette Kasson House
1442 N. Astor St.
1891, POND & POND

The doorway's pointed stone arch is echoed in tracings of arches in brick above the windows.

33| Horatio N. May House
1443 N. Astor St.
1891, JOSEPH LYMAN SILSBEE

HORATIO N. MAY HOUSE

The quarry-faced granite blocks of the rigidly symmetrical facade are on a colossal scale.

34| George W. Meeker House
1431 N. Astor St.
1894, HOLABIRD & ROCHE

Although reminiscent of Boston's Federal-style houses, it has suffered from the unsympathetic additions of a pedimented porch, disproportionate shutters, and a discordant paint scheme. The best original feature is the metal cornice with its garlands of balls.

35| Eugene R. Hutchins House
1429 N. Astor St.
1891, POND & POND

This quirky design combines rough Romanesque masonry with such Gothic details as the pointed arch above the door and the crocketed dormers with small-paned windows.

36| Rensselaer W. Cox House
1427 N. Astor St.
1889, WILLIAM LE BARON JENNEY

The rock-faced brick is an unusual feature of this otherwise mundane design.

37| Thomas W. Hind House
1412 N. Astor St.
1892, DOUGLAS S. PENTECOST

This unusually decorated facade still evokes the French Renaissance, mixing classical elements with diamond-paned windows and medieval motifs.

38| Joseph T. Ryerson, Jr., House
1406 N. Astor St.
1922, DAVID ADLER
1931, ADDITION, DAVID ADLER

Adler fluidly adapted French style to the Chicago town house formula. His mansarded fourth-floor addition accommodated a large collection of Chicago memorabilia later donated to the Chicago Historical Society. Note the owner's initials in the decorative ironwork over the entrance.

39| Perry H. Smith House
1400 N. Astor St.
1887, COBB & FROST
1991, ADDITION, HAMMOND, BEEBY & BABKA

The Astor St. side is handsome but underplayed; it is along Schiller St. that the house sprawls, punctuated by a magnificent Romanesque arch. So beautifully matched that it is almost indistinguishable from the original is the 3,000-square-foot rear addition, which contains the kitchen and a master bedroom suite.

40| James Charnley House
1365 N. Astor St.
1892, ADLER & SULLIVAN
1988, RESTORATION, SKIDMORE, OWINGS & MERRILL

This is a landmark in the early career of Frank Lloyd Wright, who as an Adler & Sullivan employee was chiefly responsible for its design. The interplay of planes shows Wright beginning to break down the solidity of the mass, and the flattened Sullivanesque ornament is deemphasized. A central light well runs the full height of the house, which despite its size has only eleven well-proportioned rooms.

JAMES CHARNLEY HOUSE

41| Astor Court
(*William O. Goodman House*)
1355 N. Astor St.
1914, HOWARD VAN DOREN SHAW

In this very formal exercise in neo-Classical/Georgian Revival

ASTOR COURT

composition, the details are alternately robust (the second-floor window surrounds) and delicate (the design of stacked urns around the central window, the feathery pilaster capitals, and animal heads and skulls topped with fruit baskets forming keystones). The entrance on the south, originally a drive, leads to a landscaped court and entries to several units.

42 | Edwin J. Gardiner House
1345 N. Astor St.
1887, TREAT & FOLTZ

The sandstone from Dunreath quarry, Ohio, in a mélange of fruit sherbet colors, is one of the street's most vivid materials —and the only notable element of this otherwise ordinary Romanesque town house.

43 | Houses for Potter Palmer
1316–1322 N. Astor St. and 25 E. Banks St.
1889, CHARLES M. PALMER

Four of this group are textbook examples of rustication, especially the striated or banded variety on 1316 and 1320.

44 | James L. Houghteling Houses
1308–1312 N. Astor St.
1887–1888, BURNHAM & ROOT

Root designed four town houses (1306 was demolished) for Houghteling and moved into 1310. The large second-floor bay is not part of his original design, which had a series of three arched windows. The group of

JAMES L. HOUGHTELING HOUSES

houses shows a remarkably coherent combination of stylistic influences.

45| 1301 N. Astor St.
1932, PHILIP B. MAHER

46| 1260 N. Astor St.
1931, PHILIP B. MAHER

These severe, decorous Art Moderne apartment buildings were among the first Gold Coast high rises west of Lake Shore Dr.

1301 N. ASTOR ST.

47| Astor Tower
(*Astor Tower Hotel*)
1300 N. Astor St.
1963, BERTRAND GOLDBERG
1996, FACADE, DESTEFANO AND PARTNERS

Concrete columns raise the lowest floors above the rooflines of surrounding houses. The metal jalousies, which originally screened the windows in this design experiment, were replaced with plain glass in the massive facade renovation of 1996.

48| 65 E. Goethe
2002, LUCIEN LAGRANGE ARCHS.

Another Gallic bit of luxury from the current master. The roofline and massing fit well into the neighborhood. The structure incorporates four town houses on the first two floors, with traditional condominiums above.

49| Renaissance Condominiums
(*McConnell Apartments*)
1200 N. Astor St.
1897, HOLABIRD & ROCHE

Perhaps the ultimate Chicago School apartment building, this is a forthright composition in red brick with strong bays that echo the firm's Old Colony Building and many demolished hotels.

50| Frank F. Fisher Apartments
1209 N. State Pkwy.
1937, ANDREW N. REBORI; EDGAR MILLER, DESIGN ASSOC.

Ignoring the street's parade of Revival styles, Rebori wrote a new chapter with this coolly masterful Art Moderne block. Onto a long, narrow, unpromising lot, he shoehorned thirteen duplex apartments oriented around a sliver of private space. The terra-cotta plaques (some are missing) are by Edgar Miller.

FRANK F. FISHER APARTMENTS

51| Charles Henry Hulburd & Charles C. Yoe Double House
1243–1245 N. State Pkwy.
1880, ARCHITECT UNKNOWN

This Second Empire design uses a contrasting stone to join window heads and sills. The abstract foliate ornament in the keystones has a neo-Grec crispness.

52| 1328 N. State Pkwy.
1938, ANDREW N. REBORI
1956, REMODELING, BERTRAND GOLDBERG

A simple brick zigzag unites the facade and leads the eye to the small entry sculpted from the severe front. Two houses were built on opposite ends of this narrow lot, each with the main second-floor living space designated a "studio." Goldberg made the houses into a home and studio for his mother-in-law, sculptor Lillian Florsheim. Look for Rebori's tiny initials in the wooden spandrel.

53| George S. Isham House
1340 N. State Pkwy.
1899, JAMES GAMBLE ROGERS

The leaden sobriety of this stiff, French-inspired mansion became an odd backdrop for later owner Hugh Hefner's 1960s *Playboy* excesses.

54| 1411 N. State Pkwy./10 E. Schiller St.
1914, ANDREW SANDEGREN

This unique Tudor-Craftsman hybrid smoothly incorporates generous balconies, not only enhancing the floor plans but also strengthening the facades.

55| George A. Weiss House
1428 N. State Pkwy.
1886, HARALD M. HANSEN

The deep pockets of Gold Coast clients enabled the use of highly worked, unusual materials such as this pink Georgia marble and the copper crockets, crests, and parapets.

56| Charles K. Miller House
1432 N. State Pkwy.
1884, A. M. F. COLTON

CHARLES K. MILLER HOUSE

Remarkable individual elements give the facade that vigorous incoherence so typical of the early Queen Anne Style. Most peculiar is the terra-cotta plaque, where florid Sullivanesque ornament appears to spew from a flaming brazier.

57| Graham Foundation for Advanced Studies in the Fine Arts
(*Albert F. Madlener House*)
4 W. Burton Pl.
1902, RICHARD E. SCHMIDT
1963, RESTORATION, BRENNER, DANFORTH & ROCKWELL

Heaven's gate can be no more finely crafted than this doorway. The building's cubical massing and Teutonic severity owe a debt to the early nineteenth-century villas of Karl Friedrich Schinkel, but the precise ornament is pure Chicago. Schmidt's employee Hugh M. G. Garden is credited with the design. A collection of architectural fragments is on display in the rear court.

GRAHAM FOUNDATION FOR ADVANCED STUDIES IN THE FINE ARTS

58| J. Lewis Cochran House
1521 N. State Pkwy.
MID-1890S, GEORGE W. MAHER

Developer Cochran selected Maher from among the many architects who designed for his Edgewater subdivision and elsewhere. What he got is ordered, disciplined, and mainline—and a little dull.

59| 1550 N. State Pkwy.
1912, MARSHALL & FOX

This was the ultimate in luxury when it was built, by architects who set the standards for early twentieth-century hotels and apartments. Each apartment originally had fifteen rooms and occupied an entire floor—over 9,000 square feet. From the bowed windows and metal balconies to the *orangerie*, it is the *dernier cri* in French elegance. There is an ordered rhythm to the lively facade, with more dimension to the wall plane.

1550 N. STATE PKWY.

60| Residence of the Roman Catholic Archbishop of Chicago
1555 N. State Pkwy.
1880, ALFRED F. PASHLEY

This early Queen Anne residence still has Italianate windows but is dominated by the busy, picturesque roofline typical of the style, punctuated by nineteen chimneys.

61| George E. Rickcords House
1500 N. Dearborn Pkwy.
1889, WILLIAM W. CLAY

The Richardsonian Romanesque style frequently gives substance and street presence to a house squeezed onto a narrow lot. The entry is carved from the body of the house and is framed by low-springing arches. Look past the age-darkened patina on the granite to see the fine banded rustication.

62| Joseph C. Bullock House
1454 N. Dearborn Pkwy.
1877, EDBROOKE & BURNHAM

63| John P. Wilson House
1450 N. Dearborn Pkwy.
1877, ARCHITECT UNKNOWN

64| Philo R. King House
1434 N. Dearborn Pkwy.
1876, ARCHITECT UNKNOWN

The Bullock House is a fine rare example of a full-blown Second Empire town house. In addition to the characteristic mansard roof (still shingled in slate), there is abundant Classical detail. A pavilion effect was created by setting back the entrance bay and emphasizing the north corner with pilasters and incised quoins. The Wilson and King houses share many of the details, with crisp incised ornament giving them even more of a French flavor.

65| St. Chrysostom's Episcopal Church
1424 N. Dearborn Pkwy.
1913, BROWN & WALCOTT
1922, ADDITION TO CHURCH & PARISH HOUSE, CLARK & WALCOTT
1925, ONE-STORY ADDITION & BELFRY, CHESTER H. WALCOTT
1925, REMODELING, CHESTER H. WALCOTT AND BENNETT, PARSONS & FROST

The intimate church has the feeling of a campus chapel. The complex swallowed a house by William Le Baron Jenney to the south to create the parish house.

66 | Luther McConnell House
1401 N. Dearborn Pkwy.
1877, ASA LYON

One of Chicago's oldest Queen Anne houses exhibits the style's characteristic variety. A rotated corner bay enlivens the irregular but not excessively polygonal facade. The severe planar surfaces are enriched with carved terra-cotta plaques—like the griffin crouched in a niche under the chimney.

67 | 40–50 W. Schiller St.
1922, REBORI, WENTWORTH, DEWEY & MCCORMICK

To envision the original aspect of this elegant small apartment building, picture the garden opening onto the street where a low wall now partially fills the arches. The primary entrances used to face this garden, and the doors that now serve as street entries were for servants and tradesmen.

68 | Augustus Warner House
1337 N. Dearborn Pkwy.
1884, L. GUSTAV HALLBERG

The deep overhanging bay is the major design element, making the house look as if it had been plucked from a narrow European street.

69 | Lucius B. Mantonya Flats
1325 N. Dearborn Pkwy.
1887, CURD H. GOTTIG

The facade is bedecked with seventeen Moorish arches, many infilled with rich leaded glass.

70 | Three Arts Club
1300 N. Dearborn Pkwy.
1914, HOLABIRD & ROCHE

This residence for female art students was John A. Holabird's first design after he joined his father's firm on his return from Paris. The musical, dramatic, and pictorial arts have been expanded to include architecture, film, and fashion, but the club's mission is unchanged: to provide safe, inexpensive accommodations for women studying them.

The vaguely Mediterranean exterior hints at the lovely courtyard within. The ornament is highly eclectic, drawn from a variety of European sources. On the inside, note especially the stenciling in the dining hall and on the chandeliers. The sculptural panels on the east facade were inspired by Jean Goujon's Fontaine des Innocents (1549) in Paris.

71 | R. Philip Gormully House
1245 N. Dearborn Pkwy.
1884, ARCHITECT UNKNOWN

The pink slate is a foil to the magnificent copper work of the second-floor windows and third-floor dormer. It must have served as a billboard-size advertisement for Gormully's business, galvanized iron cornices and metalwork.

72 | 1211 N. LaSalle Blvd.
1929, OLDEFEST & WILLIAMS
1981, RENOVATION, WEESE SEEGERS HICKEY WEESE

An old apartment hotel with one decorated facade was converted to an apartment building whose walls became a canvas for artist Richard Haas. His *Homage to the Chicago School of Architecture* arranges the windows into trompe l'oeil bays on the eastern facade. On

1211 N. LASALLE BLVD.

the south wall, Louis H. Sullivan's round, terra-cotta–encrusted window from the Merchants' National Bank in Grinnell, Iowa, rises above the Golden Doorway of his Transportation Building at the 1893 World's Columbian Exposition. Between them, the Board of Trade Building two miles south is "reflected" in painted windows.

73| First St. Paul's Evangelical Lutheran Church
1301 N. LaSalle Blvd.
1970, FREDERICK W. WOLF

Severe on the outside but serene and comfortable inside, the church has an inward focus; north windows bring gentle, clear light to the extremely simple chancel.

Severe on the outside but serene and comfortable inside, the church has an inward focus; north windows bring gentle, clear light to the extremely simple chancel.

74| Carl Sandburg Village
Clark St. and LaSalle Blvd. between Division St. and North Ave.
1960–1975, LOUIS R. SOLOMON AND JOHN D. CORDWELL & ASSOCS.

A blighted area of run-down housing was demolished for this new urban neighborhood, part of the Clark-LaSalle Redevelopment Project. Most prominent are the high rises, which do not match the charm of the low-rise apartments or town houses.

Here is a fragment of fashionable LaSalle Blvd., once the western fringe of the Gold Coast, walled off from old neighbors to the east by Carl Sandburg Village. Most of the houses were demolished or else converted to apartments or commercial use. Many survivors were badly remuddled, but several have been restored.

75| Anna A. Wolf House
1338 N. LaSalle Blvd.
1888, FREDERICK W. WOLF

The tiny copper turret has gusto, from its engaged column "leg," to its fish-scale panels, to its bell-shaped roof. In the gable is a wolf's head, a pictorial reference to the owners' name.

76| Double House for John McEwen
1340–1342 N. LaSalle Blvd.
1888, BURLING & WHITEHOUSE

Mirror images up to their mis-matched gables, these choco-late brown sandstone houses are distinguished by fine crafts-manship on the bays and in the stonework.

77| John McEwen House
1346 N. LaSalle Blvd.
1872, ARCHITECT UNKNOWN

Although altered, this grand mansard-roofed villa with its

CARL SANDBURG VILLAGE

projecting central pavilion still reveals a French influence. In the late nineteenth and early twentieth centuries, the neighborhood was heavily Swedish; the house was both a Swedish Lutheran hospice and a home for the elderly before its 1986 rehabilitation as luxury housing.

78 | John F. Jelke House
1352 N. LaSalle Blvd.
1895, BEERS, CLAY & DUTTON
1981, RENOVATION, MARVIN ULLMAN

This facade playfully exaggerates its Classically derived elements. The Palladian window stretches to five panes across, while a low row of rolling swan's-neck pediments forms the parapet. The appendage to the north is a 1980s elevator.

79 | Schiller Street Town Houses
141–149 W. Schiller St.
1988, NAGLE, HARTRAY & ASSOCS.

Bulging exaggerated bays grab for the maximum north light.

80 | Frederick Keller House
1406 N. LaSalle Blvd.
1882, ARCHITECT UNKNOWN

Far from the spartan "octagon front" formula of the 1870s is this finely crafted fussbudget. It has a distinctly French flavor with its mansard roof, stringcourses, and colonnettes.

81 | W. Burton Pl.
(Carl St.)

Across the street from the ordered universe of Carl Sandburg Village is a small, happily slapdash dreamworld, credited as the birthplace of Old Town as an artists' community. In 1927 a lively group of artists and craftspeople began to reinvent W. Burton Pl., then called Carl St. This neighborhood of "tumbledown old flats and cheap rooming houses," as the Chicago Daily News described it in 1940, became their urban canvas.

Entrepreneur and artist Sol Kogen and artist Edgar Miller had met at the School of the Art Institute in 1917. Chicagoan Kogen then worked several years in his family's yard goods business before moving to Paris. Miller grew up in Idaho, where he was influenced by Native American artists and developed a love for animals—including the antelopes, horses, and weasels that populate his work. After returning to Chicago, Kogen began his conversions by inviting Miller to join him in the work at 155 W. Burton Pl.

Kogen and the others began with Victorian houses like those still visible at 147 or 164–166 W. Burton Pl. (both built in 1881) and remade them in a richly decorative, freehand Art Deco style. Some were merely embellished; others were entirely slipcovered with brick and sported additions and new profiles.

Much was done without building permits, and when architects were retained, they apparently had only a minor influence on the designs, which were directed by the artist-owners and their artist-craftsmen friends. Andrew N. Rebori, for instance, who worked with Kogen on 155 W. Burton Pl., recalled, "Yes, I was the consulting architect, but only when I was consulted—which was damned little."

Low on capital but high on vision, the owners went scavenging in Maxwell St. flea markets for tiles, copper tubs, wooden doors, and hardware. Construction was often limited to one apartment at a time, using rents to capitalize slow unit-by-unit conversions. Some were never really finished, as their owners continued to add new art objects. Appreciative tenants and owners care for and continue to carefully embellish their buildings.

82 | Theophil Studios
143 W. Burton Pl.
1940, RENOVATION, FRANK J. LAPASSO

With Kogen's advice, artist Theophil Reuther rebuilt an 1892 house to a Moderne look with stucco facades sporting red brick trim, porthole windows, and Milleresque decorative plaques. Note the leaded-glass windows.

83 | 151 W. Burton Pl.
1932–1935, REMODELING, ARCHITECT UNKNOWN

Self-confident pizzazz transformed an 1887 house into this stylish apartment building. Kogen served as an advisor to owner and rehabber William Giuliani, a former opera singer. A front addition brought the house out to the street, while at the rear it grew to engulf the old coach house. The deliberately rough brick walls, set with flagstones and tiles, serve as artful foils to three sets of rounded corner windows. Glass and tile scavenged from the 1933 World's Fair form the curving windows and line the stairway and halls.

151 W. BURTON PL.

84 | 155 W. Burton Pl.
(*Carl Street Studios*)
1927, REMODELING, SOL KOGEN, ARTIST/CONTRACTOR; EDGAR MILLER, ARTIST; ANDREW N. REBORI, CONSULTING ARCH.

Lovingly detailed and devotedly maintained, this apartment complex is intriguing, beguiling, unpredictable, and visually bounteous. A mansarded Victorian was converted to seventeen (now sixteen) idiosyncratic studio apartments. Corridors and spaces open up in unanticipated directions, with a surprise

155 W. BURTON PL.

around every corner. Miller's beloved animals, especially weasels, enliven the stained-glass windows and wooden carvings, while Kogen's vigorous hand can be seen in the mosaic sidewalk.

85 | 161 W. Burton Pl.
1940, REMODELING, WILLIAM WENDLAND

An 1879 Italianate house with a Joliet limestone front (the brick side wall is still visible on the alley) was rebuilt into a snazzy four-unit apartment building. The enclosed stair is lit by four slit windows that climb the facade. The two-story windows on the front and side lend the stylistic cachet of artists' studios, though the owner, Norman E. Johnson, intended the dwellings "for the average person in commercial life."

86 | 160 W. Burton Pl.
1887, ARCHITECT UNKNOWN
1938, REMODELING, LAWRENCE MONBERG

The original window locations on this 1887 house still show through the paint and the patching on the severe facade. Miller maintained that Kogen duplicated some existing sculptured plaques by Miller without his permission and installed them on several Burton Pl. buildings, including this one.

87| 152–156 W. Burton Pl.

1933–1939, REMODELING, ARCHITECTS UNKNOWN; SOL KOGEN, CLIVE RICKABAUGH, AND CARL PETER KOCH, ARTISTS/CONTRACTORS

The resident artists created a courtyard complex by combining two rooming houses and three coach houses. They bricked up old windows and added new ones, leaving a roundheaded third-floor dormer on 156 as a clue to the original, nineteenth-century look.

88| 1500 N. LaSalle Blvd.

1892, EDMUND R. KRAUSE

Bays serve this apartment building as well as they did the skyscrapers downtown, providing light, ventilation, and a pleasingly rhythmic facade.

GERMANIA PLACE

89| Germania Place
1536 N. Clark St.

1888, AUGUST FIEDLER

This ethnic meeting hall is a symbolic gateway to the Old Town Triangle, settled by German immigrants in the late 1840s. The club was built by the Germania Maennerchor, organized in 1865 to sing a requiem for President Lincoln when his bier rested in Chicago. The elaborate terra-cotta ornament includes lyres centered on the Ionic capitals. Step inside the bank lobby to see the stained-glass windows.

90| Latin School of Chicago
59 W. North Ave.

1969, HARRY WEESE & ASSOCS.
1993–1994, FIRST-FLOOR INFILL AND LOBBY RENOVATION, NAGLE, HARTRAY & ASSOC.
1995–1996, TOP-FLOOR CLASSROOM ADDITION AND ALLEY EXPANSION, NAGLE, HARTRAY & ASSOC.

This concrete-and-brick structure houses the upper grades of the private Latin School, founded in 1888. Completely filling its limited site, the school also uses the playing fields of Lincoln Park for recreation.

91| Chicago Historical Society
Clark St. at North Ave.

1932, GRAHAM, ANDERSON, PROBST & WHITE
1988, ADDITION, HOLABIRD & ROOT

It's grown in all directions—but, happily, in the hands of skillful designers respectful of precious park space. The major remaining GAPW facade faces Lincoln Park in a sober Federal Revival style. The plaza surmounts underground storage areas that accommodate growing collections without infringing on

CHICAGO HISTORICAL SOCIETY

open space. The Clark St. addition, which consumed a previous addition, blends with the original's massing, colors, and materials, but with a more open and welcoming appearance at the entry under its precisely gridded pediment and curtain wall. Sheila Klein's sculpture *Commemorative Ground Ring* (1989) honors Chicago's architectural past with suggestions of the Getty Tomb and a Prairie School roof. It invites inspection, but aggressive southbound positioning seems to suggest that architecture is on the attack!

92| Moody Memorial Church
1609 N. LaSalle Blvd.
1925, FUGARD & KNAPP

Evangelist Dwight L. Moody came to Chicago in 1856 as a businessman but soon devoted his life to uplifting working people and the poor. According to the dedication-day program, the church design was inspired in part by the Byzantine Hagia Sophia in Istanbul; the offices and meeting rooms on the LaSalle Blvd. side were based on various Romanesque churches from Lombardy. A brick structure with sparing use of terracotta ornament, the building provided a large gathering place at limited cost.

93| BP Gas Station
Clark St. and LaSalle Blvd.
1971, STANDARD OIL OF INDIANA (NOW BP AMOCO); GEORGE W. TERP, JR., SUPERVISING ARCH.

Standard Oil used the prominent location to make a bold corporate statement with a space-age gas station, while placating developer Arthur Rubloff, who did not want unattractive views from his planned high rise across the street. A shipyard welded steel beams into the desired curves, and an innovative white material—since replaced by the standard tar and gravel—covered the roof.

94| Emma Fernow House
1620 N. LaSalle Blvd.
1883, FROMMANN & JEBSEN

While delighting modern eyes, this type of early Queen Anne eclecticism drove critics to exasperation: French Second Empire roof; an almost Gothic third-floor window; slate-, brick-, stone-, and metalwork; and a carved stone head commonly found on homes of this period designed or owned by Germans.

The streets of Old Town are inviting but narrow and difficult to navigate by car. The area between Wells St. and Cleveland Ave. is best seen on foot or by bicycle.

95| Piper's Alley Commercial Mall
Wells St. north of North Ave.
1974–1977, STANLEY TIGERMAN & ASSOCS.

The renovation of a bakery on the west side of Wells St. and new construction on the east created a retail complex around this busy intersection. While Tigerman's building for the Walgreens drugstore chain has functioned successfully, the building to the west has been through many changes. One part that has remained constant is Second City, the popular theater company, which occupies space behind a terra-cotta frieze salvaged from Adler & Sullivan's demolished Schiller Theatre. Designed for the third-floor balcony, it features the heads of great German writers and philosophers and is the largest of several Schiller fragments scattered around the near North Side. At Walgreens, the exterior light fixtures of crouching frogs supporting light globes are from Navy Pier.

96| Crilly Ct. Development
North Park Ave. and Wells St., St. Paul Ave. and Eugenie St.

This late nineteenth-century mixed-use Queen Anne development offered many housing

CRILLY CT. DEVELOPMENT

options and convenient retail space. Real estate developer Daniel F. Crilly purchased this block in 1885, cut a street (Crilly Ct.) through it, and built the row houses on the west side. Three years later 1717–1719 N. North Park was moved to its present site from Germania Pl., just south of North Ave. The combination commercial and apartment building at 1700–1718 N. Wells St., designed by Flanders & Zimmerman (1888), was followed in 1893 by the three apartment buildings designed by that firm at 1701 to 1713 N. North Park Ave. Crilly's undertaking culminated in 1895 with four apartment buildings on the east side of Crilly Ct., named after his children, Isabelle, Oliver, Edgar, and Erminie.

97 | Olsen-Hansen Row Houses
164–172 W. Eugenie St.
1886, HARALD M. HANSEN

Of the twelve houses that the Norwegian-born Hansen designed for Adolph Olsen at this corner, only five survive; 164 was the architect's own residence. The fanciful facades of these Queen Anne structures, together with their irregular rooflines and combinations of materials and colors, typify the most exuberant Victorian design.

98 | Kogen-Miller Studios
1734 N. Wells St.
1928–1932, REMODELING, SOL KOGEN, CONTRACTOR/ARTIST; EDGAR MILLER, ARTIST

As with their W. Burton Pl. collaborations, Kogen and Miller designed and built with great enthusiasm and imagination but little documentation. They built onto the front in 1928, raised the building in 1931, and put on a top addition in 1932. Their handiwork includes carved doors and windows, Miller's stained glass, small decorative plaques, and ceramic tiles from Kogen's scavenged collection.

99 | Houses for John B. Mallers
1834–1836 N. Lincoln Ave.
1876, JOHN J. FLANDERS
1838 N. Lincoln Ave.
1879, JOHN J. FLANDERS

An Italianate variation popular in post-Fire Chicago is this triangular bayed type, usually executed—as it was here—in Joliet limestone.

100 | Row Houses for Edwin B. Sheldon
1841–1849 N. Lincoln Ave.
1881–1882, ARCHITECT UNKNOWN

These well-preserved Second Empire houses feature sunburst pedimented dormers and corbeled brick cornices.

101 | 301–315 W. Wisconsin St.
1878, ARCHITECT UNKNOWN

102 | John N. Young House
317 W. Wisconsin St.
1879, ARCHITECT UNKNOWN

Here is a long row of the classic "octagon front" Italianates that sprang up all over Chicago after the Fire. The bays not only increase light and ventilation but also set up a lively rhythm. The remodelings show the many approaches to altering the facade that result from changing the entrance from the very high first floor to the English-basement level.

103 | House of Light
1828 N. Orleans St.
1983, BOOTH HANSEN ASSOCIATES

The widely imitated plan overcomes the disadvantages of the narrow city lot with a central stairwell that floods the interior with daylight. The limestone facade has prominent joint lines, echoed by the window mullions, that describe its proportional elements and call attention to its Classical derivation.

104 | 325 through 345 & 348
W. Menomonee St.

These nine cottages, all in various states of remodeling, give a good idea of what the community looked like before the Fire of 1871. The tiny cottage at 348, on the edge of the alley, is a rare surviving example of a "fire relief cottage." Immediately after the Fire, the Relief & Aid Society supported the construction of these one-room dwellings, which could be moved

by wagon to a burned-out lot. This one has been slightly enlarged and has new siding.

105 | Henry Meyer House
1802 N. Lincoln Park West
1874, ARCHITECT UNKNOWN

The narrow end, on Lincoln Park West, has window hoods with carved wooden keystones that imitate those on more expensive masonry buildings.

106 | 1829 N. Lincoln Park West
1875, 1882, ARCHITECT UNKNOWN

107 | 1835 N. Lincoln Park West
1874, ARCHITECT UNKNOWN

These Italianate wood houses have very well preserved trim. The structure at 1829 has a pilaster and pediment surround on all the window and door openings, as well as incised scrolling designs. The trim on 1835 is mostly of the bull's-eye type found in many interiors, but it also has pierced work above the door and rope molding around the attic window.

108 | Houses for Ann Halsted
1826–1828 N. Lincoln Park West
1884, ADLER & SULLIVAN
1830–1834 N. Lincoln Park West
1885, ADLER & SULLIVAN

Built as rental property, these houses are rare examples of the early Picturesque phase of the firm's work. The bold ornament shows the influence of Sullivan's early employer, Frank Furness of Philadelphia. The three houses were designed as a symmetrical group.

HOUSES FOR ANN HALSTED

109| Charles H. Wacker House
1836 N. Lincoln Park West
EARLY 1870S; 1884, REMODELING,
ARCHITECT UNKNOWN

The Wackers' coach house, in which the family lived while 1838 was under construction, was relocated from the rear of the property to this position and remodeled by Frederick's son, Charles. The namesake of Wacker Dr., Charles was the youngest director of the World's Columbian Exposition of 1893 and a vigorous promoter of Daniel H. Burnham's 1909 Plan of Chicago.

110| Frederick Wacker House
1838 N. Lincoln Park West
1874, ARCHITECT UNKNOWN

A Swiss-born brewer, Wacker built his frame house just before new regulations prohibited wood construction in that part of the city destroyed by the Great Fire of 1871. The form is typical of a Chicago cottage, but the ornament is unusually elaborate, with incised pilasters around the doors and windows and a large overhanging porch that recalls a Swiss chalet.

111| "The Beauty Pageant"
1811 to 1847 N. Sedgwick St.

In the early 1970s the Department of Urban Renewal closed Ogden Ave., a major southwest thoroughfare, from North Ave. at Larrabee St. to Armitage Ave. at Clark St. The former roadbed and some adjacent property was offered for development, including ten lots on the east side of Sedgwick St. that were sold in 1977. Efforts were made by the buyers to consider design guidelines for their new houses, but each ultimately preferred to go his own way. Of the resulting diversity, Stanley Tigerman, who designed 1847, said, "This is an American street . . . It's quiet, dumb, Wild West, egocentric, and typically American. Americans have always seen themselves as individuals, and that individual imperative governs everything."

Booth Hansen Associates did 1843 and 1829, while Wilbert O. Rueter, a former protégé of Walter A. Netsch, Jr., at Skidmore, Owings & Merrill, designed 1841, whose angled bay looks southwest down the abandoned street. In one of several small parks aligned with the former street is a sculpture of two horses by Chicago artist John Kearney, who uses old car bumpers to create creatures with great character.

112| Belgravia Terrace
W. Wisconsin St. between
Sedgwick St. and Hudson Ave.
1989, GELICK FORAN ASSOCS.

In a gracious urbanistic gesture, these row houses come out to the lot line with split staircases designed to invite entry rather than repel intruders. The absence of high brick walls is a welcome change from the usual formula.

113| Midwest Buddhist Temple
435 W. Menomonee St.
1971, HIDEAKI ARAO

The base contains classrooms and meeting rooms and also serves as a terrace for ceremonial precessions. The temple's combination gable and hip roof is traditionally Japanese. A rectory stands to the west.

114| Menomonee Lane
Town Houses
1801–1813 N. Mohawk St.
1986, MICHAEL LUSTIG & ASSOCS.

English row houses were the inspiration for this fourteen-unit project. Lines of contrasting brick are laid over Flemish bond, uniting the windows and doors and enlivening the surfaces with a crisply articulated grid.

115| Steel and Glass House
1949 N. Larrabee St.
1981, KRUECK & OLSEN ARCHITECTS

It's aloof and mechanically pristine—but at night, when the light shines alluringly through the windows and steel grating, who'd turn down an

STEEL AND GLASS HOUSE

invitation to step inside this beautiful cage? This 5,000-square-foot house is made of shop-fabricated steel angle frames joined to form structural bays. The U-shaped plan has two levels with a two-story living space. A central court and an informal garden provide private outdoor space.

116| 1900 N. Howe St.
1991, MAX GORDON; OFFICE OF JOHN VINCI, ASSOC. ARCH.

This 10,000-square-foot house meets the neighborhood standard of lavishness but is a quiet island of understatement and good taste. Executed in rosy brick, with long, taupe window frames divided into small panes, it was designed to accommodate the owners' art collection.

117| 636 W. Willow St.
1995, PETER DE BRETTEVILLE, ARCHITECT

Designed around a glassy courtyard, this corner-lot house presents a private face to the street. Roman brick and horizontal mullions reinforce the overall horizontal massing. Vertical piers on the entrance facade suggest the double height space concealed within, lit with clerestory windows.

636 W. WILLOW ST.

118| City Commons
W. Willow St. between N. Orchard and Vine Sts.
1986, PAPPAGEORGE/HAYMES

Trendsetting developers Horwitz-Matthews worked with the architects to devise a project that organizes town houses around a private, secured courtyard. Walled gardens act as a buffer between the street and the unbroken perimeter wall and increase the fortresslike quality. But through the tinseltown entrance with its backlit glass block is a ring of row houses that honor their Italianate grandparents, complete with a long flight of stairs up to the stoop.

119| House with a Bay
1873 N. Orchard St.
1986, NAGLE, HARTRAY & ASSOCS.

In Adler & Sullivan's work of a century earlier, several examples of which survive in Old Town and Lincoln Park, severe red brick facades serve as backdrops for bold, prominently placed, geometric or "organic" terra-cotta ornament. This modern interpretation of that historic precedent focuses attention on the bay window, whose ornamental casting in fiberglass is an enlargement of the design of the terra cotta.

HOUSE WITH A BAY

120| YMCA—New City Center
1515 N. Halsted St.
1981, METZ, TRAIN & YOUNGREN

Glazed brick in bright colors covers the exterior, which has very few openings for security and functional reasons. The design is far from fortresslike, however, with the mass broken up by a varied roofline.

121| Yondorf Block and Hall
758 W. North Ave.
1887, FREDERICK AHLSCHLAGER
1989, RENOVATION, FITZGERALD ASSOCS.; OFFICE OF JOHN VINCI, ASSOC. ARCH.

This combination retail and hall building was constructed by the owners of a clothing business that occupied a nearby storefront on North Ave. In 1910 the store-fronts were remodeled with a white terra-cotta facade for a bank, and roof cresting at the corner was removed. The largest of the six halls is complete with a stage and gallery. They were rented for social gatherings and meetings by unions and fraternal organizations. The building has stylistic elements of both the Victorian Gothic and the Romanesque Revival.

YONDORF BLOCK AND HALL

122| St. Michael's Roman Catholic Church
447 W. Eugenie St.
1869; 1872, REBUILDING, AUGUST WALLBAUM
1888, ALTERATIONS AND STEEPLE, ADAM F. BOOS
1889, CLOCK, SCHWALBACH CO.
1913, REMODELING AND BRICK FACADE, HERMANN J. GAUL

Generations of German architects, craftspeople, designers, and parishioners made St. Michael's a Romanesque monument with a Bavarian Baroque interior. The church was largely destroyed in the Fire, but the exterior walls survived, and the church was rebuilt within them. The grandest single element is the high altar, designed and installed along with four sub-sidiary altars by E. Hackner & Sons of La Crosse, Wisc. Within an arched niche, flanked by the archangels Gabriel and Raphael, St. Michael stands high above a defeated Lucifer. The stained-glass windows, by the Mayer Window Art Institute of Munich, were installed, as was the altar, in celebration of the parish's golden jubilee in 1902.

123| Walter A. Netsch, Jr., House
1700 N. Hudson St.
1974, WALTER A. NETSCH, JR.

This is a rare example of the domestic work of the former general partner at Skidmore, Owings & Merrill best known for his design of the Air Force Academy Chapel in Colorado Springs and the University of Illinois at Chicago. While ensuring privacy from the street, the interior offers a lofty, open central space, thirty-three feet high, under skylights covered with a passive solar collector.

124| Anton Franzen House
1726 N. Hudson Ave.
1880, ARCHITECT UNKNOWN

The form of the Chicago cottage lent itself to brick construction, although it was more typically built of economical wood.

ANTON FRANZEN HOUSE

125| 421–423 W. Willow St.
1982, FREDERICK PHILLIPS & ASSOCS.

Two divided by three equals these twin town houses, joined behind a white steel frame that suggests the shape of a third.

126| 319 & 315 W. Eugenie St.
1874, ARCHITECT UNKNOWN

These well-preserved frame cottages have lively woodwork, including dentils and paired brackets below the gabled cornices.

127| 235 W. Eugenie St.
1962, HARRY WEESE & ASSOCS., BEN WEESE, DESIGNER

The varied layouts were intended to lure renters to this pioneering example of modern design in Old Town. Constructed of Chicago common brick, it maintains a nineteenth-century scale all the way up to its mansard roof.

235 W. EUGENIE ST.

128| Old Town Triangle Association Building
1763 N. North Park Ave.
1922, GRAHAM, ANDERSON, PROBST & WHITE

Throughout the Triangle are brick buildings designed as garages with apartments above. They were chauffeurs' quarters for employees of Gold Coast residents whose narrow lots could not accommodate cars. The garage space of this building was remodeled to house meeting rooms and classrooms.

129| Willow St. Town Houses
312–318 W. Willow St.
1974, HARRY WEESE & ASSOCS.

The architect and three friends built these row houses for themselves. Their inspiration was London's row house "terrace" altered to accommodate the automobile. Their plan has become standard: garage,

entrance foyer, family room, and garden at street level; living room, dining room, and kitchen on the second floor; and bedrooms on the third and fourth floors.

130| 225, 219, 217 & 215 W. Eugenie St.
1874, ARCHITECTS UNKNOWN

This unusual concentration of one- and two-story frame cottages was built just before the 1874 ordinance banning wooden construction. They all have high basements (in some cases a full story), gabled roofs with bracketed cornices, and simple trim that reflected the prevailing Italianate style.

215 W. EUGENIE ST.

131| Cobbler Square
(*Western Wheel Works*)
1350 N. Wells St.
1889, BLOCK ON W. SCHILLER ST. AT NORTH PARK AVE.: HENRY SIERKS
1891, BLOCK ON W. EVERGREEN ST. AT NORTH PARK AVE.: HENRY SIERKS
1895, BLOCK ON W. EVERGREEN ST. AT WELLS ST.: JULIUS H. HUBER
1985, RENOVATION, KENNETH A. SCHROEDER & ASSOCS.

This residential and retail complex was created from some twenty buildings built from 1880 to 1959. The oldest structures, of heavy wooden-beam mill construction, belonged to the Western Wheel Works, bicycle manufacturers, and reflect the vertical organization of the manufacturing process. In 1911 the company founded by Dr. William M. Scholl acquired the property for the

COBBLER SQUARE

manufacture of his foot-care products, adding structures in the 1940s and 1950s. After the company vacated the site in 1981, some of the interior buildings were demolished, and a slice was cut out of a building on Wells St. to create an entry to the 295 residential units. An engaging series of courtyards, hollowed out of the center of the site, is ringed by steel walkways and entered through a three-story atrium.

132| **Marshall Field Garden Apartments**
N. Sedgwick St., W. Evergreen Ave., N. Hudson Ave., and W. Blackhawk St.
1928–1929, ANDREW J. THOMAS; GRAHAM, ANDERSON, PROBST & WHITE, ASSOC. ARCH.

1993, RENOVATION, DUBIN, DUBIN & MOUTOUSSAMY

Under the direction of Marshall Field III, the Marshall Field Estate built this low-income housing complex of ten buildings on two city blocks with a large central courtyard, communal interior spaces, and retail space on Sedgwick St. One of the nation's largest such efforts, it was an attempt to see if private initiatives could eliminate slum housing and become economic successes. A New York architect, Thomas was a preeminent designer of housing projects; his spartan, almost Art Deco complex was a success on aesthetic grounds. But it failed to provide housing to low-income tenants because costs proved greater than anticipated and required moderate, rather than low, rents.

133| **Tower House**
1306 N. Cleveland St.
2001, FREDERICK PHILLIPS & ASSOCS.

This modern urban "tree house" has two floors of interior space sandwiched between a roof terrace and an open carport. Much is achieved with a small building footprint. An exterior circular stair provides code-required redundancy to the concrete block stair tower. The living spaces are on the third floor in order to take advantage of the best views.

MARSHALL FIELD GARDEN APARTMENTS

LINCOLN PARK

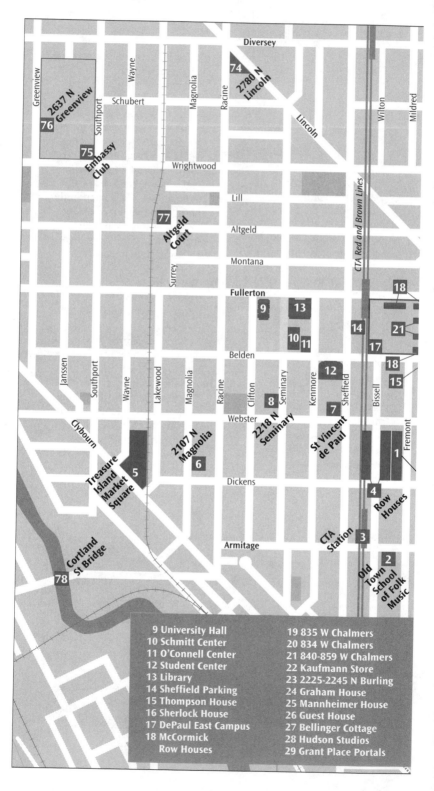

9 University Hall
10 Schmitt Center
11 O'Connell Center
12 Student Center
13 Library
14 Sheffield Parking
15 Thompson House
16 Sherlock House
17 DePaul East Campus
18 McCormick
   Row Houses

19 835 W Chalmers
20 834 W Chalmers
21 840-859 W Chalmers
22 Kaufmann Store
23 2225-2245 N Burling
24 Graham House
25 Mannheimer House
26 Guest House
27 Bellinger Cottage
28 Hudson Studios
29 Grant Place Portals

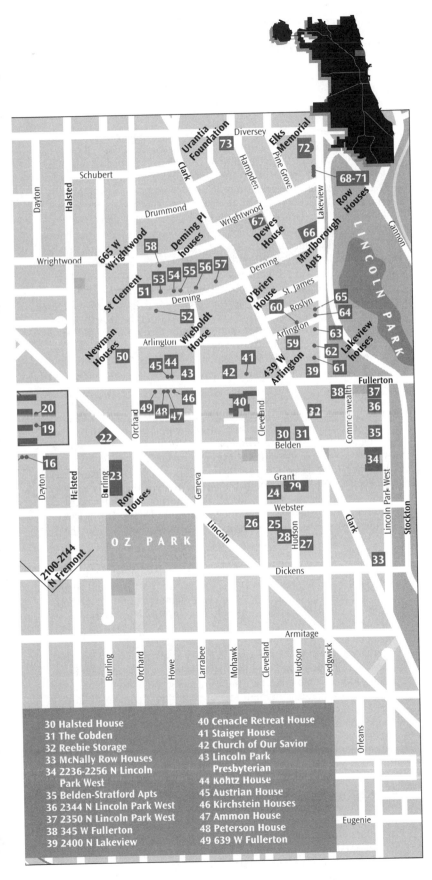

30 Halsted House
31 The Cobden
32 Reebie Storage
33 McNally Row Houses
34 2236-2256 N Lincoln
    Park West
35 Belden-Stratford Apts
36 2344 N Lincoln Park West
37 2350 N Lincoln Park West
38 345 W Fullerton
39 2400 N Lakeview

40 Cenacle Retreat House
41 Staiger House
42 Church of Our Savior
43 Lincoln Park
    Presbyterian
44 Kohtz House
45 Austrian House
46 Kirchstein Houses
47 Ammon House
48 Peterson House
49 639 W Fullerton

LINCOLN PARK

NO OTHER CHICAGO NEIGHBORHOOD HAS WITNESSED AS DRAMATIC A RESUR-
gence as Lincoln Park. The 1950 *Local Community Fact Book*, the city's
decennial oracle of sociological trends, predicted "the end of much of
Lincoln Park as a residential community." Today it is for many people
the most desirable neighborhood—with real estate prices to match.
The density and congestion that constitute its chief drawbacks are the
inevitable side effects of its popularity. Yet unlike the Gold Coast, the
only neighborhood with higher median home values, high-rise construction has invaded only a small area, and the vast majority of streets
retain their late nineteenth-century character.

Lincoln Park had distinctly inauspicious origins. Like the rest of the
North Side, it was less accessible to the central city because of the intervening river. The lakefront just beyond North Ave. was considered
remote enough for use as the city's cemetery, until the growth of the
North Side population (still primarily farmers) led public health cru-
saders like Dr. John H. Rauch to demand the removal of the bodies to
cemeteries farther north. This was accomplished in 1864, and the city
established in its place Lake Park, renamed for the assassinated president the following year.

The Fire of 1871 destroyed the North Side as far as the city limits at
Fullerton Ave., and an 1874 ordinance extended the fireproof building
codes to the entire city. The growth of industry along the north branch
of the river in the 1880s provided an impetus for the construction of
workers' housing to the west. Cable cars arrived on Clark St. and Lincoln
Ave. later in the decade, increasing middle-class settlement near those
streets. The 1889 annexation of Lake View bumped the city boundary
well north of Fullerton Ave., ending the construction of wooden houses,
which had flourished just north of the former city limits. Construction
of the Northwestern Elevated Railroad Company's tracks along Sheffield
Ave. in the late 1890s spurred further commercial development.

By 1900 ethnic patterns were well established, with wealthy Germans
living in large houses near the lake, and middle- and working-class
Irish and Poles in modest flats farther west. The 1920s and 1930s
brought an extensive turnover, with poorer immigrants moving in and
buildings subdivided to accommodate them. New construction was
limited to the ever-desirable lakefront, while west of Halsted St. rooming houses were carved out of already modest dwellings.

After World War II most of Lincoln Park was considered a slum. The
housing stock was similar to that of most other close-in neighborhoods: fifty-year-old buildings that were aging badly through neglect
and subdivision into tenement-size units. But because the situation
was less desperate than in other neighborhoods, such as the Near
South Side, urban renewal arrived at a slower, more measured pace.
Funds were not allocated until 1964, eight years after most of the community had been included in a 226-acre urban renewal area. By then
there was less enthusiasm—and money—for the wholesale replacement of the housing stock with clusters of high rises. Private owners
had already begun to renovate their property—if sometimes in a way
that horrifies today's preservationists. An influx of Baby Boomers in
the 1970s filled the rehabbed graystones, vintage apartments, and new
high rises, bolstering the demand for shopping and entertainment.
Restaurants, bars, theaters, and boutiques would quickly make this
one of the city's liveliest neighborhoods.

Gentrification proceeded slowly westward, crossing Halsted St. in the early 1980s. Deconversion became the rage: not only were rooming houses returned to their original configuration of large apartments, but structures built as two- and three-flats were remodeled into luxurious single-family residences. The passion for preservation also led to the increasingly authentic restoration of facades, even where the interiors (whose original features were sometimes unsalvageable) have been redone in white-on-white modern.

Retail and entertainment establishments have followed the westward expansion, creating a new frontier along the formerly industrial Clybourn Ave. The availability of large parcels of land hard by the Chicago River's north branch led to the creation of suburban-style strip malls that offer the abundant free parking that is in woefully short supply closer to the lake.

The demographic dip in the number of twenty- to thirty-five-year-olds and the white-collar recession of the late 1980s have chastened the area's gold rush mentality, but suburban empty nesters returning to the city provide a whole new source of homeowners. Lincoln Park unequivocally has entered the twenty-first century as one of the city's most vital residential communities.

—PATRICIA MARKS LURIE WITH LAURIE MCGOVERN PETERSEN

1| 2100–2144 N. Fremont St.
1875, EDWARD J. BURLING

Rebuilding after the Fire filled entire blocks with Italianate houses and flats. The ritzier dwellings were termed marble fronts, because they were built of Joliet limestone. For this more modest project, common brick walls and cast stone (concrete) sills and hood molds were used all around. An elaborate cornice unites this monolithic block with end houses set slightly forward. The porches closest to original are probably those with a simple bracketed canopy over the door.

2| Old Town School of Folk Music
(*The Aldine*)
909 W. Armitage Ave.
1896, JOSEPH BETTINGHOFER
1987, RENOVATION AND
STOREFRONT RESTORATION,
LISEC & BIEDERMAN

In anticipation of the Northwestern Elevated Railroad Company's Center St. (Armitage Ave.) station, business blocks sprang up here during the mid-1890s; 917, 919, 921, and 925 all date from 1895–1897. Their Baroque embellishments—cherubs, figures, and banded pilasters—and elaborate corner bays compete for shoppers' attention.

3| CTA—Armitage Ave. Station
944 W. Armitage Ave.
1900, WILLIAM R. GIBB;
J. A. L. WADDELL, CONSULTING ENG.

This station of the Northwestern Elevated line from the Loop to Wilson Ave. is similar to five others by Gibb at Belmont, Fullerton, Diversey, Sedgwick, and Chicago. The brick walls are trimmed with cast stone tinted to look like terra cotta.

4| 2100–2144 & 2101–2145 N. Bissell St.
1883, IVER C. ZARBELL

John Davis developed these rental row houses, which are clustered in pairs and triplets to resemble grand homes. Second Empire mansard roofs and central pavilions blend with the Queen Anne's quirky variety of shapes, colors, and materials.

OLD TOWN SCHOOL OF FOLK MUSIC

5 | Treasure Island Market Square
Clybourn, Wayne, Lakewood, and Webster Aves.
1987, BOOTH HANSEN ASSOCIATES

This complex is notable less for its design, a serviceable postmodern composition of industrial materials, than for its site plan, which places shops on the periphery and parking in the middle. Regrettably, the other shopping centers lining Clybourn Ave. did not follow this pattern, offering instead the standard sea of surface parking between sidewalk and storefronts.

2107 N. MAGNOLIA ST.

6 | 2107 N. Magnolia St.
(*Joel T. Headley Public School*)
1875, ARCHITECT UNKNOWN
1985, CONVERSION TO APARTMENTS, BAUHS & DRING

The city's oldest public school building now houses condominium lofts, but the Italianate exterior and spartan lobby are little changed.

7 | St. Vincent de Paul Roman Catholic Church
1004 W. Webster Ave.
1897, JAMES J. EGAN

Egan's smooth and graceful interpretation of the Romanesque does not evoke the sense of shelter associated with the style's fortresslike Richardsonian version. The high altar (1903–1909), of Carrara marble, is inlaid with mother-of-pearl and mosaics.

8 | 2218 N. Seminary Ave.
1996, SCHROEDER MURCHIE LAYA

What at first may appear to be a renovation/addition is all new construction, built on a double lot. The limestone portion of the house was designed to relate to its late nineteenth-century neighbors, while the steel-and-glass box that intersects it at a 12-degree angle provides a multistory interior space.

DePaul University— Lincoln Park Campus
Webster Ave., Fullerton Ave., Halsted St., and Clifton Ave.

Founded as St. Vincent's College in 1898 and chartered under its current name in 1907, DePaul's small Lincoln Park campus was until recently dominated by a pair of megabuildings dating from a 1960s and 1970s expansion. The campus east of the elevated tracks originally belonged to the McCormick Theological Seminary, which sold it to DePaul in 1973. In 1988 Lohan Assocs. developed a master plan for future development that has guided the creation of a more campuslike environment. A campus building boom beginning in the late 1980s has brought new life to DePaul. The architecture of the new dormitories, classroom, and athletic facilities has emphasized contextual and low-profile respectful neighbors rather than signature architecture. The heart of the campus is the landscaped quadrangle created by closing the 2300 block of Seminary Ave to traffic in 1992.

9 | University Hall
2345 N. Clifton Ave.
1986, LOHAN ASSOCS.

Architect and client worked to create housing with massing and materials sympathetic to surrounding nineteenth-century houses and flats. The window hoods are inspired by the Italianate, although the openings that they top are almost square rather than tall and narrow.

10 | Arthur J. Schmitt Academic Center
2323 N. Seminary Ave.
1968, C. F. MURPHY ASSOCS.

DEPAUL UNIVERSITY LIBRARY

This brutalist concrete building is a relic of the "university as fortress" image that DePaul has successfully shed.

11| Michael J. O'Connell Center (*Hall of Science*)
1036 W. Belden Ave.
1938, SHAW, NAESS & MURPHY

This modest Art Moderne building denotes chemistry, biology, and physics in spandrel panels that depict laboratory beakers, splayed frogs (presumably awaiting dissection), and engines and gears.

12| DePaul Student Center
2250 N. Sheffield Ave.
2002, WTW ARCHITECTS WITH VMC ARCHITECTS

This three-story block is big, but respectful to the street and neighbors. Two main entrances at opposite corners are linked by a curved interior street of student services.

13| Library
2350 N. Kenmore Ave.
1992, LOHAN ASSOCS.

The first major building designed in accordance with the 1988 master plan is this signature building. The red brick trimmed in pale masonry establishes a strong presence yet blends well with the neighborhood. Piers suggestive of buttresses lend a collegiate air, while the towers anchor the building. The eclectic vocabulary—Classical keystones, Gothic buttresses, and Chicago School towers—fails to speak with a clear voice, although it is too subdued to be cacophonous.

14| Sheffield Parking Garage
2331 N. Sheffield Ave.
1993, ANTUNOVICH ASSOCS.

One of four buildings on the east side of Sheffield that Antunovich designed for DePaul, it is particularly successful in its brick and limestone detailing and sensitivity to the scale of the neighborhood.

15| Hiram J. Thompson House
851 W. Belden Ave.
1885, BURLING & WHITEHOUSE

This Queen Anne house retains the flat-fronted sobriety of the Italianate style on the first two floors but explodes in scale at the top, where the huge dormer pierces an oversized cornice ornamented with giant shells between brackets. These bulky elements and the wide variety of materials (red brick trimmed in brownstone, hung with a metal bay) are typical of the uninhibited if awkward early Queen Anne style.

16| James P. Sherlock House
845 W. Belden Ave.
1895, LOUIS BRODHAG

Sedate and cohesive compared to its next-door neighbor, it shows the relative quietness and monochromatic palette of the later Queen Anne style, here executed in the Romanesque mode. The once-popular variety of brown sandstone known as Lake Superior raindrop stone shows characteristic "spattering."

17| DePaul University—Lincoln Park Campus (East Portion) (*McCormick Theological Seminary*)
Halsted St., Belden Ave., Fullerton Ave., and the El tracks

The Presbyterian Theological Seminary was founded in Indiana in 1829, moved to Chicago in 1859, and relocated here in 1864. All of the original academic buildings, which faced Halsted St. and Belden Ave., were demolished, most of them during a 1960s building campaign. The most notable remnant is the collection of Queen Anne row houses, now a designated landmark district. Dissatisfied with the return produced by investing the endowment in bonds and mortgages, the seminary began constructing row houses in 1882 to produce rental income and create a comfortable island of Protestants in a sea of German Catholics.

The next building phase began in 1929, when architect Dwight G. Wallace created a grand plan to redesign the entire campus in the Collegiate Gothic style. What are now DePaul's Gymnasium (1929) and Commons Building (1932) are the sole offspring of Wallace's efforts. After moving to Hyde Park in 1973, the seminary sold its institutional buildings to DePaul University and the houses to private owners.

18| McCormick Row Houses
832–840, 844–858 W. Belden Ave., 833–841, 845–859, 901–913, 917–927 W. Fullerton Ave.
1884–1889, A. M. F. COLTON

These modest Queen Anne dwellings have lively rooflines, a

MCCORMICK ROW HOUSES

street wall that steps in and out, and ornamental brick patterns. Construction proceeded from east to west, and the later buildings in the 900 block of Fullerton Ave. differ slightly.

19| 835 W. Chalmers Pl.
1882, WILLIAM LE BARON JENNEY

20| 834 W. Chalmers Pl.
1889, A. M. F. COLTON & SON

These two freestanding houses were built for the seminary's faculty members; 835 was for high-rankers and was moved from its original location on Belden Ave. when a library (now demolished) was constructed there in 1894.

21| 840–858 & 841–859 W. Chalmers Pl.
1889–1891, A. M. F. COLTON & SON

The row houses surrounding the greensward on Chalmers Pl. are more subdued than their predecessors on the avenues. Each group shares a long gabled roof broken by a symmetrical pattern of round and triangular cross gables. They have smooth brick facades with recessed windows and deep arches sheltering the doorways. The dark color, arched entries, and corner tourelles convey a Victorian—or is it Presbyterian?—sobriety.

22| Ferdinand Kaufmann Store & Flat Building
2310–2312 N. Lincoln Ave.
1883, 1887, ADLER & SULLIVAN

FERDINAND KAUFMANN STORE & FLAT
BUILDING

The south portion is earlier,
although the design for the
entire building was probably
done at the same time. The
only element distinguishing it
as the firm's work is the robust
ornament in the stone moldings
and terra-cotta lunettes and the
small lotus flowers topping the
first-floor pilasters.

23| 2225–2245 N. Burling St.
1879, EDWARD J. BURLING

These row houses are almost
identical to those at 2100–2144
N. Fremont St. A large cornice
joins an undifferentiated group
of common brick Italianates,
with the two houses at each end
breaking forward only slightly.

24| Bruce Graham House
2215 N. Cleveland Ave.
1969, BRUCE GRAHAM

Unabashedly different and
fiercely private is this home
designed by and built for a
former SOM partner. It tries no
harder to fit in here than does
his Sears Tower in the Loop.
Lacking streetside windows, it is
oriented around a walled garden; the steel gate is the only
opening on the street facade.

25| Leon Mannheimer House
2147 N. Cleveland Ave.
1884, ADLER & SULLIVAN

The outsized chunks of lotuslike
metal ornament are close to the
scale of decoration on the firm's
business buildings downtown.
Along with the idiosyncratic
semicircle topping the window

and the triangular bay, they are
the only clues to Sullivan's involvement.

26| Walter Guest House
2150 N. Cleveland Ave.
1932, REMODELING, EDGAR MILLER,
ARTIST

The Art Deco streetside and
topside additions of buff brick
gave this old house a face-lift.
The facade is dominated by
large expanses of Miller's characteristic chevron-patterned
leaded-glass windows. The
screen on the front door displays another Miller favorite:
animals from antelopes to
sea horses.

WALTER GUEST HOUSE

27| Richard Bellinger Cottage
2121 N. Hudson Ave.
1869, WILLIAM W. BOYINGTON

Like Boyington's Water Tower,
this house survived the Fire and
became a legendary landmark.
Located near the northernmost
edge of the Fire's reach, it was
saved when Bellinger allegedly
soaked the roof with cider
(his wife claimed it was water).
This superb example of an 1860s
Chicago cottage is clapboarded
and shingled and was ultimately
raised for a new foundation.

28| Hudson Studios
2134–2138 N. Hudson Ave.
1948-1952, REMODELING AND
ADDITIONS, FRANK LAPASSO

Attorney Lawrence S. Adler and
commercial artist Clive Rickabaugh developed this courtyard
complex with the bohemian,
do-it-ourselves charm of

W. Burton Pl., where Rickabaugh lived near his friend Sol Kogen. A long-vacant burned-out shell at 2138 was replaced by four apartments in 1948, with duplexes on the second and third levels. The building at 2134 was converted next and still has the bricked-in windows of its earlier incarnation as a Victorian house. In 1952 additions were built on the back of each, with diamond-shaped bays and "Miami windows." The maple railings, doors, carvings, and fireplaces were scavenged from the La Salle St. Methodist Church, which had burned.

29| Grant Place Portals
415–443 W. Grant Pl.
1972, BOOTH & NAGLE

These stacked town houses meet the street with the walled yards typical of others nearby, but within is a village atmosphere. Despite the density (fifty houses on less than an acre), the slice of landscaped space knits them together.

30| Ann Halsted House
440 W. Belden Ave.
1883, ADLER & SULLIVAN

The lotus motif that decorates many Sullivan houses and business buildings of this era adorns the gable of this severely simple, early Queen Anne house.

31| The Cobden
418–424 W. Belden Ave.
1892, CHARLES S. FROST

On busy Clark St. it is a typical flats-above-storefronts building, while the facade on residential Belden Ave. derives its picturesque variety from its bays and the shaped gable that breaks the roofline.

32| Reebie Storage & Moving Company
2325 N. Clark St.
1923, GEORGE S. KINGSLEY

"If Old King Tut were alive today, he'd store his goods the Reebie way!" Thus did the enterprising Reebie Brothers capitalize on the Egyptomania occasioned by the opening of King Tut's tomb in 1922. The well-preserved polychrome terra-cotta facade (missing only its cavetto cornice, similar in shape to those above the second-floor windows) is guarded by two statues of Ramses II, representing William C. and John C. Reebie. The hieroglyphics at the base say, "Forever I work for all of your regions in daylight and darkness" (left statue) and "I give protection to your furniture." Much of the elaborate sculptural program, which extends to the interior foyer and office lobby, was devised by Northwestern Terra Cotta Co. sculptor Fritz Albert.

THE COBDEN

REEBIE STORAGE & MOVING COMPANY

33 | Row Houses for Andrew McNally
2103–2115 N. Clark St./310–312
W. Dickens Ave.
1885, JOSEPH LYMAN SILSBEE

Queen Anne variety enlivens this corner block, designed by one of Frank Lloyd Wright's first employers.

34 | 2236–2250 N. Lincoln Park West
1910, SIMEON B. EISENDRATH

The influence of Eisendrath's former employer, Louis H. Sullivan, shows in the hearty foliate terra cotta surrounding each entrance.

35 | Belden-Stratford Apartments
(*Belden Hotel*)
2300 N. Lincoln Park West
1922, FRIDSTEIN & CO.

This elegant apartment building seems almost to have been plucked from a Parisian boulevard and enlarged to Chicago scale. The mansard roof dominates the skyline, and the smooth limestone facade is embellished with quoins and Classical carving.

36 | 2344 N. Lincoln Park West
1917, KARL M. VITZTHUM
1991, PENTHOUSE ADDITION,
FREDERICK PHILLIPS & ASSOCS.

A small sixth-floor apartment was remodeled and a 2,000-square-foot seventh floor added to create a dazzling penthouse that is still low enough to be seen from the street. With its twin limestone belvederes, it fits securely atop this Beaux Arts facade.

37 | 2350 N. Lincoln Park West/
305 W. Fullerton Ave.
1916, ANDREW SANDEGREN

A master of quiet elegance, Sandegren created signature sunrooms with million-dollar views of Lincoln Park.

38 | 345 W. Fullerton Ave.
1973, HARRY WEESE & ASSOCS.

The concrete frame surrounding the dark glass windows is made less severe by the gradual stepping back of each facade.

39 | 2400 N. Lakeview Ave.
1963, LUDWIG MIES VAN DER ROHE

This is the last residential high rise that Mies designed for Chicago.

40 | Cenacle Retreat House
513 W. Fullerton Ave.
1967, CHARLES POPE

Siting the parking lot on Fullerton Ave. was unfortunate, but it lessens the impact of the tall buildings behind, which house sleeping rooms. The complex is a terrific example of the warm side of clean, quiet modernism in brick, with narrow brick piers forming strong verticals. Go inside the chapel to see the same sensibility, augmented with boldly abstract windows.

41 | Carl M. Staiger House
520 W. Fullerton Pkwy.
1891, LAMSON & NEWMAN

All the bang is in the bay. With a swan's-neck pediment and large acroterion, it projects from the facade like a corsage.

42 | Church of Our Savior
(Episcopal)
530 W. Fullerton Pkwy.
1888, CLINTON J. WARREN

The tourelled Romanesque facade blends seamlessly with the rector's house on the west. The nave has walls of unglazed terra-cotta tiles and a beautifully trussed ceiling. Some of the original, geometrically patterned leaded-glass windows were replaced with figural stained glass, several by Tiffany Studios.

43| Lincoln Park Presbyterian Church

(*Fullerton Avenue Presbyterian Church*)
600 W. Fullerton Pkwy.
1888, JOHN S. WOOLLACOTT
1898, ADDITION, WILLIAM G. BARFIELD

Every corner on this massive Richardsonian Romanesque church is soft and rounded. Fat disks of greenish sandstone are stacked to form giant tourelles, and blocks of many sizes are knit into a tall tower (minus its steeple since 1970). This variety of green stone, called Michigan buff sandstone, was popular from the mid-1880s to the mid-1890s. From the pulpit on the west wall the aisles radiate in a semicircle on an ascending grade as in "all the first-water Presbyterian churches of the city," as the *Daily Inter Ocean* noted. Barfield's addition pushed the west wall back twenty-five feet but maintained this orientation.

44| Louis O. Kohtz House
620 W. Fullerton Ave.
1886, ARCHITECT UNKNOWN

45| Leo Austrian House
624 W. Fullerton Ave.
1886, THEODORE KARLS

LEO AUSTRIAN HOUSE

The Austrian House sets itself apart from its neighbor with a flattened Romanesque castle front that includes a corner tower, parapet, and shallow machicolations.

46| Herman Kirchstein Houses
621 & 627 W. Fullerton Ave.
1888, JULIUS H. HUBER
623–625 W. Fullerton Ave.
1887, JULIUS H. HUBER

Awkwardly massed but beautifully detailed, the two slightly later houses stiffly bookend the double house. All are enlivened by robust wooden porches whose cornices feature disks that look like flying saucers impaled on spikes.

47| Ernest Ammon House
629 W. Fullerton Ave.
1889, FROMMANN & JEBSEN

48| Peter Peterson House
631 W. Fullerton Ave.
1889, JULIUS H. HUBER

Look closely at 629 for an extroverted Queen Anne palette; although begrimed, the red-and-green sandstone still peeks through.

49| 639 W. Fullerton Ave.
EARLY 1890S, ARCHITECT UNKNOWN

This house is saved from formula by the fabulous acanthus-leaf symphony at the entry. The fingered leaves swirl and twist, framing jesters' faces at the bottom. At the top they become spiky collars that frame facing dog faces—or are they caricatures of humans?

639 W. FULLERTON AVE.

NEWMAN BROTHERS HOUSES

50| Newman Brothers Houses
2424, 2430 & 2434 N. Orchard St.
1895, JOHN M. VAN OSDEL II

S. S. Beman popularized the Châteauesque locally with his Kimball House of 1891; many elements of his design are squeezed here into a narrower, high-shouldered version. This trio was to have been done in shades of red stone, but the middle house was executed in limestone. Van Osdel was the nephew of John Mills Van Osdel, Chicago's first architect.

51| St. Clement Roman Catholic Church
646 W. Deming Pl.
1918, BARNETT, HAYNES & BARNETT
1989, RESTORATION, HOLABIRD & ROOT

The architects of the St. Louis Cathedral produced a scaled-down version here, complete with a Byzantine dome inspired by Istanbul's Hagia Sophia. Trompe l'oeil mosaic, plaster-work, and marble make the interior a riot of colors and faux textures.

52| William A. Wieboldt House
639 W. Deming Pl.
1896, ROBERT C. BERLIN

The plain but vaguely Italian façade is topped by a deter-minedly German Baroque third-floor gable.

53| Jacob Gross House
632 W. Deming Pl.
1892, EDMUND R. KRAUSE

Krause prized the massiveness and geometries of the Queen

ST. CLEMENT ROMAN CATHOLIC CHURCH

Anne style, while eschewing its fussiness. This facade is a balance of squares and rectangles, topped by triangles and cones. The monochromatic palette quiets the clamor.

54| William Schmidt House
618 W. Deming Pl.
1889, FREDERICK FOEHRINGER

Tourelles on the third-floor dormer, a Classical cornice with modillions and brackets, a mansard roof, a rusticated stone facade, and Ionic porch columns create a house with an identity crisis.

55| Frederick J. Lange House
612 W. Deming Pl.
MID-1890S, THOMAS W. WING

The handsomest stone detailing on the street is on the porch parapet.

56| 546 W. Deming Pl.
(*Chateau VI*)
1968, JEROME SOLTAN

Ranging from banal to bruising, the curse of city neighborhoods in the 1960s and 1970s was the infamous four-plus-one, invented by Soltan in 1960. Here twenty-four apartments on four floors are squeezed onto a space that originally accommodated a single-family home. The ground-level parking is partially screened by decorative concrete blocks. All but filling the lot, the four-plus-one not only provides little light to the units on the sides and back but also cuts off light to neighboring buildings. They were never built with sufficient parking, and streets were clogged with the overflow cars. The lack of parking was their ultimate downfall.

57| William C. Groetzinger House
526 W. Deming Pl.
1895, FREDERICK B. TOWNSEND

Ponderous but comfortably cavelike and beautifully detailed, the Romanesque facade is Gothicized with pointed arches.

WILLIAM C. GROETZINGER HOUSE

58| 665 W. Wrightwood Ave.
1998, TADAO ANDO ARCHITECTS AND ASSOCS., BOOTH HANSEN ASSOCIATES, ASSOC. ARCHS.

The high quality of Ando's exacting concrete work is apparent in this, his first building in the United States. Typical of Ando's houses in Japan, this minimalist residence focuses inward and reveals nothing of its interior life to the street. The intensely private house occupies three lots, though close to half of that area is devoted to a walled garden with reflecting pool.

59| 439 W. Arlington Pl.
1908, ARCHITECT UNKNOWN

The owner of this Georgian house maintains the wooded lot to the west as a bird sanctuary, protected from development by an easement given to the Chicago Audubon Society.

60| William V. O'Brien House
426 W. Arlington Pl.
1894, FLANDERS & ZIMMERMAN

Built for an art dealer, this house is one of the city's most unusual for its era. The band of windows tucked under the eave was a favorite device of Frank Lloyd Wright, although it predates his use of the motif. The enormous dormer that continues the wall plane in an upward surge is also an anomaly, perhaps inspired by Adler & Sullivan's towered Victoria Hotel (1892) in Chicago Heights. The house is well preserved, al-

WILLIAM V. O'BRIEN HOUSE

though at some point (possibly in 1921) the front entrance was moved to the side, and the eastern arch was transformed from a door to a window.

61| 2430 N. Lakeview Ave.
1927, REBORI, WENTWORTH, DEWEY & MCCORMICK

Although Rebori's most distinctive work is his interpretation of the Deco and Moderne styles, he was also a fluent translator of the Georgian idiom so beloved of his wealthy clients. The horizontal separation of living spaces and bedrooms is evident in the window arrangement.

62| 2440 N. Lakeview Ave.
(*Lake View Avenue Apartments*)
1927, RISSMAN & HIRSCHFELD

Despite its frilly facade, six units per floor make for less luxury than in its more sober neighbors.

2440 N. LAKEVIEW AVE.

63| 2450 N. Lakeview Ave.
1924, HOWARD VAN DOREN SHAW

Servants lived on the second floor of this simplified Georgian building, which was designed with only one unit per floor. Shaw was one of the original owners, but he died only two years later at the age of fifty-six, having just been awarded the gold medal of the American Institute of Architects.

64| Joseph Theurer/Philip K. Wrigley House
2466 N. Lakeview Ave.
1897, RICHARD E. SCHMIDT

The monochromatic scheme of orange brick and terra cotta and the palazzo form have a kinship with Stanford White's Patterson-McCormick Mansion, but the asymmetrical bays and exaggerated quoins add a German neo-Classical flavor. This was Schmidt's first major commission.

65| 2474 N. Lakeview Ave.
1993, LOHAN ASSOCS.

The architects describe the elevation as "an abstract collage on which the spatial and constructive elements are realized." The most prominent element is a sinuous skylighted galleria that runs the length of the interior.

66| Marlborough Apartments
400 W. Deming Pl./2608 N. Lakeview Ave.
1923, ROBERT S. DEGOLYER

The clever massing and delicate Adamesque ornament diminish the bulk. Apartments on the Lakeview Ave. side were for the building's investors; the much smaller units on Deming Pl. were rented to others.

67| Francis J. Dewes House
503 W. Wrightwood Ave.
1896, CUDELL & HERCZ
1998, RENOVATION, HAMMOND BEEBY RUPERT AINGE

This Prussian confection can't decide whether to be neo-Classical, Baroque, or Rococo,

FRANCIS J. DEWES HOUSE

but it does succeed in being impressive. The rich carving includes statues supporting a balcony above the entrance.

68| Mrs. Arthur Ryerson House
2700 N. Lakeview Ave.
1917, DAVID ADLER

69| Abram Poole House
2704 N. Lakeview Ave.
1917, DAVID ADLER

70| Henry C. Dangler House
2708 N. Lakeview Ave.
1917, HENRY C. DANGLER

71| Ambrose C. Cramer House
2710 N. Lakeview Ave.
1917, AMBROSE C. CRAMER

Although designed by different architects, this cohesive block seems straight out of Georgian London—up to the cornice line, at least. The houses share an Adamesque sensibility in the details as well. Dangler was Adler's partner, and he stamped all of the construction drawings because Adler had never passed the engineering test needed to obtain an architect's license.

72| Elks National Memorial Building
2750 N. Lakeview Ave.
1923–1926, EGERTON SWARTWOUT
1967, MAGAZINE BUILDING, HOLABIRD & ROOT

This memorial to fallen Elks of World War I (rededicated after subsequent conflicts to include latter-day heroes) contains one of the city's grandest public spaces. The Memorial Rotunda is a riot of colored marble and mural painting, dazzling in opulence if not taste. Eugene Savage painted the enormous and rather cryptic murals here and in the reception room (on axis with the main entrance); Edwin H. Blashfield was responsible for the more subdued wall paintings in the small lobby between the two rooms. Adolph A. Weinman sculpted the gesticulating figures in the niches; James Earle Fraser was responsible for the sculpture in the entry vestibule; and Laura Gardin Fraser designed the life-size elks that flank the steps where they meet the sidewalk on Lakeview Ave. Weinman also designed the monumental bronzes in the pair of exterior niches.

73| Urantia Foundation
(*Sylvan Kunz Flats*)
533 W. Diversey Pkwy.
1908, FROMMANN & JEBSEN

Light-years from the firm's turgid, tourelled stone-front houses on Fullerton Ave. is this grand flat, the star of this graceless south-side stretch of

ELKS NATIONAL MEMORIAL BUILDING

URANTIA FOUNDATION

Diversey Pkwy. Lavish ornament grows out of the wall organically, recalling Art Nouveau and Jugendstil masters. The integration of the metal railing with the stone balcony is the jewel in the crown of this sculptured facade.

74| 2780 N. Lincoln Ave.
(*John E. Hufmeyer Building*)
1888, CHARLES F. HERMANN

The diagonal path of Lincoln Ave. creates dozens of six-point intersections that are a motorist's nightmare but provide high-visibility sites for storefronts. This mansard-roofed block is one of the city's most elaborate flatiron flats-above-shops buildings.

75| Embassy Club
Southport Ave., Greenview Ave., and Wrightwood Ave. just south of Diversey Pkwy.
1989–1992, PAPPAGEORGE/HAYMES
2609 & 2613 N. Greenview Ave.
1992, DIAMOND PHILLIPS

One of Chicago's grandest yupscale developments has narrow row houses grouped around cobbled streets. The elaborate facades feature the bay windows and lively street-wall rhythms of their Queen Anne ancestors but with a Georgian formality. The resulting Queen George amalgam conveys a Disneyland ambience of virtual reality, with none of the quirks or messiness—or vitality—of a true cityscape.

76| 2637 N. Greenview Ave.
1996, KRUECK & SEXTON ARCHITECTS

The modernist planes of brick and glass are a rebuke to the traditionalism of the surrounding Embassy Club. On the west elevation, a slot window extends as a continuous skylight across the roof. The interior offers an open plan centered around a two-story living space.

77| Altgeld Court
1300 W. Altgeld St.
1992, PAPPAGEORGE/HAYMES

Courtyards carved out of a one-story 1960s industrial building form the entries for new loftlike units. The original masonry building forms the perimeter walls of the complex. On the courtyard facades, corrugated galvanized siding and colorful canopies playfully reinterpret the industrial aesthetic.

78| Cortland St. Bridge
(*Clybourn Place Drawbridge*)
Cortland St. (1400 W.) at the Chicago River
1902, JOHN E. ERICSON, CITY ENG.; THOMAS G. PIHLFELDT, CITY BRIDGE ENG.

This was the nation's first trunnion bascule bridge. The leaves are hinged at the shore end on a trunnion, or shaft. Chicago's conception and execution of this type of bridge became a textbook example around the world.

Lincoln Park
Oak St. to Ardmore Ave.; Lake Michigan to N. Lake Shore Dr., N. Clark St., Lincoln Park West, Lakeview Ave., Lake Shore Dr., Marine Dr.
1865–1880S, SWAIN NELSON & OLAF BENSON
1903–1921, OSSIAN C. SIMONDS
1920S–1960, ERNST G. SCHROEDER
1936–1938, ALFRED CALDWELL

Chicago's largest and busiest park has more noteworthy features than any other and offers a variety of landscapes, buildings, and activities. It reflects more than a century of design and the work of many talents, but each succeeding designer knit his contributions into the existing fabric, resulting in an overall unity of appearance. The landscape also reflects a century of competing interests and ideas about how parkland should best be used.

Lincoln Park's history is unusually complex. Much of its 1,212 acres, which stretch along almost six miles of shoreline, were created from landfill. The southern section, from North to Webster Aves., comprised the municipal cemetery, established in 1837. The first area used as parkland was sixty vacant acres of the cemetery between Wisconsin St. and Webster Ave. As the population of surrounding neighborhoods increased, pressure grew to relocate the bodies for health reasons. In 1864 the Common Council prohibited the sale of burial plots and designated the land for a Lake Park, although reinterment in private cemeteries outside the city limits did not begin until 1871 and took three years to complete. In 1865 the park was renamed for the recently assassinated president, and three years later a zoo was established when New York City's Central Park donated two pairs of swans. In 1869 state legislation created the Lincoln Park Commission to manage the park and permitted its northward expansion.

Landscape gardener Swain Nelson drew up the first plan for the park in 1865. Its naturalistic style, derived from eighteenth-century French landscaping, featured small lawn areas outlined with winding pathways and interspersed with three ponds. The Waterfowl Lagoon in the Zoo is the principal surviving feature of his tenure. His colleague Olaf Benson took over as landscape gardener in 1870 and expanded on Nelson's plan to encompass the entire area from North Ave. to Diversey Pkwy., adding a few formal elements and the first park structures. The first landfills were created in the 1880s, including the narrow extension south of North Ave.

In 1903 Ossian C. Simonds began to promote a midwestern style of naturalistic landscaping inspired by the landforms, rock outcroppings, waterways, and native plants of the prairies. Simonds proposed extending the park all the way to Devon Ave., a mile past its present terminus, and during his tenure it grew north to Cornelia St.

Beginning in the 1920s engineer Ernst G. Schroeder directed the park's growth to its termination in 1957 at Ardmore Ave./Hollywood Beach. The newly created sections were laid out in a naturalistic style that incorporated interesting rockwork elements. The most important designer during this period was Alfred Caldwell, a disciple of landscape architect Jens Jensen. During his two-year tenure Caldwell brought the Prairie School spirit into the park, most dramatically in the Lily Pool. His work can also be seen in the broad open spaces defined by groves of hawthorn trees in the Montrose Point area.

The most dramatic changes since the 1950s have been made to accommodate the ever-increasing demands of the automobile. Wheeled traffic has been an issue since 1873, when a speed limit was established for the park's roadways; two years later a separate speeding track was built. Encroachment on park land began in earnest in 1938, when La Salle Dr. was extended through the park's south end. Lake Shore Dr. now cuts a wide swath through its entire length, separating the lakefront from the rest of the city. The many issues concerned with the use of Lincoln Park—cars vs. pedestrians, passive vs. active recreation, buildings vs. open space—continue to generate lively dialogue and inspire strong passions.   —JOAN POMARANC

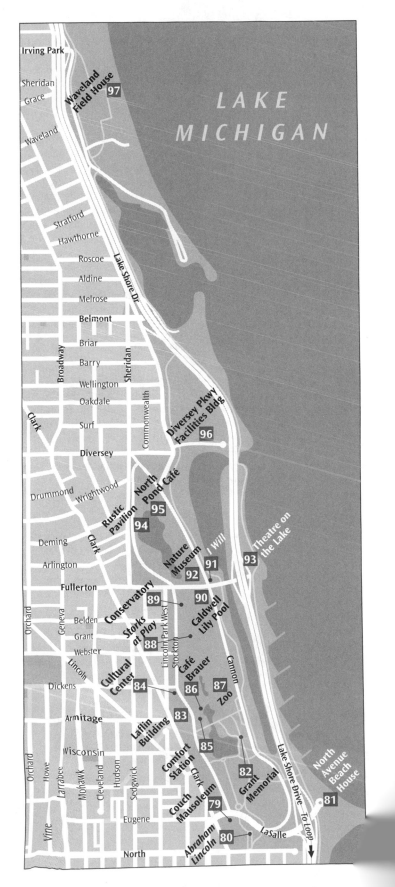

LINCOLN PARK

79| Couch Mausoleum
Northwest of *Abraham Lincoln*
1857–1858, JOHN VAN OSDEL

The only tomb left from the park's early days as the municipal cemetery is here because the family refused to move it. Construction excavations have uncovered adjacent remains unknowingly left behind.

80| *Abraham Lincoln*
("The Standing Lincoln")
East of the Chicago Historical Society
1887, AUGUSTUS SAINT-GAUDENS;
BASE AND EXEDRA MCKIM,
MEAD & WHITE

One of America's greatest nineteenth-century sculptures and widely considered Saint-Gaudens's most significant work, this imposing statue commands its handsome setting. The face and hands are based on life casts by sculptor Leonard W. Volk, but Saint-Gaudens had also seen Lincoln, once in life and when his body lay in state. The great orator is portrayed in the penultimate moment before a speech, as he gathers his thoughts to step forward and address the crowd.

ABRAHAM LINCOLN
("THE STANDING LINCOLN")

81| North Ave. Beach House
Lakefront at North Ave.
1999, G.E.C. DESIGN GROUP WITH
WHEELER KEARNS ARCHITECTS

When the popular 1939 beach house just north of this location had deteriorated to the point of necessitating its replacement, public sentiment was strongly in favor of a new facility that would capture the playful nautical spirit of the original. The new, more durable cast-in-place concrete "steamship" updates and reinterprets many original elements and adapts them to a larger scale. Elliptical "smokestacks," functional counterparts of the decorative originals, contain open-air stairs to the rooftop restaurant. Nautical imagery pops up in playful details throughout the building. The building's new siting relieves congestion and opens up vistas of the lake from North Ave.

82| Ulysses S. Grant Memorial
1891, LOUIS T. REBISSO; FRANCIS M.
WHITEHOUSE, ARCH.

The aesthetic quality of this ponderous monument has been the subject of debate since its unveiling. One early newspaper account called it suitable only for impressing country cousins.

83| Matthew Laflin Memorial Building
(Chicago Academy of Sciences)
2001 N. Clark St.
1893, PATTON & FISHER
1996, RENOVATION FOR OFFICES,
SOLOMON CORDWELL BUENZ &
ASSOCS.

The building is named after the pioneer businessman who provided this Renaissance Revival home for Chicago's oldest museum, founded in 1857 to promote knowledge of the region's natural history. That museum became the Notebaert Nature Museum.

84| Lincoln Park Recreation & Cultural Arts Center
2045 N. Lincoln Park West
1927, EDWIN H. CLARK

This Georgian Revival building recalls the architect's contemporaneous work for the Lincoln Park Zoo.

85 | Comfort Station
(*Carlson Cottage*)
Stockton Dr. southwest of Café Brauer
1888, JOSEPH LYMAN SILSBEE

One of the earliest park structures, it was first identified as Men's and Ladies' Cottage. Inappropriate alterations and loss of the berm into which its north side originally nestled have diminished the appearance of this picturesque structure.

86 | Café Brauer
(*South Pond Refectory*)
2021 N. Stockton Dr.
1908, PERKINS & HAMILTON
1989, RENOVATION, LAWRENCE B. BERKLEY & ASSOCS.; MEISEL & ASSOCS.; WISS, JANNEY, ELSTNER ASSOCS.

On the banks of the South Pond the Lincoln Park Commission constructed a new refectory financed by restaurateurs Paul and Caspar Brauer. The building is a masterpiece of designer Dwight H. Perkins, a leader of the Prairie School.

The massing includes a large closed central pavilion flanked by two graciously curving loggias. A broad expanse of green tile roof with deep overhangs, combined with earthy red brick, subtle terra-cotta details, and polychromatic mortar, settles the building into the landscape. Viewed from Stockton Dr. to the west, the large block of the central pavilion dominates, while the curving loggias recede. But on the lagoon side the main pavilion is opened up with large expanses of glass, and the two loggias are seen to wrap around the end of the pond. Simultaneously the loggias contain the water, and the lagoon's form controls their curves.

The centerpiece of the building is the Great Hall, located on the second floor of the pavilion. It is accessed from a lobby that has low ceilings and rich, earth-toned colors. At the top of the stair the Great Hall rises thirty-four feet to the peak of the skylight that bathes the room in sunlight. The large glass doors on the lagoon side also provide soothing natural light to the room. Two art-glass chandeliers hang from the trusses. The walls are buff speckled brick, and Rookwood mosaics enhance recessed corner alcoves and a musicians' gallery. From the loggias, which open off the Great Hall, the skyline unfolds to the south.

The café was a favored establishment during its early years and throughout Prohibition. The dining room fell into decline, however, after repeal, because state law forbade the sale of liquor in the parks. The Great Hall closed in 1941, and throughout the late 1950s and 1960s the space was used as a winter theater.

CAFÉ BRAUER

Not until legislation in 1989 permitted the sale of liquor at Café Brauer could a viable restoration plan be undertaken. At that time the clay tile roof and skylight, which both had been removed in the 1940s, were reinstalled; the original wall sconces, which were also missing, were reproduced; and all the original paint colors were re-created. The two chandeliers, which had hung in place throughout the hall's incarnations, remarkably required only cleaning and minor repairs. They are the centerpieces of that room as restored to its original elegance.

Café Brauer is an outstanding example of the Prairie School style in a public building.

—WILLIAM W. TIPPENS

---

87 | Lincoln Park Zoo
Armitage to Fullerton Aves., Stockton to Cannon Drs.

Early zoo buildings, little more than decorative cages for the separation of species, evolved into settings designed to appropriately frame the animal for human eyes. Modern design stresses the re-creation of natural habitats with human intrusion kept to a minimum. The beasts in the beautifully detailed **Lion House** *(1912, Perkins, Fellows & Hamilton; 1986, renovation, Hammond, Beeby & Babka)* had indoor and outdoor quarters, not just for their own comfort but to increase their visibility. The Georgian Revival architecture popular in the 1920s is represented by the **Reptile House** *(Aquarium & Fish Hatchery, 1923; renovation 1998, Valerio Dewalt Train)* and **Primate House** *(Small Animal House, 1927)*, both by Edwin H. Clark and renovated by John Macsai & Assocs. in 1984 and 1992, respectively. The **McCormick Bird House** *(1900, Jarvis Hunt)* has been completely renovated to house naturalistic habitats. The **Waterfowl Lagoon** *(1865, Swain Nelson; 1978, renovation, Chicago Park District)* re-creates the naturalistic landscape planned by the park's original designer.

In the 1990s the zoo undertook a major building campaign to provide more visitor services. Entrance from the Cannon Dr. parking lot is through the whimsical **Entrance Gate** by David Woodhouse Architects. On the north side of the landscaped plaza are the **Gateway Pavilion** (1995, Kathryn Quinn) and the **Mahon-Theobald Pavilion** (1999, Valerio Dewalt Train), which houses the Wild Things! Gift Shop and Big Cats Café. A new bridge (1996, Teng & Assocs.) spans the Swan Pond. A new **Ape House** by Lohan Caprile Goettsch is expected to open in 2005.

WILD THINGS! GIFT SHOP

88 | *Storks at Play*
(The Bates Fountain)
1887, AUGUSTUS SAINT-GAUDENS AND FREDERICK WILLIAM MACMONNIES

Saint-Gaudens received this commission together with that for the *Standing Lincoln*, which so absorbed him that he called upon a former student to work on the fountain. He later gave MacMonnies primary credit for this popular work.

89 | Lincoln Park Conservatory
Stockton Dr. between Belden Ave. and Fullerton Pkwy.
1894, JOSEPH LYMAN SILSBEE, ASSISTED BY MIFFLIN E. BELL

The Crystal Palace–inspired conservatory (its entrance was enlarged in the 1950s) overlooks a formal French garden to the south and an English-style perennial garden on the west, across Stockton Dr. Both gardens have been in place at least since 1887.

90 | Alfred Caldwell Lily Pool
Fullerton Pkwy. between Stockton and Cannon Drs.

1937, ALFRED CALDWELL
2001–2002; RESTORATION, CHICAGO PARK DISTRICT AND THE FRIENDS OF LINCOLN PARK; WOLFF CLEMENTS AND ASSOCS., LANDSCAPE ARCH; EIFLER & ASSOCS., ARCH.

Caldwell redesigned a Victorian lily pool to evoke the midwestern landscape by way of Japan and the Prairie School, with stratified stonework, a wooden pavilion, and native plants. After years of overuse and insensitive maintenance, a $2.5 million rehabilitation brought Caldwell's vision back to life. Non-native invasive trees and plants were replaced with native prairie and woodland plants. Trees, shrubs, and grasses now protect from erosion, enabling the removal of slabs of concrete and stone. A council ring, a favorite element of both Caldwell and Jens Jensen, adds seating for conversation and contemplation. The Lily Pool

once again takes its place as one of the loveliest pockets of nature in the city.

91 | *I Will*
Cannon Dr. at Fullerton Pkwy.

1981, ELLSWORTH KELLY

The park's first contemporary sculpture honors Chicago's unofficial motto of the 1890s, recalling the rebuilding after the Fire of 1871.

92 | Peggy Notebaert Nature Museum
2430 N. Cannon Dr.

1999, PERKINS & WILL

The color and angular massing are meant to recall the shifting sand dunes that earlier occupied the site. The building is composed of a series of paths, some breaking through the wall to be exterior walkways, layered atop one another. Large expanses of glass emphasize the close relationship of building to landscape.

93 | Theatre on the Lake
(*Chicago Daily News* **Fresh Air Sanitarium**)
Lakefront northeast of Lake Shore Dr. and Fullerton Pkwy.

1920, PERKINS, FELLOWS & HAMILTON

Major changes to Lake Shore Dr. and Fullerton Pkwy. in 1937 necessitated significant

ALFRED CALDWELL LILY POOL

alterations to this Prairie School structure, later remodeled into a theater.

94| Rustic Pavilion
Lakeview Ave. at St. James Pl.
1883, MIFFLIN E. BELL

An artesian well once briefly bubbled up nearby. The site's naturalness has been obscured, but the structure has been restored to its original color. The Adirondack twig detailing recalls a bygone era of pleasure grounds and picturesque vistas.

95| North Pond Café
(*Warming House*)
2610 N. Cannon Dr.
1914, PERKINS, FELLOWS & HAMILTON
1998 AND 2002, CONVERSION TO RESTAURANT, NANCY WARREN

This warming shelter for skaters was set into the slope of the landscape and given a flat roof and very simple facade. It now has a new life as an Arts & Crafts–style restaurant.

96| Diversey Pkwy. Facilities Building and Driving Range
(*Golf Course Shelter*)
Diversey Pkwy. east of Lake Shore Dr. West
1916, 1919, ANDREW N. REBORI
1998, DRIVING RANGE, DESTEFANO AND PARTNERS

Originally open to the golf course, the north side of the shelter was filled in by Rebori's expansion.

At the north end of Lincoln Park is one of Clark's finest park buildings.

97| Waveland Field House
(*Refectory*)
East of Lake Shore Dr. opposite Waveland Ave.
1932, EDWIN H. CLARK

The Collegiate Gothic field house includes a clock tower with the Wolford Memorial Chimes. In 1992 a dedicated group of volunteers finished restoring the long-silent chimes and the clock's immobile hands.

LAKEVIEW/RAVENSWOOD/UPTOWN

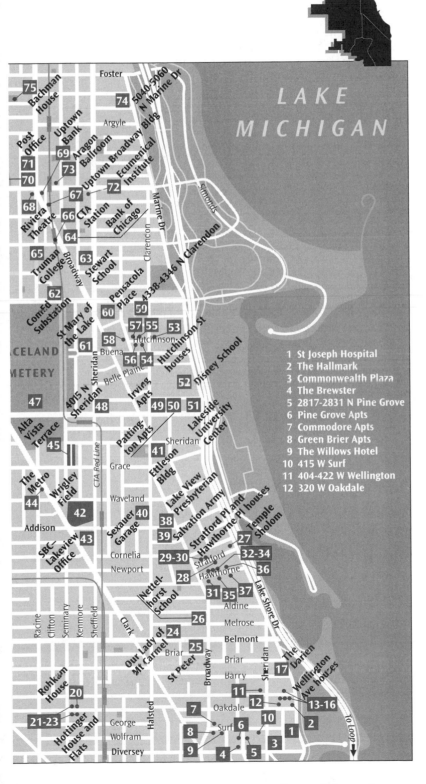

LAKE MICHIGAN

75 Bachman House
Foster
74 5040-5060 N Marine Dr
Argyle
Post Office
Uptown Bank
69 Aragon Ballroom
71 73 Uptown Broadway Bldg
70 Ecumenical Institute
67 72
68 Riviera Theatre
66 CTA Station
64 Bank of Chicago
Marine Dr
Simonds
Clarendon
65 Truman College
63 Stewart School
Broadway
62 ComEd Substation
Pensacola Place
St Mary of the Lake
60 50 4338-4346 N Clarendon
57 55 53
58 Hutchinson St
LACELAND CEMETERY
61 Buena
56 54 Hutchinson St houses
Belle Plaine
52 Disney School
47 Irving Apts
4015 N Sheridan
Sheridan
48 49 50 51
Lakeside University Center
Alta Vista Terrace
Patting-ton Apts
45
CTA Red Line
Sheridan
41 Ettleson Bldg
Grace
Lake View Presbyterian
The Metro
Wrigley Field
Waveland
44
Salvation Army
42
Sexauer Garage
40
Stratford Pl and Hawthorne Pl houses
Addison
38
27 Temple Sholom
SBC–Lakeview Office
43
39
Cornelia
29-30 Stratford
32-34
28 Hawthorne
36
Newport
Nettel-horst School
31 35 37
Aldine
26 Melrose
Racine
Clifton
Seminary
Kenmore
Sheffield
Clark
Our Lady of Mt Carmel
24
25
Briar
Belmont
St Peter
Briar
Barry
Sheridan
The Darien
17
Broadway
Lake Shore Dr
11 Wellington Ave houses
Rohken House
20
12
13-16
21-23
Hottinger House and Flats
George
Wolfram
Halsted
7 Oakdale
8 Surf
6
10
1
2
9
4
5
3
Diversey

1 St Joseph Hospital
2 The Hallmark
3 Commonwealth Plaza
4 The Brewster
5 2817-2831 N Pine Grove
6 Pine Grove Apts
7 Commodore Apts
8 Green Brier Apts
9 The Willows Hotel
10 415 W Surf
11 404-422 W Wellington
12 320 W Oakdale

LAKEVIEW/RAVENSWOOD/UPTOWN

THE NORTH SIDE COMMUNITIES OF LAKEVIEW, UPTOWN, AND RAVENSWOOD carved themselves over time out of a much larger government entity, the township of Lake View. When organized in 1857 Lake View Township extended north from Fullerton Ave. to Devon Ave. and from the lake to Western Ave. Today the name Lakeview survives only for the neighborhood from Diversey Pkwy. to Addison St. Communities to its north include Wrigleyville (Addison to Irving Park Rd.), Buena Park (east and west of Graceland Cemetery), Uptown (north of Montrose Ave.), and Ravenswood (west of Ashland Ave. from Addison to Lawrence Ave.). The history of the area can be divided easily into the nineteenth-century saga of Lake View Township and the twentieth-century stories of the individual communities.

Throughout the nineteenth century Lake View Township resembled the garden in Chicago's motto, *Urbs in Horto* (City in a Garden). Farms dominated the landscape to the west, and country estates lined the lakefront. In 1836 Conrad Sulzer established a farm near the present intersection of Clark St. and Montrose Ave., and the truck farmers who followed his lead made Lake View Township the center of the Midwest's greenhouse industry and the nation's largest shipper of celery.

Along the lakeshore developers James B. Rees and Elisha E. Hundley acquired 225 acres between Belmont Ave. and Irving Park Rd. in 1852. Two years later they opened a first-class lakefront hotel, the Lake View House. When the state of Illinois conferred township status on the area three years later, Lake View became the first North Side community named for a resort hotel. Rees and Hundley subdivided their acres into spacious residential lots, and wealthy Chicagoans, such as real estate investor Samuel H. Kerfoot, laid out beautifully landscaped lakefront estates that attracted visitors from miles around. To the west in Ravenswood other developers built frame houses near the Chicago & North Western right-of-way to attract families displaced by the Chicago Fire of 1871. Beer gardens in the vicinities of Clark and Diversey and Broadway and Lawrence, and a baseball park at Sheffield and Addison placed an emphasis on outdoor entertainments.

Lake View Township went out of existence in 1889, when annexation by Chicago brought improved municipal services and increasing urbanization. Lakeview developed a split personality as early frame houses remained concentrated west of Halsted St. while graystone and brick houses, flats, and apartments predominated to the east. Pockets of spacious homes, such as those found at Buena and Sheridan parks, continued to bear witness to the area's suburban origins, even after elegant 1920s apartments filled Sheridan Rd. Outdoor amusements now centered on Riverview Amusement Park at Belmont and Western and National League baseball at Wrigley Field. In Ravenswood the residential neighborhoods were pierced by an industrial corridor along the railroad line.

The pace of urbanization accelerated northward to Wilson Ave. after 1900, along with new elevated train service. By the 1920s the area around Wilson and Broadway had been christened Uptown, a name that reflected the glamour and urbanity of a vibrant commercial and entertainment district. Uptown never really recovered from the Depression. Its famous movie palaces and dance halls went dark and poverty overtook its once-fashionable neighborhoods. Although it continued to attract weekend crowds of the young and the restless, for decades Uptown lagged ever further behind adjacent neighborhoods. Private renewal began slowly in the 1980s, just as the area began to benefit from the vitality that immigrants invest into port-of-entry neighborhoods.

Postwar construction initially concentrated on the ever-desirable lakefront, creating canyons of concrete high rises and infill pockets of "four-plus-one" apartments. The 1990s tear-down mania latched onto the miles of aging frame dwellings in all of the communities. Density soared everywhere as new multiple units, often keeping something of the high-stooped look of the early houses, packed the lots of lost single-family homes.

—MARY ALICE MOLLOY

ST. JOSEPH HOSPITAL

1 | St. Joseph Hospital
2900 N. Lake Shore Dr.
1963, BELLI & BELLI

Forgive the blue walls with their diamond-shaped windows and the dark glass cylinder that hangs like a uvula from the front. The eleventh-floor Dan Ryan Memorial Chapel, open every day, is a great treat. It may be the city's most perfectly preserved 1960s interior, from the mosaic-lined, concrete baldachin to the pointy-legged altar furniture. Architects would like to think the 1960s looked like Mies's Federal Center, but this is what that era *really* looked like.

2 | The Hallmark
2960 N. Lake Shore Dr.
1990, JOHN MACSAI & ASSOCS.

Competing with St. Joseph Hospital in the aggressive-palette category is this red brick high rise banded in glossy blue and white. The sill line of this upscale residence for the elderly dips down to twenty inches in the living room bays to provide views for those in a chair or wheelchair.

Walk this densely built lakefront neighborhood from Diversey Ave. to Wellington Ave. to see a variety of Chicago housing types from the 1890s to now.

3 | Commonwealth Plaza
(Commonwealth Promenade Apartments)
330–340 W. Diversey Pkwy.
1953–1956, LUDWIG MIES VAN DER ROHE; FRIEDMAN, ALSCHULER & SINCERE, ASSOC. ARCHS.

This is curtain-wall modernism in full stride. The project was commissioned by developer Herbert S. Greenwald, Mies's early and influential client, whose death in 1959 halted

COMMONWEALTH PLAZA

development of two additional towers planned for the site. The glass-and-aluminum skin is suspended in front of the columns, which comprise two different structural systems (reinforced concrete on the lower floors and steel above). The space between the columns and the skin contains vertical ventilation shafts, allowing for more efficient heating and cooling than in Mies's previous buildings.

4| The Brewster
(*Lincoln Park Palace*)
2800 N. Pine Grove Ave.
1893, ENOCH HILL TURNOCK
1972, RENOVATION, MIEKI HAYANO

It looks like a brooding high-rise armory from the outside, but beg your way indoors to see the "sky lobby," a fantasy in steel and glass block. Every apartment opens onto a gabled, skylighted court. Turnock's early years in the office of William Le Baron Jenney may account for

THE BREWSTER

the steel frame and the atrium design, which resembles bridge construction. The rugged "Jasper stone" (quartzite) walls set off an outstanding Sullivanesque terra-cotta frieze on the top floor. The polished granite entry on Pine Grove Ave. was originally the ladies' entrance.

5| 2817–2831 N. Pine Grove Ave.
1891, OSTLING BROS.

The use of a uniform building material increases the apparent size of the units, while varied bay shapes, rooflines, and stone cuts provide individuality.

6| Pine Grove Manor Apartments
(*Pine Grove Apartment Hotel*)
2828 N. Pine Grove Ave.
1924, LOEWENBERG & LOEWENBERG

Upper-class vintage apartment buildings frequently have re-markably understated entrances, to downplay the communal nature of the accommodations. But apartment hotels, which offered dining, recreation, and other services, flaunted their congregate nature. Playing up the grand public spaces, an octagonal entry pavilion leads to an enormous lobby, and an ornate belt course separates the monumental and heavily detailed first floor (which contained the public spaces) from the private residential floors above.

7| Commodore Apartments
550–568 W. Surf St.
1897, EDMUND R. KRAUSE
1985, RENOVATION, NAKAWATASE,
RUTKOWSKI, WYNS & YI

This exemplary Chicago School apartment building owes as much to the skyscrapers of Holabird & Roche as to the flats of the era. A massive building, it is broken into smaller blocks to increase ventilation and light. The Roman brick facade is crisply edged and sparingly ornamented, with oculi at the top story and an Ionic temple front entrance.

COMMODORE APARTMENTS

8| Green Brier Apartments
559–561 W. Surf St.
1904, EDMUND R. KRAUSE
1985, RENOVATION, ARCHITECTS
INTERNATIONAL—CHICAGO

Familiar from the Commodore are the temple front entrance and the use of Roman brick, but the flat facades—with their pox of brackets—are repetitious by comparison.

9| The Willows Hotel
555 W. Surf St.
1925, RISSMAN & HIRSCHFELD

Behind the ornate terra-cotta facade is an apartment hotel shaped like a bowling alley: the footprint is 36′ x 216′!

10| 415 W. Surf St.
1910, SAMUEL N. CROWEN

Crowen was more successful than most in marrying Prairie School detailing to apartment-house formulas. This brick three-flat has Wrightian geometric decoration and an unusual stepped elevation ending in a large square bay.

11| 404–422 W. Wellington Ave.
1939, LOEBL & SCHLOSSMAN

The enduring desirability of this lakefront community called for the successful reintroduction of a decades-old housing type, the row house. These ten stream-lined Lannon stone examples, each with from five to seven rooms, are densely packed on the site. The courtyard is an important amenity, made private by its half-story elevation from the street.

12| 320 W. Oakdale Ave.
1953, MILTON M. SCHWARTZ

The concrete overhangs of this high rise, which make the building look like a stack of plates, were designed to control heat gain and prevent rain infiltration. Charitable observers call it a hybrid of Mies van der Rohe and Frank Lloyd Wright.

On this short block of Wellington Ave. are elegant single-family houses dating from the 1920s. This area developed later than the Gold Coast because much of the land east of Sheridan Rd. between Diversey and Belmont Aves. had been created by an ongoing process of filling in the shoreline. In the early twentieth century, Lincoln Park expanded north of Diversey, and the streets immediately to the west filled up with stately homes in fashionable revival styles.

13| Arthur H. Apfel House
341 W. Wellington Ave.
1925, E. H. FROMMANN

14| Oscar Mayer Houses
333 & 335 W. Wellington Ave.
1926, RISSMAN & HIRSCHFELD

15| Philip T. Starck House
330 W. Wellington Ave.
1925, MAYO & MAYO

16| Lester Armour House
325 W. Wellington Ave.
1915, HOWARD VAN DOREN SHAW
1925, REMODELING,
HOWARD VAN DOREN SHAW

ARTHUR H. APFEL HOUSE

PHILIP T. STARCK HOUSE

These houses are as substantial and bourgeois as their owners, bastions of the business community. Individual but not eccentric, they exude fine craftsmanship while blending nicely in the streetscape. Starck's French neo-Classical house is the most elegant; Apfel's Tudor Revival, the most charming.

17| The Darien
(*Darien Apartment House*)
3100 N. Lake Shore Dr. West
1948–1951, LOEBL, SCHLOSSMAN & BENNETT

Bennett folded the masonry curtain wall like paper, arranging the floor plans to maximize lake views. The metal-framed windows are laid almost flush with the brick, emphasizing the wall's thinness.

Farther west in Lake View were more ethnic neighborhoods. Two reminders of the large German community still stand on Southport Ave.

18| Schuba's
3159 N. Southport Ave.
1903, FROMMANN & JEBSEN

At the turn of the century, the Joseph Schlitz Brewing Company bought many corner lots and built its own saloons in order to increase its market share and ensure maximum distribution. A busy street in a German neighborhood was a prize location. Vice president Edward G. Uihlein purchased

the properties and hired the architects. Although no emphasis was placed on unique design, the Schlitz trademark, the terra-cotta globe, was always prominent on the facade.

19| St. Alphonsus Roman Catholic Church
2950 N. Southport Ave.
1889–1897, ADAM BOOS AND JOSEPH BETTINGHOFER, SCHRADER & CONRADI

The unusual central placement of the large tower follows a German Gothic precedent that was later translated to a smaller scale in nineteenth-century English parish churches. The small lantern windows high atop the roof were a popular feature in nineteenth-century German neo-Gothic churches. In the nave, a steel support system with exposed rivets tops the ornate decor.

ST. ALPHONSUS ROMAN CATHOLIC CHURCH

From 1048 to 1059 W. Oakdale Ave. is "Terra-Cotta Row," a group of houses and flats built for executives of the Northwestern Terra Cotta Company. Established in 1877, the company opened a large plant at Clybourn and Wrightwood Aves. in 1883 and became a leader in the booming industry of architectural ornament.

20| Henry Rohkam House
1048 W. Oakdale Ave.
1887, THEODORE KARLS

Built for one of the founders of Northwestern Terra Cotta, this exuberant brick house and ornate fence display the company's products with great flair. A full range of wares is on display, from small geometric stock prices to elaborately sculpted plaques, tympana, and chimney pots. The wild eclecticism of the ornament is held in check by a monochromatic color scheme. Don't miss the relief of a woman at a spinning wheel on the west side.

HENRY ROHKAM HOUSE

21| Gustav Hottinger House
1054 W. Oakdale Ave.
1886, JULIUS H. HUBER

This more modest house, built for Northwestern's founder and president, has been substantially altered but retains a terracotta panel at the peak of the gable and volutes bracketing the east window.

22| Adolph Hottinger Flat
1057 W. Oakdale Ave.
1916, MORITZ F. STRAUCH

23| Gustav Hottinger Flat
1059 W. Oakdale Ave.
1901, THEODORE ANDRESEN

Terra-cotta's ability to ape any material in any style made it equally appropriate for the banded Ionic columns at 1059 and the geometric ornament on 1057.

24| Our Lady of Mt. Carmel Roman Catholic Church
700 W. Belmont Ave.
1914, EGAN & PRINDEVILLE

An imposing English Gothic edifice of Indiana limestone, this rib-vaulted Catholic church has two organs and frequently hosts concerts of sacred and modern music. The reredos behind the altar continues the Gothic vocabulary in a backdrop for statues of the four evangelists.

25| St. Peter's Episcopal Church
615 W. Belmont Ave.
1895, WILLIAM A. OTIS

This small and beautifully detailed structure looks like the top stories of a regulation-sized church, but it is whole and complete according to the architect's plans.

26| Louis Nettelhorst Public School
3252 N. Broadway
1892, JOHN J. FLANDERS
1911, ARTHUR F. HUSSANDER

The public schools' Queen Anne period was shaped by Flanders, who between 1884 and 1893 designed over fifty projects for the Board of Education. His earliest formula was gloomy and Flemish-gabled, but after William Carbys Zimmerman joined him in practice in 1886 his designs brightened, with lively ornament and larger, more varied windows. Flanders's portion faces Broadway; its polygonal forms and bands of ornament typify Chicago's public school of the early 1890s. Hussander's addition defers to the original.

27| Temple Sholom
3480 N. Lake Shore Dr.
1930, LOEBL, SCHLOSSMAN & DEMUTH AND COOLIDGE & HODGDON

Loebl, Schlossman & Demuth conceived this project while in graduate school at the Armour Institute. Byzantine in inspiration, the octagonal limestone synagogue is elaborately ornamented with friezes, ornate column capitals, and a portal with stained-glass windows over three-paneled doors. The sanctuary is illuminated with indirect light, and a movable wall doubles the seating capacity.

28| Albert B. Towers House
551 W. Stratford Pl.
1894, GEORGE W. MAHER

A great gambrel roof and enormous boulders at ground level hint at the rustic grandeur of this much altered house.

29| George M. Harvey House
600 W. Stratford Pl.
1888, ADLER & SULLIVAN

Though greatly altered, this is of interest as one of only two frame houses designed by Adler & Sullivan.

30| 606 W. Stratford Pl.
1912, HUEHL & SCHMID

This is a two-flat masquerading as an urbane single-family house. The monochromatic color scheme suits the severity of the pared-down facade, which seems to anticipate the angular crispness of Art Deco architecture.

Hawthorne Pl. between Broadway and Lake Shore Dr.

Subdivided in 1883 by John and Benjamin F. McConnell, this tree-lined street is a rare and cohesive remnant of the single-family-house district that once stretched for miles along the lakefront.

31| Nicholas J. Sheridan House
587 W. Hawthorne Pl.
1906, BORST & HETHERINGTON

The battered sides, art glass, and balcony roof with exposed supports are all Craftsman touches.

32| Alfons Bacon House
580 W. Hawthorne Pl.
1937, MAYO & MAYO

This house presents an elegant Art Deco interpretation of the Georgian style.

33| George E. Marshall House
574 W. Hawthorne Pl.
1886, BURNHAM & ROOT
1896, ADDITION, ARCHITECT UNKNOWN
1938, ALTERATIONS, ARCHITECT UNKNOWN

The original Queen Anne design is visible only in the half-timbered third-floor gables. Subsequent alterations, such as the pedimented front door and Palladian window, were mostly Classical Revival.

34| Benjamin F. McConnell House
568 W. Hawthorne Pl.
1884; 1887, REMODELING, GEORGE BEAUMONT
1987, ADDITION, SCHROEDER MURCHIE LAYA

The oldest house on the block has been spectacularly transformed by the rear addition of a fun house for people and plants. Inside this luxuriously modern version of a Victorian conservatory are a swimming pool and a hot tub.

BENJAMIN F. MCCONNELL HOUSE

35| Herman H. Hettler House
567 W. Hawthorne Pl.
1892, JOSEPH LYMAN SILSBEE
1899, ADDITION AND REMODELING, JULIUS H. HUBER

This lavish Queen Anne, built by a wealthy lumber merchant, is pierced and anchored by a great round bay.

36| John McConnell House
546 W. Hawthorne Pl.
1885, ARCHITECT UNKNOWN

This brick and limestone villa with rotated corner bay seems like the city cousin of the rambling clapboard house at 568.

CHICAGO CITY DAY SCHOOL

37 | Chicago City Day School Additions
541 W. Hawthorne Pl.
1990 AND 1997, WEESE LANGLEY WEESE

The clock tower and low canopy create a modest civic presence and an inviting entrance. An addition to a classroom facility built in 1969 and 1973, the building was sited on the rear of the property to lessen the impact on the residential streetscape. The architects expanded the school westward again in 1997, this time matching the brick of the earliest buildings in order to bracket and emphasize the central stone facade.

38 | Lake View Presbyterian Church
716 W. Addison St.
1888, BURNHAM & ROOT

This simple Shingle Style structure—now unfortunately sided—has a high pitched roof and octagonal tower with conical steeple. Built shortly before the annexation of Lake View, it features the wood frame construction that had been prohibited in Chicago after the Fire. In the 1890s the church was enlarged, shifting the axis to north–south.

39 | Salvation Army College for Officers' Training
(*Joseph E. Tilt House*)
700 W. Brompton Ave.
1914, HOLABIRD & ROCHE

This grand Tudor Revival mansion, built for the owner of a shoe company, has been almost obscured by later buildings and a brick wall.

40 | Sexauer Garage
3640 N. Halsted St.
1924, DAVID SAUL KLAFTER

The winged wheel in polychrome terra-cotta is both advertising and decoration.

41 | Isaac G. Ettleson Building
3837–3845 N. Broadway
1911, HARRY HALE WATERMAN

Wingtip to wingtip, terra-cotta eagles flap in formation across the top of this otherwise typical retail and office building.

ISAAC G. ETTLESON BUILDING

42 | Wrigley Field
(*Weeghman Park*)
1060 W. Addison St.
1914, ZACHARY TAYLOR DAVIS

Chicago's beloved "Cubs Park" is the oldest surviving National League ballpark and one of the few survivors of baseball's golden age (1910–1925). Key features from that era include the use of permanent materials (steel and concrete instead of wood); large seating capacity (usually over 10,000); post-and-beam construction, which allowed spectators to be close to the action; and an urban context that frequently determined the dimensions of the playing field (as was the case here). Davis had designed several other ballparks (including Chicago's demolished original Comiskey Park), and his knowledge and foresight facilitated the park's constant enlargements and remodelings. Little of the original structure remains visible, but Wrigley still has the ambience of an old-time ballpark, offering views of surrounding three-flats instead of parking lots.

43 | SBC—Lakeview Office
(*Chicago Telephone Company—Lakeview Office*)
3532 N. Sheffield Ave.
1914, HOLABIRD & ROCHE

In the early twentieth century Holabird & Roche developed a generic Georgian brick box to house telephone switching equipment throughout Chicago and its suburbs. This example is less altered than most, with a pedimented entrance and simple limestone lintels, cornice, and base.

44 | The Metro
(*Northside Auditorium Building*)
3730 N. Clark St.
1928, MICHAELSEN & ROGNSTAD

Spanish Baroque Revival, with its exotic connotations and exuberant ornament, was the style of choice for many Roaring Twenties entertainment halls.

45 | Alta Vista Terrace
3800 block of N. Alta Vista Terr.
1904, JOSEPH C. BROMPTON

This tiny street is well worth the circuitous route needed to reach it. Alta Vista Terrace was one of the last real estate developments of Samuel Eberly Gross, a prominent developer of working-class housing during the 1880s and 1890s. Inspired by a European sojourn, Gross recreated the character of London row houses on newly purchased land. As with Georgian terraces, the street wall is designed as a unit—but with a wealth of contrasts in color, rooflines, and stylistic detail. Twenty small row houses on each side of the narrow street create an intimate streetscape; the designs are mirrored diagonally across the block. All are two-story buildings of Roman brick except for a quartet of three-story graystones in the center. In 1971 Alta Vista Terrace was designated Chicago's first historic district.

ALTA VISTA TERRACE

LAKEVIEW HIGH SCHOOL

46| Lakeview High School
4015 N. Ashland Ave.
1898, NORMAND S. PATTON
1916, ARTHUR F. HUSSANDER
1939, JOHN C. CHRISTENSEN

The influence of Oxford and Cambridge is evident in American college and university designs of the 1890s (see University of Chicago). This magnificent complex, intended to emulate the style and quality of a university building, was Chicago's first public high school in the Tudor style. Patton's design comprises the section running from the gatehouse tower (with 1898 carved above the entry) north to the center of the block, it was an addition to a building (now demolished) on Irving Park Rd. Patton's design was echoed by Hussander's quarter blocks to the north and south; note especially the fine doorway on Irving Park Rd. The extreme northern quarter came last. Gables, crenellated towers, ornamentation, and fenestration create a unified whole.

47| Graceland Cemetery
4001 N. Clark St.
These 121 acres were a rural area when the cemetery was founded in 1860 by Thomas B. Bryan, a lawyer and real estate investor who received a state charter in 1861 exempting the property from condemnation for public purposes. The first designers were William Saunders, who also worked at Rosehill, assisted by Swain Nelson and followed by Horace W. S. Cleveland, who may also have worked on the design for Oak Woods Cemetery. Bryan's nephew, Bryan Lathrop, served for many years as president and was a self-taught naturalist. Under his influence, architects William Le Baron Jenney and Ossian Cole Simonds were brought in to improve the site in 1878. Simonds decided to devote his practice to landscape design and was superintendent from 1881 until his death in 1931. His harmonious settings using native flora presaged the Prairie School Movement. —JOAN POMARANC

Holabird & Roche designed the **A| Entrance Gates and Fence** as well as the adjacent **B| Administration Building and Waiting Room** in 1896. The firm received many commissions at Graceland from Simonds, who had been a founding partner of the architecture firm in 1880. Eifler & Assocs. designed the renovation of the Waiting Room in 2002 and the Administration Building in 2003.

C| Howard Van Doren Shaw designed his family plot with a tall central column and separate stones for the families of two of his daughters. A traditionalist in his architectural work, Shaw created a flat-sided column

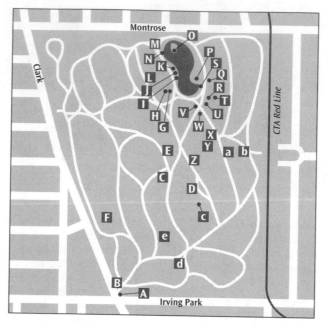

topped by a bronze ball, cast with the words of the Twenty-third Psalm.

The rusticated red granite **D| Chapel and Mortuary Crypt** was designed by Holabird & Roche and constructed in 1888 (with several later additions). Adjacent to the chapel is a columbarium and fountain completed in 1996, the work of architect Eifler & Assocs. and landscape architect Wolff Clements and Assocs., who have collaborated on many improvements at the cemetery since the early 1990s. Look for the plaque marking the interment of **Marion Mahony Griffin,** designed by Eifler and incorporating a flower copied from one of her renderings for Frank Lloyd Wright. Along with her husband, Walter Burley Griffin, and her cousin, Dwight H. Perkins, Marion Griffin was an architect of the Prairie School movement, known for her beautiful Japanese-influenced drawings.

E| William A. Hulbert founded the National League of Professional Baseball Clubs in 1876. The names of the league's eight teams are carved into the giant baseball that marks his grave.

The columnar monument with an urnlike top, designed by Richard E. Schmidt for his parents, **F| Ernst and Therese Schmidt,** is a handsome and personal example of his Prairie School style.

The grave of structural engineer **G| Fazlur Rahman Khan,** whose work at Skidmore, Owings & Merrill included the John Hancock Center and the Sears Tower, is marked by a square stone of red granite, snugly surrounded by low, tight greenery.

Photographer **H| Richard Nickel** was an early crusader for architectural preservation, renowned for his efforts to document and save the great works of Chicago architecture. While salvaging ornament from Adler & Sullivan's Stock Exchange Building during its demolition in 1972, he was killed by falling masonry. His black granite stone was designed by architects John Vinci and Lawrence Kenny.

Architect **I| Bruce Goff** was influenced by Louis Sullivan and the Prairie School architects. Although he lived in Chicago for only a few years, Graceland Cemetery was an appropriate place in which to place his ashes in 2000. The marker, designed by Seattle architect Grant Gustafson, incorporates a chunk of cullet glass from the house Goff designed for Joe Price in Oklahoma (1956), which was destroyed by arson in 1996.

The flat slab of black granite that marks the grave of **J| Ludwig Mies van der Rohe** was designed by his grandson, architect Dirk Lohan. Mies came to Chicago from Germany in 1938 to direct the architecture department of the Armour Institute, which became the Illinois Institute of Technology. His designs for steel-and-glass buildings revolutionized modern architecture and established the International Style.

Architect Peter Weber designed the **K| Lucius Fisher** columbarium in 1916, and sculptor Richard W. Bock designed the hooded figure.

Architect Henry Bacon and sculptor Daniel Chester French designed the monument for **I| Marshall Field,** which French titled *Memory*. On the base of the statue is the emblem of the caduceus, the staff of Mercury, Roman god of commerce. Bacon and French later collaborated on the design of the Lincoln Memorial in Washington, D.C.

Louis H. Sullivan designed the **M| Getty Tomb** for lumber merchant Henry Harrison Getty after the death of his wife, Carrie Eliza, in 1890. Getty was a partner of Martin Ryerson, whose nearby tomb was also Sullivan's work. Freed from addressing the normal practical requirements of a working building, Sullivan gave free rein to his decorative talents in designing this monument, planning the ornament in full-scale drawings. The frilly acanthus leaf, a favorite plant form of Sullivan and his contemporaries, is lushly but delicately rendered in Bedford limestone and bronze. Look through the gates to the explosion of ornament on the massive door. Frank Lloyd Wright said of this work, "Outside the realm of music, what finer requiem?"

N| Ernest Robert Graham was one of Daniel Burnham's partners who established the firm of Graham, Anderson, Probst & White in 1917, after Burnham's death.

O| Daniel Burnham and his family are buried on an island in the lake, reached by a plain concrete footbridge; boulders mark the burial sites. As an architect, chief of construction for the 1893 World's Columbian Exposition, and coauthor of the 1909 Plan of Chicago, Burnham was a central figure of the Chicago School.

New York architects McKim, Mead & White designed the **P| Potter and Bertha Palmer** tomb, tall twin sarcophagi set within an open-air temple of Ionic columns.

Across the road from the Palmers, McKim, Mead & White designed a French Gothic tomb for Bertha's parents, **Q| Henry H. and Eliza Honoré.** Southeast of the Palmer tomb is an equally grandiose McKim, Mead & White monument to piano manufacturer **R| William Kimball.**

The **S| Goodman Family** tomb, designed by Howard Van Doren Shaw in 1918, nestles into the lakeshore, its top appearing as an overlook and its entrance reached by a flight of stairs leading to the water's edge.

GETTY TOMB

The grave of **T| Louis H. Sullivan** was designed by Thomas Tallmadge in 1929, five years after Sullivan's death. Upon a wide boulder Sullivan's profile is set in one of his own ornamental designs; Tallmadge wrote the tribute on the back of the stone. On the narrow sides, a setback skyscraper seems to be emerging, reflecting Sullivan's role in the development of the high rise. Tallmadge wrote a history of nineteenth-century Chicago architecture and coined the term "Chicago School."

MARTIN RYERSON TOMB

Lumber merchant and real estate speculator **U| Martin Ryerson** died in 1887; his son, Martin A. Ryerson, commissioned this mausoleum from Louis H. Sullivan, who had designed four downtown office buildings for the senior Ryerson. The polished black granite tomb is inspired by Egyptian funerary forms, the mastaba for the lower portion and the pyramid for the top. Unlike most Egyptian-style tombs, the design calls on Egyptian precedents not for detailing but for the dark and massive form, which seems as timeless as the concept of eternity itself.

Solon S. Beman, who was responsible for the design of the company town of Pullman, also designed the **V| George M. Pullman** monument, a very tall Corinthian column placed in a terraced setting with an exedra on either side. Pullman died after a bitter and violent strike had disrupted his town. Fearing that his remains might be vandalized, the family had him interred below the monument

inside a concrete block topped with railroad ties set in concrete.

Brewer **W| Peter Schoenhofen** rests in a steep-sided pyramid, entered through an Egyptian portal with a sun disk. A sphinx and a rather out-of-place Victorian angel stand guard, the latter holding a key and gazing heavenward.

JOHN WELLBORN ROOT MONUMENT

Burnham's partner **X| John Wellborn Root** died of pneumonia while their firm was planning the World's Columbian Exposition. Included among the abstract ornament on the Celtic cross that marks his grave is his last drawing, a design for the entrance to a building proposed for the fair. The cross was designed by Jules Wegman, a member of the firm.

Y| William Holabird, another central figure of the Chicago School, is buried in a family plot tucked into a low ridge.

The work of **Z| George Grant Elmslie** is a highly personal interpretation of the Chicago and the Prairie schools. His name is engraved on a flat slab of black granite along with the names of members of his wife's family.

"Above All Things Truth Beareth Away the Victory" are the only words on this monument to **a| Victor F. Lawson.** Lorado Taft sculpted the larger-than-life, polished black granite figure of a medieval Crusader. The statue was erected in 1931, six years after the death of the philanthropic publisher of the *Chicago Daily News*.

b| Peirce Anderson was one of Daniel Burnham's partners who became a founding member of Graham, Anderson, Probst & White. Anderson's profile is featured on a large pink granite monument, with his name and dates in very small letters near the lower edge.

Designer **c| László Moholy-Nagy** came to Chicago in 1937, after the Bauhaus had been closed by the Nazis. Here he opened the New Bauhaus, renamed the Institute of Design and later merged with the Illinois Institute of Technology. His cremated remains are buried under a small, standardized granite square behind the chapel.

The family plot of pioneer Chicagoan and hotel owner **d| Dexter Graves** features a mysterious and haunting bronze sculpture, *Eternal Silence*, by Lorado Taft.

e| Dwight H. Perkins played an important role in the Prairie School movement, designing innovative schools and park buildings. He also helped to establish the Cook County Forest Preserves.

Other architects buried at Graceland include: David Adler, Augustus Bauer, L. Gustav Hallberg, Richard G. Schmid, James J. Egan, Alfred Shaw, and Edward Burling.

48| 4015 N. Sheridan Rd.
(*Marmon Hupmobile Showroom*)
1920, PAUL GERHARDT

Things Egyptian were very popular in this era of archaeological marvels, which culminated in the opening of King Tut's Tomb in 1922. Gerhardt was so enamored of Egyptian motifs that he incorporated them into two entries for the Chicago Tribune Competition.

49| Irving Apartments
(*Kellshore Apartment Hotel*)
718–756 W. Irving Park Rd.
1915, E. NORMAN BRYDGES

In the description of this project, *The Book of the North Shore* said, "Much as one may regret the necessity of people living in apartments instead of in attractive vine-covered houses, the problem is with us and so has to be met in a manner which will insure the maximum of comfort, light, air, and pleasing composition." Although basking in the reflected glory of the grand Pattington Apartments, the units here are small studios and one-bedrooms designed to appeal to young marrieds and single office workers. Shallow urns that flank the courtyard entryways and top the corner piers provide a Prairie School touch.

50| Pattington Apartments
660–700 W. Irving Park Rd.
1902–1903, DAVID E. POSTLE

Chicago's best courtyard building is the largest built to that time. All seventy-two units were capacious apartments with servants' quarters, marketed to upper-middle-class families as an alternative to single-family residences. The two courtyards each have five elaborate neo-Classical entrances. The design provides complete cross-ventilation for each apartment, enhanced by bay windows that flood the rooms with light and air.

PATTINGTON APARTMENTS

51| Lakeside University Center
(*Immaculata High School*)
640 W. Irving Park Rd.

Former Mary Hall
600–634 W. Irving Park Rd.
1922, BARRY BYRNE

Former Convent
4030 N. Marine Dr.
1955, BARRY BYRNE

Former St. Joseph's Hall
636 W. Irving Park Rd.
1956, BARRY BYRNE

This important early modern school displays Byrne's characteristic combination of Prairie School massing and forms with a very personal interpretation of Gothic detailing. Shared facilities such as the assembly hall and the gymnasium dominate the pavilion, which breaks out slightly from the southeast corner; the window treatment here reflects the scale of the interior spaces. Classroom windows are arranged in groups of three, enframed by slender pointed arches rising the building's full height. The spare ornament (which originally included sculpture by Alfonso Iannelli) is concentrated at the entrances.

LAKESIDE UNIVERSITY CENTER

52| Walt Disney Magnet School
4140 N. Marine Dr.
1973, PERKINS & WILL

Chicago's first magnet school draws students from large areas rather than just the surrounding neighborhood. Innovations include flexible classroom space organized into nine "pods."

Hutchinson St. Landmark District
Hutchinson St. between Marine Dr. and Hazel St.

This two-block area, a showcase for residential architecture of the late nineteenth and early twentieth centuries, is particularly rich in designs by George W. Maher, spanning two decades of his career.

53| Edwin J. Mosser House
750 W. Hutchinson St.
1902, GEORGE W. MAHER

The cream-colored Roman brick walls flower with luxuriant Sullivanesque ornament, especially around the main entrance facing west. The south facade is dominated by a one-story sunporch, with a projecting roof that forms a porte cochere.

54| Claude Seymour House
817 W. Hutchinson St.
1913, GEORGE W. MAHER

Maher's last house on Hutchinson St. is broad, monumental, and dignified. It includes a favorite motif, the flanged segmental arch over the door, and features such Prairie Style characteristics as a hipped

CLAUDE SEYMOUR HOUSE

roof, pronounced horizontality, and bands of windows under deep eaves.

**55| William H. Lake House
826 W. Hutchinson St.**
1904, GEORGE W. MAHER

Asymmetrical but formal and subtly balanced, the monumental facades are topped by great overhanging low-hipped roofs.

**56| Grace Brackebush House
839 W. Hutchinson St.**
1909, GEORGE W. MAHER

This mature design combines the straightforwardness and severity that Maher admired in such English contemporaries as C. F. A. Voysey with the long horizontals of the Prairie School.

**57| John C. Scales House
840 W. Hutchinson St.**
1894, GEORGE W. MAHER

This is the earliest house in the district, designed for the street's developer in the Queen Anne style of Maher's early career. Complex roof forms, beautifully reshingled, and high chimneys top heavily textured walls of boulders and half-timbering.

**58| Louis Wolff House
4234 N. Hazel St.**
1904, RICHARD E. SCHMIDT

Long attributed to Schmidt's chief designer, Hugh M. G. Garden, this house is now credited to another employee, William Drummond. The very closed facade, with small windows and large brick walls, has beautifully carved stone around the front door.

59| 4338–4346 N. Clarendon Ave.
1905, SAMUEL N. CROWEN

Crowen frequently blended Prairie Style elements with a dash of the Egyptian in his blocky apartment buildings. The delicate Sullivanesque frieze contrasts with robust entrance canopies.

**60| Pensacola Place Apartments
4334 N. Hazel St.**
1981, STANLEY TIGERMAN & ASSOCS.
WITH ROBERT FUGMAN, ASSOC. ARCH.

The eastern facade of this "two-faced" structure mirrors the Boardwalk Apartments at 4343 N. Clarendon Ave. (1974, Stanley Tigerman & Assocs.). The western facade is an essay in pop architecture. Semicircular balconies are intended to suggest the shafts of gigantic columns that culminate in huge Ionic volutes—a visual joke more clearly read in drawings than on the building. A ground floor of retail space and a mezzanine of aluminum-sided town houses form the base.

**61| St. Mary of the Lake
Roman Catholic Church
4200 N. Sheridan Rd.**
1913–1917, HENRY J. SCHLACKS
1915, SCHOOL, JOSEPH W. MCCARTHY
1939, CONVENT, MCCARTHY, SMITH & EPPIG

Unlike an earlier generation of church designers who knew

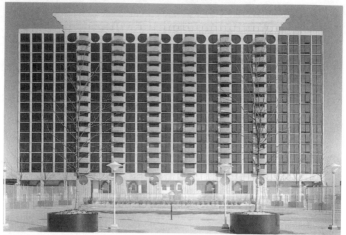

PENSACOLA PLACE APARTMENTS

historic architecture more through drawings and photos than direct experience, Schlacks traveled extensively in Europe in search of inspiration. This Renaissance design freely combines several major fourth- and fifth-century Roman churches: the freestanding campanile was patterned after that of St. Pudentiana, while the facade borrows from the Basilica of St. Paul Outside the Walls. The richly painted interior, decorated by Arthur Hercz, features fine stained-glass windows by F. X. Zettler.

ST. MARY OF THE LAKE
ROMAN CATHOLIC CHURCH

62| Commonwealth Edison Electric Power Substation
4401 N. Clifton Ave.
1916, HERMANN V. VON HOLST

Like many of von Holst's power stations, this strong, blocklike design is enriched with brickwork in geometric patterns.

63| Graeme Stewart Public School
4525 N. Kenmore Ave.
1907, DWIGHT H. PERKINS

Pairs of enormous copper brackets support the massive hipped roof of this imposing brick and limestone structure. Features in common with Perkins's other schools include the robust consoles serving as keystones atop the large arched windows of the central block and, on the end pavilions, vertical pairs of windows with only the lower of the two pedimented.

64| Bank of Chicago Lakeshore (*Standard Vaudeville Theater*)
1050 W. Wilson Ave.
1909, WILLIAM F. BEHAN
1989, RENOVATION, MAYES-VOSTAL ARCHITECTS

A building with many lives, the original theater closed in 1922 and was replaced by a series of banks. Bank of Chicago arrived in 1947 and added a trompe l'oeil mural that hides a wall left bare by the demolition of an adjacent building in the 1980s. Through the "arch" is a southern Italian formal garden!

65| Truman College
1145 W. Wilson Ave.
1977, DUBIN, DUBIN, BLACK & MOUTOUSSAMY

This city college in a gritty neighborhood has an appropriately sturdy, hard-edged Miesian campus.

Because Northwestern University's original charter specified a "four-mile limit" banning liquor sales, for many years no alcohol could be served north of Devon Ave.—making Uptown the city's northernmost outpost for taverns and the first spot south of suburban Highwood to get a drink. With the advent of Prohibition, the booze just went underground, making this neighborhood a bootlegging and roadhouse center, filled with young people and entertainment complexes.

66| CTA—Wilson Avenue Elevated Station
(*Uptown Union Station*)
4604–4634 N. Broadway
1923, A. W. GERBER

This small building served as a transfer point between suburban railroads and elevated trains that ran downtown. The Beaux Arts arcade (which replaced one designed by Frank Lloyd Wright) was designed for a glamorous era of train travel but now reflects the grimy reality of public transportation.

67| Uptown Broadway Building
4707 N. Broadway
1927, WALTER W. AHLSCHLAGER

Uptown boomed when terra cotta was at its peak of popularity, and this commercial building is a visual encyclopedia, with human faces, animal heads, foliage, columns, and ribbons rendering in yellow and gray the Spanish Baroque style. A popular claim that the building was built by Al Capone is unsubstantiated.

68| Riviera Theatre
4746 N. Broadway
1918, C.W. AND GEORGE L. RAPP

This was the second theater built by Balaban & Katz and the first for which they used Rapp & Rapp. Its success led B & K to use Rapp & Rapp almost exclusively. Originally started by another owner, the project went broke during construction. The facade and adjacent commercial building were by another architect (unknown) and were probably left intact by the Rapps; the facade is tame by comparison with the firm's subsequent work.

69| Uptown National Bank of Chicago
(*Uptown Bank Building*)
4753 N. Broadway
1924, MARSHALL & FOX
1928, ADDITION, HUSZAGH & HILL

Originally constructed with only eight floors and later expanded, the building has two cornices. The base reflects the importance of the second and third floors, which contain the main banking spaces. Step inside to see original fixtures and ornamental work. The plaster ceiling was originally cast in Italy and shipped in pieces for installation.

UPTOWN NATIONAL BANK OF CHICAGO

70| Uptown Theatre
4814 N. Broadway
1925, C.W. AND GEORGE L. RAPP

Eight stories tall and with 4,381 seats, it was the largest theater ever for both the architects and the developers, Balaban & Katz. The Uptown was an important addition to the entertainment district, which included the Aragon Ballroom and the Green Mill Lounge. The Spanish Baroque Revival style, with its emphasis on the grandly ornamented portal, was perfect for a movie palace. Through

UPTOWN THEATRE

those doors lay a world much grander and more exotic than the neighborhood's cramped apartments and smoky bars.

71| U.S. Post Office—Uptown Station
4850 N. Broadway
1939, HOWARD L. CHENEY

Polished granite eagles guard this small Moderne post office. Inside, murals (1943) by Henry Varnum Poor depict Carl Sandburg and Louis H. Sullivan, who holds a model of the Carson Pirie Scott store.

72| Ecumenical Institute
(*Mutual Insurance Building*)
4750 N. Sheridan Rd.
1921, FUGARD & KNAPP
1926, ADDITION AND ALTERATIONS, B. LEO STEIF

Handsomely clad in gleaming terra cotta, this office building was originally a four-story retail building with an arcaded corridor; its facade was "stretched" to insert three more floors.

73| Aragon Ballroom
1106 W. Lawrence Ave.
1926, HUSZAGH & HILL

The golden age of ballroom dancing came to life in this Moorish dreamland. A grand entrance lobby, running the length of the building, culminated in a wide staircase flanked with plaster dragons. Double-tiered, ornate terracotta arches, mosaics, tiles, palm trees, and a promenade surrounded the dance floor.

Lights from Spanish-style fixtures glowed under the twinkling stars in the cobalt blue dome. Ceilings that imitated the night sky were key features of 1920s "atmospheric" theaters and dance halls, transporting snowbound Midwesterners to warm Mediterranean landscapes. The Spanish or Moorish—or sometimes Oriental—decor enhanced the appealing exoticism.

When ballroom dancing faded after World War II, the Aragon was used for a series of unsuccessful ventures before becoming a concert hall in the 1970s.

74| 5040–5060 N. Marine Dr.
(*Marine Drive Apartments*)
1939, OMAN & LILIENTHAL

This development followed close on the heels of the Granville Gardens and Wolcott Gardens and shows the same simple Art Moderne detailing: corner windows (originally metal casements), multicolored stripes of brick, and a very thin wall plane, with windows set close to the surface. Six staggered blocks are arranged to take advantage of lake views and maximize ventilation.

75| Myron Bachman House
1244 W. Carmen Ave.
1948, REMODELING, BRUCE GOFF

If the Jetsons had remodeled a house after World War II, it might have looked like this. Goff had designed Quonset huts during the war and applied his interest in corrugated metal to this renovation of an old house, incorporating a recording-studio control room in front. Though

MYRON BACHMAN HOUSE

WOLCOTT GARDENS

hardly contextual, it is fascinating—especially the combination of corrugated metal and weeping mortar.

76| Wolcott Gardens
4901–4959 N. Wolcott Ave.
1939, MICHAELSEN & ROGNSTAD

A full block of twenty-one modest Art Moderne apartment buildings is arranged around open space, creating courtyards that are more private than those in traditional U-shaped flats of the 1920s. The detailing varies subtly, usually around the doorways. This was another project made possible by FHA mortgage insurance, and construction was not started until Granville Gardens on N. Hoyne Ave. had been successfully leased.

77| Carl Sandburg House
4646 N. Hermitage Ave.
EARLY 1890S, ARCHITECT UNKNOWN

Sandburg moved into the second-floor flat in 1912 with his wife and infant daughter and wrote "Chicago" while living here.

78| Wallace C. Abbott House
4605 N. Hermitage Ave.
1891, DAHLGREN & LIEVENDAHL

One of the finest Victorian homes lining Hermitage and Paulina Aves. is this one built for the founder of Abbott Laboratories. Beautifully restored and maintained, it also retains a nineteenth-century stable.

79| All Saints Episcopal Church
4550 N. Hermitage Ave.
1883, JOHN C. COCHRANE

This distinctive Stick Style structure may be the city's oldest frame church. The bell in the corner tower summoned the volunteer fire department and announced services, which Carl Sandburg attended here.

ALL SAINTS EPISCOPAL CHURCH

80| Ravenswood United Methodist Church
(Ravenswood Methodist Episcopal Church)
4501 N. Hermitage Ave.
1890, JOHN S. WOOLLACOTT

Behind the prim rusticated facade is a sculpted space inspired by H. H. Richardson and Louis H. Sullivan. A great roundheaded arch filled with organ pipes dominates the almost square worship space. A hammer-beam ceiling rises

above gently curving amphitheatrical seating and a balcony.
The church was designed to
accommodate these leaded-glass
windows, which were brought
from an earlier church nearby.

81| Ravenswood Public School
4332 N. Paulina Ave.
1892, JOHN J. FLANDERS
1912, ARTHUR F. HUSSANDER

The broad-eaved Flanders
design was echoed by copycat
Hussander; cut-stone ornament
is reproduced in terra cotta on
later sections.

82| Museum of Decorative Art
(*Krause Music Store*)
4611 N. Lincoln Ave.
1922, WILLIAM C. PRESTO WITH
LOUIS H. SULLIVAN, ASSOC. ARCH.

Unlike his professional fortunes,
Sullivan's talent never waned, as
this, his final design, testifies.
William Krause asked his neighbor, Presto, to design a building
to house his music store showroom below and his family
above. Presto, in turn, asked
former employer Sullivan to
design the facade, which he did
while working out of an office
of the American Terra Cotta
Company. With the help of their
modeler Kristian Schneider,
Sullivan's characteristic foliate
ornament bloomed as beautifully on this modest project as
it had on the magnificent Auditorium Theater over thirty years
before. The elaborate system

MUSEUM OF DECORATIVE ART

of ornament culminates in
a large cartouche rising three
feet above the parapet. The
facade was restored by the
current tenant.

83| Old Town School of Folk Music
(*Chicago Public Library—Frederick H. Hild Regional Branch*)
4544 N. Lincoln Ave.
1931, PIERRE BLOUKE
1998, ADAPTIVE REUSE, WHEELER/
KEARNS ARCHITECTS WITH MORRIS
ARCHITECTS PLANNERS

The restrained Art Deco facade
on Lincoln Ave. is smooth and
blocky, a discreet owl the only
playful element. The centerpiece of the transformation
from library to music center is
the semicircular concert hall
that once housed four floors of
book stacks. Large sliding doors
in the backstage wall open the
space to the lobby, creating an
informal gathering space at the
hub of the complex. Highlights
of the interior are two reused
WPA murals by Francis F. Coan.

84| Chicago Public Library—Conrad Sulzer Regional Branch
4455 N. Lincoln Ave.
1985, HAMMOND BEEBY & BABKA
WITH JOSEPH W. CASSERLY, CITY
ARCH.

This friendly, whimsical, and
inviting public building is worth
exploring for its decorative
delights. The long facade continues the street wall of Lincoln
Ave. and ends in a graceful
curve. The entrance is subtly
indicated by a large gabled
window that opens into the
second-floor reading room.
Inspired by neo-Classical architecture, the building is nonetheless modern in its revelation of
metal structure with infills of
glass or brick. The division of
functions is logical, with noisy
activities (circulation desk,
audio and video materials,
children's library) concentrated
on the first floor. Whimsically
painted furniture, originally
intended for the children's area,
now delights patrons throughout the building.

CHICAGO PUBLIC LIBRARY—
CONRAD SULZER REGIONAL BRANCH

85 | St. Benedict's Roman Catholic Church
2201 W. Irving Park Rd.
1918, HERMANN J. GAUL

The large German congregation built their church in the Rundbogenstil, a nineteenth-century revival of Romanesque forms that predates the more robust Richardsonian Romanesque. It is exuberantly studded with short columns outside as well as inside. The interior is also Germanic and features art-glass windows by F. X. Zettler.

ALBERT G. LANE TECHNICAL HIGH SCHOOL

86 | Albert G. Lane Technical High School
2501 W. Addison Rd.
1934, PAUL GERHARDT
1940, STADIUM, JOHN C. CHRISTENSEN

The Board of Education took technical education seriously, creating special facilities for these schools and endowing them with the dignity and focused purpose of a college campus. Lane Tech looks like an Industrial Gothic factory, with its large glazed areas, clock tower, and smokestack. A light court gives outside exposure to all classrooms and shops. The interior is worth a visit to see sculptures in the library by Peterpaul Ott and frescoes in the auditorium lobby glorifying *The Teaching of Art* (late 1930s, Mitchell Siporin). The concrete football stadium, a 1930s version of Gothic, was built by the WPA.

87 | Friedrich Ludwig Jahn Public School
3149 N. Wolcott Ave.
1907, DWIGHT H. PERKINS

This is a Prairie form with simplified Gothic details. The depth of the facade and the Secession-style entrance link it with Perkins's other powerfully modeled schools of this period.

FRIEDRICH LUDWIG JAHN PUBLIC SCHOOL

88 | Brundage Building
3325 N. Lincoln Ave.
1923, WILLIAM G. UFFENDELL

The robust neo-Classical facade of this elegant flatiron building (note the four-foot-wide pilasters) looks like limestone but is entirely of terra cotta. Avery Brundage, famous as the longtime head of the International Olympic Committee, acquired properties that he had built as a contractor and that went under in the 1930s

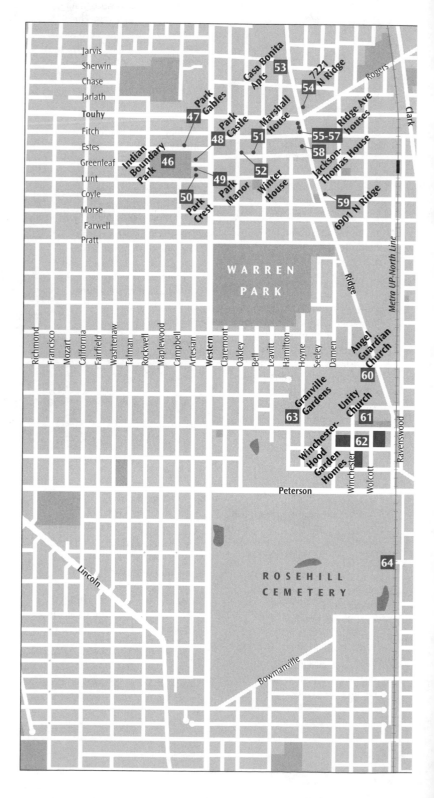

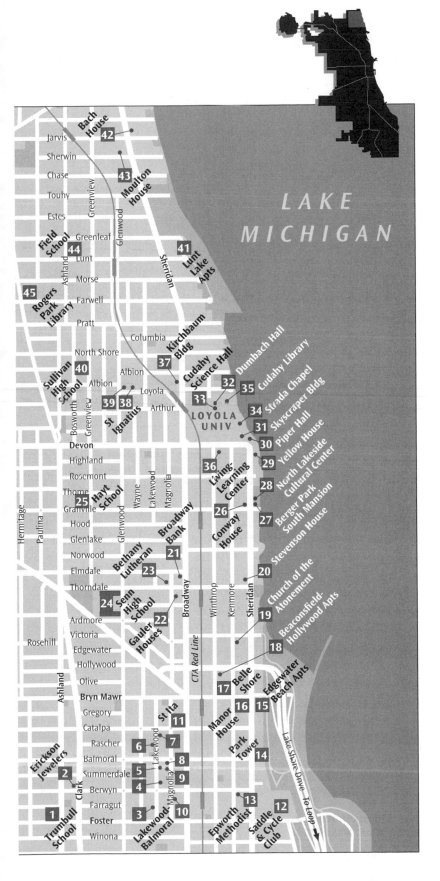

LAKE
MICHIGAN

Jarvis
Sherwin
Chase
Touhy
Estes

Bach
House **42**

43 Moulton
House

Greenview
Glenwood

Field
School **44**
Greenleaf
Lunt
Morse

45
Rogers
Park
Library
Farwell
Pratt

Ashland

Sheridan

41
Lunt
Lake
Apts

Columbia
North Shore

Kirchbaum
Bldg
37

Cudahy
Science Hall

Dumbach Hall

Cudahy Library

Albion

40
Sullivan
High
School
Albion
Loyola

39 38
St
Ignatius
Arthur

32
33
35 Strada Chapel

Skyscraper Bldg

34
31 Piper Hall

Bosworth
Greenview

LOYOLA
UNIV

30 Yellow House

29 North Lakeside
Cultural Center

Devon
Highland
Rosemont
Thome

25 Hayt
School
Granville
Hood
Glenlake

Wayne
Lakewood
Magnolia

36
Living
Learning
Center

28 Berger Park
South Mansion

Stevenson House

27

26
Conway
House

Hermitage
Paulina

Glenwood

Broadway
Bank

Norwood
Elmdale

21

23

20 Church of the
Atonement

Bethany
Lutheran

Broadway

Winthrop
Kenmore

Sheridan

Thorndale

24 Senn
High
School
Ardmore
Victoria
Edgewater

22
Gauler
Houses

19 Beaconsfield-
Hollywood Apts

Rosehill

18

Edgewater
Beach Apts

Hollywood
Olive

Bryn Mawr

Ashland

St Ita
11

17 Belle
Shore

Lake Shore Drive to Loop

Gregory
Catalpa
Rascher

6
Lakewood

7

16
Manor
House

15

Erickson
Jewelers

2

Balmoral
Summerdale

5

8

9

Park
Tower

14

Clark

Berwyn
Farragut

4

3

Magnolia

13 Epworth
Methodist

12 Saddle
& Cycle
Club

1
Trumbull
School
Foster
Winona

Lakewood-
Balmoral
10

EDGEWATER/ROGERS PARK

THE HISTORY OF EDGEWATER AND ROGERS PARK TELLS OF THE METAMORPHOSIS from genteel suburb to urban neighborhood. As usual, the catalyst was the extension of a transit line, making the community more accessible to legions of Loop office workers. Highway construction brought further changes, turning quiet streets into congested thoroughfares. But behind the row of Sheridan Rd.'s high rises are pockets of elegance that hint at the area's enduring appeal.

Edgewater and Rogers Park began as farming communities but originally belonged to different townships, separated at Devon Ave. Edgewater joined the city as part of the Lake View annexation in 1889; four years later Rogers Park voted to secede from Evanston and become part of Chicago.

Edgewater's landscape of celery farms began its suburban transformation in 1885, when J. Lewis Cochran purchased lakefront property—the first of his many subdivisions—bounded by Foster Ave., Broadway, and Bryn Mawr Ave. Known as the "father of Edgewater," Cochran installed roads, sidewalks, drainage, and electricity; gave the area its name; and built about fifty "stylish mansions" on streets named for towns along the Main Line of his native Philadelphia. By 1910 Sheridan Rd. had become an exclusive stretch lined with mansions, while developments west of Broadway (such as Cochran's Lakewood-Balmoral) retained the suburban ambience on a more modest scale. Farther west, working-class Swedes and Germans built single-family homes and two-flats near industries clustered along the Chicago & North Western tracks. The extension of the Northwestern Elevated Railroad (now the CTA Red Line) through Edgewater in 1908 spurred further residential growth, and by the 1920s some of the original houses had yielded to high-rise hotels and apartments.

Rogers Park was incorporated as a village in 1878. It was named by its chief promoter, Patrick L. Touhy, for his father-in-law, Phillip Rogers, an early settler. Development took place first along the Ridge, a shelf of land left by the receding lake shore and the site of an Indian trail that was the area's only north–south road for decades. Farmers, especially Luxembourgers and Germans, built cottages here, and wealthier families like the Touhys built substantial homes in the picturesque styles. Even after the coming of two railroads, development was slow until the 1908 extension of the elevated line to Evanston. With stops every three blocks, the El set off a boom in apartment and hotel building adjacent to the lakefront.

In the southeastern corner of Rogers Park, Loyola University opened in 1922 on sand dunes acquired by the Jesuits in 1906, and Mundelein College (now part of Loyola) opened its skyscraper campus in 1930. With less public transportation, West Ridge (west of Ridge Blvd.) was sparsely settled until after World War I, when brick bungalows and flats sprouted along its streets. For decades the site of nurseries, truck farms, and greenhouses, it was extensively developed after World War II.

—WILLIAM B. HINCHLIFF

1| **Lyman Trumbull Public School**
5200 N. Ashland Blvd.
1910, DWIGHT H. PERKINS

Shorn of traditional ornament and showing the influence of the progressive Prairie School

LYMAN TRUMBULL PUBLIC SCHOOL

movement, this massive block has the power and purity of form that distinguishes Perkins's work as Chicago Board of Education architect. Towering and percussive, the walls roll from pier to pier, punctuated with deep vertical window reveals. The strong entrance pavilion rises above the busy intersection, marking the site as a community anchor. Innovations of this era include a ground-floor (rather than top-story) auditorium to facilitate community use of the space, generous corridors to improve circulation, washrooms on every floor instead of in the basement, and skylights. The grimy brick, once creamy, and the lunar landscape of the grassless playground now cast a pall.

2 | Erickson Jewelers
5304 N. Clark St.
EARLY 1940S, REMODELING, ARCHITECT UNKNOWN

In 1935 America's aging and dowdy retail areas were suffering from the effects of the Depression; for years merchants had put little money into remodeling. That year the Federal Housing Administration began insuring loans for store improvements up to $50,000, and in June *Architectural Record* announced a competition sponsored by the Libbey-Owens-Ford Glass Co. to "Modernize Main Street," with a jury that included Albert Kahn, William Lescaze, and John W. Root. Architects were directed to rethink the typical cluttered storefront as a merchandising device: "The store front with its plate glass show windows establishes the character of the store . . . It must serve to make the passer *buy*, inviting him or her to stop and shop." L-O-F sponsored the competition to promote Vitrolite, their opaque, pigmented structural glass (marketed under different names by other companies). Attached by adhesive to masonry, Vitrolite was a perfect modernizing material for storefronts: low maintenance, extremely durable, sleek and shiny. According to the *Record*, the properly "modernized" storefront should feature a prominent sign or logo against an unadulterated surface. Fragments of these storefronts survive in many neighborhood shopping districts; few are as well preserved as this example. The black-glass background still sets off the brushed metal name and the diamond ring, almost two feet in diameter—enticing us to stop, look . . . and buy.

ERICKSON JEWELERS

Lakewood-Balmoral Neighborhood
Lakewood, Magnolia, and Wayne Aves. from Foster to Bryn Mawr Aves.

Developer J. Lewis Cochran began energetically promoting his Edgewater subdivisions in the mid-1880s. The grandest houses, built on lots east of the railroad (now CTA) tracks, have almost all been replaced by apartments. These more modest dwellings, substantial yet often half the price of those closer to the lake, form a still-desirable neighborhood of single-family residences. Cochran sold unimproved lots and also built houses on speculation, frequently five or ten at a time. Between 1885 and 1896 he commissioned designs from Joseph Lyman Silsbee, L. Gustav Hallberg, Henry H. Sprague, George W. Maher, J. N. Tilton, Joseph C. Brompton, Julius H. Huber, Church & Jobson, and Handy & Cady. Attributions are difficult because of the number of architects Cochran commissioned and the extensive remodeling that many houses have undergone. But even the unattributable Victorians are of interest, as they reemerge under the care of owners who remove artificial siding, repair the porches, and strip the woodwork.

3| Herman C. Lammers House
5222 N. Lakewood Ave.
1898, JULIUS H. HUBER
1901, ADDITION; 1911, REMODELING

The Hansel and Gretel remodeling was intended to make the house look more "European."

4| 5313 N. Lakewood Ave.
1903, ARCHITECT UNKNOWN

The pinched verticality of the dormers gives a piquant silhouette to Cochran's speculative house.

5| Angelica Holzaffel House
5347 N. Lakewood Ave.
1910, LEON E. STANHOPE

Features typical of the Craftsman Style include diamond-paned windows and a pergola-like porch.

6| 5426 N. Lakewood Ave.
1893, ARCHITECT UNKNOWN

Cochran built this Queen Anne with an unusual lidded third-floor window surround.

7| Patrick H. McNulty House
5453 N. Lakewood Ave.
1898, HOLABIRD & ROCHE

The centrally placed door and second-floor bay of this Classically inspired house are a play on Palladian window composition.

PATRICK H. MCNULTY HOUSE

8| Arthur Deppman House
5356 N. Magnolia Ave.
1904, GEORGE W. MAHER

Maher's simple, rectilinear design is firmly rooted in the twentieth century.

9| H. Mark Flat
5344 N. Magnolia Ave.
1913, HENRY L. NEWHOUSE

The huge two-story bay makes both floors equally grand, revealing this house's true nature as a two-flat. Corinthian columns as attenuated as toothpicks rise the full height of the bay.

10| 5247 N. Magnolia Ave.
1899, HARVEY L. PAGE & CO.

The Classical language is bold and self-confident; Ionic columns support a double-height porch.

11| St. Ita's Church
1220 W. Catalpa Ave.
1927, HENRY J. SCHLACKS

The M carved in the stone parapet honors the powerful Cardinal Mundelein, whose preference for French Gothic was not lost on Schlacks: he made it solidly thirteenth-century inside and out. The graceful, cohesive interior is warmed by wood wainscoting with Gothic detailing.

Lincoln Park and Lake Shore Dr. ended at Foster Ave. until the early 1950s, when a huge landfill project extended them to Hollywood Ave. On the lake north of Foster Ave. were the private beach areas of the Saddle and Cycle Club and the Edgewater Beach Apartments and hotel complex.

12| Saddle and Cycle Club
900 W. Foster Ave.
1898, JARVIS HUNT
1904, 1909, ADDITIONS, JARVIS HUNT
1968, ADDITION, C. F. MURPHY ASSOCS.

You can catch a fleeting glimpse of this private club from Sheridan Rd. or Lake Shore Dr. In the mid-1890s the main club facilities were downtown; the Edgewater location was originally for cyclists and equestrians riding on the lakefront. The Shingle Style clubhouse and its first additions, designed by club member Hunt, are now barely visible; the tower with its bell-shaped cap is their most prominent remaining feature. The private beach was originally only 100 feet from the veranda and at the end of the nineteenth century had a boathouse and pier.

13| Epworth United Methodist Church
(Epworth Methodist Episcopal Church)
5253 N. Kenmore Ave.
1890, FREDERICK B. TOWNSEND
1930, ADDITION AND RENOVATION, THIELBAR & FUGARD

The massive boulders that form the craggy, random-coursed stone walls were floated down Lake Michigan from Wisconsin to a shoreline slip. The composition is beautifully balanced by three towers: square, round, and octagonal. An early drawing shows entries in the square and octagonal towers; the current one dates from the 1930 addition and sanctuary renovation.

14| Park Tower Condominiums
5415 N. Sheridan Rd.
1974, SOLOMON CORDWELL BUENZ & ASSOCS.

The beautifully detailed and proportioned curtain wall stands out among Edgewater's lakeside cliff of largely dreary high rises.

15| Edgewater Beach Apartments
5555 N. Sheridan Rd.
1928, BENJAMIN H. MARSHALL

This is the sole survivor of the Edgewater Beach Hotel complex, a sophisticated luxury resort and center of Roaring Twenties nightlife. A central octagonal tower and four Y-shaped wings rise from a rectangular base. When built, three out of four apartments had a view of the lake.

EDGEWATER BEACH APARTMENTS

16| Manor House
1021–1029 W. Bryn Mawr Ave.
1908, J. E. O. PRIDMORE

British-born Pridmore designed this elegant Tudor Revival apartment building with only six units (later subdivided) of twelve to sixteen rooms—and two of the apartments had ballrooms. Once the home of the British consul and known as the Prince of Wales House, it bears the royal coat of arms in terra cotta at the rear of the courtyard. Other upscale features were the rounded sunporch on the corner (the *Orangerie*) and the private "family room" at the rear.

17 | Belle Shore Apartment Hotel
1062 W. Bryn Mawr Ave.
1929, KOENIGSBERG & WEISFELD

Behind the Art Deco terra-cotta facade are 138 one-room/kitchenette apartments. Sculptural embellishments include an Egyptian frieze above the storefronts and Art Nouveau–influenced figures.

18 | Beaconsfield-Hollywood Apartments
1055–1065 W. Hollywood Ave.
1913, J. E. O. PRIDMORE

This complex of connecting three-flats has fanciful terracotta ornament that culminates in an elaborate portal with diamond-patterned columns and a crest modeled on that of Castile, Spain.

19 | Church of the Atonement
5749 N. Kenmore Ave.
1919, 1924, J. E. O. PRIDMORE

The use of red sandstone ran counter to the tidal wave of Bedford limestone covering most Gothic churches of the era, but the overall design is conservative and elegant. The towering nave is a uniform vision, with pale colors and rich

CHURCH OF THE ATONEMENT

wood. Buried within the north transept is a piece of the original church, designed in 1890 by Henry Ives Cobb.

20 | Harry M. Stevenson House
5940 N. Sheridan Rd.
1909, GEORGE W. MAHER

Signature details include the dormer window, a complex play on a Palladian theme, and the second-floor window recessed behind colonnettes. At the rear, the broad cornice unites the garage, porte cochere, and house.

21 | Broadway Bank
(*Riviera-Burnstine Motor Sales*)
5960 N. Broadway
1925, R. BERNARD KURZON

Terra cotta is spun like sugar across a brick facade to form French Gothic lancets, finials, and drop-pendant window hoods. The interior is a fine example of a 1920s automobile showroom. The Mediterranean decor, with its stuccoed walls, columns, and grand staircase,

BROADWAY BANK

JOHN GAULER HOUSES

was meant to suggest an out-door setting such as a plaza or courtyard—which was considered the most appropriate backdrop for displaying cars.

22| John Gauler Houses
5917–5921 N. Magnolia Ave.
1908, WALTER BURLEY GRIFFIN

Griffin achieved maximum impact by carefully placing these twin Prairie School houses on their narrow lots. Framed by embracing porches, the intervening space—a gangway in less skillful hands—offers an additional architectural experience. The visitor is deep into this space before even seeing the very private front doors. Griffin's characteristic touches are the wood-mullioned windows and unbroken vertical piers.

23| Bethany Evangelical Lutheran Church
1244 W. Thorndale Ave.
1914, GRANT C. MILLER
1908, BIBLE CHAPEL, PATTON & MILLER

Patton & Miller was among the few firms that designed churches in the informal, domestically scaled, simply but beautifully detailed Craftsman Style. The Tudor Revival–Craftsman Bible chapel (now a Montessori school), which served as the first church, blends well with the larger Craftsman church on the corner. Religious motifs are limited to the stone crosses on the bell tower and small medallions in the grapevine-patterned leaded-glass windows. Inside, an unsympathetic paint scheme

obscures some of the original charm, but a few pieces of vintage Craftsman furniture remain.

24| Nicholas Senn High School
5900 N. Glenwood Ave.
1912, ARTHUR F. HUSSANDER
1931, ADDITIONS, PAUL GERHARDT

Grand but bland, it is greatly enhanced by the broad lawn, a rarity on Board of Education properties. Hussander's block, the north–south rectangle, contains a 2,000-seat auditorium. Gerhardt's perpendicular additions form a broad U-shaped court.

25| Stephen K. Hayt Public School
1518 W. Granville Ave.
1906, DWIGHT H. PERKINS

Bold arches top vertical rows of windows in this school, which is closely related to the Francis Scott Key School in the Austin neighborhood.

26| Richard F. Conway House
6200 N. Sheridan Rd.
1906, WILLIAM CARBYS ZIMMERMAN

27| Berger Park South Mansion
(*Joseph Downey House*)
6205 N. Sheridan Rd.
1906, WILLIAM CARBYS ZIMMERMAN
1988, RENOVATION, CHICAGO PARK DISTRICT

28| North Lakeside Cultural Center
(*Samuel H. Gunder House*)
6219 N. Sheridan Rd.
1910, MYRON H. CHURCH
1988, RENOVATION, ROULA ASSOCS. ARCHITECTS AND SIMON & CO.

This prestigious residential area resembled neighboring North Shore suburbs until high rises replaced most of the mansions during the 1950s and 1960s. A hint of grandeur survives in the lavish, historically inspired detail of the Conway House, in contrast to the more sober Downey House.

On Sheridan Rd. are the buildings of Mundelein College, a women's school that merged with Loyola University in 1991.

29| Yellow House
(*Adolf Schmidt House*)
6331 N. Sheridan Rd.
1917, GEORGE W. MAHER

The decorative motif on this late work of Maher is the water lily, used on the capitals of the octagonal columns.

30| Piper Hall
(*Albert G. Wheeler House*)
956 W. Sheridan Rd.
1909, WILLIAM CARBYS ZIMMERMAN

Wheeler, chief engineer of the Chicago Tunnel Company, provided the architect with a lavish budget, enabling him to create Classical, Romanesque, Tudor, and Prairie details from rough-textured white Vermont marble. Mundelein retained the interior detail and first-floor grandeur. A breathtaking art-glass window fills the wall behind the stair landing.

SKYSCRAPER BUILDING

31| Skyscraper Building
(*Mundelein College*)
6363 N. Sheridan Rd.
1930, NAIRNE W. FISHER AND JOSEPH W. MCCARTHY

The first "skyscraper college," Mundelein's thoroughly modern school for women was head-quartered in the impressive fifteen-story tower. With its Art Deco massing and zigzags, curves, and stylized floral patterns, it could house the *Daily Planet*—were it not for the colossal archangels flanking the entrance. Uriel (Light of God) holds a book inscribed with a cross and points skyward; Jophiel (Beauty of God) holds aloft the torch of knowledge and grasps a celestial globe.

Loyola University Chicago Lake Shore Campus
6525 N. Sheridan Rd.

In 1906 the Jesuits of St. Ignatius College on Roosevelt Rd. purchased a twenty-acre site between Devon and Loyola Aves. and Sheridan Rd. They established Loyola Academy, a high school, in 1909. The first college building followed in 1912; the university moved from Roosevelt Rd. in 1922. Several buildings of the 1930s are memorable, but those of the 1960s building boom are eminently forgettable. A long-standing plan for campus expansion on a landfill project was shelved in 1990 after environmentalists raised objections.

The Loyola campus occupies the lakefront north and east of Sheridan's right-angle turn at Broadway and Devon. Major entries are on the north side of W. Sheridan Rd. at Winthrop Ave., on N. Sheridan Rd. just north of the elevated tracks, and on Loyola Ave. at Winthrop Ave. Street addresses are of little help in locating buildings, which are best found by checking the prominently posted campus maps.

Loyola's earliest years are best represented by

32| Dumbach Hall
(*Loyola Academy*)
1909, WORTHMANN & STEINBACH

33| Michael Cudahy Science Hall
1912, ATTRIB. TO WORTHMANN & STEINBACH

These near twins blend Spanish Mission Style with Renaissance details such as elaborately decorated arched windows. Dumbach was originally the high school, Cudahy the first college building.

34| Madonna della Strada Chapel
6525 N. Sheridan Rd.
1939, ANDREW N. REBORI

35| Elizabeth M. Cudahy Memorial Library
1930, REBORI, WENTWORTH, DEWEY & MCCORMICK
1968, ADDITION, BARRY & KAY

In vivid contrast to the historical styles of the early buildings, Loyola's Library and Chapel are fresh and bold. Facing each other across a broad lakefront lawn, they offer a striking display of Rebori's distinctive interpretation of modernism. Although designed as an ensemble in the late 1920s, the buildings were constructed nearly ten years apart due to the Depression.

The artless library addition, with its aluminum sculpture by Steven Urry—at one point titled *Erection* by the artist, later re-christened *Resurrection*—obscures most of Rebori's work. But walk around to the lake side to view the carved frieze with Latin names of subjects, the tower with its ziggurat, and the sundial. Go inside to see the main reading room with its large mural by John Warner Norton, who also painted the murals in the Board of Trade and Chicago Daily News Buildings. It celebrates the seventeenth-century French explorers of the region and re-creates Father Marquette's map of Illinois.

Rebori reworked his earlier design of the Chapel in the late 1930s. The curving Art Moderne form is reminiscent of a small dirigible or airplane hangar. The walls of the apse are "accordioned"—the folds filled with glass blocks, which admit slim slices of light. Names of famous Jesuits are crisply incised along the roofline; the tall tower is flat-topped and windowless. The Chapel has fared better than the Library with recent changes. The sanctuary was reoriented from the west to the north side

MADONNA DELLA STRADA CHAPEL

SIMPSON LIVING-LEARNING CENTER

of the church, creating a cozier and more intimate feeling and opening up a lake view through the glass doors on the east.

36| Simpson Living-Learning Center
6333 N. Winthrop Ave.
1991, SOLOMON CORDWELL BUENZ & ASSOCS.

This residence hall is a model of architectural collegiality, fitting well into this dense residential neighborhood. The varied roof heights of the interconnected buildings signal different functions, which include student housing as well as a conference and study center.

37| Kirchbaum Building
6560 N. Sheridan Rd.
1922, RONNEBERG, PIERCE & HAUBER

Look above the cluttered storefronts to see the Northwestern Terra Cotta Company's panorama of Chicago's growth. The long panel between Fort Dearborn, on the left, and the newly completed Wrigley Building, on the right, shows the contemporary skyline and features many of Northwestern's greatest hits, including the Railway Exchange Building and the Blackstone Hotel.

38| St. Ignatius Auditorium
1320 W. Loyola Ave.
1931, REBORI & WENTWORTH

Art Deco lettering over the entrance hints at Rebori's authorship.

39| St. Ignatius Roman Catholic Church
6559 N. Glenwood Ave.
1917, HENRY J. SCHLACKS

Here is a monument to God and to Bedford limestone; the giant columns of the Roman Renaissance portico are each carved from a single block of stone. A six-story campanile anchors the eastern end.

40| Roger C. Sullivan High School
6631 N. Bosworth Ave.
1927, JOHN C. CHRISTENSEN

Low and laid out close to the sidewalk, Sullivan was designed to a residential scale. Take in the delightful Tudor details—finials, quoins, medallions, and gargoyles—in a trip around the block. Gothic-lettered panels identify various sections, from boiler room to assembly hall.

41| Lunt Lake Apartments
1122–1140 W. Lunt Ave.
1949, HOLSMAN, HOLSMAN, KLEKAMP & TAYLOR

The same issue of *Architectural Forum* (January 1950) that featured Mies van der Rohe's Promontory Apartments and his 860–880 N. Lake Shore Dr. (for which Holsman's firm was consulting architect) gave equal

ROGER C. SULLIVAN HIGH SCHOOL

space to this project and the firm's Winchester-Hood Garden Homes. What most impressed the magazine were the innovative construction techniques, especially the use of "rowlock bond" brickwork, developed by structural engineer Frank Kornacker. Steel rods reinforce concrete poured in the cavity between outer and inner courses of brick, creating a very strong, very thin bearing wall.

42 | Emil Bach House
7415 N. Sheridan Rd.
1915, FRANK LLOYD WRIGHT

One of the few Wright houses within Chicago, this is also one of the last small urban commissions of his Prairie Style period. It is a compact version of Wright's suburban residences, with a cantilevered second story. The floor plan is a con-

densed version of the open layouts pioneered by Wright.

43 | J. Benjamin Moulton House
1328 W. Sherwin Ave.
1908, WALTER BURLEY GRIFFIN

The massing follows a scheme developed by Frank Lloyd Wright, Griffin's employer from 1901 to 1905: the first-floor living room wing projects from the main two-story block, creating a tiered effect. Griffin preferred windows with thick wood mullions to the more delicate, leaded art glass favored by most Prairie School architects.

44 | Eugene Field Public School
7019 N. Ashland Blvd.
1898, NORMAND S. PATTON
1916, ADDITION, ARTHUR F. HUSSANDER
1940, ADDITION, JOHN C. CHRISTENSEN

J. BENJAMIN MOULTON HOUSE

EUGENE FIELD PUBLIC SCHOOL

Many elementary schools in older neighborhoods were built over several decades, and until the 1960s the Board of Education's architects designed additions to match. The oldest part is the central section facing Ashland Ave.; it was built as an addition to Rogers Park's pre-annexation East Side School, which faced Greenleaf Ave. The proportions, the hipped roof, and the rusticated base were all respected when the complex was expanded to a harmonious block-long campus.

45| Chicago Public Library— Rogers Park Branch
6907 N. Clark St.
1999, ANTUNOVICH ASSOCS. LTD.

Prairie School influences are evident in this building's massing, horizontal band of lime-stone, and the slablike clock tower. This is the first of four "prototype" buildings that were developed by four architectural firms in collaboration with the CPL. The interior offers a variety of well-lighted spaces, enlivened by details such as the CPL's motto—Read, Learn, Discover—rendered in brass in the lobby's terrazzo floor.

46| Indian Boundary Park
2500 W. Lunt Ave.
1929, FIELD HOUSE, CLARENCE HATZFELD

Through this thirteen-acre park runs the northern boundary of an 1816 Indian treaty ceding the Chicago area to the federal government. In 1922, when the park opened, the surrounding area was almost completely undeveloped. The small zoo at

CHICAGO PUBLIC LIBRARY—ROGERS PARK BRANCH

PARK GABLES

the northwest corner is the city's only remaining neighborhood zoo. A 1989 addition to the park is an elaborate playground designed by Robert Leathers and constructed by local residents. The field house combines Tudor and American Indian motifs. In the assembly hall, the beamed ceiling features chandeliers sporting peace pipes, drums, and arrowheads.

47| Park Gables
2438–2484 W. Estes Ave.
1927, JAMES F. DENSON

48| Park Castle
2416–2458 W. Greenleaf Ave.
1925, JENS E. JENSEN

49| Park Manor
2415–2437 W. Greenleaf Ave.
1926, MELVILLE GROSSMAN

50| Park Crest
2420–2434 W. Lunt Ave.
1925, JAMES F. DENSON

This magnificent ensemble is crowned by Park Gables, a Tudor Revival double-courtyard complex with enormous projecting gables, slate roofs, tall casement windows, and ornamented chimney pots. Cathedral ceilings grace the upper-floor apartments. Park Castle reaches back to the medieval castle for its machicolations, crenellations, and gargoyles. The two smaller buildings to the south are less flamboyant but reiterate the English theme.

51| Fred B. Marshall House
2238 W. Greenleaf Ave.
1915, FRED B. PRATHER

52| Fred Winter House
2246 W. Greenleaf Ave.
1928, FRED WINTER

Marshall's house is monastically simple, honest, and unadorned, while down at the corner Winter pulled out all the stops when he designed his own massive bungalow. The red-tiled roof, Tudor half-timbering, battered walls, and Georgian windows are a raucous blend of colors, textures, and materials.

53| Casa Bonita Apartments
7340–7350 N. Ridge Ave.
1928, ALEXANDER CAPRARO & MORRIS KOMAR
1974, RENOVATION, WARNER, BREJCHA, EVANS AND ASSOCS.

Glistening white terra-cotta facades define the deep courtyard.

54| 7221 N. Ridge Ave.
1914, REMODELING, NIELS BUCK

Ridge Ave. follows the still-discernible contour of an ancient beach. Because the lower land to the east was frequently swampy, many of the first houses in Rogers Park were built on this street. A few cottages, some from the 1870s, remain. This one was remodeled in the Craftsman Style popular before World War I. Characteristics include the exposed rafters under overhanging gables, bands of casement windows, and wood strips decorating stucco walls. Another Craftsman house is next door at 7215.

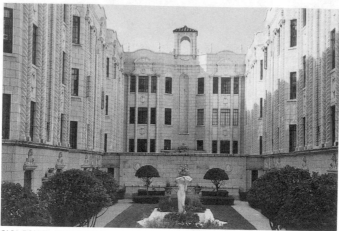
CASA BONITA APARTMENTS

55| 7114 N. Ridge Ave.
1913, ROBERT E. SEYFARTH

56| 7106 N. Ridge Ave.
1913, ROBERT M. HYDE

57| 7100 N. Ridge Ave.
1916, A. J. SMITH

Built during Ridge Ave.'s heyday as a fine residential street, 7100 has elaborate Craftsman Style brackets under a gabled roof. The house at 7106, similar to Hyde's Charles A. Carlson House in the Austin area, has an asymmetrical gabled roof that extends over the recessed entrance with battered piers. Other Craftsman features include decorative brickwork, exposed rafters, and floral-design leaded windows on the south wall. The Dutch Colonial house at 7114 presents an unusual treatment of a common style, with its gambrel roof exaggeratedly broadened to hold down the entire house, which is built at grade.

58| Jackson-Thomas House
7053 N. Ridge Ave.
EARLY 1870S, ARCHITECT UNKNOWN

Commissioned by Andrew B. Jackson, a founding trustee of Rogers Park, this was one of the first generation of grand houses on Ridge Ave. that rose above the modest cottages in bracketed splendor. The symmetrical facade with its central pavilion, the tall windows, and the bracketed hood molding and eaves make this a fine example of the Italianate style at its zenith.

59| 6901 N. Ridge Ave.
1959, DONALD E. ERICKSON

While many neighborhood apartment buildings were being built to a watered-down Geor-

JACKSON-THOMAS HOUSE

gian Revival formula, former Frank Lloyd Wright Foundation fellow Erickson curved this flagstone and curtain-wall building to give every apartment a view of open space. The steel-rod stairway gave the building its nickname, "the birdcage," and originally rose above a fish pond whose reflections doubled its pizzazz.

60 | Angel Guardian Croatian Catholic Church
(St. Henry's Roman Catholic Church)
6346 N. Ridge Ave.
1906, HENRY J. SCHLACKS

This towered and gabled church is Schlacks's most folkloric design. St. Henry's parish was founded in the early 1850s by German-speaking Catholics, many from Luxembourg, who decided in 1904 to replace their church buildings with this brick and limestone Gothic edifice. Clocks fill in the tops of the tower's louvered arches, and in a niche above the round window on Ridge Ave. is a statue of St. Henry standing next to a model of Bamberg Cathedral, which he built.

61 | Unity Church in Chicago
(Chicago Town and Country Tennis and Swim Club)
1925 W. Thome Ave.
1925, GEORGE W. MAHER & SON

The chimney of this grand Tudor manor house bears a limestone shield sporting the club's emblem: tennis racquets flanking intertwined initials. Though best known for his modern Prairie School–influenced work, Maher also did revivalist buildings between World War I and his death in 1926. Given the late date of this building, his son Philip may have been responsible for the design.

62 | Winchester-Hood Garden Homes
1823–1825 W. Granville Ave.,
1908–1922 & 1940–1960
W. Hood Ave., 6149–6175 N.
Wolcott Ave., 6113–6129 N.
Winchester Ave., 1920–1922
W. Norwood Ave.
1949–1951, HOLSMAN, HOLSMAN, KLEKAMP & TAYLOR

This ambitious project encompasses twenty-two four- and five-story apartment buildings and contains some 800 units. Like the similar Lunt Lake Apartments by the same architect-developer-engineer team, Winchester-Hood combines innovative construction techniques—including concrete-reinforced brick walls and radiant-heated ceiling beams—with a "Scandinavian Modern" look that recalls the work of Eliel Saarinen and Alvar Aalto. Ornament is used sparingly but effectively. The stair halls rise behind walls punctuated by a series of three concrete panels depicting stylized signs of the zodiac, designed by architect Coder Taylor.

WINCHESTER-HOOD GARDEN HOMES

63 | Granville Gardens
6200–6242 N. Hoyne Ave.
1938, RISSMAN & HIRSCHFELD

FHA mortgage insurance stimulated a slow resumption of residential construction in the few years before America's entry into World War II halted nonessential building. Several stripped-down Art Deco housing projects were built on the Far North Side, where undeveloped land was still available. Granville Gardens was Chicago's first large, privately financed housing complex since the onset of the Depression and the first built under direct government supervision. The carefully tailored design kept construction costs low enough to charge a monthly rent of no more than $15 per room. Fourteen buildings, each containing fourteen units, face two garden courts. To increase the sense of spaciousness, steel-framed casement windows were placed at the corners of each unit. The wall planes are very flat, with windows recessed only slightly. Decoration is limited to horizontal brickwork, which defines the ground floor and enhances the corners. Amazingly, the entire complex is in close to original condition.

64| Rosehill Cemetery
5800 N. Ravenswood Ave.

The Chicago area's largest nonsectarian cemetery was established in 1859 on a rural 350-acre site over four miles north of the existing city limits. The name came from an error in the charter documents that referred to Hiram Roe's tavern on a nearby hill as Roe's Hill. The cemetery's founders ensured the success of their investment by placing the entrance adjacent to the Chicago & North Western Railroad line. They also sought advice from John Jay Smith, founder of Philadelphia's Laurel Hill Cemetery. He recommended his associate, William Saunders, who provided the initial landscaping in a parklike setting of drives and walkways amid artificial lakes and well-tended grounds.

—JOAN POMARANC

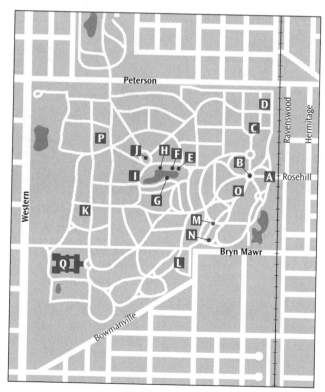

A| Entrance Gate and Office Building
1864, WILLIAM W. BOYINGTON

Built of Joliet limestone, these structures were designed in the "castellated Gothic" style, which employed the forms of medieval English architecture for picturesque effect.

Mid-nineteenth-century rural cemeteries were located on the outskirts of the city near rail lines. Railroads owned special funeral cars that could be rented to transport funeral parties to and from the city center. When the train tracks were elevated after 1900, a new Rosehill station and an elevator (for caskets) were designed to match the nearby entrance. The station has been demolished, although part of the platform remains. The elevator tower remains but is no longer in use.

ROSEHILL CEMETERY ENTRANCE GATE AND OFFICE BUILDING

Atop the hill is the **B| Civil War Soldiers Memorial,** in the grassy center of a circular driveway ringed with other memorials to the Civil War. The columnar monument, designed by sculptor Leonard Volk and titled *Our Heroes*, is topped by a figure of a Union soldier. Four bronze plaques near the base represent the four service branches: army, navy, artillery, and cavalry.

C| George S. Bangs invented the railway mail car that made it possible to collect and sort mail on a moving train. His

GEORGE S. BANGS TOMB

monument depicts a dead tree that represents the deceased; despite death, the trunk continues to support life in the form of plants and animals. A "fast mail" rail car emerges from a tunnel at the base of the trunk.

D| "Long John" Wentworth, one of twelve mayors buried at Rosehill, has a seventy-two-foot obelisk, the cemetery's tallest monument.

Around the lake, near the center of the cemetery, is an impressive row of mausoleums representing the popular styles of the late nineteenth century. The Egyptian temple for railroad president **E| Darius Miller** reflects the popularity of a cultural style whose greatest monuments focused on death and eternity.

DARIUS MILLER TOMB

A Greek temple with Doric columns marks the resting place of **F| Charles Gates Dawes,** the nation's vice president under Calvin Coolidge.

Look across the lake for the best view of banker **G| Norman W. Harris's** mausoleum, with its Corinthian columns and copper-clad dome. The tomb is a perfect Classical tempietto in the eighteenth-century manner. The burial chambers lie below the floor of the structure.

H| Charles M. Hewitt, a manufacturer and financier, has a rusticated Romanesque mausoleum.

Another very impressive temple form, for I| **Adam Schaaf,** has two lions resting at the front steps.

J| Horatio N. May Chapel
1899, JOSEPH LYMAN SILSBEE

The picturesque design combines Gothic and Romanesque elements. The chapel is generally kept locked, but walk through the porte cochere and note the handsome mosaic ceiling.

HORATIO N. MAY CHAPEL

K| **William B. Mundie** was William Le Baron Jenney's partner from 1891 to 1907 and worked on the design of the Manhattan Building.

The mausoleum of banker L| **Oscar G. Foreman** is noteworthy for its unusual Art Nouveau architecture (designer unknown) and because it is empty; the Foremans are buried in Graceland Cemetery.

Sculptor M| **Leonard W. Volk** carved the life-size statue of himself that marks his family plot. His wife's cousin, Senator Stephen A. Douglas, and his political opponent, Abraham Lincoln, were frequent and popular subjects for Volk's work.

N| **John M. Van Osdel,** Chicago's first professional architect, was responsible for more than seventy commercial and public buildings in the Loop alone.

O| **William W. Boyington,** an early Chicago architect, was a leading designer of Chicago railroad stations and other public buildings.

The grave of architect P| **George W. Maher** is marked with a small unadorned block of granite. Maher's work is generally classified with that of the Prairie School, but his was a highly personal interpretation of ideas from various contemporary sources.

Q| Rosehill Mausoleum
1914, SIDNEY LOVELL

Within its marble-lined hallways, family crypts open off long corridors embellished with stained-glass windows; the most impressive is the Tiffany window in the John G. Shedd Memorial Room.

NORTHWEST SIDE

NORTHWEST SIDE

CHICAGO—O'HARE
INTERNATIONAL AIRPORT

NORTHWEST SIDE

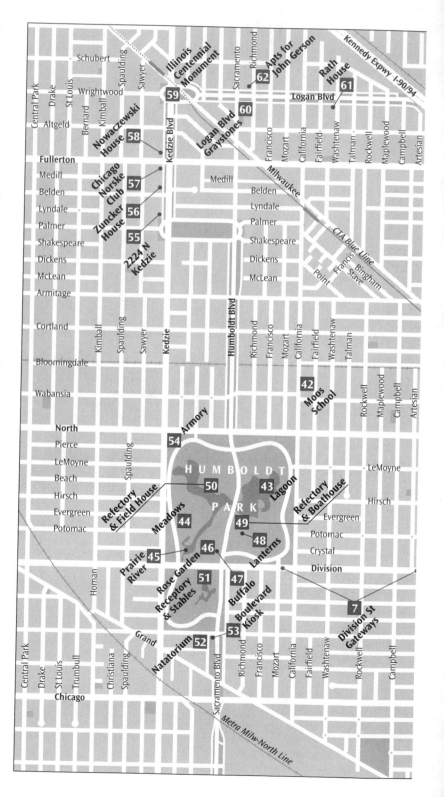

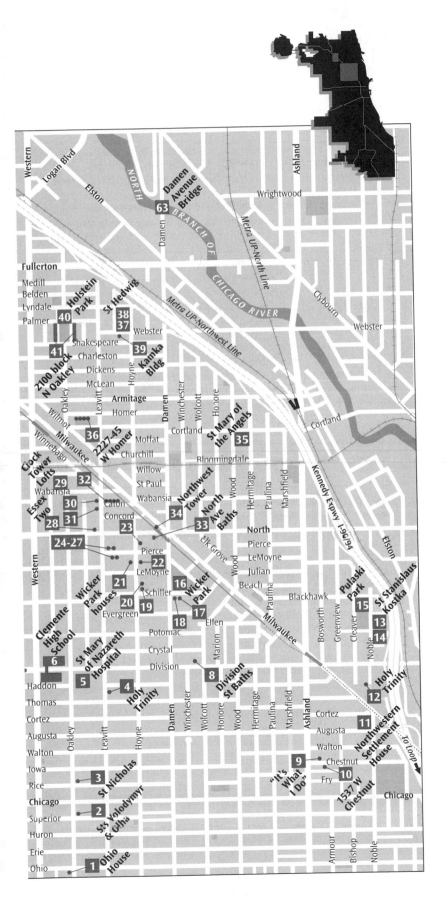

NORTHWEST SIDE

THE NORTHWEST SIDE COMPRISES DISPARATE NEIGHBORHOODS UNITED BY THE important artery of Milwaukee Ave. Like many of Chicago's diagonal streets, it began as an Indian trail, was developed as a plank road and streetcar route, and remains a heavily traveled commercial thorough-fare. The many changes in neighborhood names and boundaries along the Milwaukee Ave. corridor reflect the area's shifting populations and their various motives of ethnic pride, historical interest, and real estate promotion.

The major community areas, which extend west from the north branch of the Chicago River for about two miles, are West Town, from Kinzie St. to about Bloomingdale Ave.; Logan Square, from Blooming-dale to Diversey Aves.; Avondale, from Diversey Ave. to Addison St.; and Irving Park, from Addison St. to Montrose Ave. West Town includes the neighborhood of Wicker Park; the section of Logan Square east of Western Ave. is known as Bucktown.

In 1851 Chicago's boundaries were extended to Western and North Aves. The earliest housing in West Town was built by German Catholics who came after the 1848 revolutions in Europe and settled around Mil-waukee Ave. and Division St. By the mid-1860s they were joined by large numbers of Polish immigrants, and animosities between nation-alities caused conflicts. Germans and Poles both emphasized the estab-lishment of "national" parishes and built large churches that served as both community and religious centers.

The boulevard system radiating from Humboldt Park is a major fea-ture of the area. An 1869 act of the State Legislature established the West Park Commission, one of three municipal bodies responsible for creating a system of peripheral boulevards and pleasure grounds in-tended to ring the city. William Le Baron Jenney, better known as the father of the skyscraper, was hired in 1870 to design the West Side parks and boulevards. Conceived as an ensemble and originally named Upper, Central, and Lower parks, these landscapes are now known as Humboldt, Garfield, and Douglas parks and are linked by broad boule-vards lined with stately houses and apartments.

The creation of Humboldt Park attracted real estate speculators, and the Fire of 1871 was another impetus to population growth, driving many workers from damaged areas to this expanding industrial and residential corridor. Much of what is now the Northwest Side lay be-yond the city limits, with the housing stock consisting of inexpensive wooden buildings free from the ban on frame construction enacted within Chicago itself.

In 1870 Charles G. and Joel H. Wicker donated a small triangle of land at the center of their subdivision to become a city park. By the late 1880s and early 1890s the surrounding area had developed as fashionably middle and upper class. The construction of streetcar lines and the ex-tension of the elevated line to Logan Square in 1895 fostered growth north along the boulevards. Many of the successful immigrants who ran businesses on Milwaukee Ave. and had lived there in "flats above the store" built elegant graystones, brick town houses, and two- and three-flats emulating single-family homes on Kedzie and Logan Blvds.

In the great annexation of 1889 Chicago added 125 square miles, and the extension of the city's north and west boundaries placed the boule-

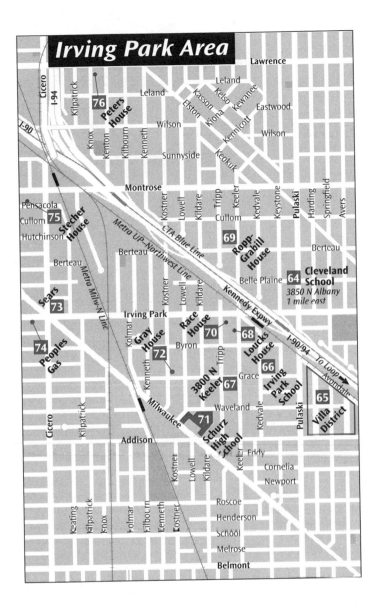

Irving Park Area

Lawrence

Cicero
I-94
I-90

Kilpatrick

76 Peters House

Leland
Leland

Kasson
Kelso
Kiona
Kewanee
Kennicott
Keokuk

Eastwood

Wilson
Wilson

Knox
Kenton
Kilbourn
Kenneth

Sunnyside

Montrose

Pensacola
Cullom
75 Stecher House
Hutchinson

Berteau

Kostner
Lowell
Kildare
Cullom

Tripp
Keeler
Kedvale
Keystone
Pulaski
Harding
Springfield
Avers

Berteau

Berteau

69 Ropp-Grabill House

Belle Plaine

64 Cleveland School
3850 N Albany
1 mile east

Metra UP–Northwest Line

CTA Blue Line

Metra Milw-N Line

Sears
73

Kennedy Expwy

I-90/94   To Loop

Irving Park

Kostner
Lowell
Kildare

74 Peoples Gas

Kolmar

Gray House
72

Race House
70

68

Loucks House

66

Byron

Kenneth

3800 N Keeler
67

Tripp

Grace

Irving Park School

65 Villa District

To Loop
Avondale

Milwaukee

71 Schurz High School

Waveland

Kedvale

Pulaski

Cicero
Kilpatrick

Addison

Kostner
Lowell
Kildare

Keeler

Eddy
Cornelia
Newport

Keating
Kilpatrick
Knox

Kolmar
Kilbourn
Kenneth
Kostner

Roscoe

Henderson
School

Melrose

Belmont

---

vard system in the center of the city, rather than on its periphery. North along Milwaukee Ave. the annexation of part of Jefferson Township added the suburb of Irving Park. Evidence of this nineteenth-century community is still visible in the cluster of fine Victorian homes in the area of Irving Park Rd. and the Kennedy Expressway. Many of them have shed their siding to emerge as clapboard Cinderellas. Electric streetcar lines were established along Irving Park Rd. and Milwaukee and Elston Aves. in the 1890s, and the neighborhood began to develop as part of the city. But even greater development occurred between 1910 and 1920, when Irving Park's population more than doubled.

Early settlers of West Town included not only Germans and Poles but also Scandinavians and Italians. After World War I a tremendous influx of Russian Jews replaced some of the Poles and Germans. The newest wave of newcomers includes Hispanics as well as Polish immigrants. St. Stanislaus Kostka now offers masses in English, Polish, and Spanish, testifying to the area's continuing diversity.

—JULIA SNIDERMAN BACHRACH

1| Ohio House
2301 W. Ohio St.
1989, 1999, VALERIO DEWALT TRAIN

The square masonry base was part of the first project and houses all of the public spaces. The forty-two-foot-diameter aluminum-clad cylinder was added to the second floor a decade later. It shimmers in the right light. The two front doors, at right angles to each other, lead to the same space.

OHIO HOUSE

2| Sts. Volodymyr & Olha Church
739 N. Oakley Blvd.
1975, JAROSLAW A. KORSUNSKY

3| St. Nicholas Ukrainian Catholic Cathedral
2238 W. Rice St.
1915, WORTHMANN, STEINBACH & PIONTEK

Liturgical differences split St. Nicholas's congregation, leading the traditionalists to build their own church. The cathedral's thirteen domes represent Christ and the Apostles; the application of intricate mosaics derives from the Cathedral of St. Sophia in Kiev. The church has a simpler profile but still includes five domes and an enormous mosaic commemorating the conversion of Grand Duke Vladimir of Kiev to Christianity in 988, an occasion also marked by the sculpture of the two saints northwest of the church. The mosaics and paintings are dazzling.

HOLY TRINITY RUSSIAN ORTHODOX CATHEDRAL

4| Holy Trinity Russian Orthodox Cathedral
1121 N. Leavitt St.
1899–1903, LOUIS H. SULLIVAN

Sullivan synthesized Orthodox iconography and Byzantine tradition with his own design ideals and the theories of the nineteenth-century Gothic Revival architect Eugène-Emmanuel Viollet-le-Duc. The portal's ogee-arched canopy derives from Russo-Byzantine precedent, while the decorative sheet metal under the canopy, though subsidiary, is as fine and fluid as Sullivan's contemporaneous work on the Carson Pirie Scott & Co. Building. The Eastern Orthodox central plan creates an intimate interior; the congregation stands in a square space surmounted by a painted octagonal dome. The sacred apse is screened from view by an elaborate iconostasis. Although most of the decoration is stenciled, it is not by Sullivan.

5| St. Mary of Nazareth Hospital
2233 W. Division St.
1975, PERKINS & WILL

The fluted exterior resembles the AT&T Long Lines Building in New York and could have inspired the sets of the futuristic movie *Brazil*.

6| Roberto Clemente High School
1147 N. Western Ave.
1974, FUJIKAWA, CONTERATO, LOHAN & ASSOCS.

DIVISION ST. GATEWAYS

To squeeze a large high school onto a limited site split by a major street, Clemente's instruction building rises nine stories and is connected to the athletic building by a steel bridge over Division St.

7| Division St. Gateways
Division St. at Artesian Ave. and Mozart Dr.
1995, DESTEFANO AND PARTNERS

The Puerto Rican flag, abstracted and rendered in forty-five tons of steel, spans the street in two places to celebrate the neighborhood's ethnic identity. Related street ornamentation includes seating with game tables as well as metal light-pole banners with laser-cut silhouettes of Puerto Rican cultural themes.

8| Division St. Russian & Turkish Baths
(*Kaplan Baths*)
1916 W. Division St.
1907, MAURICE SPITZER

Unlike the municipal baths, these provided more than just hygiene; behind the Classically derived limestone facade they were a luxurious retreat.

9| "It's What I Do"
1544 W. Chestnut St.
BEGUN 1979, EDWIN SZEWCZYK, ARTIST

Despite the crosses, this bold, layered installation bespeaks the artist's devotions not to religion but to film stars. The artist says his work is not architectural or religious: "It's what I do."

"IT'S WHAT I DO"

10| 1537 W. Chestnut St.
1994, FREDERICK PHILLIPS & ASSOCS.

To stay in scale with other houses on the block, this residence on a double lot is articulated as two volumes, allowing room for a side garden. The eastern wing is a steel structure that houses a top-floor bedroom from which a screen porch is suspended. To increase security, there are indoor parking and a minimum of ground-floor openings.

11| Northwestern University Settlement House
1400 W. Augusta Blvd.
1910, POND & POND

The solid massing and finely detailed brickwork are typical of the settlement houses designed by these architects. Geometric trim on piers and diaper brickwork are their trademarks.

12| Holy Trinity Roman Catholic Church
1120 N. Noble St.
1906, HERMAN OLSZEWSKI AND WILLIAM G. KRIEG

The exuberant pilastered facade with its balustrades, urns, and obelisks is based on Roman Baroque models, with additional homage to the Pantheon's pedimented portico. Under the iron-vaulted ceiling, the column-free space is adorned with unusual ceiling paintings and windows by F. X. Zettler and Mayer & Co.

13| St. Stanislaus Kostka Roman Catholic Church
1327 N. Noble St.
1876–1881, PATRICK C. KEELEY
1892, TOWERS, ADOLPHUS DRUIDING

The dazzling interior focuses on the apse, with richly embel-

ST. STANISLAUS KOSTKA CHURCH

lished paintings of the life of St. Stanislaus by Thaddeus Zukotynski. In 1923 the brick walls were covered with stucco in an economical if gritty imitation of stone. The southern tower was destroyed by lightning in 1964.

14| St. Stanislaus Kostka School
1255 N. Noble St.
1959, BELLI & BELLI

The John F. Kennedy Expressway was routed around the church but displaced many parishioners and destroyed the old school. The replacement is a slightly kitschy take on Corbusian modernism with a classroom block atop *pilotis*.

15| Pulaski Park
Blackhawk St., Potomac Ave., Noble St., and Cleaver St.
1912, JENS JENSEN
1913, LOCKER BUILDING;
1914, FIELD HOUSE, WILLIAM CARBYS ZIMMERMAN

The West Park Commission carved this Progressive Reform movement park out of a densely populated neighborhood and programmed it to meet a wide range of needs. The bathing facilities of the Locker Building, intended for men and boys, served 500 patrons per hour. Dominated by a multiplaned, clipped gable roof, the Tudor Revival/Craftsman–style field house is as grand as a manor house, its generous scale and high style contrasting sharply with the modest flats nearby. It housed men's and women's gyms (with separate entrances), an auditorium, and, originally, a branch of the Chicago Public Library, hinted at by the sculptured owl and open book in the western gable.

16| Wicker Park
Damen, Schiller & Wicker Park Aves.

The 1880s fountain was rebuilt in 2002 (DeStefano and Partners) from castings made from the original molds. The field house (1985, Chicago Park District) is reminiscent of John S. Van Bergen's Oak Park playground shelters of the 1920s (now remodeled or demolished), built to a domestic scale with Prairie School lines.

Often called Chicago's ethnic Gold Coast, Wicker Park housed many prosperous Scandinavian and German immigrants who could have afforded to live farther east and south but chose to build here, alongside other successful compatriots.

17 | Harris Cohn House
1941 W. Schiller St.
1891, THEODORE LEWANDOWSKI

A standout among its more sedate Italianate neighbors, this costly Queen Anne has a rusticated and towered stone facade with granite columns—a fine display of the style's forms, materials, and window shapes.

18 | Nels T. Quales House
1951 W. Schiller St.
CA. 1873, ARCHITECT UNKNOWN
1890, ADDITION AND REMODELING, THIEL & LANG

The original, Italianate house was set far back from the street; its stone window hoods are still visible on the sides. The Queen Anne front addition, complete with Moorish arch, is a stylish update. It distinguished the house from adjacent properties such as 1955–1957 (1883, Charles O. Hansen), which Quales, a Norwegian immigrant who became a Chicago city physician, developed.

19 | 1407 N. Hoyne Ave.
1879, ARCHITECT UNKNOWN

This high-shouldered Second Empire house is tall and exuberantly French, with its curbed mansard roof, incised foliate detailing, sawtooth window hoods, and cast iron porch details.

1407 N. HOYNE AVE.

20 | Louis Hanson House
1417 N. Hoyne Ave.
1879, ARCHITECT UNKNOWN

The side porch on this Italianate house has nothing to do with entry but was intended as a frame for viewing the garden.

21 | Henry Grusendorf House
1520 N. Hoyne Ave.
1886, GUSTAV BLOEDNER

22 | Adolph Borgmeier House
1521 N. Hoyne Ave.
1895, HENRY T. KLEY

Bloedner's Second Empire design is embellished with a carved portrait of a woman, of the type frequently seen on houses designed by or built for Germans. Kley's turreted Queen Anne has an intricately detailed stoop framed with wooden "lace."

23 | Albin Greiner House
1559 N. Hoyne Ave.
1876, ARCHITECT UNKNOWN

This elaborate gabled brick cottage with Italianate window hood moldings is one of the area's oldest houses, featuring the side garden porch common in this neighborhood.

24 | Hermann Weinhardt House
2135 W. Pierce Ave.
1889, WILLIAM OHLHABER

Fancy houses in neighborhoods of successful immigrants often looked to Europe for inspiration and ingenuously used elements that had gone out of style elsewhere. The side porch with

HERMANN WEINHARDT HOUSE

the garden view is a holdover; the rich and heavy metal barge-boards recall northern Europe.

25| John D. Runge House
2138 W. Pierce Ave.
1884, FROMMANN & JEBSEN

The elaborate two-story porch beautifully frames the views through robust posts and finely worked motifs, such as the Masonic insignias under the eaves of the gabled dormer.

JOHN D. RUNGE HOUSE

26| Theodore Juergens House
2141 W. Pierce Ave.
1895, HENRY T. KLEY

27| 2146, 2150 & 2156
W. Pierce Ave.
1890, LUTKEN & THISSLEW

These fine examples of rusticated Romanesque show how the style was better adapted in the long run to the more durable limestone (2141 and 2150) than to the softer sandstone (2146 and 2156).

28| Essex Two Live/Work Structure
2210 W. North Ave.
1995, WHEELER KEARNS ARCHITECTS

The clean, simple elevation could be the business card of the two graphic designers who live and work here. To construct a solid, high-quality house on a restricted budget, a prefabricated structure of insulated concrete beams, walls, floors, and a roof was erected in four days atop six site-cast concrete caissons. Concrete is left exposed, although it is visually softened on the interior floors with integral pigment.

29| Clock Tower Lofts
2300 W. Wabansia Ave.
1919, ALFRED ALSCHULER
1995, CONVERSION TO LOFTS, HARTSHORNE & PLUNKARD

This unusually fine loft conversion leaves the best of the old building and beautifully complements it with new material. It fits well into its side street.

30| Flats for Iver Christianson
1658 N. Leavitt St.
1893, CHARLES F. SORENSEN

31| Flats for Gustaf Murbach
1644 N. Leavitt St.
1896, CHARLES THISSLEW

Using high-quality materials such as stone, cast iron, and art glass, the owners built many handsome flats, such as these rusticated Romanesque graystones, in this prestigious area of single-family houses.

32| 2138, 2142, 2146, 2152
& 2156 W. Caton St.
1891, FABER & PAGELS

2156 W. CATON ST.

53| Boulevard Kiosk

1995, DLK ARCHITECTURE

Map station kiosks and additional new signage were designed as part of an improvement project for the city's twenty-eight-mile boulevard system. The kiosks reinterpret nineteenth-century forms in contemporary materials.

ILLINOIS NATIONAL GUARD, THIRTY-THIRD DIVISION—NORTHWEST ARMORY

54| Illinois National Guard, Thirty-third Division— Northwest Armory
1551 N. Kedzie Ave.

1940, CHATTEN & HAMMOND

Late nineteenth-century armories were fortified like castles to preserve public order against possible workers' demonstrations and other civil unrest. By the 1930s the typical armory was more civil, with more entrances and windows, because its drill hall could also serve as a convention hall or sports arena. This strong Art Deco limestone block gives the reassurance of a fort—but with the modern styling of an office building or movie palace. The panels of men in uniform are by John J. Szaton.

Humboldt and Kedzie Blvds. and Logan Square

No part of the twenty-six-mile boulevard system offers more pleasure than the drive from Humboldt Park to Logan Square, a trip that would be even more pleasant at a nineteenth-century pace. The 250-foot-wide roadways were designed with central "carriage drives" and service roads framed by formal lines of elm and catalpa trees. The roadway widens to 400 feet at Palmer Square, a popular raceway for nineteenth-century carriage drivers and cyclists.

55| 2224 N. Kedzie Blvd.

1915, JEAN B. ROHM & SON

A stolid square facade is enlivened by inventive Art Nouveau stone trim, especially the cartoonish human face.

56| Peter M. Zuncker House
2312 N. Kedzie Blvd.

1911, HUEHL & SCHMID

The quirkiness of the unusual dormer, with its ski slope profile, ornaments a conservative Prairie School design.

57| Chicago Norske Club
2350 N. Kedzie Blvd.

1916, GIAVER & DINKELBERG

CHICAGO NORSKE CLUB

"No two alike!" the architects could boast. When built, 2152 was described as Renaissance; 2146 was called Swiss.

33| North Ave. Baths Building
2039 W. North Ave.

1921, LLOYD & KLEIN
1997, RESTORATION, JAY R. KAISER

Bathhouses often served as social centers in ethnic neighborhoods, and this building has found new life as a restaurant and residential structure.

34| Northwest Tower
1608 N. Milwaukee Ave.

1929, PERKINS, CHATTEN & HAMMOND

The peaked tower of this neighborhood skyscraper was to have housed a revolving red, green, and white beacon. The first two floors were designed for retail, with medical offices on the middle floors.

NORTHWEST TOWER

35| St. Mary of the Angels Roman Catholic Church
1850 N. Hermitage Ave.

1914–1920, WORTHMANN & STEINBACH
1992, REHABILITATION, HOLABIRD & ROOT

An ambitious pastor's architectural ambitions, combined with a devout and generous congregation's funds, created this neo-Renaissance "Polish cathedral," where angels tread on the parapets and hover in the massive nave. The tile and terra-cotta dome recalls the silhouette of St. Peter's in Rome.

36| 2227 through 2245 W. Homer Ave.

1888, THEODORE N. BELL

Still remarkably well preserved, these tiny Queen Anne cottages miniaturized the style for the budget conscious.

37| St. Hedwig Roman Catholic Church
2100 W. Webster Ave.

1899–1902, ADOLPHUS DRUIDING

In this high-octane Renaissance Revival design for a Polish congregation, the geometric facade is anchored by square corner piers topped by robust cupolas. The aedicula above the entry is echoed by a pedimented reredos behind the altar.

38| St. Hedwig Rectory
2226 N. Hoyne Ave.

1892, ADOLPHUS DRUIDING

This kind of Second Empire grandeur was already out of style in more fashionable neighborhoods. Essentially a boardinghouse, the rectory is masquerading as a mansion, its breadth visually diminished by setbacks.

39| Joseph Kamka Building
2121 W. Webster Ave.

1910, WORTHMANN & STEINBACH
1940, REMODELING, ARCHITECT UNKNOWN

The first-floor funeral parlor was modernized with a pigmented, structural glass facade that is sleek and elegant—and completely at odds with the prim slice of dull flats above it.

40| Holstein Park
Shakespeare Ave., Oakley Ave., and Lyndale St.

1912, FIELD HOUSE, WILLIAM CARBYS ZIMMERMAN

In 1854 three developers donated just under two acres of their Holstein District property in the hope that a city park would increase the value of their surrounding land. But development did not pick up until after the city had given the land in 1901 to the West Park Commission, which began improvements five years later. Clunky compared to the refined Pulaski Park field house, this blockwide recreation center contained many of the same elements: gymnasiums, a library, assembly rooms, showers, and lockers.

41 | 2100 Block of N. Oakley Ave.

Tall, narrow, and stiff, the gabled brick cottages and two- and three-flats ringing Holstein Park are curious anachronisms created between 1901 and 1908 by neighborhood architect

Humboldt Park
W. North Ave., N. Kedzie Ave., W. Augusta Blvd., N. Sacramento Blvd., W. Division St., N. California Ave.
1912, ADDITION: W. AUGUSTA BLVD., N. WHIPPLE ST., W. WALTON ST., WEST OF N. SACRAMENTO BLVD.
1871–1877, WILLIAM LE BARON JENNEY
1877–1890s, OSCAR F. DUBUIS
1906–1909, JENS JENSEN

The most impressive of the three great nineteenth-century West Side parks, Humboldt Park gives no hint of its originally flat and boggy site. As did his colleagues in the naturalistic landscape movement, such as Frederick Law Olmsted, Jenney strove to create man-made vistas that aspired to the beauty of the natural. His work is best seen in the section east of Humboldt Dr., where the irregularly shaped **43 | Lagoon & Islands** typify the picturesque ideal. The concrete bases of lamp standards marking Jenney's northeast entrance to the park still stand at the corner of California and North Aves. His southeast entrance, at Division St. and California Ave., marked by the *Miner and Child* sculpture (1908, Charles J. Mulligan), was

Joseph A. Wilkowski and contractor John Konczik. Their monotonous uniformity is relieved only by slightly varying colors and setbacks. German names were originally given to the park and surrounding streets, but by 1901 many Germans had moved out, replaced by Poles.

42 | Bernard Moos Public School
1711 N. California Ave.
1910, DWIGHT H. PERKINS

Best described as castellated Chicago School, with crenellated parapets above the projecting stair towers, this is a close cousin of the architect's contemporaneous George M. Pullman School.

eliminated during Jensen's era.

Humboldt Park played a significant role in the development of Jensen's style. Early in his career, he served here as park superintendent, returning to it after being named chief landscape architect of the West Park System in 1905. The area west of Humboldt Dr. shows his hand in the three large **44 | Meadows,** sheltered from Kedzie Ave. by berms and heavy landscaping. He narrowed the western section of the **Lagoon** (called the "New Lake") to form a signature **45 | Prairie River** that imitates one of his beloved native Illinois landscapes. Nearby he bermed and set below grade the formally designed **46 | Rose Garden,** which in 1911 gained bronze castings of Edward Kemeys' **47 | Buffalo** sculptures originally created for the 1893 World's Columbian Exposition.

Jensen also introduced Prairie School architecture into Humboldt Park, hiring Schmidt, Garden & Martin and William Carbys Zimmerman. The former firm's **48 | Lanterns** (1907), identical to those in Columbus Park, have been virtually destroyed by vandals.

HUMBOLDT PARK REFECTORY & BOAT HOUSE

49 | Refectory & Boat House
East side of Humboldt Dr. north of W. Division St.
1907, RICHARD E. SCHMIDT, GARDEN & MARTIN
2002, RESTORATION, BAUER LATOZA STUDIO

The hovering hipped roof and the three great arches are bounteously reflected in the lagoon to the north. This great Prairie School amenity encouraged visitors to stay outdoors, sheltering summer guests on the terraced open-air room and their rental boats below, and serving as a warming house for ice-skaters in the winter. The parking lot to the south was once the Music Court.

50 | Refectory & Field House
1400 N. Sacramento Blvd.
1928, MICHAELSEN & ROGNSTAD

Georgian and Tudor details combine in this eclectic facility, grandly historic in derivation.

51 | Receptory & Stables
South side of W. Division St. west of Humboldt Dr.
1896, FROMMANN & JEBSEN
1998, RESTORATION, MCCLIER

Domestically detailed but lavishly scaled, this was intended to resemble "the old German Style of country house architecture," according to the West Park Commission. Renovation to house a Hispanic Cultural Arts Museum was severely set back by a fire in 1992. The nearby Lily Pond (1897) is thought to be an early Jensen project.

52 | Natatorium
W. Augusta Blvd. west of N. Sacramento Blvd.
1914, WILLIAM CARBYS ZIMMERMAN

This simple Prairie School pool house provided other recreational opportunities as well.

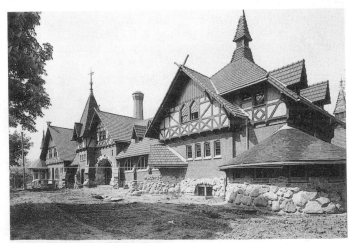

HUMBOLDT PARK RECEPTORY & STABLES

The stylized dragons and heavy brackets are borrowed from Norwegian vernacular architecture.

58 | William Nowaczewski House
2410 N. Kedzie Blvd.
1897, ARCHITECT UNKNOWN

One can only wonder at the appetite for display that funded this virtuoso panorama of carved limestone. Flemish stepped gables, a medieval crenellated tower, Gothic crockets and window hood molds, and Classical capitals and modillions compete for attention on the ashlar front.

59 | Illinois Centennial Monument
Logan Square
1918, HENRY BACON, ARCH.; EVELYN BEATRICE LONGMAN, SCULPTOR

Around the base range Native Americans, explorers, workers, and farmers, an honor roll of citizens from the state's first century of statehood. Longman frequently collaborated with Bacon, the designer of the Lincoln Memorial in Washington, D.C.

60 | Logan Blvd. Graystones

After the Fire and through the early 1890s, architects experimented with a variety of decorative sedimentary stones, from yellow Joliet-Lemont limestone to Minnesota's pink Kasota stone to the dark red sandstones of the northern Wiscon-

3024 W. LOGAN BLVD
(LOGAN BLVD. GRAYSTONES)

sin shores of Lake Superior. But by the mid-1890s Chicago's proximity by rail to Indiana's limestone quarries and a shift to simpler styles had created a demand for Bedford limestone not only among developers of skyscrapers and mansions but also first-generation citizens building homes and flats.

The ace of sedimentary stones, limestone is hard and durable, takes carving beautifully, and holds its crisp lines even through Chicago's vicious freeze-thaw cycles. Smooth or rusticated, it weathers well, discoloring little and adapting to any style of masonry.

Logan Blvd. has the city's finest and most easily viewed collection of graystones. Classical detailing abounds, as at **2955** (1908, Douglas S. Pentecost) and **2947**, **2949**, and **2951** (1907, Albert J. Fischer). Groups are frequently built to a uniform height, usually with roofline emphasis above the bay. Checkerboard patterning, alternating solids and open spaces, is popular for balcony walls. Curious amalgams abound: at **2959** (1909, Hermann I. Gaul) the porch piers are embellished with stripes that are apparently Prairie School at the corners but become meander patterns on the central

2959 W. LOGAN BLVD
(LOGAN BLVD. GRAYSTONES)

piers. Classical and Gothic details combine at **2715** and **2741** (1905, Burtar & Gassmann), which bracket **2735** and its pronounced Richardsonian Romanesque porch arch. Even the grandest buildings are flats masquerading as houses, like the immense gabled and balconied examples at **2820** (1904, Fred & John Ahlschlager) and **3024** (1908, John Ahlschlager).

Because of limestone's durability, there has been little replacement on these homes, which retain unusual integrity. The front porches and steps alone deserve landmark designation—perhaps as a historic Stoop District, to celebrate the six- to eight-inch-wide railings and eight-foot-wide treads.

61| John Rath House
2701 W. Logan Blvd.
1907, GEORGE W. MAHER

The low, Prairie School profile and characteristic Maher detailing, such as the flanged segmental arch shapes of the entrance bay and doorway, are resolutely individual. The floral-patterned art glass is remarkable, as is the carved wood and stone. Under the exaggeratedly deep eaves of the low, hipped roof, the curious boulevard facade features impressive second-floor artglass windows across the immense porch opening.

62| Apartments for John Gerson
2934–2936 W. Logan Blvd.
1909, FREDERICK R. SCHOCK

The Art Nouveau doorway leads through a mosaic-lined hall to Craftsman Style apartments lavishly decorated with art glass and decorative tiles. The stacked porches make the facade rhythmic, while capturing the boulevard's beauty for outdoor living rooms.

63| Damen Ave. Bridge
Damen Ave. south of Diversey
1998, TRANSSYSTEMS ENG.,
J. MULLER INTERNATIONAL,
BRIDGE ENG.; MULLER &
MULLER, ARCHS.

APARTMENTS FOR JOHN GERSON

The bright red arches of the modern bridge rise above the former industrial landscape and promise to become a new neighborhood landmark. The thin road deck is suspended from two four-foot-diameter curved steel pipes, which are self-supporting and require no cross-bracing. The result is a light, open, and graceful structure.

64| Grover Cleveland Public School
3850 N. Albany Ave.
1910, DWIGHT H. PERKINS

The bold, almost intimidating massing is warmed by bands of subtly colored brick that run like a tapestry along the edges of the elevations.

65| The Villa District
**Bounded by Addison St.,
Hamlin Ave., Avondale Ave.,
and the alley east of Pulaski Rd.**

In 1907 Albert Haentze & Charles M. Wheeler subdivided the land of this historic Villa District, stipulating single-family homes "of bungalow appearance." Two popular types appear here. The "Chicago" bungalow is narrow, long, and built of brick with a side entrance; it is represented at 3700 N. Avers Ave. and on the west side of the 3600 block of N. Hamlin Ave. The "California" bungalow is usually wider and has a front entrance, an open front porch, wide eaves, and more varied materials; 3700 N. Springfield Ave. (1920, John C. Christensen) is a good example. Prairie

School touches enliven 3646 N. Avers Ave. (1912, Hatzfeld & Knox), while generic Sullivanesque ornament, such as that on many Irving Park Rd. storefronts, graces the facade at 3608 N. Avers Ave. (1917, Harley & Aga).

THE VILLA DISTRICT

66| Irving Park Public School
3815 N. Kedvale Ave.
1912, DWIGHT H. PERKINS

Best viewed from the corner of Grace St., the assembly hall is treated like a separate block, with massing similar to a Louis H. Sullivan bank.

67| 3800 N. Keeler Ave.
BEFORE 1870, ARCHITECT UNKNOWN

The earliest houses on these blocks can be identified by their brick foundations. This delicate villa combines Gothic Revival (steeply pitched gabled roofs), Italianate (high corner tower), and Second Empire (mansard roof) elements.

68| Charles N. Loucks House
3926 N. Keeler Ave.
1889, CLARENCE H. TABOR

Despite alterations, this remains one of the area's finest Queen Annes, especially for its rich art glass and idiosyncratically capped turret.

69| Ropp-Grabill House
4132 N. Keeler Ave.
BEFORE 1871, ARCHITECT UNKNOWN

This lovely Italianate house still has its cupola, an ornamental feature useful as a "chimney" for drawing fresh air up through the house.

70| Stephen A. Race House
3945 N. Tripp Ave.
CA. 1870, ARCHITECT UNKNOWN

This Italianate house originally faced Irving Park Rd., but was turned on the lot in 1905.

71| Carl Schurz High School
3601 N. Milwaukee Ave.
1908–1910, DWIGHT H. PERKINS
1915, ADDITION, ARTHUR F. HUSSANDER
1924, ADDITION, JOHN C. CHRISTENSEN
1993–2000, RENOVATIONS, ROSS BARNEY + JANKOWSKI

Schurz High School is an ideal model for urban development and for its expression in architectural form.

Commissioned by a reform-minded school board headed by Jane Addams, the project was one highlight of a broad program for rescuing

CARL SCHURZ HIGH SCHOOL

the immigrant poor from the ignorance and isolation engendered by the industrial city.

One revolutionary aspect of this program was linking the development of schools with the development of neighborhood parks. In 1904 Perkins, in partnership with landscape designer Jens Jensen, had written Chicago's first citywide park plan, promoting a network of "breathing holes" that would bring the social and health benefits of natural landscapes to the common citizen. Perkins was thus the ideal choice to bring these qualities to the expanding school system as architect of the Board of Education.

Chicago's typical Dickensian public school before 1905 was a poorly lighted and ventilated box, set into the city grid with no significant playgrounds. Toilet facilities were archaic and located in the basement. The forty-odd schools that Perkins designed between 1905 and 1910 changed all that, creating a building type with grass and trees, sunlight and fresh air, safety from fire, and good sanitation.

At the same time that these functional transformations were taking place, a similar revolution was developing in the art of architecture. A circle of young architects, including Perkins, Frank Lloyd Wright, Hugh M. G. Garden, Purcell & Elmslie, Walter Burley Griffin, Pond & Pond, Robert Spencer, and others, was transforming the concepts of the Arts & Crafts movement into the indigenous Prairie School.

Schurz High School represents the translation of what was mainly a domestic vocabulary into an institutional one. A centralized composition that telescopes out from a dominant center, it sits astride its site. Its syncopation of horizontal sills and eaves with vertical piers, together with its hovering roofs and earth-toned brick and terra-cotta trim, place it squarely among the contemporaneous Prairie School explorations of Perkins's colleagues. The interiors and decoration are somewhat generic Prairie designs. Lighting fixtures, trim, and other details are highly geometric, often reflecting stylized natural forms; the auditorium, which benefited from recent alterations, was a cubic volume with spatial, planar, and linear transparencies similar to—if not as bold as—Frank Lloyd Wright's spectacular Unity Temple.

Carl Schurz High School asserted that the urban public school belongs much higher on the architectural hierarchy than had been allowed. Beyond its task of providing a safe, healthy, and beautiful place to learn, it towers over the trees, sheltering the entire community, an immense Prairie house for the new citizens of its immigrant, working-class neighborhood. —ERIC EMMETT DAVIS

72| John Gray House
4362 W. Grace Ave.
BEFORE 1870, ARCHITECT UNKNOWN

The nearby Chicago, Milwaukee & St. Paul Railroad station was named Grayland after this early settler, as was the neighborhood created when his farm was subdivided in 1873 and this country villa became a suburban home.

73| Sears, Roebuck & Co.
4730 W. Irving Park Rd.
1938, NIMMONS, CARR & WRIGHT

In the early 1930s Sears established a department to design stores built around the presentation of merchandise; this was one of the first five constructed to their specifications. Windows, intended as a kind of transparent billboard, were for display, not illumination; products inside were better lit artificially. The plain, vaguely Art Moderne concrete facades are a backdrop to these windows and to a giant logo.

PEOPLES GAS CO.—IRVING PARK STORE

74 | Peoples Gas Co.—Irving Park Store
4839 W. Irving Park Rd.
1926, GEORGE GRANT ELMSLIE AND HERMANN V. VON HOLST

Elmslie was Louis H. Sullivan's chief draftsman, and this finely carved facade shows his mastery of the Sullivanesque ornamental style. Bedford limestone blooms in delicately embellished carvings atop the side piers and across the cornice. The vestigial display of gas appliances recalls the days when Peoples Gas sold and rented them at neighborhood stores.

Within a mile of this area are two unusual houses by a leading Prairie School architect.

75 | Karl Stecher House
4840 W. Pensacola Ave.
1910, WALTER BURLEY GRIFFIN

The soaring roof seems poised for takeoff from its ground-hugging base. Horizontal board-and-batten siding, stucco, and corner windows with geometric mullions are prominent Prairie School motifs.

76 | Harry V. Peters House
4731 N. Knox Ave.
1906, WALTER BURLEY GRIFFIN

A broad side-gabled roof dominates this small house, with eaves extending far beyond the wall plane. The front door is tucked into a tunnel-like entry passage.

CHICAGO–O'HARE INTERNATIONAL AIRPORT

IN JUNE 1942 THE FEDERAL GOVERNMENT BOUGHT 1,000 ACRES SURROUNDING the small Orchard Place Airport to establish the Douglas Aircraft Co. factory, which built C-54 transport planes there during World War II. In 1945 an urgent search to replace Midway Airport, then the world's busiest, led to this wartime factory site. Although fifteen miles northwest of the Loop, and burdened with an existing infrastructure of streets and railroads, it offered the best chance for rapid development. The federal government gave the site to the city, retaining 280 acres for the Army Air Force, and the first commercial flight left the following year. In 1948 City Engineer Ralph H. Burke published his phased master plan for a commercial airport, which was renamed in 1949 to commemorate Edward H. ("Butch") O'Hare, a flying ace lost over the Pacific in 1942. "Orchard" lives on, however, as ORD, the call letters appearing on all inbound luggage tags.

The introduction of commercial jet service in Europe in 1952 and the anticipated debut of American jets demanded a facility with different terminal and concourse configurations as well as longer runways. By 1955 city money had funded rerouting of railroads and highways, and construction of a terminal building, new runways, and a control tower, enabling several airlines to operate regularly scheduled flights. In 1956 recently elected Mayor Richard J. Daley invited the architectural and engineering firm Naess & Murphy (which became C. F. Murphy Associates in 1957 and Murphy/Jahn in 1981) to examine the existing master plan for O'Hare development. More important, Daley successfully established an airport funding mechanism whereby landing fees would be used to pay revenue bonds, allowing a series of connecting but separate terminals to be constructed.

Naess & Murphy, consulting with others—most notably airport specialists Landrum & Brown—focused on the design concepts of "concentration, consolidation, and connections." The airport's original terminal was the International Terminal, whose site is now the current United Airlines Terminal. The location of the new terminals (now Terminals 2 and 3) was determined by the airlines' requirements for five

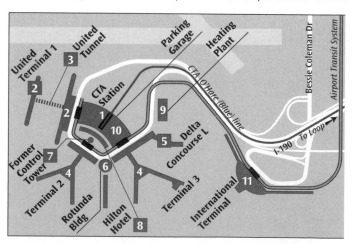

two-story concourses, radiating like fingers, with covered "accordion" ramps to planes. The boarding functions would be on the terminals' upper levels, arrival functions on the lower levels, and the administrative services on a mezzanine level. The three terminals would form a half hexagon, with parking in the center.

In 1958, as the Air Force Academy project was completed in Colorado, many members of the Skidmore, Owings & Merrill design team left that firm to join this project. Among them was Stanislav A. Gladych, who became O'Hare's chief designer. The new terminals were Miesian in concept, exploiting concrete, steel, and specially fabricated glass as the principal exterior materials.

Construction of the $120 million airport, the largest public works project ever undertaken in Chicago, began in 1959. Most of the work was completed within thirty-three months, much of it under adverse weather conditions. In 1946 Ralph Burke had predicted an almost unbelievably high 12 million passengers at O'Hare by 1960, but his estimate proved low; although the airport was still under construction, traffic that year topped 13 million.

As the airlines added jet aircraft, operations were shifted from Midway to O'Hare, serving passengers from temporary facilities that were quickly demolished as the project progressed. Construction included two terminals, a restaurant pavilion, an underground utilities tunnel, a fire station, fuel farm, two new runways, a post office, telephone exchange, heating plant, and hangars. Existing runways, portions of which are still in use, were reinforced and lengthened in their east–west configuration, and the parking lot was enlarged. The design was unusually consistent throughout, from baggage handling to furnishings and signage, with high-quality materials and craftsmanship.

At the dedication in March 1963, Mayor Daley hailed the terminals as an "engineering and administrative wonder," and they have proved durable and surprisingly flexible, even under post-9/11 security conditions. Forty years later, the adjacent terminals are now connected only for ticketed passengers, while the walk-in visitor is left with no convenient airport amenities.

Increasing traffic and bigger planes have constantly challenged the terminal facilities. Initiated by the city's Department of Aviation, O'Hare's current configuration was forged in the $2 billion O'Hare Development Plan for 1982–1995. Among those improvements are the United Airlines Terminal and the separate International Terminal. These expanded terminal areas are linked to parking facilities by the Airport Transit System (ATS), an automated, high-speed "people mover," 3.2 miles long with five stations at each of the terminals and the parking lot. American Airlines acquired the G Concourse, and rebuilt it to a design by Teng & Associates; it now has six clerestory vaults and more capacity for American's aircraft. A new $28 million FAA prototype control tower, embedded in front of the former restaurant rotunda building, was designed by Holmes & Carver Inc. of California and customized with a glass skin by Murphy/Jahn; it opened in 1996. The old FAA tower remains in place; however, it is now used for managing airfield operations. Traveling children were accommodated in 1996 in Terminal 2 with a play area designed by Peter J. Exley of the architecture firm architectureisfun.

Concern about O'Hare's congestion again became a national issue in the 1990s leading to the announcement of the $10 billion World Gateway program in 1998. Two new terminals and gate modifications to 2 and 3, a new maintenance facility, hangars and cargo depots, parking for the International Terminal, and extension of the ATS were planned in addition to reconfigured runways. T6-Partners, a consortium led by Bechtel Infrastructure Corporation, completed 30 percent of the design of the first terminal by October 2002 when the project was put on hold by the financially strapped airlines. Variations of the original plan have been promised.

Improved runway infrastructure is, however, a key component of Chicago's economic development. Two new runways and the reconfiguration of the older ones for use in all-weather conditions by the heavier planes of the future are considered necessary. The airport footprint will be enlarged by 5 percent with the controversial purchase of 141 acres on the northwest side and 292 acres on the southwest side to accommodate this growth. For now, new north and south runways are most likely to be constructed.

With its award-winning buildings spanning forty years, Chicago–O'Hare International Airport still provides a constantly changing "Design Gateway" to the city.　　　　　　　　　　　　　　　—ANNE ROYSTON

O'HARE CTA STATION

O'Hare is exciting on many levels, and is well integrated with connecting terminals, underground moving sidewalks, and the Airport Transit System. It is easier on Chicagoans, who never change flights here, than on out-of-towners, frequently seen sprinting across the great plains of terrazzo to make a connecting flight. But the airport is logical, well signed, and suitable for an indoor walking tour.

1| Chicago Transit Authority—O'Hare Station
1984, CITY OF CHICAGO, DEPT. OF PUBLIC WORKS, BUREAU OF ARCHITECTURE; MURPHY/JAHN, ASSOC. ARCH.

If only air travel could live up to the glamour of this subway terminal! The backlit glass-block walls undulate slowly to deaden sound and please the eye. The abrupt transition into the basement of the parking garage is eased by the Jahn-designed wall treatments.

2| United Airlines Terminal One Complex
1982–1988, MURPHY/JAHN; A. EPSTEIN & SONS, ASSOC. ARCH.

United's terminal is that rarest of species, an instant landmark: conspicuously, singularly, and clearly an expression of its time, place, and function.

Any terminal initially designed to serve 35 million passengers a year would have to be conspicuous, but designer Helmut Jahn and his colleagues confounded expectations by refusing to match the two handsome structures already in place around O'Hare's tight U-shaped core —a move that would have completed the three-part configuration as originally conceived. Far from being capricious, the new architectural expression derived from changes in air travel. In the early jet age terminal designers had used the logic of railroad and bus stations, with their large waiting rooms in which passengers arrived, bought tickets, and

UNITED AIRLINES TERMINAL ONE COMPLEX

waited to depart. Such configurations proved unsatisfactory as air traffic grew and as greater distances between ticket counters and planes encouraged passengers to cluster at woefully underscaled gates.

One way out of the impasse, used by Eero Saarinen at Dulles International Airport outside Washington, D.C., was to reinforce the terminal's centrality and to provide access to aircraft with shuttle buses. Although this created a magnificent architectural space, it raised new functional problems and ducked the issue of using architectural form to express the linkage between automobile and airplane. The more common solution was to decentralize, pulling apart terminals so that cars could deliver passengers close to airplanes. At its extreme this produced Dallas–Fort Worth, one of the nation's newer and more impressive airports. But the enormous distances between terminals created functional problems, and the possibility of significant interior spaces was almost ruled out.

United's Terminal represents a cross between the two approaches. It is necessarily compact because of its position within the tight O'Hare horseshoe, but it is split into two main concourses connected by an underground tunnel to increase the interface with airplanes. Its longer, lower profile along the curb gives maximum access to automobiles. The straightforward, steel-framed simplicity of the earlier terminals is brilliantly fused with a more elaborate development of the building's section and a richer palette of materials. The resulting monumentality is as grand as Dulles's but much lighter and more luminous. It also expresses more directly the reality of the contemporary airport as the place where the automobile meets the plane.   —ROBERT BRUEGMANN

3| United Airlines Terminal Pedestrian Tunnel

Connecting Concourses B and C is an 860-foot-long pedway submerged thirty-five feet below the apron with its parked and taxiing jets. An integral part of the United complex, it is a gigantic version of the undulating glass-walled tube of the CTA O'Hare Station. The colored walls ripple over white vertical bands symbolizing trees whose canopies cover the walkways.

The passage compels forward motion with a four-lane moving sidewalk and a neon-on-Dexedrine ceiling sculpture entitled *Thinking Lightly* by Michael Hayden.

4 | Terminals 2 & 3; Concourses E, F, G, H & K

1961, C. F. MURPHY ASSOCS.

1990, AMERICAN AIRLINES CONCOURSES H & K REMODELING, KOBER/BELLUSCHI AND WELTON BECKET ASSOCS.

1995, AMERICAN AIRLINES CONCOURSE G REMODELING, TENG & ASSOCS.

5 | Delta Airlines Concourse L

1982, PERKINS & WILL; MILTON PATE & ASSOCS., ASSOC. ARCH.

The terminals' vintage "glass box" look is best seen on street sides; concourse sides have been more altered with security gates, kiosks, and concession stands. Originally identical, the concrete-framed, column-free, 770-foot-long terminals spin off the Rotunda. Specially formulated tinted glass, terrazzo floors, and Charles Eames–designed waiting-area chairs have worn exceptionally well, visually and practically. Because of changes in baggage handling, ticketing, and seat-assignment procedures, passengers now spend less time in the terminals and more time in the concourses. E and F are no fun; they are still spartan 1960s in style. By comparison, the concourses stamped by a particular airline's signature (and money) look sybaritic; waiting travelers linger in a variety of bars, restaurants, stores, and spruced-up lounges. American Airlines' Concourses H and K, started by one firm and finished by another, are pleasant but read as a weak echo of the stunning United Airlines Terminal. American's G Concourse is more original and better communicates the sense of imminent flight. Delta Airlines' expansive steel-framed Concourse L was the first of the 1980s generation. Its greater width allows more spacious passage as well as more efficient handling at the ground level. The glass-walled gate at the far end is popular with plane watchers.

6 | Rotunda Building

1962, C. F. MURPHY ASSOCS.

When O'Hare opened, jet travel was a spectator sport as well as a means of transportation. The Rotunda, with its bars, restaurants, and expansive views, was the airport's social center. The circular building, which links Terminals 2 and 3 and Concourse G, not only relieves the rectilinearity but is also a practical connecting shape. To enhance circulation, the building is column-free, with a precast-concrete slab roof suspended by steel cables from a central steel ring—Chicago's only such structural tour de force.

7 | Former Control Tower

1970, I. M. PEI

O'Hare's original central nervous system was built from Pei's prototype designed for the FAA. The glass bubble 200 feet in the air was the radome.

8 | O'Hare Hilton Hotel

1972, C. F. MURPHY ASSOCS.

The slight curve relieves its immense (720-foot) length.

9 | Heating Plant

1961, C. F. MURPHY ASSOCS.

Another Stanislav Gladych design, this is Chicago Modern at its best. Considered O'Hare's finest Miesian building, it undergoes a transformation at night, when the dark glass curtain wall vanishes and the mechanical equipment inside appears as if on a giant TV screen.

O'HARE HEATING PLANT

O'HARE INTERNATIONAL TERMINAL

10| Parking Garage

1973, C. F. MURPHY ASSOCS.

The largest construction contract ever awarded by the city and the world's largest garage when built, it has a total of seventy-nine acres of parking on six levels.

11| International Terminal

1993, PERKINS & WILL

Long underserved at O'Hare, the international airlines fill this gateway building. The gentle arc of the long curvilinear roof recalls old hangars while evoking an "architecture of movement." The transparency, intended to enhance the traveler's orientation and conserve energy, makes the terminal dazzling at night.

WEST SIDE

NEAR WEST SIDE

GARFIELD PARK | AUSTIN

NEAR WEST SIDE

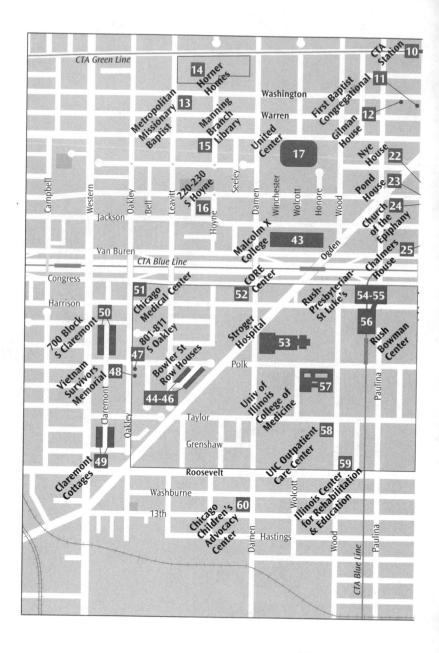

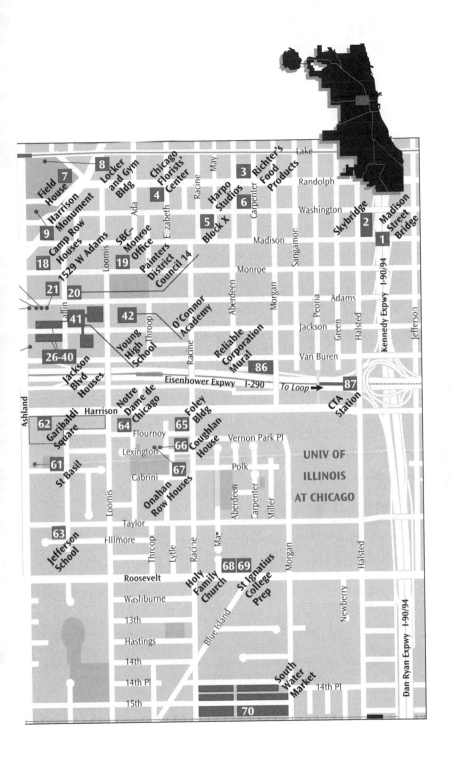

Lake

May

Randolph

Richter's
Food
Products

8 Locker
and Gym
Bldg

3

Washington

7 Field
House

4 Chicago
Florists'
Center

Racine

Harpo
Studios

6

Carpenter

Skybridge

2

Madison
Street
Bridge

Harrison
Monument

Ada

Elizabeth

5 Block X

1

9 Camp Row
Houses

Madison

Sangamor

18 1529 W Adams

SBC-
Monroe
Office

19

Loomis

Painters
District
Council 14

Monroe

Morgan

Adams

Peoria

Halsted

Kennedy Expwy I-90/94

Jefferson

21

20

Tatin

O'Connor
Academy

Aberdeen

Green

Jackson

41

42

Throop

Racine

Reliable
Corporation
Mural

Van Buren

26–40

Young
High School

Jackson
Blvd
Houses

86

Eisenhower Expwy I-290

To Loop →

87

CTA
Station

Ashland

62 Garibaldi
Square

Harrison

Notre
Dame de
Chicago

Foley
Bldg

64

65

Flournoy

Coughlan
House

Vernon Park Pl

UNIV OF

61 St Basil

Lexington

66

67

Polk

ILLINOIS

Cabrini

Onahan
Row Houses

Aberdeen

Carpenter

Miller

AT CHICAGO

Taylor

Loomis

63 Jefferson
School

Hillmore

Throop

Lytle

Racine

May

Morgan

Halsted

Roosevelt

68 **69**

Holy
Family
Church

St Ignatius
College Prep

Newberry

Washburne

13th

Hastings

Blue Island

Dan Ryan Expwy I-90/94

14th

14th Pl

South
Water
Market

14th Pl

15th

70

NEAR WEST SIDE

THE NEAR WEST SIDE IS A PATCHWORK OF PAST AND PRESENT: HISTORIC blocks separated by vast stretches of urban renewal and pockets of blight. From a Civil War–era residence and church to newly converted industrial lofts and modern institutional complexes, the area displays the cycles of growth, decline, and rebirth that characterize mature industrial cities. Exclusive Victorian residential districts that devolved into blight have been reborn, while immigrant ghettos have yielded to brutally modern university buildings.

The area is split east–west by the Eisenhower Expressway (I-290), completed in 1960. To the south, the former immigrant area around Hull House continues to be replaced by the growing University of Illinois at Chicago, which recently demolished the historic Maxwell St. Market for redevelopment. A pocket of an Italian neighborhood survives between this campus and the massive Medical Center, which occupies the half mile from Ashland Blvd. west to Damen Ave. Modern residential construction fills the eastern flank of the Medical Center, while the gentrifying Tri-Taylor Historic District forms its western boundary.

North of the Eisenhower Expressway, the expanding central business district grows toward Greek Town on Halsted St. and the Randolph St. Market area, where some wholesale grocers have been replaced by trendy restaurants. Industrial loft buildings predominate, and many of these have been converted to residences, offices, and art galleries. Historic districts near Union Park and along Jackson Blvd. recall some of Chicago's premier addresses of the Gilded Age. West of this narrow strip are vast stretches of vacant land, parking, and replacement housing built during the construction of the United Center Stadium. As in other areas, new town houses are replacing public housing high rises, using the same neo-Victorian styling popular with more upscale town house and loft developments. Churches represent a wide variety of faiths and provide stability amid the whirling winds of the Near West real estate market.

The Near West Side is witness to the history of immigrant struggle at Hull House and immigrant success in Tri-Taylor, to Yankee prosperity along Ashland Ave., and 1960s racial strife and frustration along Madison St. It reflects the social engineering implicit in large-scale urban renewal at the University of Illinois campus, and it affirms Chicago's enduring commercial vitality in the Randolph St. Market. Eternally half-made and half-mad, the Near West Side is Chicago's private face, a thousand miles distant from its lakefront profile.

—VINCENT MICHAEL

1| **Madison St. Bridge**
Madison St. and the Kennedy Expressway
1996, DESTEFANO AND PARTNERS

This bridge was a prototype for the other bridges over the Kennedy. The red handrail sports motifs drawn from the Chicago flag, and a curbside barrier wall protects pedestrians. Unique to this bridge is the decorative fascia mounted with a strip of 300 bright blue pinpoint lamps. The bridge was rebuilt in this decorative style just in time for the 1996 Democratic convention, which was held farther west on Madison in the United Center. When the convention was coming and the Chicago Bulls were winning, local wags called this bridge "The Road to Oz."

2| Skybridge
1 N. Halsted St.
2003, PERKINS & WILL

This residential high rise is so far west of the bulk of tall downtown buildings that it is a powerful sculptural presence from almost any direction. There are two towers connected by glass-enclosed walkways. The facades are rich compositions with opaque and transparent, solid and void elements coming to a balance. The giant roof trellis creates a distinct profile and shelter for outdoor recreation and entertainment.

3| Richter's Food Products
1040 W. Randolph St.
1933, H. PETER HENSCHIEN

This rare local example of an Art Deco factory produced sausages as well as smoked and boiled meats; Henschien's specialty was meat-packing facilities. The closely spaced piers frame striking geometric designs; the elegant entrances

RICHTER'S FOOD PRODUCTS

are framed in black terra cotta flecked with gold.

4| Chicago Florists' Center
1313 W. Randolph St.
1928, FOX & FOX

Large Art Deco posies grace this concrete loft structure, which concentrated the wholesale floral trade in the Randolph St. Market area of meat and produce distributors.

5| Block X
1141–1151 W. Washington St., 15, 23 & 27 N. Racine St., 16, 24 & 26 N. May, and the alley north of Madison St.
1999, PAPPAGEORGE/HAYMES

By the late 1990s developers ran short of the most suitable industrial loft buildings for residential conversions, so new construction resumed in this area after a hiatus of almost a

BLOCK X

century. While many of these structures are literal re-creations of converted factories, this project is clearly modern even as the materials and massing respond to its context. Parking is hidden beneath the buildings and grassy interior courtyard.

6| Harpo Studios
1058 W. Washington Blvd.
1989, REMODELING, NAGLE, HARTRAY & ASSOCS.

Pieces of this block-long Art Deco Revival office and studio complex have served as a stable, a bowling alley, and a film studio. The remodeled whole is owned by the palindromic Oprah (read it backward) Winfrey, who tapes her popular talk show here.

Union Park
Lake St., Randolph St., Ogden Ave., Warren Blvd., Ashland Ave.
1853

The history of Union Park reflects the changing fortunes of its neighborhood. In 1853 local landowners seeking to increase the value of their property successfully lobbied the city to make this area a park. Named in honor of the Union cause, the park was the centerpiece of a wealthy residential area. Described as the "Bois de Boulogne of the West Side" in the 1870s, it included a band shell, gazebos, and a bridged lagoon. By the 1920s the surrounding streets were no longer fashionable, and many mansions on Ashland Ave. had become labor union headquarters—lending an ironic twist to the name Union Park.

7| Field House
(West Park Commission Headquarters)
1888, WILLIAM LE BARON JENNEY
1909, NORTH ADDITION, WILLIAM A. OTIS

Jenney's original Shingle Style building has been defaced by subsequent remodelings; only the stair tower suggests his original design. Since 1934 brick facades have concealed the original wood structure. The West Park System was headquartered here from 1888 until it moved to Garfield Park in 1928.

8| Locker and Gym Building
1917, JAMES B. DIBELKA

Most notable is the large pergola of concrete columns.

9| Carter Henry Harrison Monument
1907, FREDERICK C. HIBBARD

A relentless city booster, Harrison was the Richard J. Daley of his era, serving five terms as mayor (1879–1887, 1893) and fathering Carter H. Harrison II, who was elected in 1897. The quote on the monument's base, taken from Harrison's speech at the World's Columbian Exposition on October 28, 1893, captures the city's 1890s spirit: "Genius is but audacity, and the audacity of Chicago has chosen a star. It has looked upward to it and knows nothing that it fears to attempt and thus far has found nothing that it cannot accomplish." Later that day, Harrison was assassinated in his home at the southwest corner of Ashland and Jackson Blvds. The statue's pose is mayoral but the rendition is naturalistic, especially the drape of the trousers and the soft felt hat clutched in the mayor's hand.

10| Chicago Transit Authority— Ashland Ave. Station
1601 W. Lake St.
1893, ARCHITECT UNKNOWN

Look north as you cross Ashland Ave. to see a relic of the Metropolitan West Side Elevated Railroad's early days. The station is sided with stamped metal panels and crowned with an ornate metal cupola.

11| First Baptist Congregational Church
(Union Park Congregational Church)
60 N. Ashland Ave.
1869–1871, GURDON P. RANDALL

FIRST BAPTIST CONGREGATIONAL CHURCH

The attenuated spire and yel-
lowed, rusticated Joliet limestone mark one of Chicago's
oldest churches. But the prim
and dignified Gothic facade
won't prepare you for the warm
and encircling interior, the oldest
remaining amphitheatrical nave
in Chicago. The speaker is surrounded by the congregation,
in contrast to the celebrant-
worshiper division apparent
in Catholic and Episcopalian
churches. The enormous Kimball
organ still joyfully rocks the
trussed ceiling during services.

12| William Gilman House
1635 W. Washington Blvd.
1887, LOUIS J. BOURGEOIS

This essay in Gothic is smoothly
finished and lavished with
crocketed arches, a corner oriel,
and an elaborate third-floor
dormer.

13| Metropolitan Missionary
Baptist Church
(*Third Church of Christ, Scientist*)
2151 W. Washington Blvd.
1901, HUGH M. G. GARDEN

Garden combined the Greek
Revival forms favored by Christian Scientists with his own
Prairie Style details, especially
the window surrounds on the
west facade and the art glass.
Gray granite columns have inverted capitals reminiscent of
Secessionist architecture—and
of Wright's Heller House in
Hyde Park.

METROPOLITAN MISSIONARY
BAPTIST CHURCH

14| Henry Horner Homes
W. Washington Blvd., Leavitt St.,
Lake St., and Damen Ave.
1998, LEAVITT ST. TO HOYNE AVE.,
SOLOMON CORDWELL BUENZ &
ASSOCS.

1999, HOYNE TO DAMEN AVES.,
JOHNSON & LEE, MASTER ARCH.;
BROOK ARCHITECTURE AND
HAMMOND BEEBY RUPERT AINGE,
ASSOC. ARCHS.

Horner was one of the first
Chicago Housing Authority
properties to have its high rises
replaced by town houses. It is
also an early example of the
CHA encouraging a variety of
architectural signatures rather
than a single look. The development's least successful elements are the cul-de-sacs that
isolate it from the surrounding
community.

15| Chicago Public Library—
Mabel Manning Branch
6 S. Hoyne Ave.
1994, ROSS BARNEY + JANKOWSKI

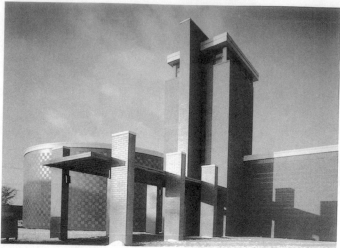

CHICAGO PUBLIC LIBRARY—MABEL MANNING BRANCH

The forty-foot tower glows at night, but even during the day, this small civic gem is a beacon in its busy neighborhood. Directed by the city to give the library a Prairie School appearance, the architects honored that intention while creating a modern composition that holds the street wall and plays off its contrasting horizontal and vertical, rectangular and circular elements. The diversity of spaces and uses within the small building is expressed with varied fenestration and massing.

16| 220 to 230 S. Hoyne Ave.
1992, LANDON ARCHITECTS

Dubbed "the houses the Bulls built," this tidy row of capacious two-flats was erected for home-owners displaced by construction of the new stadium. Each is pleasingly neo-Victorian, complete with a low stoop and an embellishing tickle of decoratively laid brick in the gable.

17| United Center
1800 W. Madison St.
1994, HOK SPORTS FACILITIES GROUP

This buttoned-down corporate sports mall is a weak echo of the "madhouse on Madison" that was the old Chicago Stadium. It is, however, far superior to the same architects' design for Comiskey Park, both in appearance and comfort. Although surrounded by surface parking on three sides, this arena extends all the way to the sidewalk on Madison St. and has large windows that provide views in and out of the spacious upper lobbies. Among the long list of staggering statistics about this building is the fact that the "megatruss" roof support system required 3,000 tons of steel.

18| Isaac N. Camp Row Houses
1526–1528 W. Monroe St.
EARLY 1870S, ARCHITECT UNKNOWN

The height of each story diminishes as these exaggeratedly vertical town houses rise; large blocks of Joliet limestone are striated to appear as many stacked, smaller blocks. The robust bracketed cornice and window trim are currently overdone in Painted Lady colors.

19| SBC—Monroe Office
1340 W. Monroe St.
1932, HOLABIRD & ROOT

This cool, severe, but lovely Art Deco switching office is trimmed with black granite and cast aluminum. Abstract bas-relief panels above the entrance and first-floor windows depict the transmission of sound.

20| Painters District Council 14
1456 W. Adams St.
1956, VITZTHUM & BURNS

A pristine echo of the Art Deco style, this blocky little corner building is one of thirty union headquarters in the neighborhood. It provides an artful show of the beauties of limestone and polished granite—with not a painted surface in sight.

21 | 1529 W. Adams St.
1888, ARCHITECT UNKNOWN

This 520-ton house was purchased for $1 on the condition that it be relocated from its original site at 1706 W. Jackson Blvd. The arduous move was chronicled by Home and Garden Television (HGTV).

22 | Iram Nye House
1535 W. Adams St.
1874, ARCHITECT UNKNOWN

The flat, crisp wall of large unbroken blocks of Joliet limestone is treated like a canvas on which incised ornament is stiffly embroidered. The ornament is a miniaturized element adapted from more lavish, overtly "French"-style homes; incised ornament was also cheaper than carved hood molds and keystones.

23 | Walter M. Pond House
1537 W. Adams St.
1879, ARCHITECT UNKNOWN

The profusion of pilasters and engaged columns, together with the mansard roof with its pedimented dormers, mark this as a rare surviving example of a full-blown Second Empire town house.

24 | Church of the Epiphany
201 S. Ashland Blvd.
1885, BURLING & WHITEHOUSE

Here is one of Chicago's earliest and best examples of the Richardsonian Romanesque, a style known as "Norman" in the 1880s. The basic forms are simple and geometric—broad gables, a stocky tower, and roundheaded doors and windows—while the wall surfaces are complex. Rich, ruddy Lake Superior sandstone is carved into rectangles, squares, slivers, voussoirs, and colonnettes that fit together like an intricate jigsaw puzzle. Although the interior has taken some hard hits, including stained-glass theft and water infiltration, it remains a comfortable Victorian cave, punctuated by rows of deep-set windows. The wall treatment is most unusual: unglazed terra-cotta tiles in alternating squares of fluid ribbons and pods that seem to have been squeezed from a pastry tube. Against the dark backdrop of wood and terra-cotta, the remaining windows and the Venetian glass mosaic murals in the sanctuary glow softly, visual feasts of Victorian polychromy.

CHURCH OF THE EPIPHANY BEFORE COMPLETION OF TOWER

25| William J. Chalmers House
315 S. Ashland Blvd.
1885, TREAT & FOLTZ

Uniform in material but richly varied in form, this house exhibits in stone many elements of the Queen Anne style in wood: a turreted corner tower, windows (some mullioned) of many shapes and sizes, and a complex, irregular roof. Although only brownstone is used, it is carved, rusticated, planed smooth, and set in a checkerboard pattern for the stringcourse.

26| B. Dorr Colby House
1539 W. Jackson Blvd.
1894, RUSSELL B. POWELL

The robust Richardsonian Romanesque personality derives from the prominent turreted entry tower, with second-floor loggia.

27| Richard Norman Foster House
1532 W. Jackson Blvd.
1892, PATTON & FISHER

The formula for this elegant limestone Romanesque town house includes a shallow facade, off-center entry, combination of smooth and rusticated stone, eaveless gable, and acanthus leaf carvings.

28| Mortimer & Tapper Houses
1533–1537 W. Jackson Blvd.
1881, ARCHITECT UNKNOWN

The flat fronts and emphasized roofline of these Italianate row houses set the stylistic tone for the developing block.

29| Flora M. Chisholm House
1531 W. Jackson Blvd.
1886, JOHN M. VAN OSDEL

Queen Anne breaks through the Italianate with a broadened bay and two-tone brickwork.

30| Norman Bridge House
1529 W. Jackson Blvd.
1883, ARCHITECT UNKNOWN

31| William Messenger House
1527 W. Jackson Blvd.
1884, ALFRED SMITH

32| Mary J. Dodge Houses
1526–1530 W. Jackson Blvd.
1885, WILLIAM STRIPPELMAN & CO.

These early Queen Anne designs retain the flat fronts and mansard roofs of slightly earlier styles.

33| William P. Henneberry House
1520 W. Jackson Blvd.
1883, FURST & RUDOLPH

The Second Empire facade is ironed almost flat, with shallow pilasters and incised ornament surrounding the door and windows. An aggressively over-scaled dormer interrupts the mansarded tower.

WILLIAM P. HENNEBERRY HOUSE

34| Henry C. Morey House
1519 W. Jackson Blvd.
1884, JOHN J. FLANDERS

Queen Anne exuberance bubbles up at the roofline, with a pink slate mansard and unusual semicircular metal pediments filled with symmetrical flowering plants.

35| John C. Nicol House
1515 W. Jackson Blvd.
1879, ARCHITECT UNKNOWN

The gargantuan blocks of Joliet limestone and the high level of the first floor are hallmarks of one of the block's oldest houses.

36| Andrew T. Merriman House
1516 W. Jackson Blvd.
1884, JOHN M. VAN OSDEL

37| George Ross House
1514 W. Jackson Blvd.
1884, JOHN M. VAN OSDEL

Not a match but balanced, the slopes of the mansard roofs are the perfect foil for the robustly pedimented dormers.

38| Matilda Hale House
1513 W. Jackson Blvd.
1883, L. GUSTAV HALLBERG

Even this three-story residence wears a shallow mansard lid.

39| 1506 & 1508 W. Jackson Blvd.
1884, EDWARD BAUMANN

Designed by Baumann for himself, these are late examples of "marble front" (Joliet stone) Italianates.

40| 1501–1509 W. Jackson Blvd.
1882, ARCHITECT UNKNOWN

These Second Empire town houses are united by wide cornices and a broad string-course with grape leaf decoration. At 1501 was the home of lumber merchant Benjamin Franklin Ferguson, who left almost $1 million upon his death in 1905 to establish a fund for public sculpture to be administered by the Art Institute.

Apart from a brief spurt of public and semipublic construction in the late 1920s, there was very little development in the area north of Congress St. for decades. In the early 1970s three large government-funded projects in the Miesian style put a stamp of brawny modernism on these rough-edged precincts.

41| Whitney M. Young Magnet High School
211 S. Laflin St.
1971, PERKINS & WILL PARTNERSHIP

This steel-framed trio has the cold efficiency of a factory for learning. The enclosed truss bridge spanning Jackson Blvd. links the fine arts building to the south with the academic and physical education buildings.

42| Timothy J. O'Connor Training Academy (*Chicago Police Training Center*)
1300 W. Jackson Blvd.
1976, JEROME R. BUTLER, JR., CHICAGO CITY ARCH.

Haymarket Riot Monument
1889, JOHN GELERT

The only tangible reminder of the 1886 disturbance is the sculpture now in the courtyard of this modernist training center. The police officer, his arm upraised, restrains an invisible mob, commanding peace "In the name of the people of Illinois." The controversy that surrounded the riot continued to plague this statue, which was erected near the site. The plaques at the base were stolen in 1903, and later a streetcar motorman rammed into the statue, claiming to be sick of looking at it every day. Moved to Union Park in 1928, the statue remained unmolested until the civil unrest of the 1960s, when it was defaced with black paint and twice blown up by a bomb. The statue was placed under twenty-four-hour guard and moved to Central Police Headquarters, from which it was transferred to its present site in 1976.

43| Malcolm X College
1900 W. Van Buren St.
1971, C. F. MURPHY ASSOCS.

This state-operated junior college was designed to serve a student population of 10,000 as well as the local community. The steel frame has brick and glass infill; in contrast with Whitney Young and the Training Academy, the building's structural expression is limited to the first-floor columns. The third floor has two open-air courtyards.

South of the Eisenhower Expressway (I-290), the steady growth of the University of Illinois and the Medical Center has spurred residential redevelopment since the mid-1980s. Historic buildings have been renovated, and clusters of town houses have sprouted. Of special note is the pocket between Polk St., Ogden Ave., and Western Ave., part of the Tri-Taylor Historic District. A "second settlement" community, it received upwardly mobile immigrants graduating from the Maxwell St. area on the Near West Side. Tri-Taylor contains many examples of 1880s working- and middle-class housing.

44| 2125–2133 W. Bowler St. & 2135-2145 W. Bowler St.
1881, ARCHITECT UNKNOWN

45| 2147–2159 W. Bowler St. & 2136–2146 W. Bowler St.
1882, ARCHITECT UNKNOWN

46| 2148–2158 W. Bowler St.
1882, EDBROOKE & BURNHAM

This remarkable ensemble was developed by James L. Campbell. With the exception of the red brick row houses with Gibbsian quoins framing the windows and doors at 2148–2158, all are Italianate with neo-Classical details. The Joliet limestone facades are of massive ashlar blocks, and each row shares a pressed-metal cornice with brackets and dentils.

47| 801–811 S. Oakley Blvd.
LATE 1870S, ARCHITECT UNKNOWN

The Italianate row houses at 801 and 811 were moved from a site two blocks north and now "bookend" similar neighbors.

48| Vietnam Survivors Memorial
815 S. Oakley Blvd.
1987, WILLIAM S. LAVICKA

One of the city's quirkiest pieces of folk art is this assemblage of ten cast-iron columns, taken from the interior of the Page Brothers Building and arranged around a granite marker. Structural engineer, Vietnam veteran, and preservationist Lavicka erected the memorial on his property with the help of other volunteer veterans.

49| Claremont Cottages
1000 block of S. Claremont Ave.
1884, ARCHITECT UNKNOWN

Turn west on Grenshaw St. and north on Claremont Ave. for an unexpected delight: a block of small Queen Anne brick cottages. A speculative development by Turner & Bond, they feature projecting gables, dormers, and overhanging eaves with slightly recessed entrances—and, at 1016, 1024, 1042, and 1045, excellent integrity.

50| 700 Block of S. Claremont Ave.
1886–1887, ARCHITECT UNKNOWN

This is an unusually cohesive streetscape of Queen Anne two-flats. Almost all of them were developed by George N. Hull and feature deep red face brick, stringcoursing, and pressed-metal cornices. Much rehabilitation took place on this block after 1983, when it was added to the National Register of Historic Places as part of the Tri-Taylor Historic District.

2148–2158 W. BOWLER ST.

CLAREMONT COTTAGES

51| Chicago Medical Center
Ashland Ave. to Oakley Blvd.; Congress Pkwy. to Roosevelt Rd.

In 1941 the state legislature created the Chicago Medical Center Commission and empowered it to acquire land on a 305-acre tract surrounding existing medical buildings. The commission was charged with clearing blighted slum areas, allocating sites to medical institutions (five hospitals and ten professional schools), encouraging them to expand their facilities and create new housing for their employees, and relegating land for small parks. The scheme's promoters envisioned a "Garden of Health," a very different image from what confronts the visitor to this gritty urban complex.

Over a century of health-care architecture is represented here. Most of it is fairly undistinguished, burdened by the strained budgets and ever-changing needs that beat the beauty out of most hospital architecture. But there are a few gems—and several curiosities. Almost every facility has been expanded and remodeled, some of them many times. Only the original architects of major visible sections are noted here.

52| CORE Center
2020 W. Harrison St.
1998, PERKINS & WILL, CAMPBELL TIU CAMPBELL, ASSOC. ARCHS.

This specialized outpatient clinic for the treatment of HIV/AIDS and related infectious diseases is organized vertically around a light-filled atrium that serves as a community room. Each floor offers an increasingly higher level of patient treatment, from a first-floor screening clinic behind the curved brick wall to the infusion room at the top of the building, where the most seriously ill benefit from abundant space and daylight.

53| John H. Stroger Hospital of Cook County
1901 W. Ogden Ave.
2002, CCH DESIGN GROUP (LOEBL SCHLOSSMAN & HACKL; MCDONOUGH ASSOCS., GLOBETROTTERS ENGINEERING CORPORATION, HDR INC.)

An assortment of modules in handsome materials form this replacement for an eighty-nine-year-old hospital. The arrangement of the interconnected modules was programmed for improvements in patient flow through the complex. In 2003 the County Board delayed demolition of the original hospital (1913, Paul Gerhardt) and requested proposals for its adaptive re-use.

54| Rush–Presbyterian–St. Luke's Cohn Research Bldg.
1753 W. Harrison St.
2000, PERKINS & WILL

55| Rush–Presbyterian–St. Luke's Medical Center Atrium Building
1653 W. Congress Pkwy.
1982, HANSEN LIND MEYER; SOLOMON CORDWELL BUENZ & ASSOCS.

56| Rush–Presbyterian–St. Luke's Johnston R. Bowman Health Center
West side of S. Paulina St. between Harrison & Polk Sts.
1976, 1977, METZ, TRAIN, OLSON & YOUNGREN

Presbyterian Hospital was established here in 1883 and merged with St. Luke's in 1956. Rush Medical College, the first of its kind in Illinois, was founded in 1837, deactivated in 1942, and revived in 1969 as part of Presbyterian–St. Luke's. Still visible on Congress Pkwy. are the 1888 Presbyterian Hospital (a mangled Queen Anne structure by Stephen V. Shipman) and the 1956 Presbyterian–St. Luke's. The constricted site led to dramatic solutions for the 1970s and 1980s expansions. Paulina St. was closed; the block-long metal-paneled Rush Medical College and Bowman Health Center bestride Harrison St. and the elevated tracks. These are further enclosed by the Atrium Building, which emulates a modern hotel, with many patient rooms facing pleasant atria.

57| University of Illinois College of Medicine Complex
(*Research & Educational Hospitals of the State of Illinois*)
Bounded by Polk St., Wolcott Ave., Taylor St. and Wood St.

College of Medicine West Addition
(*Medical & Dental College & Laboratories*)
1853 W. Polk St.
1931, GRANGER & BOLLENBACHER

College of Medicine West
(*Research Laboratory & Library*)
1819 W. Polk St.
1924, RICHARD E. SCHMIDT, GARDEN & MARTIN

Clinical Sciences North Building
(*General Hospital & Clinical Institute*)
1819 W. Polk St., inside courtyard
1925, RICHARD E. SCHMIDT, GARDEN & MARTIN

College of Medicine East
(*Medical & Dental College Laboratories*)
808 S. Wood St.
1937, GRANGER & BOLLENBACHER

UIC COLLEGE OF MEDICINE COMPLEX

Clinical Sciences Building
(*Hospital Addition*)
820–840 S. Wood St.
1954, HOLABIRD, ROOT & BURGEE

Neuropsychiatric Institute
912 S. Wood St.
1941, C. HERRICK HAMMOND

**Biological Resources
Laboratory**
(*Medical Research Laboratory*)
1840 W. Taylor St.
1959, SKIDMORE, OWINGS &
MERRILL

The original scheme for this
two-square-block complex,
developed in 1920 by Richard E.
Schmidt, Garden & Martin, was
followed closely for the northern half of the site, which was
built out by later architects
working in an Art Deco–influenced version of the 1920s
English Gothic. The south half
was to have contained one huge
courtyard, but this plan was
abandoned in 1930 with the
construction of a nurses' residence; the 1954 Hospital Addition further injured the scheme.
The hidden treasures among
these red brick buildings are the
secluded courtyards. On Polk St.
near Wood St., enter the picturesque north courtyard
through an arched entryway
lined with WPA mosaics of
astrological motifs. Sculptures
of Aesculapius (the Greek god
of medicine) and Hygeia (his
daughter, the goddess of
health) by Edouard Chassaing
grace the west end of the court.
In the Neuropsychiatric Institute
courtyard above the entrance,
a bas-relief of a brain is surrounded by names of famous
brain researchers.

58| UIC Outpatient Care Center
1801 W. Taylor St.
1999, PERKINS & WILL

This building with fine proportions and muted colors fits
gracefully into a neighborhood
of buildings of many materials.
A three-story, glassy pedestrian
bridge over Taylor St. links
several facilities and provides
a focal point.

**59| Illinois Center for
Rehabilitation and Education**
1151 S. Wood St.
1965, HARRY WEESE & ASSOCS.

This small-scale village of linked
brick buildings has a welcoming
presence sorely lacking among
its large institutional neighbors.

**60| Chicago Children's Advocacy
Center**
1240 S. Damen Ave.
2001, TIGERMAN MCCURRY
ARCHITECTS

To create a nonthreatening,
noninstitutional environment
for the Center's young clients,
the exterior includes glazed
brick in pastel tones, windows
shaped as a child would draw
them, and, facing the parking
lot, a colorful mural by Christine
Tarkowski with abstract images
of stuffed animals.

**61| St. Basil Greek Orthodox
Church**
(*Temple Anshe Sholom*)
733 S. Ashland Blvd.
1910, ALEXANDER L. LEVY

The Greek Revival temple front
made the synagogue well suited
for conversion to a Greek Orthodox church in 1927, after the
original congregation had moved
to Lawndale (now the Independence Boulevard Seventh-Day
Adventist Church). The dome,
originally ribbed but now asphalt-
shingled, gives the building
the height of a spired church,
while maintaining the Classical
language of the ensemble.

62| Garibaldi Square
**1400–1600 W. Harrison St.,
south side**
1984–1988, NAGLE, HARTRAY
& ASSOCS.

An unfussy low-rise development fits eighty-six town
houses, forty-two condominiums, and a hotel onto an irregular seven-and-a-half-acre site.
The red brick and Indiana
limestone buildings fit the
neighborhood well.

63| Thomas Jefferson Public School
1522 W. Fillmore St.
1884, JOHN J. FLANDERS

As Board of Education architect, Flanders designed dozens of schools during the 1880s and early 1890s; only a handful from the era before his partnership with William Carbys Zimmerman (1886–1898) are still in use. Tall and foreboding, most of them have even lost Flanders's signature Flemish gables, replaced with a flat parapet requiring lower maintenance.

64| Notre Dame de Chicago Church
1336 W. Flournoy St.
1887–1892, GREGORY VIGEANT
1982, RENOVATION, HISTORIC BOULEVARD SERVICES

French Catholics built this nearly circular church, whose transept walls are almost entirely filled with stained glass. The bronze Virgin Mary atop the dome replaced a lead-coated wooden version struck by lightning.

65| James Foley Building
626 S. Racine Ave.
1889, PATRICK J. KILLEEN

This Queen Anne "flats above the store" sports pressed-metal bays, terra-cotta panels, a cast-iron storefront, and a foliate cornice.

66| John Coughlan House
1246 W. Lexington St.
1871, ARCHITECT UNKNOWN

67| William J. Onahan Row Houses
1254–1262 W. Lexington St.
MID-1870S, ARCHITECT UNKNOWN

The street was an Irish stronghold named Macalister Pl. when these Italianate houses were built. The row houses' huge blocks of yellow Joliet limestone are scored to resemble smaller blocks, a technique that enlivened the surface and saved on labor costs.

68| Holy Family Church
1080 W. Roosevelt Rd.
1857–1859, ATTRIBUTED TO DILLENBURG & ZUCHER
1860, INTERIOR AND FACADE, JOHN M. VAN OSDEL
1874, UPPER STEEPLE, JOHN PAUL HUBER
1886, SOUTH ADDITION, ARCHITECT UNKNOWN
1991–2002, RESTORATION, OFFICE OF JOHN VINCI AND WISS, JANNEY, ELSTNER ASSOCS.

A hardy survivor, the church is a tribute to the craftsmanship of neighborhood workers and to the leadership of Jesuits from the parish's founder, the Reverend Arnold J. Damen, to Father George Lane, the head of a 1990s restoration campaign. The phlegmatic German Gothic structure is bent with age; some of the tall Gothic pillars are as much as eighteen inches out of plumb, displaced by the weight of the slate roof. But generations of embellishments crowd the nave and sanctuary. The spired and crocketed wooden reredos (1865), painted white to imitate marble, was crafted

WILLIAM J. ONAHAN ROW HOUSES

ST. IGNATIUS COLLEGE PREP

by nearby resident Anthony Buscher, a carver of cigar store Indians. The altar front features a folksy Last Supper—down to carved knives and forks.

69| St. Ignatius College Prep
(*St. Ignatius College*)
1076 W. Roosevelt Rd.
1866–1874, TOUSSAINT MENARD
1895, NORTHWEST ADDITION,
ARCHITECT UNKNOWN

The upstanding and disciplined façade is decidedly French, from the mansard roof to the projecting pavilion, to the stringcourses and quoining. The formal five-part facade features a columned entry atop a double-axial staircase. A typical feature of late nineteenth-century schools is the assembly room or library on the top floor, where a clear span space was structurally easier to include. The fourth floor here contains a fabulous example. Now known as the Brunswick Room, it was originally a natural history museum donated in 1873 by John M. Brunswick, a leading manufacturer of billiard tables and bowling equipment.

70| South Water Market
W. 14th Pl. and W. 15th St., between S. Morgan St. and S. Racine Ave.
1925, FUGARD & KNAPP

The sprawling open-air poultry and garden markets along the south bank of the Chicago River were displaced by the construction in 1925 of Wacker Dr., but they kept their name when they moved to this landlocked site served by trucks, not ships. The six neo-Classical terra-cotta buildings are virtually identical and share a continuous canopy above the first-floor loading docks. In 2003 the tenants moved to a new location and the complex was purchased by a residential developer.

University of Illinois at Chicago
(*University of Illinois at Chicago Circle*)
East Campus: Eisenhower Expressway to Roosevelt Rd.; Halsted to Racine Sts.
1965, 1967, SKIDMORE, OWINGS & MERRILL

Hailed as the college of the future when it opened in 1965, UIC is one of Chicago's strongest individual architectural statements—and one of the most violently disliked. The opening salvo was fired by architecture critic M. W. Newman, who shortly after its opening dubbed it "Fortress Illini."

UIC is an unmistakable product of an era proud of grand schemes and social engineering; few college campuses have been so strongly shaped by their original architect, designer Walter A. Netsch, Jr. Although many of the social and aesthetic principles that guided the design are now considered outdated, the university itself has prospered far beyond original expectations. Planned as an undergraduate branch of the well-established University of Illinois, it is now a major research institution, with a third of its 25,000 students enrolled in graduate and professional programs.

The first and most lasting controversy surrounding the school was its location. In 1946 the university had opened a Chicago branch at Navy Pier to provide a two-year college course for returning servicemen. The predicted crush of Baby Boomers created a need for a permanent site for a four-year college; the search began a decade later. Garfield Park, Meigs Field, and several suburban sites were considered and discarded. Mayor Richard J. Daley favored a South Loop location, in what is now Dearborn Park, but negotiations with the railroads that owned the land could not be concluded quickly enough; in 1959 Daley proposed a fifty-five-acre site at Harrison and Halsted Sts. The densely populated neighborhood, already designated for urban renewal, was variously considered an expendable slum or a vibrant community—depending on the source. Community activists in the affected area tried to fight City Hall, but almost everyone else—including other West Siders—favored the site. The 1960 Democratic electoral landslide (President Kennedy was a grateful Daley supporter) gave the mayor the backing he needed to acquire the site and finance the project.

In 1961 Skidmore, Owings & Merrill presented a campus master plan, and construction began when the U.S. Supreme Court removed the last legal hurdle two years later. The university opened in February 1965, and five more buildings were added in Phase II by 1967. After this initial burst of construction, the pace slowed somewhat but never stopped, and a 1990 master plan envisioned considerable growth.

Probably the only university named for a traffic interchange, the campus was originally known as the University of Illinois at Chicago Circle, for the "spaghetti bowl" freeway tangle just to the east. In 1982 this campus was merged with the university's long-established medical center to the west, and the combined institution was renamed the University of Illinois at Chicago. The earlier name was not inappropriate, however, as SOM designer Netsch had taken many cues from his own theories of transportation and movement.

The campus had two main organizing principles: a double-level system of walkways and a central hub consisting of a raised plaza surrounded by the most heavily used buildings. Netsch described the plan as "concentric rings with elements of most intense usage in the center; activity decreases and specialization increases with outward movement." The walkway system and the raised plaza at the campus core were demolished in 1995. A few vocal fans of the original work cried foul, but most students and faculty welcomed the friendly ground-level plaza that forms the new center of campus.

Grouping buildings by function rather than discipline gave great flexibility to the newly developing university but decreased teacher-student contact and increased the sense of anonymity. This scheme was gradually abandoned as more specialized graduate divisions were added, but the core continues to function as planned,

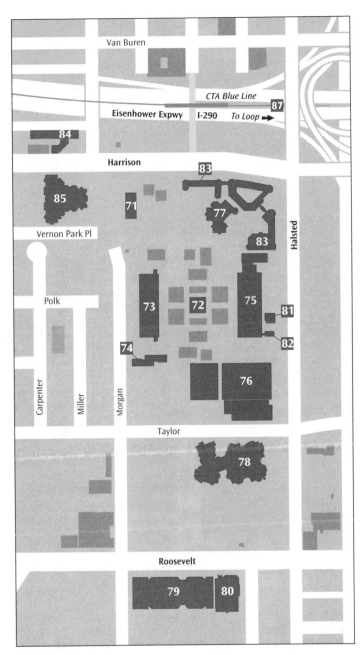

Van Buren

CTA Blue Line

Eisenhower Expwy   I-290   To Loop ➡   87

84

Harrison

83

85   71   77

Vernon Park Pl   83   Halsted

Polk   73   72   75   81

82

74   Carpenter   Miller   Morgan   76

Taylor

78

Roosevelt

79   80

with a central area of lecture halls flanked by the library and student union.

The entire original campus is built of exposed concrete, dark brick, and brown-tinted glass, which eliminated the need for window treatments. The reinforced-concrete structure is exposed on all the early buildings except Science & Engineering, and the decision to use concrete of uniform strength everywhere led to huge amounts of it in buildings with heavier structural loads. In an excessive refinement of the visible-structure principle, the concrete that carries heavier loads is sandblasted more to give it a coarser aggregate. The brutalism is extended inside the buildings, where concrete ceilings support exposed mechanical and lighting elements.

A major expansion of the campus got under way in 2002 with the creation of University Village on a sixty-eight-acre site south of Roosevelt Rd. This raised almost as great an uproar as when the original construction was proposed in 1959, because it entailed demolition of the lively Maxwell St. Market. Designs of the new parking and retail facilities along Halsted St. include twenty-one of the street's historic facades. The major architects of University Village, which includes town houses, mid rises, two dormitories, academic buildings, shops, restaurants, and parking facilities, are Roy H. Kruse & Assocs., Pappageorge/Haymes, FitzGerald Assoc., and Solomon Cordwell Buenz & Assocs.

Explore the campus on foot.

71| University Hall
601 S. Morgan St.
1965, SKIDMORE, OWINGS & MERRILL

Looming over the campus is its only skyscraper—the campanile, to use Netsch's metaphor —this twenty-eight-story office building for faculty and administration. In a paradoxical display of structuralism, the building becomes wider as it rises, with fewer columns creating bays of increasing width. The number of stories in each of the upper tiers—five, eight, and thirteen—was derived from another of Netsch's aesthetic principles: use of the golden section.

Continue south toward the center of campus. The blocky structure on the left is the Commonwealth Edison Vernon Park substation, a vivid reminder of the logistical difficulties of planning a new campus over a century-old grid of city utilities. Just past the substation is a cluster of classrooms around an informal court.

72| Campus Core
821 S. Morgan St.
1965, SKIDMORE, OWINGS & MERRILL
1995, REDESIGN, DANIEL P. COFFEY & ASSOCS.

An amphitheater and plaza originally covered the core of the campus, but both were removed in the early 1990s renovation; they also composed the common roof for several lecture halls. The new elliptical "piazza," designed to a human scale and furnished with benches, planters, and torchieres, has finally created the casual social environment originally envisioned.

73| Richard J. Daley Library
801 S. Morgan St.
1965, SKIDMORE, OWINGS & MERRILL

The library was among the first buildings constructed.

74| Science & Engineering Offices
851 S. Morgan St.
1965, SKIDMORE, OWINGS & MERRILL

75| Chicago Circle Center
710 S. Halsted St.
1965, C. F. MURPHY ASSOCS.

Circle Center is the only one of the original buildings designed by a firm other than SOM. Walk through it for a shortcut to Hull House.

76| Science & Engineering Laboratories
840 W. Taylor St.
1965, SKIDMORE, OWINGS & MERRILL
1990, ADDITION, HANSEN LIND MEYER

This hulk forms the south wall of the campus core. The giant structural bays are divided by concrete columns five feet square at the base. The bricks are twice as large as those on other campus buildings, and the concrete aggregate is coarser.

77| Architecture & Art Building
845 W. Harrison St.
1967, SKIDMORE, OWINGS & MERRILL

In contrast to the earlier buildings, Netsch developed his "field theory" of rotated squares here. In drawings, the plans look like lovely snowflakes, but in three dimensions, they are dark and confounding, with no perceptible spatial logic. The

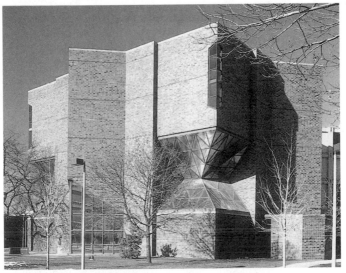

UIC ARCHITECTURE & ART BUILDING

raw walls on the exterior indicate where a planned expansion never happened.

78| Science & Engineering South
801 W. Taylor St.
1968, SKIDMORE, OWINGS & MERRILL

The last of Netsch's "field theory" trio of buildings was based on a complex geometry that Netsch developed while collecting op art paintings.

79| Physical Education Building
901 W. Roosevelt Rd.
1967, HARRY WEESE & ASSOCS.

Remarkable chiefly for its enormous bulk, the building was reoriented by Weese from its north-south axis on the plan to close the campus off on the south.

80| Flames Athletic Center
839 W. Roosevelt Rd.
2000, MEKUS STUDIOS; SASAKI ASSOCS., CONSULTING ARCH.

A new glass entrance and circulation space join the Physical Education Building to this converted ice rink, which houses administrative and support space and has a southern addition containing basketball courts.

81| Jane Addams's Hull House Museum
(*Charles J. Hull House*)
1856, ARCHITECT UNKNOWN

JANE ADDAMS'S HULL HOUSE MUSEUM

82| Hull House Dining Hall
800 S. Halsted St.
1905, POND & POND
1967, RECONSTRUCTION OF BOTH,
FRAZIER, RAFTERY, ORR & FAIRBANK

Representative more of Hull than of Addams is this rebuilding of a first-generation Italianate "cube and cupola." The Italianate reigned in Chicago from the 1850s to the 1880s. The symmetry, low foundations, arched windows, shallow sloped roof, and heavy bracketed eaves offer a rare view of a pleasing composition of the pre–Civil War era.

By the 1880s rapid expansion had overtaken the area, and the house was a furniture shop prior to its conversion to a settlement house by social reformers Jane Addams and Ellen Gates Starr in 1889. During the 1890s and early 1900s thirteen buildings covering two city blocks were built around the house. The resulting complex, which offered social, cultural, and educational facilities for the urban poor and underprivileged, was inspired by the Progressive Reform movement and Toynbee Hall settlement house in London. The Dining Hall, a simple Craftsman Style building, is the sole survivor of the complex; its architect, Allen Pond, was a social activist and supporter of the settlement. The house was substantially altered prior to Addams's death in 1935, gaining a third story and losing its wide veranda.

In 1963 the property was acquired by the University of Illinois and dedicated to a museum of Jane Addams's good works. As the other buildings in the Hull House complex were demolished, the house itself reemerged and was reconstructed. Furnishings from Addams's era were restored, and others were gleaned from antique stores, creating an interior that is a comfortable Victorian mélange. The fireplaces and moldings are original; the chandeliers were reproduced from photos. The Dining Hall, relocated from its nearby site, is now used for exhibits and presentations.

83| University Center Housing & Commons
700 S. Halsted St.
1988, SOLOMON CORDWELL BUENZ & ASSOCS.
1993, WEST ADDITION SOLOMON CORDWELL BUENZ & ASSOCS.; LOEBL, SCHLOSSMAN & HACKL, ASSOC. ARCHS.

A marked departure for the campus in form and function, these buildings are the first undergraduate housing here, and the first complex to create a street wall and a grassy courtyard. They face the central city with a welcoming gateway, displaying a visual richness and logical form missing in much of the campus.

84| Education, Communications & Social Work
1040 W. Harrison St.
1968, HARRY WEESE & ASSOCS.

This balconied bunker meets the standard of bleakness set by the first phase of campus construction.

85| Behavioral Sciences Building
1007 W. Harrison St.
1967, SKIDMORE, OWINGS & MERRILL

The torturous floor plan of this "field theory" building is the butt of many jokes about rats in a maze.

86| Reliable Corporation Mural
1001 W. Van Buren St.
1984, RICHARD HAAS

If the Burnham and Bennett plan of 1909 had been realized, this area would have been the site of a grand civic center. It exists today in this trompe l'oeil tour de force, best seen from the UIC campus. Haas illustrates both Burnham's visions and the actual skyline, complete with a peekaboo illusionist "cutout" view of the Sears Tower, visible from the west. The medallions contain visual odes to Chicago's importance as a transportation center.

87 | Chicago Transit Authority— Halsted St. Station
S. Halsted St. at the Eisenhower Expressway
2001, ROSS BARNEY + JANKOWSKI

A snazzy stainless-steel sign is just the beginning of the improvements here. A high roof runs from the platform into the station, and clear glass walls on station and ramp make the station and platform feel safer while enhancing their appearance.

GARFIELD PARK/AUSTIN

TO THOSE TRAVELING FROM WESTERN AVE. TO THE CITY LIMITS—PAST EMPTY
lots, crumbling six-flats, well-maintained graystones, battered retail
areas, and sturdy churches—the suburban origins of these neighborhoods may seem remote and invisible. But the area from Western Ave.
to Harlem Ave. in Oak Park, and from North Ave. to Pershing Rd., was
once Cicero Township, an independent political entity founded in 1857.
Its villages, which grew up along the train lines, were coveted by
Chicago politicians eager to add their public properties and tax assess-
ments to the city's holdings.

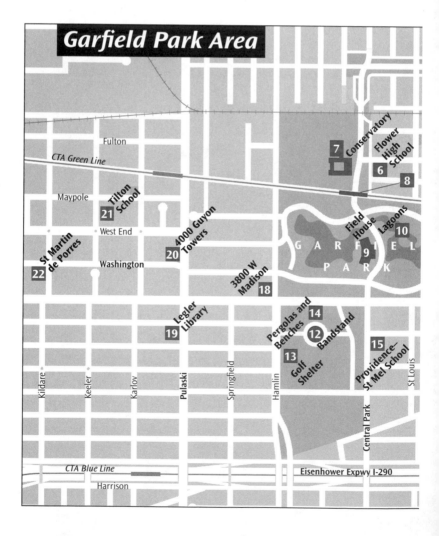

Garfield Park Area

In 1869, a seminal year for the West Side, Chicago annexed most of the easternmost two miles of Cicero Township, from Western Ave. to what is now Pulaski Rd. That year also saw the establishment of the West Park Commission, which immediately began acquiring property for what are now Humboldt, Garfield, and Douglas parks. Selection of the Garfield Park site spurred speculation in surrounding properties, but construction accelerated only after transportation had improved. A station on the Chicago & North Western Railroad at Kedzie Ave. led in the early 1870s to residential development there; but not until the 1890s, with the advent of the Metropolitan West Side Elevated and better streetcar service, did the area begin to burgeon.

In the huge 1889 annexation that quadrupled Chicago's size, the city bit off another chunk of Cicero Township: Central Park and Moreland, the two communities immediately west of Garfield Park. Pulaski Rd. (then 40th St.) was already a transportation center; at Kinzie were the carbarns for the Chicago & North Western Railroad and, at Madison, the transfer point from city streetcars to suburban lines such as the Cicero

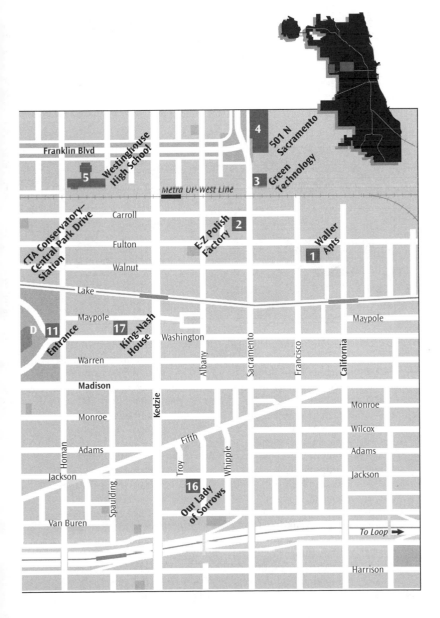

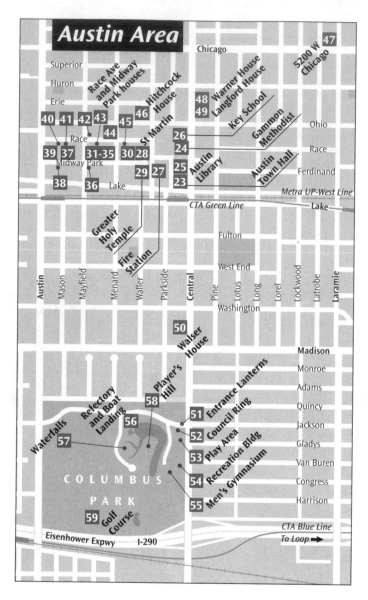

Austin Area

Chicago

5200 W Chicago — 47

Superior
Huron
Erie

Race Ave and Midway Park houses

Hitchcock House

Warner House
Langford House

Key School

40 41 42 43 45 46

44

St Martin

48
49

Gammon Methodist

Ohio

Race

39 37 31-35 30 28

Midway Park

26
24

Austin Library

Austin Town Hall

Ferdinand

38 36 Lake

29 27

25
23

Metra UP-West Line

CTA Green Line — Lake

Greater Holy Temple

Fire Station

Fulton

West End

Austin · Mason · Mayfield · Menard · Waller · Parkside · Central · Pine · Lotus · Long · Lorel · Lockwood · Latrobe · Laramie

Washington

50

Walser House

Madison
Monroe

Player's Hill

Adams

Refectory and Boat Landing

58

Entrance Lanterns

Quincy

Waterfalls

56

51 Council Ring

Jackson

57

52 Play Area

Gladys

53 Recreation Bldg

Van Buren

COLUMBUS PARK

54 Men's Gymnasium

Congress

55

Harrison

59 Golf Course

CTA Blue Line
To Loop ➡

Eisenhower Expwy   I-290

& Proviso Street Railway. The latter intersection grew into a vibrant urban center, a minidowntown halfway between the Loop and Oak Park shopping areas. In the 1920s developers put up high-rise hotels, apartments, dance halls, and clubs. But the area was hard hit by the riots and fires that erupted after the 1968 assassination of Dr. Martin Luther King, Jr. Despite massive disinvestment in the area, the intersection remains a retail hub, one of the few shopping centers between the West Loop and the city limits.

Annexation's pros and cons were long debated in Austin, which retained its autonomy as a village in Cicero Township until 1899. Austin and Oak Park, the township's two largest villages, battled for decades over allocations of funds in a rivalry that came to a head in the 1890s. Although not in the majority, there was some sentiment in Austin for annexation, largely among developers and investors in the Metropolitan West Side Elevated. Antiannexation fervor was much stronger in Oak Park, but seceding was difficult, with a majority of the entire township needed. When Austin thwarted Oak Park's efforts to secede in an 1895 election, bitterness increased and Oak Parkers redoubled their efforts to become independent. The *Oak Park Vindicator* editorialized, "the larger the municipality the greater are the opportunities for boodlers—vile men, who can no more appreciate the fine sentiments of patriotism than can Satan the sweet melodies of heaven. The Chicago boodler is the worst type in existence. The question before fair Cicero is, will she willfully put her head into his yoke?" The majority of Austin residents felt the same way. But in the decisive election of April 1899, Oak Park vanquished its rival, leading the township's villages in voting Austin into Chicago, despite Austin's 972-to-516 vote to remain.

Austin retains preannexation features such as Merrick and Town Hall parks, many churches and widely spaced homes, and the fire station on Waller Ave. During the 1920s apartment and commercial buildings replaced single-family homes along major arteries such as Lake St., Central Ave., and Jackson and Washington Blvds. The 1920s also saw the completion of Jens Jensen's masterpiece, Columbus Park.

The West Side shows typical inner-city scars of age and blight. There is little new construction, and empty lots outnumber buildings on some blocks; the building stock is aging faster than money becomes available to save it. But the positive effects of dedicated institutions and strong individuals are seen in every neighborhood, from the well-tended church and school complexes of Garfield Park, to the rehabilitated homes of central Austin, to the restored sections of Garfield and Columbus parks. —ALICE SINKEVITCH

Two lesser-known works of Frank Lloyd Wright are nearby in an area east of Garfield Park that is difficult to navigate due to railroad embankments and street conditions.

1| Edward C. Waller Apartments
2840–2858 W. Walnut St.
1895, FRANK LLOYD WRIGHT

Real estate developer Waller was interested in low-income housing; of his several schemes, these were among the few actually built. Four of the five units remain; all once backed up to Waller's more famous Wright-designed project, the Francisco Terrace Apartments, demolished in 1974 and partially re-created in Oak Park.

2| E-Z Polish Factory
3005 W. Carroll Ave.
1905, FRANK LLOYD WRIGHT
1913, ADDITION, HARRY H. MAHLER

This greatly altered factory is Wright's earliest essay in re-inforced concrete. After commissioning him to design their homes, William E. Martin of Oak Park and his brother Darwin E. Martin of Buffalo hired him to design this stove- and shoe-polish factory. The windows have been bricked in and two floors have been added; the only exterior suggestion of Wright's involvement is the detailing around the entries and the ordered geometry of the facade.

3| Chicago Center for Green Technology
(Sacramento Stone Co.)
445 N. Sacramento Blvd.
2002, FARR ASSOCS.

A small abandoned factory on a former brownfields site was transformed into a showcase for energy efficiency. Photovoltaic panels are on the roof and in the place of awnings. High-performance insulation, as well as HVAC using ground source heat technology, and a rooftop planted with sun- and drought-tolerant greenery all help the building achieve its LEED (Leadership in Energy and Environmental Design) Platinum rating, the first building in Chicago to earn such a rating. The barrels on the front of the building catch the rain for reuse on the landscape.

4| 501 N. Sacramento Blvd.
(*Sprague, Warner & Co.*)
1941, A. EPSTEIN

The Art Deco tower anchors this stretch of the boulevard system, developed as an industrial area because of nearby railroads. Food processors Sprague, Warner brought in raw materials and shipped out finished goods via a railway siding directly connected to the first floor. The tower housed offices and concealed the water tank.

5| George Westinghouse Vocational High School
(*Bunte Brothers Candy Co.*)
3301 W. Franklin Blvd.
1921, SCHMIDT, GARDEN & MARTIN
1969, REHABILITATION FOR BOARD OF EDUCATION, SAUL SAMUELS
1982, PHYSICAL EDUCATION BUILDING, KENNETH GROGGS

One of the largest (400,000 sq. ft.) Chicago School buildings ever designed, this blunt and forthright factory/office building shuns the prettifying Industrial Gothic details popular for post-World War I factories. Horizontal bands of windows are rhythmically punctuated by powerful piers, whose verticality is echoed by the eight-story tower. The office wing faced the boulevard;

WESTINGHOUSE HIGH SCHOOL

the factory was the block-long wing paralleling the tracks.

6| Lucy L. Flower Vocational High School
3545 W. Fulton Blvd.
1927, JOHN C. CHRISTENSEN

The structurally expressive facade has light touches of Gothic detailing, a favorite design type of Board of Education architect Christensen. "Flower Tech" first opened in 1911 on the South Side as an open-enrollment high school for girls. Technical education included sewing, millinery, the "home arts," and, later, business classes.

Some of the activities in Garfield Park might be termed "underground economies" and are hostile to strangers. The park is best explored by automobile.

Garfield Park
(*Central Park*)
From the Chicago & North Western Railroad tracks to Fifth Ave. between Hamlin Blvd. and S. Central Park Blvd.; central section extends east to Trumbull Ave.

The middle of the West Park System's three great parks (see Humboldt and Douglas parks) still clearly shows the work of William Le Baron Jenney and Jens Jensen, two of the commission's major talents. Starting in 1869 with a 185-acre *tabula rasa*, Jenney began transforming the flat and treeless site into a picturesque landscape of winding lagoons and romantic vistas. Among the first improvements was the "pretty little inland sea," a fifteen-acre lagoon with excursion boats and flocks of ducks. Although he resigned as West Park Commission chief engineer in 1874, Jenney was retained as a consultant until the 1890s.

From 1877 to 1893 Oscar F. DuBuis continued developing acreage, somewhat modifying Jenney's plans. When Jens Jensen became general superintendent and chief landscape architect in 1905, his vision of a prairie landscape shaped the park's unfinished southern portion and altered the central section. Jensen also introduced Prairie School architecture into the park, hiring William Carbys Zimmerman and Schmidt, Garden & Martin for major improvements.

Only a portion of Garfield Park's structures remains, but several—such as the Bandstand, Conservatory, and West Park Commission Headquarters—are prime examples of their styles.

The park's most interesting historic landscape features are between Lake St. and Jackson Blvd. The area north of Lake St. was intended by Jenney as an open green meadow for "croquet parties, military parades, and baseball games." It became the site of several of the park's largest buildings, housing the Conservatory and a cluster of much-altered service buildings that are difficult to see and in varying states of repair. The **Power Plant** (West Park Light Plant, 1896, Solon S. Beman) was designed to serve a large part of the West Park system but became obsolete only a decade later, when it proved cheaper to purchase power from a utility than to generate it. The pair of ventilators atop the roof of the **Garage** (Stable, 1890, William Le Baron Jenney, with a 1915 addition) is a clue to its initial use.

7| Conservatory
300 N. Central Park Blvd.
1906–1907, JENS JENSEN AND SCHMIDT, GARDEN & MARTIN; HITCHINGS & CO., ENG.;
1998, ENTRY PAVILION AND LANDSCAPING, BOOTH HANSEN ASSOCIATES
1995–2000, PLANNING AND RESTORATION, EIFLER & ASSOCS.

Considered revolutionary when it opened, the Conservatory was conceived by Jensen as a work of landscape art under glass and was designed in collaboration with a New York engineering firm that specialized in greenhouse design. Unlike Victorian hothouses—which had showy floral displays that often included potted plants, benches, and exposed pipes—this conservatory was designed as a series of internal landscapes of tropical plantings, stonework, and water features.

Those who know Jensen as the dean of the Prairie landscape style might conclude that this work strayed from his usual efforts to convey symbolically the Midwest's indigenous landscape. Some of the gardens, however, were meant to emulate poetically the tropical appearance of the Chicago region during prehistoric times. In addition, according to

GARFIELD PARK CONSERVATORY

Jensen, the structure's form was inspired by "the great haystacks which are so eloquent of the richness of prairie soil." Jensen, who was the West Park System's chief landscape architect from 1905 to 1920, had recommended replacing small greenhouses in Humboldt, Douglas, and Garfield parks with one economical, centrally located facility, which is thought to be one of the world's largest.

The Conservatory plan consists of a large rectangular palm house and several small square rooms configured around the structure's premier space, the fern room. In the center of this compelling landscape is a small naturalistic lagoon framed by lush ferns on stratified stonework meant to emulate the outcroppings found along Illinois's Rock River. A path winds past the lagoon to the far end of the room, where stepping-stones cross a rocky brook fed by a "prairie waterfall." In a 1930 interview Jensen explained that when the waterfall was being constructed he was consistently dissatisfied with the stonework and required the mason to dismantle and rebuild it several times. When the workman became frustrated, Jensen suggested that he listen to Mendelssohn's "Spring Song." After hearing the music, the mason constructed the waterfall perfectly, so that the "water tinkled gently from ledge to ledge, as it should in a prairie country."

The Conservatory's original vestibule and decorative art-glass features in the palm house were designed by Schmidt, Garden & Martin. Unfortunately, they were lost in 1958, when the palm room's elegant, lacy truss system was demolished and replaced with a bolder structure of I-beam construction.

Although the Conservatory's annual attendance had reached a half million visitors in the 1920s, within the following decades, the facility began to deteriorate. Construction projects in the 1950s were insensitive to the structure's historic character. The neighborhood began declining and attendance went down.

Fortunately, in 1994, the Chicago Park District began turning that cycle around with multimillion-dollar improvements to the building, its collections, and its grounds. The newly formed Garfield Park Conservatory Alliance has upgraded educational programs and visitor services. The Conservatory has become one of Chicago's most popular attractions once again.

—JULIA SNIDERMAN BACHRACH

8| Chicago Transit Authority—Conservatory and Central Park Dr. Station
3630 W. Lake St.
2001, CHICAGO TRANSIT AUTHORITY

Portions of the canopies and the station houses came from a former station at nearby Homan Ave. These preserved and restored pieces were fashioned into a new station meant to look like the oldest stations on the line, those built for the Lake St. elevated railroad of the early 1890s.

Modern technology was also incorporated into this increasingly busy station, which serves several schools and the Garfield Park Conservatory.

9| Field House
(*West Park Commission Administration Building*)
100 N. Central Park Ave.
1928, MICHAELSEN & ROGNSTAD

Bertram Goodhue's Spanish Baroque Revival creations for the 1915 Panama-California Exposition in San Diego were cream-hued, grand, and bristling with sculpture. Their popularity changed the direction of architecture in Southern California and filtered east to inspire a new decorative vocabulary. Goodhue's California State Building from the exposition was the inspiration for this headquarters of the politically powerful West Park Commis-

FIELD HOUSE

sion; it housed their administrative offices, engineering department, and police force.

The facade is exuberantly if rather breathlessly punctuated with a Churrigueresque entry pavilion of spiral Corinthian columns, cartouches, and portrait sculptures. The gold terra-cotta dome shelters a rotunda with a geometric terrazzo floor. Four panels sculpted by Richard W. Bock pay homage to Art and Architecture (figures hold a model of this building), Chicago's parks and playgrounds, and the Illinois highway system. After the 1934 consolidation of the city's park districts, the building served as a field house and the meeting room to the north was the commissioner's boardroom.

From the front of the Field House are excellent views of the eastern Lagoon and Suspension Bridge, the park's oldest elements.

10| Lagoons and Island
1870, WILLIAM LE BARON JENNEY

Suspension Bridge
1870, WILLIAM LE BARON JENNEY

The lagoons are the most notable remnants of Jenney's landscape design, and the area east of Central Park Blvd. is the oldest preserved landscaped space in a Chicago park. Done on an intimate, romantically miniaturized scale, the very irregular shoreline creates many inlets and changing vistas. Here

one can imagine Chicagoans escaping to the city's edge to promenade, view the landscape, and partake of such amenities as the healthful water from the artesian well (which ran dry and was later removed by Jensen). Jenney's Suspension Bridge, the sole survivor of a group of ornamental bridges, is a miniature display of his engineering talents and an elegant adornment. Steel cables support a wooden deck hung from concrete piers, which have replaced the stone originals.

Look across the Lagoon to see the park's eastern entrance, at Washington Blvd.

11| Washington Blvd. Entrance
Washington Blvd. at Homan Ave.
1907, WILLIAM CARBYS ZIMMERMAN

Originally laid out in a semicircle by Jenney, the entrance was reemphasized by Jensen, who hired Zimmerman to design the architectural enhancement. In their current deteriorated condition, the short concrete bollards arranged in a semicircle appear more Druidic than Prairie School, although they are still sheltered by hawthorns, a tree favored by Jensen for its horizontal branching.

12| Bandstand
Music Ct. east of Hamlin Ave.
1896, JOSEPH LYMAN SILSBEE

Nineteenth-century park planners chose the site for this white marble octagon, part of a never-completed scheme for the park's southern portion. A 100-piece orchestra could fit on its broad platform, sheltered by the fantastic copper roof. The inspiration was Arabian for the trefoil arches and the calligraphic mosaic panels. No longer host to music lovers, it is frequently surrounded by jitney cabs and idling chartered buses waiting to pick up Conservatory visitors.

13| Golf Shelter

1907, ATTRIB. TO HUGH M. G. GARDEN

While greatly altered, the area south of Madison St. shows Jensen's contribution to the landscape. He placed a semicircular earth berm south of the Bandstand to create a gently sloped amphitheater and a spot from which to view the golf course (now eradicated) that he created to the south. The now vacant Golf Shelter that served the course had a full-width pergola across its southern facade.

14| Pergolas and Benches

1907, ATTRIB. TO HUGH M. G. GARDEN

Jensen linked the Bandstand to the western Lagoon by the siting of a large formal garden with reflecting pools running north. They were on axis with the Boathouse (burned in 1981; a fragment of the stair remains on Washington Blvd.), which stood on the southern edge of the western Lagoon. A second formal garden paralleled Madison St. to the south, flanked by Pergolas and Benches. The Pergolas are now fragmentary and merely suggest their original role as pleasant walkways and frames for the pedestrians' views of the park.

15| Providence–St. Mel School
(*Providence High School*)
119 S. Central Park Blvd.
1929, MORRISON & WALLACE

The Tudor style, particularly that of Oxford and Cambridge universities, was a popular model for Chicago public high schools from 1898 through the 1930s. The Central Park Blvd. entrance, derived from a fifteenth-century Gothic gatehouse, features carved reliefs of young scholars. One peers at a plant through a magnifying glass; the other, her hair in a fashionable 1920s bob, studies in a library.

16| Our Lady of Sorrows Basilica
3121 W. Jackson Blvd.
1890-1902, HENRY ENGELBERT, JOHN F. POPE, AND WILLIAM J. BRINKMAN

It's Bramante on the Boulevard—with a coffered, barrel-vaulted ceiling rising above the long nave. The stolid Classical facade is enlivened by an English Baroque steeple (its mate was destroyed by lightning).

17| King-Nash House
(*Patrick J. King House*)
3234 W. Washington Blvd.
1901, GEORGE W. MAHER

An interesting counterpoint to Maher's smooth, finely finished, Roman brick and stucco houses is the occasional appearance of a megalithic work. The influence is Richardsonian in this husky limestone city house, with its exquisitely carved columns, capitals, and urns. The rhythmically recurring motif is the thistle, seen in the capitals and dormer and used extensively inside. The monochromatic palette originally offset jewel-like glass mosaic panels, fragments of which remain beneath the second-floor window. Elongated Roman tray shapes, a favorite Maher motif, form the tall fence. Patrick Nash, a later owner, was a prominent politician.

KING-NASH HOUSE

LEGLER LIBRARY

18| 3800 W. Madison St.
(*Midwest Athletic Club*)
1926, MICHAELSEN & ROGNSTAD

The Spanish Baroque Revival palette and decorative vocabulary translated beautifully into terra cotta. The fifth-floor shields commemorate the short-lived athletic club, which offered West Side businessmen all the amenities of a Loop club—including two ballrooms, an Olympic-size pool, a gym with a running track, plus a fabulous view across the park to the city skyline—before sinking into receivership in 1930.

19| Chicago Public Library—Henry E. Legler Regional Branch
115 S. Pulaski Rd.
1919, ALFRED S. ALSCHULER

This dignified Beaux Arts building, with its elegant raked brickwork, was Chicago's first regional library. The seventeenth-century priest/explorer Father Marquette is portrayed on the wall of the study room in a WPA mural by R. Fayerweather Babcock.

20| 4000 Guyon Towers
(*Guyon Hotel*)
4000 W. Washington Blvd.
1928, JENS J. JENSEN
1988, REHABILITATION, HEARD & ASSOCS., LTD.

"The Land of the Moors" was the inspiration for this pleasure palace guarded by avian gargoyles. The poured-concrete structure is faced with cream and red brick and ornamented with flora and fauna in terra cotta and tile. West Side dance hall entrepreneur J. Louis Guyon developed this stretch of Pulaski Rd. as an entertainment center and occupied the hotel's southernmost penthouse.

21| George W. Tilton Public School
4152 W. West End Ave.
1908, DWIGHT H. PERKINS
1965, ADDITION, SAUL SAMUELS

It was "the most successful of all Mr. Perkins's designs" in the opinion of *Architectural Record* (1910). The architect's bold hand sculpted a strong, geometric facade deriving drama from the articulate layering of planes, from windows to walls to towering piers. The virtuoso masonry is in unusually rich tones of mustard and burnt orange brick.

TILTON SCHOOL

22| St. Martin de Porres Roman Catholic Church
(*St. Thomas Aquinas Church*)
4301 W. Washington Blvd.
1923–1925, KARL M. VITZTHUM

Austinite Vitzthum's grandest local project is Gothic Moderne, a house of worship yearning to be a soaring skyscraper. The Celtic cross atop the tower is the clue that this church was built for a predominantly Irish congregation. Inside, extensive gold mosaic work and opalescent *grisaille* glass make the nave worth a visit.

23| Austin Town Hall Park Field House
5626 W. Lake St.
1929, MICHAELSEN & ROGNSTAD
1992, RENOVATION, CHICAGO PARK DISTRICT

From 1871 to 1928 the Cicero Town Hall stood on this site, which was donated by Henry W. Austin. When the West Park System took over the property in 1927, planning began for a "patriotic memorial hall for Austin organizations." This Georgian Revival recreational facility, with a tower modeled on Independence Hall in Philadelphia, once contained a swimming pool, auditorium, and shooting range.

24| Gammon United Methodist Church
(*Austin Methodist Church*)
502 N. Central Ave.
1900, SIDNEY R. BADGLEY
1909, BADGLEY & NICKLAS

A staid facade in plain-Jane Gothic hides an unusual rotated plan with the altar in the northwest corner. The west wall of the nave could be raised to increase the size of the worship space. When the church burned in 1909, the congregation again hired Cleveland architect Badg-

ley and rebuilt to his original design.

25| Chicago Public Library— Henry W. Austin Branch
5615 W. Race Ave.
1928, ALFRED S. ALSCHULER

This Beaux Arts library subtly integrates Egyptian forms in the papyriform capitals.

26| Francis Scott Key Public School
517 N. Parkside Ave.
1906, DWIGHT H. PERKINS

This solid, unfussy design is from Perkins's early years as Board of Education architect.

27| Fire Station
(*Cicero Township Fire and Police Station*)
439 N. Waller Ave.
1899, FREDERICK R. SCHOCK

The last municipal building erected before Austin's annexation to Chicago is now one of the West Side's oldest firehouses. The eclectic facade is dominated by the very flat, vaguely Gothic stone trim around doors and windows.

Begin a tour of Austin's finest residential area on the other side of the cul-de-sac of Midway Park at Waller Ave., where the Congregationalists and the Episcopalians had a stylistic face-off.

FIRE STATION

The Episcopalians clung more tightly to tradition, while the Congregationalists threw caution to the winds.

28| St. Martin's Episcopal Church (*St. Paul's Methodist Episcopal Church*)
5700 W. Midway Park
1901, ALLAN M. BARROWS

The interior of this simplified Tudor Revival church is a small glory, with a beautiful timbered ceiling and rich stained glass. In the chapel are five stained-glass windows saved from the wooden church (1880) that originally occupied this site. The rectory, at 5710, echoes the Gothic church in the pointed-arch forms of the side entry, the dormer windows, and the porch piers.

29| Greater Holy Temple, Church of God in Christ (*First Congregational Church of Austin*)
5701 W. Midway Park
1908, WILLIAM E. DRUMMOND

Drummond's first independent commission owes much in plan and massing to employer Frank Lloyd Wright's design for Unity Temple in Oak Park. After you enter through a small, low-ceilinged vestibule, the worship space at the top of the stairs seems very spacious. A central nave with an ornamental colored-glass skylight is flanked by lower side aisles. Unlike Wright's design, the social hall and kitchen here are underneath the raised worship space, in a variation of the typical "church basement" style.

30| 5744 W. Midway Park
1988, JOHN KRAII

Donated materials and services made possible this unique home built by West Side Habitat for Humanity and the Home Builders Association of Greater Chicago. It was designed for a quadriplegic child and her family; ease of access was a prime consideration. The simple gable and the veranda enable it to slip unobtrusively into the nineteenth-century streetscape.

31| Frederick R. Schock House
5804 W. Midway Park
1886, FREDERICK R. SCHOCK

The empress of Queen Annes, this richly inventive design was Schock's home for almost fifty years. Schock purchased the property just when central Austin was beginning to boom as a desirable residential location. The house was his architectural calling card, announcing his talents to new residents buying lots in the area, and it remains a traffic stopper. The rusticated stone base supports a riot of materials and forms, from slate shingles to arched window surrounds that look like wood but are actually pressed metal. The extremely varied roofline is topped by a large crest shaped like a handle—an invitation, perhaps, to carry this dollhouse

GREATER HOLY TEMPLE

FREDERICK R. SCHOCK HOUSE

away. Inside, the architect finished or remodeled rooms during different eras; there is a Queen Anne entry hall, a French parlor, and a Craftsman dining room.

32| Frederick Beeson House (2)
5810 W. Midway Park
1892, FREDERICK R. SCHOCK

Manneristic excesses abound in this Queen Anne house—from the wooden "keystone" piercing the Palladian window form, to the cartoonish broken pediments atop the second-floor bay windows, to the stable's peculiar gable. The lavish budget was a step up from Beeson's modest Schock-designed first house in South Austin, and it paid for the stone and leaded colored glass, as well as interior finishes such as African mahogany and walnut.

FREDERICK BEESON HOUSE (2)

33| Frederick Beeson House (4)
5830 W. Midway Park
1922, FREDERICK R. SCHOCK

With the construction of this amiable Georgian residence, the peripatetic Beeson ceased his restless architectural wandering of Midway Park.

34| Frederick Beeson House (3)
5840 W. Midway Park
1901, FREDERICK R. SCHOCK

The rounded second-floor bay and the Baroque gable whisper nineteenth-century eclecticism, while the hipped roof, deep eaves, urns, and Roman brick herald the emerging Prairie Style.

35| Edward Funk House
5848 W. Midway Park
1886, HOLABIRD & ROCHE

Originally a shingled, turreted counterweight to Schock's extravaganza on the eastern end of the block, this house is now greatly altered.

36| Alvin F. Davis Flats
5849 W. Midway Park
1912, FREDERICK R. SCHOCK

Austinites favored the suburban look even after annexation to the city in 1899. Although the depth of the building bespeaks a multifamily residence, the facade—with its geometric detailing popularized in nearby Oak Park—could pass for that of a single-family home.

37 | William Ford House
5928 W. Midway Park
1893, JAMES BEVINS

Some embellishments on this Queen Anne are of recent vintage, but all are in the spirit of the original style.

38 | Frank Barrett House
5945 W. Midway Park
MID-1890S, ARCHITECT UNKNOWN

Almost every kind of window appears on this Queen Anne, most notably the circular series atop the turret.

39 | Charles A. Carlson House
5964 W. Midway Park
1910, ROBERT M. HYDE

This lovely Craftsman house is enriched by leaded-glass doors and windows, arched corner entry, and battered dining room bay at the rear. The chimney bisects the facade, an indication of the importance of the fireplace, a key element in the Craftsman Style.

40 | Benjamin Wikoff House
5939 W. Race Ave.
1894, OLIVER C. SMITH

The picturesque tower and gambrel dormer pierce the gambrel roof of this large but snug Queen Anne.

41 | Elwood Riggs House
5929 W. Race Ave.
1895, ARCHITECT UNKNOWN

Although neo-Classical on the front, with a curiously dissected Palladian dormer, the sides are more stubbornly irregular and eclectic. With its billowing wall plane, the third-floor dormer on the east side could have been plucked from a Shingle Style house.

42 | 5850 W. Race Ave.
1901, JOHN D. CHUBB

Builder Henry Hogan and owner Henry W. Austin, Jr., developed the property with this very late Queen Anne style house.

43 | Francis Pray House
5837 W. Race Ave.
1904, ARCHITECT UNKNOWN

This fine example of a transitional style is still Queen Anne in plan and overall proportions but simpler and more rectilinear. Across the street at 5824 and 5830 are two more of the same era.

44 | Catherine Schlecht House
5804 W. Race Ave.
1887, FREDERICK R. SCHOCK

It could have been assembled from two different kits—it has two prominent entries, sides flat

CATHERINE SCHLECHT HOUSE

and sides rounded, and porches on several levels. The best element is on the west side: the high and hooded third-floor balcony flanked by shingled tourelles.

45 | Marie Schock House
5749 W. Race Ave.
1888, FREDERICK R. SCHOCK

Schock designed it for his mother, then had it published in *Building Budget* as "A Cheap Suburban Residence." All wall surfaces and roofs were originally covered in stained shingles.

46 | Charles Hitchcock House
5704 W. Ohio St.
1871, ARCHITECT UNKNOWN

This archetypal suburban Italianate house is strongly vertical and frosted with elaborate paired brackets and a fretsawn porch balustrade. Most suburban Italianates were built in wood, and many mimic grander masonry homes. Here the wooden window molding imitates incised keystones.

CHARLES HITCHCOCK HOUSE

Before continuing south on Central Ave., a detour east to Laramie Ave. will take you to one of the city's finest terra-cotta neighborhood business blocks.

47 | 5200 W. Chicago Ave.
(*Laramie State Bank*)
1928, REMODELING, MEYER & COOK

What started out as a one-story addition and remodeling of a modest 1909 building grew into a major overhaul. The celery, mustard, and off-white facades are terrific examples of the craftsmanship of the Northwestern Terra Cotta Company. Decorative panels portray men

5200 W. CHICAGO AVE.

SETH P. WARNER HOUSE

at work, clouds of gigantic coins, and bees and squirrels—familiar symbols of industry and thrift.

48| Seth P. Warner House
631 N. Central Ave.
1869, ARCHITECT UNKNOWN

Compare this symmetrical Italianate with the Charles J. Hull House (1856) on S. Halsted St. to see how slowly architectural styles changed in the mid-nineteenth century. The projecting central pavilion, pediment, central stair-hall plan, and cupola typify this phase of the style.

49| Thomas J. Langford House
621 N. Central Ave.
1895, ARCHITECT UNKNOWN

On their property the Langfords spanned the architectural generations. The roundheaded windows in the Queen Anne turret echo the cupola of the Seth P. Warner House to the

THOMAS J. LANGFORD HOUSE

north. To the south stands the Langford, an English Gothic six-flat developed by Langford in the 1920s.

50| Joseph J. Walser House
42 N. Central Ave.
1903, FRANK LLOYD WRIGHT

One of the last single-family houses built on Central Ave. during its heyday as a fine residential street, it has been altered by the removal of leaded-glass windows and by the addition of side porches.

Columbus Park
W. Adams Blvd., S. Central Ave., Eisenhower Expressway, and S. Austin Blvd.
1920, JENS JENSEN
1992, RESTORATION, CHICAGO PARK DISTRICT

Jensen's prairie vision for Chicago's parks was most com-pletely realized here, and the spirit lives on. The landscape, natural and man-made, was filled with emotional content for Jensen, who wrote of this work, "Looking west from the river bluffs at sundown across a quiet bit of meadow, one sees the prairie melt away into the stratified clouds above . . . this gives a feeling of breadth and freedom that only the prairie landscape can give to the human soul."

Concerns that nearby Oak Parkers would use a park on their border argued against a city park at this location. The West Park Commission explored the expansion of its tax district to include the neighboring village but was defeated by the Oak Park lobby. Because it was the last large piece of land in the area, the property was acquired anyway; the Knights of Columbus suggested the name. Noting the lingering resentment toward Oak Park, sociologist W. R. Ireland commented, "Memorializing the great explorer and the patron saint of travelers, the park's name links to one another the Italian and Irish coreligionists of nearby populations and looks across the city limit to the Protestant 'Indians' of Oak Park who failed in their part of a projected bargain."

A shared public space that portrayed the beauties of the country was of great spiritual value to city dwellers, Jensen felt. Although largely man-made, the lines of the park feel natural and informal. When Jensen began work, the land was almost flat, rising only seven feet from east to west, an elevation he interpreted as an ancient glacial beach. Drawing inspiration from the landscape of northern Illinois, Jensen created a symbolic "prairie river": the Lagoon that flows south and east from the Refectory and features two rock-ledge Waterfalls. Dirt excavated to form the river was used to create a ridge shielding the body of the park from the city to the east and, originally, from the railroad to the south. Jackson Blvd. was rerouted slightly to flow through the park's north end. North of Jackson Blvd. is an area intended by Jensen for casual strolling and tennis courts.

The sheltering ridge and lagoon were truncated when the park's southern end was destroyed during construction of the Eisenhower Expressway in the 1950s. The extreme tip of the original lagoon still exists as a small pond just behind the athletic fields north of the expressway. A parking lot and bus turnaround have also been carved from the park's southeastern corner.

Though heavily used for swimming, golf, and other sports, the park also harbors less-healthful activities. Major buildings are heavily programmed and welcome visitors; the paths around the Lagoon should be explored in groups.

51| Entrance Lanterns
Jackson Blvd. at Central Ave.
1918, SCHMIDT, GARDEN & MARTIN

Hipped-roof copper lanterns hover atop the concrete bases of the massive light fixtures, which are identical to those designed for Humboldt Park.

COLUMBUS PARK ENTRANCE LANTERN

52| Council Ring
Central Ave. and Jackson Blvd.
EARLY 1920S

The Council Ring, one of Jensen's trademarks, was a large circular bench intended to inspire fellowship and storytelling in the Native American tradition of gathering around a campfire. Most are circles of layered flagstone piers, originally topped by solid slabs of stone.

53| Children's Play Area
S. Central Ave. near Gladys Ave.
EARLY 1920S

The playlot shelter (with modern metal roof), wading pool edge, and Council Ring are all built from stratified limestone, one of Jensen's favorite materials.

54| Recreation Building
(*Locker and Shower Building*)
S. Central Ave. south of
Van Buren St.
1918, JOHN C. CHRISTENSEN

An eclectic English brick building with a spreading U plan, it originally contained changing facilities for Jensen's rock-ledged swimming pool (since replaced by a modern pool).

55| Men's Gymnasium
(*Stable*)
West of Recreation Building
1917, JAMES B. DIBELKA
1936, CONVERSION TO GYMNASIUM

One of the handsomest remaining stable buildings in the Chicago Park District reveals its intended function on the west wall, where outlines of the

original doors are still visible. Built on Central Ave. at Lexington St., it was moved here from the path of the expressway in 1953, when it was connected to the Fieldhouse. Columbus Park's bridle paths were the only ones on the West Side; visitors rented horses at the Stable.

56| Refectory and Boat Landing
South of Jackson Blvd. between
Waller and Menard Aves.
1922, CHATTEN & HAMMOND
1992, RESTORATION, CHICAGO PARK DISTRICT

Jensen envisioned Prairie School architecture in his park and was dismayed at the commissioners' insistence on more traditional styles. He may have been disappointed by the revivalist design chosen for the Refectory, but the rolling arches are romantic and rhythmic. The Refectory and the "prairie river" are each a beautiful vista for the other. The primary space is a light-filled dining room/meeting hall, where the Columbus theme is evoked by a mural on the west wall depicting his three ships. On the Refectory's eastern end is a concrete boat landing and dining terrace. On the lower level, forty boats were available for rental in the summer—and 1,000 pairs of ice skates in the winter.

COLUMBUS PARK REFECTORY

COLUMBUS PARK WATERFALLS

57| Waterfalls

EARLY 1920S

The sources of Jensen's "prairie river" are two waterfalls built of stratified limestone and designed to resemble an Illinois river bluff in miniature.

58| Player's Hill

EARLY 1920S

Jensen was committed to the idea of education through community theater, with open-air performances heightening communication with nature. The grassy slope between the two Waterfalls was the stage, which the audience looked up to from the meadow to the southeast. Originally the hill was much more heavily planted; clearings provided natural dressing rooms shielded from the audience by greenery.

59| Golf Course

EARLY 1920S

Under Jensen's hand the nine-hole golf course occupying the park's western half became a miniaturized prairie—broad and expansive, dotted with clusters of vegetation. The starter shed, first tee, and concession stand were moved to their present locations in 1953.

OAK PARK

OAK PARK

OAK PARK

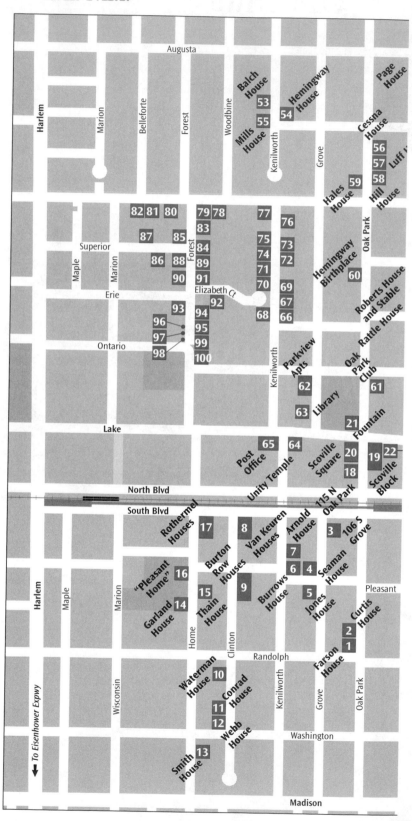

Augusta

Harlem

Marion

Belleforte

Forest

Woodbine

Balch House
53

Hemingway House
54

Page House

Kenilworth

Mills House
55

Cessna House

Grove

56
57
58
Luff

Hales House
59

Hill House

82 **81** **80**

79 **78**

77

76

Oak Park

87

85

83

75
73

Superior

Marion

86 **88**

Forest

84
89

74
72

Hemingway Birthplace

Maple

90

91

71
70

60

Erie

Elizabeth Ct

92

69

Roberts House and Stable

93

94

68

67
66

Rattle House

96

95

97

99

Kenilworth

Oak Park Club

Ontario

98

100

Parkview Apts

61

62

Lake

Library

63

21
Fountain

65

64

Scoville Square

20

19 **22**

Post Office

18

Scoville Block

Unity Temple

115 N Oak Park

North Blvd

South Blvd

Rothermel Houses

17

8

Van Keuren Houses

Arnold House

3
106 S Grove

Harlem

Maple

Marion

"Pleasant Home"
16

Burton Row Houses

7

Seaman House

Pleasant

Garland House
14

15
Thain House

9

6 **4**

Burrows House

5

Jones House

Curtis House

Home

Clinton

2
1

Farson House

Grove

Oak Park

Randolph

Waterman House
10

Conrad House

Kenilworth

Wisconsin

11

12
Webb House

Washington

Smith House
13

Madison

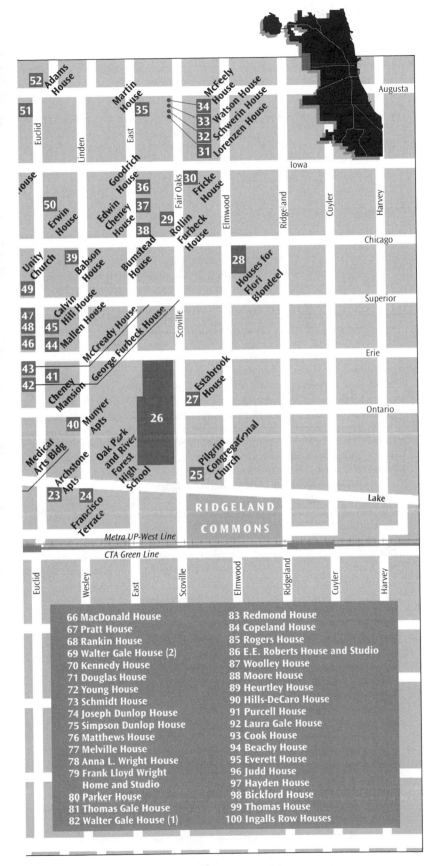

52 Adams House
51
Martin House
35
34 McFeely House
33 Watson House
32 Schwerin House
31 Lorenzen House

Euclid
Linden
East

Iowa

Augusta

30 Fricke House
36 Goodrich House
37 Edwin Cheney House
38
29 Rollin Furbeck House
Fair Oaks
Elmwood
Ridgeland
Cuyler
Harvey

Chicago

39 Babson House
Unity Church
49
Bumstead House
28 Houses for Flori Blondeel

Superior

47/48 Calvin Hill House
45 Mallen House
44
McCready House
George Furbeck House
Scoville

Erie

43
41 Cheney Mansion
42

Estabrook House
27

Ontario

40 Munyer Apts

26 Oak Park and River Forest High School

Medical Arts Bldg
Archstone Apts
23 24 Francisco Terrace

25 Pilgrim Congregational Church

Lake

RIDGELAND COMMONS

Metra UP-West Line
CTA Green Line

Euclid
Wesley
East
Scoville
Elmwood
Ridgeland
Cuyler
Harvey

OAK PARK

ARRIVING IN WAVES AFTER THE CHICAGO FIRE, SETTLERS CAME BY THE THOUSANDS to build homes: freestanding, sun-filled, hygienic, secure. Fleeing the city's crowded, combustible flats and row houses, cholera epidemics, and corruption, they sought to create a community in harmony with God and with the help of like-minded souls.

Today, tens of thousands come to tour their houses, for it was in Oak Park that the modern American home was born. Twenty-seven designs by Frank Lloyd Wright still stand, from the fanciful experiments of his early years, through his own Home and Studio, to mature Prairie School masterpieces. The geometric lines, the nature-inspired ornament, the hovering deep-eaved roofs, and the artful plans reflected a cohesive aesthetic vision and were Wright's heartfelt response to the need for shelter.

The twenty-two-year-old Wright moved here in 1889, brought by his mother, who distrusted "the raw winds of the lake." Oak Park was a borderland community, separated from similar settlements by stretches of prairie, connected to the city and to other suburbs by train lines. Realtors extolled the artesian wells, the many churches, and the public library, but the streets were largely unpaved and houses were just being numbered. Wright chose for his homesite an overgrown lot on the edge of an undeveloped prairie where he often went for nature walks.

During Wright's formative years in Oak Park, the community was dominated by hard-nosed British immigrants and transplanted Yankees. Disciplined, resourceful, and inventive problem-solvers, they sought to shape their own environment and to have local control of taxes, school, transportation, and development. Threatened by annexation to Chicago, which had already swallowed up townships such as Lake View and Hyde Park, determined Oak Parkers stopped the city's westward movement. They created and pushed through the state legislature a law enabling towns to withdraw from townships and set up independent village governments. The new village of Oak Park was incorporated in 1902.

Up to 1880 settlers had built cottages and small villas with Greek Revival, Italianate, or Gothic detailing. As the population boomed, the prairie filled with subdivisions of wooden houses, from the structurally expressive Stick Style to the heavily ornamented Queen Anne and Classical Revival. No one style prevailed; unschooled architects and builders delighted in miniaturizing elements from grand houses and uninhibitedly combining them for maximum picturesque effect.

Later in his career Wright would blast such designs: "These over-dressed wood house walls had cut in them, or cut out of them to be precise, big holes for the big cat and little holes for the little cat . . . The whole exterior was be-deviled, that is to say, mixed to puzzle-pieces with corner-boards, panel-boards, window-frames, corner-blocks, plinth-blocks, rosettes, fantails, and jiggerwork in general . . . Simplicity was as far from this scrap-pile as the pandemonium of the barnyard is far from music." But the designs themselves stimulated him, and he himself in the 1890s worked with some of their forms before synthesizing his own ideas.

Like most middle-class suburbs of its era, Oak Park was a conservative community, a temperance town nicknamed Saint's Rest for its many churches. But the young architect thrived in this atmosphere—nourished by the town's rapid growth, emphasis on the home, and respect for resourceful individualists. His neighbors became his friends and clients; their commissions constitute the nation's most amazing open-air museum of houses. Their freshness of concept and beauty of form, their modernity and originality, are strikingly set amidst not only their Victorian predecessors but also their offspring designed by Wright's employees and contemporaries.

Wright entered a new phase of his life when he broke the bonds of Oak Park propriety with his 1909 trip to Germany. He had gone there to oversee the preparation of the Wasmuth edition of his work, taking with him his lover, Mamah Borthwick Cheney, wife of his Oak Park client Edwin H. Cheney. It was a turning point in many respects. Now in midlife, with a new love, he was seeking fresh challenges and an international profile. In the two decades of his residence the population of 4,500 had quadrupled. No longer a suburban frontier, Oak Park had become an established center of its own, concerned less with innovation than with the status quo. Along the streets of his village, Wright could see his own ideas interpreted and re-hashed not only by younger architects who had worked in his studio but also by speculative builders cashing in on "the look."

The frontier had disappeared; locally, his aesthetic was mainstream. Seeking new horizons, he moved on to Taliesin, his home in Wisconsin, leaving behind his family, his friends, and a dazzling body of built work.

—ALICE SINKEVITCH

---

1 | John Farson House (1)
237 S. Oak Park Ave.
1888, ARCHITECT UNKNOWN

Farson's Queen Anne was a comfortable, commodious, and picturesque home for an up-and-coming young investment banker. After rapid financial success, he sought something more avant-garde, and in 1897 commissioned the modern "Pleasant Home" a few blocks to the west.

2 | Edward P. Curtis House
231 S. Oak Park Ave.
1889, FRANK ELLIS

Considered Oak Park's first architect, Ellis was actually a builder with a certain flair. This rectilinear Queen Anne house differs from his slightly earlier Stick Style houses only in the addition of a rounded corner bay with an exotic onion-shaped cap.

3 | 106 S. Grove Ave.
1914, JOHN S. VAN BERGEN

A former Wright employee, Van Bergen excelled at designing small houses with flowing plans and horizontal lines for deep but narrow lots. Tucked into the side, the entry brings the visitor directly into the heart of the house.

106 S. GROVE AVE.

4 | John A. Seaman House (1)
139 S. Grove Ave.
1894, HODELKE & ELLIS

The Columbian Exposition of 1893, a gleaming White City built to an awesome scale,

EDWARD P. CURTIS HOUSE

JOHN A. SEAMAN HOUSE (1)

created an enormous appetite for the Classical Revival style; this grand wedding cake was one of the first homes in Oak Park to reflect the fair's influence. A profusion of garlands decorate porch and dormer pediments. A plainer sibling, also designed by Fiddelke, was built diagonally across the corner in 1899.

5| John I. Jones House
209 S. Grove Ave.
1887, CICERO HINE

From the second-floor row of miniature Moorish arches, to the Tudor half-timbering, to the multitude of window shapes and styles, this picturesque snapshot captures the uninhibited freedom of the Queen Anne style. How fresh, lively, and inventive the robust porch and well-broken skyline and wall surfaces still appear! Originally, the exterior walls and the roof were covered with stained shingles, making them read like a uniformly fuzzy fabric.

6| Asa W. Burrows House
142 S. Kenilworth Ave.
1887, FRANK ELLIS

Devoid of historical references, geometrically paneled frame houses like this were in their era called modern and are now called Stick Style. The exterior cladding suggests the underlying balloon frame, with bands of wood dividing all wall planes into a series of clapboard and shingle rectangles. The wooden porch echoes the house's structure, framing the view of the world outside. The banded, rotated corner bay is a rectilinear version of the rounded Queen Anne tower.

7| Wesley A. Arnold House
130 S. Kenilworth Ave.
1888, WESLEY A. ARNOLD

Many homes of the 1880s that became Painted Ladies in the 1980s have been bedecked in colors that would have been chemically impossible and aesthetically undesirable at the time of construction. Here is a rare opportunity to study a true Victorian color palette. Built with unusually expensive materials, such as Darlington sandstone and slate, Arnold's own home promoted his talents. The pleasing but sober colors of nature favored in the late 1880s are displayed in the hard materials, which Arnold bent to his will, rounding off every corner. The richest element is the doorway, framed by beveled-glass sidelights and a Moorish arch.

WESLEY A. ARNOLD HOUSE

8| William J. Van Keuren Houses
100 & 102 S. Clinton Ave.
1896, WILLIAM J. VAN KEUREN

Oak Park architect Van Keuren built these late Queen Anne houses himself as an investment.

9| Edmund F. Burton Row Houses
200–208 S. Clinton Ave.
1892, WILLETT & PASHLEY

Five Queen Anne dwellings with Romanesque details are shoehorned into a space that could have accommodated only two freestanding houses. The most elaborate occupies the eye-catching corner plot; its first tenant was Wright's future client Arthur Heurtley. A disastrous fire in 1979 destroyed 202 and damaged the others; sensitive rebuilding has brought them back.

10| Henry B. Waterman House
309 S. Clinton Ave.
1894, WILLIAM J. VAN KEUREN

Oak Parkers were fond of the no-nonsense Stick Style, with clapboards and rotated corner bay, which persisted here well into the era of Queen Anne and Classical Revival.

11| Isaac N. Conrad House
321 S. Clinton Ave.
1902, EBEN E. ROBERTS

Roberts created dozens of versions of this classic Oak Park house. Typical elements include the exaggerated breadth, the very low hipped roof and deep eaves, the manneristic brackets scrolling down the walls, and the disproportionately large abacus between the porch roof and columns.

12| George D. Webb House
329 S. Clinton Ave.
1896, ARCHITECT UNKNOWN

Showing the influence of the then-recent Columbian Exposition, this high-shouldered house features a New England curbed gambrel roof, dentils, and decorative columns.

13| George W. Smith House
404 S. Home Ave.
1898, FRANK LLOYD WRIGHT

Designed in 1895, this house of contrasts looks forward and backward. The walls are subtly broken into rectangular planes like a Stick Style house but are covered in shingles rather than clapboard. Although as tall as its Queen Anne and Classical Revival neighbors, the house has proto–Prairie School elements: the entry is hidden from view and the house hugs the ground. Originally shingled like the walls, the steep double-pitched roof is now covered with pink asphalt, making the house look like a crazed pagoda.

14| Garland House
241 S. Home Ave.
EARLY 1850S, ARCHITECT UNKNOWN

Beneath the stucco, which dates from around 1910, is one of Oak Park's oldest houses. According to local lore, it was moved from Lake St. in the mid-1880s. The symmetry, the rows of modillions, and the cornice return on the sides hint at the Greek Revival design.

15| Richard S. Thain House
210 S. Home Ave.
1892, PATTON & FISHER

The tall roof with the eaveless edge, and the combination of robust forms with thin, crisp, clapboard siding, are hallmarks of this firm's version of the Queen Anne style. Every room on the first two floors, except the kitchen, was designed with a bay, providing expansive views and a charmingly irregular form.

RICHARD S. THAIN HOUSE

16| "Pleasant Home"
(*John Farson House 2*)
217 S. Home Ave.
1897–1899, GEORGE W. MAHER

Designed in 1897 for investment banker John Farson, "Pleasant Home" was named for the streets that bound it. Maher considered it a "type for an American style," representative of the indigenous architecture that

"PLEASANT HOME" EXTERIOR

"PLEASANT HOME" DINING ROOM

he and other Prairie School architects were creating. It would become a prototype for many of Maher's houses.

"Pleasant Home" is approached by a formally landscaped, raised garden that emphasizes the facade's symmetry. The original ornamental fence and garden urns are preserved; the stable and greenhouse are not. Many aspects of the house relate to the William H. Winslow House in River Forest (1893) by Frank Lloyd Wright, with whom Maher had apprenticed in the office of Joseph Lyman Silsbee. Its low-pitched roof, horizontality, buff-colored Roman brick, and simple stone enframements for the windows respond to Wright's work. Maher introduced the emphasis on symmetry, the broad front porch, the elaborate centralized dormer, and the use of a floral motif in the decoration.

The house's decoration introduced a personal design philosophy that Maher later called motif-rhythm theory. Selecting three decorative motifs—the American honeysuckle, the lion's head, and the shield—Maher unified the exterior details with art glass, mosaics, woodwork, light fixtures, and furniture. The art-glass door and windows at the entry repeat the honeysuckle pattern and shield of the porch medallions; lion's heads appear on the porch and are carved into the hall's oak mantel. Maher designed the dining room table, chairs, and sideboard that are on view.

Maher developed a highly successful residential practice in the Chicago suburbs, especially in Kenilworth; his Chicago work is best represented on Hutchinson St. He developed his motif-rhythm theory to create visual unity in later commissions, exploiting the thistle in the James Patten House (Evanston, Ill., 1901), the coral lily at Rockledge

(Homer, Minn. 1911), both demolished, and the poppy in the Ernest Magerstadt House (Chicago, 1908).

His subsequent furniture and interior decorations link his work to modern European design after 1900.

Herbert S. Mills, the house's second owner, sold the house to the Park District of Oak Park in 1939. —KATHLEEN CUMMINGS

17| Samuel A. Rothermel Houses
100–110 S. Home Ave.
1891, WILLIAM J. VAN KEUREN

South and North Blvds. were originally the Boulevard, a broad street split by train tracks at grade and one of the village's earliest residential streets. With increasing traffic on the train lines, lots on the Boulevard became less desirable for fine homes and were developed as rental properties. Miniaturizing a variety of Queen Anne fronts, the design maximizes the number of units and features a style whose "stage set" quality is literally only skin-deep.

18| 115 N. Oak Park Ave.
(Cicero Gas Company Building)
1893, PATTON & FISHER

This narrow business block springs from a base of beautifully detailed Roman brick. An upstairs hall was available for rental to local fraternal organizations.

19| Scoville Block (1)
116–132 N. Oak Park Ave.
1899, PATTON, FISHER & MILLER
1901, NORTH ADDITION, EBEN E. ROBERTS
1929, GROUND-FLOOR REMODELING, ROY J. HOTCHKISS

With this project, developer Charles B. Scoville accelerated the change of the Oak Park Ave./Lake St. district from single-family residential to commercial. Unusual for Oak Park are the Flemish stepped gables and the rich burnt-orange Roman brick and terra cotta. Scoville is memorialized in medallions under the bays on the south wall. The original design was echoed beautifully in Roberts' Lake St. addition. The building remains a "flats above, stores below" complex.

20| Scoville Square
(Scoville Block 2)
137 N. Oak Park Ave.
1908, EBEN E. ROBERTS
1982, RESTORATION, OFFICE OF JOHN VINCI

This business block contained offices and a Masonic hall above shops. Bands of windows are divided by piers and topped by a row of roundheaded windows, a Sullivanesque organization of the wall popular with Oak Park architects Roberts and Normand S. Patton. The hipped roof and overhanging eaves are distinctly Prairie Style. Step inside to see a bright and breezy arcade.

21| Horse Show Association Fountain
Lake St. at Oak Park Ave.
1969 REPLICA OF 1909 ORIGINAL, RICHARD W. BOCK, SCULPTOR

Man's relationship to his four-legged friends was a favorite sentimental theme of the period; this sculptured fountain symbolically and practically united them. People were to drink from the highest level, horses and dogs from the lower two. Bock showed a preliminary design to his friend and professional associate Frank Lloyd Wright, whose buildings frequently featured Bock's sculpture. Wright suggested the opening in the middle, a contribution that grew into the apocryphal story that Wright had designed the fountain.

22| Medical Arts Building
715 W. Lake St.
1929, ROY J. HOTCHKISS

If Raymond Chandler's private eye Philip Marlowe had prowled the streets of Oak Park, his office would have been in this

Art Deco miniskyscraper. In contrast to the overgrown domesticity of much suburban commercial architecture of the 1920s, the unrestrained verticality and geometric decorative panels suggest that Oak Parker Hotchkiss looked to Loop high rises for inspiration. The simple interior has been altered very little and is worth a look, especially for the light fixtures.

23| Archstone Apartments
675 W. Lake St.
1987, NAGLE, HARTRAY & ASSOCS.

This handsome, modern interpretation of the Prairie School idiom privatizes as much open space as possible, creating a tranquil spot that turns its back on the noise of Lake St. and the train tracks. Careful massing and choice of materials visually diminish the bulk. The lobby continues the look, featuring a fireplace with inglenook and Prairie Style light fixtures and leaded glass.

ARCHSTONE APARTMENTS

24| Francisco Terrace
W. Lake St. at N. Linden Ave.
1978, HARRY WEESE & ASSOCS.

This was among the first—and remains one of the best— Prairie School Revival projects in Oak Park. In 1973, as Frank Lloyd Wright's Francisco Terrace apartments in Chicago were about to be demolished, quick action on the part of Realtor John Baird, attorney and historian Devereux Bowly, and architect Ben Weese salvaged the

terra-cotta arch, cornice, decorative panels, and other ornamentation. Adapting Wright's plan, Weese created a courtyard complex of seventeen town houses, replicating the original massing and details. The entry arch forms a beautiful terminus to Linden Ave.

25| Pilgrim Congregational Church
(*Second Congregational Church*)
460 W. Lake St.
1889, SOUTH HALF, PATTON & FISHER
1899, NORTH HALF, PATTON, FISHER & MILLER

The design bends a knee not to God but to H. H. Richardson, emulating his materials, polychromatic palette, bold forms, and confident vision. The rockfaced walls are trimmed in red brick, an inexpensive stand-in for Richardson's favored reddish Longmeadow stone. The Lake St. facade is unaltered; the remodeled office and chapel retain only the leaded-glass windows and fireplace. The addition to the north blends seamlessly, the stone base supporting a tall, rectilinear tower and an immense gable filled with a roundheaded window. Over 1,100 worshipers could be seated by raising the wall between the body of the church and the galleried Sunday school rooms to the east.

26| Oak Park and River Forest High School
201 N. Scoville Ave.
1906, NORMAND S. PATTON AND ROBERT C. SPENCER; 1908, 1911, PATTON & MILLER; 1913, ERIE ST. ADDITION, EBEN E. ROBERTS; 1921, HOLMES & FLINN; 1924, PERKINS, FELLOWS & HAMILTON; 1928, FIELD HOUSE AND GYMNASIUM, CHILDS & SMITH; 1968, ONTARIO ST. INFILL ADDITION, EVERETT I. BROWN & ASSOCS.

The clumsy late 1960s addition linking the field house and gym to the original school north of Ontario St. obscures the design, best seen from the Scoville and East Aves. sides. This project was a political marriage for Oak

OAK PARK AND RIVER FOREST HIGH
SCHOOL (ERIE ST. ADDITION)

Parker Patton and River Forest
resident Spencer: the school
board split the design commission between them. Sometimes
described as Italian Renaissance, the school actually descends directly from Richardson's and Sullivan's organization
of a large building block and
strongly resembles Patton's best
work as Chicago Board of Education architect in 1897–1898. A
school designer with twenty
years' experience, Patton had
favored roundheaded windows
since the 1880s; combined with
the deep eaves and hipped
roofs, the whole has a Prairie
spirit. The additions filling out
the block from Ontario St. north
to Erie St. emulate the original
design.

27| Torrie S. Estabrook House
200 N. Scoville Ave.
1909, TALLMADGE & WATSON

The gabled roofs and projecting
vertical piers are typical of this
firm's work. Like many bungalows of the era, it has a large
footprint; the cruciform plan
included not only kitchen,
living, and dining rooms on
the first floor but also a den,
a music room, and two bedrooms. This house was considered noteworthy in its time for
the basement garage, entered
from the rear of the property.

28| Houses for Flori Blondeel
426, 432 & 436 N. Elmwood Ave.
1913–1914, JOHN S. VAN BERGEN

This pleasing trio of Prairie
School houses is symmetrical
and simply detailed. The center
house is one of Van Bergen's
many versions of Frank Lloyd
Wright's "Fireproof House for
$5,000," an economical design
published in the *Ladies' Home
Journal* in April 1907 and imitated by Van Bergen and others
for years.

29| Rollin Furbeck House
511 N. Fair Oaks Ave.
1897, FRANK LLOYD WRIGHT

Wright's first emphatically forward-
looking design in Oak Park
excites with its remarkable ex-
perimentation. The variety and
broken roofline of the Queen
Anne style would have been
comfortably familiar to any
nineteenth-century viewer, while

HOUSES FOR FLORI BLONDEEL

CHARLES F. LORENZEN HOUSE

the dynamic composition and geometric detailing catapult boldly into the twentieth century. With its towering central pavilion, the design was an odd choice for this already elevated lot, which rolls over the remnants of an ancient glacial beach. Despite the placement of the first floor low on a water table, and the horizontal banding of materials, the house reads as very tall—getting shyer as it rises. The very open "picture window" on the first floor contrasts sharply with the recessed diamond-paned windows above.

30| William G. Fricke House
540 N. Fair Oaks Ave.
1902, FRANK LLOYD WRIGHT
1907, GARAGE (FOR EMMA MARTIN), FRANK LLOYD WRIGHT

This dazzling and dynamic arrangement of planes was originally anchored by a loggia and porch that ran to the south. Without them, the massive tower pulls the composition vertically. Even so, the interplay of wall and roof planes and the diamond-shaped entry bay on the north are the work of a rapidly maturing visionary.

31| Charles F. Lorenzen House
635 N. Fair Oaks Ave.
1906, EBEN E. ROBERTS

32| Charles Schwerin House
639 N. Fair Oaks Ave.
1908, EBEN E. ROBERTS

These typical Foursquare houses are refracted through the Oak Park prism, their exaggerated breadth and horizontality adorned with geometric Prairie School details from the front porch to the chimneys. Roberts frequently inflated the third-floor dormers on hip-roofed houses to give them maximum flair. The dormer at 639 owes a debt to George W. Maher, particularly to his nearby house for Charles R. Erwin.

33| Vernon S. Watson House
643 N. Fair Oaks Ave.
1904, VERNON S. WATSON

Watson designed this modest house before he joined Thomas Tallmadge in practice. Built for $2,000, it is sided with horizontal board-and-batten and clapboard. Watson later added bays at front and rear.

34| Otto H. McFeely House
645 N. Fair Oaks Ave.
1905, VERNON S. WATSON

Architects and owners valued concrete's fireproof qualities, especially after Chicago's disastrous Iroquois Theater fire of 1903. But the cost of constructing the forms was high, necessitating simple repetitive shapes and little or no ornament. This severe little experiment in concrete is softened somewhat by the porch and the Prairie-influenced stringcourse and wide eaves.

WILLIAM E. MARTIN HOUSE

35 | William E. Martin House
636 N. East Ave.
1903, FRANK LLOYD WRIGHT

"Here entered the important new element of Plasticity . . . The windows would sometimes be wrapped around the building corners as inside emphasis of plasticity and to increase the sense of interior space. I fought for outswinging windows because the casement window associated house with the out-of-doors, gave free openings outward."—Frank Lloyd Wright

This mature Prairie School design offsets its great height by three layers of hipped roofs, which emphasize the horizontal and shield sparkling ribbons of leaded glass.

36 | Harry C. Goodrich House
534 N. East Ave.
1896, FRANK LLOYD WRIGHT

The steeply pitched fedora roof with flared edges and the off-center porch are in the same vein as the George W. Smith House. The thin, crisp clapboard that covers so many Queen Anne houses in Oak Park reaches its true rectilinear potential here.

37 | Edwin H. Cheney House
520 N. East Ave.
1904, FRANK LLOYD WRIGHT

Eye-catching in its dramatic horizontality, yet guarding the path to penetration, this house protects as it entices. Even the location of the front door (in the middle of the south wall) is difficult to guess; the route to entry is circuitous and engaging. The lot slopes down to the east; the house snuggles into the same slight ridge that Wright's nearby Rollin Furbeck House (1897) surmounts. From the street, the terrace walls and the massive, low hipped roof hide most of the facade with its dazzling art glass. No wonder Cheney's wife, Mamah Borthwick, fell in love with Wright! Their trip to Europe in 1909 was the beginning of the end for their marriages and for Wright's Oak Park life and Chicago practice; they moved together to Spring Green, Wisc., in 1911. She is buried there at Wright's home, Taliesin East, where she and her two children were among those murdered by a servant in 1914.

38 | Dale Bumstead House
504 N. East Ave.
1909, TALLMADGE & WATSON

This successful design, with its signature narrow vertical piers and emphasized entry bay, became a formula for the firm.

39 | Gustavus Babson House
415 N. Linden Ave.
1913, TALLMADGE & WATSON

By the time this split-level house was built, the Prairie School had become mainstream Oak Park, mingling with massive Georgians on Linden Ave.

40| Salem E. Munyer Apartments
175– 181 N. Linden Ave./643–645
W. Ontario St.
1916, JOHN S. VAN BERGEN

Stripped and spare, this Prairie School building has a severity that looks ahead ten years to the International Style. It gracefully rounds the corner, balancing the horizontals of roof, raked mortar joints, and stone lintels with piers, chimneys, and stacks of sunporches.

41| Cheney Mansion
(*C. A. Sharpe House*)
208 N. Euclid Ave.
1913, CHARLES E. WHITE, JR.

This mansion, now owned by the Park District of Oak Park, is distinguished chiefly for its size and craftsmanship.

42| George W. Furbeck House
223 N. Euclid Ave.
1897, FRANK LLOYD WRIGHT

This snug exercise in symmetry has a prominently placed door (in an enclosed porch, altered in the 1920s) but gives little indication of the interior layout. Wright loved to play with the viewer's sense of anticipation by giving false clues. A favorite subtly confusing device used here is the visual "stretching" of the first floor and shortening of the second by placing the string-course very high on the facade, directly under the second-floor windows. The textured surface, complex but well ordered,

features Chicago common brick that interlocks and projects at the corners. Diagonal piers projecting from the sides of the bays resemble those on the front of the Rollin Furbeck House, done the same year for his brother. The house was a wedding present from the resident's father, investor Warren Furbeck.

43| Edward W. McCready House
231 N. Euclid Ave.
1907, SPENCER & POWERS

This work—perhaps the firm's greatest—derives its grace from a subtle balancing of details: low urns, the high stringcourse, the deep-set door framed by glittering art-glass windows. The palette is simple but rich, the raked masonry joints of the orange brick emphasizing horizontality. It's a practical plan for a corner, often compared to H. H. Richardson's plan for the John J. Glessner House on Prairie Ave. The north wall continues straight back to the garage, shielding the yard from the street.

44| Herman W. Mallen House
300 N. Euclid Ave.
1905, GEORGE W. MAHER

Damaged by fire and greatly altered, the house was originally stuccoed and sported open porches on the east and west. But beautiful art glass still adorns the second-floor bays of the Euclid Ave. facade.

EDWARD W. MCCREADY HOUSE

45| Calvin H. Hill House
312 N. Euclid Ave.
1904, PATTON & MILLER

The style is Colonial Revival, but the massiveness is characteristic of the firm's Queen Anne work.

46| Thomas S. Rattle House
315 N. Euclid Ave.
1885, GEORGE O. GARNSEY

As editor of the monthly *National Builder*, a pattern-book magazine, Garnsey was one of Chicago's influential architects. This simple Queen Anne house has Stick Style details.

47| Charles E. Roberts House
321 N. Euclid Ave.
1883, BURNHAM & ROOT
1896, REMODELING, FRANK LLOYD WRIGHT

Most of Wright's work was on the interior; some of his leaded glass can be glimpsed from the alley. Roberts was a great champion of the young architect and a prominent member of the Building Committee for Unity Temple.

48| Charles E. Roberts Stable
317 N. Euclid Ave.
1896, FRANK LLOYD WRIGHT
1929, CONVERSION TO A HOUSE, WHITE & WEBER

Perhaps Wright remodeled an existing stable; if so, it was a complete remodeling. From the front, it reads as stacked volumes; from the sides, as decorated planes.

49| Unity Church
(*James Hall Taylor House*)
405 N. Euclid Ave.
1912, GEORGE W. MAHER

This formal house resembles Maher's grand designs for Hutchinson St. in Chicago. The colossal flanged segmental arch over the door was one of his favorite details of this period. The deep, unusually detailed roofline features wide soffits and fascia.

50| Charles R. Erwin House
530 N. Euclid Ave.
1905, GEORGE W. MAHER

Look at the tall narrow windows above the scalloped door arch to see the pattern in the art glass that once graced all the windows. It was echoed in a beautiful wrought-iron gate and fence.

51| George G. Page House
637 N. Euclid Ave.
1896, HARVEY L. PAGE

The grandeur and formality of this Federal Revival residence contrast sharply with other Oak Park houses of the era. Page had recently moved from Washington, D.C., and his academically correct cornice, pilasters, dentils, and Palladian windows have a measured and almost exotic beauty amid the efforts of Wright and Maher.

GEORGE G. PAGE HOUSE

52| Harry S. Adams House

710 W. Augusta St.

1914, FRANK LLOYD WRIGHT

The unusual width of the lot allowed Wright to sprawl beyond his usual limits in this, his last Oak Park house. The breadth of the low chimney echoes the sweeping lines of the roof, stringcourse, and porte cochere. The sheltered entry features one of Wright's loveliest front doors.

53| Oscar B. Balch House

611 N. Kenilworth Ave.

1911, FRANK LLOYD WRIGHT

Wright had remodeled a store on Lake St. for decorator Balch and his partner Frank Pebbles in 1907. The music, living, and dining rooms flow straight across the front of the house, which is similar in first-floor plan to the Edwin H. Cheney House.

54| Clarence E. and Grace Hall Hemingway House

600 N. Kenilworth Ave.

1906, HENRY G. FIDDELKE

Mrs. Hemingway collaborated with the architect on the design, which included offices for Dr. Hemingway and a large music room. Ernest Hemingway lived here from the age of six until he left home at eighteen.

55| Walter Thomas Mills House

601 N. Kenilworth Ave.

1897, PATTON & FISHER

The simplicity and lack of fuss, the reliance on powerful forms already characteristic of the firm's Queen Anne style work, are edging here toward something more modern and rectilinear. Note the symmetrically placed corner windows on the second floor.

56| Charles E. Cessna House

524 N. Oak Park Ave.

1905, EBEN E. ROBERTS

Roberts indulged in rich materials: clay tile for the roof, a brick base, stone trim and brackets, and dazzling art glass. The emphasis on the horizontal is greatly exaggerated by the generous hipped roofs. The dormers are so deep that they subvert their function of admitting light into the attic space, much as the cavelike porch darkens the living room. A small price to pay for such a grand house.

57| William M. Luff House

520 N. Oak Park Ave.

1886, THEODORE V. WADSKIER

Even on this street of excessive architectural personality, this rare, well-preserved Swiss chalet version of the Stick Style holds its own. The wooden members

WILLIAM M. LUFF HOUSE

that frame the rectangular panels of shingles and clapboard break through the plane of the wall, forming picturesque balconies. These, in turn, increase the complexity of the surface as the sun moves across the house, casting bars of shadow across its face.

58| Walter C. Hill House
516 N. Oak Park Ave.
1897, HARVEY L. PAGE

As strict an exercise in Federal Revival as can be seen in Oak Park, it is rigidly symmetrical and well proportioned.

59| Burton F. Hales House
509 N. Oak Park Ave.
1904, HENRY G. FIDDELKE

Oak Park's grandest mansion is this sober brick and Bedford limestone Gothic house.

60| Ernest Hemingway Birthplace
(*Ernest Hall House*)
339 N. Oak Park Ave.
1890, WESLEY A. ARNOLD

Ernest Hemingway was born in the second-floor turret bedroom in 1899. Hall was his maternal grandfather.

61| Oak Park Club Condominiums
721 W. Ontario St.
(*Oak Park Club*)
1923, MILLER, HOLMES & FLINN
156 N. Oak Park Ave. (*YMCA*)
1904, POND & POND
1991, CONVERSION TO CONDOMINIUMS, BAUHS & DRING

The Georgian YMCA and the Renaissance/Prairie Oak Park Club served diverse social needs for decades. The club is the last major local descendant of the handsome building blocks seen in Oak Park and River Forest High School and Scoville Square. Designed by Normand S. Patton's successor firm, it shifts to a more overtly revival style with Palladian detailing.

62| Parkview Apartments
173–181 N. Grove Ave.
1922, EBEN E. ROBERTS

As developer of this quality apartment house, Roberts billed it as "late English Gothic" and marketed it as "owner-occupied." Included were maids' rooms in the basement, a vacuum-cleaning system, "sound deafening" between floors, and "radio-receiving apparatus" on the roof with outlets in each unit. Note the looming faces at the parapet, styled on the north side as an iceman and a deliveryman to identify the service entrances.

63| Oak Park Public Library
834 W. Lake St.
2003, NAGLE HARTRAY DANKER KAGAN MCKAY

The third library to stand on this site still faces Lake St. but is oriented more toward Scoville Park.

64| Unity Temple
875 W. Lake St.
1905–1908, FRANK LLOYD WRIGHT

Throughout his life, Wright was absorbed with pathways of discovery. At Unity Temple, the experience is both physical and spiritual. The route from the radical and uncompromising Lake St. facade to the warm and intimate Temple is a sequence of spaces as compelling as any Wright ever created.

After their Gothic Revival church burned in June 1905, Oak Park's Universalists asked Wright to design a new building for four hundred members. The chosen site was prominent but small and close to noisy streetcar and train tracks. The budget was a modest $45,000.

UNITY TEMPLE—EXTERIOR

UNITY TEMPLE—INTERIOR

These limitations, and a deep understanding of the principles of the Universalist faith, stimulated Wright's creativity. For reasons of economy, the architect selected reinforced concrete, usually used for important buildings only if covered with another material or molded to resemble stone. Construction technology and economics dictated broad, unornamented expanses and repetitive shapes. High walls and side entries set far back would shield worshipers from as much noise as possible.

Two similar but unequal blocks—"Unity Temple" for worship and "Unity House" for social-service functions—are joined by a low entry link. The deep overhang of the slab roof covers the walkway; the monumentally scaled planter cuts off the view of the street as one ascends the short flight of stairs. The visitor is sheltered and then encircled by the building before ever crossing the threshold. Facing the doors, the sheer walls of the two blocks and the entry parapet dramatically emphasize the sky, presaging the Temple space. The inscription above each entry, "For the Worship of God and the Service of Man," reflects the Universalist belief that a house of worship must serve both sacred and secular needs.

Inside, the low-ceilinged entry area leads circuitously to even more confining cloisters from which one enters the dramatic Temple space. Only thirty feet from the clamor of Lake St. is another world, flooded with light from amber-colored skylights which create the impression of what Wright called a "happy cloudless day." Three sets of galleries for the congregation and an alcove for the choir create a Greek cross within the square, with the corners occupied by square stair towers. No seat is more than forty-five feet from the pulpit, and most seats are just barely above or below the speaker's eye level. There are no religious symbols; the Universalists chose to focus all attention on the speaker. Wright placed doors to either side of the pulpit so the congregants would exit toward the minister.

Even before it gained worldwide renown, Unity Temple was widely praised both by the congregation and by local newspapers. Despite the unorthodox form and materials, they recognized that Wright had given form to a deeply rooted spirituality. It remains a transcendent work, bound to the earth and open to the heavens.

—ALICE SINKEVITCH

65| U.S. Post Office—Oak Park Station
901 W. Lake St.
1933, WHITE & WEBER

Here sober Art Moderne is enlivened with amusing details, like the sculptured panels over the entries documenting the world of mail delivery: birds carrying letters, a mail bag and cap, the Pony Express, a mail truck, a covered wagon, a train and plane. Studded with patriotic stars, Art Deco sconces and chandeliers light the pale interior.

66| William J. MacDonald House
300 N. Kenilworth Ave.
1890, WESLEY A. ARNOLD

Although added in 1911, the porch with its rock foundation complements the Queen Anne house.

67| George B. Pratt House
308 N. Kenilworth Ave.
1886, ARCHITECT UNKNOWN

This fine Stick Style house is modest in scale but boldly articulated on both front and sides.

68| John Rankin House
245 N. Kenilworth Ave.
1891, PATTON & FISHER

A grand parade of Kenilworth Ave. Queen Annes begins with this behemoth. The massive bays are tightly wrapped in thin clapboards. The octagonal corner turret appears to bulge from the effort of containing the great spaces within.

69| Walter H. Gale House (2)
312 N. Kenilworth Ave.
1905, HENRY G. FIDDELKE

This symmetrical Colonial Revival work has a detailed cornice and front door with sidelights.

70| David J. Kennedy House
309 N. Kenilworth Ave.
1888, PATTON & FISHER

Kennedy was a real estate investor and part owner of the Cicero & Proviso St. Railway. His barnlike Queen Anne features a layered gable front with flared edges.

71| William A. Douglas House
317 N. Kenilworth Ave.
1893, PATTON & FISHER
1908, ADDITION, PATTON & MILLER

Capacious, rambling, and generously scaled, the Douglas House has one of Oak Park's best porches. As in the John Rankin House, shingled, rolled edges frame the third-floor dormer.

72| Harrison P. Young House
(*W. E. Coman House*)
334 N. Kenilworth Ave.
1870s, ARCHITECT UNKNOWN
1895, REMODELING, FRANK LLOYD WRIGHT

The porch and the leaded diamond-paned windows are the most visible part of Wright's work.

73| John Schmidt House
400 N. Kenilworth Ave.
EARLY 1870s, ARCHITECT UNKNOWN

AMERICUS B. MELVILLE HOUSE

This early Oak Park cottage has Italianate detailing. The wood molding around the exaggeratedly vertical windows imitates masonry.

74| Joseph K. Dunlop House
407 N. Kenilworth Ave.
1897, EBEN E. ROBERTS

75| Simpson Dunlop House
417 N. Kenilworth Ave.
1896, EBEN E. ROBERTS

The Dunlop brothers were real estate developers and capitalists who established a bank in Oak Park in 1886. These magnificent houses are often labeled Rectilinear Queen Anne, because although quite geometric on the outside, the plans still open out from the Queen Anne "great hall."

76| Charles E. Matthews House
432 N. Kenilworth Ave.
1909, TALLMADGE & WATSON

The facade is sedate and formal, focusing on the entry, with its art-glass windows that illuminate the stair hall.

77| Americus B. Melville House
437 N. Kenilworth Ave.
1904, EBEN E. ROBERTS

Roberts abandoned the box for this free-flowing stucco house, which is complex in elevation and sophisticated in plan. His characteristic brackets don't really support anything but have grown to gigantic proportions, dripping down the walls and porch piers.

78| Anna L. Wright House
(*John Blair House*)
931 W. Chicago Ave.
BEFORE 1873, ARCHITECT UNKNOWN

Wright bought the steeply gabled Gothic Revival house and large lot from Blair, a landscaper. On the Forest Ave. side of Blair's property Wright built his own house; Wright's mother continued to live in "Grandmother's Cottage."

79| Frank Lloyd Wright Home and Studio
951 W. Chicago Ave.
1889–1911, FRANK LLOYD WRIGHT
1976–1986, RESTORATION, RESTORATION COMMITTEE OF THE FRANK LLOYD WRIGHT HOME AND STUDIO FOUNDATION

Wright's love was designing houses, and in seventy-two years of architectural life created over 270 of them. This was his earliest—and also the first that he called home. Containing the seeds of all the rest, it was built on a corner lot acquired in 1889. The shingle-clad houses that Wright saw in architectural magazines gave aspect to the Forest Ave. facade; but the forms are sharply cut, crystal-clear products of the childhood training in geometric shapes that infused his entire career.

FRANK LLOYD WRIGHT HOME AND STUDIO

FRANK LLOYD WRIGHT HOME AND STUDIO—INTERIOR

In keeping with the Shingle Style tradition, Wright's house is divided into three horizontal bands of base, walls, and roof. The base of Chicago common brick not only provides a protective wainscot but also roots the house in the suburban prairie. With what would be characteristic care for the setting, Wright retained most of the lot's tangle of native and exotic plants as a nest for his cottage. The wood-shingled middle zone almost disappears in the undulations of its wings and octagonal bays and in the transparency of its wide casement windows—a hint at the dissolution of the wall that characterized the Prairie School. The great gabled roof dominates the composition with proclamations of "shelter" and "home," as it always would for Wright. A dining room addition to the south and a kitchen/playroom addition to the rear completed the home about 1895.

Wright's studio addition (1898), facing Chicago Ave., shows a bold massing that came out of his love for pure geometric grammar. The exterior is a direct expression of the octagonal spaces within—a cubic two-story drafting room to the east of the entry and a library to the west. Commercial in scale, as befits an architectural office, the studio is nonetheless visually coupled to the house by its use of the same materials. Decorative elements by Wright and sculptor Richard W. Bock highlight the studio's elevations.

The organic, flowing, harmonious, and reposeful qualities that pervaded Wright's interiors can be found throughout, especially in the dining room, playroom, drafting room, and library. The heating and lighting as well as the furnishings are everywhere integrated into the architectural environment.

After leaving Oak Park, Wright remodeled the studio as living quarters for his family, and the home was rented out; the complex was later remodeled into six apartments. The property was acquired by the National Trust for Historic Preservation in 1974. A National Historic Landmark, restored by the Frank Lloyd Wright Home and Studio Foundation to its 1905–1909 appearance, it offers an intriguing look at the early home life and workplace of a master architect.

—DONALD G. KALEC

---

80 | Robert P. Parker House
1019 W. Chicago Ave.

81 | Thomas H. Gale House
1027 W. Chicago Ave.
1892, FRANK LLOYD WRIGHT

These "bootlegged" houses were designed by the moonlighting Wright while he was still employed by Adler & Sullivan; local Realtor Thomas Gale probably knew Wright through the Unitarian community. Both houses are a slight variation on a popular Queen Anne style, with a two-story corner bay topped by a turret. Wright's version is more geometric; the octagonal bay is a prominent element on both front and back, and the windows are massed in a band.

82 | Walter H. Gale House (1)
1031 W. Chicago Ave.
1893–1894, FRANK LLOYD WRIGHT

Construction of a cottage by architect L. D. Beman began in the spring of 1893 but apparently had not gotten far when Gale bought the lot later that year. This Queen Anne with its sweeping roof offers a rare example of Wright's skillful handling of spindles, an ele-

WALTER H. GALE HOUSE (1)

ment frequently used to define interior spaces. Unusually tall and thin, they are so closely spaced that they appear as a solid wall as you approach. Not until you are directly in front does the view of the wall behind suddenly emerge.

83 | Andrew J. Redmond House
422 N. Forest Ave.
1900, EBEN E. ROBERTS

A giant step past the Victorianism of the Dunlop Houses, this is the first of a fifteen-year series of low, broad, beautifully detailed boxes. Maher's influence emerges in the urns, the emphasized third-floor dormer, the broad porch, and the formal symmetry.

84| William H. Copeland House
(*William Harman House*)
400 N. Forest Ave.

EARLY 1870S, ARCHITECT UNKNOWN

1908, GARAGE, FRANK LLOYD WRIGHT

1909, REMODELING, FRANK LLOYD WRIGHT

Known in Wright literature for later owner Copeland, this was originally an Italianate home in a yellowish "Milwaukee brick." An earlier renovation had already raised the roof when Wright remodeled the entry and interior, adding wood-mullioned windows and sidelights.

85| Sampson Rogers House
401 N. Forest Ave.

1890, FRANK ELLIS

This immense Queen Anne is made even larger by layers of porches, at least some of which were additions.

86| Eben E. Roberts House and Studio
1019 W. Superior St.

1911, REMODELING, EBEN E. ROBERTS

It has a cozy, hand-built look; most of the interest is in the interior, which is filled with detailed woodwork, art glass, and a built-in grandfather clock

87| Francis J. Woolley House
1030 W. Superior St.

1893–1894, FRANK LLOYD WRIGHT

A curiosity in Wright's development, it bears a greater resemblance to Oak Park builders' houses of 1910 than to his later work.

88| Nathan G. Moore House
333 N. Forest Ave.

1895, FRANK LLOYD WRIGHT

1923, REMODELING, FRANK LLOYD WRIGHT

This generously scaled and lovingly detailed house is the product of two stages of Wright's career. Moore came to him in 1894 for a remodeling of his frame house on this site, then decided it would be too small and directed Wright to give him something "Elizabethan." The bold and impressive Tudor Revival house was imitated by local architects for the next twenty years. Wright wrote in his autobiography, "Anyone could get a rise out of me by admiring that essay in English half-timber. 'They' all liked it and I could have gone on unnaturally building them for the rest of my natural life."

In December 1922 the house burned down to the top of the first floor. Wright, who happened to be in Chicago, contacted Moore and received the commission to rebuild. This opulent hybrid, with touches of Gothic, Sullivanesque, and Mayan design, was the result. Charles E. White, Jr., was

NATHAN G. MOORE HOUSE

ARTHUR HEURTLEY HOUSE

Wright's local coordinator for the project and is credited with the very traditional interior.

89 | Arthur Heurtley House
318 N. Forest Ave.
1902, FRANK LLOYD WRIGHT

Rich, challenging, and satisfying, open yet mysterious, firmly rooted to the ground yet removed from prying eyes, this is one of Wright's most magnificent homes. The raised living rooms enable occupants to look out through uncurtained art-glass windows without fear of being seen. An overscaled brick half-wall shields the roundheaded portal, rendering the front door invisible. The great hipped roof, utterly simplified, hovers over bands of richly leaded casement windows and a variegated battered brick wall laid in a complex, textured pattern.

90 | Edward R. Hills–Thomas DeCaro House
313 N. Forest Ave.
1883, CHARLES C. MILLER
1900–1906, REMODELING, FRANK LLOYD WRIGHT
1976, RECONSTRUCTION (FOR THOMAS DECARO), JOHN TILTON ASSOCS.

After several reincarnations, this gift from Nathan Moore to his daughter, Mary, is in excellent condition. The original Stick Style frame house stood just to the north with its narrow end facing Forest Ave. Wright and Moore moved it, turned it ninety degrees, and overhauled it so dramatically that they might as well have started from scratch. Although built in 1906, it had apparently been designed in 1900, which partially accounts for the roofline with

its flared eaves. The restored shingled roof is one of its most interesting features. Even here Wright emphasizes the horizontal, with every fifth row of shingles a double layer.

91 | Charles A. Purcell House
300 N. Forest Ave.
1893, ARCHITECT UNKNOWN

This sober Queen Anne was built for architect William Gray Purcell's father, who once commented to his family, "If that Wright don't quit, he'll have our street ruined."

92 | Laura Gale House
6 Elizabeth Ct.
1909, FRANK LLOYD WRIGHT

A stylistic step beyond even the boldest of Wright's Forest Ave. homes, this cantilevered composition looks forward twenty-five years to Fallingwater in Pennsylvania. Wright wrote, "In integral architecture the room-space itself must come through. The room must be seen as architecture or we have no architecture." Here the porches are not applied appendages but "room-spaces" thrust through the wall, uniting exterior and interior. The leaded windows are screens, not barriers, protecting from the weather while enhancing the view.

93 | Edgar Cook House
231 N. Forest Ave.
1870S, ARCHITECT UNKNOWN

One of the first generation of Forest Ave. houses, this simple cottage is vertically oriented, with jigsawed bargeboards under the eaves. Most of the other cottages from this era were either remodeled beyond recognition or moved after 1885 to other, less expensive sites.

94 | Peter A. Beachy House
238 N. Forest Ave.
1906, FRANK LLOYD WRIGHT

The original commission was to remodel a modest cottage, which was ultimately obliterated by this grand Prairie Style work. The thick lines of the eaves, lintels, and corner piers and the wood-mullioned windows have led to speculation that the talented hand of Wright's employee Walter Burley Griffin contributed much to the design.

95| Joseph D. Everett House
228 N. Forest Ave.
1888, WILSON, MARBLE & LAMSON

An overriding preference for the rectilinear once again harnesses the Queen Anne style.

JOSEPH D. EVERETT HOUSE

96| Henderson Judd House
219 N. Forest Ave.
1881, ARCHITECT UNKNOWN

The Italianate was in its final years of popularity when this house was built. In plan it resembles the emerging Stick Style, with an entry and stair hall pushed to the side. A very similar house was built at the same time at 223; remodeled after 1900, it is now unrecognizable as Italianate.

97| George T. Hayden House
209 N. Forest Ave.
1893, W. K. JOHNSTON

The riot of materials includes brick, stone, and shingles. The turret, porch, and shingled colonnettes display more round forms than most Queen Annes in Oak Park.

98| R. K. Bickford House
203 N. Forest Ave.
1885, ARCHITECT UNKNOWN

This Stick Style house retains a feature long lost on most houses of the era: the scrolling open brackets that enhance the second-floor porch and corners and cast moving shadows on the clapboard.

99| Frank W. Thomas House
210 N. Forest Ave.
1901, FRANK LLOYD WRIGHT
1922, REAR ADDITION, TALLMADGE & WATSON
1975, RESTORATION

Turning a blind eye to the Victorian timidity on its flanks, the Thomas House is considered Wright's first constructed Prairie School house. "First thing in building the new house, get rid of the attic, therefore the dormer," Wright wrote in *An Autobiography.* "Get rid of the useless false heights below it. Next, get rid of the unwholesome basement, yes

FRANK W. THOMAS HOUSE

absolutely—in any house built on the prairie. Instead of lean, brick chimneys bristling up everywhere to hint at Judgment, I could see necessity for one chimney only." This house meets the ground with a simple water table above which the walls rise unbroken to the line of dazzling art glass. The entry sequence is complex and unpredictable. The roundheaded portal appears to shield a door but actually conceals a stair leading up and back to the real front door.

100| Emerson Ingalls Row Houses
200–208 N. Forest Ave.
1892, WILLIAM J. VAN KEUREN

Looking like an overgrown Queen Anne house, this symmetrical composition is interesting mainly for its sharp contrast with the Prairie Style, which emerged on the lot next door in 1901.

LOWER
WEST SIDE

LOWER WEST SIDE

LOWER WEST SIDE

THE LOWER WEST SIDE GREW UP WITH CHICAGO'S INDUSTRY, THRIVING IN THE 1870s when the city was becoming an industrial powerhouse, and declining a century later as the manufacturing base withered away. The flats, cottages, and commercial buildings that met the needs of generations of factory workers suffer from decay and neglect, but lively areas persist in the immigrant neighborhoods, which continue to attract the newly arrived.

The Lower West Side comprises Pilsen, Heart of Chicago, Little Village, and Lawndale. Pilsen, the oldest community, is bounded on the south by the Illinois & Michigan Canal (1848) and was developed with lumberyards and breweries; on the north it ends at railroad tracks laid in the 1860s. Its major development occurred after the Great Fire of 1871, when burned-out industries and workers moved west. Immigrants from Bohemia were the earliest settlers, and they named the community for their homeland's second-largest city. Polish and Yugoslavian immigrants arrived in the early twentieth century and were replaced beginning in the 1950s by Mexicans and Puerto Ricans. Pilsen's early role as a "port of entry" called for flats, apartments, and combination retail-residential buildings, built mostly by investors for rental. Its continued status as a "first-stop" immigrant neighborhood has restricted development. The area has a concentration of buildings from the 1870s and 1880s, many of which feature the mansard roof characteristic of those decades. In 1875 the city's ongoing sewer project reached the Pilsen area. This process of raising streets and sidewalks above new sewer and drainage systems left many buildings with their first floors eight to ten feet below street level.

Heart of Chicago, which is west of Ashland Ave., also boomed after the 1871 Fire, when industries began to cluster along the river. Ger-

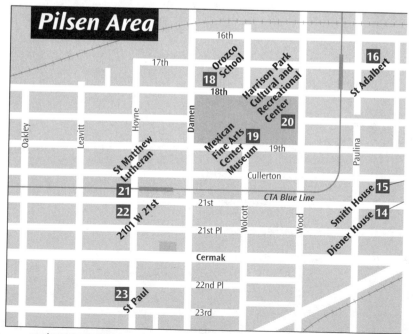

mans, Poles, and northern Italians were the major ethnic groups. The leading industry was the McCormick Reaper (later International Harvester) works at Western and Blue Island Aves.; like other large employers, it is long gone. The southern stretches of both Pilsen and Heart of Chicago contain many barren former industrial sites, but the residential portions remain vital.

Little Village, or Pueblo Pequeño, was originally known as South Lawndale and was renamed in the mid-1970s by its Mexican-American majority. Both Lawndales were primarily open swamplands west of the city limits at Western Ave. in 1863, when the Chicago, Burlington & Quincy Railroad was laid out on a southwesterly course that became the boundary between the two areas. Annexed by Chicago in 1869, South Lawndale witnessed residential development around 1885, with the general westward expansion of the built-up city, but it was contained on the south and west by the accelerating development of industry. Immigrants from Bohemian Pilsen were among the first occupants of the area's small brick houses, followed in the 1930s by Poles and, since 1960, by increasing numbers of Hispanics. By 1980 the community had the city's largest concentration of Mexicans.

Lawndale (originally North Lawndale) is crossed diagonally by Ogden Ave., built in the 1850s as a plank road along the portage trail linking Lake Michigan to the Des Plaines River. Residential development progressed westward along Roosevelt Rd., the commercial street at Lawndale's northern edge, after 1895, when the Garfield Park elevated train inaugurated service to Cicero Ave. The bulk of the residential construction—primarily rental apartments and two-flats—took place between 1910 and 1925. The earliest occupants were Russian Jews moving from the Near West Side; in the 1920s the area had seventy synagogues. After World War II African-Americans began following the same westward route and constituted 90 percent of the population by 1960. The West

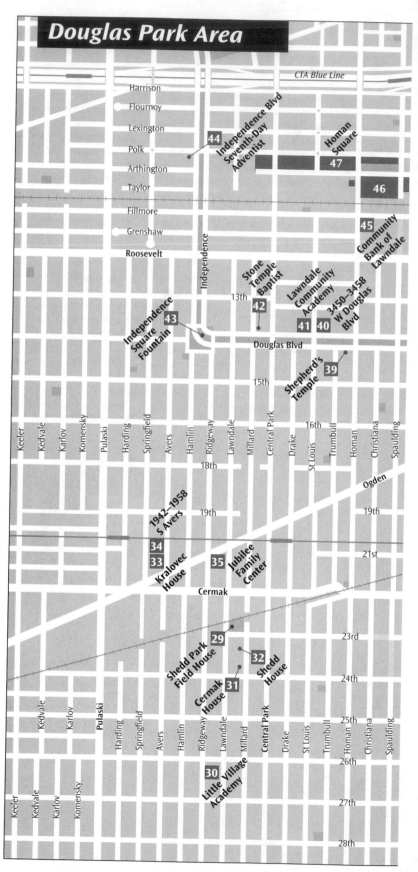

Douglas Park Area

CTA Blue Line

Harrison
Flournoy
Lexington
Polk
Arthington
Taylor
Fillmore
Grenshaw
Roosevelt

Independence Blvd
Seventh-Day
Adventist

44

Homan
Square

47

46

45

Community
Bank of
Lawndale

Stone
Temple
Baptist

Independence

13th

42

Lawndale
Community
Academy

3450–3458
W Douglas
Blvd

Independence
Square
Fountain

43

41 **40**

Douglas Blvd

15th

Shepherd's
Temple

39

Keeler
Kedvale
Karlov
Komensky
Pulaski
Harding
Springfield
Avers
Hamlin
Ridgeway
Lawndale
Millard
Central Park
Drake
St Louis
Trumbull
Homan
Christiana
Spaulding

16th

18th

Ogden

1942–1958
S Avers

19th

19th

34
33

Kralovec
House

35

Jubilee
Family
Center

21st

Cermak

23rd

29

Shedd Park
Field House

32

Shedd
House

24th

Cermak
House

31

Kedvale
Karlov
Pulaski
Harding
Springfield
Avers
Hamlin
Ridgeway
Lawndale
Millard
Central Park
Drake
St Louis
Trumbull
Homan
Christiana
Spaulding

25th

26th

30

Little Village
Academy

27th

Keeler
Kedvale
Karlov
Komensky

28th

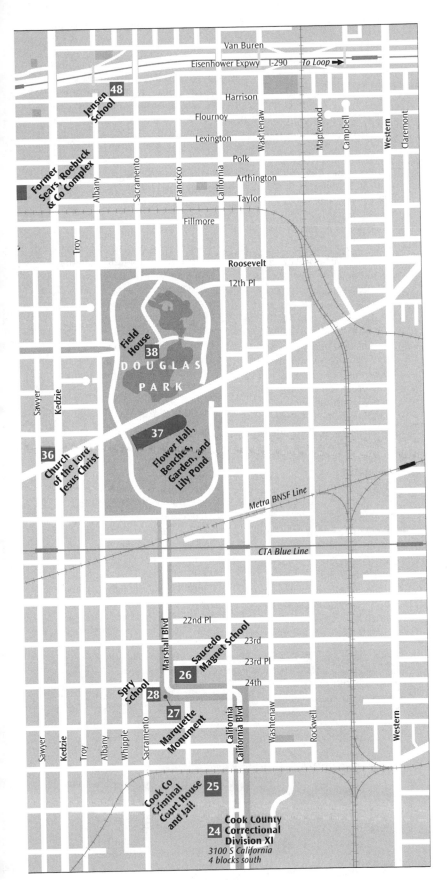

Side riots following the 1968 assassination of Dr. Martin Luther King, Jr., closed some businesses, and the refusal of insurance companies to extend their policies closed many more. Industrial properties have been vacated as the city shifted from a manufacturing to a service orientation. Lawndale's landscape is now characterized by aging housing stock, with blocks of neat graystones interspersed with vacant lots and crumbling buildings. Infill housing projects have begun to appear but have not kept pace with the rate of decay.   —VINCENT MICHAEL

1| St. Procopius Church
18th St. at Allport St.
1883, JULIUS H. HUBER

The design of this "mother church" of Chicago's Bohemian parishes was inspired by the Romanesque Revival of early to mid-nineteenth-century Germany and eastern Europe, translated into inexpensive local materials. As in nearby flats and commercial buildings, walls of common brick are trimmed with Joliet limestone, sparely embellished with incised ornament. The leaded-glass windows are filled with plant forms and fleurs-de-lis, with religious imagery limited to small medallions.

2| Thalia Hall
1807 S. Allport St.
1893, FABER & PAGELS

This husky Romanesque mixed-use building served Pilsen's Bohemian community as a social and political center and hosted musical and theatrical productions. Apartments and stores helped support the Hall, named for the Greek muse of comedy. Above the entry hovers a "green man," with hair, beard, and mustache of acanthus. A popular pagan figure co-opted by Christians, he can be traced to the head-hunting and -worshiping Celts. He enjoyed a revival on turn-of-the-century buildings, particularly those faced with limestone, along with other elements borrowed from the Romanesque.

3| Iglesia Presbiteriana Emmanuel
(*Emmanuel Presbyterian Church*)
1850 S. Racine Ave.
1965, LOEBL, SCHLOSSMAN, BENNETT & DART

Although small, modestly towered, and set back from the street, this church has a powerful, intriguing presence. The thin, angular, brick wall planes appear idiosyncratic until you step inside to see how their careful placement catches the light. Inspired rather than hamstrung by the small budget, designer Edward D. Dart made morning light the most powerful architectural element, casting it across the angled chancel wall to create a sense of shelter

THALIA HALL

and spirituality. Pews fan out around the altar, and the angled ceiling focuses attention on the chancel.

4 | Dvorak Park
**Cullerton to 21st Sts.;
Carpenter to May Sts.**
1908, WILLIAM CARBYS ZIMMERMAN
AND RICHARD E. SCHMIDT, GARDEN
& MARTIN

Surviving features of this Progressive Reform movement park—used by 2,500 people a day during its first decade—include Zimmerman's original field house and fence posts; Schmidt, Garden & Martin's iron lamp standards; and 1920s fencing. Zimmerman's pool building has been heavily altered.

5 | Benito Juárez High School
2150 S. Laflin St.
1977, BERNHEIM, KAHN & LOZANO

Built for Pilsen's growing Mexican-American community, this school was designed in consultation with Pedro Ramírez Vázquez, a Mexican architect. The geometry of the elevations was meant to evoke pre-Columbian temples but unfortunately has none of their drama or rich narrative details.

6 | St. Pius V Roman Catholic Church
1901 S. Ashland Ave.
1885–1892, JAMES J. EGAN

Egan brought a light touch to the Romanesque Revival style, preferring smooth masonry to the rough ashlar favored by other Chicago church architects such as Burling & Whitehouse and Edbrooke & Burnham. The finely detailed arched entrances and windows are echoed on the interior, which, although modernized, retains a powerful trio of roundheaded arches in the sanctuary, embellished with Norman carving and stencils. On the facade, the flowing geometric designs of the impost blocks and the band connecting the upper windows are in the vein of Frank Furness and Louis H. Sullivan.

7 | U.S. Post Office— Pilsen Station
1859 S. Ashland Ave.
1935, JOHN C. BOLLENBACHER

The Pony Express goes Moderne in the reliefs above the windows of this blocky post office, one of the finest of its era.

Both sides of 18th St. from Ashland Ave. west to Damen Ave. are lined with well-worn but still heavily used retail, recreational, and residential buildings. Although many of them are remuddled and hung with modern signs, they are still vividly eclectic.

8 | John Novak Store and Flats
1501 W. 18th St.
1887, ARCHITECT UNKNOWN

This deep tenement (with a fourth floor squeezed under the mansard roof) above a storefront grabs for glory with an effusively ornamented pressed-metal corner tower.

9 | Francis D. Nemecek Studio
1439 W. 18th St.
1907, FRANK RANDAK

This tiny Baroque storefront for a photographer had a well-lit studio space above a metal and leaded-glass storefront, which has been well preserved.

10 | Chicago Public Library— Rudy Lozano Branch
1805 S. Loomis St.
1990, JAY CAROW ARCHITECTS

Bands of red and blue terra-cotta ornament pierce the curved glass facade to run through the library's interior. The motif of the decorative tile is derived from pre-Columbian structures at Mitla, in Oaxaca.

LOZANO LIBRARY

11| Store and Flats
1870 S. Blue Island Ave.
1899, FROMMANN & JEBSEN

For Schlitz agent Edward G. Uihlein, the architects bent their Germanic Queen Anne taproom formula around this oblique corner to visually command the intersection.

12| Jan Kralovec Stores and Flats
1923–1929 S. Blue Island Ave.
1886, ARCHITECT UNKNOWN

Note the cast-iron columns with foliate capitals and the ornate spandrels between the second and third floors. The cornice, which is of pressed metal with paired brackets on Blue Island Ave., changes to a simpler brick corbel table around the corner on Cullerton St.

13| George Van Dolen Stores and Flats
2008–2010 S. Blue Island Ave.
1879, ARCHITECT UNKNOWN

Half of the storefront of this Italianate building is relatively unaltered, with cast-iron pillars carrying elaborate capitals and stone window hoods bearing prominent keystones.

14| Gustave Diener House
1529 W. Cullerton St.
1886, ARCHITECT UNKNOWN

15| Frank Smith House
1530 W. Cullerton St.
1887, ARCHITECT UNKNOWN

This street of late Italianate two- and three-flats is notable for the "boomtown" fronts (straight cornices disguising gable fronts) with straight or arched pediments projecting from the center. Here the cornice line leaps over an attic window, forming a semicircle, a characteristic of Pilsen two-flats.

16| St. Adalbert Roman Catholic Church
1656 W. 17th St.
1914, HENRY J. SCHLACKS

On a street so narrow that the 185-foot towers reach almost out of sight stands Schlacks's basilica-plan masterpiece. Grand and formal, intended to inspire awe rather than familiarity, the facade and worship space are Renaissance Revival, typical of Chicago's Polish churches. The imposing colonnaded porch combines granite columns and door surrounds with terra-cotta capitals and pediment. Inside, the long nave is filled with golden light from tall clerestory windows. The sanctuary wall, painted with scenes from Polish history, frames a fabulous Baroque baldachin over the marble altar. Polish saints including Casimir and Stanislaus Kostka are commemorated in the rich stained-glass windows, made by F. X. Zettler.

17| Pilsen Academy School
1420 W. 17th St.
1898, NORMAND S. PATTON

The arches and stone carvings give an unusual interest to this small school, which was designed during Patton's employment as Board of Education architect.

18| José Clemente Orozco Community Academy
1940 W. 18th St.
2000, ALPHONSE GUAJARDO ASSOCS.; URBAN WORKS, ASSOC. ARCHS.

Art teacher Francisco Mendoza worked with students to do drawings of Mexican and Mexican-American icons and scenes. The drawings were then digitized and turned into mural panels with mosaics. The resulting band of images, which distinguishes this school, is a stunning display of talent and history.

19| Mexican Fine Arts Center Museum
(*Harrison Park Natatorium*)
1852 W. 19th St.
1914, WILLIAM CARBYS ZIMMERMAN
1978, RENOVATION, ADRIAN LOZANO

Brick, concrete, and glass block transformed an aging natatorium into a museum.

20| Harrison Park Cultural and Recreational Center
S. Wood St. at W. 18th Pl.
1992, CHICAGO PARK DISTRICT

The facade is bent like an exedra to welcome visitors, while respecting the park's original grid plan and maximizing the green space.

21| St. Matthew Lutheran Church
(*Evangelische Lutherische St. Matthäus Kirche*)
2100 W. 21st St.
1888, FREDERICK AHLSCHLAGER

The *Chicago Inter-Ocean* noted in 1888 that Ahlschlager "is getting the retainer for about everything Lutheran." His church is a rare surviving example of the off-the-shelf late nineteenth-century Gothic Revival that so many congregations replaced with larger, more academically correct buildings. Common brick and Lemont limestone are joined by pressed metal that pinch-hits for stone in places like the arcaded corbel table. The three entrances are topped by the original tympana of colored leaded glass, and the main door is surrounded by eight cast-iron columns.

22| 2101 W. 21st St.
(*Evangelische Lutherische Schule*)
1882, ARCHITECT UNKNOWN

A very early private school is rendered in the Italianate style of the neighborhood's flats and storefronts. Look up at the roof to see a pressed-metal cupola with delicate cresting.

23| St. Paul Roman Catholic Church
(*St. Paulus Kirche*)
2234 S. Hoyne Ave.
1897–1899, HENRY J. SCHLACKS

ST. PAUL ROMAN CATHOLIC CHURCH

The parish dreamed beyond reason, the architect designed beyond budget—and St. Paul's became Chicago's greatest Gothic leap of faith. In a working-class neighborhood of modest homes and flats, the 245-foot towers soared higher than the Loop's Reliance and Monadnock buildings. Thrillingly out of scale in both size and expense, the construction left the parish deeply in debt and led Archbishop James Quigley to replace the pastor. The church was completed in just two years by an architect acting as contractor and by parishioners donating their skilled labor. Its strength lies in the boldness of scale, the integration of interior and exterior, and the selective embellishment that achieves maximum drama. Most of the building (and the surrounding parish complex) is modest common brick; the east facade and interior are a light brown face brick. Molded brick is used where Schlacks would have used stone on a more expensive design, such as the colonnettes and rib vaulting; only where absolutely necessary did he resort to terra cotta.

St. Paul's held Schlacks's interest for several decades. He designed the main altar (1910), communion railing (1912), and side altars and pulpit (1916) in a complementary Gothic style in white marble. The luminous Venetian mosaics that decorate the interior and facade were the final major element. Installed in 1930, they combine natural forms with symbolic and pictorial content. Completing the lush but harmonious decoration are stained-glass windows. The transept windows, which depict six scenes in the life of Christ, are particularly fine, with unusually well detailed architectural backdrops and plant forms. Across the street to the north is St. Paul Parochial School (1892), also designed by Schlacks and connected by a second-story bridge to Casa Claret, once St. Paul's convent.

24 | Cook County Maximum Security Facility Division XI
3105 S. California Blvd.
1995, ROULA ASSOCS. ARCHITECTS; KNIGHT ARCHITECTS ENGINEERS PLANNERS, ENGINEERING AND PROGRAM MANAGEMENT; PHILLIPS SWAGER ASSOCS., SECURITY CONSULTANTS

With a capacity of 1,600 inmates, this jail is one of the nation's largest. The X-shaped configuration provides a master control center for four self-sustaining "pods," each of which has a control area and outdoor yard for 200 two-person cells.

25 | Cook County Criminal Court House and Jail
2600 S. California Blvd.
1927, HALL, LAWRENCE & RATCLIFFE

Although far from the Loop's Cook County headquarters, this site was chosen because it adjoined the Bridewell House of Correction and offered room for expansion. This severe monument to criminal justice is realized in a brand of flat Classicism most notable for its rich sculptural program, which is largely the work of Peter Toneman of Joseph Dux Studios in conjunction with the Indiana Limestone Co. Above each of the giant Doric columns rises an allegorical figure: Law, Justice, Liberty, Truth, Might, Love, Wisdom, and Peace. S.P.Q.C., inscribed under the adjacent eagle panels, is Chicago's variant of the classical S.P.Q.R. (the Senate and People of Rome). The bisons above the doors grow their pelts in a Greek meander pattern.

26 | Maria Saucedo Magnet School (*Carter H. Harrison Technical High School*)
2850 W. 24th Blvd.
1912, ARTHUR F. HUSSANDER

Ponderous classicist Hussander succeeded Prairie School designer Dwight H. Perkins as architect for the Chicago Board of Education in 1910. The roofline of this heavily ornamented structure bristles with acroteria, the shell-shaped protrusions generally found only at the apex and corners of a pediment.

COOK COUNTY CRIMINAL COURT HOUSE AND JAIL

27| Jacques Marquette Monument
S. Marshall Blvd. at W. 24th Blvd.
1925, BASE, HOLABIRD & ROCHE
1926, HERMON A. MACNEIL, SCULPTOR

Explorers Marquette and Louis Joliet are accompanied by an Algonquin Indian. Chicago's first known European inhabitant, Father Marquette spent the winter of 1674–1675 near what is now the intersection of Damen Ave. and 26th St. Bronze tablets at the bridge's northeast corner commemorate his stay.

28| John Spry Public School
2400 S. Marshall Blvd.
1899, NORMAND S. PATTON
1919, ADDITION, ARTHUR F. HUSSANDER

Patton's gently Romanesque central section was the Board of Education's first fireproof school.

Subdivided in 1870 by Alden C. Millard & Edwin J. Decker, Millard Ave. south of the Chicago, Burlington & Quincy Railroad tracks was fashionable in the late nineteenth century. It retains a whisper of elegance in a sampling of Gothic Revival, Italianate, and Queen Anne houses, most of which have been greatly remod-

eled. The railroad had a station at what is now Shedd Park.

29| Shedd Park Field House
(*Recreation Building*)
3660 W. 23rd St.
1917, WILLIAM DRUMMOND
1928, GYMNASIUM ADDITION,
MICHAELSEN & RUGNSTAD

By 1885 John G. Shedd had re-subdivided part of Millard & Decker's subdivision and set aside just over an acre for a private park. After unsuccessful efforts to assess local homeowners for improvements, the land was transferred to the city in 1888 and to the Chicago Board of Park Commissioners ten years later. Although nothing remains of Jens Jensen's landscape (1917), the field house is one of the best examples of Prairie School architecture in the Chicago Park District. Above the south entrance, a large but delicately detailed wood pediment contains a fine tympanum with thin glass windows between vertical wooden slats. The sensitively realized gymnasium is recessed forty feet behind the main entrance and repeats the horizontal massing and stringcoursing of Drummond's original.

SHEDD PARK FIELD HOUSE

LITTLE VILLAGE ACADEMY

30| Little Village Academy
2620 S. Lawndale Ave.

1996, ROSS BARNEY + JANKOWSKI

A tight site dictated an efficient, compact building, but this public school building is no blank box. Sculptural elements seem to burst out of the facades, symbolizing an energy generated from within. These include the white trapezoidal library, horizontal sunscreens outside the computer room, and the angled fiberglass walls of the science room. The most dramatic punctuation is the entry and skylit stair tower, the functional and symbolic heart of the school. Its flat interior wall features a precisely oriented sundial. The sun motif, symbolic of the community's Mexican heritage, is carried through in the lobby flooring and extends outdoors to the plaza. Color and playful elements carried out in economical materials create a sense of fun throughout the building.

31| Anton J. Cermak House
2348 S. Millard Ave.

1920, RANDAK & REZNY

This stolid essay in Bohemian Bourgeois was built by a solid citizen, a state senator, chairman of the Cook County Board, and Chicago's mayor from 1931 until an assassin's bullet intended for President-elect Franklin D. Roosevelt felled him in 1933.

32| John G. Shedd House
2316 S. Millard Ave.

1888, ARCHITECT UNKNOWN
1886, STABLE, CHARLES A. WEARY

Shedd rose from stockboy to partner to president of Marshall Field & Co. His robust Queen Anne house is remarkably intact, retaining its original porch with simple turned columns.

Just a few blocks northwest of Shedd Park, somewhat isolated by Ogden Ave. and one-way streets, is a cluster of unusually fine rusticated limestone homes.

33| Jan Kralovec House
2102 S. Avers Ave.

1892, FREDERICK B. TOWNSEND

34| 1942 through 1958
S. Avers Ave.

1893–1894, ATTRIBUTED TO FREDERICK B. TOWNSEND

In anticipation of a new streetcar line on Cermak Rd., the Czech-born Kralovec began developing homes nearby. His own house is an imposing example of the Richardsonian Romanesque style and has a matching coach house. The four adjacent houses he built are also of rusticated limestone, although only two of them continue the Romanesque style; those at 1942 and 1950 are Classically inspired.

1952 S. AVERS AVE.

35| Jubilee Family Center
3701 W. Ogden Ave.
2002, ROSS BARNEY + JANKOWSKI

Creative use of durable, cost-effective materials makes this child-care center a source of neighborhood pride. Masonry on the north and south facades is patterned to resemble Kente cloth, an African fabric originally worn only by royalty. At the entrances to the building and to classrooms, colored floor tiles form "floor mats" that look like Zairian raffia cloths. A central courtyard provides protected play space and abundant daylight.

36| Church of the Lord Jesus Christ
of the Apostolic Faith
(*Douglas Park Auditorium***)**
3202 W. Ogden Ave.
1910, RUSY & REZNY

Stores, offices, clubrooms, and a dance hall filled this massive, *retardataire* Second Empire structure lavished with terra cotta.

Douglas Park
California Ave., Roosevelt Rd.,
Albany Ave., W. 19th St.
1071, WILLIAM LE BARON JENNEY
1885, OSCAR F. DUBUIS
1906, JENS JENSEN

Also originally laid out by Jenney, Douglas Park is best seen by car from its inner drive and along Ogden Ave. Created along with Humboldt and Garfield parks by the West Park Commission in 1869, Douglas Park was developed and redesigned over the next forty years. The most glaring of many subsequent alterations was the intrusive siting of George W. Collins High School (1968, Andrew Heard & Assocs.), just north of the Douglas Blvd. entrance. Jenney was starting from scratch; the park had to be raised to grade level by filling it in with manure and sand. The *Land Owner* reported on progress in 1874: "To enhance the beauties of the place, there have been 40,000 yards of Stock Yards' manure deposited there in an imposing mass, not to speak of the thousands of yards of the same romantic material scattered broadcast over the other parks . . . The manure is magnificent soil medicine and its effects can be plainly traced in the improved vegetation and general fertility of a region that two years ago was not much removed from 'a howling wilderness.'"

The most important surviving element of Jenney's design is the northernmost portion of the Lagoon, framed by the Iron Bridge (1893, Adolph Gottlieb) to the south and by the Stone Bridge (1897, designer unknown) to the north. Later neighborhood residents put this lagoon to good use; the Federal Writers Project's *Illinois Guide* (1939) noted that annually "in early autumn, orthodox Jews gather at the lagoon for a ritualistic casting away of their sins."

Jensen's work is visible in the southern half of the park. At the Marshall Blvd. entrance at 19th St. are the wooden pergola and reflecting pools. The other surviving features of his design are the bermed Prairie Meadow, with its hawthorn trees, and the formal flower garden ensemble that parallels Ogden Ave. The Stable & Shop Building (1892, Jenney & Mundie; alterations

DOUGLAS PARK FLOWER HALL

1897 and 1907) is a rare surviving structure by Jenney in the West Parks, although changes have rendered his hand all but invisible.

37| Flower Hall, Benches, Garden, and Lily Pond
CA. 1907

The reinforced-concrete Flower Hall (covered walkway) is Classical in form but Prairie Style in its integrated execution, with copper coping, extended cornice lines, and linear benches reinforcing the horizontality. The rectangular lily pond was designed to reflect the Hall and enhance the structure by serving as an entrance to Jensen's long, linear formal garden.

Benches and lantern standards mark the east end of the garden, which is now planted with species similar to but less invasive than Jensen's original choices. The Flower Hall, gardens, and major elements such as lights were restored in 2001.

38| Douglas Park Cultural and Community Center
(*Field House*)
1928, MICHAELSEN & ROGNSTAD

The southern half of the lagoon was made into a beach area with the construction of the field house, a virtual twin to the Humboldt Park field house in both Georgian style and siting.

Douglas Blvd. is lined with former synagogues and other remnants of the area's past as a Jewish community. Jews began moving here just before World War I, and between the wars Lawndale and Garfield Park were known as "Chicago's Jerusalem." Most of Chicago's synagogues built during the 1910s and 1920s were Classically inspired, but Byzantine motifs surfaced with increasing frequency.

39| Shepherd's Temple Missionary Baptist Church
(*Anshe Kenesseth Israel*)
3411 W. Douglas Blvd.
1913, ARONER & SOMERS

The unusual organization of the facade, with a Byzantine semi-

circular pediment flanked by chunky wings, was derived from mid-to late nineteenth-century European synagogues. Above the doors are marble spandrels and the original stained-glass windows with geometric borders.

SHEPHERD'S TEMPLE MISSIONARY BAPTIST CHURCH

40 | Former Lawndale Community Academy
(*Hebrew Theological College*)
3450–3458 W. Douglas Blvd.
1923, LOEWENBERG & LOEWENBERG

In the 1920s Greek Revival styles became more popular than Renaissance designs for synagogues. The entrance features classical Greek decorative patterns, stylized in an angular, almost Art Deco fashion. Papyrus leaves below the Corinthian capitals add an Egyptian motif to the eclectic mix.

41 | Lawndale Community Academy
(*Jewish People's Institute*)
3500 W. Douglas Blvd.
1927, KLABER & GRUNSFELD

The Moorish capitals, religious symbols, glazed polychrome terra-cotta tile, abstract medallions, and ornamental brickwork evoke Judaism's Middle Eastern origins.

42 | Stone Temple Baptist Church
(*Congregation Anshe Roumania*)
3622 W. Douglas Blvd.
1926, J. W. COHN & CO.

Classical facades lent themselves to discreet ornamental clues about a building's use and purpose. Here the Star of David is included on the modified Composite capitals, and a menorah and the Torah are depicted on stone medallions below the blind arcade.

43 | Independence Square Fountain
(*American Youth and Independence Day Fountain*)
Independence Sq. at W. Douglas and Independence Blvds.
1902, CHARLES J. MULLIGAN

Bronze children joyously celebrate Independence Day with Roman candles (the fountain's original waterspouts), musical instruments, and a flag.

44 | Independence Boulevard Seventh-Day Adventist Church
(*Anshe Sholom Synagogue*)
3803 W. Polk St.
1926, NEWHOUSE & BERNHAM

The congregation's history vividly illustrates the rapid westward migration of the neighborhood's Jewish community. This synagogue replaced one built only sixteen years earlier on Polk St. at Ashland Blvd. (now St. Basil Greek Orthodox Church). Here the austere Classical style of its predecessor continues, with a stone entablature bearing a Hebrew inscription.

45 | Community Bank of Lawndale
1111 S. Homan Ave.
1982, WEESE HICKEY WEESE

Louis H. Sullivan's National Farmers' Bank (1906–1908) in Owatonna, Minn., inspired this crisp, blocky bank, one of the first new buildings in this neighborhood.

46 | Former Sears, Roebuck & Co. Complex
900–930 S. Homan Ave.
1905–1906, NIMMONS & FELLOWS

Girded by scaffolding that replaced the massive building bracing it, the tower stands sentinel over remnants of the former Sears complex and the new housing that has sprung up in its shadow.

In 1906 the world's largest mail order company moved into the world's largest commercial building. Founded in 1886, Sears sent out its first large general catalog ten years later and within another ten years was mailing catalogs and orders to 35,000 customers a day. The business was then conducted exclusively with a rural clientele; according to *Architectural Record*, "No business is solicited with people living in large cities, and, in fact, this firm refuses to fill any order from a citizen of Chicago." Two hundred carloads of freight went out each day; all goods were shipped within twenty-four hours after the order was received.

The centerpiece of this monument to efficiency and speed was the Merchandise Building, with 1.7 million square feet of optimally planned space. The

FORMER SEARS, ROEBUCK & CO. COMPLEX

second floor of the nine-story (plus tower) building was the central shipping location. Pneumatic tubes carried orders from the Administration Building to the upper floors, where workers sent goods down to the second floor on spiral conveyors controlled by gravity and centrifugal force. Orders were loaded onto freight cars waiting in a train shed that spanned the space between the building's west wings. Completing the complex are the five-story (originally two-story) Administration Building, the four-story Printing Building to the east, and the Power Plant to the south. All are of brown brick trimmed in white terra-cotta with blue accents. The only elaboration is at the pedimented entrance to the Administration Building and at the entrance and top of the tower—the original "Sears Tower," in fact, with an observation room for visitors. The large arcades and red-tiled roof were inspired by the Tuscan style that the architects thought most appropriate to the simple materials.

In 1925 Sears expanded into retail operations and opened their first store in this complex. They maintained their dominance as the nation's largest retailer and in 1974 moved to the world's tallest building, the Sears Tower. Their 1992 move to suburban Hoffman Estates brought them full circle—back to a sprawling low-rise complex in a residential area.

47| Homan Square
W. Lexington to W. Fillmore Sts.,
S. Kedzie Ave. to S.
Independence Blvd.
Phase I, S. Homan to
S. St. Louis Aves., W. Polk to
W. Lexington Sts.
1995, NAGLE HARTRAY DANKER KAGAN MCKAY

A joint venture of Sears and the Shaw Company, this residential development represents the first large-scale investment in North Lawndale since the 1960s. Targeted to low-income buyers and renters, the Phase I town houses and apartments have a clean, modern look that was not consistently maintained in subsequent residences. The community center at 3559 W. Arthington St. (1999, Booth Hansen Associates) provides neighborhood amenities.

48| Jens Jensen Public School
3030 W. Harrison St.
1961–1963, HARRY WEESE & ASSOCS.

Built of warm, natural materials and on a human scale, the hexagonal classrooms establish the unusual geometry of this villagelike school complex rendered in brick.

SOUTH SIDE

BRIDGEPORT | CANARYVILLE | MCKINLEY PARK | BACK OF THE YARDS

OAKLAND | KENWOOD

NEAR SOUTH SIDE

BEVERLY | MORGAN PARK

HYDE PARK | SOUTH SHORE

PULLMAN

NEAR SOUTH SIDE

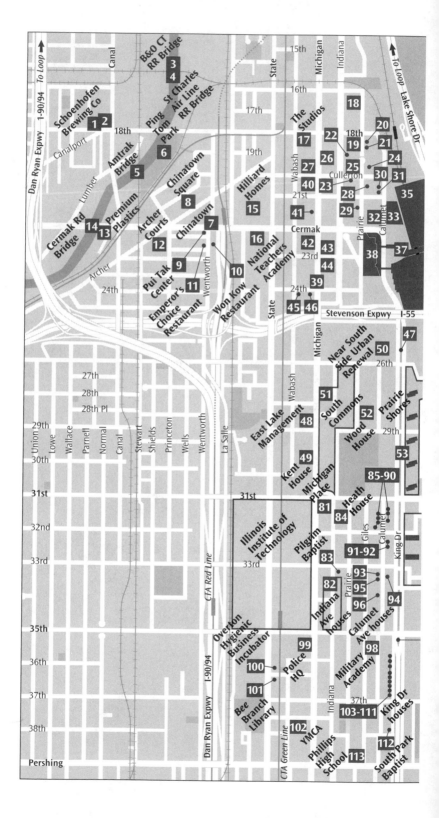

18 Metra Substation
19 Glessner House
20 Kimball House
21 Coleman House
22 Clarke House
23 213, 215 & 217 E Cullerton St
24 Field House
25 Keith House
26 Vue 20
27 Second Presbyterian Church
28 Reid House
29 Rees House
30 Wheeler House
31 320 E 21st St
32 330 E Cermak Rd
33 Lakeside Technology Center
34 Lakeside Center at
   McCormick Place
35 McCormick Place North
36 McCormick Place South
37 Hyatt Regency
38 McCormick Place Parking, Office,
   and Conference Center
39 Motor Row
40 Locomobile Lofts
41 Willie Dixon's Blues Heaven
42 2222-2228 S Michigan
43 2255 S Michigan
44 2309-2313 S Michigan
45 Quinn Chapel
46 *Chicago Daily Defender* Building

LAKE

MICHIGAN

NEAR SOUTH SIDE

AS ONE OF CHICAGO'S EARLIEST SETTLEMENTS, THE NEAR SOUTH SIDE WAS ONE of the first areas to experience the typical urban cycles of prosperity, decay, and renewal, and it now contains the city's most intensely polyglot collection of buildings and neighborhoods. Beyond the conventioneers' mecca that is McCormick Place, and the tourist magnet of Chinatown, lies a mix of rehabbed mansions, glassy lakefront high rises, decaying residential areas, and thriving institutions.

When the City of Chicago was incorporated in 1837, its southern boundary was at Cermak Rd. (22nd St), but the area south of the original riverfront settlement was still a wilderness. Small encampments were scattered along the two Indian trails now traced in part by Vincennes and Cottage Grove Aves., and Henry B. Clarke's house stood at what is now 16th St. and Michigan Ave. But the area remained undeveloped countryside for over a decade.

The arrival of the railroads in the 1850s brought the first major change to the area, with industry and working-class houses clustering near the train tracks. In 1853 the city limits were extended a mile south to 31st St.; a decade later they moved another eight blocks farther south, where they remained until the 1889 annexation of Hyde Park Township. Politician and real estate speculator Stephen A. Douglas created the area's first planned residential development. He bought sixty acres of lakefront property between 33rd and 35th Sts. in 1852 and three years later recorded his Oakenwald subdivision, with lots fronting on two private parks. Two short-lived institutions helped attract attention to the area: the first University of Chicago, whose Baptist founders accepted Douglas's donation of ten acres and had a small campus here from 1859 until going bankrupt in 1886; and Camp Douglas, which opened as an army training camp in 1861 and housed prisoners of the Civil War.

Because the north and west sides were separated from the central city by the Chicago River, the south side was the most accessible and quickly became the neighborhood of choice for wealthy homeowners. After the Fire of 1871 burned virtually everything to the north and west, businesses rebuilt in or near their original locations, but displaced residents moved south. Prairie Ave. between 16th and 22nd Sts. was soon lined with mansions, and Michigan Ave., designated a boulevard in 1880, also became a very fashionable address; meanwhile, the area west of State St. filled up with working-class housing. The abundance of transportation brought many new residents, with the Illinois Central Railroad along the lakefront, horsecars on Cottage Grove Ave. and State St., and in 1892 the city's first elevated line.

By the late 1890s the area had already peaked as a residential community and was beginning a long process of decay. The city's growth and the concentration of railroad terminals on the Loop's southern flank pushed industry and commerce (including the thriving vice business) farther south. The process accelerated after the turn of the century; by 1910 Michigan Ave. was known as Automobile Row, and the lakefront was crowded with railroad tracks, breweries, and industrial complexes.

As the city's social elite created a new Gold Coast on the North Side, upwardly mobile German Jews, Irish, and Norwegians moved farther south and west. They were replaced by Chinese and African Americans moving from the south edge of the Loop. There had been a black community centered at 22nd and State Sts. since the 1870s, and the building frenzy that preceded the 1893 World's Columbian Exposition resulted in increased housing opportunities for middle- and upper-class African Americans. The neighborhoods remained integrated until the great influx of African Americans during the two world wars. Restricted from settling in other areas, the newcomers were forced into increasingly crowded and dilapidated housing, accelerating the transformation of once-fashionable houses into slum dwellings.

In the 1940s two of the area's major institutions, Michael Reese Hospital and the Illinois Institute of Technology, joined forces to plan a program of urban renewal, eventually redeveloping seven square miles. Dilapidated housing was razed, and shiny new Modernist buildings rose like beacons from the rubble. The Chicago School of Architecture Foundation (now the Chicago Architecture Foundation) was founded in 1966 to save Richardson's John J. Glessner House, sparking a movement that led to the creation of the Prairie Avenue Historic District in the 1970s. In the 1980s restoration of historic housing began around Calumet Ave. and 32nd St., including the only extant row houses designed by Frank Lloyd Wright. From the Prairie Avenue District, with two of the city's most important house museums, to the bastion of Miesian modernism that is IIT, this area has a diversity of landmarks that suits its varied character.

—JOSEPH D. LA RUE WITH LAURIE MCGOVERN PETERSEN

1| Peter Schoenhofen Brewing Co. Administration Building
Northwest Corner W. 18th St. at S. Normal Ave.
1886, ADOLPH A. CUDELL

2| Powerhouse-Warehouse
1770 S. CANALPORT AVE.
1902, RICHARD E. SCHMIDT
1992, RENOVATION, NORMAN KOGLIN & ASSOCS.

Beermaking was a thriving industry in Chicago, with over fifty breweries in operation by 1890; the proximity of rail lines and the river made this a logical spot for industry. These surviving buildings sum up the startling leap made by Chicago architects between the mid-1880s and 1900. The fussy Administration Building has Renaissance and Baroque detailing, with an elaborate cornice, terra-cotta keystones, and medallions sporting sheaves of grain. In contrast, the Powerhouse is a spare, strong statement in brick that fully exploits the expressive potential of masonry. On the west facade the dual functions of the building are clearly visible in the organization of

SCHOENHOFEN BREWING CO.—POWERHOUSE-WAREHOUSE

the wall. The north half of this rectilinear trapezoid housed the boiler rooms; the Canalport Ave. side was the hops warehouse. Shooting through the roof is the tower, which hid the water tanks and surmounted the stairs and elevator. Although longer than it is tall, the Canalport Ave. facade appears proudly vertical with full-height brick panels on the ends and recessed windows divided by thin brick piers. The powerful Bedford limestone arch, with voussoirs up to seven feet long, is gracefully beribboned with the company name, sheltering what was surely the city's most graphically blessed loading dock.

3| Baltimore & Ohio Chicago Terminal Railroad Bridge
S. Branch Chicago River at 1500 south
1930, B&O RAILROAD AND STRAUSS BASCULE BRIDGE CO.

4| St. Charles Air Line Railroad Bridge
S. Branch Chicago River at 1500 south
1919, ILLINOIS CENTRAL RAILROAD, A. S. BALDWIN, CHIEF ENG.; 1931, RELOCATION

After 1900 the obstructive center-pier swing bridge was replaced by the trunnion bascule type, whose leaves swing up like one end of a seesaw. The "seam" in the middle of a double-leaf bridge is a potential pivot point as a heavy train begins to cross; movable railway bridges are usually single spans, which also require only one set of machinery.

On these single-leaf Strauss trunnion bascules, the trunnions are very high and balanced by concrete counterweights that slip in underneath. The St. Charles Air Line bridge was originally 260 feet, the longest of its type in the world, and weighed 3,500 tons. When it was built, the straightening of the south branch of the river was already anticipated. The bridge was designed to pivot to its new position but instead was dismantled, shortened (to 200 feet), and rebuilt in 1931. The B&O Bridge led to a large train yard on the east side of the river and to Grand Central Station at Wells and Harrison Sts., demolished in 1971.

5| Amtrak Bridge
(*Pennsylvania Lines—South Branch Chicago River Bridge*)
S. Branch Chicago River east of Canal St. at 2000 south
1915, WADDELL & HARRINGTON; FABRICATED BY THE PENNSYLVANIA STEEL CO.

With a pair of 195-foot towers, it's the kinetic cathedral of this railyard area, carrying southbound freight and passenger traffic out of the city. Engineers J. A. L. Waddell and J. L. Harrington of Kansas City were the masters of the vertical lift bridge, designing two dozen between 1907 and 1914. Because of its dominating profile, this type was never popular downtown; remaining examples are in industrial areas. The entire center span lifts straight up and is balanced by heavy counterweights, visible here on the sides of the towers. A vertical-lift configuration was chosen for this site because it was more economical than a bascule for this long span. Because the tracks cross the river at an angle, the towers are trapezoidal to hug the shoreline and make the movable span no longer or heavier than necessary. The span is a 1,500-ton riveted steel Pratt through truss, which is 272 feet long and lifts to a height of 130

AMTRAK BRIDGE

feet over the river. The original tenders' cabin on the upper chord of the lift span now houses only the electric drive motors that operate the span. Attendants in a control tower five blocks away at 14th and Lumber Sts. operate the span via television monitors.

6| Ping Tom Memorial Park
S. Branch Chicago River, east side, 18th St. to 20th St.
1999, SITE DESIGN GROUP (ALSO MCCLIER, LAND DESIGN COLLABORATIVE, E. C. PURDY & ASSOCS.)

Old railyards along the river edge have been transformed into a park that celebrates the neighborhood's Chinese heritage. Gingko trees and a bamboo grove on a terraced site evoke a Chinese landscape. A courtyard entry and columns with dragon details are other traditional Chinese elements.

7| Chinatown

In 1912 a large group of Chinese were displaced from the South Loop by new construction. The On Leong tong (benevolent association) was responsible for the establishment of this Chinatown, arranging for their members fifty leases in the 22nd St. and Wentworth Ave. area, a neighborhood of modest stores and flats. Wentworth Ave. south of 22nd St. is lined with typical nineteenth-century buildings remodeled to look more Chinese. Many of the buildings constructed after 1912 are inspired by traditional Chinese architecture, in which the wall is not load-bearing. Instead, columns ascend toward the roof to support elaborately cantilevered brackets below wide eaves that extend far beyond the building's envelope. The wall is treated as a screen, and attention is focused on the brackets, which are often highly painted. The wall of the top floor is often recessed behind the columns to create a loggia.

8| Chinatown Square
Archer Ave., Cermak Rd., Chicago River, 18th St., and Wentworth Ave.
1992–1994, HARRY WEESE & ASSOCS.

Hemmed in for years by highways and railroad tracks, Chinatown was finally unleashed when the Santa Fe Railroad abandoned its yards north of Archer Ave. The first buildings to rise on the thirty-acre site were brick retail strips, followed by a variety of housing.

9| Pui Tak Center
(On Leong Chinese Merchants' Association Building)
2216 S. Wentworth Ave.
1928, MICHAELSEN & ROGNSTAD

After relocating from downtown, the On Leong tong carried on their activities—a hostel for immigrants, a Chinese-language school, business, job-placement, and dating services—in various nearby locations. For their new building they turned to Michaelsen & Rognstad, who had done restaurant remodelings for a prominent member. Although unfamiliar with Chinese architecture, they were willing students. Rognstad was responsible for the sculptural program, executed in terracotta, a very good substitute for the *liu li* glazed ceramic of traditional Chinese architecture. Polychrome terra-cotta flowers, vases, and moths cover the walls. Lions guard the doorway, their heads twisted so they face us but do not turn their backs on each other, which would be bad luck.

PUI TAK CENTER

10| Won Kow Restaurant
2233 S. Wentworth Ave.
1928, MICHAELSEN & ROGNSTAD

Look up at the top two stories, with recessed balconies supported by brick piers. Decorative roundels display herons and parrots; again, stylized lions guard the doorway. The building's central portion is flanked by square towers that symbolize the pagoda form but are flat-topped, with enameled urns at the corners.

11| Emperor's Choice Restaurant
2238 S. Wentworth Ave.
1928, MICHAELSEN & ROGNSTAD
1932, TWO-STORY ADDITION,
MICHAELSEN & ROGNSTAD

Graceful terra-cotta herons fold sinuously around the door frame, while snakes encircle a pair of columns. More Chinese details appear at the top, which has a traditional Chinese profile.

12| Archer Courts
2220 S. Princeton Ave.
2000, RENOVATION AND
COMMUNITY CENTER, LANDON BONE
ARCHITECTS

This is the city's most dramatic renovation of a dismal public housing project into an attractive complex. The simple gesture of placing a curtain wall over the long, exposed corridors was enhanced by dividing the glass into panels, some clear and some frosted, and by painting the entry doors in bright hues that make the wall a tapestry of color, especially at night. A new community building provides a simple but light-filled gathering space for residents, all former Chicago Housing Authority tenants who now use Section 8 vouchers to pay rent to the private owner. Asian design motifs are integrated into features such as the fence and gateway. To complete the transformation of the property into a mixed-income community, the western portion of the site has town houses (2003, Landon Bone Baker Architects), of which the majority are market rate.

13| Premium Plastics
(*William M. Hoyt Co.*)
465 W. Cermak Rd.
1909, NIMMONS & FELLOWS

Chicago's premier designers of industrial buildings created this sturdy but elegant concrete-frame office and warehouse for a wholesale grocer. The long facade on Cermak Rd. and the lovely chamfered corner (shades of the Schoenhofen Powerhouse) turn a civilized, corporate face to customers and guests. It's one of the firm's liveliest facades, with pronounced vertical piers that rise to Prairie Style "capitals." The warehouse functions are more visible on the river side and the south facade (which now faces an urban no-man's-land), where two railroad tracks enter the building. Wedged between the tracks and the river, the site was perfect for the easy shipment of goods.

14| Cermak Rd. Bridge
Cermak Rd. and the Chicago River
1906, SCHERZER ROLLING LIFT
BRIDGE CO.

Designed by William Scherzer, the rolling lift bridge was the first of the two bascule types to replace the cumbersome nineteenth-century center-pier swing bridges. The bridge was patented in 1893; the Chicago-based Scherzer Co. designed bridges constructed around the world. The Scherzer bridge works like a rocking chair, utilizing overhead counterweights to balance its truss double leaves, which roll into place on large steel girder rockers at their bases. The counterweights slide into the slots between roadway and sidewalk, as the teeth on the rounded tracks engage holes in the rockers. Despite its global success, the Scherzer type was soon surpassed locally by the trunnion bascule bridge. The Cermak Rd. Bridge is the last Scherzer-type owned and operated by the city.

HILLIARD HOMES

15| Chicago Housing Authority—Raymond M. Hilliard Homes
2030 S. Slate St.
1966, BERTRAND GOLDBERG & ASSOCS.
2003, REHABILITATION, LISEC & BIEDERMAN

The revolutionary design theories that Goldberg developed for Marina City were applied here to the problem of public housing, creating what is still regarded as one of the city's best examples of humane high rise living for low-income families. In a parklike setting, a pair of twenty-two-story curving slabs accommodate families, and two sixteen story cylindrical towers are devoted to seniors. The curved walls and windows express the character of poured concrete, while providing structural stability; curved windows also distribute stress in the building's "skin." The floor plan of the round towers, with wedge-shaped apartments ringing the elevator core, minimizes the corridor distances for the elderly occupants. The complex's national landmark status and continued appeal to tenants inspired an exterior restoration paired with a gut rehab of the interiors to give it another half century of life.

16| National Teachers Academy—Professional Development School
55 W. Cermak Rd.
2002, DESTEFANO AND PARTNERS

This unusual four-story building houses a functioning elementary school (preschool through 8) that also serves as a showcase center for professional teacher training. An adjacent community center connected by a pedestrian bridge contains a natatorium, gymnasium, and day-care center.

17| The Studios at 1801 S. Wabash Ave.
1997, MCBRIDE & KELLEY

As gentrification proceeded south from the Loop in the 1990s, many single-room-occupancy residences were lost to demolition or conversion. This was the first of three new SROs constructed in the last half of that decade. It offers common areas for the provision of social services such as substance abuse counseling.

18| Metra (Metropolitan Rail) Substation
(Commonwealth Edison E. 16th St. Substation)
1620 S. Prairie Ave.
1925, HERMANN V. VON HOLST

Many substations are found near the Chicago Transit Authority's elevated tracks or Metra electrified rail lines. They were built by Commonwealth Edison between about 1900 and 1930 to supply power to the traction conglomerate of Samuel Insull, who also controlled Commonwealth Edison. They are usually of brick, with details that run the gamut of styles; many exhibit Prairie School massing and were designed by von Holst. This delightful polychromatic substation has whimsical limestone trim with reliefs of a 1920s electric locomotive and other traction devices.

19| John J. Glessner House
1800 S. Prairie Ave.
1885–1887, HENRY HOBSON RICHARDSON

Glessner House is the finest urban residence of Henry Hobson Richardson. Richardson used a corner site to create a dwelling of extraordinary distinction, one eloquently expressing his desire for a modern American architecture. The house has two powerful facades. The primary Prairie Ave. one calls upon American Colonial design; the subsidiary 18th St. one has an English prototype. Two striking arched doorways were derived from the Romanesque sources that Richardson favored. The seemingly symmetrical main facade includes a porte cochere leading to a walled courtyard. Norcross Bros. constructed the building with facade walls of pink-gray granite and courtyard elevations of rosy brick with limestone trim. The roof is terra-cotta.

John Jacob Glessner, the vice president of a company that manufactured farm implements, and his wife, Frances Macbeth Glessner, commissioned the house in 1885 for use primarily as a winter residence. Richardson finished the design before his death in 1886, and his succes-

JOHN J. GLESSNER HOUSE

JOHN J. GLESSNER HOUSE—INTERIOR

sors, Charles A. Coolidge and George F. Shepley, carefully carried it to completion in 1887. The functional plan is one of Richardson's best: principal living spaces face the southern courtyard and have large windows to capture the winter sun, while a service passage to the north mitigates Chicago's chilliest winds. The house served the Glessners perfectly for the next half century. Daniel H. Burnham, one of their earliest dinner guests, observed that it was in Chicago that the great Boston architect took new departures and did his most successful work.

The settings, furniture, and decorative objects assembled within Glessner House are a cohesive grouping of items designed by architects or designers with architectural training. These include masterpieces of Modern Gothic case goods by Isaac E. Scott; a library double desk, dining room chairs, and a grand piano by Charles A. Coolidge and Francis Bacon, both designing for the A. H. Davenport firm; and wallpapers, upholstery and hanging fabrics, chairs, lamps, carpets, and ceramic tiles and vases from the British workshops of William Morris and William De Morgan, both known and admired by Richardson. Woodwork for paneling, doors, and mantels is primarily quartersawn oak. Wall colors were terra-cotta red, gold, and green, while gold leaf highlighted the dining room ceiling.

Understanding of the Glessners' uniquely close relationship with their architect, their home, and their lives is enhanced by extensive documentation, much of it used by restoration architects who have worked on the house such as John Thorpe, Wilbert R. Hasbrouck, John Vinci, and Walker Johnson.

The Glessner House Museum is private, not-for-profit, and open to the public. —ELAINE HARRINGTON

20| William W. Kimball House
1801 S. Prairie Ave.
1890–1892, SOLON S. BEMAN

As the Second Empire's influence faded in the 1880s, wealthy clients increasingly abandoned the eccentricities of the Queen Anne style in favor of more historically correct designs, such as those imitating the great French châteaus of the reign of Francis I (1515–1547). The "châteauesque" was an ideal choice for an era of pastiche. Its prototype was a polyglot style that had applied Classical motifs newly introduced from Renaissance Italy onto the irregularly massed forms of the medieval castle. Following the lead of New York architect Richard Morris Hunt on the Vanderbilt châteaus, Beman here recalled picturesque, fragmented sixteenth-century French facades with pavilions and windows of varied shapes and sizes. His immediate inspiration was the design of the sixteenth-century dormers of the Château de Josselin in Brittany, the model for the massing for the three-story bay on the main facade.

21| Joseph G. Coleman House
(*Miner T. Ames House*)
1811 S. Prairie Ave.
1885, COBB & FROST

The entrance is a superb example of contrasting surfaces. Huge sandstone blocks form roundheaded arches atop squat, clustered, smooth columns with Romanesque capitals, while in the second story a window-filled bay of smooth stone stands out against the rusticated walls.

WILLIAM W. KIMBALL HOUSE

HENRY B. CLARKE HOUSE

22| Henry B. Clarke House
1855 S. Indiana Ave.
1836, ARCHITECT UNKNOWN
1981, RESTORATION, JOSEPH W.
CASSERLY, CHICAGO CITY ARCH.;
WILBERT R. HASBROUCK,
RESTORATION ARCH.

Chicago's only visibly Greek Revival building is very possibly the city's oldest structure (a contender for the title has emerged in Norwood Park). Originally built at 1700 S. Michigan Ave., it was moved twice, returning in 1977 to this, its original neighborhood. Its colonnaded grandeur still projects an aura of the civilizing influence that pioneers attempted to bring to frontier Chicago. The ancient forms of pedimented porticoes, Doric columns, and pilasters (although Roman, not Greek), and the "entablature" were considered most appropriate for a growing democracy. Greek Revival buildings were invariably white, regular, and symmetrical, with a central-hall plan. The Greek Revival style reigned from 1820 to 1860, and rebellion against its ordered predictability stimulated the development of the picturesque and irregular Gothic Revival and Italianate styles.

23| 213, 215 & 217 E. Cullerton St.
213: 1891, THOMAS & ROPP
215 AND 217: LATE 1860s,
ARCHITECTS UNKNOWN

Insurance atlases show the smallest and earliest of this curious trio, the Italianate home at 215, in the center of two identical buildings. They probably date from after the 1865 closing of nearby stockyards, which increased the area's appeal. The two flanking houses are either replacements or enveloping additions built between 1886 and 1892.

24| Marshall Field, Jr., House
(*William H. Murray House*)
1919 S. Prairie Ave.
1884, SOLON S. BEMAN

This example of Beman's Queen Anne work is so heavily altered that, in novelist Arthur Meeker's words, "it's impossible to say any longer what it thought it was originally trying to be."

25| Elbridge G. Keith House
1900 S. Prairie Ave.
1870, JONATHAN W. ROBERTS
CA. 1880, MANSARD ADDITIONS,
ARCHITECT UNKNOWN

This is the quintessential "marble front" of the 1870s, a brick house whose main facade is faced with Joliet limestone, then known as "Athens marble." This type almost universally has a single projecting bay running the full three-story height. The stable at the rear of the property may hint at the house's original roofline.

26| Vue 20
1845 S. Michigan Ave.
2003, BRININSTOOL & LYNCH

The five-story base, containing the requisite multilevel parking garage above retail, is enlivened with a palette of clear, perforated, translucent and opaque materials. Floor-to-ceiling glass on the east and west elevations exposes the building's structure, which is of post-tension concrete that allows for column-free residences and a minimal number of caissons. Balconies are concentrated on the north and south shear walls, maintaining the clean lines of the principal facade on Michigan Ave.

27 | Second Presbyterian Church
1936 S. Michigan Ave.
1874, JAMES RENWICK, JOHN ADDISON ASSOCIATED
1900, REBUILDING, HOWARD VAN DOREN SHAW

Renwick, architect of the Smithsonian Institution and St. Patrick's Cathedral in New York City, had in 1849 designed for this congregation the city's first Gothic Revival church, destroyed in the Fire of 1871. This replacement was built of a local limestone with bituminous mottling accented with strong horizontal bands of black rock from the same quarry. The strongest elements of Renwick's Gothic vocabulary, a steeply pitched roof and rose window, were altered after a fire in 1900. The interior is imbued with the Arts & Crafts and Pre-Raphaelite influences introduced in Shaw's rebuilding and by muralist Frederic Clay Bartlett. A tree of life mural on the west wall, a screen with four heralding angels, the strapwork ceiling, and a palette of muted red, blue, green, and gold against buff and dark oak are a backdrop for an unrivaled collection of nineteenth-century stained glass, with examples from every phase

SECOND PRESBYTERIAN CHURCH

of Louis C. Tiffany's career. The two windows in the entry were designed by the British Pre-Raphaelite painter Edward Burne-Jones and executed by the William Morris studio.

28 | William H. Reid III House
2013 S. Prairie Ave.
1894, BEERS, CLAY & DUTTON

This lonely slice of a vanished block has a central, first-floor skylit room in an open plan made possible by the building's steel frame.

29 | Harriet F. Rees House
2110 S. Prairie Ave.
1888, COBB & FROST

The twenty-five-foot Richardsonian facade formula is polished and emboldened by the team that introduced it to Chicago. The smooth facade features an elegantly controlled use of ornamentation.

30 | Calvin T. Wheeler House
(*Joseph A. Kohn House*)
2020 S. Calumet Ave.
1870, O. L. WHEELOCK

Style sleuths will delight in Second Empire details and the mansard roof. The incised hood moldings around the windows are typical of the Italianate style; the matching incised pilasters are unusual.

31 | 320 E. 21st St.
(*Columbian Colortype Co.*)
1920, ALFRED S. ALSCHULER

A pivotal building in the career of a prolific factory designer features innovations that became standard. Entrance, docks, stairwells, and all services were pushed to the west wall to minimize interference with clear floor spaces and natural lighting. Economical flat-slab concrete construction reduced vibration. The concrete columns were exposed on the main elevations so that—when used in combination with terra-cotta detailing at the base, entry, and cornice—the effect of a totally brick and terra-cotta facade was achieved without its expense.

32 | 330 E. Cermak Rd.
(*American Book Company*)
1912, N. MAX DUNNING

This company shared with the other South Side presses the notion that books deserved to be made and stored more artistically than other goods. This red brick and terra-cotta warehouse features excellent surface-shadow effects accomplished by slight vertical and strong horizontal projections. Rooftop tanks and sprinkler equipment assume the usual tower disguise.

33 | Lakeside Technology Center
(*R. R. Donnelley & Sons Co. Calumet Plant*)
350 E. Cermak Rd.
1912–1924, HOWARD
VAN DOREN SHAW
1929, WEST-CENTRAL AND SOUTH
SECTIONS (INCLUDING TOWER),
CHARLES Z. KLAUDER
2000, ADAPTIVE REUSE,
PDA ASSOCS.

The Donnelleys had commissioned Shaw to design their Lakeside Press Building on S. Plymouth Ct., and they returned to him for a master plan and design for a new printing facility, to be built in stages over two decades. Shaw took the opportunity to create one of the city's—perhaps the nation's—finest essays in Industrial Gothic. Buttresslike piers separate large vertical bands of windows capped by limestone arches. Stone medallions and terra-cotta plaques depict stylized marks and devices of early printers like Johannes Gutenberg, William Caxton, and John Baskerville. At the main entry are six seals, three with the initials of the architect and owners, and carved relief panels of a Prairie Indian and a frontiersman. The taller tower, designed after Shaw's death by collegiate Gothicist Klauder, contained a two-story Gothic library.

34 | Lakeside Center at McCormick Place
2301 S. Lake Shore Dr.
1971, C. F. MURPHY ASSOCS.

This structural tour de force, which brutally interrupts the sweep of the lakefront, is one of Chicago's biggest planning gaffes. As early as 1954 the South Side Planning Board had proposed an exposition hall, to be designed by Mies van der Rohe, for a site on the south side of Cermak Rd. between King Dr. and Michigan Ave. The Metropolitan Fair and Exposition Authority, established in 1955 by the state, instead accepted the city's offer of a Burnham Park site east of the 23rd St. viaduct. Howls of protest, ignored by City Hall, greeted this proposal, which violated the dreams of city visionaries from A. Montgomery Ward to Daniel H. Burnham to keep the lakefront "forever open, clear and free." When the first McCormick Place (1960) burned in 1967, civic groups mounted a campaign to relocate it, but the economic pressures of getting the lucrative convention hall back in operation as quickly as possible dictated remaining on

LAKESIDE TECHNOLOGY CENTER

this site, where the foundations could be reused.

Designer Gene R. Summers, who had worked for Mies from 1950 to 1966, brought to life an airy, powerful hall. The statistics are staggering. The 1,360-foot roof, which cantilevers so gracefully seventy-five feet beyond supporting columns, covers nineteen acres and weighs 10,000 tons. Yet the 300,000-square-foot main exhibit space contains only eight columns. The cross-shaped columns of reinforced concrete poured into steel shells form a superstructure of 150 x 150-foot bays of unencumbered space and carry the roof fifty feet above the floor level. It's an impressive engineering feat and a keystone of the city's convention business— but neither built to nor intended for human scale.

35 | McCormick Place North
450 E. 23rd St.
1986, SKIDMORE, OWINGS & MERRILL

The diamond patterning symbolizes the hidden truss system and is a faint echo of Mies's convention hall project of the 1950s. As in the Lakeside Building, the roof is the dramatic focal point, using a fifteen-foot-deep truss system, supported by seventy-two four-inch, 450-strand cables hung from twelve concrete pylons. The system is designed to withstand abrupt changes in temperature, high winds, or broken cables. The pylons contain conduits for air-conditioning and heating, making ceiling vents unnecessary. The fixed vertical pipes on the long sides are designed to help stabilize the roof when it moves (normally up or down an inch or so) in certain kinds of weather.

36 | McCormick Place South
2301 S. King Dr.
1996, THOMPSON, VENTULETT, STAINBACK & ASSOCS., DESIGN ARCH.; A. EPSTEIN AND SONS INTERNATIONAL, ARCH. OF RECORD

The most graceful of all the buildings in this complex, it engages well with the outdoors, both at the entrance and on the east side. Because it is not meant solely for trade shows but for meetings as well, windows are plentiful.

37 | Hyatt Regency McCormick Place
2233 S. King Dr.
1998, MC3D, INC.

38 | McCormick Place Parking, Office, and Conference Center
301 E. Cermak Rd.
1996, MC3D, INC.

The Hyatt is better composed than its predecessor hotel, and its extended roof strengthens its identity from the Loop.

The western elevation of the parking garage incorporates the facade of Howard Van Doren Shaw's 1907 Platt Building.

39 | Motor Row
S. Michigan Ave., originally Roosevelt Rd. to 29th St.

In the 1880s the fashionable residential area of S. Michigan Ave. acquired a "magnificent stretch" of asphalt pavement "as level as a billiard table." After 1900 car dealers were eyeing the wide, deep (180 feet) lots for showrooms and by 1910 had created

MCCORMICK PLACE NORTH

what *Architectural Record* called "the longest and best automobile course in any city of this country," with at least forty new buildings selling or servicing cars.

The earliest showroom buildings were only slightly more elaborate than factories, typically three stories high, on corner lots, and almost invariably three bays wide. Spans of up to thirty feet permitted windows low and wide enough to show an entire car. Construction methods varied from semi-mill to steel and reinforced-concrete framing. Interior finishes were kept close to utilitarian even in the salesrooms, which had easily maintained red terrazzo floors and inexpensive wood wainscotings. Exteriors were initially brick with terra-cotta trim and logos.

In the 1920s designers began addressing the problem of how to effectively display indoors an item meant to be seen outdoors. Interiors, often with offices tucked away on mezzanines, were made to look like exteriors, with walls of stucco or stone. Mediterranean and California Spanish styling were deemed highly suitable.

Since the 1960s most Motor Row buildings have been converted to other uses, many of which are associated with activities at McCormick Place. Most buildings between 22nd St. and the Adlai E. Stevenson Expressway are vacant and ripe for redevelopment. Ground-floor remuddlings have dimmed most of the facades; look up to see the broad windows and fanciful terra-cotta logos.

40| Locomobile Lofts
(*Locomobile Showroom*)
2000 S. Michigan Ave.
1909, JENNEY, MUNDIE & JENSEN

Here is a quintessential early auto facility: a three-story corner building of reinforced concrete, trimmed in brick and terra-cotta. The showroom windows have been filled in.

41| Willie Dixon's Blues Heaven
(*formerly Chess Records; originally McNaull Tire Co.*)
2120 S. Michigan Ave.
1911, HORATIO R. WILSON
1957, REMODELING, JOHN S. TOWNSEND, JR., AND JACK S. WEINER

This is Chicago's only building to inspire a Rolling Stones song, which was named for the building and recorded here in 1964 as a tribute to Chess Records. The company's headquarters from 1957 to 1967 were in this building, which—like its neighbors—began life "in the motor trade."

42| 2222–2228 S. Michigan Ave.
(*Hudson Motor Co. of Illinois*)
1922, ALFRED S. ALSCHULER

H (for Hudson) medallions sit above the Palladian window in the central bay. Exuberant terra cotta imitates stone in twisted columns and rope moldings.

2222–2228 S. MICHIGAN AVE.

43| 2255 S. Michigan Ave.
(*Thomas Flyer Garage & Service Building*)
1910, HOLABIRD & ROCHE
1916, ADDITION, ALFRED S. ALSCHULER

Although two stories have been added, the base still reveals its origins as a classic auto-sales facility; varieties of brickwork and multicolored terra-cotta panels articulate the structural system.

44| 2309–2313 S. Michigan Ave.
(*Automobile Buildings for Alfred Cowles*)
1915, HOLABIRD & ROCHE

Two small automotive buildings reveal lively uses of terra-cotta, in the jagged blind arcade of the northern building and in the three-dimensional geometric patterning entirely covering the southern one.

45| Quinn Chapel
(*African Methodist Episcopal*)
2401 S. Wabash Ave.
1891–1894, EXTERIOR, HENRY F. STARBUCK; INTERIOR, CHARLES H. MCAFEE

Named for William P. Quinn, bishop of the Midwest diocese of the African Methodist Episcopal Church in the 1840s, the Chapel houses the city's oldest black congregation. Brick walls are faced with gray stone; the Victorian Gothic facade is distinguished by the north tower, with its belfry and tourelle. The church proper is a second-floor amphitheater, with seating arranged in a fan pattern and a balcony wrapping around three sides. The William H. Delle pipe organ was purchased from the German Pavilion at the Columbian Exposition.

46| *Chicago Daily Defender* Building
(*Illinois Automobile Club*)
2400 S. Michigan Ave.
1936, PHILIP B. MAHER

Built on the site of Adler & Sullivan's Standard Club (1887) and using the abandoned foundations of a predecessor organization's planned clubhouse, this two story brick building with its lantern-topped clock tower employs a simplified Spanish Mission styling. Many of the social aspects of automobile clubs vanished after World War II, when cars became more readily available to the average person. This building has housed one of the nation's leading African-American newspapers since the 1950s.

47| *Monument to The Great Northern Migration*
King Dr. at 26th St.
1994, ALISON SAAR

This fifteen-foot bronze statue of a man carrying a worn suitcase in his left hand and gesturing toward the north with his right symbolizes the migration of African Americans from the rural South to Chicago and other northern cities in the early 20th century. The sculpture can also be viewed as a gateway to the Black Metropolis–Bronzeville Historic District, the city's oldest African American neighborhood. A close look at the figure's bronze suit reveals that it is made of the soles of shoes, suggesting the arduous journey to Chicago many had to endure. This statue is part of the effort to repave and landscape King Dr. from 25th to 35th Sts. Other King Drive Gateway Project elements that are worth seeing include the many artist-designed benches and sidewalk plaques that make up the Bronzeville Walk of Fame and the Historic Bronzeville Street Map (on the median at 35th St.).

48| East Lake Management Development Co.
(*Vista Accumulator Co.*)
2850 S. Michigan Ave.
1919, PUCKEY & JENKINS

CHICAGO DAILY DEFENDER BUILDING

This was initially a deep, one-story sales and service building that housed a shock absorber business. A shallow second floor is now hidden behind a blind facade. The elaborate terra cotta, which includes tympana of paired griffins, demonstrates the exuberance that enlivened auto-related architecture in the 1910s.

49| Sidney A. Kent House
2944 S. Michigan Ave.
1883, BURNHAM & ROOT
1982, CONVERSION TO APARTMENTS, SWANN & WEISKOPF

"Subdued richness" aptly describes this mansion. The ornamentation and styling, including the enhanced central pavilion carried above the cornice line, were consciously drawn from the châteaus of Francis I. But the essentially cubic massing, the unusual expanses of plate glass, the wide undecorated Philadelphia pressed-brick wall surfaces, and the uniform color all provide repose. Built when its neighbors were similar in size (60 x 100 feet), this house is now a rare example of the residential work of a major Chicago firm, surviving as five luxury apartments. The wrought-iron fence is truly French, having been purchased by Kent from a Columbian Exposition display.

50| Near South Side Urban Renewal

The character of the area between 26th and 35th Sts. is the result of decisions made in the 1940s, when the area's anchor institutions considered moving but instead stayed and exercised their influence on the neighborhood. The newly created Illinois Institute of Technology (formed in 1940 by a merger of two schools) was building a new campus, and Michael Reese Hospital needed room to expand. In 1945 the hospital created a planning staff with a mandate to devise a campus plan and also to improve the character of its urban surroundings. The director was Reginald R. Isaacs, and Walter Gropius was architectural consultant. In what was perhaps the most comprehensive and ambitious essay in urban planning since Daniel H. Burnham's 1909 scheme for the entire city, the final report envisioned the complete redevelopment of seven square miles, from the lake west to the Pennsylvania Railroad tracks, and from 12th St. south to 47th St. Taking a cue from Le Corbusier's model cities of the 1920s and 1930s, the planners advocated the abandonment of the urban grid in favor of towers set in open expanses of greenery.

NEAR SOUTH SIDE URBAN RENEWAL

It was also during this decade that local, state, and federal governments resolved to address the lack of affordable urban housing. The housing shortage of the 1930s and 1940s, combined with a large influx of African-Americans from the South whose areas of settlement were restricted by prejudice and covenant, had resulted in intolerable slum conditions on the South Side. In 1947, when Reese completed its two-year study, the city had just established a land-clearance program that made possible many of the study's recommendations. Lake Meadows became the city's first racially integrated, middle-income housing, and Prairie Shores continued the success story. However, the "towers in a park" concept proved disastrous when governmental housing authorities applied it to low-income units. West of the lakefront, the State St. slum was demolished only to make way for a more vicious reincarnation, the high-rise projects of Stateway Gardens (State St. from 35th St. to Pershing Rd.) and the Robert Taylor Homes (State St. from Pershing Rd. to 54th St.), whose own demolition began in the late 1990s.

51| South Commons
26th to 31st St., Michigan to Prairie Aves.
1966–1970, EZRA GORDON–JACK M. LEVIN & ASSOCS.; L. R. SOLOMON, J. D. CORDWELL & ASSOCS.

Planned as a small village with ambitious goals of racial and economic balance, this was one of the final building blocks in the grand plan of postwar urban renewal on the Near South Side. The town houses turn their backs on cars and streets, clustering around quiet, neighborly open courts, playgrounds, and stores.

52| George Ellery Wood House
2801 S. Prairie Ave.
1885, JOHN C. COCHRANE

The sole reminder of elegant "Lower Prairie Avenue," this Queen Anne house survives because its 1950s owners fought orders for the wholesale demolition of what was regarded as one of the city's worst slums.

53| Prairie Shores
2801–3001 S. Martin Luther King, Jr., Dr.
1958–1962, LOEBL, SCHLOSSMAN & BENNETT

This was Michael Reese Hospital's own contribution to the plan they advocated. Comprising five apartment towers, with a total of 1,677 units, the complex was intended primarily for hospital employees who wanted to live nearby. The narrow buildings are oriented north-south to maximize daylight, and each is massed as a pair of overlapping slabs. The curtain walls have ribbon windows and louvered spandrels of a different color on each building.

54| Michael Reese Hospital and Medical Center
S. Lake Shore Dr. and E. 31st St.
BEGUN 1907, VARIOUS ARCHITECTS

PRAIRIE SHORES

Established at this site in 1881, the nonsectarian institution replaced the city's old Jewish hospital, destroyed in the Fire a decade earlier. The campus, which has thirty buildings surrounding four parks, owes its look to the modernist design influence of Walter Gropius. There are no individual masterpieces, but they form a pleasing group; **2929 S. Ellis Ave.** (1907, Richard E. Schmidt, Garden & Martin) is the oldest. Schmidt gave the building a Prairie Style look, with strong verticals balanced by continuous moldings at the sill and lintel lines. The unusual massing repeats that of the prior Michael Reese building at this corner site: two wings at right angles are joined by a pavilion that cuts across the corner. The hospital has converted the mechanical top floor to two floors for offices and research, and has removed the projecting cornice. **The Kaplan Pavilion** (the Psychosomatic and Psychiatric Institute, 1951, Loebl, Schlossman & Bennett) has distinctive continuous slatted canopies over each window— clean, handsome detailing with good energy sense, reducing heat gain through the wide windows. The hospital's owners declared bankruptcy in 2002, leaving the complex to an uncertain fate.

55| Lake Meadows
S. Martin Luther King, Jr., Dr. between 31st and 35th Sts.
1950–1960, SKIDMORE, OWINGS & MERRILL

The overwhelming impression is of green, open space; the buildings cover only 9 percent of the land. The first housing constructed under the aegis of the Michael Reese plan, it was built on land assembled by the Chicago Land Clearance Commission and sold to New York Life Insurance Co. for about one-sixth of what the city paid for it. In 1946 *Architectural Forum* claimed that it would be "one of the first private housing projects to allow mixed Negro and white occupancy," an important ad-

vance in an area where as late as the 1930s properties carried covenants excluding sales to nonwhites. The 70-acre, 2,033-unit complex includes ten apartment buildings, an office building, a small shopping center, and a community club.

56| Lake Meadows, 601 Building
601 E. 32nd St.
1960, SKIDMORE, OWINGS & MERRILL

The last and most luxurious building of the complex is the only one with floor-to-ceiling windows. Miesian influence is evident in the columns set behind the glass-and-steel curtain wall, the recessed brick or tile infill panels between the piers, and the inset wall on the ends.

57| Lake Meadows Tennis Club
3211 S. Ellis Ave.
1960, SKIDMORE, OWINGS & MERRILL

The second floor is the primary social space. The delightfully graceful pyramidal roof admits light through louvered corners and hangs far beyond the completely glazed exterior wall.

LAKE MEADOWS TENNIS CLUB

58| Groveland Park
S. Cottage Grove Ave. at E. 33rd Pl.

In 1847 Senator Stephen A. Douglas moved to Chicago and began acquiring property, including a sixty-acre tract spreading from Lake Michigan west to King Dr. between 33rd and 35th Sts. His shrewd investment was made all the more valuable in the early 1850s when the Illinois Central Railroad—whose right-of-way Douglas had encouraged politically—built its tracks along the lakeshore. Douglas recorded the subdivision, Oaken-wald, in 1855, setting aside the portion east of Cottage Grove Ave. for his own home and for two residential parks, Groveland and Woodland, with fifty-foot lots facing central open spaces. The depression of 1857 reduced the value of his holdings, which he mortgaged in order to finance his political campaigns. He was unable to redeem them before his death in 1861.

The property was developed only after years of lawsuits had been settled in favor of Douglas's sons in 1873, when a Groveland Park homeowners' association could finally be formed to oversee the maintenance of the common parklands. The first houses, clustered along the northern side of the park, have all been destroyed. Many of the others are altered, but all enjoy frontage on this small, quiet park. The drives are a graveyard of demolished homes, lined with slabs and blocks of limestone, sandstone, and terra-cotta.

59 | Groveland Park Gardener's Lodge
601 E. Groveland Park Ave.
EARLY 1870S, ARCHITECT UNKNOWN

This Gothic Revival dollhouse was originally trimmed with fancy bargeboards.

GROVELAND PARK GARDENER'S LODGE

60 | Charles W. and Edwin Pardridge Houses
607, 609 & 611 E. Groveland Park Ave.
LATE 1870S, ARCHITECT UNKNOWN

Three houses remain of the five built on lots subdivided in 1878. The "Athens marble" fronts, heavy pressed-metal cornices, and incised neo-Grec carving proved attractive to professors at the first University of Chicago, which was located on the west side of Cottage Grove Ave. from 1859 to 1886.

61 | Hamilton Borden and William E. Selleck Houses
613 & 615 E. Groveland Park Ave.
1882, ARCHITECT UNKNOWN

Built by partners in a scales business, these rusticated sandstone houses have brown-stone panels with robust leaf-and-tendril designs.

62 | Frank N. Gage House
637 E. Groveland Park Ave.
1879, ARCHITECT UNKNOWN

Gothic details, such as the trefoil carved over the entrance and the pointed relieving arches in the windows, enliven an otherwise Italianate facade.

63 | Edward S. Hunter and John B. Mallers Houses
639 & 641 E. Groveland Park Ave.
1886, FLANDERS & ZIMMERMAN

Mallers developed this double house with its brown sandstone facade; one half still has the original slate roof.

64 | John M. Gartside House
663 E. Groveland Park Ave.
1885, WILLETT L. CARROLL

This brick two-story and attic residence has a Euclid stone front.

65 | Stephen A. Douglas Tomb & Memorial
636 E. 35th St.
1863–1881, LEONARD W. VOLK

This is a monument as much to its era as to its subject, the Little Giant, Stephen A. Douglas. A larger-than-life bronze figure perches ninety-six feet in the air surveying Lake Michigan—or preparing to dive in, according to more than one critic. To offset the height, sculptor Volk placed four allegorical figures on freestanding plinths around the vault that contains Douglas's sarcophagus. The grounds were intended for Douglas's own elegant home. Lack of funds delayed the statue's completion.

ST. JOSEPH CARONDELET CHILD CARE CENTER (SOLDIERS' HOME)

66 | St. Joseph Carondelet Child Care Center
(*Soldiers' Home*)
739 E. 35th St.
1864, NORTH HALF OF EAST BUILDING, ATTRIBUTED TO WILLIAM W. BOYINGTON
1866, MAIN BUILDING (35TH ST.), WILLIAM W. BOYINGTON
1873, SOUTH HALF OF EAST BUILDING, ARCHITECT UNKNOWN
1878, NORTHWEST BUILDING, ARCHITECT UNKNOWN
1923, SOUTHWEST BUILDING, ARCHITECT UNKNOWN
1957, SOUTH BUILDING, ARCHITECT UNKNOWN

A rare example of a surviving Civil War–era building in Chicago, this home was intended to serve soldiers who were sick, wounded, or merely in transit. Its intended function as a permanent home for disabled soldiers was made obsolete when Congress established national veterans' care in 1869, and it has been operated since 1872 as a Catholic child-care facility. The simple Italianate style of Boyington's first buildings set the tone for all subsequent construction. The Northwest Building, which contains the entrance, has a second-floor chapel.

Illinois Institute of Technology (IIT)
S. Michigan Ave. to the Metra tracks, 31st to 35th Sts.

IIT presents a remarkable example of a university campus that was shaped by a single architectural sensibility. It may be one of the nation's last bastions of modernism in both its design and teaching philosophy. Ludwig Mies van der Rohe's original plan (as well as the buildings) has continued to serve the campus well, especially in his choice of steel, brick, and glass materials; additions vanish seamlessly into the fabric of the original buildings. The design of the campus was his first American commission, and his buildings here develop ideas that he and his many students would apply throughout the world.

In the late 1930s, as the Nazis tightened their grip on Germany's cultural life, many of the most talented artists fled to the United States. One of the most prominent of the Bauhaus architects, Ludwig Mies van der Rohe, was persuaded by Chicago architect John A. Holabird (son of William Holabird) to accept the directorship of the architecture department of the Armour Institute of Technology. Mies immigrated in 1938 and began his American career as a teacher and architect, a potent combination that exerted lasting influence. In 1940 Armour merged with Lewis Institute, a West Side technical school, to form the Illinois Institute of Technology.

Mies's campus plan for the new institution consisted of twenty buildings arranged

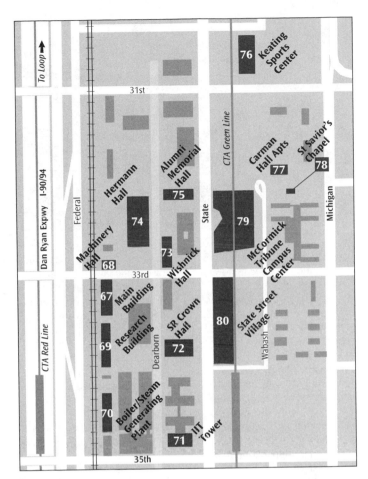

To Loop ↑

31st

Dan Ryan Expwy I-90/94

Federal

CTA Red Line

CTA Green Line

State

Michigan

Dearborn

Wabash

33rd

35th

76 Keating Sports Center

St Savior's Chapel 78

Carman Hall Apts 77

Hermann Hall

Alumni Memorial Hall 75

74

79

McCormick Tribune Campus Center

Machinery Hall 68

73

Wishnick Hall

67 Main Building

Research Building

SR Crown Hall

69

72

80

State Street Village

70

Boiler/Steam Generating Plant

71 IIT Tower

---

symmetrically around 33rd St. between State St. and the railroad tracks to the west. Mies chose a module of 24 feet x 24 feet bays, 12 feet high, to determine both the bay size of individual buildings and the distances between them. The uniformity of the twenty-four-foot length, a standard dimension for American classrooms at the time, allowed economies of construction and ensured a certain uniformity in campus design over time. The buildings are sited to form open spaces that are implied rather than defined. The buildings provided Mies with the opportunity to explore and elaborate on a new architectural vocabulary of skeletal steel construction. Welded steel frames, painted black, have infill panels of glass or tan brick. Guiding principles for all buildings are clarity of structure, appropriate use of materials, and sensitivity to proportions. Of his greatest

achievement, Crown Hall, he said, "I think this is the clearest structure we have done, the best to express our philosophy."

After Mies retired as professor in 1958, he was replaced as campus architect by Skidmore, Owings & Merrill, one of the firms that had adopted his tenets most completely. Mies's twenty-two buildings were joined by others in the same vein, although many lacked the subtlety and refinement that had characterized his work. Results of a revitalization effort that began in the mid 1990s include two dramatic buildings that opened in 2003.

67 | Main Building

(*Armour Institute of Technology*)
3300 S. Federal St.
1891–1893, PATTON & FISHER

IIT's roots as a no-frills workingman's school began here, when Philip D. Armour, Sr., commissioned this manual training school. Designed as a

IIT MAIN BUILDING

companion piece to Burnham & Root's Armour Mission, a now-demolished settlement house across the street, it is rock solid and Romanesque. The rhythmic wall composition with its round-arched windows owes, along with many of this firm's masonry buildings, a great debt to Louis H. Sullivan. The fourth story, served by its own elevator, housed the "girls' department," with cooking and dressmaking workshops. Walk inside to see the Philip Danforth Armour, Jr., memorial window by Edwin P. Sperry on the stair landing.

68| Machinery Hall
100 W. 33rd St.
1901, PATTON, FISHER & MILLER

This simplified version of the Main Building segregated noise-generating activities behind its Romanesque walls.

69| Minerals and Metals Research Building
3350 S. Federal St.
1943, 1958, LUDWIG MIES VAN DER ROHE; HOLABIRD & ROOT, ASSOC. ARCHS.

This was the first campus building designed by Mies, and it established the basic concepts of subsequent classroom buildings. Stripped down and startlingly severe, the glassy east side is now the only original piece easily seen.

70| Boiler Plant & Steam Generating Plant
3430 S. Federal St.
1945–1950, LUDWIG MIES VAN DER ROHE; ALSCHULER & SINCERE, ASSOC. ARCHS.; FRANK J. KORNACKER, STRUCT. ENG.; SARGENT & LUNDY, MECH. ENG. 1964, NORTH ADDITION, SARGENT & LUNDY

The six north bays follow Mies's original specifications. Steam is generated in the 1990 Co-Generation Building, a smaller version of the original.

71| IIT Tower
10 W. 35th St.
1963–1964, SCHMIDT, GARDEN & ERIKSON

The tallest building on campus is the least sympathetic to earlier buildings.

72| S. R. Crown Hall
(*College of Architecture, Illinois Institute of Technology*)
3360 S. State St.
1956, LUDWIG MIES VAN DER ROHE; PACE ASSOCS. AND C. F. MURPHY ASSOCS., ASSOC. ARCHS.
2003, SOUTH PORCH RESTORATION, KRUECK & SEXTON; MCCLIER

During his American career, Mies came to believe that structure and space were the essential elements of architecture; as a result, his American reputation has centered on the expression of those concepts. In Crown Hall he exposed the structure and enclosed the space with a powerful balance of steel, glass, and light.

S.R. CROWN HALL

Mies's building for the College of Architecture was in design as early as 1950 and was completed in 1956. It is dominated by the steel frame and glass pavilion of its upper level. Effectively a one-room school, the space is 120 by 220 feet and 18 feet high.

Crown Hall's greatness derives from both its clarity and its comprehensive solution of all the problems it set out to solve. The building reads as a largely transparent glass box floating between its translucent podium and its roof, which is suspended from the four plate girders that punctuate its silhouette. The podium is actually a concrete frame on a twenty-by-thirty-foot module, set with eight feet below grade and with four feet above grade glazed with translucent glass.

During the day Crown Hall seems a precisely defined, translucent, and transparent volume in perfect repose. At night it becomes a reliquary of light, as its interior illumination appears to make the building seem almost to float on a cushion of light. The travertine main entrance stairs, centered on a long side of the building, also seem to float, serving to invite the visitor inside, through entrances marked by floor-to-ceiling glass. Upon entering, one faces a central space defined by eight-foot-high oak partitions; the cross axis that divides this core into two parts helps orient the visitor to the richly developed spaces of a building that seems initially to be without a plan. One could easily locate the physical center of the building only to discover that much of the greatness of the space comes from its development whereby no single place is seen to have priority.

Crown Hall departs from the module that Mies established for the campus in his master plan. As a result, it—rather than a more traditional campus structure, such as a library, administration building, or student union—becomes what Mies called representational. Such a building, Mies had maintained, must declare the highest purposes and ideals of the institution. At the dedication of Crown Hall he said, "Let this building be the home of ideas and adventure" that would be "in the end a real contribution to our civilization."

—KEVIN HARRINGTON

73| **Wishnick Hall**
(*Chemistry Building*)
3255 S. Dearborn St.
1946, LUDWIG MIES VAN DER ROHE;
ALFRED S. ALSCHULER AND R. N.
FRIEDMAN, ASSOC. ARCHS.

Using the same materials and structure as Alumni Memorial Hall, but with smaller windows (four per bay), this building became the standard for subsequent classroom buildings.

74| Grover M. Hermann Hall
3241 S. Federal St.
1962, SKIDMORE, OWINGS & MERRILL

This was originally the student union building; together with the Library to the south it follows Mies's plan for two large buildings on this site. But both are done with a heavier hand; beams lie across the roof like logs, instead of being gracefully integrated with the wall as at Crown Hall. The original precast concrete porch, similar to that of Crown Hall, has been replaced with granite. Unlike that building, the structure here is hidden behind the glassy skin. To the north is Morton Park, landscaped by faculty member Alfred Caldwell.

75| Alumni Memorial Hall
(*Navy Building*)
3201 S. Dearborn St.
1946, LUDWIG MIES VAN DER ROHE; HOLABIRD & ROOT, ASSOC. ARCHS.
1972, ADDITION, MITTELBUSHER & TOURTELOT

The first academic building completed after the war, this is also the first in which the glass panes fill the width of an entire twenty-four-foot bay. It was an archetype, with a primary structural frame of steel beams and a secondary structure of I-beams attached to the exterior to support brick infill and window frames. The hidden structural system is expressed in the reentrant corners, showing the secondary I-beam welded to the primary column.

76| Arthur S. Keating Sports Center
3040 S. Wabash Ave.
1966, SKIDMORE, OWINGS & MERRILL

Here is another SOM building that hides the structure behind the walls, although nighttime illumination reveals the steel columns. The first floor is raised, and windows below it provide clerestory lights for the lower level.

77| Carman Hall Apartments
60 E. 32nd St.
1951–1953, LUDWIG MIES VAN DER ROHE; PACE ASSOCS., ASSOC. ARCHS.

IIT built these apartments for faculty and married students. Rare for this campus, the concrete-frame buildings show Mies's signature receding columns, which carry less weight as they rise.

78| Robert F. Carr Memorial Chapel of St. Savior
65 E. 32nd St.
1952, LUDWIG MIES VAN DER ROHE

Known on campus as the "God box," this is the only church that Mies ever designed. A nondenominational, meditational chapel, it is all glass on the east facade and enclosed by brick walls on the others.

ROBERT F. CARR MEMORIAL CHAPEL OF ST. SAVIOR

79| McCormick Tribune Campus Center
3201 S. State St.
2003, OFFICE OF METROPOLITAN ARCHITECTURE; HOLABIRD & ROOT, ASSOC. ARCHS.

Rem Koolhaas presented his design proposal for the IIT Campus Center as a critique of the planning philosophy that led to clearing the land for Mies's academic campus. The design intent was to restore, within the building, the density of the historic housing that had been demolished during the urban renewal era.

The Koolhaas design has incorporated Mies's 1953 Commons Building into the fabric of the new building. An inside corner of two of the Commons's exterior walls forms part of the enclosure of an interior courtyard within the Campus Center.

The Center departs from architectural norms by not having conventional facades. Its floor plan is simply cut off at the edge of the building so that the glazed exterior walls display sections of its varied interior spaces.

The Center passes under the Green Line elevated tracks to unite the academic and residential zones of the IIT campus. Its primary visual element is the acoustic tube that encloses the trains as they pass over the Center. Diagonal paths within the Center connect the academic and residential destinations beyond. The spaces that remain between these paths house student and community activities.

80| State Street Village
3303, 3333, 3353 S. State St.
2003, MURPHY/JAHN

The 550-foot-long dormitory is actually three separate buildings with passageways between. The school hopes that a new dorm on the west side of the CTA tracks will help unify the campus.

81| Michigan Place
3115 S. Michigan Ave.
2002, OPTIMA, INC.

Two mid-rise towers are sited to the north to provide maximum sun exposure for these town homes and their courtyard. Parking for the town houses is concealed beneath landscaped berms creating a rolling courtyard.

82| Single-Family Houses
3326, 3328 & 3337 S. Indiana Ave.

Two-Flats
3312, 3320, 3335, 3347, 3349, 3357, 3359, 3403 & 3405 S. Indiana Ave.
1989, PHILLIP KUPRITZ & ASSOCS.
WITH JOHNSON & LEE, ROULA ASSOCS.
AND RAY/DAWSON ARCHITECTS

Twelve of the houses built for those displaced by the new Comiskey Park are clustered near 34th St. and Indiana Ave. Owners were offered a choice of two building types and four designs. Common to all are red brick facades with white wood trim and concrete block sides. Because sites of varying sizes were chosen by lottery, some of the two-flats had to be adjusted to fit on cramped lots.

83| Pilgrim Baptist Church
(Kehilath Anshe Ma'ariv Synagogue)
3301 S. Indiana Ave.
1890–1891, ADLER & SULLIVAN
1986, INTERIOR RESTORATION,
OFFICE OF JOHN VINCI

KAM (Congregation of the Men of the West) was Chicago's oldest Jewish congregation, founded in 1847; Adler's father had been rabbi from 1861 to 1883. The architects responded to programmatic needs by designing an auditorium (their specialty) expressed as two stacked rectangles—one for the worship space and the other for the clerestory necessary for good acoustics. Terra-cotta panels hint at the richness of the interior. The original design for an entirely limestone-clad building was over budget; economy made necessary a pressed-metal cladding for the top cube, now sided. The wide entrance of broad expanding arches gives a sense of the grandeur originally envisioned. But there is no skimping visible on the interior, a thrilling worship space. A balcony completely surrounding the seating space required a tunnel vault overhead, rather than the firm's usual ceiling of expanding curves. The lower walls are russet, the upper ones cream. Colorist Louis Millet combined both tones in a rubbed effect on the gallery face, blended cream and the ceiling's oak on the clerestory frieze, and incorporated all of these tones in the Healy & Millet art-glass windows. The discovery during restoration of the precision of

PILGRIM BAPTIST CHURCH

this coloration inspired scholars to reexamine the Sullivan-Millet palette on other buildings.

84| Ira A. Heath House
3132 S. Prairie Ave.
1889, ADLER & SULLIVAN

The long-standing attribution of this house to Adler & Sullivan has been called into question ever since Frank Lloyd Wright asserted that the house Heath built was not the one Adler & Sullivan designed.

85| Samuel B. Steele House
3123 S. Calumet Ave.

Isaac Wedeles House
3127 S. Calumet Ave.
1890, CHARLES S. FROST

Carefully controlled Romanesque houses for partners in a wholesale grocery business, these stone-front dwellings feature two-story, gently projecting bays and strong stringcourses above their battered bases.

86|Thomas D. Stimson House
3132 S. Calumet Ave.
1886, GEORGE H. EDBROOKE

A scalloped roofline distinguishes this Romanesque house, a virtual duplicate of the one the architect had designed for himself up the block at 3314-3316.

87| Carl D. Bradley House
3140 S. Calumet Ave.
1884, CHARLES M. PALMER

On the cusp of stylistic change, here is an Italianate house breaking out in a Queen Anne pox. This hybrid has the flat front, tall narrow windows, and bracketed cornice of the older style—but with the rounded elements, decorative roof peak, and varied materials of the new fashion.

88| Joseph Deimel House
3141 S. Calumet Ave.
1887, ADLER & SULLIVAN

This is the lone survivor of over twenty residential commissions for Adler & Sullivan's Jewish clientele in this part of town. Like many of the firm's residences, it lacks the flair of their larger commissions.

89| 3144–3148 S. Calumet Ave.
1881, ARCHITECT UNKNOWN

Investors John J. Curran and Maximillian and Isaac Wolff were partners in a lumber-drying business and invested in several row house developments along Calumet Ave. This set, in which three of the eight units survive, was home to the Wolffs; it features angular neo-Grec styling, incised ornament of Joliet limestone facing, and strong metal cornices.

90| 3154 S. Calumet Ave./ 320 E. 32nd St.
1988, JOSEPH J. HOENDERVOOGT & ASSOCS.

This complex attempts to blend with its Victorian neighbors by assuming a single-family-house disguise, with towerlike corners and a pedimental roofline.

91| Robert W. Roloson Houses
3213–3219 S. Calumet Ave.
1894, FRANK LLOYD WRIGHT
1980, RENOVATION, FITCH/LAROCCA ASSOCS.

The only Wright row houses ever built date from the early years of his independent practice. In them he reduced the Jacobean gable to a simple geometric form. The Roman brick wall is a severe but lovely backdrop for Sullivanesque terra-cotta panels.

92| Thomas Brown Houses
3221–3223 S. Calumet Ave.
1885, JULIUS H. HUBER

Terra-cotta spandrel panels featuring putti, masks, and foliage enliven this mansarded brick double house.

93| George H. Edbrooke Houses
3314–3316 S. Calumet Ave.
1884, GEORGE H. EDBROOKE

A Romanesque facade with a Flemish roofline marks Edbrooke's own home at 3316. The attached house is smaller, simpler, and set back in deference to its showier neighbor.

94| Morris Cohn House
3321 S. Calumet Ave.
1891, KLEY & LANG

A gently rounded second-floor bow window and arched first-floor openings compose a nicely varied facade, disturbed by a pedimented dormer and a turret above the roofline.

95| Clarence A. Knight House
3322 S. Calumet Ave.
1891, FLANDERS & ZIMMERMAN

The unusual palette and materials—pink-veined, rusticated orange Kasota stone and orange rock-faced Roman brick—contribute to a very lively design by architects known for their picturesque work. The

ROBERT W. ROLOSON HOUSES

CLARENCE A. KNIGHT HOUSE

combination of burly Romanesque corner towers and fine Gothic detailing in the ogee arches is skillfully handled.

96| John B. Cohrs, Albert R. Southard, and Chauncey E. Seaton Houses
3356–3360 S. Calumet Ave.
CA. 1890, ARCHITECT UNKNOWN

A trio of Richardsonian Romanesque town houses strike a harmonic chord in sandstone, greenstone, and limestone. The elaborate carving on 3360 portrays dragons and enigmatic men.

Dr. Martin Luther King, Jr., Dr. (*Grand Blvd.*)

In 1869 Frederick Law Olmsted and Calvert Vaux were commissioned to survey and plan two boulevards, eventually named Drexel and Grand. They were intended to link a park to be created in the township of Hyde Park with the city of Chicago, whose southern boundary was then at 39th St. As built, only Grand Blvd. was a continuation of an actual Chicago street. It ran from 35th St. to 51st St., curving gently into Washington Park for an impressive view of the huge meadow. Extensions to the north and south of the boulevard segment were named South Pkwy., and in 1968 the entire eleven-mile thoroughfare was renamed Dr. Martin Luther King, Jr., Dr. Unlike the other boulevards that converge on Washington Park, King Dr. has no central planted median. Its six wide central lanes are flanked by slim grassy strips, which are in turn bordered by local drives.

CHAUNCEY E. SEATON HOUSE

97 | *Victory*
S. King Dr. at 35th St.
1928, 1936, LEONARD CRUNELLE

Three life-size figures—a soldier, a mother, and Columbia—carved in high relief around a shaft honor the dead of the U.S. Army 370th Infantry, 93rd Division, a black World War I unit. Unveiled in 1928, it was topped by the three-dimensional doughboy in 1936.

98 | Chicago Military Academy—Bronzeville
(*Eighth Regiment Armory*)
3519 S. Giles Ave.
1915, JAMES B. DIBELKA
1999, EXTERIOR RESTORATION, INTERIOR REMODELING, WENDELL CAMPBELL ASSOCS., LTD.
2002, NORTH ADDITION, MAUREEN REAGAN ARCHITECTS, LTD.

The long-abandoned armory has been reborn as the home for an innovative Chicago Public School program with a strong military emphasis. The original building, now the southern part, has a long, three-story facade of brown brick with limestone trim. Punctuated by broad arches at street level and a series of gables and towers at the roofline, the facade conveys strength and monumentality. The link between the addition and existing building further celebrates the history of Bronzeville and the armory by incorporating a clock tower with a historical informational plaque and military insignia plaques representing the five branches of the service.

99 | Chicago Police Department Headquarters
3510 S. Michigan Ave.
2000, LOHAN ASSOCS.

A modern brick and curtain wall building with a cantilevered canopy houses a technologically advanced police facility with an emphasis on community involvement and ease of use for the staff.

100 | Overton Hygienic Business Incubator
(*Overton Hygienic/Douglass National Bank Building*)
3617 S. State St.
1923, Z. EROL SMITH
2000, RESTORATION OF FACADE, BAUER LATOZA STUDIO

Located close to the intersection of 35th and State, which was the heart of Bronzeville in the 1920s, the Overton Hygienic Building became the prime business address of the community for a number of years. The four-story structure was built by Bronzeville's leading entrepreneur, Anthony Overton, to house his successful cosmetics enterprise (the Overton Hygienic Co.), his Douglass Bank, and a variety of other shops and professional offices. It was promoted during construction as "a monument to Negro thrift and industry." Supported by a reinforced concrete frame, the Overton has street facades of dark red brick with extensive trim in white-glazed terra cotta. An impressive terra-cotta plaque in the center of the fourth-floor facade proudly carries the name OVERTON HYGIENIC COMPANY. The Mid South Planning and Development Commission acquired the badly deteriorated building in 1998, restored the facade, and made plans to renovate the interior for offices and ground-floor retail.

101 | Chicago Public Library—*Chicago Bee* Branch
(Chicago Bee *Building*)
3647 S. State St.
1931, Z. EROL SMITH
1995, RESTORATION OF EXTERIOR AND REMODELING OF INTERIOR, MCCLIER CORP.

Overshadowed for years by the massive public housing towers to the west, by the general bleakness of the streetscape, and by its own dilapidated condition, this colorful three-story building was easy to overlook. A recent award-winning restoration of the exterior has brought the green, black, and tan terra-cotta panels, as well as the intricately incised ornamentation, back to their original look and revealed the *Chicago Bee* Building to have one of the city's niftiest Art Deco facades. Built to be the headquarters of a newspaper started in 1926 by Bronzeville entrepreneur Anthony Overton, and then later used by his cosmetics firm, the building was vacant for a number of years, until the recent remodeling and restoration turned it into a branch of the Chicago Public Library.

102| Wabash Ave. YMCA
3763 S. Wabash Ave.
1913, ROBERT BERLIN
2000, RESTORATION AND
REMODELING, WEESE LANGLEY
WEESE ARCHITECTS LTD.

The great philanthropist Julius Rosenwald led the effort to build this and many other YMCAs in African American communities in Chicago and elsewhere; architect Berlin designed several of them. This handsome building with bold piers and recessed spandrels features a subdued Arts & Crafts style on the interior, with a brick fireplace, oak trim, cast-metal balusters, ceramic tile, wood floors, and a 1936 mural by African American artist William Edouard Scott.

WABASH AVE. YMCA INTERIOR

103| Double House for Albert Mendel and James S. Toppan
3558–3560 S. King Dr.
1889, WILSON, MARBLE & LAMSON

104| Double House for John F. Finerty and Edward J. Mendel
3562–3564 S. King Dr.
1888, WILSON, MARBLE & LAMSON

Four rusticated limestone facades combine Gothic and Romanesque motifs.

105| John F. Whiting House
3568 S. King Dr.
1888, THOMAS W. WING

The great Queen Anne bay is robust and highly detailed, studded and pointed, serving as a signpost for this narrow house.

106| John J. Hill House
3608 S. King Dr.
1889, E. CLARKE JOHNSON

This dignified Romanesque house has a beautiful entry, with a curving wall of small beveled windows, whose squares are echoed in the paneled wooden door.

107| John Tait House
3614 S. King Dr.
1888, HOLABIRD & ROCHE

The simple facade is made interesting by the lively use of a single material, a variegated brownstone. This house was an excellent advertisement for its owner, a stone collector, as well as for its architect, Tait's brother-in-law, Martin Roche. Both men lived here. Roche documented the construction in his diary.

108| John McCormick House
3616 S. King Dr.
1886, CHARLES E. KAUFFMANN

An idiosyncratic stone house, it has the tall, narrow proportions of the much earlier Gothic Revival.

109| Ida B. Wells House
(*Martin Meyer House*)
3624 S. King Dr.
1889, JOSEPH A. THAIN

This house is noteworthy for its 1920s owners. Wells was a black-rights activist and a crusading journalist who exposed the ugly reality of lynching. Her husband was the lawyer and journalist Ferdinand Lee Barnett. This was the earliest and largest of a succession of somewhat fussy

Romanesque houses on this stretch of the boulevard by a prolific but little-known architect.

110| Charles H. Nichols House
3630 S. King Dr.
1886, RAE & WHEELOCK

Queen Anne exuberance is manifested in rich detailing in pressed metal, an elaborate iron porch rail, carved brownstone animal masks and terra-cotta panels, a foundation of novel Hummelstown striated brownstone, two very different oriels, and a high picturesque roof.

111| D. Harry Hammer House
3656 S. King Dr.
1885, WILLIAM W. CLAY

It's the king of King Dr., a rare surviving example of the large houses that anchored many corners of the South Side boulevards by the 1890s. Striking color—orange brick, brownstone, and copper trim—enhances the more usual corner features of two impressively gabled sides and an angled tower element. Terra-cotta detailing, wrought-iron grilles, and art glass abound on this design, by one of the era's most flamboyant architects.

112| South Park Baptist Church
3722 S. King Dr.
1953, HOMER G. SAILOR

Here is a lingering postwar blast of Art Moderne styling. A broad expanse of narrow bright orange brick, broken only by the vertical thrust of a limestone tower, dips inward at the street-level portal and outward as ribbon windows are introduced to light the office wing.

113| Wendell Phillips High School
244 E. Pershing Rd.
1902, WILLIAM B. MUNDIE FOR JENNEY & MUNDIE

Hailed as one of Chicago's first modern high schools, Wendell Phillips was intended to grace an affluent neighborhood with a "stately presence" of red brick and a colossal Ionic order and to provide "everything that can vitalize and energize the school work." Initially it had forty-eight classrooms fully equipped for the manual and academic training of 1,700 students, a gymnasium, a lunchroom, spaces for extracurricular activities, and—recognizing the new notion that schoolhouses should be civic centers open day- and year-round—a large auditorium.

D. HARRY HAMMER HOUSE

BRIDGEPORT/CANARYVILLE/
MCKINLEY PARK/
BACK OF THE YARDS

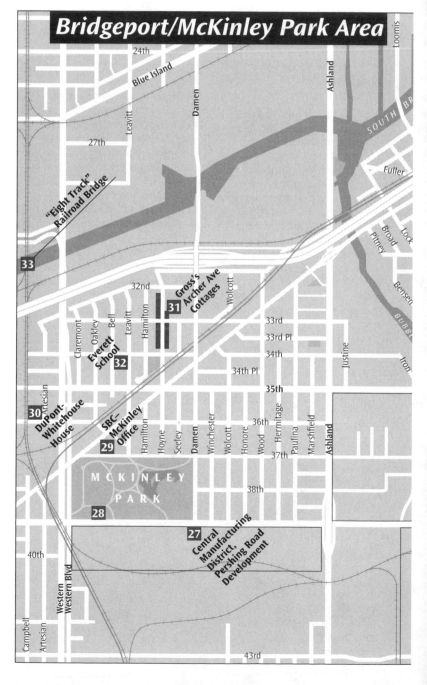

Bridgeport/McKinley Park Area

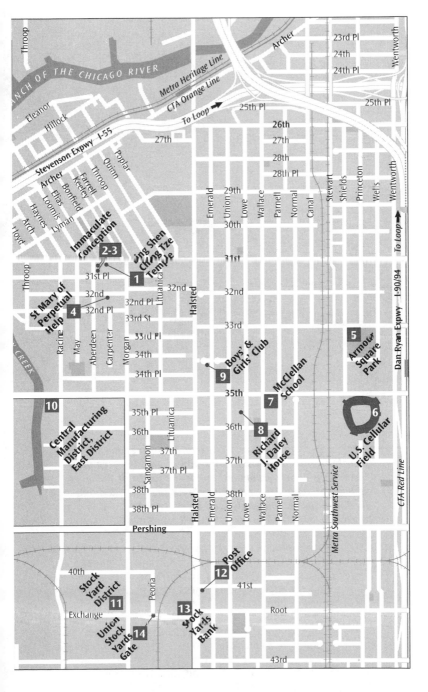

Throop

BRANCH OF THE CHICAGO RIVER

Eleanor

Hillock

Metra Heritage Line

CTA Orange Line

Archer

To Loop →

23rd Pl

24th

24th Pl

25th Pl

Wentworth

Stevenson Expwy I-55

Archer

Throop
Quinn
Poplar
Farrell
Keeley
Elias
Bonfield
Loomis
Lyman
Haynes
Arch
Hoid

27th

26th

27th

28th

28th Pl

Emerald
Union
Lowe
Wallace
Parnell
Normal
Canal

29th

30th

Stewart
Shields
Princeton
Wells
Wentworth

To Loop →

Immaculate
Conception

Ung Shen
Ching Tze
Temple

2-3

1

31st Pl

31st

Lituanica

32nd

St Mary of
Perpetual
Help

4

32nd

32nd Pl

32nd Pl

Halsted

32nd

33rd St

33rd

Dan Ryan Expwy I-90/94

Throop

Racine
May
Aberdeen
Carpenter
Morgan

33rd Pl

33rd Pl

34th

34th Pl

Boys' &
Girls' Club

9

5

Armour
Square
Park

CREEK

35th

35th

McClellan
School

7

10

Central
Manufacturing
District,
East District

Lituanica

Sangamon

35th Pl

36th

37th

37th Pl

36th

37th

8

Richard
J. Daley
House

6

U.S. Cellular
Field

CTA Red Line

Metra Southwest Service

Halsted

Emerald
Union
Lowe
Wallace
Parnell
Normal

38th

38th

38th Pl

Pershing

40th

Stock
Yard
District

Peoria

Exchange

11

Post
Office

12

41st

Halsted

Root

13

Stock
Yards
Bank

Union
Stock
Yards
Gate

14

43rd

Canaryville/Back of the Yards Area

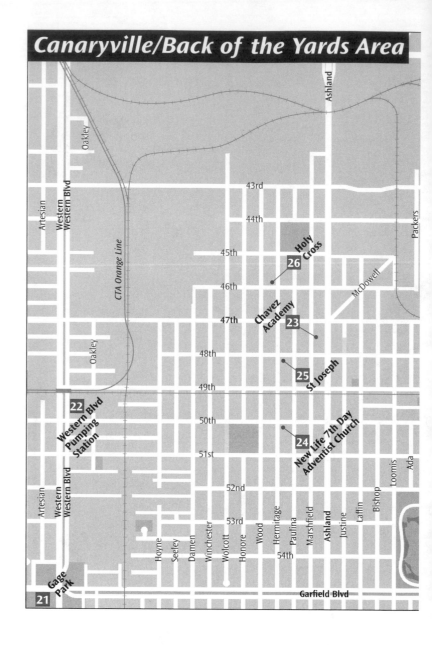

> "They were left standing upon the corner, staring; down a side street there were two rows of brick houses, and between them a vista: half a dozen chimneys, tall as the tallest of buildings, touching the very sky—and leaping from them half a dozen columns of smoke, thick, oily, and black as night . . . stretching a black pall as far as the eye could reach."

THE GREAT SMOKING CHIMNEYS THAT SO AWED AND ULTIMATELY OVERWHELMED the young Lithuanian immigrants in Upton Sinclair's *The Jungle* (1906) no longer blacken the sky over this industrial neighborhood. But church spires still rise above modest homes and apartments, commemorating the waves of immigrants that poured into the South Side beginning in the 1830s, pursuing the American Dream. The Lithuanians were only the most recent group in Sinclair's time. Canal construction and railroads, stockyards and slaughterhouses, steel mills and breweries had already brought the Irish, then the Germans, followed by Slavs and Balts in the 1880s and 1890s and, after World War II, Hispan-

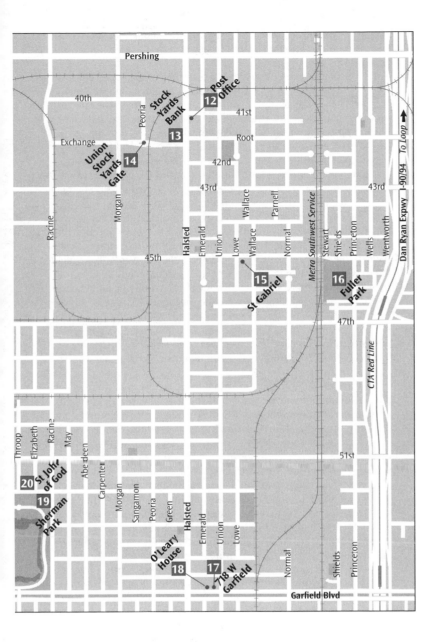

ics and African Americans. These waves of newcomers flowed into an area rigidly divided by the physical barriers of the river branches, the canal, railroad tracks and embankments, and, later, highways, creating a series of neighborhoods whose boundaries are more visibly defined than in many other parts of Chicago.

Bridgeport, the first community to be settled, is one of the city's oldest. The Illinois & Michigan Canal, begun in 1836 to connect the Chicago and Illinois rivers, offered construction jobs to Irish and later German immigrants, who settled along the Chicago River's south branch at the northern terminus of the canal. Originally referred to as Hardscrabble, Bridgeport was named for the port area created by a bridge near Ashland Ave. built so low that it obstructed river traffic and made it necessary to unload and reload cargo. The narrow diagonal streets perpendicular to Archer Ave. still retain the atmosphere of this workers' community; though not the original shanties and frame houses, many are quite old and little changed. After the canal opened in 1848, Bridgeport attracted many new industries, primarily slaughterhouses and supporting businesses. The area east of Halsted St. and north of 31st St. was incorporated into the City of Chicago in 1853; the area from 31st to 39th Sts. was annexed in 1863.

The opening of the Union Stock Yards in 1865 consolidated Chicago's livestock trade between 39th and 47th Sts., Halsted St. and Racine Ave. The Union Stock Yard & Transit Company (backed largely by the railroads' investors) purchased 345 acres and laid the Chicago Junction Railway to link the yards with all major lines entering the city: "as far as the eye can reach," Sinclair wrote, "there stretches a sea of pens. And they were all filled—so many cattle no one had ever dreamed existed in the world . . . The sound of them here was as of all the barnyards of the universe." The stockyards and train lines that served them created physical barriers that still mark the divisions between ethnic and racial groups.

To the east of the yards' entrance at Halsted St. and Exchange Ave., Canaryville was originally middle-class. The Swifts, Libbys, and Hutchinsons settled on Emerald Ave., and the Irish community gradually expanded south from Bridgeport to be closer to the stockyards. St. Gabriel's parish was established in 1880 to serve them. In the 1890s the upwardly mobile began to move south, with many of them building large houses on Garfield Blvd., still within easy distance of the stockyards.

West of Bridgeport lies McKinley Park, also settled by Irish canal workers. Originating as a farming community in the 1840s, it grew into an industrial center incorporated as the Town of Brighton in 1851. Samuel E. Gross created several developments of small-scale workers' cottages that still exist.

By the 1870s, after the introduction of the refrigerated railroad car, packing plants had moved to the area immediately west of the yards, creating Packingtown, isolated by industrial sites, garbage dumps, and railroads. Living conditions in Back of the Yards epitomized the worst of industrialization. The noxious stench of Bubbly Creek, a stagnant fork of the river's south branch, permeated the area. Essentially an open sewer, it carried offal from the slaughterhouses and packinghouses. There were few or no services in these congested neighborhoods.

It was to these inhumane working and living conditions that progressive reformers turned their attention. Their emphasis on open areas, or "breathing spaces," led to the development of a significant type of public space, the neighborhood park, which combined recreational and social facilities. Not surprisingly, due to the severity of local conditions, the South Park Commission led the way. After their first success with McKinley Park, the Commission hired D. H. Burnham & Co. and the Olmsted Brothers to design a series of small parks, of which Sherman and Fuller are perhaps the finest examples.

By 1900 another industry was contributing to the area's development. In 1890 a group of investors headed by Frederick H. Prince had purchased the Union Stock Yard & Transit Co. and the Chicago Junction Railway and, in 1902, began to acquire land north of the yards. In 1905 they announced the Central Manufacturing District (CMD), a planned industrial site that housed manufacturing and warehousing operations and employed thousands of local residents.

Since the 1950s, there has been little new construction. The Union Stock Yards closed in August 1971, after years of declining trade. The eclipse of related industries and the replacement of most of the International Amphitheater's uses by McCormick Place effectively curbed the area's growth. The stockyards' land was turned over to the CMD for development into the Donovan Industrial Park. Low warehouse and light industrial buildings now sprawl out behind the old Stock Yards Gate, a sanitized relic of a pungent past. The neighborhood retains the varied ethnic character established throughout its development.

—KATHLEEN NAGLE

Archer Ave. began as a path along the Illinois & Michigan Canal, named for canal commission member Colonel William B. Archer. Bridgeport's oldest neighborhoods are nearby and still contain early cottages and flats. Through Bridgeport, the Adlai E. Stevenson Expressway (I-55) runs along the site of the canal.

1| Ling Shen Ching Tze Temple (*Immanuel Presbyterian Church*)
1035 W. 31st St.
1892, BURNHAM & ROOT

Look past the recent additions to see the severe simplicity of one of John Wellborn Root's last designs.

2| Immaculate Conception Roman Catholic Church
3101 S. Aberdeen St.
1909, HERMANN J. GAUL AND ALBERT J. FISCHER

3| Immaculate Conception Rectory
3109 S. Aberdeen St.
1901, ALBERT J. FISCHER

The charming rectory creates a pleasing Gothic ensemble with the slightly later church, founded to serve a German parish.

4| St. Mary of Perpetual Help Roman Catholic Church
1035 W. 32nd St.
1889–1892, HENRY ENGELBERT

The dull brick Romanesque exterior gives no hint of the lavishly shaped and decorated nave enriched with stations of the cross and stained-glass windows with Polish inscriptions. Three domes sail high above, the central one lit by a ring of lantern windows and sheathed in a copper roof. The nave is further decorated with fine scagliola work, three elaborate marble altars, and a suspended pulpit topped by a wedding-cake cupola.

5| Armour Square Park
33rd to 34th Sts., from S. Wells St. to S. Shields Ave.
1904–1905, OLMSTED BROS.
1905, FIELD HOUSE,
D. H. BURNHAM & CO.

Of the parks proposed by the South Park Commission in 1903, eight were to be "small parks" of up to 100 acres, and six were to be "squares" of ten acres or less. The site plan is unusual for its placement of the field house across one corner; the park was designed symmetrically along this diagonal axis. Unfortunately, subsequent alterations have diminished the visual impact of this plan, and the poured-in-place concrete field house is unremarkable.

6| U.S. Cellular Field (*Comiskey Park*)
333 W. 35th St.
1991, HELLMUTH, OBATA & KASSABAUM

This 43,000-seat stadium, built strictly for White Sox baseball, bows to tradition but responds chiefly to modern sports realities. With eighty-four skyboxes, broad walkways, and assorted clubs and restaurants it seems more like a suburban mall than a city ballpark. All the seats are blue, to achieve what the stadium architects call a "subtle womb of color," like the "great old stadiums." Each seat was positioned by computer and is free from visual obstructions to the playing field. To keep the sight lines clear, supporting columns were placed outside the lower deck. This, plus the need to make room for skyboxes, resulted in a steep upper-deck pitch of 34 degrees (compared to 14 degrees in the lower deck).

The designers were mindful of their directive, "Don't turn your back on old Comiskey," the beloved home of the White Sox since 1910. The most obvious tribute to the old park is the series of broad, reddish-brown concrete arches (filled with colored glass) that form the exterior structure. Unfortunately, they are often obstructed from view by large ramps. With its self-conscious regard for both baseball history and modern economics, new Comiskey Park may have tried too hard, but its heart is in the right place— when it can be glimpsed.

7| George B. McClellan Public School
3505 S. Wallace St.
1881, ARCHITECT UNKNOWN
1896, SOUTH ADDITION, AUGUST FIEDLER

One of Chicago's oldest remaining public schools is in the popular, all-purpose, pedimented Italianate style.

8| Richard J. Daley House
3536 S. Lowe Ave.
1939, ERIC E. HALL

Although built after the 1920s vogue for bungalows had peaked in Chicago, this is a modest continuation of the formula. Daley was born at 3602 and was a lifelong resident of S. Lowe Ave.

9| Boys' & Girls' Clubs of Chicago—Louis L. Valentine Unit
(*Valentine Chicago Boys' Club*)
3400 S. Emerald Ave.
1938, CHILDS & SMITH

The entrance to this Art Moderne temple to boyhood adventure is flanked by replicas of Alaskan Coastal Indian totem poles and is topped by a terracotta overhang suggesting a cliff cave entrance. The apparently romantic name is actually that of the donor, a retired furniture manufacturer.

BOYS' & GIRLS' CLUBS OF CHICAGO—
LOUIS L. VALENTINE UNIT

10| Central Manufacturing District, East District
35th St. to Pershing Rd., Morgan St. to Ashland Ave.
1905–1915

The first American industrial park was established here in 1905 by a group of investors headed by Frederick H. Prince. They began acquiring land, mostly vacant except for three established industries, in 1902. By 1908 the 265 acres were serviced by individual switch-tracks from the Chicago Junction Railways, and utilities, services, and street improvements were in place. The CMD built manufacturing buildings and warehouses designed by their own staff architects and engineers (until 1921 by S. Scott Joy, then A. Epstein) and financed the lease or purchase by tenant companies. The CMD's architectural standards dictated design basics, whether companies used Joy's services or another architect's. Among the companies that located here were William Wrigley, Jr., Co., American Luxfer Prism Co., Westinghouse Electric & Manufacturing Co., and Spiegel, May, Stern & Co. (later Spiegel, Inc.).

11| Stock Yard District
Clustered around the intersection of Halsted St. and Exchange Ave. are only a few structures recalling the days when Chicago was "hog butcher to the world." The city's location made it a natural trading hub and, after the invention of the refrigerated car, a processing center for many forms of livestock—a position further consolidated by the opening in 1865 of the Union Stock Yards. The stockyards attracted not only workers and livestock traders but also tourists, who marveled at the scale and efficiency of the operation. But by the mid-twentieth century, business was declining as trucking supplanted rail for transporting livestock products, and modern,

decentralized packinghouses sprang up farther west. When the stockyards closed in 1971, the CMD began development of Donovan Industrial Park, a series of single-story, light-industrial buildings.

12| U.S. Post Office— Stock Yards Station
4101 S. Halsted St.
1936, HOWARD L. CHENEY

The U.S. eagle meets the stock-yards cow on reliefs ornamenting this small Art Moderne post office.

13| Stock Yards Bank Building
W. Exchange Ave. and S. Halsted St.
1924, A. EPSTEIN

Philadelphia's Independence Hall inspired this anchor of the business district.

14| Union Stock Yards Gate
850 W. Exchange Ave.
1879, ATTRIBUTED TO BURNHAM & ROOT

A lonely symbol of the vanished stockyards, the Stone Gate is almost certainly the work of Burnham & Root, who did other projects for the stockyards' own-

ers (including a house for its organizer, John B. Sherman, Burnham's father-in-law). This tripartite gate marked the entrance to the animal pens, providing a large central arch for livestock and wagons flanked by pedestrian arches. The great copper roof concealed an iron grille that was lowered each night over the main arch; the southern arch has its original, hinged iron gate. Above the central arch is a relief head of another Sherman, the steer that won the American Fat Stock show in 1878.

15| St. Gabriel Roman Catholic Church
4501 S. Lowe Ave.
1887, BURNHAM & ROOT

St. Gabriel's parish was organized by the Reverend Maurice J. Dorney in 1880 to serve Irish immigrant stockyard workers. According to Harriet Monroe, Root's biographer and sister-in-law, Root felt that "people too often attempted to build 'little cathedrals,' instead of being content with parish churches . . . the Romanesque was more suitable [than the Gothic style]

ST. GABRIEL ROMAN CATHOLIC CHURCH

to a simple home of the people." Monroe considered the church one of Root's most characteristic works, "as personal as the clasp of his hand."

The preliminary design was for a centrally planned stone church with a low, massive tower over the crossing. For cost reasons the material was changed to brick, and the tower was moved to the side but made much higher. The north facade was altered in 1914 by the addition of a portico and vestibule; it originally had a taller arch in the middle, as seen in the window arrangement on the west transept. In 1944 the 160-foot tower was shortened by fourteen feet and lost its high pyramidal roof. The interior of the church has been substantially altered.

16| Fuller Park
45th St. to 46th Pl., S. Princeton Ave. to S. Stewart Ave.
1905, OLMSTED BROS.
1910, BUILDINGS,
D. H. BURNHAM & CO.

The creative plan fits many recreational amenities onto a tight site, even making use of the railway embankment for spectators' seating. The buildings are of poured-in-place concrete with integrally cast ornament, an economical alternative to cut stone known as "marblecrete" or "popcorn concrete" due to the roughness of the aggregate. Two open

loggias connect the field house to the U-shaped gymnasium to the north. The wading pool to the east of the buildings, a common feature in Olmsted parks, is more intact than most.

17| 718 W. Garfield Blvd.
(*Chicago Bicycle Club*)
1898, ANDERS G. LUND

Club members departed from this late Queen Anne house on velocipede tours and other jaunts.

JAMES J. O'LEARY HOUSE

18| James J. O'Leary House
726 W. Garfield Blvd.
1901, ZACHARY T. DAVIS

O'Leary, whose mother owned Chicago's most famous cow, was a gambling king who operated from his saloon across from the Stock Yards. His busy, châteauesque house has Renaissance details such as the dormers and balustrades.

FULLER PARK FIELD HOUSE

SHERMAN PARK FIELD HOUSE

19| Sherman Park
W. 52nd St. to Garfield Blvd.,
S. Racine Ave. to S. Loomis St.
1904, OLMSTED BROS.
1904–1905, BUILDINGS,
D. H. BURNHAM & CO.

This sixty-acre oasis achieves
the pastoral qualities of much
larger parks by the gentle berm-
ing of its perimeter, which
creates a tranquil spot focusing
on a large lagoon. The extensive
use of water is unusual in the
South Parks but was suitable for
this poorly drained site. Unlike
Jenney's picturesque, frilly-
edged lagoons in the great West
Side parks, the landscape here
is tranquil, broad, and modern.
The island encircled by the
lagoon accommodates playing
fields, reached by four bridges
at the corners of the park.
The buildings at the north end
create a strong axis and an impressive view from the south.
The field house contains an auditorium, meeting rooms, and a
refectory.

20| St. John of God
Roman Catholic Church
1234 W. 52nd St.
1920, HENRY J. SCHLACKS

The park's green foreground
beautifully sets off the grand
balance of the Renaissance
facade, a Schlacks masterpiece.
Although dimly lit, the barrel-
vaulted nave is worth a look.
Trompe l'oeil painting imitates
mosaics and marble.

21| Gage Park
W. 54th to W. 56th Sts.,
Claremont to Artesian and
Maplewood Aves.
1905, SOUTH PARK COMMISSION
1928, FIELD HOUSE AND POOL
HOUSE, SOUTH PARK COMMISSION

At the southwest corner of the
original plan for the South Park
System, Gage Park anchors the
corner of Garfield and Western
Blvds. The field house follows
the earlier pattern established
by D. H. Burnham & Co. Tom
Lea's interior mural (1931) depicts a pioneer scene.

22| Western Blvd. Pumping
Station
4919–4943 S. Western Blvd.
1927, CHARLES KALLAL, CHICAGO CITY
ARCH.; G. DWIGHT TOMPKINS, ASST.
ENG., DEPT. OF PUBLIC WORKS

This dignified little box, encrusted with shells and crabs,
is a decorative cap on a large
node of Chicago's vast water
system. At an intake crib three
miles out into the lake, fresh
water enters a tunnel running
to the South District Filtration
Plant. The purified water flows
west through tunnels to this
station (and others), where
steam engines pump it to the
area between Pershing Rd.,
Indiana Ave., 79th St., and the
city limits, as well as to some
southwestern suburbs. This
station is one of the city's
largest, with a capacity of
320 million gallons a day.

CÉSAR CHAVEZ ACADEMY

23| César Chavez Academy
4747 S. Marshfield Ave.
1993, ROSS BARNEY + JANKOWSKI

Joyful and playful, this building creates wonder and a heightened sense of anticipation to see what is inside. To meet the challenges of a long, narrow lot, the architects sited the building to shelter classrooms and outdoor play spaces from the alley to the east. A cube-shaped library pavilion topped with a translucent fiberglass skylight and a gymnasium/lunchroom building are broken out from the single-loaded classroom wing, saving on structural costs while enlivening the design. Bright colors and differing shapes suggest that school can be fun.

24| New Life Seventh Day Adventist Church
(*Sts. Cyril and Methodius*)
5001 S. Hermitage Ave.
1913, JOSEPH MOLITOR

25| St. Joseph Roman Catholic Church
1729 W. 48th St.
1914, JOSEPH MOLITOR

26| Holy Cross Roman Catholic Church
1736 W. 46th St.
1913–1915, JOSEPH MOLITOR

Molitor, an immigrant from Bohemia, shaped the Back of the Yards skyline with this trio of towered churches. The Renaissance-style New Life Seventh Day Adventist, formerly a Bohemian Catholic church, is anchored by an Italian bell tower. The Romanesque St. Joseph, which still houses a Polish congregation, has twin Baroque towers and an exquisitely lit interior with rings of brass sconces and a leaded-glass chandelier. The Renaissance Revival Holy Cross features Lithuanian religious iconography, including facade sculptures of favorite saints George and Isidore, and rises to twin Baroque towers.

27| Central Manufacturing District, Pershing Rd. Development
Pershing Rd. between Ashland and Western Aves.

The brick and terra-cotta water tower at Damen Ave., flanked by massive warehouses, stands as a powerful signpost for this early industrial park. By 1915 the original East District was full, and the CMD purchased the entire south frontage of 39th St. from Ashland Ave. to Western Ave., extending 700 feet south to the Chicago Junction Railways' classification yards. The site included the infamous Bubbly Creek, which the CMD and the Sanitary District filled in and replaced with a sewer in the early 1920s.

CENTRAL MANUFACTURING
DISTRICT—PERSHING RD.
DEVELOPMENT

The Pershing Rd. Develop-
ment extended the industrial-
park concept to include such
comprehensive services as a
central power plant and sprinkler plant, central union freight
stations, comprehensive railroad track arrangements, concrete traffic and utility tunnels
connecting all buildings, brick-
paved streets with water and
sewer systems, sidewalks and
grass parkways, and street
lighting. The standardized
buildings were constructed of
concrete or heavy timber, with
pressed brick and terra-cotta
exteriors. Most of them had six
stories and basement, with
uniform floor areas of about
30,000 square feet. They epito-
mize the multistory "gravity"
system of manufacturing, which
lost favor to the "straight line
production" system, which
called for single-story buildings.

The first four units of the
Union Freight Station and Loft
Buildings (A, B, C, D) were built
between March and October
1917, faster than any other
buildings of their kind. The
CMD architect for almost all of
the work up to 1921 was S. Scott
Joy, who was replaced by engineer A. Epstein in July 1921.

The view down Pershing Rd.
is impressive, with the water
tower dominating the mile of
cohesive development. The
terra-cotta logos such as Goodyear Tire & Rubber Co., Albert
Pick & Co., and L. Fish Furniture
Co. identify the original tenants.

28 | McKinley Park
**Damen Ave. to Western Ave.,
37th St. to Pershing Rd.**
1902–1906, SOUTH PARK
COMMISSION
1916, FIELD HOUSE, SOUTH PARK
COMMISSION

The lovely foreground to the
Pershing Rd. Development is
idyllic McKinley Park, the first
of the South Park Commission's
neighborhood parks and a
model for the progressive park
movement. Designed by the
commissioners and staff, the
park was a laboratory for testing
new ideas, with a swimming pool
and changing rooms equipped
with showers—an important
amenity for occupants of cold-
water buildings. When the commission retained the Olmsted
Brothers and D. H. Burnham &
Co. to design the next series of
parks and park buildings, their
designs were partially a result of
experiments here.

Planning began in 1900
under South Park Commission
General Superintendent J. Frank
Foster. The park was enlarged in
1906 to include a lagoon, bathhouse, wading pool, and music
pavilion (demolished); the old
swimming pool building is currently a service building. The
field house was designed by
staff architects, who adapted
models originated by D. H.
Burnham & Co. The Damen Ave.
Viaduct truncated the park's
eastern end. President McKinley, assassinated in 1901, is
commemorated with a statue
by Charles J. Mulligan.

29 | SBC—McKinley Office
(*Chicago Telephone Company*)
2240 W. 37th St.
1917, HOLABIRD & ROCHE
1938, ADDITION, HOLABIRD & ROOT

Eschewing their "Phone Company Georgian" formula, the
architects delivered a Renais-

sance Revival building with rusticated base and Venetian windows. When first built, the building was only three stories tall and three bays (the easternmost) wide.

30 | DuPont-Whitehouse House
3558 S. Artesian Ave.
1876, OSCAR COBB & CO.

This unusually well documented house is a relic of the era when manufacturers stored explosives and gunpowder in what was then a sparsely populated area. E. I. DuPont de Nemours & Co.'s local agent, Junot J. Whitehouse, commissioned Cobb to design this residence, moved from 3616 S. Western Ave. in 1920. Gray cement parging partially conceals the original brick, but the incised stone hood moldings and the pedimented pavilion mark the house as a rare example of the Italianate country-house style that reigned from the 1850s through the 1870s.

31 | Samuel E. Gross's Archer Ave. Cottages
3200–3300 S. Hoyne Ave.
1887, ARCHITECT UNKNOWN

The P. T. Barnum of working-class housing, developer Gross boasted that these houses, "for the price, are the handsomest, best built brick cottages in the city, with stone and brick trim-mings, seven-foot basement, lake water and large lot." But, he admonished, "you must be quick if you want one at these prices and terms. They go fast. Go and see them and take your wife with you." He was right: they sold out. But fortunately there was almost always another one under construction; his annual catalog for 1889 cites five developments in the Bridgeport/Back of the Yards area alone.

The uniformity of the long rows of rooflines hints at the development's original cohesiveness. The plain facades have served as blank canvases for widely varied remodelings. In this modest subdivision, Gross not only provided the lot and infrastructure but built the house as well, selling it for $1,050–$1,200, payable on "easy terms" of $50–$100 down and $8 a month (equivalent to the cost of renting). To save excavation and drainage costs, houses had basements aboveground; exterior stairs led to the main level, comprising a parlor, kitchen, two bedrooms, and a small pantry. The street level was later raised, placing the first floor virtually at grade. Many are now reached by a small footbridge between the sidewalk and the front door.

SAMUEL E. GROSS'S ARCHER AVE. COTTAGES

32| **Edward Everett Public School**
3419 S. Bell Ave.
1891, JOHN J. FLANDERS
1914, ARTHUR F. HUSSANDER

The corner towers of this archetypal Queen Anne school are visible from many nearby bridges and viaducts.

A worthwhile side trip lies west along the Adlai E. Stevenson Expressway (I-55) from Western Ave., where a textbook collection of bridges spans the Sanitary & Ship Canal north of the highway. These are of special note.

33| **"Eight Track" Railroad Bridge**
Chicago Sanitary & Ship Canal,
west of Western Ave.
1901, 1909–1910, SCHERZER
ROLLING LIFT BRIDGE CO.

The inclined top chords of these parallel single-leaf bridges and their alternating orientations create a dramatic sculptural

profile. The bridges, no longer movable, alternated north–south to better distribute the weight and allow room for each span's operating machinery.

34| **Illinois Central Gulf**
Railroad Bridge
Chicago Sanitary & Ship Canal,
east of Kedzie Ave.
1899

This is the easternmost of the canal's seven remaining center-pivot swing bridges, rare examples of Chicago's first generation of movable-bridge design. They opened and closed to river traffic by rotating around a central pier. Although now fixed, the stone pivot and its turntable are clearly visible. The drawbacks of this bridge type were the narrowing of the navigable space and the danger that vehicles, pedestrians, or trains would fall off the road edge after the bridge had swung open.

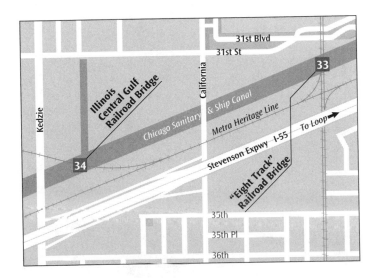

OAKLAND/KENWOOD

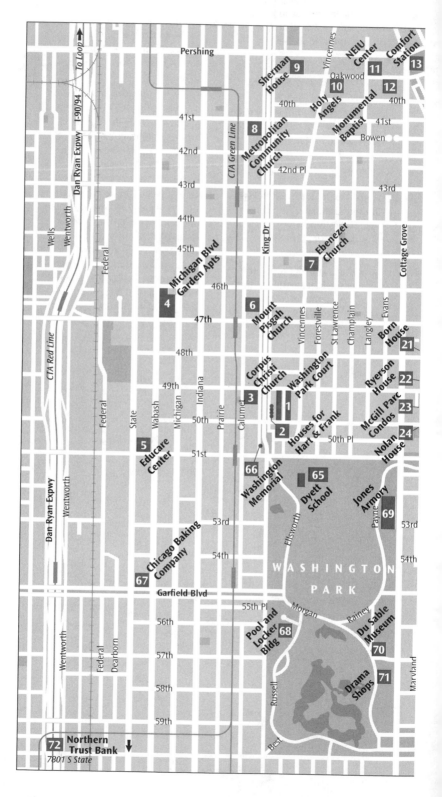

Pershing

Vincennes

NEIU Center

Comfort Station

Sherman House

9

Oakwood

11

13

To Loop

I-90/94

Dan Ryan Expwy

10

Holy Angels

Monumental Baptist

12

40th

40th

41st

Bowen

41st

8

Metropolitan Community Church

42nd

CTA Green Line

42nd Pl

43rd

43rd

44th

Cottage Grove

45th

Michigan Blvd Garden Apts

Ebenezer Church

7

King Dr

46th

4

6

Mount Pisgah Church

Evans

47th

Vincennes

Forestville

St Lawrence

Champlain

Langley

Born House

21

48th

Corpus Christi Church

3

Washington Park Court

Ryerson House

22

49th

1

McGill Parc Condos

23

Indiana

50th

2

Houses for Hart & Frank

Nolan House

24

Prairie

Calumet

5

Educare Center

50th Pl

51st

66

Washington Memorial

65

Dyett School

Jones Armory

69

Wabash

Michigan

State

52nd

Payne

53rd

53rd

Chicago Baking Company

54th

54th

67

W A S H I N G T O N

Garfield Blvd

Ellsworth

55th Pl

Morgan

P A R K

56th

Pool and Locker Bldg

68

Rainey

Du Sable Museum

Wentworth

Federal

Dearborn

57th

70

Russell

58th

Drama Shops

71

Marlyand

59th

72

Northern Trust Bank

Best

7801 S State

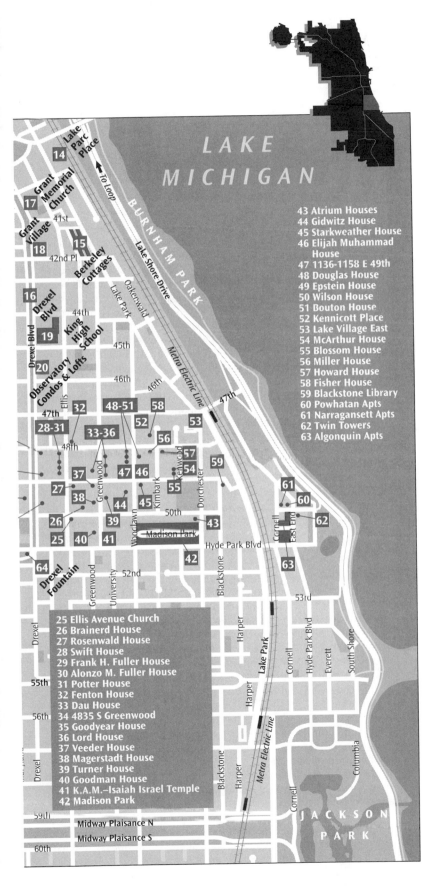

LAKE MICHIGAN

14

Lake
Parc
Place

Grant
Memorial
Church

17

Grant
Village

18

41st

15

Berkeley
Cottages

42nd Pl

16

Drexel
Blvd

44th

19

King
High
School

Drexel Blvd

20

Observatory
Condos & Lofts

46th

Ellis

47th

32

28-31

48th

48-51

33-36

58

52

53

56

47

46

57

54

59

37

Greenwood

44

45

Kimbark

55

Kenwood

Dorchester

27

38

50th

43

61

60

Cornell

East End

62

26

39

25

40

41

Madison Park

42

Hyde Park Blvd

63

64

Drexel
Fountain

52nd

Greenwood

University

Blackstone

Harper

Lake Park

Cornell

Hyde Park Blvd

Everett

South Shore

53rd

Drexel

55th

56th

Drexel

Blackstone

Harper

Metra Electric Line

Cornell

Columbia

JACKSON
PARK

59th

Midway Plaisance N

Midway Plaisance S

60th

Oakenwald

Lake Park

Lake Shore Drive

BURNHAM PARK

Metra Electric Line

To Loop

47th

43 Atrium Houses
44 Gidwitz House
45 Starkweather House
46 Elijah Muhammad
   House
47 1136-1158 E 49th
48 Douglas House
49 Epstein House
50 Wilson House
51 Bouton House
52 Kennicott Place
53 Lake Village East
54 McArthur House
55 Blossom House
56 Miller House
57 Howard House
58 Fisher House
59 Blackstone Library
60 Powhatan Apts
61 Narragansett Apts
62 Twin Towers
63 Algonquin Apts

25 Ellis Avenue Church
26 Brainerd House
27 Rosenwald House
28 Swift House
29 Frank H. Fuller House
30 Alonzo M. Fuller House
31 Potter House
32 Fenton House
33 Dau House
34 4835 S Greenwood
35 Goodyear House
36 Lord House
37 Veeder House
38 Magerstadt House
39 Turner House
40 Goodman House
41 K.A.M.–Isaiah Israel Temple
42 Madison Park

OAKLAND/KENWOOD

THE RESIDENTIAL DEVELOPMENT OF THIS AREA REFLECTS TWO CONTRASTING ideals: the urban boulevard house and the country retreat. Chicago's earliest boulevards were established just north of Washington Park, and their popularity with wealthy homeowners set the pattern for other areas. Along the lake, Kenwood's large wooded lots created a secluded suburban setting that contrasted with the see-and-be-seen urbanity of the broad streets to the north and west. The fate of these neighborhoods began to diverge sharply as early as 1900, and today they have little in common. While the boulevards offer examples of past grandeur in decayed circumstances, the enclave of Kenwood south of 47th St. has retained its affluent character to a remarkable degree.

West of the lakefront communities of Oakland and Kenwood are the neighborhoods of Grand Boulevard, which lies north of 51st St., and Washington Park, which includes the park itself and the streets to its west. Kenwood was the first to develop and closely followed Paul Cornell's establishment in 1853 of the village of Hyde Park. In 1856 Jonathan A. Kennicott, a dentist and horticulture enthusiast, bought eight acres of countryside near the Illinois Central Railroad tracks south of 43rd St. and named his estate Kenwood after his mother's ancestral home in Scotland. A few wealthy families joined him in the area, and when the railroad added a station at 47th St. in 1859, it was named Kenwood.

In 1861 the area east of State St. from 39th to 63rd Sts. was incorporated as the township of Hyde Park. Separated by 43rd St. and sharing a western boundary at Cottage Grove Ave., Oakland and Kenwood grew as desirable lakefront suburbs throughout the next three decades. Kenwood outshone all its competitors, however, and was already known by 1874 as the Lake Forest of the South Side.

The neighborhoods west of Cottage Grove Ave. developed slightly later, receiving their impetus from the establishment of the boulevard and park system. Frederick Law Olmsted's 1870 plan for the South Park Commission, established in 1869, included a grand circuit of boulevards. Garfield Blvd. was planned as a link to the West Parks, and to the north Grand (now Martin Luther King, Jr., Dr.) and Drexel Blvds. were connected by Oakwood Blvd. to form a four-mile circuit popular for fashionable carriage promenades. In 1874 improvements began on Grand Blvd., which soon became lined with mansions whose styles were emulated by the more modest houses on the side streets. The area north of 51st St. was built up by the 1890s, when development spread south to the Washington Park neighborhood.

The 1890s witnessed the decline in fashionableness of the mature neighborhoods. The City of Chicago had swallowed the township of Hyde Park in 1889, and the elevated train line was extended to Jackson Park in time for the 1893 World's Columbian Exposition. Apartment construction began to exceed that of single-family houses, and the original Protestant residents moved on to other neighborhoods. By 1900 Grand Blvd. had become a second settlement area for German Jews, and large houses in Oakland were being subdivided to provide apartments for Irish stockyard workers. The establishment of a streetcar line on 47th St. created a commercial strip that forms the present boundary between Oakland and Kenwood. To the south, Kenwood remained an exclusive neighborhood of single-family houses, and its status became more closely tied to that of Hyde Park.

During and after World War I, the Great Migration of African Americans from the rural South greatly increased population densities in the traditional African American neighborhoods to the west and south. By the 1920s middle-class African Americans began to move into the Grand Boulevard and Washington Park neighborhoods, creating a thriving city within a city. Known variously as Black Metropolis or Bronzeville (the latter commemorated in the title of a 1945 collection of poems by Gwendolyn Brooks), the original community centered on 35th and State Sts. Later in the decade it moved to 47th St., where the old Regal Theatre hosted nationally famous entertainers. In the wake of another African American influx that occurred during World War II, overcrowding spilled into this neighborhood from the north, and middle-class residents fled. Decay overtook the area in the 1950s, and the absence of large institutions left a vacuum filled by the Chicago Housing Authority, which constructed the Federal St. corridor, a narrow but long strip of high rises west of State St. The sad result is that these two neighborhoods had among the highest concentrations of public housing in Chicago while many privately owned buildings continued to succumb to abandonment and decay. On the positive side, local institutions such as churches, social agencies, and community groups began fighting back with subsidized housing of their own. A public-private initiative was established to provide funds for the repair and renovation of boulevard properties. This encouraged similar activities on adjacent streets.

Oakland had shared the fate of its impoverished neighbors to the north and west. Success stories included the upgrading of a pair of CHA lakefront properties and the subsequent reform of public housing. Hundreds of new market-rate and subsidized housing units began appearing in the late 1990s. South of 47th St., Kenwood has benefited from its proximity to Hyde Park and the stabilizing influence of the University of Chicago, which spurred extensive redevelopment in the 1950s and 1960s. Kenwood remains one of the city's most racially integrated and economically stable neighborhoods.

—JOSEPH D. LA RUE WITH LAURIE MCGOVERN PETERSEN

1| Washington Park Court
**S. Washington Park Ct.
from 49th to 50th Sts.**
1895–1905, HENRY L. NEWHOUSE, AND OTHERS
ANDREW SANDEGREN, AND OTHERS

The T. G. Dickinson real estate company created this one-block subdivision in 1892, specifying a ten-foot setback and selling the lots in clusters of two or three. Andrew and John M. Dubach developed at least twenty-five of the fifty-one lots, and Henry L. Newhouse was their architect for at least twelve designs. They set the tone of the street as an enclave of brick and limestone houses with common porch and cornice lines (third stories are often mansarded or recessed) and, almost invariably, with bay fronts.

2| Houses for the Hart & Frank Co.
4941–4959 S. Martin Luther King, Jr., Dr.
1901, PEABODY & BEAULEY

The subdivision that created Washington Park Court allowed Robert & Emil Hart and their partner in a mortgage-loan business, David L. Frank, to create an unusually harmonious streetscape. Details are drawn from Gothic and Châteauesque idioms in three cases and from Classical and Renaissance Revival in the other four.

3| Corpus Christi Roman Catholic Church
4920 S. Martin Luther King, Jr., Dr.
1916, JOSEPH W. MCCARTHY
1976, RESTORATION, PAUL J. STRAKA

Built by affluent Irish Catholics just before racial change swept the South Side boulevards, this twin-spired Renaissance Revival church has support buildings grouped around an adjacent cloister. The church features a magnificent coffered ceiling, a main altar that is a mosaic replica of that in Leonardo da Vinci's *The Last Supper*, and windows by F. X. Zettler depicting the church's members in procession with Pope Pius X. This was McCarthy's first major commission; as Cardinal Mundelein's favorite architect, he went on to build twenty-eight churches, most of them during the 1930s.

4| Michigan Boulevard Garden Apartments
4610–4646 S. Michigan Ave. and 40–78 E. 47th St.
1929, ERNEST A. GRUNSFELD, JR.

Sears, Roebuck & Co. president Julius Rosenwald, one of Chicago's greatest philanthropists, planned the project to provide sound housing within the black community and a small return on investment. His inspiration was post–World War I municipal housing in Vienna (for example, the Metzleinstaler-Hof, 1921–1923; the more famous Karl-Marx-Hof, 1927–1930, was contemporaneous with Rosenwald's

effort). The architect was his nephew, who shared the design of numerous subsequent housing developments; his son-in-law, Alfred K. Stern, was in charge of the plan. For decades the apartments were extremely attractive to working-class renters, but the profit was only 2.4 percent over seven years on a $2.7 million investment. After Rosenwald's death in 1932, Stern conceded that low-income housing required government support.

Five-story walls of cream brick are relieved with red brick banding. Storefronts line the base along 47th St., and eight Art Moderne terra-cotta doorways lead into a spacious inner court of gardens and playgrounds that provides access to the 421 walk-up apartments.

5| Educare Center
5044 S. Wabash Ave.
2000, TIGERMAN MCCURRY ARCHITECTS

This villagelike complex is designed to provide a sense of security in an impoverished neighborhood formerly dominated by towers of public housing. Intended as a national model for day-care centers, it has a large interior courtyard surrounded by colorful classroom pavilions with sheltering gable roofs.

MICHIGAN BOULEVARD GARDEN APARTMENTS

6| Mount Pisgah Missionary Baptist Church
(*Sinai Temple*)
4622 S. Martin Luther King, Jr., Dr.
1909–1912, ALFRED S. ALSCHULER

Alschuler capitalized on lessons learned as a tyro on Adler's Isaiah Temple to establish a widely copied formula for Reform synagogues: separate but linked community and worship buildings isolated daily activities from formal weekly ones. The freely adapted Classical styling was regarded as expressing the broad views of the congregation. The temple proper is a wide, shallow space, cross-axial to a broad lobby and entrances. Alschuler conceded that they were modeled on those of the Auditorium Theater, emulating the ease of ingress and egress.

7| Ebenezer Missionary Baptist Church
(*Isaiah Temple*)
4501 S. Vincennes Ave.
1899, DANKMAR ADLER

Adler's last commission was an auditorium-style synagogue featuring a vaulted ceiling to create the "very nearly perfect" acoustics for which he was famous. Although the building sold out stylistically to the Georgian Revival, it was innovative in elevating school and community services from the basement to a separate but connected annex.

8| Metropolitan Community Church
(*41st Street Presbyterian Church*)
4100 S. Martin Luther King, Jr., Dr.
1891, JOHN T. LONG
1913, SOUTH GABLE REMODELING, CHARLES S. FROST

A Romanesque church, with a Greek-cross plan to accommodate semicircular seating, presents gable end walls with round arched openings that get smaller as they move up the variegated red sandstone faces.

Oakwood Blvd. provides a short, spacious link between Grand Blvd. (now King Dr.) and Drexel Blvd.

that allowed carriages and riders to make a four-mile grand circuit to Washington Park without backtracking. As a major thoroughfare, it was a natural location for neighborhood churches.

9| Isaac N. W. Sherman House
442 E. Oakwood Blvd.
1889, BURNHAM & ROOT

The severity of John Wellborn Root's Monadnock Building imbues this large house, which is dominated by a huge front gable.

10| Holy Angels Roman Catholic Church
607 E. Oakwood Blvd.
1991, SKIDMORE, OWINGS & MERRILL

When fire destroyed his 1896 church, Father George Clements recruited SOM to donate this design for the nation's first church heated and cooled by solar energy. Simplicity, flexibility, and energy efficiency characterize this concrete basilica with a pitched roof supported by exposed steel trusses. Stucco covers virtually all of the street elevations, while the south side has a glass-filled wall and a roof of solar collectors. The architects, the artists (Englebert Nveng, Richard Hunt, and Roy Lichtenstein), and most of the contractors worked pro bono.

11| Northeastern Illinois University—Center for Inner City Studies
(*Abraham Lincoln Center*)
700 E. Oakwood Blvd.
1898–1903, FRANK LLOYD WRIGHT AND DWIGHT H. PERKINS
1903–1905, DWIGHT H. PERKINS
1971–1976, RENOVATION, HEARD & ASSOCS.

A crusty client with a broad agenda of social reform had a major hand in shaping this high-rise settlement house. Jenkin Lloyd-Jones, Wright's uncle, was pastor of nearby All Souls Unitarian Church (demolished) and conceived the idea for this religious social center. Wright lived nearby when he first arrived in Chicago in 1887; it was

NORTHEASTERN ILLINOIS UNIVERSITY—CENTER FOR INNER CITY STUDIES

at his uncle's church that he met his first wife, Catherine Tobin.

Pastor Lloyd Jones's interests ranged far beyond Unitarianism; his desire for a nonsectarian facility led him to shun historic styles for his church center. The brick base housed activity rooms and a library. The second and third floors, the site of the galleried auditorium-church, were identified by groups of windows united vertically. The three upper floors, devoted to meeting rooms, the pastor's quarters, and a top-floor gymnasium and domestic science rooms, were marked by decreasing window heights. Strong corner piers strengthen the elevations; the dark floor-line bandings cross the piers only four times. The 1970s renovation made extensive changes to suit the university's needs.

12 | Monumental Baptist Church (*Memorial Baptist Church*)
729 E. Oakwood Blvd.
1899, PATTON, FISHER & MILLER

This is one of Chicago's finest surviving examples of the central lantern church, a type popularized by H. H. Richardson's Trinity Church in Boston.

13 | Mandrake Park Comfort Station
3900 S. Cottage Grove Ave./ 900 E. Pershing Rd.
2001, JOHNSON & LEE

The heavy timber structure that is typical of similar Park District buildings is embellished here

with African-inspired motifs, including semicircular porches at each end and geometric patterns in the masonry, metal grilles, and roof shingles. A high pitched roof makes the small building more prominent from the street.

14 | Lake Parc Place (*Victor A. Olander Homes and Olander Homes Extension*)
3939 & 3989 S. Lake Park Ave.
1953 AND 1956, SHAW, METZ & DOLIO
1991, RENOVATION, DAVID A. SAUER

In a remarkable demonstration of how the Chicago Housing Authority can redevelop its dreary 1950s properties, two fifteen-story Y-shaped public housing blocks, distinguished only by their views of Lake Michigan, were meticulously rehabbed, imaginatively landscaped, and secured with attractive fencing that emblazons their trendy new name. The project's success in attracting a mixture of market-rate and public housing tenants led the CHA to adopt ambitious plans for creating mixed-income communities out of all of its holdings. One of these, Lake Park Crescent (begun 2003, Campbell Tiu Campbell, master arch.), is immediately to the south, from 40th St. to 42nd Pl.

15 | Berkeley Cottages
4119 through 4169 S. Berkeley Ave.
4130 through 4162 S. Lake Park Ave.
1886–1887, CICERO HINE

Sited back to back are twenty-six freestanding cottages with wood "simple work" and detailed with Queen Anne elements. They are the survivors of a development that was entirely the work of the English-born Hine, who had a brief solo practice before becoming staff architect for the Brunswick, Balke, Collender Co., where he designed pool halls and bowling alleys.

16 | Drexel Blvd.

The most elegant of the South boulevards, Drexel was planned by Olmsted & Vaux in 1871 as a drive with traffic lanes on either side of a 100-foot-wide median, landscaped by H. W. S. Cleveland in 1873–1874 with winding walks and formal plantings. The land was donated by the Drexel banking family of Philadelphia, which reaped the benefits of greatly increased value for their South Side holdings.

17 | Grant Memorial African Methodist Episcopal Church
(*First Church of Christ, Scientist*)
4017 S. Drexel Blvd.
1897, SOLON S. BEMAN

The first of Beman's Christian Scientist churches, this set the Classical Greek pattern followed for decades. The architect of Pullman was invited to submit plans for a 1,500-seat church with a "large vestibule hall" on a long, narrow site. He modeled his main elevation on the Ionic facade of the Erechtheion, on the Acropolis in Athens. A foyer is wrapped around three sides of the building, providing stairways to a column-free auditorium fitted with theater seats under a low Tiffany "fish scale" dome. The plan and styling were hailed for creating a distinctive architecture for the young religion.

18 | Grant Village
4161 S. Drexel Blvd.
1991, JOHNSON & LEE

Grant Church developed this housing for senior citizens. To downplay the vertical block formula dictated by government guidelines while suiting the boulevard context, this eighty-unit, six-story development has two-tone brick banding and a third color on the windows, doors, grilles, and entrance canopy.

19 | Martin Luther King, Jr., High School
4445 S. Drexel Blvd.
1971, CAUDILL, ROWLETT & SCOTT

The concrete-framed school has its main entrance at the rear of an inner courtyard that flows toward the street, around the slab columns and beneath the second floor at the school's southwest corner. Glazing in metal frames is placed behind the deep columns as well as flush with their front planes. It was rehabbed and given a fresh color scheme in 2002.

20 | The Observatory Condos and Lofts
(*William E. Hale House*)
4545 S. Drexel Blvd.
1885–1886, BURNHAM & ROOT
1925, SCHOOL ADDITION, E. NORMAN BRYDGES

This vigorous house gets bigger as it rises, with ledges and corbels thrusting successive floors beyond the planes of lower ones.

21 | Moses Born House
4801 S. Drexel Blvd.
1901, FROST & GRANGER

This smooth-faced limestone house demonstrates Charles S. Frost's masterly adaptation of historic styles.

22 | Martin A. Ryerson House
4851 S. Drexel Blvd.
1887, TREAT & FOLTZ

This Richardsonian mansion was built shortly after the marriage of the lumber-fortune heir. The stern massiveness was at odds with the qualities of the French Impressionist masterworks that once hung here.

23 | McGill Parc Condominiums
(*John A. McGill House*)
4938 S. Drexel Blvd.
1890, HENRY IVES COBB
1928, ANNEX FOR CARRIE MCGILL MEMORIAL YWCA, BERLIN & SWERN
1982, CONVERSION TO APARTMENTS, CARL R. KLIMEK & ASSOCS.

Cobb's penchant for picturesque styles led him to a medieval French model for this limestone-clad mansion. McGill left the land, house, and funding to the YWCA, which added the annex of concrete and stucco with

MCGILL PARC CONDOMINIUMS

limestone details. After decades of use as a nursing home and cultist hangout, its derelict hulk was adapted to hold thirty-four units, some duplexed.

24 | John H. Nolan House
4941 S. Drexel Blvd.
1887, BURNHAM & ROOT

This simply massed house of variegated brick dates from the last phase of Root's career, when strong gable facades characterized much of his work. The satisfied client wrote, "You not only can make a good picture of a house, but . . . when it comes to delivering up the keys make a man happier . . . than he expected he would be."

25 | Ellis Avenue Church
(*William M. Crilly House*)
5001 S. Ellis Ave.
1908, WILLIAM CARBYS ZIMMERMAN

In partnership with John J. Flanders or on his own, Zimmerman designed houses in various styles for the Crilly family of developers and contractors. This one, in the mode of Richard E. Schmidt's Madlener House, might best be called Chicago School Residential.

26 | Ezra S. Brainerd House
1030 E. 50th St.
1867, ARCHITECT UNKNOWN

Built by a Civil War soldier with his mustering-out money, this back-lot frame house with an extensive veranda evokes Kenwood's era as a community of lakefront cottages.

27 | Julius Rosenwald House
4901 S. Ellis Ave.
1903, NIMMONS & FELLOWS

The head of Sears, Roebuck gave the commission for his house to the pair of masterful designers who became Sears's virtual house architects. Perhaps they had some trouble ratcheting down to the domestic scale; apart from such Prairie School elements as the hipped roof and Roman brick, it's otherwise a grand styleless galoot.

28 | Gustavus F. Swift House
4848 S. Ellis Ave.
1898, FLANDERS & ZIMMERMAN

This meat-packer's palazzo features sweeping verandas, Palladian windows, and at each corner of the third floor, a terra-cotta lion bearing a shield emblazoned with a huge S.

GUSTAVUS F. SWIFT HOUSE

29 | Frank H. Fuller House
4840 S. Ellis Ave.
1891, FREDERICK W. PERKINS

30 | Alonzo M. Fuller House
4832 S. Ellis Ave.
1890, FREDERICK W. PERKINS

A society architect who had been trained in Paris at the École des Beaux-Arts, Perkins combined rock-faced stone and steep roofs here for different effects. Alonzo's imposing house works tan stone into towers, gabled pavilions, and verandas wrapped around a hip-roofed core. Frank's uses a version of the gambrel roof, a battered rubblestone tower, and varied window shapes in a most pleasing, relaxed manner.

31 | Edward C. Potter House
4800 S. Ellis Ave.
1892, CHARLES S. FROST

This brick house has the double-tower facade popularized by Charles F. McKim at East Coast resorts.

32 | William T. Fenton House
1000 E. 48th St.
1899, WILSON & MARSHALL

All of the exuberance and care that were to characterize Benjamin H. Marshall's flamboyant career appear in this Georgian Revival study.

33 | J. J. Dau House
4807 S. Greenwood Ave.
1897, GEORGE W. MAHER

Designed while Maher was working on his innovative "Pleasant Home" in Oak Park, this house demonstrates that the style, drawn from Colonial American themes, was better served by a full-width veranda than by this hulking extended porch. The reddest of Roman brick is offset by limestone details, some of which introduce Maher's signature "motif-rhythm"—in this case a round shield and berry-laden leaves.

34 | 4835 S. Greenwood Ave.
2001, VINCI/HAMP ARCHITECTS

A modern, volumetric composition is executed in rich Roman brick.

35 | Charles A. Goodyear House
4840 S. Greenwood Ave.
1902, WILLIAM CARBYS ZIMMERMAN

An elaborate stone facade, which invokes such Tudor details as a broad arched entryway and a sort of strapwork on the second-story balustrade, also pairs lions within the tympanum and angels beside the arch.

36 | John B. Lord House
4857 S. Greenwood Ave.
1896, CHARLES S. FROST

Frost again proves his deftness at picking up on McKim, Mead & White's free handling of historical styles.

4835 S. GREENWOOD AVE.

37| Henry Veeder House
4900 S. Greenwood Ave.
1907, HOWARD VAN DOREN SHAW

The site allowed Shaw to place the entrance on the long 49th St. facade. It is organized symmetrically, with full-height bays at each end, but the door is off-center, occupying a space between four engaged columns. Shaw's free use of the Classical vocabulary comes through in the Lego-like metope blocks on the cornices.

ERNEST J. MAGERSTADT HOUSE

38| Ernest J. Magerstadt House
4930 S. Greenwood Ave.
1908, GEORGE W. MAHER

This is one of Maher's finest designs, sympathetic to the demands of a house whose narrow lot requires a side entrance. The carved poppies on the porch columns introduce the selected "motif-rhythm," repeated inside in moldings, mosaics, and leaded glass.

39| Edward H. Turner House
4935 S. Greenwood Ave.
1888, SOLON S. BEMAN

This Queen Anne house, built entirely of masonry, has the style's characteristic solidity but little of its picturesque variety.

40| William O. Goodman House
5026 S. Greenwood Ave.
1892, TREAT & FOLTZ

The heavy hand of Fritz Foltz robs all possible grace from the Italian palazzo form.

41| Kehilath Anshe Ma'ariv–Isaiah Israel Temple
(*Temple Isaiah Israel*)
1100 E. Hyde Park Blvd.
1924, ALFRED S. ALSCHULER
1973, ADDITION, JOHN H. ALSCHULER

To be "distinctive in style, majestic in appearance, and Jewish by suggestion," the architect chose "Byzantine lines" for this synagogue. The walls are polychromatic brick in various shapes laid up randomly to suggest old, sun-baked walls, while the smokestack is disguised as a minaret. The acoustically perfect auditorium has a spherical Guastavino dome and a stone treatment also intended to suggest age. The addition, designed by the architect's son, adds a chapel and social facilities around a courtyard, one wall of which is the old building. Brick is again the main material, but in a single shape.

KEHILATH ANSHE MA'ARIV–ISAIAH ISRAEL TEMPLE

42 | Madison Park
Entrances on S. Woodlawn and Dorchester Aves. between 50th and 51st Sts.

In December 1883 John H. Dunham, a sugar merchant and banker who had acquired considerable property in Kenwood shortly after the Civil War, filed a subdivision of his holdings. Mostly he provided spacious lots for suburban homes but—apparently emulating Stephen A. Douglas's Woodland and Groveland parks—he also set out very small city-size lots around an open common ground in Madison Park and along 50th St., which backs up against the park's lots. In no hurry to develop the tracts, he built a few rental houses along 50th St. but specified in his will that his holdings could not be sold until his last surviving heir had died. His heirs supplied a number of single and duplex rental houses, but major development was not possible until the 1920s, after the death of Dunham's daughters. Lots were then combined for the apartment construction that had become the norm in Hyde Park–Kenwood.

43 | Atrium Houses
1366–1380 E. Madison Park
1961, Y. C. WONG

The windowless street facades give no clue to the light-filled interiors of these Modernist town houses. Each is oriented to a glass-walled atrium deep within. With their severe tan brick walls, beams for cornices, and simple doors, they have been praised as "the ultimate in reticence." Wong also designed the town house complex at 1239–1243 in 1966.

44 | Willard Gidwitz House
4912 S. Woodlawn Ave.
1947, RALPH RAPSON AND JOHN VAN DER MEULEN

In the immediate postwar years, young architects wishing to build in the Modernist manner of Walter Gropius and Marcel Breuer sometimes chose traditional materials to ensure acceptance. Here the architects used the stone and wood of the existing house on the site—but completely transformed them. The rubble-stone of the recessed base came from the porch; stones from its huge piers were reused in the chimney. Other materials on the new elevations are wood panels, steel supports, and a glass-enclosed cantilevered steel stair.

45 | Charles H. Starkweather House
4901 S. Woodlawn Ave.
1902, HOWARD VAN DOREN SHAW

As with Shaw's Veeder House one block to the west, this house faces 49th St. and offsets the symmetrical composition of the main block with an off-center entrance. The entrance contrasts with the house's Georgian vocabulary with a pier-and-slab frame

ATRIUM HOUSES

JAMES DOUGLAS HOUSE

topped by a half-round window, creating a forced perspective that dramatizes the entrance.

46| Elijah Muhammad House
4855 S. Woodlawn Ave.

47| 1136–1158 E. 49th St.
1971, MEESI

The leader of the Nation of Islam, his children, and his chief aides occupied this complex, a mix of Mediterranean and Modernist elements. The stained-glass windows incorporate Muslim emblems.

48| James Douglas House
4830 S. Woodlawn Ave.
1907, HOWARD VAN DOREN SHAW

This is an archetype of the formal, symmetrical Georgian Revival house that set the pattern for countless thousands of center-entry Colonials. A balustrade originally ran the length of the roof ridge from chimney to chimney.

49| Richard Epstein House
4824 S. Woodlawn Ave.
1980, NAGLE, HARTRAY & ASSOCS.

The street side is a good neighbor, recalling the red brick and fanlight door of the Colonial Revival home it replaced. The private side is a sculptural facade of stucco and large window openings.

50| Thomas E. Wilson House
4815 S. Woodlawn Ave.
1910, HOWARD VAN DOREN SHAW

By 1910 Shaw was better known for palatial suburban estates than for city houses in Kenwood and Hyde Park. Despite its urban location, this house has much in common with those rambling, artfully asymmetrical Tudor-inspired country houses.

51| Christopher B. Bouton House
4812 S. Woodlawn Ave.
1873, ARCHITECT UNKNOWN

Built as a substantial country villa on a large tract, this is regarded as the least altered 1870s house in Kenwood–Hyde Park. While the window shapes suit the Italianate roofline, their framing suggests another, indeterminate, era.

52| Kennicott Place
4701 and 4721 S. Woodlawn Ave.
1991, DAVID SWAN

These eighteen single-family and duplex "cottage style" town houses have either high stoops or English basement entries (slightly below grade). The Queen Anne houses on Kimbark Ave. near 48th St. were their prototypes.

LAKE VILLAGE EAST

53| Lake Village East
4700 S. Lake Park Ave.
1971, HARRY WEESE & ASSOCS.;
EZRA GORDON–JACK M. LEVIN
ASSOCS., ASSOC. ARCH.

The slim silhouette changes constantly as you move around its thirty-eight brick-and-glass facets. The twenty-five-story tower with eight units per floor is one of several Ben Weese designs from the early 1970s that used "minimum perimeter" floor planning in response to demands for short corridors, interesting layouts, and structural economy. The multifaceted shape tends toward the circular—the most economical ratio of perimeter to floor area—but it also permits rectangular rooms. Window tiers were placed to capture the best lake and Loop views. The brick sections provide interior walls that welcome the large furniture that Modernist apartment design generally found anathema and did not accommodate. The additional cost of the irregular (rather than rectangular) concrete structural system was offset by the lower cost of enclosing a reduced perimeter.

54| Warren McArthur House
4852 S. Kenwood Ave.

55| George W. Blossom House
4858 S. Kenwood Ave.
1892, FRANK LLOYD WRIGHT

The most important of the "bootlegged" commissions done while he was working for Adler & Sullivan prove that the highly inventive Wright could create successful traditional designs. On the McArthur House, the gambrel roof and the porch with arched corner sections are Colonial motifs; the bay windows nestle under the eaves and gable as they do on Wright's own Oak Park home; and the molding dividing the brick base from the stucco wall becomes part of the entrance arch.

The Blossom House appears coldly symmetrical on the front, with three Palladian openings on each street facade, but its plan is not the traditional central hall. A living room and hall combination spans the midsection from north to south; the first floor ends in a glassy, sunlit, half-circular dining area

GEORGE W. BLOSSOM HOUSE

GEORGE L. MILLER HOUSE

in the southwest corner. Note the coach houses; McArthur's is a miniature of the main house set at an angle while Blossom's is a 1907 design exhibiting Wright's Prairie School themes.

56| George L. Miller House
4800 S. Kimbark Ave.
1888, GEORGE O. GARNSEY

Garnsey unabashedly appropriated and miniaturized H. H. Richardson's William Watts Sherman House (1874–1876) in Newport, R.I., almost detail for detail; he also advertised the plans for a double-house version of it in his magazine, *National Builder*.

57| Joseph H. Howard House
4801 S. Kimbark Ave.
1891, PATTON & FISHER

Every peak, plane, dormer, and turret above the stone base is sheathed in the pink slate tiles found on numerous Queen Anne houses in Hyde Park and Kenwood but in few other places locally.

58| Reynolds Fisher House
4734 S. Kimbark Ave.
1890, PATTON & FISHER

The thin, tight clapboarding, high gables, and eaveless roof edges of the architect's own house are all typical Patton & Fisher elements.

59| Chicago Public Library—
Blackstone Branch
(*T. B. Blackstone Memorial Library*)
4904 S. Lake Park Ave.
1902, SOLON S. BEMAN

Executed in Concord granite, this Beaux Arts cupcake was modeled after Beman's Merchant Tailors Building. That miniature domed temple, facing the lagoon at the 1893 World's Columbian Exposition, had pleased both Blackstone and a critic who found it "one of the beauty spots of that grand architectural display."

60| Powhatan Apartments
1648 E. 50th St.
1928, ROBERT DEGOLYER AND CHARLES L. MORGAN

61| Narragansett Apartments
1640 E. 50th St.
1929, LEICHENKO & ESSER WITH CHARLES L. MORGAN

In the late 1920s developers attempted a South Side version of the North Side's fashionable Streeterville on landfill holdings of the Chicago Beach Hotel (demolished), a longtime resort at the foot of Hyde Park Blvd. (51st St.). Five apartment buildings were begun before the stock market crash, the jewels of which are the Powhatan and the Narragansett; both were developed by the Garard Trust,

POWHATAN APARTMENTS

with Morgan in charge of aesthetics. Native American names and themes were chosen, primarily because they were untapped sources for the Art Deco designs that embellish the black bas-relief spandrels in the limestone bases and the earth-toned tile panels inserted in the upper elevations. The Narragansett also features goofy, flat-faced pachyderms solemnly gazing down on visitors and residents. The Powhatan is a reinforced-concrete structure with outer walls that could have been flat surfaces but are instead composed of a rhythmic pattern of projecting piers and mullions. It is the only large-scale Chicago apartment building that fully exhibits the "stripped architecture" of recessed spandrels and continuous piers introduced by Eliel Saarinen's entry for the Chicago Tribune Tower Competition of 1922.

62 | Twin Towers
1645 and 1649 E. 50th St.
1951, A. EPSTEIN

The recessed spandrels, finished in horizontally striated metal, stretch the entire distance between strongly expressed corner piers, contrasting with their earlier neighbors' vertical orientation.

63 | Algonquin Apartments
Hyde Park Blvd., E. 50th St., Cornell Ave., and East End Ave.
1950–1952, PACE ASSOCS. AND HOLSMAN, HOLSMAN, KLEKAMP & TAYLOR

These spartan, fourteen-story concrete-frame units perpetuate the Native American theme of the 1920s Chicago Beach development properties in name only. Ludwig Mies van der Rohe was associated with this complex—but removed his name when plans were altered to include first-floor residences.

64| Francis M. Drexel Fountain
Drexel Sq. (Drexel Blvd. and
E. 51st St.)
1881–1882, HENRY MANGER,
SCULPTOR

Drexel Sq. serves as a transition space between Drexel Blvd. and Washington Park, a truncated version of the sweeping approach envisioned by Frederick Law Olmsted. The family of the Philadelphia financier donated the land and the fountain.

65| Walter H. Dyett Middle School
555 E. 51st St.
1972, DAVID N. HAID

Between 1968 and 1973 the Public Buildings Commission, headed by architect Jacques C. Brownson, hired private architects to build twenty-six inner-city schools according to careful guidelines seeking universal modules and flexible plans. Park sites were sought to give under-privileged children the advantages of landscaped suburban schools, provoking protests from open-land advocates. The courts upheld the controversial invasion, but only three schools were eventually built on Chicago Park District property.

Sensitive to arguments against the site, Haid designed two large-span steel structures with identical modules and dark, fully glazed skins with the transparency to fit into their green setting; the front building is below grade. The instructional building accommodates four "learning houses" for team teaching around two open courts. It is connected underground to the sports facility, which is spanned by four plate girders.

66| George Washington Memorial
S. Martin Luther King, Jr., Dr.
at E. 51st St.
1904, DANIEL CHESTER FRENCH
AND EDWARD CLARK POTTER

French's rather stolid figure, in contrast to Potter's spirited horse, is meant to indicate Washington's rocklike support of freedom. The work is a second casting of a Paris monument.

67| Chicago Baking Company,
International Brands
Corporation
(*Schulze Baking Company*)
40 E. Garfield Blvd.
1914, JOHN AHLSCHLAGER & SON

Paul Schulze planned his bakery as part of an aggressive campaign to sell his "better than homemade" bread to tradition-bound, cleanliness-conscious housewives. Five-story walls of glazed cream terra cotta suggest hygienic conditions. Blue lettering, stringcourses of rosettes, and foliated cornice ornament all carry associations of sunlight, fresh air, and purity, as do the 700 windows grouped in unified ranges. The ornamentation is abstract, Sullivanesque, and modern, not overtly classical and old, because Schulze's product relied on modern technology.

Washington Park
(*South Park*)
E. 51st St., S. Martin Luther King,
Jr., Dr., E. 60th St., and
S. Cottage Grove Ave.
1871 PLAN, OLMSTED & VAUX,
LANDSCAPE ARCHS.; EXECUTED
BY H. W. S. CLEVELAND

Washington Park was designed in 1871 by Olmsted & Vaux as the Upper Division of a great "South Park" that also included a Lower Division (now Jackson Park) and a connecting strip, the Midway Plaisance. In contrast to Jackson Park's swampy lakefront site, Washington Park was flat prairie, which would not "elsewhere be recognized as well adapted to the purpose." It was also to be the terminus of three boulevards, Garfield from the west and Drexel and Grand (now Martin Luther King, Jr., Dr.) from the north.

WASHINGTON PARK AND MIDWAY PLAISANCE

Making an advantage of what they had, Olmsted & Vaux established in the park's northern half a "large meadowy ground," 100 acres of open space perceptible without break from all three approaches. The southern end was to be more verdant, with a pond that would connect—via a canal down the Midway—with the lagoon in Jackson Park. In 1872 park commissioners entrusted the plan's execution to an Olmsted associate, H. W. S. Cleveland, stipulating that he avoid "extensive alterations of the natural surface," thereby putting an end to the Midway's waterway linkage.

Washington Park today retains its naturalistic character, with buildings restricted to the perimeter and with the main traffic lanes raised slightly, so that visitors must descend into the park proper. The casting pond and the islanded lagoon are the sole reminders of the intended emphasis on water.

68| Pool and Locker Building
(*Refectory*)
Pool and Russell Drs.
1891, D. H. BURNHAM & CO.
1992, EXTERIOR RESTORATION,
A. EPSTEIN & SONS WITH DUBIN,
DUBIN & MOUTOUSSAMY AND
HASBROUCK PETERSON ASSOCS.

This elegant, Classically derived refectory was built near the site chosen by Olmsted for a pavilion to overlook his "Southopen Ground." It features a deep ground-level colonnade and four open rooftop corner towers. The much-needed restoration was done in conjunction with the creation of adjacent pool facilities.

69| General Richard L. Jones
Armory
5206–5310 S. Cottage Grove Ave.
1928, PERKINS, CHATTEN &
HAMMOND

The cubic, hard-edged profile of one of the nation's largest urban armories is softened by a crisply detailed bas-relief frieze of soldiers, vertical fluting, giant pilasters every fourth bay, and towers marking the entrances on the north and east sides. Ancient and modern (World War I) sentries emerge from the stone to guard the vehicular entrance.

70| DuSable Museum of African-
American History
(*South Park Commission—*
***Administration Building*)**
740 E. 56th Pl.
1910, D. H. BURNHAM & CO.
1992, ADDITION, WENDELL
CAMPBELL ASSOCS.

The most elaborate of the firm's concrete buildings designed for the South Parks shows how a poured material can be manipulated to imitate a carved one; only the terra-cotta Ionic capitals at the main entrance are added on. The lightly sanded precast-concrete addition duplicates the original's color and fenestration, adding galleries, a theater, and exhibit space.

71| Drama and Rigger Shops (*Stable*)
Payne Dr. south of 57th St.
1880, BURNHAM & ROOT

This rare roundhouse stable and its attendant buildings, all built of random ashlar Joliet limestone, survive as the scenery shops for Chicago Park District theaters.

72| Northern Trust Bank South Financial Center
7801 S. State St.
1996, JOHNSON & LEE

The Prairie School style is a nod to the neighborhood's residential character while the clock tower gives the building high visibility from the Dan Ryan Expressway. Loggias and overhanging roofs mitigate solar heat gain on the south and west exposures.

HYDE PARK/SOUTH SHORE

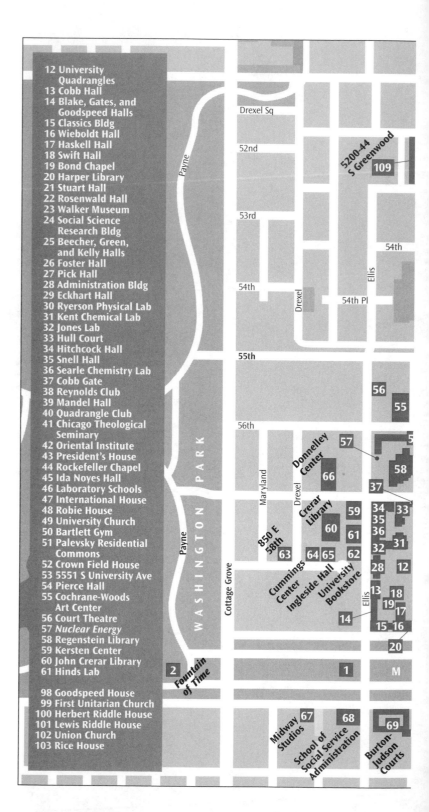

12 University
   Quadrangles
13 Cobb Hall
14 Blake, Gates, and
   Goodspeed Halls
15 Classics Bldg
16 Wieboldt Hall
17 Haskell Hall
18 Swift Hall
19 Bond Chapel
20 Harper Library
21 Stuart Hall
22 Rosenwald Hall
23 Walker Museum
24 Social Science
   Research Bldg
25 Beecher, Green,
   and Kelly Halls
26 Foster Hall
27 Pick Hall
28 Administration Bldg
29 Eckhart Hall
30 Ryerson Physical Lab
31 Kent Chemical Lab
32 Jones Lab
33 Hull Court
34 Hitchcock Hall
35 Snell Hall
36 Searle Chemistry Lab
37 Cobb Gate
38 Reynolds Club
39 Mandel Hall
40 Quadrangle Club
41 Chicago Theological
   Seminary
42 Oriental Institute
43 President's House
44 Rockefeller Chapel
45 Ida Noyes Hall
46 Laboratory Schools
47 International House
48 Robie House
49 University Church
50 Bartlett Gym
51 Palevsky Residential
   Commons
52 Crown Field House
53 5551 S University Ave
54 Pierce Hall
55 Cochrane-Woods
   Art Center
56 Court Theatre
57 *Nuclear Energy*
58 Regenstein Library
59 Kersten Center
60 John Crerar Library
61 Hinds Lab

98 Goodspeed House
99 First Unitarian Church
100 Herbert Riddle House
101 Lewis Riddle House
102 Union Church
103 Rice House

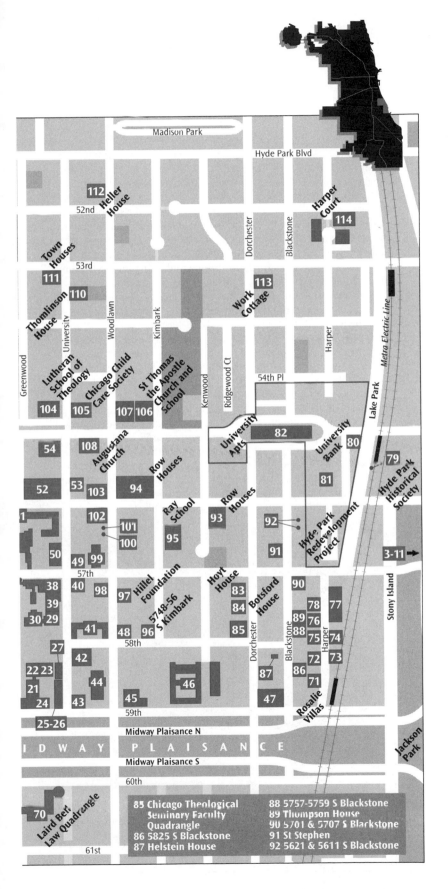

Madison Park

Hyde Park Blvd

112 Heller House

52nd

Harper Court

114

Dorchester

Blackstone

Town Houses

53rd

111

Thomlinson House

110

Work Cottage

113

Woodlawn

Kimbark

Metra Electric Line

Greenwood

University

Lutheran School of Theology

Chicago Child Care Society

St Thomas the Apostle Church and School

104

105

107 **106**

Kenwood

Ridgewood Ct

54th Pl

Harper

54

108

Augustana Church

Row Houses

University Apts

82

University Bank

80

Lake Park

79

Hyde Park Historical Society

52

53

103

94

81

1

102

101

100

Ray School

Row Houses

93

95

92

91

Hyde Park Redevelopment Project

3-11

50

49 **99**

57th

Hillel Foundation

5748-56 S Kimbark

Hoyt House

90

Stony Island

38

40

98

97

83

Botsford House

78 **77**

39

84

89 **76**

30 **29**

85

Dorchester

Blackstone

88

75

Harper

74

41

48

96

58th

72

73

27

87

86

22 23

42

44

46

47

71

21

24

43

45

59th

Rosalie Villas

Jackson Park

25-26

Midway Plaisance N

I D W A Y   P L A I S A N C E

Midway Plaisance S

60th

70

Laird Bell Law Quadrangle

61st

85 Chicago Theological Seminary Faculty Quadrangle
86 5825 S Blackstone
87 Helstein House

88 5757-5759 S Blackstone
89 Thompson House
90 5701 & 5707 S Blackstone
91 St Stephen
92 5621 & 5611 S Blackstone

HYDE PARK/SOUTH SHORE

THE WORLD'S COLUMBIAN EXPOSITION OF 1893 HAD A POWERFUL AND LASTING impact on Chicago's urban development, and nowhere was this felt as strongly as in Hyde Park. The enormous annexation of 1889, in which the city swallowed up huge townships like Lake View, Jefferson, and Hyde Park, was prompted in part by the theory that the larger the city's population, the better its chances of being named the site of the fair. Once Chicago had won this prize, in April 1890, civic pride demanded the creation of institutions befitting the nation's second most populous city. One of these was the University of Chicago, founded in 1890. Other preparations for the exposition included the long-postponed landscaping of Jackson Park (chosen as the site of the fair), the extension and expansion of public transportation from the Loop, and massive construction of hotels and apartments. Hyde Park would never again be the quiet suburb envisioned by its founder.

In 1853 Paul Cornell, a Chicago lawyer newly arrived from New York, bought 300 acres of lakefront land between 51st and 55th Sts. and deeded sixty of those acres to the Illinois Central Railroad in return for a train station located in his new community of Hyde Park. He knew that his hopes for a prosperous residential development would depend in equal measure on perceived seclusion from urban woes and easy access to the city's commercial and cultural institutions. Hyde Park was incorporated as a township in 1861 (its boundaries vastly exceeding those of the small settlement by that name) and as a village in 1872. Originally concentrated around 53rd St. and Hyde Park Blvd. (near the train station at 53rd St. and Lake Park Ave.), commercial development continued to follow the train's southward path, with districts emerging along Stony Island Ave. and East 71st, 75th, and 79th Sts.

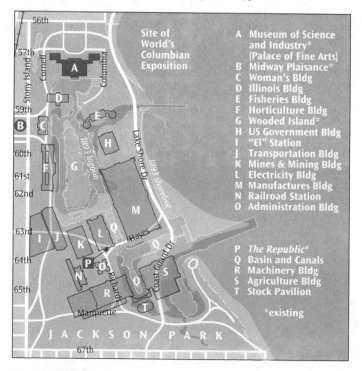

Site of World's Columbian Exposition

A Museum of Science and Industry* (Palace of Fine Arts)
B Midway Plaisance*
C Woman's Bldg
D Illinois Bldg
E Fisheries Bldg
F Horticulture Bldg
G Wooded Island*
H US Government Bldg
I "El" Station
J Transportation Bldg
K Mines & Mining Bldg
L Electricity Bldg
M Manufactures Bldg
N Railroad Station
O Administration Bldg

P The Republic*
Q Basin and Canals
R Machinery Bldg
S Agriculture Bldg
T Stock Pavilion

*existing

Local businesses were the only nonresidential users of land in Hyde Park; industry was deliberately excluded. Cornell hoped that a large institution would become an anchor for the area, but this did not come to pass until after his death, when the University of Chicago was founded. The lakefront location, although swampy and not very attractive in its unimproved state, gave the area great potential as both a resort location and a year-round suburban community. Hotels were among the earliest large buildings, and housing ranged from villas and cottages to row houses and apartment buildings.

The area's most ambitious landscape improvements resulted from the 1869 creation of the South Park Commission, of which Cornell was a member. The commission established an extensive system of connected parks and landscaped boulevards, and hired Frederick Law Olmsted and Calvert Vaux to design the enormous South Park (now Washington and Jackson parks and the connecting Midway Plaisance). Although several features of the original plan were altered or omitted, the overall character of these parks is remarkably close to Olmsted's pastoral vision.

The slow pace of land acquisition and a lack of money delayed the landscaping of Jackson Park. Not until it was chosen in 1890 as the site for the World's Columbian Exposition did work progress—but then at a breakneck pace that made up for two decades of neglect. The White City created here was intended to show how parks, boulevards, and buildings could be planned in a unified manner that would bring harmony and order to the chaos of the industrial city. It sowed the seeds of the City Beautiful movement, which culminated in Daniel H. Burnham's 1909 Plan of Chicago. Two of the plan's features that had the greatest impact on this area were the dedication of all lakefront land to public use and the creation of wide thoroughfares to facilitate access to and from the central city.

The increasing ease of transportation to the Loop—frequent train service would be supplemented in the twentieth century by automobile and bus access—brought greater density to Hyde Park and also spurred development to the south. The South Shore became a fashionable middle-class area, with an elegant country club and a planned subdivision called Jackson Park Highlands.

The diverse architecture of Hyde Park comprises excellent examples of almost every urban building type and style, from modest frame cottages to luxurious lakefront high rises. The area is particularly rich in houses from the 1890s, the era of its most feverish development. Many of them were designed by architects later grouped as the Chicago School, a term that includes both the Prairie School and less radical colleagues such as Pond & Pond and Howard Van Doren Shaw. All were experimenting with new forms and rethinking what the house should be. Frank Lloyd Wright's Robie House is the most outstanding example.

Some of Hyde Park's finest houses were designed for faculty members of the university, which has continued to play a pivotal role in the community and was instrumental in the large-scale redevelopment of the 1950s. Its reassuring presence has helped to maintain the desirability of the Hyde Park neighborhood for the last century. It will, no doubt, continue to do so for at least the next hundred years.

—R. STEPHEN SENNOTT

1| Midway Plaisance
Between E. 59th & 60th Sts
from Washington Park east to Jackson Park

Although its name is a contradictory mix of the tawdry and the elegant, the Midway Plaisance is actually a broad boulevard with a vast sunken grassy median. The first half of its name resulted simply from its location midway between the two large parks that it connected. Its use as a grounds for the Ferris wheel and other amusements during the 1893 World's Columbian Exposition—in contrast to the high-minded, educational quality of the exhibits farther east—made "Midway" synonymous with carnival grounds everywhere. A plaisance was one of Frederick Law Olmsted's landscape types and referred to a pleasure grounds with winding, shrub-lined paths for strolling and picnicking. Ironically, the Midway was never developed with such a landscape. Nor did it ever become the great water link between parks that Olmsted had envisioned, with its median canal planned to unite Jackson Park's lagoons to a lake in Washington Park. Today it serves as a broad greensward that sets off the neo-Gothic grandeur of the University of Chicago campus.

2 | *Fountain of Time*
Midway Plaisance at entrance to Washington Park
1922, LORADO TAFT
BASE DESIGN,
HOWARD VAN DOREN SHAW
2002, RESTORATION, CHICAGO PARK DISTRICT AND BAUER LATOZA STUDIO

One of Chicago's most impressive monuments anchors the west end of the Midway, which Taft wanted balanced by a Fountain of Creation at the east end. Inspired by lines from an Austin Dobson poem:

Time goes, you say? Ah no!
Alas, Time stays, we go. . . .

Taft depicts a hooded figure leaning on a staff and observing a panorama of humanity that rises and falls in a great wave. The statue's ambitious theme, size, and scope overshadow its original purpose, which was to commemorate a century of peace between England and the United States that resulted from an 1814 treaty resolving Canadian border conflicts. Taft envisioned the group sculpted from marble, but the material's high cost and vulnerability to Chicago's weather made it impractical. Bronze, his second choice, was also prohibitively expensive, leading to the selection of a pebbly concrete aggregate. The hollow-cast concrete form reinforced with steel was cast in an enormous, 4,500-piece mold. Taft himself appears among the figures that line the west side of the monument; he is wearing a smock, head bowed and hands clasped behind him.

Jackson Park
(*South Park*)
E. 56th-67th Sts., S. Stony Island Ave. to Lake Michigan
1871, OLMSTED & VAUX
1895, OLMSTED, OLMSTED & ELIOT

Although Olmsted & Vaux had prepared a comprehensive plan for the South Parks in 1871, Jackson Park did not receive major improvements for two

FOUNTAIN OF TIME

decades. The primary features of the plan were aquatic: a channel cut through the beach would link a 200-foot pier with a series of lagoons that would lead to canals along the Midway and eventually to a small lake in Washington Park. During the 1870s dredging of the swampy land began, and in the 1880s a permanent beach was completed from 56th to 59th Sts. and later paved with granite blocks down to 63rd St. When planning began in 1890 for the World's Columbian Exposition, it finally created an impetus to complete work on Jackson Park, the main site of the fair. Frederick Law Olmsted designed the fairgrounds, and his vision of a watery paradise was fulfilled with a ceremonial basin called the Court of Honor, canals, a lagoon with a wooded island, and a pond. The only tangible reminders of the fair's glory are the Museum of Science and Industry, the Lagoon and Wooded Island with its Japanese garden, and Daniel Chester French's statue *The Republic.*

The third and most influential plan for the park was drawn up by Olmsted, Olmsted & Eliot in 1895. The theme of water was central to the plan and can still be seen despite the loss of several links between ponds and lagoons. Improvements were made on a grand scale, so that by 1904 Jackson Park contained beautifully scenic greens, shrubbery, trees, walks, bridges, and driveways. The encroachment of the automobile has destroyed much parkland, but the essential character remains.

3 | Museum of Science and Industry
(*Palace of Fine Arts*)
S. Lake Shore Dr. at E. 57th St.
1893, D. H. BURNHAM & CO.
1929–1940, RECONSTRUCTION, GRAHAM, ANDERSON, PROBST & WHITE
1998, GARAGE AND UNDERGROUND ADDITION, E. VERNER JOHNSON
AND ASSOCS., A. EPSTEIN AND SONS INTERNATIONAL, JACOBS/RYAN ASSOCS.

Built as the Palace of Fine Arts of the World's Columbian Exposition, this is the sole remnant of the great 1893 fair and its only fireproof structure. Designed by Charles B. Atwood (1849–1895) to display paintings and sculpture assembled from all over the world, the Palace of Fine Arts was the greatest of Atwood's structures at the exposition.

Following the fair, the building housed the Field Museum of Natural History until 1920. It then stood empty and deteriorating while architect George W. Maher, who called its neo-Classical architecture "unequaled since the Age of Pericles," spearheaded an effort by the AIA to save it. In 1930 Julius Rosenwald, philanthropist and president of Sears, Roebuck & Co., contributed $5 million to rehabilitate the structure and to establish a world-class museum. The rebuilding, completed in 1940, produced a stylistic anomaly. The original exterior of staff, a hemp-and-plaster compound, was replaced exactly in marble and limestone, while the interior received Art Moderne streamlining.

Handsome changes at the museum's imposing grand entrance facade occurred in 1998. An unsightly 1,300-car surface lot was transformed by Jacobs/Ryan into six acres of green space. The garage was transferred below; exhibition space was expanded, and a dashing new underground

MUSEUM OF SCIENCE AND INDUSTRY

MUSEUM OF SCIENCE AND INDUSTRY —DETAIL

entry was designed by Epstein to complement the museum's 1930s Moderne interior.

With its Ionic colonnades, caryatid porches, and domed roofs, the Palace of Fine Arts represented the acme of the Classicism that made the fair a White City of marble temples. After Chicago won out over New York in a fierce rivalry to host the fair, Frederick Law Olmsted was hired to plan the grounds on a 700-acre site in Jackson Park. John Wellborn Root was selected the architect in charge of design; and his partner, Daniel H. Burnham, was to be chief of construction. Buildings of "high architectural importance" were to be designed by East Coast establishment architects, some of whom had been educated at the École des Beaux-Arts in Paris. These men included Richard Morris Hunt, third president and a founder of the AIA; Atwood; and the firm of McKim, Mead & White.

Root's sudden death in January 1891, however, and his replacement by Charles Atwood, left the architects free to agree among themselves that Classical motifs would be stressed throughout. This choice not only secured the reputation of academically trained architects for decades to come but also ensured that Classicism would become the standard dress for practically every city's major cultural, commercial, and municipal institutions virtually until the Depression. Burnham's role, as coordinator left totally in charge of the exposition, launched him as the nation's top city planner. —SUSAN S. BENJAMIN

4| Columbian Basin

This reflective pool, designed as part of the 1895 plan, replaced an informal pond but conveys the character of the fair's Court of Honor, which had been farther south in the park. At the south end of the basin is the Clarence S. Darrow bridge, named for the lawyer who lived nearby and had his ashes scattered over the bridge into the lagoon.

5| Music Court

Decorative lampposts are the only clue that this parking lot was once a Music Court, built to the 1895 plan.

6| Wooded Island and Lagoon, Japanese Garden

A survivor of the 1893 Exposition, the island was the site of the Ho-o-den, a group of three Japanese pavilions that strongly impressed Frank Lloyd Wright

with their inventive organization of space. In 1981 the gardens were restored and a new Japanese teahouse built. The island is now a nature sanctuary, and its planting of native midwestern foliage framed by the lagoon strongly evokes Olmsted's turn-of-the-century vision for the park.

7| *The Republic*

1893, DANIEL CHESTER FRENCH (CAST 1918)
1992, RESTORATION, CHICAGO PARK DISTRICT

The "Golden Lady" is, surprisingly, Jackson Park's only sculpture. It was cast from a plaster model of the original, which was almost three times as big and graced the eastern end of the fair's Court of Honor. Now located on the site of the fair's Administration Building, which terminated the western end of the Court of Honor, the

THE REPUBLIC

statue symbolized the advanced state of civilization on the 400th anniversary of Columbus's landing.

8| Jackson Park Beach House (*64th St. Beach Pavilion*)

1919, SOUTH PARK COMMISSION
1999, RESTORATION, MANN, GIN, DUBIN & FRAZIER; DLK ARCHITECTURE

This enormous, classically inspired concrete bathhouse was modeled on the many buildings of this type designed by D. H. Burnham & Co. It included a covered promenade and an infirmary in addition to the lockers and showers. As restored, it is again a grand lakeside amenity.

9| Former U.S. Coast Guard Station

1906, ARCHITECT UNKNOWN
1992, RESTORATION, CHICAGO PARK DISTRICT

This was commissioned by the federal government to serve the crowds of bathers and boaters flocking to the park. The shingled surfaces and roof terrace are like those of other, more remote Great Lakes Coast Guard stations.

10| Hayes Dr. and Coast Guard Dr. Bridges

These are two of the four rusticated stone bridges erected in Jackson Park around 1904, when walkways, boulevards, meadows, and other landscape features were being completed. Part of the 1895 plan, the bridges are decorated with figures and reptiles meant to evoke the theme of wind and water.

11| La Rabida Children's Hospital & Research Center
65th St. and Lake Michigan

1931, GRAHAM, ANDERSON, PROBST & WHITE
1952–1959, ADDITIONS, FRIEDMAN, ALSCHULER & SINCERE AND PACE ASSOCS.
1992, ADDITION, VOA ASSOCS.

The name comes from the Spanish pavilion at the 1893 Exposition, which replicated the convent where Columbus awaited Queen Isabella's decision about his voyage to the New World. Converted to a children's hospital, it was later replaced by the present structure.

University of Chicago Campus

Because campus buildings are organized around landscaped quadrangles with little or no automobile access, the campus is best seen on foot. This walking tour begins at the southwest quadrangle of the central campus, where the earliest buildings are located.

12| University of Chicago Quadrangles
Bounded by Ellis and University Aves. and E. 57th and E. 59th (Midway Plaisance) Sts.

1891–1930
PLAN AND BUILDINGS TO 1900: HENRY IVES COBB
LANDSCAPE DESIGN. OLMSTED BROS., BEATRIX FARRAND, AND OTHERS

The Gothic quadrangles of the University of Chicago were built on land donated by or purchased from Marshall Field in 1890, the year of the university's charter. With three exceptions the site's thirty-four buildings employ various interpretations of the Gothic that are faithful to the

UNIVERSITY OF CHICAGO QUADRANGLES

spirit of the initial plan and to the trustees' dream of a unified, organic, self-contained campus that would nurture and sustain the ideal of a great research university.

Henry Ives Cobb, creator of the Fisheries Building at the 1893 World's Columbian Exposition, as well as structures for the Chicago Historical Society and the Newberry Library, designed the original scheme and its early modifications. It consists today of six broken quadrangles, three on the north side, three on the south, paralleling a larger, less defined central rectangle that runs between University and Ellis Aves. (Other academic buildings and complexes, many also wearing Gothic dress, are on adjacent streets.) Most of the structures built during the university's first ten years were designed by Cobb, including complexes running along the west and east sides of the southern half of the quadrangles and in the center on the northern half. Cobb also designed the university's Yerkes Observatory in Wisconsin and its President's House on University Ave. He was succeeded as master designer in 1901 by Shepley, Rutan & Coolidge, whose more elegant and elaborate structures include the Hutchinson Court complex in the northeast corner and Harper Memorial Library to the south. Other contributors of variations of campus Gothic included Dwight H. Perkins, Charles Z. Klauder, and Coolidge & Hodgdon.

Adorned with carved references to history, ancient and modern, to classical mythology, Christianity and folklore, featuring lancet windows, hammer-beam ceilings, loggias, corbels, gargoyles, and all the other elements of the Gothic, the picturesquely assertive buildings define a symmetrical plan whose scale and clarity recall the Beaux Arts vision of the Columbian Exposition. The beauty of these structures has also been enhanced by the work of an important series of landscape designers.

Derided by modernists for their archaic conceits, the quadrangles survive as one of the country's most remarkable expressions of commitment to a scholarly or priestly dream, one containing great stylistic variety within the larger Gothic vocabulary. The forty years of construction now seem all of one piece, the only jarring elements projected by three structures put up after World War II. By then, fortunately, this central campus was almost complete, and modern designers could build only in surrounding areas.

—NEIL HARRIS

13| Cobb Lecture Hall
5811–5827 S. Ellis Ave.
1892, HENRY IVES COBB

This was the university's first building, one of eighteen

designed by Cobb during his tenure (1891–1901) as campus architect. Named for donor Silas B. Cobb (no relation to the architect), it established the

Gothic style that would be adhered to for the next four decades—but with a chunky, robust character that hints at Cobb's attraction to the Romanesque (as do the red tile roofs). Cobb, in fact, had to be persuaded to adopt the Gothic instead of the Romanesque style of his Newberry Library. The trustees felt strongly that the ecclesiastical and educational associations of the Gothic made it more appropriate to a university than the Romanesque, which was then so popular for commercial structures. Despite his initial hesitancy, Cobb executed a masterful rendition of the Gothic style, with gables and dormers piercing steeply pitched roofs and crowned with vigorous crockets. Oriels, bays, and pavilion-like projections break the wall planes and give a suitably medieval impression of picturesque irregularity despite the buildings' essential symmetry.

The fourth floor contains the Bergman Gallery, where for many decades the Renaissance Society has exhibited important modern art.

14| Blake, Gates, and Goodspeed Halls
(*Graduate, Middle Divinity, and South Divinity Halls*)
5845 S. Ellis Ave.
1892, HENRY IVES COBB

Originally dormitories for fifty men each, they contained suites of two bedrooms on either side of a study. They continue the style of Cobb Hall, with an extra story added to Gates Hall to break up the roofline. A former reading room is now a recital hall and features its original windows and wood-trussed ceiling.

15| Classics Building
1010 E. 59th St.
1915, SHEPLEY, RUTAN & COOLIDGE

After the initial flurry of the 1890s, campus construction was heavily concentrated within three periods: 1901–1904 (see the Tower Group), 1912–1916, and 1926–1932. The second of these building booms, heralded by the long-awaited completion of Harper Memorial Library, was a period of increasing attention to architectural symbolism. No longer content with crockets and gargoyles, the university requested carved ornament indicative of activities inside the buildings, in an obsession that would culminate a decade later. The Classics Building is ornamented on the south with the heads of Homer, Cicero, Socrates, and Plato; characters from Aesop's fables; and depictions of the labors of Hercules.

16| William Wieboldt Hall
1050 E. 59th St.
1928, COOLIDGE & HODGDON

Dating from the last efflorescence of campus Gothic, Wieboldt is similar to its earlier neighbor, the Classics Building. The west wall of the archway linking them had embedded in it a stone from the old University of Chicago, which went bankrupt in 1886. The authors represented on this building for the study of modern languages are Lessing, Goethe, Schiller, Ibsen, Dante, Molière, Hugo, Cervantes, Chaucer, Shakespeare, Milton, and Emerson.

17| Frederick Haskell Hall
(*Haskell Oriental Museum*)
5836–5846 S. Greenwood Ave.
1896, HENRY IVES COBB

The building's original purpose as a museum is signaled by the unusual roof, which had skylights to illuminate the galleries. The university's collection of ancient Near Eastern art and artifacts was displayed here until the completion of the Oriental Institute in 1931. Note the trilingual cornerstone, with inscriptions in Hebrew, Latin, and Greek.

18| Swift Hall
1025–1035 E. 58th St.
1926, COOLIDGE & HODGDON

Its central campus location, planned long before construction or even design of the buildings began, was meant to symbolize the centrality of religious belief to all fields of study at the university. The richly decorated interior includes a carved, hammer-beam ceiling in a third-floor lecture hall, which was a reading room for the Divinity School library.

19| Joseph Bond Chapel
1926, COOLIDGE & HODGDON

The intimate interior is a jewel; if it is dark, look for light switches to the left of the front door. Appropriately connected to Swift Hall by a cloister, this small and beautifully ornamented chapel narrates a wide range of Christian doctrine on the exterior as well as interior. Adam and Eve flank a window on the west, while angelic and devilish figures play tag across the roofline and cornices. An orchestra of angels plays above a pierced inscription of the Beatitudes that scrolls across the walls. The designers (including Charles J. Connick, whose Boston firm executed the windows) had expert iconographical guidance from the Divinity School faculty, especially Edgar J. Goodspeed, chairman of the Department of New Testament and Early Christian Literature.

20| William Rainey Harper Memorial Library
1116 E. 59th St.
1912, SHEPLEY, RUTAN & COOLIDGE
1972, RENOVATION, METZ, TRAIN, OLSON & YOUNGREN

Punctuating the skyline with two massive towers, this library formed the first important component in the southern wall of buildings oriented toward the Midway. Its location resulted from a comprehensive campus plan formulated in 1902 that called for concentrating the humanities and social sciences buildings in the southern part of the quadrangles, which would henceforth be academic and not residential. As other buildings in the plan were completed (the last one in 1929),

second-story bridges linked the library to reading rooms and department libraries in Haskell and Stuart halls. Visit the third-floor reading room, a grand space marked on the exterior by the long row of arched, double-height windows. Look for the university's coat of arms, devised during this time so that it could be included in the room's iconography along with those of other distinguished institutions. Cross the bridge into another reading room, modernized but retaining an elaborate ceiling, that is actually part of Stuart Hall.

WILLIAM RAINEY HARPER MEMORIAL LIBRARY

21| Harold Leonard Stuart Hall
(*Law School*)
5835 S. Greenwood Ave.
1904, SHEPLEY, RUTAN & COOLIDGE

The building is carved with figures of kings and magistrates (pre-democratic dispensers of justice) and features Moses and the Ten Commandments atop the roof.

22| Julius Rosenwald Hall
1101–1111 E. 58th St.
1915, HOLABIRD & ROCHE
1972, RENOVATION, SAMUEL A. LICHTMANN

The shield next to the door proclaims DIG AND DISCOVER. Better yet, look up and discover; take out your binoculars and telephoto lens to capture all the beasts on this building. This was the home of the geology and geography departments, and the carvings reflect the interests

JULIUS ROSENWALD HALL—EXTERIOR
DETAIL

was designed to bring together the departments of history, sociology, economics, and political science in order to foster the interdisciplinary study of society. The elaborate program of ornament, which by this era of campus design was less concerned with historicism than with representational imagery, includes measuring devices such as calculators and calipers.

of these disciplines and honor the donor, Sears, Roebuck magnate Julius Rosenwald, with a frieze of roses around the entrance. The octagonal tower originally held meteorological instruments, and its gargoyles represent the four winds and four birds of the air. The square tower has four symbols of continents, with the buffalo, bull, elephant, and lion representing North America, Europe, Asia, and Africa.

23| George C. Walker Museum
1115–1125 E. 58th St.
1893, HENRY IVES COBB
1980, RENOVATION, NAGLE,
HARTRAY & ASSOCS.

Cobb designed this to be a natural history museum, pushing the stair tower out the south wall to allow space in the exhibition hall for prehistoric skeletons. It was used instead for desperately needed classrooms, laboratories, and offices; the prehistoric collection was eventually given to the Field Museum of Natural History. When the Graduate School of Business moved into the building, they took advantage of the generous ceiling heights to squeeze five floors of space into the three-story structure.

24| Social Science Research Building
1126 E. 59th St.
1929, COOLIDGE & HODGDON

When this building completed the south wall of buildings in 1929, it represented the fulfillment of the 1902 plan for the original campus quadrangles. It

25| Beecher, Green, and Kelly Halls
5848 S. University Ave.
1893 AND 1899 (GREEN HALL),
HENRY IVES COBB

26| Foster Hall
1130 E. 59th St.
1893, HENRY IVES COBB
1902, WESTERN ADDITION,
WILLIAM A. OTIS

Coeducational since its founding, the university provided women's dormitories on the southeastern edge of the main quadrangle, mirroring the original four buildings to the west. Green Hall, which was completed later for financial reasons, is a story higher than its neighbors, just as Gates Hall stands out on the opposite side. Cobb emphasized the prominent Midway corner of Foster Hall with a profusion of crockets and gargoyles on the corner turret. Marion Talbot, dean of women from 1892 to 1925, influenced Cobb's plans for the so-called Women's Quadrangle. She recommended four smaller buildings rather than one large one, and single rooms rather than the two-bedroom-and-study arrangement used for the men. She also assured that there would be parlors and dining rooms for socializing; the men's dormitories had woefully inadequate public spaces.

27| Albert Pick Hall for International Studies
5020 S. University Ave.
1971, RALPH RAPSON & ASSOCS.;
BURNHAM & HAMMOND; J. LEE
JONES

A modern attempt to evoke the Gothic tradition, this limestone building shares the materials, vertical proportions, and irregular profile of its earlier neighbors. Unfortunately, the prominent caulk lines make it look like a suit with the tailor's chalk marks still showing.

28| Administration Building
5801 S. Ellis Ave.
1948, HOLABIRD & ROOT & BURGEE

Cobb originally envisioned a library and "university hall" for this prominent site, and later plans called for a Gothic administration building. When final planning for this building began in earnest in 1945, the Gothic style was not considered aesthetically or economically appropriate, and so this utilitarian structure was erected. Truly a wallflower, it modestly directs attention to its more elaborate neighbors.

29| Bernard Albert Eckhart Hall
1118 E. 58th St.
1930, CHARLES Z. KLAUDER

A late Gothic addition to the main quad, Eckhart Hall offers further proof of the style's power to unify the work of different architects. Klauder was nationally known for his Collegiate Gothic buildings at Princeton, the University of Pennsylvania, and the University of Pittsburgh. During the 1926–1932 campus construction boom, each building design was assisted by a faculty committee on symbolism. The ornament of this building related to the physics, astronomy, and mathematics departments housed within.

30| Ryerson Physical Laboratory
1110–1114 E. 58th St.
1894, HENRY IVES COBB
1913, NORTH ANNEX, SHEPLEY, RUTAN & COOLIDGE

31| Kent Chemical Laboratory
1020–1024 E. 58th St.
1894, HENRY IVES COBB

This pair of ornate science buildings had complex interior requirements that combined with the lavishness of architectural ornament to drive the cost way over budget. Inside is a bronze relief of the donor, Sidney A. Kent, designed by Lorado Taft. The octagonal Kent Theatre to the north was the university's assembly hall until the completion in 1903 of Mandel Hall.

32| George Herbert Jones Laboratory
5747 S. Ellis Ave.
1929, COOLIDGE & HODGDON

Room 405 is a National Historic Landmark, because it was where plutonium, the first man-made element, was first isolated and weighed.

33| Hull Court & Biological Laboratories
1025–1103 E. 57th St.
1897, HENRY IVES COBB

Entered from the south through the wrought-iron Hull Gate, this courtyard contains four laboratory buildings (anatomy, botany, physiology, and zoology) designed as a group in a simpler and less costly style than Kent and Ryerson laboratories. Joined by loggias and arcades, the buildings surround but do not actually face Hull Court and Botany Pond, both planned by landscape architect John C. Olmsted, as was the nearby Hutchinson Court.

34| Charles Hitchcock Hall
1009 E. 57th St.
1902, DWIGHT H. PERKINS

Here is the university's most original interpretation of the Gothic style prior to World War II. Perkins's application of Prairie School principles can be seen in the low pitched roof, low dormers, and generally horizontal character of the building. The ornament was also a departure, with geometric stained-glass windows and corncobs and other prairie vegetation substituting for abstracted English flora. Perkins was a family friend of the donor, Mrs. Charles Hitchcock, and was one of the few outside architects brought in to design a campus building.

35| Snell Hall
5709 S. Ellis Ave.
1893, HENRY IVES COBB

The only undergraduate dormitory for men until 1901, Snell is one of just two central-campus residence halls still used as such.

36| Searle Chemistry Laboratory
5735 S. Ellis Ave.
1967, SMITH, SMITH, HAINES, LUNDBERG & WAEHLER

Elements that relate to the existing campus include limestone, window and spandrel size, and building height.

37| Cobb Gate
South side of E. 57th St. between Ellis and University Aves.
1900, HENRY IVES COBB

After budgetary constraints had curbed his use of ornament on campus buildings, Cobb let his decorative impulses run wild on this fanciful ornamental gate, which he donated to the university. It ended up being his swan song, as he was replaced as campus architect the following year. The trustees felt that his attention was being diverted by efforts to build a national practice out of his newly opened

COBB GATE

office in Washington, D.C. Ironically, the successor firm of Shepley, Rutan & Coolidge was based in Boston.

Hutchinson Court and the Tower Group:

38| John J. Mitchell Tower, Charles L. Hutchinson Hall, Joseph Reynolds Student Clubhouse

39| Leon Mandel Assembly Hall
Southwest corner of E. 57th St. and University Ave.
1903, SHEPLEY, RUTAN & COOLIDGE
1981, MANDEL HALL RENOVATION, SKIDMORE, OWINGS & MERRILL WITH THE OFFICE OF JOHN VINCI

Shepley, Rutan & Coolidge made a significant campus debut with this monumental group of buildings, which anchors the northeast corner of the main quadrangle. It marks an

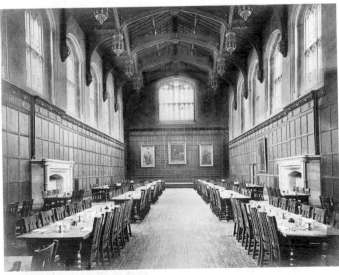

CHARLES L. HUTCHINSON HALL

increasing emphasis on historicism, including an effort to make the interiors correspond with the style of the facades. SRC's buildings generally have more elaborate wall planes than Cobb's, with arched and traceried windows. The rooflines, however, are simpler, with rows of crenellations replacing the profusion of gables and dormers.

Seeking early on to associate their fledgling institution with significant historic European (especially English) universities, donor Charles L. Hutchinson and architect Charles A. Coolidge traveled to Oxford to study its collegiate architectural tradition. The design of Mitchell Tower, the first purely ornamental building on campus, was derived from the bell tower of Magdalen College. The ten Palmer chimes, named for the first dean of women, Alice Freeman Palmer (see the Daniel Chester French plaque in the lobby), are still used for change ringing, a traditional English style of play that some find cacophonous. Originally a men's dining hall, Hutchinson Commons was modeled after Oxford's Christ Church Hall. Enjoy a modestly priced meal in the grand dining room, remarkable for the hammer-beam ceiling and the many portraits of trustees and benefactors, including John D. Rockefeller and Martin Ryerson.

Reynolds Club was derived from St. John's College at Oxford, and its domestic feeling is enhanced by a stair hall that could have come straight out of an English manor house.

40| Quadrangle Club
1155 E. 57th St.
1922, HOWARD VAN DOREN SHAW

Shaw deliberately designed this faculty club in red brick with a multicolored slate roof to contrast with the surrounding gray limestone buildings.

41| Chicago Theological Seminary
5757 S. University Ave.
1926, RIDDLE & RIDDLE

Two wings are connected by a second-story arched corridor that spans the alley. The east wing contains residential quarters; the west wing houses two chapels, a library, and classrooms. Step inside to bask in the cloistered ambience, and visit the Hilton Memorial Chapel, a tiny gem built a few years before the rest of the complex was constructed. The Chicago newspaper publisher Victor F. Lawson financed the tower that bears his name.

42| Oriental Institute
1155 E. 58th St.
1931, MAYERS, MURRAY & PHILLIP
1997, ADDITION, HAMMOND, BEEBY & BABKA

This building was designed by the successor firm to Bertram Grosvenor Goodhue Assocs. (architects of Rockefeller Memorial Chapel) with an Art Deco simplicity that tempers the Gothic gables, bays, and buttresses. Egyptologist James H. Breasted, director of the Institute from 1919 to 1935, designed the symbolic bas-relief over the north entrance. It illustrates elements of civilization from the ancient Near East and the Western world, including the Sphinx and architect Goodhue's Nebraska State Capitol.

43| University President's House
5855 S. University Ave.
1895, HENRY IVES COBB

The pale Roman brick, less expensive than limestone, blends with the surrounding buildings, as does the peaked tile roof with dormers. Many alterations have been made over the years.

44| Rockefeller Memorial Chapel
(*University Chapel*)
1156–1180 E. 59th St.
1925–1928, BERTRAM GROSVENOR GOODHUE ASSOCS.

Towering over the Midway, this massive limestone church of load-bearing masonry employs traditional Gothic structural devices of arches and buttresses.

ROCKEFELLER MEMORIAL CHAPEL

Goodhue was a nationally famous proponent of the Gothic Revival and the Arts & Crafts movements, and this design is his interpretation of Modern Gothic. The university administration was heavily involved in the design process, and its president, Ernest DeWitt Burton, toured famous English cathedrals to satisfy himself that the design was appropriate. The greatest departure from medieval Gothic is in the proportions, with unusually wide bays and tall clerestory windows over low side aisles, and in the abundance of smooth, flat surfaces. Lee Lawrie designed the facade sculpture up to thirty feet from the ground; Ulric H. Ellerhusen was responsible for the higher designs. The interior has a cool, restful palette (except for some unfortunate brightly colored modern windows) and an unusual example of Guastavino tile vaulting, a technique in which the tile is actually structural rather than merely ornamental. The sculpture includes religious as well as al-

legorical and historical figures, along with coats of arms and inscriptions. A statue of Goodhue on the east transept wall personifies architecture (opposite him is Bach representing music), with Rockefeller Chapel in his hands and West Point Chapel behind him.

45| Ida Noyes Hall
1212 E. 59th St.
1916, SHEPLEY, RUTAN & COOLIDGE
1986, MAX PALEVSKY CINEMA, VICKREY, OVRESAT, AWSUMB ASSOCS.

Lavishly decorated in a domestic Tudor Revival style, it was designed to offer women the kind of social and recreational facilities provided to men in the Tower Group buildings. It became a general student center in 1955, when women were no longer excluded from those premises. The lounge, library, and Cloister Club contain rich ornament and fixtures. Climb the elaborately carved staircase to see a third-floor student theater with an early mural by Jessie Arms Botke, *The Masque of Youth*, depicting a performance given at the building's dedication.

IDA NOYES HALL

46| University of Chicago Laboratory Schools
1362 E. 59th St. and
5823 S. Kenwood Ave.
1992, MIDDLE SCHOOL, NAGLE, HARTRAY & ASSOCS.
2000, KOVLER GYM, NAGLE HARTRAY DANKER KAGAN MCKAY

Amid the older Lab School buildings, which are U. of C. Gothic, stand two newer projects that fit in beautifully. The middle school was built to the east of a 1960s green glass high school addition by Perkins & Will with Eero Saarinen. Courtyards separate the middle school from the high school, which is no longer visible from the street. Kimbark St. was closed off to create play space for the lower grades. Across the space is Kovler Gym, which is connected to the 1929 Sunny Gym with an arcade. Both the middle school and gym are "streamlined Gothic," a more modern interpretation designed to complement the existing buildings. A modern approach characterizes the interiors.

47| International House
1414 E. 59th St.
1932, HOLABIRD & ROOT

With the completion of this building and the Henry Crown Field House, Holabird & Root ended the first era of Collegiate Gothic with a stripped-down, Art Deco interpretation. Campus building would not resume for over fifteen years—and then in a strictly utilitarian style. "I-House" rises elegantly on its long, shallow site and has an attractively landscaped interior courtyard.

Ground was broken in 2002 for a new Graduate School of Business, designed by Rafael Viñoly, at the southeast corner of 58th St. and Woodlawn Ave.

48| Frederick C. Robie House
5757 S. Woodlawn Ave.
1908–1909, FRANK LLOYD WRIGHT
RESTORATION BEGUN 1997 BY THE FRANK LLOYD WRIGHT PRESERVATION TRUST

This house, which Frank Lloyd Wright designed in 1908 for a bicycle and motorcycle manufacturer, is one of the world's most famous buildings. Magnificently poised, like a great steamship at anchor, it is the distilled essence of Wright's Prairie School style and the culmination of his search for a new architecture. It is also among the last of his Prairie houses; during construction Wright abandoned both his Oak Park practice and his family to embark on a new phase of his long career.

The Robie House faces west and south on a lot measuring 60 x 180 feet. Its basic form consists of two parallel, rectangular two-story masses at the meeting of which rises a smaller, square third story. The massive chimney effectively anchors these separate parts. The main living quarters occupy the second floor, with three bedrooms above. There is no basement. The exterior formulation of base, wall, and cornice, common to all of Wright's Prairie houses, is repeated in every part of the elevations. Here it is expressed by thin, long Roman bricks and limestone trim. Floors and balconies are reinforced concrete, while the great overhangs are made possible by numerous concealed steel girders, some as long as sixty feet.

Space is defined not by walls, in the conventional sense, but by a series of horizontal planes intercepted by vertical wall fragments and rectangular piers. These horizontals extend far beyond the enclosures,

FREDERICK C. ROBIE HOUSE

FREDERICK C. ROBIE HOUSE—INTERIOR

defining exterior space as well and echoing the flat midwestern landscape that so inspired the architect. The chief embellishments are the exquisite leaded- and stained-glass doors and windows, which not only provide accents of color and ornament but also screen interior from exterior space while preserving the unity between outside and inside.

The Robie House's calculated asymmetry, irregular form, and striking silhouette excite our curiosity and invite us to explore its carefully arranged sequences of spaces. This Picturesque manner of composition can ultimately be traced to the freely experimental buildings of the Shingle Style that Wright had learned in the 1880s from his first significant employer, Joseph Lyman Silsbee. The beautiful abstraction of the building's surfaces, clean geometry of form, and personal manner of decoration—its emphatic style—as well as the strong central axis that orders its raised living and dining rooms, are the legacy of Wright's "Lieber Meister," Louis H. Sullivan. Only by uniting these seemingly opposing traditions was Wright able to create a personal modern style in 1900 and give it its perfect expression eight years later in the Robie House.

The Frank Lloyd Wright Preservation Trust is currently undertaking a long-range restoration plan, which it began in 1997.   —PAUL KRUTY

49| University Church
(*University Church of the Disciples of Christ*)
5655 S. University Ave.
1921, HOWARD VAN DOREN SHAW
AND HENRY K. HOLSMAN

This austere Gothic church is almost primitive. An unusual feature of its spare but lovely interior is the fireplace at the back of the west aisle.

50| Bartlett Hall
(*Frank Dickinson Bartlett Gymnasium*)
5640 S. University Ave.
1904, SHEPLEY, RUTAN & COOLIDGE
2002, CONVERSION, BRUNER/COTT
& ASSOCS.

Go to the second floor to see the romantic medieval-style mural and stained-glass window, which features a scene from *Ivanhoe*. The gym was donated by university trustee and hardware merchant Adolphus C. Bartlett in memory of his son. The mural was painted by another son, Frederic Clay, who also executed designs in the Tower Group. The first Heisman Trophy for outstanding college football players was awarded in 1935 to University of Chicago halfback Jay Berwanger and is exhibited in the trophy room that bears his name.

51| Max Palevsky Residential Commons
5630 S. University Ave., 1101 E. 56th St., 5625 S. Ellis Ave.
2002, RICARDO LEGORRETA

It is orange, and it's in Hyde Park. It also has purple, yellow, and pink elements, one for each of its three sections, and it runs for two blocks along 56th St. But inside of its wings is a pleasant new court, soaking up the sun. Large window areas bring the outside in. There isn't a dingy corner in the place. And it is right next to the library.

52| Henry Crown Field House
(Field House)
5550 S. University Ave.
1932, HOLABIRD & ROOT
1977, 1979, RENOVATIONS, HOLABIRD & ROOT

Designed and redesigned over a five-year period, the building reflects the lines of its Gothic predecessors only in the vestigial buttresses and tall, arched windows. Earlier, more elaborate designs had proved too costly, and the winds of modernism had penetrated even the ivy walls of this august institution.

53| 5551 S. University Ave.
1937, GEORGE FRED KECK & WILLIAM KECK

Here is timeless, first-generation modernism from the firm that had gained fame (but few commissions) for their futuristic House of Tomorrow at Chicago's 1933 Century of Progress Exposition. A three-flat, it is unrelated

5551 S. UNIVERSITY AVE.

to any of its predecessors. The innovative louvers make curtains unnecessary and help conserve energy. Even the garage doors are building blocks for the facade's simple geometry.

54| Stanley R. Pierce Hall
5514 S. University Ave.
1960, HARRY WEESE & ASSOCS.

Heralded by *Architectural Record* as a "Major Break-through on the Anti-Slab Front," this complex was designed by Weese at about the same time as the Hyde Park Redevelopment Project. In the unique interior configuration, groups of student rooms surround two-story interior lounges. The two-story pavilion contains dining and lounge facilities and was intended to link the tower to a nearby twin, never built.

55| Cochrane-Woods Art Center
5550 S. Greenwood Ave.
1974, EDWARD LARRABEE BARNES

56| Court Theatre
5535 S. Ellis Ave.
1981, HARRY WEESE & ASSOCS.

Planned as the nucleus of a never-completed Arts Quadrangle, Barnes's simple limestone buildings house the art department and the Smart Museum of Art. They enclose the Vera and A. D. Elden Sculpture Garden.

The Gerald Ratner Athletics Center at 55th St. and Ellis Ave. began construction in 2001. The facility was designed by Cesar Pelli and OWP/P and is part of the university's $500 million capital improvement plan (1999–2005), which includes the Pelli-designed parking structure across the street.

57| Nuclear Energy
East side of Ellis Ave. between E. 56th & 57th Sts.
1967, HENRY MOORE

Intended to suggest a human skull and a mushroom cloud, this abstract bronze form commemorates the moment on December 2, 1942, when Enrico

Fermi and his colleagues created the first self-sustaining, controlled nuclear chain reaction. This initiation into the atomic age took place in a squash court under the bleachers of the now-demolished Stagg Field, site of the Regenstein Library.

58| Joseph Regenstein Library
1100 E. 57th St.
1970, SKIDMORE, OWINGS & MERRILL

Walter A. Netsch, Jr., brought the concrete brutalism of his University of Illinois at Chicago to this traditional campus, where it landed with a thud on the site of Stagg Field. The irregular massing and profile, slit windows, and vertically grooved facade are meant to allude to the surrounding Gothic buildings but are more a product of Netsch's own idiosyncratic design concepts. Fortunately, two of the seven floors are underground.

The Science Quadrangle features several modern interpretations of the Gothic style.

59| Samuel Kersten, Jr., Physics Teaching Center
5720 S. Ellis Ave.
1985, HOLABIRD & ROOT; HAROLD H. HELLMAN, UNIVERSITY ARCH.

The Ellis Ave. facade presents the most subtle and distinguished modern contribution to the Collegiate Gothic tradition on this campus. The Science Quadrangle facade reflects the brash modernity of its neighbors with a glass curtain wall that steps back to form a series of terraces. From a narrow stair hall, designer Gerald Horn forged a dynamic atrium, a pedestrian highway that shoots across 57th St. to the physicists' offices and research facilities.

60| John Crerar Library
5730 S. Ellis Ave.
1984, HUGH STUBBINS ASSOCS.; LOEBL, SCHLOSSMAN & HACKL, ASSOC. ARCH.

The use of limestone, the window proportions, and the emphasis on the entry attempt to relate to the Gothic; while the projecting third floor provides cover, as in Gothic arcades and loggias.

61| Henry Hinds Laboratory for the Geophysical Sciences
5734 S. Ellis Ave.
1969, I. W. COLBURN & ASSOCS.; J. LEE JONES

Colburn was a consulting architect to the university from 1964 to 1973, and his quirky, expressionistic Esperanto Gothic style dominates the Science Quadrangle. Bay windows and an irregular, sculptural facade loom above surrounding buildings.

62| University Bookstore (*University Press Building*)
5750 S. Ellis Ave.
1902, SHEPLEY, RUTAN & COOLIDGE

KERSTEN PHYSICS TEACHING CENTER

Another red brick building in a sea of gray, this one sports a variety of gabled forms. The unusually open first-floor facade has rows of tall arched windows.

63| 850 E. 58th St.
(*American School of Correspondence*)
1907, POND & POND

This is one of the city's finest examples of the architects' unique version of the Arts & Crafts style. The banded piers and tower may have been inspired by Secessionist architecture that the Ponds had seen at the 1904 St. Louis World's Fair; Irving Pond wrote an early and influential essay on the movement in 1905. The American School of Correspondence offered courses in a variety of subjects including architecture and engineering, and after its 1902 move to Chicago many of its texts featured work by local designers such as Frank Lloyd Wright and Pond & Pond.

64| Cummings Life Science Center
920 E. 58th St.
1973, I. W. COLBURN & ASSOCS.; SCHMIDT, GARDEN & ERIKSON

The tallest building on campus has forty red brick towers— exhaust ducts aspiring to be medieval chimney stacks.

65| Ingleside Hall
(*Quadrangle Club*)
956–960 E. 58th St.
1896, CHARLES B. ATWOOD

Moved here in 1929 from its original location on the site of the Oriental Institute, the vaguely neo-Classical building is the only one designed for the campus in the 1890s by an architect other than Cobb.

66| Donnelley Biological Sciences Learning Center/Knapp Research Center
924 E. 57th St.
1994, THE STUBBINS ASSOCS.; LOEBL, SCHLOSSMAN & HACKL, ASSOC. ARCHS.

The window shapes and limestone cladding help this huge modern science center blend with its surroundings.

A few of the university's buildings are located on E. 60th St., south of the Midway, and are easily seen by car. Those exploring on foot are advised not to wander to the south, where the neighborhood becomes distinctly uncollegiate.

67| Midway Studios
6016 S. Ingleside Ave.
1906, POND & POND
1929, OTIS F. JOHNSON
1965, PAINTING STUDIO, LOEBL, SCHLOSSMAN, BENNETT & DART

Sculptor Lorado Taft and a group of fellow artists lived and worked in this cluster of studios and living quarters, which expanded gradually from the original converted carriage house. This is where Taft created the *Fountain of Time,* located at the west end of the Midway, and the *Fountain of the Great Lakes,* outside the Art Institute. The setting now provides studio and gallery space for the university's studio art program.

68| School of Social Service Administration
969 E. 60th St.
1965, LUDWIG MIES VAN DER ROHE

The purest example of modernism on campus was designed by the master himself. Inside the black steel and glass box is a large lobby that is an exercise in Miesian "universal space"—rather like his U.S. Post Office in the Loop.

69| Burton-Judson Courts
1005 E. 60th St.
1931, ZANTZINGER, BORIE & MEDARY

The university jumped the Midway in constructing this pair of dormitories. Plans formulated in the 1920s called for the creation of a self-contained undergraduate campus south of the Midway, but they were scrapped in favor of continued northward expansion. This remains the plan's only built component. The small landscaped quadrangles are worth a peek.

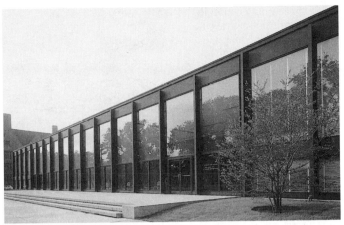

SCHOOL OF SOCIAL SERVICE ADMINISTRATION

70| Laird Bell Law Quadrangle
1111 E. 6oth St.
1959, EERO SAARINEN & ASSOCS.
1998, ADDITION, OWP/P

This complex is Saarinen's most significant contribution to the campus that resulted from his 1950s master plan. Following the tradition of clustering buildings of similar disciplines around a central court, Saarinen designed a group of four buildings (Constitution Hall, a classroom building, the law library, and the administration build-

ing) around a reflecting pool and fountain. Saarinen was quoted in *Architectural Record* in November 1960 that "By stressing a small, broken scale, a lively silhouette, and especially verticality in the library design, we intended to make it a good neighbor with the Gothic dormitories." The bronze sculpture, *Construction in Space in the 3rd and 4th Dimension*, was designed for this space by Antoine Pevsner, a Russian-born sculptor who worked in the cubist and constructivist styles.

Rosalie Villas

The 5700 and 5800 blocks of S. Harper Ave. (originally called Rosalie Ct.) contain many of the houses built as part of Rosalie Villas, the area's first planned community. Rosalie Buckingham bought this land in 1883 and subdivided it into lots for forty-two freestanding houses. She hired Solon S. Beman, fresh from his planning of Pullman, to supervise the design and construction of the houses and of the commercial buildings planned for the corner of 57th St. At that time the Illinois Central Railroad's tracks ran at grade, giving the houses on the east side of the street views of open land and the lake beyond. By the end of the decade, several of the lots had been subdivided for smaller frontages, and an apartment building anchored 57th St.,

giving the development a less rural character than originally planned. The houses are currently in various states of repair, ranging from pristine to tumbledown.

71| 5832–5834 S. Harper Ave.
1884, SOLON S. BEMAN

Beman himself was one of the first to create an exception to the detached-residence rule when he designed this double house for John A. Jackman, Jr. It is composed as a unified facade, however, with a shared chimney creating a focal point at ground level with a large terra-cotta panel. A manager at the Pullman Co., Jackman also commissioned Beman to design the house at 5824.

72| William Waterman House
5810 S. Harper Ave.
1884, HENRY F. STARBUCK

One of the few brick houses in this clapboard and shingle enclave, it has an especially fine terra-cotta cornice and the rotated bay frequently seen in Stick Style homes.

73| 5809 S. Harper Ave.
1888, E. CLARKE JOHNSON

This Queen Anne town house was turned on its side to fit an unusual site: broad and shallow rather than long and narrow.

74| 5759 S. Harper Ave.
1884, SOLON S. BEMAN

The details of this frame Queen Anne, especially on the well-preserved porch, are typically robust, showing an emphasis on cutouts and screens.

75| Charles Bonner House
5752 S. Harper Ave.
1889, WILLIAM W. BOYINGTON

This greatly altered frame house offers tantalizing glimpses of original details like the inset second-floor balcony.

76| Ernest W. Heath House
5744 S. Harper Ave.
1886, W. IRVING BEMAN

This greatly altered house is difficult to piece together. W. Irving Beman was Solon's brother and worked in the Pullman architectural offices.

77| 5719 through 5745 S. Harper Ave.
1888, ROBERT RAE, JR.

Their similarity is obscured by varying states of integrity and upkeep. The three southern-most houses (5739–5745) are from 1888, which seems a likely date for the others as well. They all offer noteworthy examples of the vigorous punched ornament popular on late nineteenth-century frame houses. Unfortunately, it is often removed or replaced by spidery mass-produced spindle work.

78| M. Cochran Armour House
5736 S. Harper Ave.
PRE-1888, ARCHITECT UNKNOWN

M. COCHRAN ARMOUR HOUSE

Then as now, this is one of the most lavish houses on the block. The exuberant forms include a two-story elliptical bay, curved corner windows, and inset balconies. Fish-scale shingles, carved plaques, and half-timbering provide a potpourri of textures.

79| Hyde Park Historical Society (*Chicago Street Railway Co. Station*)
5529 S. Lake Park Ave.
1893, ARCHITECT UNKNOWN
1981, RENOVATION, OFFICE OF JOHN VINCI

This small station once served passengers at the southern terminus of a cable car line, completed in anticipation of the 1893 World's Columbian Exposition. When the Illinois Central trains were elevated in the late 1920s, this building was tucked into their embankment.

80| University National Bank (*Ritz 55th Garage*)
E. 55th St. at Lake Park Ave.
1929, M. LOUIS KROMAN

This is an Art Deco paean to the glamour of the roadster. The terra-cotta facade cruises from one automotive image to the

UNIVERSITY NATIONAL BANK

next: engines, stoplights, tires, gearshifts—and of course a flivver itself, with jauntily clad driver. The first floor, now altered, once included a chauffeur's lounge.

81| Hyde Park Redevelopment Project
From 53rd to 57th Sts., west of the Illinois Central Railroad
1957–1959, I. M. PEI; HARRY WEESE & ASSOCS.; BARTON ASCHMAN, CIVIL & LANDSCAPING CONSULTANT

HYDE PARK REDEVELOPMENT PROJECT

82| University Apartments
1400 & 1450 E. 55th St.
1961, I. M. PEI AND LOEWENBERG & LOEWENBERG

The lush gardens and well-kept public spaces that mark the Hyde Park Redevelopment Project testify to the continuing success of a pioneering effort to combat middle-class flight from this distinguished Chicago neighborhood. They belie, however, the controversy that surrounded the project in the mid-1950s. Flight to the newly burgeoning suburbs was in full force, and the University of Chicago was threatened by the increasing decay of the once substantial neighborhood that surrounded it. In 1957 a large area of blighted buildings was torn down; they were replaced by some 150 two- and three-story town houses and two ten-story apartment buildings. The project was financed by a combination of federal, city, and private monies and was strongly backed by the university.

This effort was different from other 1950s urban renewal schemes, which cut great swaths in the existing city fabric that seldom were artfully replaced. Such projects were often like ocean liners moored in the middle of the city—separate, apart, and a world unto themselves, with little direct relationship to surrounding street patterns or building types. Here in Hyde Park great care was taken to relate the new construction to the existing neighborhood, which comprised a mixture of single-family homes from the 1880s and small pre–World War I apartment buildings.

The project was guided by an overriding concern to preserve the urban neighborhood spirit. The master plan emphasized low buildings in order to provide the strong relationship to the street characteristic of healthy and safe neighborhoods. Parklike public spaces were created, and town houses were built around inner squares. These are now filled with greenery and animated by playgrounds and basketball courts. The inclusion of a shopping center (recently replaced) recognized that traditional neighborhoods have necessary goods and services close at hand.

Probably the most radical urban planning move was placing the mid-rise University Apartments in the middle of 55th St. and splitting traffic lanes on either side, thereby creating an island to discourage high-speed traffic. This was directly inspired by planning principles of the Modern movement as espoused by Le Corbusier in *La Ville Radieuse*

UNIVERSITY APARTMENTS

(1935). The island has not had its intended effect; traffic speeds up on the split street, and pedestrians are discouraged from crossing.

Within the strong traditional forms of the overall plan, the architecture asserts a modernist design ethic. University Apartments saw the early use of fiberglass forms for poured-in-place concrete as well as a convenience unique at the time, a closed-circuit television entry system.

The two- and three-story town houses scattered throughout the area were the work of the New York office of I. M. Pei and the Chicago firm of Harry Weese & Assocs. Town houses had not been constructed in Chicago since the early 1900s and were a new element in this neighborhood. Pale brick sets them apart from their predominantly red-brick antecedents. Inspired by eighteenth-century English town house rows, or "terraces," Pei and Weese reinterpreted Georgian regularity and harmony. The strong horizontals of ground-floor recesses and third-floor clerestories unify the rows, while evenly placed door and window elements maintain symmetry throughout the project.

This project not only succeeded in combating middle-class flight but also spurred private renovation in the surrounding area. In addition, the town house form reintroduced here has been used in smaller infill sites throughout the city. The Hyde Park Redevelopment Project is notable as an outstanding example in Chicago of rebuilding a large urban area without creating a "project."

—CYNTHIA AND CATHARINE WEESE

83| William H. Hoyt House
5704 S. Dorchester Ave.
1869, ARCHITECT UNKNOWN

84| Charles H. Botsford House
5714 S. Dorchester Ave.
1860, ARCHITECT UNKNOWN

These Italianates are the grand-daddies of the block, dating from the settlement of this area. Their form is typical of the suburban or country villa of the period, with symmetrical facades, tall, narrow windows, and bracketed cornices. The

cupola (originally larger) of the Botsford House once provided a view of the lake and aided in ventilation by drawing hot air up the central stairwell.

85| Chicago Theological Seminary Faculty Quadrangle
E. 58th St. and S. Dorchester Ave.
1963, LOEBL, SCHLOSSMAN, BENNETT & DART

This cluster of three- and four-bedroom units was designed by Edward D. Dart as rental faculty housing for the seminary. Set on

CHICAGO THEOLOGICAL SEMINARY FACULTY QUADRANGLE

diagonals at the perimeter of the lot, with heights varied to increase privacy, they surround a central common intended as a children's play area. The village-like enclave recalls the work of Finnish architect Alvar Aalto.

86 | 5825 S. Blackstone Ave.
1909, MARSHALL & FOX

A building inspired by nineteenth-century Paris stands out among its Anglophile neighbors. This elegant four-flat has tall, narrow proportions (note the triple-sash windows), which had not been a prominent feature in this neighborhood since the Italianate boom of the 1860s and 1870s.

87 | Helstein House
5806 S. Blackstone Ave.
1951, BERTRAND GOLDBERG

Goldberg used his favorite materials of concrete and glass to create an uncompromisingly modern house. The placement well back on the lot provides privacy despite the expanses of glass and avoids shocking its traditional neighbors.

88 | 5757–5759 S. Blackstone Ave.
1899, NIMMONS & FELLOWS

This double house presents a handsome Chicago interpretation of the Louis XIII style, with a flattened front and slightly bowed bays.

89 | James Westfall Thompson House
5747 S. Blackstone Ave.
1899, POND & POND

The diaper pattern of bricks on the top floor was a popular motif in the 1890s among architects inspired by the Arts & Crafts movement, because the design was derived from the materials themselves rather than from applied color or ornament. Pond & Pond, who designed many settlement houses, probably used the motif more than anyone else.

90 | 5701 & 5707 S. Blackstone Ave.
1905, CARL M. ALMQUIST

This pair of typical six-flats has fluted columns supporting porches on all levels. Leaded-glass windows and brick quoins increase the grandeur.

91 | St. Stephen's Church of God in Christ
(*Tenth Church of Christ, Scientist*)
5640 S. Blackstone Ave.
1919, COOLIDGE & HODGDON

University of Chicago architects Coolidge & Hodgdon gave this church a Classical facade, in a break from their campus Gothic. The shallow inward curve of the street wall draws people in and then cuts off views of the neighboring buildings, maximizing the potential of the midblock site.

92 | 5621 & 5611 S. Blackstone Ave.
1886, FLANDERS & ZIMMERMAN

These sharply contrasting buildings were built for the same client, architect William Carbys Zimmerman himself. At 5621 is a classic example of the Shingle Style, while 5611 is almost proto-Prairie, with its deep-set door and its porch hollowed out of the building's mass and inset with square columns.

93| **5603–5615 S. Kenwood Ave. and 1357–1361 E. 56th St.**
1903, MANN, MACNEILLE & LINDEBERG

94| **5558 S. Kimbark Ave. and 1220, 1222, 1226, 1228, 1234 E. 56th St.**
1904, MANN, MACNEILLE & LINDEBERG

Several groups of cooperative row houses were designed for university faculty by this New York firm. Charles Riborg Mann was a professor of physics at the university and probably referred colleagues to his brother's firm. The group is noteworthy for its intact tile roof and for the variety of window and door treatments.

95| **William H. Ray Public School** (*Hyde Park High School*)
5631 S. Kimbark Ave.
1893, JOHN J. FLANDERS
1915, ASSEMBLY HALL, ARTHUR F. HUSSANDER
1996, SOUTH ADDITION, FOX & FOX

This highly decorated Queen Anne school is distinguished by Flanders's signature bands of ornament and full-height octagonal bays rising to an unusually lively roofline.

96| **5748, 5752, 5756 S. Kimbark Ave.**
1985, DAVID SWAN

These stucco and brick houses are starkly modern and geometric, recalling Art Deco forms in their sweeping curves and metal railings.

HILLEL FOUNDATION

97| **Hillel Foundation** (*Arthur J. Mason House*)
5715 S. Woodlawn Ave.
1904, HOWARD VAN DOREN SHAW

98| **Edgar Johnson Goodspeed House**
5706 S. Woodlawn Ave.
1906, HOWARD VAN DOREN SHAW

Shaw's Hyde Park and Kenwood houses demonstrate his admiration for the English Arts & Crafts movement, which flourished in Chicago beginning in the 1890s. Shaw had great respect for materials and craftsmanship and a deep appreciation of English vernacular residential architecture as well as classical and historical forms. At 5715 the treatment of the elaborate door surround and the inventive ornamentation on the pilaster capitals exemplify his freedom with the Classical vocabulary.

99| **First Unitarian Church of Chicago**
5650 S. Woodlawn Ave.
1931, DENISON B. HULL

This textbook example of English Perpendicular Gothic design fits in easily with the limestone facades and Gothic ornament of many Hyde Park residences and campus buildings. It was built around the Hull Memorial Chapel (1897, William A. Otis), which is now the south transept.

100| **Herbert Hugh Riddle House**
5626 S. Woodlawn Ave.

101| **Lewis W. Riddle House**
5622 S. Woodlawn Ave.
1912, RIDDLE & RIDDLE

Built for brothers who practiced architecture together, these houses share the same massing and push the entrance to one side, so that the street facade has only windows. Lewis's house is a sober Georgian composition, while Herbert's has a distinctly French flair. Don't miss the metal-and-glass entrance canopy, reminiscent of Hector Guimard's Art Nouveau design for a Paris Métro entrance.

102 | Hyde Park Union Church
(*Hyde Park Baptist Church*)
5600 S. Woodlawn Ave.
1906, JAMES GAMBLE ROGERS

The congregation of this church was closely associated with founders of the University of Chicago, and its construction was financed largely by John D. Rockefeller. The massive orange sandstone facade on Woodlawn Ave. is anchored by square entry towers marked by round arches. The round-arch motif is repeated on the interior, which also has beautiful stained-glass windows by Louis C. Tiffany of New York and Charles J. Connick Studios of Boston.

103 | Theodore F. Rice House
5554 S. Woodlawn Ave.
1892, MIFFLIN E. BELL

One of the neighborhood's best-preserved Queen Anne houses is distinguished by a wonderful color palette: the brownstone base harmonizes with the dark pink and gray tiles above.

104 | Lutheran School of Theology
1100 E. 55th St.
1966, PERKINS & WILL

A far cry from Collegiate Gothic, this triple-winged complex is a structural tour de force, with six concrete Vierendeel trusses (normally used for bridges) poured in pairs, 175 feet long and two feet thick. Three-piece steel rockers transfer the load to concrete pedestals carried on cruciform piers. The quadrangle is enclosed on the north side by the McCormick Theological Seminary (2003, M + W Zander).

105 | Chicago Child Care Society
5467 S. University Ave.
1963, KECK & KECK

The concrete floors extend beyond the glass walls and are perforated to provide a sunscreen.

106 | St. Thomas the Apostle Roman Catholic Church
5472 S. Kimbark Ave.
1924, BARRY BYRNE

107 | School
5467 S. Woodlawn Ave.
1929, SHATTUCK & LAYER

This remarkable break from traditional Catholic church design was executed by Barry Byrne, who had previously worked for Frank Lloyd Wright. This affiliation with the Prairie School may account for the naturalistic hues of the bricks, the innovative massing, and the unique design of the sculpture and ornament, especially the terra cotta surrounding the entry and windows. Alfonso Iannelli, an important sculptor who often collaborated with other Prairie School architects, worked closely with Byrne on the design of the facades and interior spaces.

Verticality has always been a meaningful metaphor in church design, and here the narrow lancet windows, doorway sculpture, and sculpted brick surfaces ascend dramatically to a richly ornamented roofline. The worship space is free of columns and has pews set close to and almost encircling the altar, which is pushed forward into the nave. The resulting proximity of celebrant and congregation anticipated Roman Catholic liturgical reforms of the early 1960s. Sculptor Alfeo Faggi designed the bronze stations of the cross with an expressive simplicity appropriate to the interior.

ST. THOMAS THE APOSTLE SCHOOL

108 | Augustana Evangelical Lutheran Church of Hyde Park
1151 E. 55th St.
1968, LOEBL, SCHLOSSMAN, BENNETT & DART

Edward D. Dart's solid design of interconnecting masses has a low and inviting entry to provide shelter from the rush of traffic on 55th St. The sculpture of Christ (*Ecce Homo*, 1939) was Egon Weiner's first important work after emigrating from Europe in 1938. He also designed the St. Paul sculpture in the 1985 Memorial Garden.

109 | 5200–5244 S. Greenwood Ave.
1903, JOSEPH C. BROMPTON

Charmingly deceptive, the entire block is lined with twenty row houses with set-back common walls mimicking detached houses. It was created by Charles Counselman, a local meat-packer, and Samuel E. Gross, an active real estate developer. Like Gross's contemporaneous Alta Vista Terrace on the North Side, the row features a variety of styles, materials, and colors—but with a remarkable effect of unity deriving from the common scale and setbacks.

110 | Joseph A. Thomlinson House
5317 S. University Ave.
1904, SOLON S. BEMAN

One of the neighborhood's most eccentric designs bears a great gambrel roof ornamented with stone brackets above a rock-faced stone facade.

111 | 53rd & University Townhouses
1119–1125 E. 53rd St.
1985, DAVID SWAN

The severe northern facade gives no clue to the personable southern side, where tiers of terraces overlook back gardens.

112 | Isidore Heller House
5132 S. Woodlawn Ave.
1897, FRANK LLOYD WRIGHT

This important early design by Wright has many of the radical features that characterize his slightly later Prairie School houses. The bands of windows

ISIDORE HELLER HOUSE

tucked under the low horizontal eaves and the potential for cross-axial spatial relationships suggest what was to follow in the Robie House. The frieze by Richard W. Bock (an important collaborator of many Prairie architects) and the two-tone brick banding of the top story emphasize the horizontal divisions of the wall plane. Despite the narrow and deep I-shaped plan, the interior space is open and expansive because Wright pulled the dining room out to the south and created a long east–west hallway axis perpendicular to the entry. Unlike the frontal entries of most 1890s houses, the all-important entries to Wright's houses—here marked by relief sculpture—are frequently set into the side for privacy and to dramatize the entry process.

113 | Henry C. Work Cottage
5317 S. Dorchester Ave.
1859, ARCHITECT UNKNOWN

Look south from 53rd St. to see what is thought to be Hyde Park's oldest house, a tiny cottage that has long been part of the larger house facing Dorchester Ave. The original board-and-batten siding has been re-created; this and the steep pitch of the roof and of the lone dormer identify the style as Gothic Revival. Work was a renowned composer of Civil War and temperance songs.

114 | Harper Court
S. Harper Ave. and E. 52nd St.
1965, DUBIN, DUBIN, BLACK & MOUTOUSSAMY

HARPER COURT

In the 1950s many Hyde Parkers feared that their community's reputation as a bohemian, artistic neighborhood was threatened by proposed urban renewal. This small-scale shopping center was meant to provide affordable space for the many artists and craftspeople working in buildings on 55th St. slated for demolition. Although the rents proved too expensive for many of those displaced, this pleasant villagelike complex has thrived as a retail center and peaceful public space.

115| 5312–5318 S. Hyde Park Blvd.
1908, ANDREW SANDEGREN

The bulging glassy bays are an early form of the boxy sunroom additions that became so popular on flat buildings in the following two decades.

116| 5451–5455 S. Hyde Park Blvd.
1907, FROMMANN & JEBSEN

The carved Art Nouveau ornament is more reminiscent of Barcelona than Chicago on this fanciful example of a luxurious six-flat, built when the street was dominated by large single-family residences.

117| 5487–5499 S. Hyde Park Blvd.
1908, DOERR & DOERR

This prototypical Hyde Park luxury six-flat has giant Classical columns supporting large open porches on the upper floors. This type of multibalconied six-flat is more common in Hyde Park than in any other area of the city.

118| 5501–5503 S. Hyde Park Blvd.
1909, HENRY W. TOMLINSON

Tomlinson's residential and commercial buildings in Hyde Park frequently exhibit flared

5451–5455 S. HYDE PARK BLVD.

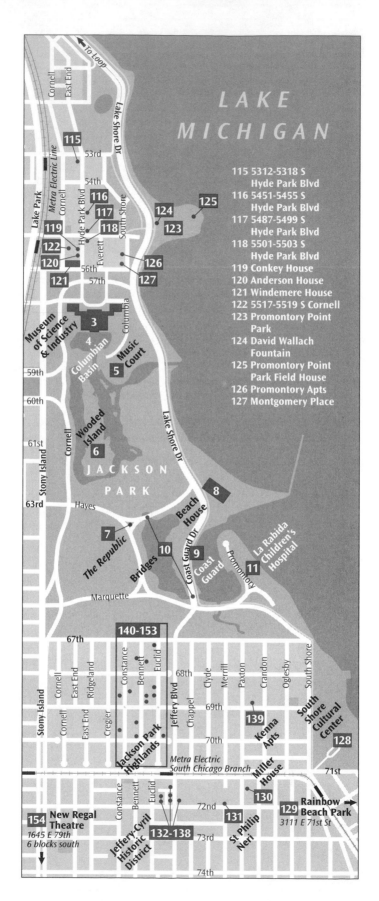

LAKE MICHIGAN

115 5312-5318 S Hyde Park Blvd
116 5451-5455 S Hyde Park Blvd
117 5487-5499 S Hyde Park Blvd
118 5501-5503 S Hyde Park Blvd
119 Conkey House
120 Anderson House
121 Windemere House
122 5517-5519 S Cornell
123 Promontory Point Park
124 David Wallach Fountain
125 Promontory Point Park Field House
126 Promontory Apts
127 Montgomery Place

To Loop

Cornell
East End
Lake Shore Dr
53rd
54th

Metra Electric Line
Lake Park
Cornell
Hyde Park Blvd
South Shore
Everett
Columbia

Museum of Science & Industry
Columbian Basin
Music Court

59th
60th
61st
63rd

Stony Island
Cornell
Wooded Island
JACKSON PARK
Lake Shore Dr
Beach House

Hayes
The Republic
Bridges
Coast Guard Dr
Coast Guard
Promontory
La Rabida Children's Hospital

Marquette

140-153

67th

Stony Island
Cornell
East End
Ridgeland
Cregier
East End
Constance
Bennett
Euclid
Jeffery Blvd
Chappel
Clyde
Merrill
Paxton
Crandon
Oglesby
South Shore

68th
69th
70th

Kenna Apts
South Shore Cultural Center
128

Jackson Park Highlands
Metra Electric South Chicago Branch

71st

Miller House

Constance
Bennett
Euclid
72nd

130
131
St Philip Neri
129 Rainbow Beach Park
3111 E 71st St

154 New Regal Theatre
1645 E 79th
6 blocks south

132-138
Jeffery-Cyril Historic District
73rd
74th

cornices and a robust modern interpretation of Classical ornament. This particular building retains the most integrity, with its basement retail shops, iron railings, intact cornice, and other original features.

119| William B. Conkey House
5518 S. Hyde Park Blvd.
1888, ATTRIB. TO GEORGE W. MAHER

This house presents several features typical of an idiosyncratic, highly decorative style. The window lintels are massive blocks of rough stone, so large that they seem structurally impossible. The second-floor window is pushed behind the wall plane, with a fat splayed column placed in front of it. The third-floor window is a variation on a Palladian theme, with the central section squeezed almost into oblivion. The rough stone and rock-faced brick are of a similar color and texture.

120| N. Anderson House
5522 S. Hyde Park Blvd.
1888, ATTRIB. TO GEORGE W. MAHER

The facade has an unusual combination of pale yellow and green sandstone.

121| Windemere House
(*Windemere East Hotel*)
1642 E. 56th St.
1924, C.W. AND GEORGE L. RAPP

The 1920s were the golden age of residential hotels, and this lakefront area is particularly rich in fine examples. Designed to house both transient and permanent guests, the Windemere offered single rooms (many with kitchenettes), as well as suites that could be combined to create apartments of up to five rooms. Typically for this building type, all the architectural exuberance is concentrated on an elaborate entry pavilion.

122| 5517–5519 S. Cornell Ave.
1891, ATTRIB. TO GEORGE W. MAHER

Built by real estate broker Alex F. Shuman, presumably to

Maher's designs, these houses have wildly original ornament, with almost no repetition of forms or detail.

Accessible only to pedestrians, via the 57th St. footbridge over S. South Shore Dr., is a spot dear to Hyde Parkers.

123| Promontory Point Park
(*55th St. Promontory*)
55th St. at S. South Shore Dr.
1937, ALFRED CALDWELL

This point of land is the highlight of Burnham Park, which stretches north all the way to Grant Park, serving as a lakefront link to Jackson Park. The area of this park had been filled in by 1926 but was not landscaped until after WPA funding became available in 1935. Alfred Caldwell, a follower of the Prairie School landscape tradition of Jens Jensen, envisioned a prairie and meadow landscape planted with native flowering trees. His design was restored following the point's fiftieth anniversary in 1987, including the previously unexecuted circular stone rings used for cookouts and benches that were modeled after Jensen's larger council rings.

124| David Wallach Fountain
1939, ELIZABETH & FRANK HIBBARD

Wallach donated money to design a fountain for "man and beast." The husband-and-wife sculptors (who designed the marble base and the bronze doe, respectively) were both students of Lorado Taft at the School of the Art Institute. Elizabeth Hibbard was also an assistant at his Midway Studios.

125| Promontory Point Park Field House
1937, EMANUEL V. BUCHSBAUM
1991, RENOVATION, CHICAGO PARK DISTRICT

This Lannon stone field house, with its circular lookout tower, was modeled after a lighthouse.

126 | Promontory Apartments
5530 S. South Shore Dr.

1949, LUDWIG MIES VAN DER ROHE;
PACE ASSOCS.; HOLSMAN, HOLSMAN,
KLEKAMP & TAYLOR

This was Mies's first constructed high rise and his first collaboration with developer Herbert S. Greenwald, who became one of his most important clients. The original design had a curtain wall of steel and glass that was the forerunner of 860–880 N. Lake Shore Dr. The columns taper as they rise, giving visual expression to their decreasing structural load.

127 | Montgomery Place
5550 S. South Shore Dr.

1991, NAGLE, HARTRAY & ASSOCS.

Crisp red brick walls are punctuated by angled bay windows that maximize light and views, in a design influenced by Richard M. Bennett's 1350–1360 N. Lake Shore Dr. This luxurious high rise for seniors was built over an existing underground garage and was sited to minimize blockage of its neighbors' light and views.

128 | South Shore Cultural Center
(*South Shore Country Club*)
7059 S. South Shore Dr.

1916, MARSHALL & FOX
1983, RENOVATION, NORMAN
DEHAAN ASSOCS.

Established in 1906, South Shore prospered along with the neighborhood to become one of the city's renowned country clubs, and Marshall & Fox's modest clubhouse (1906) was replaced with this palatial Mediterranean-style structure. Spacious and elaborately decorated corridors connect grand ballrooms to the north and south with a glazed solarium on the east, as well as dining and meeting rooms overlooking the lake. It is well worth a trip inside, especially to see the north ballroom, which is like an enormous glass box with a Wedgwood lid. The wall-to-wall windows could be raised to expand the surrounding terrace. The splendid colonnaded driveway, on axis with the entrance gatehouse (unrestored), provides a grand approach. The sixty-five-acre property, purchased by the Chicago Park District in 1974, includes a beach, golf course, tennis courts, an outdoor stage, and a riding arena, as well as traces of the original bowling green and shooting area. The stables are now used by the Chicago Mounted Police. The abandoned shooting lodge to the north was built at the same time as the main clubhouse.

129 | Rainbow Beach Park Buildings
3111 E. 71st St.

2000, DAVID WOODHOUSE ARCHITECTS

This neglected park received a jolt of creative architecture with the addition of these small but imaginative structures. The translucent oval canopies evoke clouds.

SOUTH SHORE CULTURAL CENTER

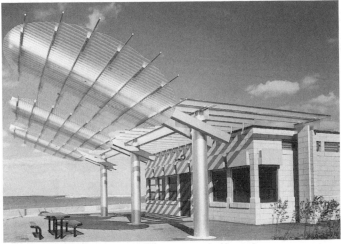

BEACH HOUSE AT RAINBOW BEACH PARK

130 | Allan Miller House
7121 S. Paxton Ave.
1915, JOHN S. VAN BERGEN

This extremely well preserved house is the only surviving building in Chicago by this Prairie School architect, most of whose work is found in the North Shore suburbs. Its open plan is derived from Wright's "Fireproof House for $5,000," but the generous seventy-five-foot lot width allowed Van Bergen to expand the cube with a large porch, giving the composition some of the expansiveness associated with suburban Prairie houses.

131 | St. Philip Neri Roman Catholic Church
2126 E. 72nd St.
1928, JOSEPH W. MCCARTHY

The golden hues of Plymouth granite set off this Tudor Revival design. Bedford limestone is used for the carving around the entrance and the tracery in the large rose windows. The copper spire adds height to this large church, which is set on a landscaped base raised above the street.

132 | Jeffery-Cyril Historic District
7100 block of S. Jeffery and S. Cyril Blvds.

The rejuvenation of this enclave provides an excellent example of the benefits available under mid-1980s tax incentives for historic preservation. The busy intersection of E. 71st St. and Jeffery Blvd. was developed in the late 1920s with six apartment buildings in widely varied styles. All but one had small to medium units (one to four rooms) marketed to middle-class tenants. Varying in height from five to thirteen stories, the buildings form a group that dominates the low-rise residential and commercial landscape. In 1987–1988 four of them were restored and modernized by a development subsidiary of South Shore Bank.

133 | E. 71st Pl. Building
1966–1974 E. 71st Pl.
1928, PAUL FREDERICK OLSEN
1987, RENOVATION, LISEC & BIEDERMAN

A Spanish colonial revival building of brick and terra cotta, it has a two-story lobby on 71st Pl. and storefronts (altered) along Jeffery Blvd.

134 | Bedford Villa Apartments
7130 S. Cyril Ave.
1929, PAUL FREDERICK OLSEN

This Gothic Revival apartment building has a distinctive entrance with gargoyles and fleurs-de-lis.

135 | Shore Manor/Eleanor Manor
7150 S. Cyril Ave.
1920, DANIEL J. SCHAFFNER

This pair of Georgian Revival apartment buildings rises over an English basement that contains the lobbies.

136| Highland Apartments
7147 S. Jeffery Blvd.
1927, MCNALLY & QUINN
1987, RENOVATION, LISEC &
BIEDERMAN

Gabled parapets and a traceried entrance give this
brick-and-limestone structure
a Tudor flavor.

137| Jeffery-Cyril Apartments
7144 S. Jeffery Blvd.
1927, JULIUS J. SCHWARZ
1988, RENOVATION, LISEC &
BIEDERMAN

The two-story entryway of this
Tudor building is decorated
with crockets. Unlike its neighbors, it was originally a cooperative, with larger apartments of
five to six rooms.

138| Jeffery Terrace Apartments
7130 S. Jeffery Blvd.
1929, PAUL FREDERICK OLSEN
1987, RENOVATION, LISEC &
BIEDERMAN

Although designed by the same
architect as two other buildings
in this group, this one represents
a complete break with their historically inspired styles. It is
a jazzy essay in Art Deco, with
ornament created only by geometric shapes. Arcades along
Jeffery Blvd. provide sheltered
entries for the commercial
spaces. Note the apartment entry
surrounded by gold glazed tile.

KENNA APARTMENTS

139| Kenna Apartments
2214 E. 69th St.
1916, BARRY BYRNE & RYAN CO.

The unusually severe composition, perhaps influenced by
Byrne's contact with California
protomodernist Irving J. Gill
in 1913, is enlivened by Alfonso
Iannelli's wonderful ornament
around the entrance and
windows.

140| Jackson Park Highlands
Euclid, Bennett, & Constance
Aves. between 67th & 71st Sts.

Named for its location atop a
ridge, this middle-class residential neighborhood was estab-

JEFFERY TERRACE APARTMENTS

lished as an eighty-acre subdivision in 1905. It was developed by Frank I. Bennett, a Chicago alderman, lawyer, and realtor, and Charles J. Bour, an "advertising agent." Most of the houses were built between 1905 and 1940, and they present an impressive array of the styles—mostly revivalist—of the period. The design standards included minimum lot widths of fifty feet, a thirty-foot setback from the street, no alleys, and buried utilities. Facade materials were restricted to brick or stone, and roof materials to tile or slate. As a group, the houses retain an unusually high degree of architectural integrity, rewarding visitors with superbly handled materials, ornamental details, and early landscape and gardening features. This subdivision grew as automobile ownership was increasing; look down the original narrow, two-track concrete driveways to see auto sheds that match the houses.

141 | 6700 S. Euclid Ave.
1952, SPITZ & SPITZ

One of the few postwar houses in this subdivision, this 1950s classic has a big front-entry fin.

142 | 6826 S. Euclid Ave.
1905, ARCHITECT UNKNOWN

The two-story temple front proclaims its Greek Revival style, but in an unusual twist, the triangular pediment is half-timbered. There is a similar house at 6931.

143 | 6840 S. Euclid Ave.
1905, ARCHITECT UNKNOWN

This is a good example of the simplification of Queen Anne forms after the turn of the century. The large bays are still present, but the massing is simpler and the facade is symmetrical.

144 | 6955 S. Euclid Ave.
1909, FRANK D. CHASE

This Tudor Revival house and matching auto shed show the influence of the English Arts & Crafts movement.

145 | 6956 S. Bennett Ave.
1936, PAUL SCHWEIKHER

This International Style house in brick has metal-framed corner windows, a low roof with a central chimney, and glass blocks in windows on the north side. Schweikher practiced in Chicago from 1933, when his work was exhibited at the Museum of Modern Art, to 1953, when he left to teach at Yale University.

146 | 6926 S. Bennett Ave.
1908, WILLIAM L. DAGELS

Maher's influence is strong in this house, with its octagonal columns and hipped roof with a flanged segmental arch dormer.

147 | 6851 S. Bennett Ave.
1909, CHATTEN & HAMMOND

One of three houses in Jackson Park Highlands by this firm

6956 S. BENNETT AVE.

(the others are at 6757 and 6855 S. Euclid Ave.), this large Tudor house has a matching auto shed.

148| 6841 S. Bennett Ave.
1915, HARLEV & AGA

Among the unusual features of this eclectic house are brickwork that imitates half-timbering, and terra-cotta plaques (more commonly found on commercial buildings) stuck like postage stamps on the first-floor piers.

149| 6737 S. Bennett Ave.
1927, CHARLES D. FAULKNER

The first-floor windows of this neo-Classical house are each framed by an arch with a coat of arms and wreaths in relief on the tympanum.

150| 6734 S. Bennett Ave.
1918, ZIMMERMAN, SAXE & ZIMMERMAN

This distinctive one-story house combines stylistic features of the Prairie School (a low profile and horizontal proportions), California Arts & Crafts (multiple roof planes), and Tudor (half-timbering). Like its neighbors, it is set back from the street and raised slightly above ground level on a terrace.

151| 6829 S. Constance Ave.
1915, EDGAR M. NEWMAN

This Craftsman bungalow has very horizontal proportions and brackets supporting low eaves.

152| 6840 S. Constance Ave.
1921, LUTHER W. MCDONALD

A more modest bungalow, this type proliferated in urban developments of the 1910s and 1920s.

153| 6946 S. Constance Ave.
1924, SAMUEL S. OMAN

This free adaptation of Classical and Gothic motifs has stylized columns, humorous animals, and a lion bearing a coat of arms.

154| New Regal Theatre
(*Avalon Theatre*)
1645 E. 79th St.
1927, JOHN EBERSON

This Austrian-born architect was known throughout the South and Midwest as "Opera House John" for his fantastic and exuberant theaters. He specialized in "atmospheric" theaters, with opulent, exotic, and evocative interiors well suited to the fantasy settings of 1920s movies. The Middle Eastern world created here was inspired by a Persian incense burner that Eberson found in a New Orleans antique shop. The exterior is equally lavish, covered with multicolored terra-cotta.

155| Oak Woods Cemetery
1035 E. 67th St.

The Oak Woods Cemetery Association was formed in 1853. Like Chicago's other historic cemeteries, Graceland and Rosehill, it was located beyond the growing city but close to a railroad line. In 1866 the Illinois Central began operating a spur line to the cemetery. The association hired Adolph Strauch, superintendent of Spring Grove Cemetery in Cincinnati, to assist in the planning, thus ensuring that Oak Woods would reflect the most up-to-date thinking. Beyond establishing a parklike environment, Strauch promoted the idea known as the lawn plan, in which no walls, fences, curbing, or coping mark the edges of the plots. His plan for Oak Woods included three lakes surrounded by curving roadways and gently rising mounds.　　—JOAN POMARANC

Oak Woods has one of Chicago's most significant concentrations of Civil War commemorations. The A| **Confederate Mound Monument,** erected in 1893 and officially dedicated on Memorial Day, 1895, marks the North's largest burial site for Southern soldiers and sailors. The two-

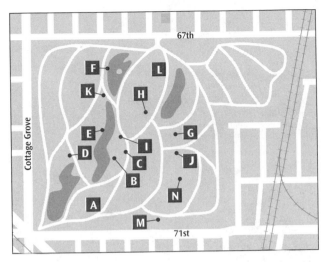

acre site, acquired by the federal government in 1867, marks the graves of 6,000 prisoners of war who died in Chicago's Camp Douglas of disease and deprivation. General John C. R. Underwood, a civil engineer and Confederate veteran, led the movement to build this memorial and designed it himself. The graves are arranged in concentric trenches around the sloping base of the forty-foot-tall monument. In 1911 bronze tablets bearing the names and ranks of the 4,275 men identified in official records were added to the mound. Atop a twelve-foot column, its capital carved to resemble a battlement, is a bronze sculpture of a Confederate infantryman, based on a figure in a painting titled *Appomattox* by Confederate veteran John A. Elder.

The 1890s saw the erection of numerous monuments to the Civil War in both the North and the South. Sufficient time had passed for the national rift to have begun to heal, and those with firsthand memories of the war wanted to commemorate their experience before it was too late. In the northwest corner of the cemetery are plots held by the Soldiers' Home, Abraham Lincoln Post No. 91, Department of Illinois, the Grand Army of the Republic, and the Chicago Veterans Association. A statue of a Union soldier with a rifle (partially missing) and a cannon and shot marks the plot of the Soldiers' Home, which still stands on E. 35th St. A 1905 replica of Charles J. Mulligan's *Lincoln the Orator (The Gettysburg Lincoln)* of 1903 marks off the plot for members of a local post of the GAR, the major Union veterans' organization.

The tallest monument is the limestone obelisk marking the burial site of B| **William Hale ("Big Bill") Thompson,** Chicago's mayor from 1915 to 1923 and from 1927 to 1931. A boorish lout with a theatrical manner, he opposed U.S. involvement in World War I and Prohibition at home, threatening to fire any policeman who interfered with a citizen's "personal liberty"—the selling or consumption of alcohol. Thompson's was one of the loudest roars in the Roaring Twenties. A gray granite mausoleum is the final resting place of C| **Harold Washington,** state legislator, Congressman, and the first African American mayor of Chicago.

A simple granite column with four sloping sides marks the grave of architect D| **Solon Spencer Beman.**

E| **George A. Fuller** was trained as an architect but achieved fame as originator of the modern contracting system in building construction. His firm, based in Chicago with a branch in New York City, built the Monadnock Building and the Rookery in Chicago and the Flatiron (originally Fuller) Building in New York. Bruce Price designed the monument, the only work in Chicago by this New York architect. It is a limestone pergola of fluted columns on which rest three layers of supporting beams representing steel, stone, and wood construction.

GEORGE A. FULLER MONUMENT

Curiously, on the underside of the topmost, or "wooden," beams, are carved stone rivets—characteristics of modern steel-frame construction. The Classical details convey an impression of a traditional, albeit somewhat peculiar, design.

The red granite monument to **F| Jesse Owens** features the Olympic rings that recall his achievements at the 1936 Games in Berlin, at which he won the broad jump and the 100- and 200-meter dash.

Crossed baseball bats and a ball mark the grave of **G| Adrian C. ("Cap") Anson,** a baseball player and manager of the Chicago White Stockings (forerunner of the Cubs) in the newly formed National League.

The monument to **H| Gale Cramer,** a young train engineer who sacrificed himself to save his passengers, features a model of the train in which he died.

I| The **Firmenich** family monument is a very tall statuary group that stands out dramatically at Symphony Lake. Atop a large, heavy base are three female figures representing Faith, Hope, and Charity.

EASTMAN MONUMENT

PAUL CORNELL MONUMENT

J| The **Eastman** monument features a life-size bronze figure of a woman in Classical dress, bearing a wreath in her right hand while she leans mournfully against a pink granite slab.

K| **Paul Cornell's** plot features a very large monument made of a material known as white bronze. In 1853 he founded the town of Hyde Park and cofounded Oak Woods Cemetery.

L| The **Chapel and Crematory** (1903, William Carbys Zimmerman) is reminiscent of a rural English Gothic church but exhibits some Prairie School elements in its steeple and entrance porch. The **Tower of Memories** (1960) is a communal mausoleum and columbarium. Prairie School architect

M| **George C. Nimmons,** who specialized in industrial buildings, is buried here.

Along the south edge of Oak Woods are a group of Jewish cemeteries, each demarcated by a fence. These plots, held by congregations or fraternal organizations, resemble traditional European graveyards with close-set headstones and no open space apart from walkways. In the cemetery proper, among another area of Jewish graves, is a monument known as the **N| Eternal Light.** In every synagogue burns an eternal light; this one is a memorial to victims of the Holocaust. Its base shaped like a Star of David, the red granite tower contains in its top a radioactive material that absorbs sunlight by day and glows at night.

OAK WOODS CEMETERY CHAPEL

BEVERLY/ MORGAN PARK

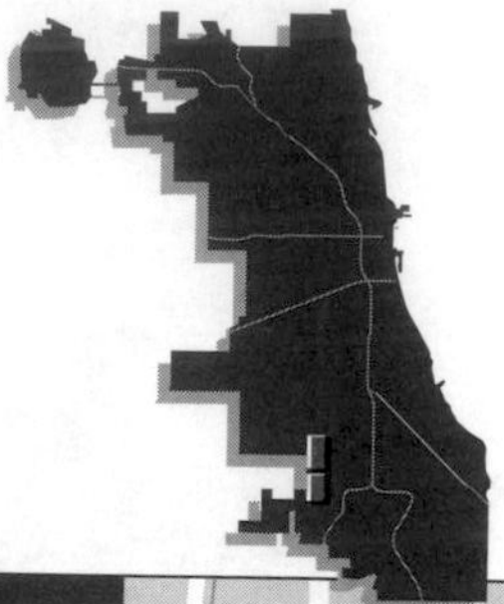

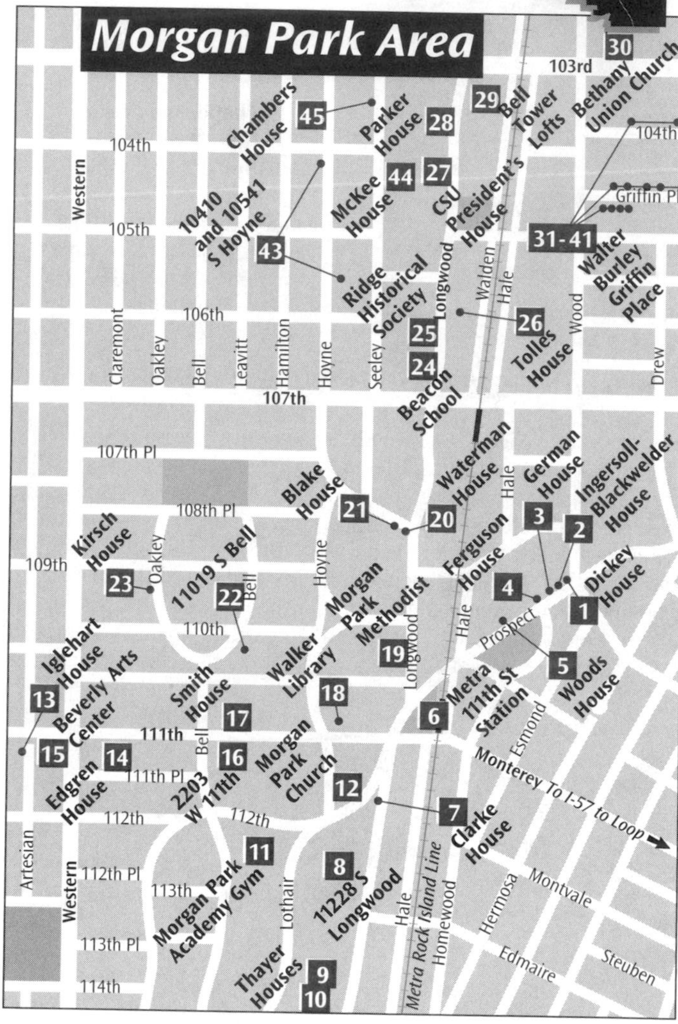

Morgan Park Area

103rd
30
Bethany
Union Church
29 Bell
Tower
Lofts
45 Parker
House
28
Chambers
House
104th
McKee
House
44
27
CSU
President's
House
Griffin Pl
104th
10410
and 10541
S Hoyne
105th
Western
43
31-41
Walter
Burley
Griffin
Place
Ridge
Historical
Society
106th
Claremont
Oakley
Bell
Leavitt
Hamilton
Hoyne
Seeley
Longwood
Walden
Hale
Wood
Drew
25
26
Tolles
House
24
Beacon
School
107th
107th Pl
Waterman
House
German
House
Ingersoll-
Blackwelder
House
Blake
House
108th Pl
21
20
3
2
Ferguson
House
Dickey
House
Kirsch
House
109th
23
Oakley
11019 S Bell
Hoyne
Morgan
Park
Methodist
4
1
22
Bell
110th
Longwood
Hale
Prospect
5
Woods
House
Iglehart
House
Walker
Library
19
Metra
111th St
Station
Esmond
13
Beverly Arts
Center
Smith
House
18
6
Monterey To I-57 to Loop →
15
14
17
16
Morgan
Park
Church
12
7
Clarke
House
Hermosa
Montvale
Edgren
House
2203
W 11th
111th
111th Pl
Bell
112th
112th
7
Artesian
Western
11
8
11228 S
Longwood
Hale
Homewood
Edmaire
Steuben
Morgan Park
Academy Gym
112th Pl
113th
Lothair
113th Pl
Thayer
Houses
9
10
114th
Metra Rock Island Line

IF COMMUNITIES STILL ADOPTED LATIN MOTTOS, BEVERLY–MORGAN PARK MIGHT bill itself as *Suburbia in Urbe*. With its towering trees, broad lawns, and sprawling old houses, it looks more like an affluent North Shore suburb than a Chicago neighborhood. The hilly topography and winding streets also set it apart from the flat urban grid to the east. The small rail stations, which retain much of their charm despite heavy-handed remodelings, recall the area's origins as a commuter suburb.

Morgan Park is the older community. In 1844 an Englishman named Thomas Morgan bought a large tract of land along the Blue Island Ridge (the hill that rises west of Longwood Dr.) from 91st to 119th Sts., which remain the north and south boundaries of the combined neighborhoods. It remained a sleepy farm community until 1869, when the Blue Island Land & Building Company bought the land and hired another English-

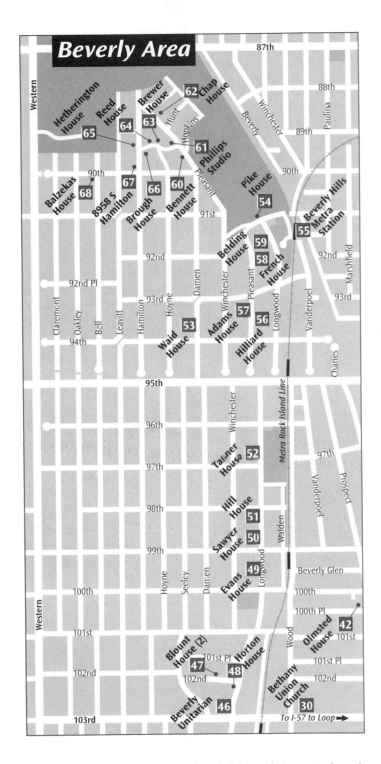

Beverly Area

Western

87th

88th

Brewer House · 62 Chap House

89th

Hetherington House · Reed House · 64 · 63 · Hunt · Hopkins · Winchester · Beverly

65

61 Phillips Studio

Pleasant

90th · Pike House · 54

Beverly Hills Metra Station · 55

Balzekas House · 68 · 8958 S Hamilton · 67 · 66 · 60 Bennett House · Brough House · 91st

90th · Marshfield

Belding House · 59 · 58 French House · 92nd

Claremont · Oakley · Bell · Leavitt · Hamilton · Hoyne · Damen · Winchester · Pleasant

92nd

92nd Pl

93rd · Adams House · 57 · 56 · Longwood · Vanderpoel · 93rd · Charles

Waid House · 53 · Hilliard House

94th

95th

96th · Winchester

Tanner House · 52 · Metra Rock Island Line · 97th · Vanderpoel · Prospect

97th

98th · Hill House · 51

Sawyer House · 50

99th · Evans House · 49 · Longwood · Welden · Beverly Glen

100th · Hoyne · Seeley · Damen · 100th · 100th Pl · Wood · Olmsted House · 42

Western

101st · Blount House [2] · 101st Pl · Horton House · 101st · 101st Pl

47 · 48 · 102nd · Bethany Union Church

102nd

Beverly Unitarian · 46 · 30 · To I-57 to Loop →

103rd

man, Thomas F. Nichols, to lay out the subdivision of Morgan Park south of 107th St. The curving streets and generous greenswards of this area result from Nichols's picturesque planning principles.

Although not incorporated as a village until 1882, Morgan Park developed significantly in the 1870s. In the first year of the decade the Chicago, Rock Island & Pacific Railroad established a branch line that provided the area with convenient service to the Loop. Three institutions were established here in quick succession: the Morgan Park Military Academy, founded in 1873, which continues—minus the military aspect—to be a prominent preparatory school; the Chicago Female College, established in 1875; and the Baptist Union Theological Seminary, which moved here from Chicago's Douglas neighborhood in 1877. The presence of the seminary, led by Thomas W. Goodspeed and William Rainey Harper, raised hopes that the proposed University of Chicago might establish its new campus here. When the more centrally located Hyde Park was chosen instead, the seminary left with them to become the university's Divinity School. Morgan Park remained a quiet residential village whose community life centered on a handful of Protestant churches. Even a fiercely fought annexation to the city in 1914 did little to alter its subdued character.

The community of Beverly, also called Beverly Hills, developed slightly later but followed a similar pattern. It was part of the village of Washington Heights to the east, which was annexed to Chicago in 1890 but retained its own small-town identity. Like Morgan Park, it developed from east to west. In 1889 the Chicago, Rock Island & Pacific Railroad opened a station at 91st St. and named it Beverly Hills, which came to be the name for the whole community north of 107th St. along the Ridge. Residential development proceeded swiftly, with the biggest boom taking place in the 1920s.

North of 95th St., an important commercial artery, the enclave of North Beverly is the area's most exclusive community. The deep wooded lots on rolling hills shelter large Revival Style houses from the 1920s and 1930s. As geographically distant from the Loop as are the suburbs of Evanston and Riverside, North Beverly shares their sylvan sense of shelter.

—LAURIE MCGOVERN PETERSEN

1| Luther S. Dickey, Jr., House
10990 S. Prospect Ave.
1912, CHATTEN & HAMMOND

Set far back on a four-acre lot is a stellar example of the Arts & Crafts–influenced eclectic house often found in the North Shore suburbs. Picturesque elements— a half-timbered double gable, sloping brick buttresses and piers, and a flanged segmental entry arch—are freely combined into a masterfully integrated composition.

2| Ingersoll-Blackwelder House
10910 S. Prospect Ave.
1874; 1887, FRONT ADDITION, ARCHITECTS UNKNOWN

3| Dr. William H. German House
10924 S. Prospect Ave.
1884, FREDERICK G. GERMAN

Ingersoll-Blackwelder is a catalog of the decorative possibilities of wood sheathing: clapboards laid horizontally, vertically, and even diagonally; applied fretwork; and shingles in three patterns. The German House is comparatively restrained but adds a touch of half-timbering to the mix.

4| William G. Ferguson House
10934 S. Prospect Ave.
1873, ARCHITECT UNKNOWN

5| Dr. Arthur W. Woods House
10970 S. Prospect Ave.
1872, ARCHITECT UNKNOWN

Deep fascia characterize these altered but charming Italianates.

6| 111th St. Metra Station
(*Chicago, Rock Island & Pacific Railroad—Morgan Park Station*)
111th St. and Hale Ave.
1891, JOHN T. LONG

Set on a large greensward, this station has a deliberately domestic scale and was meant to advertise the comfortable suburban character of early Morgan Park. The first floor was designed to be faced in brick but was constructed entirely of wood. Details such as a waiting-room fireplace survive, but overscaled asphalt siding obscures some of the charm.

Like Prospect Ave., Longwood Dr. developed early as a fashionable street. Look to the top of the hill to see many of the oldest houses, which have long front yards

MORGAN PARK CHURCH OF GOD IN CHRIST

stretching down to Longwood, frequently with newer houses on their lots at the base of the hill. Some now have addresses on Lothair Ave., one block to the west, and are best seen from this "back door" street.

7| Sarah D. Clarke House
(*W. S. Kiskaddon House*)
11156 S. Longwood Dr.
1892, JOHN GAVIN

This prim Queen Anne dollhouse miniaturizes diverse stylistic elements with bracketed charm. The Italianate corner tower shrinks as it rises.

8| 11228 S. Longwood Dr./
11213 S. Lothair Ave.
1935, REMODELING,
CHARLES D. FAULKNER

Probably dating from the late nineteenth century, this house was completely transformed with a Jacobean brick-and-stone veneer and addition.

9| Dr. Henry E. Thayer House (2)
11347 S. Lothair Ave.
1874, ARCHITECT UNKNOWN

10| Dr. Gilbert Thayer House (1)
11359 S. Lothair Ave./11410
S. Longwood Dr.
1873, ARCHITECT UNKNOWN

Almost lost to view in leafy summer are these grand hilltop Italianates with their breathtaking eastward views.

11| Morgan Park Academy
Gymnasium
2147–2155 W. 112th St.
1900, DWIGHT H. PERKINS

The geometric end gables and some of the windows hint at Perkins's Prairie School affinities. This is the oldest extant building of Morgan Park Academy.

12| Morgan Park Church of
God in Christ
(*Morgan Park Congregational Church*)
11153 S. Hoyne Ave.
1916, PATTON, HOLMES & FLYNN

Domestically scaled and comfortable, it is Chicago's best-preserved Craftsman church, here blended with Mission touches. The interior retains the original lanterns and woodwork.

13| Charles D. Iglehart House
11118 S. Artesian Ave.
1857; 1870S, FRONT ADDITION,
ARCHITECTS UNKNOWN

Tucked away on a mundane street of mid-twentieth-century brick houses is one of Chicago's earliest dwellings. The rear half of this Italianate house was a small cottage where Iglehart's daughter Mary was born in 1857—the first birth in Morgan Park. The house is in remarkably good condition for an 1870s frame building.

14| Johan Alexis Edgren House
2314 W. 111th Pl.
1882, PALLISER, PALLISER & CO.

The design for this unusually well preserved house was purchased from Palliser, Palliser & Co., producers of some of America's most influential pattern books for home owners and builders. This style is now called Stick Style, for the wood laid atop the building's clapboard walls. It articulates the structure below and was considered "modern" during its era in the 1870s and 1880s.

15| Beverly Arts Center
2407 W. 111th St.
2002, WHEELER KEARNS ARCHITECTS

One of this firm's greatest talents is to develop a noble project on only a small budget. Crisp planes of brick and glass create an imposing street presence on the busy corner and a welcoming courtyard facing the parking lot. The modest budget was stretched to include a 420-seat theater, art gallery, and studio space along with the requisite café and gift shop.

16| 2203 W. 111th St.
1873, ARCHITECT UNKNOWN

17| Justin A. Smith House
2204 W. 111th St.
1872, ARCHITECT UNKNOWN

These early, altered houses share a cross-gabled massing, triangular second-floor window hoods, and the bracketed front gables so popular in early 1870s cottages. The structure at 2203 was formerly the Morgan Park Academy Headmaster's House.

18| Chicago Public Library—
George C. Walker Branch
11071 S. Hoyne Ave.
1890, CHARLES S. FROST
1933, ADDITIONS, DOERR & DOERR
1995, RENOVATION AND NORTHERN ADDITION, VOA ASSOCS.

This is reminiscent of H. H. Richardson's suburban train stations, but the twin towers with inward-facing windows have a slightly pigeon-toed charm all their own. The end and rear rooms came later, and the interior has been completely remodeled.

19| Morgan Park United Methodist Church
(*Morgan Park Methodist Episcopal Church*)
11000 S. Longwood Dr.
1913, HARRY HALE WATERMAN
1926, ADDITION, PERKINS, FELLOWS & HAMILTON

Simple, powerful elements dominate this Craftsman church: the exaggeratedly broad gable, the anchoring tower, and the entry cut like a cave from the body of the church.

Along Longwood Dr. architects dealt with a problem rare in Chicago: the rolling lot. The houses nestle into, perch upon, strut across, or lord it over their hilltop sites with varying degrees of success.

20| Harry Hale Waterman House
10838 S. Longwood Dr.
1892, HARRY HALE WATERMAN

With its terraced entry, it snuggles more cozily into the Ridge than any house of Longwood Dr. Punctuated by an exaggerated gable at the entry porch, the high hipped roof gives a whimsical sense of disproportion to this overgrown cottage, the architect's own home.

21| J. T. Blake House
2023 W. 108th Pl.
1894, HARRY HALE WATERMAN

Typical of many of Waterman's charmingly irregular designs, the asymmetrical, steeply pitched gable roof and jutting stairway bay form an entrance facade combining stone, stucco, and wood.

22| 11019 S. Bell Ave.
EARLY 1880S, ARCHITECT UNKNOWN

Two narrow wings meet stiffly at an angled wall that grows into a tower—a massing with French precedents that is little seen in Chicago.

23| Kirsch House
10920 S. Oakley Ave.
1888, ARCHITECT UNKNOWN

Queen Anne meets the Kremlin in this exuberant house with a gilded turret.

24| Beacon Therapeutic School
(*E. J. Barker House*)
10650 S. Longwood Dr.
1910, HARRY HALE WATERMAN
1992, ADDITION, PHILLIP PEECHER & ASSOCS.

HARRY HALE WATERMAN HOUSE

The horizontal massing and simple lines show a Prairie School spirit worlds apart from the picturesque irregularity of Waterman's houses from the 1890s.

25| Ridge Historical Society
(*Herbert S. Graver House*)
10616 S. Longwood Dr.
1922, JOHN TODD HETHERINGTON

The terraces take better advantage of the dramatic hilltop site than any house on the street.

26| Harry N. Tolles House
10561 S. Longwood Dr.
1911, WALTER BURLEY GRIFFIN

Though related to the houses on Griffin Pl., it has an altered porch, a relocated main entrance, glass block, and replaced window muntins that detract from its appearance.

27| Chicago State University—President's House
(*Frank Anderson House*)
10400 S. Longwood Dr.
1924, OSCAR L. MCMURRY

This very formal, elegant rendition of 1920s Italian Renaissance Revival has simple Classical pediments above the first-floor openings.

28| Hiland A. Parker House
10340 S. Longwood Dr.
1894, HARRY HALE WATERMAN

Site and style combine here for high drama. The base of huge rusticated brownstone blocks rises from the hill to form arches on the big semicircular porch. The tall roof, pierced with steeply pitched gabled dormers, exaggerates the height.

29| Bell Tower Lofts
(*Thirteenth Church of Christ, Scientist*)
10317 S. Longwood Dr.
1916, HOWARD L. CHENEY
1992, CONVERSION TO APARTMENTS, STOWELL COOK FROLICHSTEIN

A ponderous Greek Revival box, this typical Christian Scientist church has taken on a new mission with its conversion to apartments.

30| Bethany Union Church
1750 W. 103rd St.
1927, RAYMOND M. HOOD

The narrow facade of this lovely and severely simple church has been overwhelmed by the mundane support building to the west.

31| W. 104th Pl./Walter Burley Griffin Pl.

In 1973 an article in the *Prairie School Review* revealed that detective work by architect Wilbert R. Hasbrouck and architectural historian Paul E. Sprague had uncovered a significant concentration of houses by Walter Burley Griffin in Beverly. The houses were all commissioned by Russell L. Blount, an aspiring developer whose early successes in selling houses designed by Griffin led to a string of projects. Griffin was at the height of his American career at the time; he had worked in Frank Lloyd Wright's studio from 1901 to 1905 and had a substantial solo practice, until he left for Australia in 1913 to design the capital city of Canberra.

Blount's association with Griffin began in 1909, when he commissioned a house for himself and his fiancée, to be built on her father's property on 104th Pl. Before the house was complete, he received an attractive offer for it from Edmund C. Garrity, leading him to commission a new one for himself next door (Blount House 1) and a speculative one down the block that was later sold to Harry G. Van Nostrand. In 1912–1913 Blount commissioned three more houses from Griffin: the Blount House (2), which became his by default when the intended purchaser reneged, and the Salmon and Jenkinson houses. For this last house Griffin was listed as providing "plans only," and it differs in several respects from the previous five, which are considered purer examples of his work.

Shortly after Griffin left for Australia, Blount built four other houses in the area, three based on the Van Nostrand House design (Williams, Hornbaker, Clarke) and one on the Salmon House (Furneaux). Sales of the later houses never lived up to the expectations generated by the quick offers received for the first few, and by 1915 Blount was building undistinguished rows of cracker box houses.

This remarkable street, renamed Walter Burley Griffin Pl., reflects an innovative approach to the design of small, inexpensive houses. Griffin's houses are all one and a half or two stories, built of wood and stucco on a concrete basement, and have very compact square

plans, similar to Wright's 1907 design of "A Fireproof House for $5,000." The living and dining rooms are defined, rather than separated, by a large fireplace; the kitchen is tucked into the remaining corner; and open porches extend the spaces outdoors. Griffin invariably covers the foundation with clapboards, often continuing them to the sill line of the first-floor windows. The porch's location is determined by the desire to give it at least one southern exposure. The windows are casements with robust wooden mullions in geometric patterns, sometimes quite elaborate. The roof is occasionally hipped but most often has a large open gable with extended ends that enhance its sheltering quality. Gables over the screened porches echo the main gable and add variety to the basic cube. This group is part of Griffin's rustic work, with rough brown siding, pale stucco, and naturally weathering shingles making the houses seem suited to their bucolic location.

32| Harry G. Van Nostrand House
1666 W. Griffin Pl.
1911, WALTER BURLEY GRIFFIN

The plan is a smaller version of the Garrity House and was re-used in others. Except for an added front dormer, the house is in close to original condition. It is especially rewarding to see the porch still screened—as so many of them were—rather than enclosed.

33| Edmund C. Garrity House
1712 W. Griffin Pl.
1909, WALTER BURLEY GRIFFIN

The quick and profitable sale of this newlyweds' house launched Blount on his career. The second-floor dormers were added later, although the mullion pattern was thoughtfully reproduced.

34| Russell L. Blount House (1)
1724 W. Griffin Pl.
1911, WALTER BURLEY GRIFFIN

EDMUND C. GARRITY HOUSE

RUSSELL L. BLOUNT HOUSE (1)

When Blount's first house was sold to Garrity, he commissioned this replacement. The clapboard "hoop skirt" covering the foundation exaggerates the horizontal with inexpensive flair. Griffin grouped first-floor windows to break through the wall at all four corners.

35| Walter O. Salmon House
1736 W. Griffin Pl.
1912, WALTER BURLEY GRIFFIN

The virtually unaltered exterior features an unusual two-story screened porch.

36| Arthur G. Jenkinson House
1727 W. Griffin Pl.
1912, WALTER BURLEY GRIFFIN

The partial extension of the clapboard siding above the first-floor level may be Blount's alteration to Griffin's design. It is similar to the facade treatment of the Newland House,

whose architect of record was Spencer & Powers.

37| William N. Clarke House
1731 W. Griffin Pl.
1913, WALTER BURLEY GRIFFIN

Blount shifted the Van Nostrand House plan ninety degrees here and moved the porch. The windows have lost their distinctive muntins.

38| Harry C. Furneaux House
1741 W. Griffin Pl.
1913, WALTER BURLEY GRIFFIN

This plan is a reversed version of the Salmon House but with a single-story porch and different details. The triangular roof brackets may have been inspired by those on the Newland House.

39| Harry F. Newland House
1737 W. Griffin Pl.
1912, SPENCER & POWERS

This house may have been begun by Griffin. The roof brackets and the extension of the clapboarding above the first floor are not found in his work.

40| William R. Hornbaker House
1710 W. 104th St.
1914, WALTER BURLEY GRIFFIN

This heavily altered variation of the Clarke House has had all the windows replaced and large dormers added.

41| Ida E. Williams House
1632 W. 104th St.
1913, WALTER BURLEY GRIFFIN

Despite the addition of a small dormer, this house retains much of its original appearance and still has a screened porch with the wood muntins. It is of the same plan and tiny dimensions as the Van Nostrand House.

42| Frank N. Olmsted House
1624 W. 100th Pl.
1910, WALTER BURLEY GRIFFIN

A reversal of the Blount House (1) plan, it has lost the "hoop skirt" clapboarding at the base.

43| 10410 and 10541 S. Hoyne Ave.
1917, FRANK LLOYD WRIGHT

These are products of American System-Built, a short-lived collaboration of Wright and Richards Bros. of Milwaukee that sold Wright designs prepackaged and ready to build. Novelist Sherwood Anderson was the company copywriter and touted the modestly priced houses as examples of an American architecture "as brave and direct as the country." These designs were derived from Wright's "Fireproof House for $5,000" but are far less successful schemes and were unsupervised by Wright. Other, more popular models included duplexes and bungalows.

44| James R. McKee House
10415 S. Seeley Ave.
1908, JOHN M. SCHROEDER

This house packs all its punch into one element, the projecting sunroom capped by a graceful broken arch. The simple entrance is hidden away on the side, behind the battered front wall.

JAMES R. MCKEE HOUSE

45| Chambers House
10330 S. Seeley Ave.
1874, ARCHITECT UNKNOWN

This remarkably well preserved house is a classic suburban villa, complete with "French" tower. The garden veranda on the south side was meant to frame the view and provide a suitable vantage point for the beauties of nature.

CHAMBERS HOUSE

46| Beverly Unitarian Church
(*Robert C. Givins House*)
10244 S. Longwood Dr.
1886, ARCHITECT UNKNOWN

Modeled after an Irish castle and built of Joliet limestone, this imposing edifice was the work of an early developer who wanted to give the area a fashionable image.

10541 S. HOYNE AVE.

BEVERLY UNITARIAN CHURCH

47| Russell L. Blount House (2)
1950 W. 102nd St.
1912, WALTER BURLEY GRIFFIN

The plan is the same as for the earlier Blount House (1), but the bedrooms have a cathedral ceiling that is echoed in the exterior trim. The family lived here from 1914 to 1916, when they sold it to Harry Furneaux and purchased *his* Griffin-designed house on Griffin Pl.

48| Horace Horton House
10200 S. Longwood Dr.
1890, JOHN T. LONG

This house is an imposing example of the severely academic Colonial Revival style and appears to be based on McKim, Mead & White's H. A. C. Taylor House (1886) in Newport, R.I.

49| Robert W. Evans House
9914 S. Longwood Dr.
1908, FRANK LLOYD WRIGHT

Here Wright builds onto the hill, not into it. The pinwheeling of forms around a central chimney is similar to that of his Ward W. Willitts House (1901) in Highland Park, Ill., but the stucco has been defaced with a layer of stone.

50| Frederick C. Sawyer House
9822 S. Longwood Dr.
1908, HORATIO R. WILSON

51| Bryson B. Hill House
9800 S. Longwood Dr.
1909, ALBERT G. FERREE

These Classically inspired mansions coexisted with the Prairie School and will never go entirely out of style.

52| Louis A. Tanner House
9640 S. Longwood Dr.
1909, TALLMADGE & WATSON

The simple but pleasing facade retains an element typical of this firm's smaller projects: the trellised porch with cutout balusters.

53| Dan Everett Waid House
9332 S. Damen Ave.
1894, ARCHITECT UNKNOWN
1906, ALTERATION, HENRY K. HOLSMAN

This lively Queen Anne house has an unusual triple-gable composition that is symmetrical yet highly picturesque.

54| E. S. Pike House
1826 W. 91st St.
1894, HARRY HALE WATERMAN

Expect Hansel and Gretel to come tripping past this house set on the edge of the woods. Huge blocks of sandstone anchor the first floor and contrast with the light stucco above.

E. S. PIKE HOUSE

55| Beverly Hills Metra Station
(*Chicago, Rock Island & Pacific Railroad—Beverly Station*)
91st St. & Prospect Sq.
1889, CHARNLEY & EVANS

Only the picturesque towered and gabled massing hint at the Queen Anne character. Modernizations have removed the original small-paned windows and the elaborate cladding of shingles.

56| Edwin P. Hilliard House
9351 S. Pleasant Ave.
1894, HARRY HALE WATERMAN

Like the Pike House, this small variation on Waterman's picturesque theme features a tower breaking through the curbed gambrel roof and half-

BEVERLY HILLS METRA STATION

timbered stucco over a heavy stone base. The half-timbering frames the edges of the windows, organizing the wall plane rather than fragmenting it.

57| William and Jessie M. Adams House
9326 S. Pleasant Ave.
1900, FRANK LLOYD WRIGHT
1913, REAR ADDITION, ROBERT HYDE

It is quiet by Wright standards but with a typically intriguing entry sequence.

58| William M. R. French House
9203 S. Pleasant Ave.
1894, WILLIAM A. OTIS

This Classical Revival house is sophisticated and straight-forward among its picturesque Waterman-designed and oblique Wright-designed neighbors. The second-floor central doorway treatment is as elaborate as that on the first floor.

59| Hiram H. Belding House
9167 S. Pleasant Ave.
1894, HARRY HALE WATERMAN

Described in *Inland Architect* as "Norman-French style," it has an L-shaped plan with a prominent stair tower and corner entry, favorite Waterman elements.

60| Arthur J. T. Bennett, Jr., House
8944 S. Pleasant Ave.
1937, MURRAY D. HETHERINGTON

Hallmarks of Hetherington's talents are the artfully integrated garage and the emphasis on site and landscape; the garden entrance is framed by a stone gate extending from the wall of the house. The conical corner-entrance tower and hipped roof pierced by arched dormers identify the style as French Provincial.

61| Madge Phillips Studio
8910 S. Pleasant Ave.
1954, WILLIAM CARNEGIE

This is a latter-day version of the Walter Burley Griffin idiom as seen on 104th Pl. Although a sprawling single-story house rather than a compact cottage, it has the deep eaves and patterned wooden muntins of Griffin's distinctive style.

62| Ignatius Chap House
8831 S. Pleasant Ave.
1928, HOMER G. SAILOR

A dollhouse masquerading as a hacienda, it has a miniature entrance tower with blind arches. Note the painted tiles inset into the rough stucco.

63| Everett Robert Brewer House
2078 W. Hopkins Pl.

1924, MURRAY D. HETHERINGTON

The irregular roofline, with its variegated slate hewn into random-sized slabs, evokes the craftsmanship of a preindustrial era. But the twentieth century asserts itself in the orderly arrangement of large windows in the projecting central section.

64| George W. Reed House
2122 W. Hopkins Pl.

1929, JAMES ROY ALLEN

The irregular massing of this sprawling house, with four wings spinning off the central block, was probably intended to suggest an English country house enlarged over the centuries. The style is early Renaissance, with Classical details grafted onto medieval forms.

65| Murray D. Hetherington House
8918 S. Hamilton Ave.

1924, MURRAY D. HETHERINGTON

Second-generation Beverly architect Hetherington's home is endearingly and unselfconsciously pretty. It's the perfect Cotswold cottage, from the irregular massing and roofline to the rough-hewn materials, to the flagstone-lined miniature streambed. Note the shield with the construction date in the stucco panel on the front.

MURRAY D. HETHERINGTON HOUSE

66| James Alex Brough House
8929 S. Hamilton Ave.

1927, MURRAY D. HETHERINGTON

This folksy stucco Spanish Revival home could be a stage set for *The Barber of Seville*, even down to the balcony.

67| 8958 S. Hamilton Ave.

1951, JOSEPH EMIL HOSEK

If North Beverly is a symphony of architectural styles, here's the tuba. Everything is overblown: the five-foot eaves, the picture windows, and the first-floor coat of many colors that could have been the inspiration for Perma Stone. The finishing touch is the highly manicured yard, complete with marshmallow and corkscrew topiary.

68| S. P. Balzekas House
9000 S. Bell Ave.

1935, WILLIAM SEVIC

In this multilevel Prairie and Moderne mishmash, the flat roofs projecting at many levels shelter metal-framed corner casement windows.

S. P. BALZEKAS HOUSE

PULLMAN

IN 1878 THE SWAMPY LAND NOW LOCKED BETWEEN THE DAN RYAN AND Calumet expressways contained a few Dutch farms in the community of Roseland, high ground along what is now Michigan Ave., and fewer than twenty houses in the village of Kensington, centering on the railroad junction at 115th St. and Cottage Grove Ave. Five years later the population had soared to 7,000, most of whom were laborers drawn by new industry. The leading attraction was the company town of Pullman, begun by railroad car manufacturer George M. Pullman in April 1880 on 500 acres between the western edge of Lake Calumet and the Illinois Central Railroad right-of-way. Pullman's plans called for a model town set on the north and south sides of the Pullman Palace Car Co.'s works. Superior living quarters in a healthful setting far from urban problems, he believed, would attract good workers and enhance productivity. Pullman insisted that his venture was not philanthropy but good business, and he expected everything in the town—houses, stores, stable, and even the church—to bring in a return of 6 percent on investment.

Pullman's architect was Solon S. Beman, newly launched from the office of East Coast architect Richard M. Upjohn. His landscape designer was New Yorker Nathan F. Barrett, an avowed formalist whose work contrasted with the popular naturalism of Frederick Law Olmsted. Barrett's aesthetic gave the Pullman layouts their strongly French tone, with housing units arranged in carefully balanced sets, adorned with undulating walls like French pavilions, and oriented toward garden spaces. Beman's facades, of bricks made from Lake Calumet clay, reveal the French predilection for indicating the underlying construction, even if only with a course of black brick at a floor line. Slate-covered mansard stories equaling one-third the building's height are grace notes throughout the town.

Other developers capitalized on the popularity of this famous experiment, especially the West Pullman Land Association, formed in 1890 to exploit the area west of State St. and south of 119th St. One portion, Stewart Ridge, was reserved for large houses on spacious lots. But Pullman's paternalism as well as other ambitions for the area were thwarted by the depression of 1893 and by the notorious Pullman Strike of 1894. Workers' protests that rents remained high while wages were cut escalated into a national confrontation between railroad owners and the nascent railroad union led by Eugene V. Debs. The coup de grace came in 1898, when the Illinois Supreme Court found the company in violation of a state law forbidding businesses to own land in excess of their industrial needs. By 1907 the court-ordered sale of Pullman had been completed.

The communities of Pullman, Roseland, Kensington, and West Pullman grew during the industrial buildups of the world wars and stagnated as industries departed in the 1980s. The Pullman works closed in 1981, leaving behind an area that had seen rapid racial change in the 1960s. Residents strive to maintain their landmark town, wrested from developers by the Historic Pullman Foundation, which gained national landmark status for it. Restoration of the state-owned Florence Hotel and former Pullman Administration Building, the latter almost destroyed in a 1998 conflagration, continues into the twenty-first century.

—MARY ALICE MOLLOY

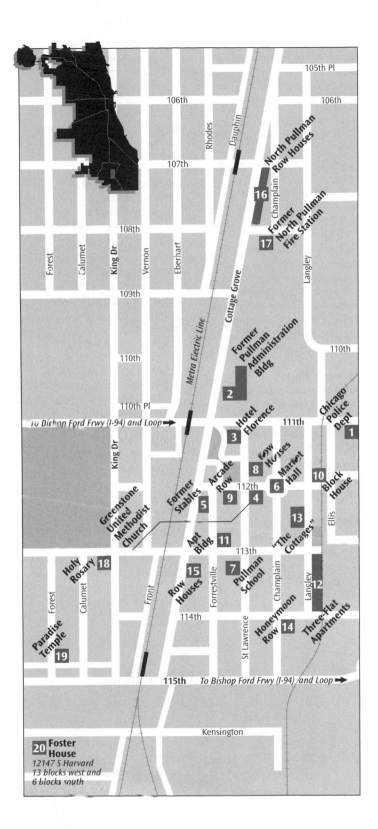

105th Pl

106th

106th

Rhodes

Dauphin

107th

North Pullman Row Houses

16

Champlain

Former North Pullman Fire Station

108th

17

Forest

Calumet

King Dr

Vernon

Eberhart

Langley

109th

Cottage Grove

Metra Electric Line

110th

Former Pullman Administration Bldg

110th

2

110th Pl

Hotel Florence

Chicago Police Dept

To Dishon Ford Frwy (I-94) and Loop ➡

111th

1

King Dr

3

Row Houses

Arcade Row

8

Market Hall

10

Block House

112th

6

Former Stables

5

9

4

Greenstone United Methodist Church

13

Ellis

"The Cottages"

Apt Bldg

11

113th

Holy Rosary

18

7

Pullman School

Champlain

Langley

12

Paradise Temple

19

Forest

Calumet

Front

Row Houses

15

Forrestville

St Lawrence

Honeymoon Row

14

Three-Flat Apartments

114th

115th   To Bishop Ford Frwy (I-94) and Loop ➡

Kensington

20 **Foster House**
12147 S Harvard
13 blocks west and
6 blocks south

1| Chicago Police Department— Area 2 Detective Headquarters

727 E. 111th St.

1981, CITY OF CHICAGO, DEPT. OF PUBLIC WORKS BUREAU OF ARCHITECTURE,

JOSEPH W. CASSERLY, CHICAGO CITY ARCH.; MURPHY/JAHN, CONSULTING ARCH.

Panels as blue as a Chicago cop's uniform, layered in long stripes with clear and opaque glass block, form the durable, low-maintenance, energy-efficient walls of this justice factory. The police headquarters and a court complex have separate entries around a shared court, enlivened by Loren Madsen's *Suspended Sentence* (1981). Composed of frosted-glass blocks, the sculpture is suspended from stainless-steel wire.

2| Former Pullman Administration Building and Clock Tower

S. Cottage Grove Ave. north of E. 111th St.

1880, SOLON S. BEMAN

The original focal point of the Pullman complex was gutted by a fire in 1998.

3| Hotel Florence

11111 S. Forrestville Ave.

1881, SOLON S. BEMAN

Named for Pullman's favorite daughter, this "large gingerbread country villa" with fifty guest rooms introduces the robust wooden embellishments on porches, gables, and stairs that characterize Beman's Queen Anne work. The trim is painted in "official" Pullman colors, two greens and a deep red, researched and reformulated by Pullman neighbor Sherwin-Williams.

4| Greenstone United Methodist Church (*Greenstone Church*)

11211 S. St. Lawrence Ave.

1882, SOLON S. BEMAN

The only significant importation of materials for Pullman was the serpentine rock quarried in New England for the town's only company-owned church. It was intended as a union church, with all denominations sharing the use and cost. This showpiece combines the peaked roofs of the Gothic with the round-arched openings and rock-faced masonry popularized by H. H. Richardson.

5| Former Pullman Stables

11201 S. Cottage Grove Ave.

CA. 1881, SOLON S. BEMAN

Time and unsympathetic readaptation have dimmed but not erased the charm of the wooden horses' heads, the wide entrance, and the shingle facing of this communal barn. It was erected to reduce town maintenance by keeping horses off most Pullman streets.

HOTEL FLORENCE

MARKET HALL AND COLONNADE
APARTMENTS AND TOWN HOUSES

6| Market Hall and Colonnade Apartments and Town Houses
E. 112th St. and S. Champlain Ave.
1892, SOLON S. BEMAN

Four excruciatingly narrow curved units with bachelor apartments above arcades are bookended with matching town houses in this touch of Italy. They were inserted into the town fabric after a market hall on this site burned down. In the center is the remaining single story of the second Pullman Market Hall.

7| George M. Pullman Public School
11311 S. Forrestville Ave.
1910, DWIGHT H. PERKINS

Beman's school was replaced by a distinctively Perkinsian stylized Gothic block, featuring thick terra-cotta copings and angle buttressing against rust brick walls.

8| Five-Room Row Houses
11145–11151 S. St. Lawrence Ave.
1880, SOLON S. BEMAN

A significant contribution to 1880s residential design was Beman's plan for a five-room worker's cottage, introduced in this block of row houses, the first to be completed in Pullman. The house, which could range in width from fourteen to twenty-two feet, features a front parlor and rear kitchen/dining room on the main floor. Upstairs are a front bedroom and two small rear ones split by a skylit stair hall that leads to a water closet. Beman pic-turesquely grouped his row houses. Here a pair that shares a dormered, mansarded second story is linked with another pair in which an enhanced central element is topped with a purlin gable. No Pullman five-room house is unaltered; additions here include porches with details drawn from the Hotel Florence.

9| "Arcade Row" Houses
533–535 E. 112th St.
1881, SOLON S. BEMAN

In Pullman the best buildings were placed in the most conspicuous locations. These two are among the best-preserved examples in a row of gambrel-dormered, three-story row houses that faces the town's park. These units, large by Pullman standards, were not restricted to middle-class tenants. They were available to anyone who could afford the rents— whether the Pullman school principal, who lived at 533 in 1889, or the collection of carpenters and foremen for whom 535 was a boardinghouse.

10| Block House
704–706 E. 112th St.
CA. 1881, SOLON S. BEMAN

Tenements anywhere else, they were called block houses in Pullman and offered individual rooms for rent. In a long row along the town's eastern edge, their low status and back-bench location called for simple common brick facades, and yet on each the third story featured an extended central section set off from the mansard roof. This building now houses two-bedroom apartments. Other surviving block houses are at 11127 S. Langley Ave. and at 614, 644–646, and 645–647 E. 113th St.

11| Corner Apartment Building
11261 S. Forrestville Ave.
CA. 1884–1886, SOLON S. BEMAN

This nearly square corner building houses its third story under an unusually high, curbed mansard roof. Others are found along 113th St. at 11260 S. St. Lawrence Ave. and 11270 S. Champlain Ave.

12| Three-Flat Apartment Buildings
S. Langley Ave. between 113th and 114th Sts.
1880–1882, SOLON S. BEMAN

An entire block of identical three-story, three-flat units stands with the backs of the units against the railroad tracks. Although built of the most modest materials, they have some of Pullman's most formal layouts. In three places, units are pulled out to the sidewalk, creating two forecourts.

13| "The Cottages"
11218–11250 S. Langley Ave.
1880–1882, SOLON S. BEMAN

Seventeen five-room row houses a mere fourteen feet wide demonstrate the great variety of facades that Beman and his associates such as Irving K. Pond designed in Pullman's early years for even the least expensive houses.

14| Flats on "Honeymoon Row"
11401–11403 S. Champlain Ave.
1888, SOLON S. BEMAN

Ingenuity faltered as building continued in Pullman. These four-flat units employ common brick picked out with red brick in the manner of industrial housing worldwide in the late nineteenth century; the only relief is in the low conical roofs at the ends and midpoints. Each trapezoidal bay has three doors. The two on the sides opened into the main-floor flats, and the central one led to stairs to two upper units. There were originally four water closets at the rear of the main floor, one for each unit.

15| Five-Room Row Houses
11307–11309 S. Cottage Grove Ave.
1888, SOLON S. BEMAN

Houses seen by the public from passing trains received special treatment, even when they were modest dwellings. These row houses have triangular bays, wide pedimented porches, and carefully balanced contrasts between light and dark brick that are unknown elsewhere in Pullman. The units to the south have the town's only round-headed windows.

16| North Pullman Row Houses
10701–10739 S. Cottage Grove Ave.
CA. 1884–1885, SOLON S. BEMAN

The first sight of Pullman from trains leaving Chicago was this picturesque row, which steps forward to follow the angle of the street. Anchored by a large corner rooming house and distinguished by particularly high false rooflines, the buildings share simple, flat, red-orange brick facades.

17| Former North Pullman Fire Station
623 E. 108th St.
1895, SOLON S. BEMAN

With a limestone pedimented truck door, ranks of arched windows, and an attenuated hose-drying tower, this Renaissance fire station was the last

"THE COTTAGES"

FORMER NORTH PULLMAN FIRE STATION

ing on the tower, and the small rose window appear to reflect the communicants' Germanic background rather than the donor's preferences.

19| Paradise Temple Church of God in Christ
(*Shomre Hadath Synagogue*)
11437–11445 S. Forest Ave.
1928, HARRY L. MORSE

This is a late example of the curved gable synagogue; the design was popularized by the Grande Synagogue of Paris, in the rue de la Victoire (1874, A. P. Aldrophe). But Morse used strictly twentieth-century Chicago materials: wire-cut brick, exposed concrete as trim, and an inset band of multi-colored tiles.

gasp in Pullman construction. It reflects the prevailing mode of the 1890s as surely as the initial Pullman buildings document the previous decade.

18| Holy Rosary Roman Catholic Church
11300 S. Martin Luther King, Jr., Dr.
1890, SOLON S. BEMAN

Built on Pullman-held land for company employees, this church replays in brick the Greenstone Church's round arched windows under peaked roofs and steep tower cap. But details such as the self-corbeling, the arched detail-

20| Stephen A. Foster Residence and Stable
12147 S. Harvard Ave.
1900, FRANK LLOYD WRIGHT

The house with the hat marks Wright's brief flirtation with Japanese variations on the Shingle Style theme. The tall, brimmed roof is echoed in the dormers and all but swamps the shingle-clad base.

TOUR INFORMATION

If you would like a knowledgeable human guide to help you explore Chicago's architecture, the following are some of the opportunities to tour the city on foot or by bus, boat, or elevated train. Note that all tours are subject to change, so always call or write first to verify times and fees.

Chicago Architecture Foundation
312/922-3432
www.architecture.org

The most extensive architectural tour program in the metropolitan area is run by the Chicago Architecture Foundation (CAF). Volunteer docents give daily downtown walking tours and weekly bus tours year-round. In warmer months, neighborhood and boat tours are added, as well as a Loop Tour Train. CAF operates the ArchiCenter visitor center, shop, and galleries in the Santa Fe Building at 224 S. Michigan Ave., with a second shop and tour center in the Hancock Building at 875 N. Michigan Ave.

Chicago Sites

Auditorium Theatre
312/431-2389, ext. 0
www.auditoriumtheatre.org;
www.roosevelt.edu/campuses/downtown.htm

Walk into the lobby of Roosevelt University, 430 S. Michigan Ave., to see the space that was the lobby of the Auditorium Hotel. Call the Auditorium Theatre Council for information on tours of the theater.

Charnley-Persky House
312/915-0105
www.sah.org

This home at 1365 N. Astor St. is now the headquarters of the Society of Architectural Historians. Tours are available April through November on Wednesdays and Saturdays; the Saturday tour can include **Madlener House** one block away.

Chicago Cultural Center
312/346-3278
www.cityofchicago.org

The city's first library, with entrances at 77 E. Randolph St. and 78 E. Washington St., offers exhibits and performances, a Chicago-themed gift shop, and a visitor center operated by the Chicago Office of Tourism. Tours are given on Wednesdays, Fridays, and Saturdays at 1:45 P.M.

Clarke House
312/745-0040
www.cityofchicago.org

Tour the city's oldest house at 1855 S. Indiana Ave., Wednesday through Sunday, at noon, 1:00, and 2:00 P.M. Glessner House is next door.

Glessner House
312/326-1480
www.glessnerhouse.org

Tour Chicago's only surviving building by H. H. Richardson at 1800 S. Prairie Ave., Wednesday through Sunday, at 1:00, 2:00, and 3:00 P.M. Clarke House is next door. Walking tours of the **Prairie Avenue Historic District** around Glessner and Clarke houses are offered May through October on the second and fourth Sundays at 1:00 and 2:00 P.M.

Pullman Historic District
773/785-3828
members.aol.com/pullmanil

At the Pullman Visitor Center at 11141 S. Cottage Grove Ave., learn more about the community, and on the first Sunday of the month, from May through October, take a guided walking tour. An annual house tour takes place in October.

Robie House
773/834-1847 or 708/848-1976
www.wrightplus.org

The Frank Lloyd Wright Preservation Trust maintains and offers tours of the house at 5757 S. Woodlawn Ave. 362 days a year. Three tours are offered on weekdays and many more on weekends.

Oak Park Sites

Oak Park Visitors Center; Oak Park Visitors Bureau
708/524-7800
www.oprf.com/opvc;
www.visitoakpark.com

Information on visiting Oak Park and its architectural and historical landmarks is available at the visitor center, 158 Forest Ave.

Frank Lloyd Wright Home and Studio
708/848-1976
www.wrightplus.org

The Frank Lloyd Wright Preservation Trust operates the Home and Studio, located at 951 Chicago Ave., which is open for tours 362 days a year. Three tours are offered on weekdays and many more on weekends. Guided tours of the **Frank Lloyd Wright Prairie School of Architecture Historic District** are offered on weekends, and self-guided tours may be taken every day. Walking tours of River Forest and Victorian Oak Park are also available from April to November. An abundance of Wright items are available at the Gingko Tree Bookshop. Wright Plus, an annual housewalk, takes place in May; tickets go on sale March 1 and sell out quickly.

"Pleasant Home" (Farson House)
708/383-2654
www.pleasanthome.org

Tours of the home designed by George Maher at 217 S. Home Ave. are offered year-round, with times varying seasonally.

Unity Temple
708/383-8873
www.unitytemple-utrf.org

Tours of the church designed by Wright at 875 Lake St. are offered year-round, with times varying seasonally.

PHOTO CREDITS

The position of photographs on a page has been abbreviated in the following manner: **T**, *top;* **B**, *bottom;* **L**, *left;* **R**, *right;* **M**, *middle.*

The Shaping of Chicago: P. 2 From Lewis University's Canal and Regional History Collection; **3T** Courtesy Chicago Historical Society (tinted); **3B** Courtesy The Art Institute of Chicago; **4** Courtesy Chicago Historical Society (tinted); **7** Courtesy Chicago Historical Society (tinted); **8** Courtesy Chicago Historical Society (cropped, tinted); **9** Courtesy of the Commission on Chicago Landmarks (tinted); **11** Courtesy Chicago Historical Society (cropped, tinted); **13** Courtesy Chicago Historical Society (cropped); **15** Courtesy Chicago Historical Society (tinted); **17** Hedrich-Blessing photograph, courtesy Chicago Historical Society (cropped, tinted); **19** Courtesy Chicago Historical Society (cropped, tinted); **20** Courtesy Chicago Historical Society (cropped, tinted); **21** Photo by Ron Gordon; **The Loop: P. 30L** Jon Miller photograph © Hedrich-Blessing; **30R** Hedrich-Blessing photograph, courtesy Chicago Historical Society (cropped, tinted); **33T** Hedrich-Blessing photograph, courtesy Chicago Historical Society (cropped); **33B** Barbara Crane for the Commission on Chicago Landmarks; **36** Courtesy Chicago Historical Society (cropped, tinted); **38** Photo: Whit Preston © Gehry Partners, LLP; **39**, Courtesy Chicago Historical Society (cropped, tinted); **40T** Hedrich-Blessing photograph, courtesy Chicago Historical Society (cropped); **40B** Bob Thall, courtesy The Art Institute of Chicago; **42** Courtesy Chicago Historical Society (cropped, tinted); **43** Chicago Park District Special Collections; **44** Barbara Karant, Karant + Associates, Inc.; **45T** Photo by Alice Sinkevitch; **45B** Barbara Crane for the Commission on Chicago Landmarks; **46** Courtesy of the Commission on Chicago Landmarks; **48** © 2002, Steinkamp/Ballogg Photography; **50** Courtesy of the Commission on Chicago Landmarks; **52L** Hedrich-Blessing, courtesy Chicago Historical Society (cropped, tinted); **52R** Hedrich-Blessing photograph, courtesy Chicago Historical Society (cropped, tinted); **53** Courtesy of the Commission on Chicago Landmarks; **55** Craig Dugan ©

Hedrich-Blessing; **57** Courtesy of the Commission on Chicago Landmarks (tinted); **58T** Courtesy of the Commission on Chicago Landmarks; **58B** Hedrich-Blessing photograph, courtesy Chicago Historical Society (cropped, tinted); **61T** Courtesy of Chicago Historical Society (cropped, tinted); **61B** Photo by Howard N. Kaplan, © HNK Architectural Photography, Inc.; **62L** Hedrich-Blessing photograph, courtesy Chicago Historical Society (cropped); **62R** Courtesy The Art Institute of Chicago (tinted); **63** Courtesy Chicago Historical Society (cropped, tinted); **64** Photo by David Clifton; **66** Photo by Howard N. Kaplan, © HNK Architectural Photography, Inc.; **67** Hedrich-Blessing photograph, courtesy Chicago Historical Society (cropped); **68** © Hedrich-Blessing; **69** Hedrich-Blessing photograph, courtesy Chicago Historical Society (cropped, tinted); **71** Hedrich-Blessing photograph, courtesy Chicago Historical Society (cropped, tinted); **72** Hedrich-Blessing photograph, courtesy Chicago Historical Society (cropped, tinted); **73** James R. Steinkamp, courtesy of Murphy/Jahn—Lester B. Knight & Associates, A Joint Venture; **75** © Hedrich-Blessing; **76** Hedrich-Blessing photograph, courtesy Chicago Historical Society (cropped, tinted); **77T** James R. Steinkamp, Steinkamp/Ballogg, Chicago; **77B** Courtesy Chicago Historical Society (cropped); **78** Nick Merrick, Hedrich-Blessing, courtesy of McClier; **79** Nick Merrick, Hedrich-Blessing, courtesy of McClier; **80** Photo by John Gronkowski; **81** James R. Steinkamp, courtesy of Murphy/Jahn; **83T** Chicago Architectural Photographing Co. for the Commission on Chicago Landmarks (tinted); **83B** Hedrich-Blessing photograph, courtesy Chicago Historical Society (cropped, tinted); **84** Jon Miller, © Hedrich-Blessing; **85** Harold A. Nelson, architect/photographer; **87L** Scott McDonald, © Hedrich-Blessing; **87R** Nick Merrick, © Hedrich-Blessing; **88** Photo by Greg Murphey; **89** Robert Shimer, Hedrich-Blessing, courtesy of Merchandise Mart Properties, Inc.; **91** Jon Miller © Hedrich-Blessing; **92** Photo by Timothy Hursley; **93** © Anthony May; **94L** © Judith Bromley; **94R** Hedrich-Blessing photograph, courtesy Chicago Historical Society (cropped, tinted); **95** Nick Merrick, © Hedrich-Blessing; **97L** William Kildow Photography; **97R** Nick Merrick, © Hedrich-Blessing; **North Michigan Avenue/Streeterville: P. 101** Steve Beal for the Commission on Chicago Landmarks; **102** Courtesy of the Commission on Chicago Landmarks (tinted); **103** Hedrich-Blessing photograph, courtesy Chicago Historical Society (cropped); **104L** Courtesy of the Commission on Chicago Landmarks; **104R** Courtesy Chicago Historical Society; **105T** Nick Merrick, © Hedrich-Blessing; **105B** Jon Miller, © Hedrich-Blessing; **106L** Courtesy of Chicago Historical Society (cropped, tinted); **106R** Photo by Alice Sinkevitch; **107T** Bob Thall for the Commission on Chicago Landmarks; **107B** Steve Hall, © Hedrich-Blessing; **108L** George Lambros Photography, courtesy of Loebl, Schlossman & Hackl; **108R** Courtesy Chicago Historical Society (cropped, tinted); **110** Courtesy Chicago Historical Society (cropped, tinted); **112** Hedrich-Blessing photograph, courtesy Chicago Historical Society; **113** Courtesy of the Commission on Chicago Landmarks (tinted); **114L** Hedrich-Blessing photograph, courtesy Chicago Historical Society (cropped, tinted); **114R** Bob Thall for the Commission on Chicago Landmarks; **115** Hedrich-Blessing photograph, courtesy Chicago Historical Society (cropped); **117** Timothy Hursley, courtesy of Holabird & Root; **118L** Photo by Greg Murphey; **118R** David A. Urschel, AIA; **119** Photo by Howard N. Kaplan, © HNK Architectural Photography, Inc.; **120** © Hedrich-Blessing photograph; **121** Hedrich-Blessing photograph, courtesy Chicago Historical Society (cropped); **River North: 128** Courtesy Chicago Historical Society (cropped, tinted); **129T** Courtesy Chicago Historical Society (cropped); **129B** © Russell Phillips Photography; **130** Bob Thall for the Commission on Chicago Landmarks; **131T** William Kildow Photography; **131M** © Russell Phillips Photography; **131B** Jon Miller, © Hedrich-Blessing; **132** Photo by William A. Rooney; **133** Barbara Crane for the Commission on Chicago Landmarks; **134** Courtesy of the Commission on Chicago Landmarks; **135** Neal A. Vogel, Restoric, LLC; **136** Courtesy of the Commission on Chicago Landmarks; **138T** Courtesy Moody Bible Institute Archives (tinted); **138M** Courtesy Chicago Historical Society (cropped); **138B** Photo by John Gronkowski; **139** Photo by Howard N. Kaplan, © HNK Architectural Photography, Inc.; **140T** Courtesy The Art Institute of Chicago (tinted); **140B** Steve Hall, © Hedrich-Blessing; **142T** Courtesy of the Commission on Chicago Landmarks (tinted);

142B Neal A. Vogel, Restoric, LLC; **143** Courtesy Chicago Historical Society (cropped); **144** Photo by Greg Murphey; **South Loop: P. 150L** Leslie Schwartz Photography; **150R** Leslie Schwartz Photography; **151** Courtesy of the Commission on Chicago Landmarks; **152** Photo by David Pilarczyk, courtesy of Schroeder Murchie Laya Associates; **155T** Photo by Ron Gordon; **155B** Photo by John Gronkowski; **156T** Ron Gordon for the Commission on Chicago Landmarks; **156B** Photo by Ron Gordon; **157** Geoffrey Goldberg, courtesy of Bertrand Goldberg Associates; **158** Hedrich-Blessing photograph, courtesy Chicago Historical Society (cropped); **159** Marco Lorenzetti, © Hedrich-Blessing. **Gold Coast/Old Town: P. 165** Courtesy of the Commission on Chicago Landmarks; **167** Photo by David Clifton; **168** Courtesy of Loebl, Schlossman & Hackl (tinted); **169T** Barbara Crane for the Commission on Chicago Landmarks; **169B** Courtesy Chicago Historical Society (cropped, tinted); **170** Nick Merrick, © Hedrich-Blessing; **171T** Courtesy Chicago Historical Society (cropped); **171B** Barbara Crane for the Commission on Chicago Landmarks; **172L** Hedrich-Blessing photograph, courtesy Chicago Historical Society (cropped, tinted); **172R** Hedrich-Blessing photograph, courtesy Chicago Historical Society (cropped); **173T** Courtesy Chicago Historical Society (cropped); **173B** Courtesy of the Commission on Chicago Landmarks; **174** Photo by Howard N. Kaplan, © HNK Architectural Photography, Inc.; **175** Paul Zakoian, courtesy of Weese Langley Weese Architects Ltd.; **176** Photo by Howard N. Kaplan, © HNK Architectural Photography, Inc.; **178L** Photo by David Clifton; **178R** Courtesy Chicago Historical Society (cropped, tinted); **179T** Kate Roth Photography; **179B** Mark Ballogg, © Steinkamp/Ballogg, Chicago; **181** Barbara Crane for the Commission on Chicago Landmarks; **182** Barbara Crane for the Commission on Chicago Landmarks; **184TL** Nick Merrick, © Hedrich-Blessing; **184BL** Alice Sinkevitch; **184R** Mark Ballogg, © Steinkamp/Ballogg, Chicago; **185L** Courtesy of Commission on Chicago Landmarks; **185R** Photograph by Sandra Peterson; **186L** Hedrich-Blessing photograph, courtesy Chicago Historical Society; **186R** Photograph by Sandra Peterson; **187T** Photo by David Clifton; **187B** Courtesy Chicago Historical Society (cropped, tinted); **Lincoln Park: P. 191** Harold A. Nelson, architect/photographer; **192** Leslie Schwartz Photography; **193** © Boschke Photo Inc.; **194** Barbara Crane for the Commission on Chicago Landmarks; **195L** Leslie Schwartz Photography; **195R** Leslie Schwartz Photography; **196** Courtesy The Art Institute of Chicago (tinted); **197** Kate Roth Photography; **198L** Courtesy Chicago Historical Society; **198R** Harold A. Nelson, architect/

photographer; **199T** Courtesy Chicago Historical Society (cropped); **199B** Lawrence Okrent; **200** Courtesy Chicago Historical Society (cropped); **201T** Courtesy of The Art Institute of Chicago (tinted); **201B** Hedrich-Blessing photograph, courtesy Chicago Historical Society (cropped); **202T** Kate Roth Photography; **202B** Elks Veterans Memorial; **203** Photo by David Clifton; **206** Courtesy The Art Institute of Chicago; **207** Courtesy of Chicago Park District Special Collections (tinted); **208**, Barbara Karant, Karant and Associates, Inc.; **209** William Kildow Photography; **Lakeview/Ravenswood/Uptown: P. 215** Photo by Howard N. Kaplan, © HNK Architectural Photography, Inc.; **216T** Hedrich-Blessing photograph, courtesy Chicago Historical Society; **216B** Bob Thall for the Commission on Chicago Landmarks; **217L** *Architectural Record*, v. 21, Feb. 1907, courtesy of The Art Institute of Chicago (tinted); **217R** Bob Thall for the Commission on Chicago Landmarks; **218L** Bob Thall for the Commission on Chicago Landmarks; **218R** Kate Roth Photography; **219** Kate Roth Photography; **220** Photostat line drawing by Schroeder Murchie Laya Associates Ltd.; **221T** Scott McDonald, © Hedrich-Blessing; **221B** Photo by David Clifton; **222** Richard Nickel for the Commission on Chicago Landmarks; **223** Courtesy Chicago Public Schools (tinted); **225** Barbara Crane for the Commission on Chicago Landmarks; **226L** Bob Thall for the Commission on Chicago Landmarks; **226R** Photo by Barry Bebart; **228T** Courtesy The Art Institute of Chicago (tinted); **228B** Bob Thall for the Commission on Chicago Landmarks (tinted); **229** Barbara Crane for the Commission on Chicago Landmarks; **230T** Photo by Howard N. Kaplan, © HNK Architectural Photography, Inc.; **230B** Leslie Schwartz Photography; **231** William Kildow Photography; **232L** Leslie Schwartz Photography; **232R** Courtesy of the Commission on Chicago Landmarks; **233T** Mark Ballogg, © Steinkamp/Ballogg Chicago (tinted); **233B** Leslie Schwartz Photography; **234** Photo by David Clifton; **235TL** © Hedrich-Blessing; **235BL** Courtesy Chicago Public Schools (tinted); **235R** Photo by David Clifton; **Edgewater/Rogers Park: P. 239T** Photo by Ron Gordon; **239B** © Fred Leavitt Photography; **240** Photo by David Vincent Forte, AIA; **241** Leslie Schwartz Photography; **242T** William Kildow Photography; **242B** Leslie Schwartz Photography; **243** Photo by Mati Maldre; **244** Photo © Lawrence Okrent; **245** Photo © by Lawrence Okrent; **246** © George Lambros/Lambros Photography Inc.; **247T** Photo by Ron Gordon; **247B** Photo by Mati Maldre; **248T** Courtesy Chicago Public Schools (tinted); **248B** Jon Miller, © Hedrich-Blessing; **249** Leslie Schwartz

Photography; **250T** Alice Sinkevitch; **250B** Alice Sinkevitch; **251** © George Lambros/Lambros Photography; **253TL** Photo by Barry Bebart; **253BL** Photo by Barry Bebart; **253R** Bob Thall for the Commission on Chicago Landmarks; **254** Photo by Barry Bebart; **Northwest Side: P. 260L** Barbara Karant, Karant + Associates, Inc.; **260R** Barbara Crane for the Commission on Chicago Landmarks; **261T** Scott McDonald, © Hedrich-Blessing; **261B** William Kildow Photography; **262** Photo © Lawrence Okrent; **263** Photograph by Felicity Rich; **264TL** Andreas Simon, *Chicago, die Gartenstadt*, 1893, courtesy of The Art Institute of Chicago (tinted); **264BL** Photo by Felicity Rich; **264R** Neal A. Vogel, Restoric, LLC; **265** James R. Steinkamp, Steinkamp/Ballogg, Chicago; **267T** Alice Sinkevitch; **267B** Charlie Mayer Photography; **268T** Barry Rustin Photography; **268B** Sean J. Reidy; **269L** Courtesy Chicago Historical Society (cropped); **269R** Sean J. Reidy; **270** Photo by Felicity Rich; **271T** Barbara Crane for the Commission on Chicago Landmarks; **271B** Steve Beal for the Commission on Chicago Landmarks; **273** © Fred Leavitt Photography; **Chicago–O'Hare International Airport: P. 276** James R. Steinkamp, courtesy of Murphy/Jahn; **277** Timothy Hursley, courtesy of Murphy/Jahn; **279T** Hedrich-Blessing photograph, courtesy of Chicago Historical Society (cropped); **279B** James Steinkamp, Steinkamp/Ballogg Chicago; **Near West Side: 285T** Leslie Schwartz Photography; **285B** George Pappageorge; **287T** Neal A. Vogel, Restoric, LLC; **287B** Elaine S. Baxton for the Commission on Chicago Landmarks; **288** Steve Hall, © Hedrich-Blessing; **289** Courtesy The Art Institute of Chicago (tinted); **290** Barbara Crane for the Commission on Chicago Landmarks; **292** Neal A. Vogel, Restoric, LLC; **293** Photo by Felicity Rich; **294** Courtesy the University of Illinois at Chicago, The University Library, University Archives; **296** Neal A. Vogel, Restoric, LLC; **297** Bob Thall for the Commission on Chicago Landmarks; **301T** Lawrence Okrent; **301B** © Judith Bromley; **Garfield Park/Austin: P. 308** Photo by Ron Gordon; **309** Courtesy of Chicago Park District Special Collections (tinted); **311** Courtesy of Chicago Park District Special Collections (tinted); **312** Bob Thall for the Commission on Chicago Landmarks; **313T** Chicago Historic Resources Survey of the Commission on Chicago Landmarks; **313B** Photo © Lawrence Okrent; **314** Photo by Josh Goldman; **315** *Western Architect*, v. 21, Feb. 1915, Courtesy of The Art Institute of Chicago (tinted); **316T** Photo by Alice Sinkevitch; **316B** Photo by Josh Goldman; **317** Photo by Josh Goldman; **318T** Neal A. Vogel, Restoric, LLC; **318B** Photo by David Clifton; **319T** Copyright © Thom Clark; **319B** Photo by Josh Goldman; **320** Neal A.

Vogel, Restoric, LLC; **321** Courtesy The Art Institute of Chicago (tinted); **322** Courtesy of Chicago Park District Special Collections (tinted); **Oak Park: P. 327L** © Suzette Bross; **327R** © Suzette Bross; **328L** Photo by Josh Goldman; **328R** Photo by Josh Goldman; **329** Photo by Josh Goldman; **330T** Leslie Schwartz Photography; **330B** Courtesy of the Historical Society of Oak Park and River Forest (tinted); **332** Marco Lorenzetti, © Hedrich-Blessing; **333T** Photo by Josh Goldman; **333B** Alice Sinkevitch; **334** © Suzette Bross; **335** Alice Sinkevitch; **336** Photo by Josh Goldman; **337** Photo by Alice Sinkevitch; **338** Photo by Josh Goldman; **340T** © Judith Bromley; **340B** © Judith Bromley; **342** Photo by Alice Sinkevitch; **343T** Donald G. Kalec, courtesy of the Frank Lloyd Wright Preservation Trust; **343B** Jon Miller, © Hedrich-Blessing, courtesy of the Frank Lloyd Wright Preservation Trust; **344** Photography by Thomas A. Heinz © 2003, Copyright Thomas A. Heinz; **345** Photo by Josh Goldman; **346** Alice Sinkevitch; **347T** Alice Sinkevitch; **347B** Alice Sinkevitch; **Lower West Side: P. 354** Photo © by Lawrence Okrent; **355** Mark Ballogg, Steinkamp/Ballogg Chicago; **357** Courtesy Chicago Historical Society (tinted); **358** Courtesy Chicago Historical Society (tinted); **359** Photo by Felicity Rich; **360** Steve Hall, © Hedrich-Blessing; **361** Chicago Historic Resources Survey of the Commission on Chicago Landmarks; **362T** Photo by Felicity Rich; **362B** Neal A. Vogel, Restoric, LLC; **364** Lawrence Okrent; **Near South Side: P. 369** Photo by Ron Gordon; **370** Photo by Ron Gordon; **371** © Lawrence Okrent; **373T** Krantzen Studio, Inc.; **374T** © Judith Bromley; **374B** Robert Shimer, © Hedrich-Blessing; **375** Hedrich-Blessing photograph, courtesy Chicago Historical Society (cropped); **376** Courtesy Chicago Architecture Foundation; **377** © Judith Bromley; **378** © Fred Leavitt Photography; **379** Nick Merrick, © Hedrich-Blessing; **380** Photo by Ron Gordon; **381** Kate Roth Photography; **382** © by Lawrence Okrent; **383** Hedrich-Blessing photograph, courtesy Chicago Historical Society (cropped); **384** Bill Engdahl for Hedrich-Blessing; **385** Neal A. Vogel, Restoric, LLC; **386** Courtesy Chicago Historical Society; **388** By permission of University Archives, Paul V. Galvin Library, Illinois Institute of Technology, Chicago; **389** Bill Engdahl, Hedrich-Blessing photograph, courtesy Chicago Historical Society; **390** By permission of University Archives, Paul V. Galvin Library, Illinois Institute of Technology, Chicago; **392** © Judith Bromley; **393** Neal A. Vogel, Restoric, LLC; **394T** Courtesy The Art Institute of Chicago (tinted); **394B** Neal A. Vogel, Restoric, LLC; **396** Bruce Van Inwegen; **397** Photo by Ron Gordon; **Bridgeport/Canaryville/ McKinley Park/Back of the Yards:**

P. 404 Neal A. Vogel, Restoric, LLC; **405** Photo by Lawrence Okrent; **406T** Neal A. Vogel; Restoric, LLC; **406B** Neal A. Vogel, Restoric, LLC; **407** Courtesy of the Chicago Park District Special Collections; **408** Steve Hall, © Hedrich-Blessing; **409** Lawrence Okrent; **410** Chicago Historical Society; **Oakland/Kenwood: P. 416** Hedrich-Blessing photograph, courtesy of Chicago Historical Society (cropped, tinted); **418** Robert Shimer, © Hedrich-Blessing; **420T** © Judith Bromley; **420B** © Judith Bromley; **421** Christopher Barrett, © Hedrich-Blessing; **422T** © Judith Bromley; **422B** Barbara Crane for the Commission on Chicago Landmarks; **423** Ernest Wong; **424** Helena Chapellín Wilson, copyright © 1993; **425T** Photo by Philip Turner, courtesy of Benjamin Weese; **425B** © Judith Bromley; **426** Barbara Crane for the Commission on Chicago Landmarks; **427** Hedrich-Blessing photograph, courtesy Chicago Historical Society (cropped, tinted); **429** Courtesy of Chicago Park District Special Collections; **Hyde Park/South Shore: P. 436** Courtesy of Chicago Park District Special Collections; **437** Courtesy of the Museum of Science and Industry, Chicago; **438** Courtesy of the Museum of Science and Industry, Chicago; **439** Courtesy of Chicago Park District Special Collections; **440** The University of Chicago Archives; **442** © Judith Bromley; **443** Kate Roth Photography; **445T** Kate Roth Photography; **445B** The University of Chicago Archives (tinted); **447L** © Judith Bromley; **447R** Steve Hall, © Hedrich-Blessing; **448** Richard Nickel for the Commission on Chicago Landmarks; **449** © Judith Bromley; **450** © Judith Bromley; **451** Nick Merrick, © Hedrich-Blessing; **453** Hedrich-Blessing photograph, courtesy of Chicago Historical Society (cropped); **454T** © Judith Bromley; **454B** © Judith Bromley; **455** Hedrich-Blessing photograph, courtesy Chicago Historical Society (cropped); **456** Hedrich-Blessing photograph, courtesy Chicago Historical Society (cropped); **457** Kate Roth Photography; **458** © Judith Bromley; **459** © Judith Bromley; **460** © Judith Bromley; **461T** © Hedrich-Blessing photograph; **461B** Photo by David Clifton; **464** Courtesy of Chicago Park District Special Collections; **465** Barbara Karant, Karant + Associates, Inc.; **466T** Dennis M. Ryan; **466B** Helena Chapellín Wilson, copyright © 1993; **467** Courtesy of Helena Chapellín Wilson, copyright © 1993; **470T** William Kildow Photography; **470B** Courtesy of the Commission on Chicago Landmarks; **471T** Courtesy of Helena Chapellín Wilson, copyright © 1993; **471B** Helena Chapellín Wilson, copyright © 1993; **Beverly/Morgan Park:** All photos in this section by Mati Maldre; **Pullman:** All photos in this section by Harold A. Nelson, architect/photographer.

GLOSSARY

Many architectural terms have several meanings. Only those primary to this book or relevant to Chicago's built environment are given here.

A | **abacus** | the slab surmounting columns that supports roof beams; also the topmost element—square or round—of a column capital

acanthus | a common Mediterranean plant whose spike-edged leaf is used for decorative purposes in Classical architecture, especially in Corinthian and Composite capitals

acroterion | a decorative element placed at the corners and peak of a roof in Classical buildings

Adam Style | architecture and interior decoration derived from the work of the British architect Robert Adam (1728–1792); based on Classical motifs, it often included Etruscan, Egyptian, and Gothic elements expressed in a light, linear, precisely detailed, and elegant manner

aedicula | the framing of a door, window, niche, or shrine with a pair of flanking columns supporting a gable

American Foursquare | a popular house type from around 1905 to 1930 that borrowed elements from the Prairie Style and is characterized by a two-story square mass, a full-width front porch, and deep eaves

anthemion | a decorative motif based on the honeysuckle, common in Greek architecture

apse | the extension of the nave, or central body, of a church that traditionally contains the altar

arcade | a line of arches resting on columns or piers, forming an interior aisle or exterior covered walkway

arcuated | supported by arches or arched vaults, as opposed to straight beams

Art Deco | a decorative style whose name derives from the Exposition Internationale des Arts Décoratifs et Industriels Modernes held in Paris in 1925; it is characterized by verticality and by geometric, stylized floral, and Native American motifs, often given a sleek, metallic, machine-made appearance

art glass | a general term for artistically designed panels of transparent or translucent pieces of leaded glass, either clear or colored

Art Moderne | an alternate term for Art Deco that has come to describe its 1930s and 1940s form, which is characterized by horizontality, curves, and streamlined forms that give an impression of speed

Art Nouveau | a decorative style of the 1890s and early 1900s, primarily in Continental Europe; it took its name from a Parisian Gallery for modern decoration, L'Art Nouveau, opened in 1895 to promote design based on natural forms expressed through sinuous lines

Arts & Crafts | A British (later American) movement of the late nineteenth century that sought to improve social conditions through the production of handmade, high-quality objects that respected indigenous traditions rather than increasingly mechanized production

ashlar | squared blocks of stone laid in horizontal rows with vertical joints

atrium | an interior space open to the sky or covered with a skylight

B | **baldachin** | an altar canopy that may be suspended from the ceiling, supported by a wall, or freestanding; frequently a dome resting on four columns

balloon frame | a wood framing system, invented in 1833, that used machine-cut two-by-fours fastened with machine-made nails, allowing for fast and easy assembly; the name was meant derisively, implying that such lightweight structures would blow away in the wind

baluster | the vertical element in a balustrade

balustrade | a decorative railing consisting of a horizontal rail atop vertical supports that are often resting on a bottom rail

bargeboard | decorative wood trim cut into curvilinear shapes and attached to the projecting gable ends of a roof

Baroque | European architecture of the seventeenth and early eighteenth centuries, characterized by effusive ornament, curved forms, and complex spatial effects; the English and French versions are more restrained and employ classical elements

bascule (French for seesaw) | Chicago's most common type of movable bridge, in which counterbalanced leaves pivot around a trunnion, or pin

basilica | a rectangular hall, divided by two rows of columns into a central aisle, or nave, and flanking side aisles; entered through a small room, or narthex, at the short end of the building, it terminates in a rounded end, or apse; also a title bestowed by the Pope on certain Roman Catholic churches of historic, artistic, or spiritual merit whereby special privileges are granted

battered | a wall that recedes as it rises

Bauhaus | a design school founded by Walter Gropius in Weimar, Germany, in 1919 in which artists and architects collaborated in developing an industrial aesthetic of worldwide influence

Beaux Arts | a style of design and planning, based on classical prototypes and often expressed on a monumental scale, named for the École des Beaux-Arts in Paris, at which many American architects, including Louis H. Sullivan, were trained

Bedford limestone | a sedimentary rock formed from shells and shell fragments cemented with calcite, quarried near Bedford, Indiana

Bedford sandstone | a sedimentary rock composed of sandlike quartz grains cemented with silica or other oxides, resulting in a variety of colors; quarried near Bedford, Indiana

belt course | a horizontal band across an exterior wall or around a building; also known as a stringcourse

berm | an earthen mound, either freestanding or adjoining a wall

beveled | cut with angled edges

blind arcade | a decorative row of arches set against a solid wall

board-and-batten | wood siding composed of flat boards laid flush, with the seam covered by a thin board, or batten

bollard | a low, thick post, often used in a series, to prevent vehicles from entering an area; also used on docks and ships for securing ropes and lines

Bower-Barff process | invented in England in the 1870s for creating a rust-resistant, gunmetal, blue-black finish on cast iron

broken pediment | a triangular gable above a door or window in which the center segment is removed

bungalow | a modest brick or stucco house, usually one-and-a-half stories high, derived from the Hindustani word *bangla*, meaning Bengalese; in Chicago it usually has a flat or segmental front and Prairie School details

Byzantine | the domed, round-arched, and colorful architecture of Greece, Turkey, and other countries; after flourishing from the fifth to the fifteenth centuries, it was revived in the nineteenth and twentieth

C| **caisson** | a foundation made by sinking a boxlike form under water or through waterlogged ground to bedrock and then filling it with concrete; also a recessed panel in a ceiling or cupola

campanile | a bell tower, usually freestanding, alongside a church

cantilever | a structural element, such as a beam, balcony, or roof, that projects beyond a supporting wall and is counterbalanced by a downward force behind the wall

capital | the uppermost, usually decorated, part of a column

cartouche | an ornamental enframement, often oval with an elaborately carved frame and central inscription

casement | a window that opens outward on side hinges mounted on the frame

center-pivot swing bridge | a bridge supported on a structural element, or pivot

chamfered | cut at an angle

chancel | that extension of the nave which lies beyond the crossing of the transepts and is the sanctuary of the church

châteauesque | a late nineteenth-century style derived from sixteenth-century French country estates and characterized by hipped and dormered roofs and finely carved ornament with a mixture of Gothic and Renaissance details

Chicago Housing Authority | a municipal not-for-profit corporation created in 1937 to manage federally subsidized or funded housing; commissioners are appointed by the mayor but it receives neither city funding nor tax levies

Chicago School | a movement (1875–1910) in which architects and engineers developed the construction technology and design aesthetic of tall, steel-framed commercial buildings

Chicago window | a three-part design, used in a steel-framed building and comprising a wide fixed pane flanked by narrow, movable sash windows

chords | the straight elements in a truss or across a curve that provide rigidity

Churrigueresque | a heavy, lavish style of late Baroque ornament popular in early eighteenth-century Spain, Mexico, and South America and named after the Churriguera family of Spanish architects

clapboard | horizontal wood siding in which the grain runs lengthwise, planed with one edge thicker than the other, and overlapping with the thicker side at the bottom

clerestory | the highest portion of the walls of a nave, pierced by windows

coffered | ornamented with recessed panels that form a continuous pattern

Colonial Revival | a historical style popular from the 1880s to the 1930s and based on the eighteenth-century American interpretation of contemporaneous, Classically derived British architecture

colonnette | a small thin column, generally used to form a clustered or compound pier

columbarium | a repository for cremated remains, containing vaults lined with recesses

common brick | inexpensive, unglazed brick intended for side and rear walls and usually painted when used on facades

Composite column | one of the five Classical orders, it combines the acanthus-leaf capital of the Corinthian order, the large scrolled volutes of the Ionic capital, and a fluted shaft

console | a decorative scrolled bracket, usually supporting a horizontal element and generally taller than its depth

corbel table | a series of projecting bricks or stones that extend progressively away from the building plane as they rise, and support a stringcourse or eaves

Corinthian column | one of the five Classical orders; the capital consists of two rows of acanthus leaves topped by narrow arched volutes

cornice | a decorative projection, generally along the edge of a roof

cornice return | the extension of a cornice as it wraps around a gable or the sides of a building

courtyard building | a U- or C-shaped building, generally three or four stories in height, constructed around a central landscaped courtyard facing the street

Craftsman | initially, a monthly magazine (1901–1916) published by furniture manufacturer Gustav Stickley in Syracuse, New York, that interpreted the theories of the English Arts & Crafts movement and published writings by Prairie School architects; by extension, a style of design, also known as "Mission"

crenellation | a defensive fortification along a roof consisting of alternating solid elements and voids; also known as a battlement

crockets | in Gothic architecture, small upward-projecting decorative elements, often floral, placed along the edge of gables, spires, and steeples

cupola | a small, often dome-shaped structure capping a roof

curtain wall | the non-load-bearing skin that encloses a building's structural framework

D| **Darlington sandstone** | a sedimentary rock quarried near Darlington, Indiana

dentils | a type of molding consisting of small, rectangular, toothlike blocks

Doric column | one of the five Classical orders, it consists of a plain, narrow, rounded capital and a fluted shaft that does not rest on a base

dormer | a vertically set window or ventilation opening that projects from a sloping roof and possesses its own roof

drop pendant | a knoblike ornamental element extending downward from the ceiling of a vault

Dryvit | a modern stuccolike material used for coating buildings

E| **eaves** | the lower edge of a roof that overhangs a wall

engaged pier | a masonry-supporting element built partially into a wall, rather than freestanding

English basement | a very high basement, almost at street level

entablature | the horizontal assemblage in Classical architecture that is carried by columns and comprises an architrave (lowest section), frieze (middle section), and cornice (upper section)

Euclid stone | a blue-gray sandstone quarried near Euclid, Ohio, and used for foundations, bridgework, and flagstones

exedra | a classical seating form, usually semicircular with a high back, either filling a niche or freestanding when outdoors

F| **face brick** | very dense brick, frequently colored or glazed, that is used as facing

fascia | a flat horizontal band or molding

Favrile | a trademark registered by the Tiffany Glass & Decorating Co. in 1894 for its blown glass, "a composition of various colored glasses, worked together while hot"

Federal Revival | a historical style popular between the 1880s and the 1930s and based on American architecture from around 1790 to 1830

finial | an ornamental termination, usually in a foliate form, atop a gable, spire, or other projection

flanged segmental arch | a curve with ends that extend out from the arch in a straight line parallel to the ground

flatiron building | a building reminiscent of an antique flatiron and shaped by its triangular site

Flemish bond | a bricklaying pattern of alternating headers (short ends) and stretchers (long sides) centered on the brick above and below

fleur-de-lis | a stylized lily originally used as an emblem of royalty and later, in churches, to represent the Holy Trinity

footprint | a building's outline on the ground

four-plus-one | a 1960s architectural phenomenon consisting of four stories of small, cheaply constructed apartments atop a floor of parking

frieze | a decorative band of molding near the top of an interior wall or within an entablature; it may be flat or enriched with figures or patterned ornament

G | **gable** | the triangular upper portion of a building's end; it may have curved, straight, or stepped sides

gambrel roof | a ridged roof with a double pitch

gargoyle | a projecting water spout carved in grotesque human or animal forms

Gibbsian surround | a door or window opening, used by James Gibbs (1682–1754), featuring a triple keystone and large and small quoins on either side

golden section | a proportion thought to have aesthetic value and universal meaning; strictly defined as the ratio (about three to five) between two parts such that the smaller is to the larger as the larger is to the sum of the two

Gothic Revival | a revival of medieval Gothic forms, such as the pointed arch and the spire, that began in the late eighteenth century and, although never dominant, persisted in changing contexts into the twentieth century

graystone | a common Chicago residential building type with a limestone front and Classical details

Greek Revival | constituting, along with the Roman Revival, an influential American architectural style, beginning in the 1820s and persisting for almost a half century; characterized by the symmetrical arrangement of parts, columned entrance or portico, and pronounced cornice

greenstone | also known as serpentine stone, essentially a hydrous silicate of magnesium that assumes various hues depending on the presence of other minerals

grisaille | painting or stained glass executed in shades of gray

H | **Hagia Sophia** | literally "holy wisdom," the epitome of Byzantine architecture, a church built in Istanbul in the fourth century, rebuilt in the sixth, and converted to a mosque in the fifteenth

half-timbering | a wood framing technique of the Middle Ages, revived as a decorative motif in the nineteenth and twentieth centuries, in which the structural members appear on the exterior with an infill of masonry or plaster

header | the short end of a brick

hip roof | a roof with four sloping surfaces, supported by a rafter extending from each corner to a top ridge

hood molding | a projecting molding above a door or window, originally intended to deflect water from the wall

I | **impost block** | a masonry element placed above the capital of a column and supporting the end of an arch

Indiana limestone | a calcite stone, virtually noncrystalline and of uniform character, quarried around Bedford and Bloomington, Indiana; its internal elasticity makes it ideal for carving; gray when freshly cut, it lightens as it dries and ages

inglenook | a semienclosed seating area around a fireplace, usually with a built-in bench

International Style | first used in a 1932 exhibit at the Museum of Modern Art in New York City, the term initially described a common design vocabulary free from regional or historical elements and characterized by cubic masses with white exterior coatings, asymmetrical compositions with cantilevered elements, and large windows, often in bands

Ionic column | one of the five Classical orders, characterized by a fluted shaft and a capital of large scrolled volutes

Italianate | typically an asymmetrical house with a tower; in Chicago usage, the typical tall and narrow house of the 1870s and 1880s usually with incised ornament in the lintels and bracketed cornices

J | **Jacobethan** (Jacobean + Elizabethan) | a revival style combining aspects of late sixteenth- and early seventeenth-century English design, characterized by varied rooflines, multiple chimneys, and clusters of tall rectangular windows with small panes

Joliet limestone | the predominant rock found in northern Illinois, quarried in the vicinity of Joliet and Lemont, is a dolomite stone similar to limestone; buff when quarried, it becomes more yellow or golden with age; formerly termed limestone or marble because of its suitability for carving and polishing, it was also known as Athens marble and Lemont limestone

K | Kasota Stone | a very strong buff or rusty pink limestone quarried near Kasota and Mendota, Minnesota

keystone | the wedge-shaped central stone, or voussoir, that locks an arch in place

L | Lake Superior sandstone | quartz cemented with silica and iron oxides that may be reddish-brown, brown, or mottled with green or gray; quarried in northeastern Minnesota

lamella truss | a truss patented in 1925 and used for large-span vaults in which the members are arranged in a diamond pattern

lancet window | a narrow, sharply peaked window

Lannon stone | limestone quarried near Lannon, Wisconsin, that has an off-white or yellowish hue with occasional darker segments; popular starting in the 1950s

lantern | a superstructure, open to the air, atop a dome or roof and used for light or ventilation

lintel | a horizontal member that traverses an opening in a wall

load-bearing | an architectural element such as a wall or column that supports weight

loggia | an arcade or gallery, roofed and open along one side, located on the front or side of a building

Longmeadow stone | a fine-grained, brick-red sandstone quarried near East Longmeadow, Massachusetts

M | machicolation | a projecting enclosure on a defensive wall or tower, supported on brackets or corbels and containing a hole for discharging missiles

mansard roof | a roof with a double pitch on all four sides, generally with ornamental dormers in the lower section; named after the seventeenth-century Parisian architect François Mansart

mastaba | the aboveground portion of an Egyptian tomb, consisting of a rectangular masonry structure with sloping walls and a flat top

meander | a decorative pattern from Greek architecture consisting of a labyrinth of lines at right angles

mews | a row of buildings, each at the back of a lot; often stables or coach houses

Miesian | pertaining to Ludwig Mies van der Rohe (1886–1969), the German architect who came to Chicago in 1938 and developed the steel-and-glass architecture with which his name is associated

Milwaukee brick | a cream-colored face brick made in Milwaukee

Moorish arch | also known as horseshoe arch, has a diameter greater than the opening that it spans

mosaic | a surface decoration created by small pieces of cemented glass, stone, or tile laid in the form of patterns or representational pictures

motif-rhythm theory | espoused by architect George W. Maher (1864–1926) in which a particular motif serves as the decorative organizing principle of a house

mullion | a vertical member that separates (and often supports) the units of a window, door, or panel and is often used for decoration on a building's surface

N | nave | the central section, or middle aisle, of a church

neo-Classical | the readaptation and reuse of the principles of Greek and Roman architecture, including the concepts of logical construction and truth to materials

neo-Grec | a mid- to late-nineteenth-century French architectural style that emulated Greek structural expressionism in masonry and cast iron

Norman | the late nineteenth-century revival of the English Romanesque architecture of the late eleventh and twelfth centuries, characterized by massive stonework, round arches, and thick columns

O | oculus | a round window or opening

ogee arch | a pointed arch formed by the meeting of two elongated, flattened S-shaped curves

oriel | a projecting bay window supported on brackets or corbels

P | Painted Ladies | wood-frame houses that display the multihued programs of authentic Victorian paint schemes or simply reflect a flair for the colorful

Palladian window | a three-part window named for the sixteenth-century Italian architect Andrea Palladio and comprising a central arched opening flanked by two shorter, narrower rectangular ones

papyriform capital | an Egyptian capital depicting or resembling papyrus flowers

parapet | the part of a wall projecting above a roof; also a low protective wall along any precipitous edge such as a balcony or bridge

parging | a plaster or mortar coating used to smooth or waterproof a brick or stone surface

pediment | the triangular end of a gable roof or a triangular or curved decorative panel over a door or window

pergola | a covered walkway consisting of columns or posts that support a lattice roof for climbing plants and vines

Perma Stone™ | a molded, exterior-cladding product that resembles stone or masonry

Phoenix column | the trade name for a nineteenth-century circular column composed of four or eight vertical segments of iron riveted together

piano nobile | the principal floor of a building, usually elevated above the ground floor and receiving the finest decoration

pier | a supporting element that carries a load

pilaster | a shallow, flattened pier that projects slightly from a wall and serves a decorative, rather than primarily structural, purpose

pilings | heavy beams used for foundations

pilotis | the French word for piling refers to a street-level column or pillar; a favorite form of the International Style

plat | a map of subdivided land, showing streets and lots

po-mo | shorthand for "postmodern," the 1970s and 1980s architectural phenomenon in which historical references were applied to contemporary buildings

porte cochere (coach door) | a door permitting vehicles to enter a building; also the covered section of a driveway that allows people to pass from a vehicle to a doorway protected from weather

portico | a colonnade or roofed entrance porch

poured-in-place | concrete components formed where they are to be used, in contrast to precast or factory-made components

Prairie Style | the Chicago-based movement, primarily in domestic architecture, of the early twentieth century, centering around Frank Lloyd Wright; it rejected historical revival styles in favor of designs reflecting the midwestern environment and the needs of the modern age

Pratt through truss | an American truss with vertical members in compression flanked by diagonal members in tension

purlin | a horizontal timber, placed parallel to the walls and ridge beam atop a peaked roof and supporting the rafters

putti | chubby cherubs with wings

Q| **quarter-sawn oak** | boards cut from timbers that have been sawn lengthwise into quarters and which show a variegated, attractive grain

quoins | decorative or reinforcing stones at the corner of a wall, frequently laid out so that small and large sides, or faces, appear in alternation

R| **rail grillage foundation** | a foundation composed of beams arranged in alternating layers so as to form a grille

raked joint | joints between rows, or courses, of brick in which the mortar is cut back with a narrow tool

rectilinear Queen Anne | eclectic Queen Anne with a proto–Prairie School appearance

reentrant corners | corners that angle inward

refectory | a hall, originally in a religious institution or university, where meals are eaten

reinforced concrete | concrete poured into forms containing steel bars or netting that strengthen the material

relieving arch | an arch built into a wall over a lintel (or another arch) to distribute the weight of the wall above

reredos | a wall or screen of wood or stone, usually tall and highly decorative, that forms the back of an altar

reveal | the side of a window or door opening lying between the frame and the outer surface of the adjacent wall

Richardsonian Romanesque | the Romanesque Revival as influenced by Boston architect Henry Hobson Richardson (1838–1886) and his followers, characterized by heavy rusticated stone walls, round arches, and thick, often squat columns with foliate capitals

Roman brick | high-quality, hard-burned face brick with thin, elongated proportions; popular with Prairie School architects

Romanesque | the architecture of Western Europe from about the tenth to twelfth centuries, derived from Roman and Byzantine architecture and characterized by the round arch and massive walls

Rookwood | the most famous American art pottery (1880–1967) of the Arts & Crafts movement, founded in Cincinnati by Maria Longworth Nichols

rose window | a circular window with tracery radiating in spokes from a central roundel

rotated bay | a corner bay placed at an angle to the adjacent walls

roundel | a small circular panel, window, or plaque

rusticated | masonry with strongly beveled and recessed borders, conspicuous joints, and often a textured finish

S| sash | the framework in which movable windowpanes are set

scagliola | a technique to imitate marble with pigmented plaster mixed with marble dust or chips and other materials

Scherzer rolling lift bridge | a movable bridge invented by Chicago engineer William Scherzer, in which two leaves come together at the center of a river, opening and closing by rolling on rockers of cogs on runners or rails

Second Empire | an eclectic style of the post–Civil War years, based on French architecture of the period of Emperor Napoleon III (1852–1870) and characterized by the mansard roof, dormers, central and end pavilions, and abundant ornamentation in the Classical mode

setback | the stepping-back of a skyscraper from property lines as it rises, the result of 1920s zoning codes that sought to maximize the light and air reaching street level

Sezession | the Austrian and German version of the Art Nouveau movement, named for the secession of its followers in the 1890s from official academies, societies, and exhibitions

sidelight | a fixed glass panel flanking a door or window

soffit | the underside of such architectural elements as an arch, eave, or cornice

spandrel | the roughly triangular area between two arches or above the curve of a single arch; in high-rise buildings, the area between a windowsill and the top of the window below

Spanish Baroque Revival | a popular 1920s style that exploited the plastic qualities of glazed terra-cotta to imitate the exuberantly ornamented architecture of seventeenth- and eighteenth-century Spain

Spanish mission | the architectural style of eighteenth-century Spanish religious settlements in the Southwest

Stick Style | a predominantly residential style of the 1860s to 1890s characterized by exterior wood boards that delineate underlying structural members, asymmetrical massing, and broad porches or verandas

strapwork | ornament composed of interlacing, folded, or ribbonlike bands

stretcher | the long side of a brick

stucco | an exterior coating material composed of portland cement, lime, and sand, generally applied wet and with a textured finish; also a fine grade of interior plaster used for decorative elements

T| teardown | a building purchased in order to be demolished and replaced with a larger one

tempietto | a small ornamental temple in the Classical style

terrazzo | a flooring made from chips of marble or other stones set into a mortar and polished to a smooth finish

terra cotta (cooked earth) | a fired clay material that can be molded or shaped, glazed with colors, or finished to resemble more expensive masonry materials

tourelle | a small, generally narrow turret projecting from the corner of a wall, supported by corbels

transept | in a cross-shaped church, the transverse arms that separate the nave from the chancel

travertine | a cream-colored, porous marble used for flooring and wall facing that became particularly popular with International Style architects in the 1950s through the 1970s

trefoil arch | a three-lobed arch

trompe l'oeil | a realistically detailed painting technique that "fools the eye" and creates the illusion of reality

truss bridge | a bridge composed of metal or wood elements arranged, in part, in triangles so as to support itself

two-flat or three-flat | a widespread residential building type having two or three stacked units and usually faced with brick

tympanum | a triangular or semicircular space, often above a door or window, enclosed by the molding of a pediment or arch

U| urban renewal | government-sponsored programs, authorized under the Federal Housing Act of 1949 and persisting until the early 1970s, of acquiring land in severely deteriorated inner-city communities, relocating residents, demolishing existing structures, and selling the cleared land to private developers or institutions for new construction

V| vision glass | transparent glass

volute | a spiral scroll on a capital or console

voussoir | one of the wedge-shaped or tapering elements making up an arch or vault

W| wainscot | a wood or stone facing applied to the lower portion of an interior wall

Warren truss | patented by the British engineer James Warren in 1848, this truss consists of diagonal members between the top and bottom chord, and was the preferred type for nineteenth-century railroad bridges

water table | a sloping horizontal element between two vertical sections of a wall, designed to deflect water

weeping mortar | excess mortar that by design has oozed out of joints between bricks

WPA murals | the federal Works Progress Administration (1935–1943), as the major New Deal relief agency, employed artists to paint murals in public buildings

Z| **ziggurat** | a pyramidal Mesopotamian temple with three to ten stepped-back levels, each smaller than the one below

FOR FURTHER READING

This list is an introduction to the many publications on Chicago's (and Oak Park's) man-made environment. It includes many of the resources most frequently used by the writers of this book.

Adelman, William. *Touring Pullman.* 2d ed. Chicago: Illinois Labor History Society, 1977.

Bach, Ira J., and Mary Lackritz Gray. *A Guide to Chicago's Public Sculpture.* Chicago: University of Chicago Press, 1983.

Bach, Ira J., Susan Wolfson, and Charles E. Gregersen. *A Guide to Chicago's Train Stations, Present and Past.* Athens: Ohio University Press, 1986.

Bachrach, Julia Sniderman. *The City in a Garden: A Photographic History of Chicago's Parks.* Chicago: University of Chicago Press, 2001.

Berger, Miles L. *They Built Chicago: Entrepreneurs Who Shaped a Great City's Architecture.* Chicago: Bonus Books, 1992.

Blaser, Werner, ed. *Chicago Architecture: Holabird & Root, 1882–1992.* Basel: Birkhausen Verlag, 1992.

Block, Jean F. *Hyde Park Houses: An Informal History, 1856–1910.* Chicago: University of Chicago Press, 1978.

———. *The Uses of Gothic: Planning and Building the Campus of the University of Chicago, 1892–1932.* Chicago: University of Chicago Press, 1983.

Bluestone, Daniel. *Constructing Chicago.* New Haven: Yale University Press, 1991.

Bowly, Devereux, Jr. *The Poorhouse: Subsidized Housing in Chicago, 1895–1976.* Carbondale: Southern Illinois University Press, 1978.

A Breath of Fresh Air: Chicago's Neighborhood Parks of the Progressive Era, 1900–1925. Chicago: Chicago Public Library and Chicago Park District, 1989.

Brooks, H. Allen. *Frank Lloyd Wright and the Prairie School.* New York: George Braziller, 1984.

———. *The Prairie School: Frank Lloyd Wright and His Midwest Contemporaries.* Toronto: University of Toronto Press, 1972.

Bruegmann, Robert. *Holabird & Roche/Holabird & Root: An Illustrated Catalog of Works, 1880–1940.* 3 vols. New York: Garland, 1991.

Burnham Library of Architecture. *The Plan of Chicago, 1909–1979.* Chicago: Art Institute of Chicago, 1979.

Chappell, Sally A. Kitt. *Architecture and Planning of Graham, Anderson, Probst & White, 1912–1936: Transforming Tradition.* Chicago: University of Chicago Press, 1992.

Chicago: An Industrial Guide. Chicago: Public Works Historical Society, 1991.

Chicago and New York: Architectural Interactions. Chicago: Art Institute of Chicago, 1984.

Chicago Architects Design: A Century of Architectural Drawings from the Art Institute of *Chicago.* New York: Rizzoli, 1982.

Chicago Issue. *Abitare* (Milan) no. 256 (July–August 1987).

"Chicago, a Special Issue." *Architectural Review* (London) no. 968 (October 1977).

Chicago Department of Public Works. *Chicago Public Works: A History.* Chicago: City of Chicago, 1973.

Cohen, Stuart E. *Chicago Architects.* Chicago: Swallow Press, 1976.

Condit, Carl W. *Chicago, 1910–1929: Building, Planning, and Urban Technology.* Chicago: University of Chicago Press, 1973.

———. *Chicago, 1930–1970: Building, Planning, and Urban Technology.* Chicago: University of Chicago Press, 1974.

———. *The Chicago School of Architecture: A History of Commercial and Public Building in the Chicago Area, 1875–1925.* Chicago: University of Chicago Press, 1964.

Cudahy, Brian J. *Destination: Loop, the Story of Rapid Transit Railroading in and around Chicago.* Brattleboro, Vt.: The Stephen Greene Press, 1982.

Darling, Sharon S. *Chicago Ceramics and Glass: An Illustrated History from 1871 to 1933.* Chicago: Chicago Historical Society, 1979.

———. *Chicago Furniture: Art, Craft and Industry, 1833–1983.* New York: W. W. Norton, 1984.

———. *Chicago Metalsmiths: An Illustrated History.* Chicago: Chicago Historical Society, 1977.

Duis, Perry R. *Chicago: Creating New Traditions.* Chicago: Chicago Historical Society, 1976.

Frueh, Erne R., and Florence Frueh. *Chicago Stained Glass*. Chicago: Loyola University Press, 1983.

Gilbert, James. *Perfect Cities: Chicago's Utopias of 1893*. Chicago: University of Chicago Press, 1991.

Glibota, Ante, and Frederic Edlemann. *Chicago: 150 Years of Architecture, 1833–1983*. Paris: Paris Art Center, Musée-Galerie de la SEITA, 1983.

Grese, Robert E. *Jens Jensen: Maker of Natural Parks and Gardens*. Baltimore: Johns Hopkins University Press, 1992.

Grube, Oswald W., Peter C. Pran, and Franz Schulze. *100 Years of Architecture in Chicago: Continuity of Structure and Form*. Chicago: J. Philip O'Hara, 1976.

Hirsch, Susan E., and Robert I. Goler. *A City Comes of Age: Chicago in the 1890s*. Chicago: Chicago Historical Society, 1990.

Hoffmann, Donald. *The Architecture of John Wellborn Root*. Baltimore: Johns Hopkins University Press, 1973.

Holt, Glen E., and Dominic A. Pacyga. *Chicago: A Historical Guide to the Neighborhoods: The Loop and South Side*. Chicago: Chicago Historical Society, 1979.

Kunz, Richard. *Overhead and Underground: A Guide to Chicago's Rapid Transit*. Andover, N.J.: Andover Junction Publications, 1991.

Lanctot, Barbara. *A Walk Through Graceland Cemetery*. 3d ed. Chicago: Chicago Architecture Foundation, 1988.

Lane, George A. *Chicago Churches and Synagogues: An Architectural Pilgrimage*. Chicago: Loyola University Press, 1981.

Lowe, David. *Chicago Interiors: Views of a Splendid World*. Chicago: Contemporary Books, 1979.

———. *Lost Chicago* Rev. ed. New York: Watson-Guptill, 2000.

Lyden, Jacki, and Chet Jakus. *Landmarks and Legends of Uptown*. Chicago: n.p., 1980.

Manson, Grant C. *Frank Lloyd Wright to 1910: The First Golden Age*. New York: Reinhold, 1958.

Mayer, Harold M., and Richard C. Wade. *Chicago: Growth of a Metropolis*. Chicago: University of Chicago Press, 1969.

McBrien, Judith Paine. *Skyline: Chicago*. Wilmette: Perspectives Press, 1991–. A series of videotapes accompanied by guidebooks.

Miller, Donald L. *City of the Century: The Epic of Chicago and the Making of America*. New York: Simon and Schuster, 1996.

Miller, Ross. *American Apocalypse: The Great Fire and the Myth of Chicago*. Chicago: University of Chicago Press, 1990.

Moffat, Bruce. *Forty Feet Below: The Story of Chicago's Freight Tunnels*. Glendale, Calif.: Interurban Press, 1982.

Molloy, Mary Alice. *Chicago Since the Sears Tower: A Guide to New Downtown Buildings*. 3d rev. ed. Chicago: Inland Architect Press, 1992.

Morrison, Hugh. *Louis Sullivan, Prophet of Modern Architecture*. New York: Peter Smith, 1952.

Museum of Science and Industry. *A Guide to 150 Years of Chicago Architecture*. Chicago: Chicago Review Press, 1986.

Pacyga, Dominic A., and Ellen Skerrett. *Chicago, City of Neighborhoods: Histories and Tours*. Chicago: Loyola University Press, 1986.

Pacyga, Dominic A., and Charles Shanabruch. *The Chicago Bungalow*. Chicago: Chicago Architecture Foundation, 2001.

Prairie in the City: Naturalism in Chicago's Parks, 1870–1940. Chicago: Chicago Historical Society, Chicago Park District, and Morton Arboretum, 1991.

Rader, James L. *Chicago Sculpture*. Chicago: University of Illinois Press, 1981.

Randall, Frank A. *The History of the Development of Building Construction in Chicago*. Urbana: University of Illinois Press, 1949.

Randall, John D. *The History of the Development of Building Construction in Chicago*. (2d ed., rev. and exp.) Urbana: University of Illinois Press, 1999.

Saliga, Pauline A., ed. *Fragments of Chicago's Past: The Collection of Architectural Fragments of the Art Institute of Chicago*. Chicago: Art Institute of Chicago, 1990.

———. *The Sky's the Limit: A Century of Chicago Skyscrapers*. Reissue with additions. New York: Rizzoli, 1998.

Schulze, Franz. *Mies van der Rohe: A Critical Biography*. Chicago: University of Chicago Press, 1985.

Schulze, Franz, and Kevin Harrington. *Chicago's Famous Buildings*. 4th rev. ed. Chicago: University of Chicago Press, 1993.

Sirefman, Susanna. *Chicago: A Guide to Recent Architecture*. London: Ellipsis Könemann, 1996.

Siry, Joseph. *Carson Pirie Scott: Louis Sullivan and the Chicago Department Store*. Chicago: University of Chicago Press, 1988.

Slaton, Deborah, ed. *Wild Onions: A Brief Guide to Landmarks and Lesser-Known Structures in Chicago's Loop*. Chicago: Association for Preservation Technology International, 1989.

Solzman, David M. *The Chicago River: A Illustrated History and Guide to the River and Its Waterways*. Chicago: Wild Onion Books/Loyola Press, 1998.

Sprague, Paul E. *Guide to Frank Lloyd Wright and Prairie School Architecture in Oak Park*. 4th ed. Oak Park: Village of Oak Park, 1986.

Stamper, John W. *Chicago's North Michigan Avenue: Planning and Development, 1900–1930*. Chicago: University of Chicago Press, 1991.

Takayama, Masami. "The Structural Architecture of Chicago." *Process: Architecture* (Tokyo) no. 102 (April 1992).

University of Chicago. *A Walking Guide to the Campus.* Chicago: University Publications Office, 1991.

Vergara, Camilo José, and Timothy J. Samuelson. *Unexpected Chicagoland.* New York: The New Press, 2002.

Viskochil, Larry A. *Chicago at the Turn of the Century in Photographs.* New York: Dover, 1984.

Wille, Lois. *Forever Open, Clear, and Free: The Struggle for Chicago's Lakefront.* 2d ed. Chicago: Henry Regnery, 1991.

Zukowsky, John, ed. *Chicago Architecture, 1872–1922: Birth of a Metropolis.* Munich: Prestel Verlag, 1987.

———. *Chicago Architecture and Design, 1923–1993: Reconfiguring an American Metropolis.* Munich: Prestel Verlag, 1993.

INDEX

Every building described in the Guide is listed as a primary entry in the index, both by the building's previous and current names. Street names beginning with "North," "South," "East," or "West" are alphabetized under those words; building and street names beginning with numbers are alphabetized as if spelled out. The names of persons, firms, organizations, and government offices involved in creating the works listed in the Guide appear in UPPER AND LOWER CASE SMALL CAPS. *Unless otherwise indicated, they are architects or associated artists. Names of towns, historic districts, and communities within Greater Chicago appear in* **boldface.** *Major divisions and tours appear in* **BOLD UPPER CASE.** *A page reference in* **boldface** *indicates that an illustration of the building, area, or other work appears on that page.*

The following abbreviations appear in the index:

adapt.	adaptation	H.S.	High School
add.	addition	Hosp.	Hospital
alt.	alteration	Intl.	International
Assn.	Association	M.S.	Middle School
Assocs.	Associates	Natl.	National
Apts.	Apartments	Pkwy.	Parkway
Ave.	Avenue	Pl.	Place
Bldg.	Building	P.S.	Public School
Blvd.	Boulevard	R.C.	Roman Catholic
Bros.	Brothers	Rd.	Road
Cem.	Cemetery	rebldg.	rebuilding
Co.	Company	recon.	reconstruction
Condos.	Condominiums	rehab.	rehabilitation
conv.	conversion	rem.	remodeling
Corp.	Corporation	renov.	renovation
Ct.	Court	res.	restoration
Dept.	Department	RR	Railroad
Dr.	Drive	St.	Street
Expy.	Expressway	Univ.	University

SAMUELS, SAUL
 Bunte Bros. Candy Co. (rehab.), 308, **308**
 Tilton (George W.) P.S. (add.), 313, **313**
 Westinghouse (George) Vocational H.S. (rehab.), 308, **308**
Sandburg, Carl, 232, 233
Sandburg (Carl) House, 233
Sandburg (Carl) Village, 164–65, 176, **176**, 177
SANDEGREN, ANDREW
 E. Schiller St., No. 10, 173
 N. Lincoln Park West, No. 2350, 197
 N. State Pkwy., No. 1411, 173
 S. Hyde Park Blvd., Nos. 5312–5318, 461
 Washington Park Ct., 415
San Miniato al Monte (Florence), 132
Santa Fe Center, 42, **42**
Santa Fe RR, 371
SARGENT & LUNDY
 Illinois Institute of Technology, Boiler Plant & Steam Generating Plant (add.), 388
SASAKI ASSOCS.
 Univ. of Illinois at Chicago, Flames Athletic Center, 301
SAS ARCHITECTS
 Columbia College—1104 Center (res. & adapt.), 151, **151**
 Columbia College Dance Center (adapt.), 150, **150**
 Columbia College Music Center (rem.), 149
 Ludington Bldg. (res. & adapt.), 151, **151**
 Paramount Pictures Film Exchange (adapt.), 150, **150**
Saucedo (Maria) Magnet School, 358
SAUER, DAVID A.
 Lake Parc Place (renov.), 418
 Olander (Victor A.) Homes & Olander Homes Extension (renov.), 418
Saunders, William, 223, 252
SAVAGE, EUGENE
 Elks Natl. Memorial Bldg., 202, **202**
Savings of America Tower, **81**–82
Sawyer, Eugene, 19
Sawyer (Frederick C.) House, 481
SBC
 Lakeview Office, 222
 McKinley Office, 410
 Monroe Office, 288
Scales (John C.) House, 229
Schaaf, Adam
 personal gravesite, Rosehill Cem., 254
SCHAFFNER, DANIEL J.
 Shore Manor/Eleanor Manor, 465
Scherzer, William, 372
SCHERZER ROLLING LIFT BRIDGE CO.
 Cermak Road Bridge, 372
 "Eight Track" RR Bridge, 411
Schiller Bldg., 9, 20, 135
Schiller St. Town Houses, 177
Schiller Theatre, 180
Schindler, Rudolf, 84
Schinkel, Karl Friedrich, 173
SCHIPPOREIT, GEORGE
 Asbury Plaza, 134

IBM Self Park, 127
SCHIPPOREIT-HEINRICH
 Lake Point Tower, 17, 121, **121**
SCHLACKS, HENRY J.
 Angel Guardian Croatian Catholic Church, 251
 Holy Name Cathedral (add.), 132–33
 St. Adalbert R.C. Church, 356
 St. Henry's R.C. Church, 251
 St. Ignatius R.C. Church, 246
 St. Ita's Church, 241
 St. John of God R.C. Church, 407
 St. Mary of the Lake R.C. Church, 229–**30**
 St. Paul R.C. Church, **357**–58
 St. Paulus Kirche, 357
Schlecht (Catherine) House, **317**–18
Schlesinger & Mayer Dept. Store, 7, 49, 56–**58**, 62
Schlitz (Joseph) Brewing Co., 218
Schmid, Richard G.
 personal gravesite, Graceland Cem., 227
Schmidt, Ernst & Therese
 personal gravesites, Graceland Cem., 224
SCHMIDT, RICHARD E.
 Graham Foundation for Advanced Studies in the Fine Arts, 173, **173**
 gravesite for Ernst & Therese Schmidt, Graceland Cem., 224
 Grommes & Ullrich Warehouse, 138, **138**
 Hulbert (William A.) gravesite, Graceland Cem., 224
 Madlener (Albert F.) House, 173, **173**, 420
 Montgomery Ward & Co. "Tower Bldg.," 39
 Montgomery Ward Warehouse & Offices, 142
 Powerhouse-Waterhouse, Peter Schoenhofen Brewing Co., **369**–70, 372
 Theurer (Joseph)/Philip K. Wrigley House, 201
 W. Illinois St., Nos. 108–114, 138, **138**
 Wolff (Louis) House, 229
SCHMIDT, RICHARD E., GARDEN & ERIKSON
 Chicago Federal Center, **64**–65, 74
 Illinois Institute of Technology, ITT Tower, 388
 La Casita Court Apts., 130
 Univ. of Chicago, Cummings Life Science Center, 452
SCHMIDT, RICHARD E., GARDEN & MARTIN
 Annex Bldg., 39
 Bunte Bros. Candy Co., 308, **308**
 Chandler Apts., 166
 Conservatory, Garfield Park, **309**–10
 Cosmopolitan Bank & Trust, 137
 Cosmopolitan State Bank, 137
 Dvorak Park, 355
 Entrance Lanterns, Columbus Park, 320, **320**
 Garfield Park, 309
 Humboldt Park, 266
 Illinois Women's Athletic Club, 111

Vietnam Survivors Memorial, 292
VIGEANT, GREGORY
  Notre Dame de Chicago Church, 296
VIGUIER, JEAN-PAUL
  Sofitel Chicago Water Tower, 130, **131**
Villa District, The, 270–71
VINCI, JOHN, 375
  Nickel (Richard) monument, Graceland
    Cem., 224
VINCI, JOHN, OFFICE OF
  Art Institute of Chicago lobby (res.), 41
  Carson Pirie Scott & Co. (res.), 56–**58**
  Chicago Street Railway Co. Station
    (renov.), 454
  Holy Family Church (res.), 296–97
  Hyde Park Historical Society (renov.),
    454
  Kehilath Anshe Ma'ariv Synagogue
    (res.), 391–**92**
  N. Howe St., No. 1900, 184
  Pilgrim Baptist Church (res.), 391–**92**
  Scoville Block (2) (res.), 331
  Scoville Square (res.), 331
  Univ. of Chicago, Mandel (Leon) As-
    sembly Hall (renov.), 444, 445–46
  Yondorf Block and Hall (renov.), 185,
    185
VINCI/HAMP
  Arts Club, The, 119–20
  S. Greenwood Ave., No. 4835, 421
  Tribune Tower (renov.), 103–**4**
Viollet-le-Duc, Eugène-Emmanuel, 260
Vista Accumulator Co., 381–82
VITZTHUM, KARL M.
  Cabrini (Frances) Homes, 141
  N. Lincoln Park West, No. 2344, 197
  St. Martin de Porres R.C. Church,
    313–14
  St. Thomas Aquinas Church, 313–14
VITZTHUM & BURNS
  Bell Bldg., 30
  N. La Salle St., No. 1, 81
  Old Republic Bldg., 30
  Painters District Council 14, 288–89
  Steuben Club Bldg., 84
  W. Randolph St., No. 188, 84
Vladimir of Kiev, 260
VMC ARCHITECTS
  DePaul Student Center, 193
VOA ASSOCS.
  Chicago Public Library—George W.
    Walker Branch (renov. & add.), 476
  Navy Pier (Municipal Pier No. 2)
    (recon.), 120–21
  Northwestern Memorial Hosp., Fein-
    berg & Galter Pavilions, 118
  S. La Salle St., No. 120 (res.), 80
  Shakespeare Theater, 120–21
  State Bank of Chicago Bldg. (res.), 80
VOLK, LEONARD W., 206
  Civil War Soldiers Memorial (*Our He-
    roes*), Rosehill Cem., 253
  Douglas (Stephen A.) Tomb & Memor-
    ial, 385
  family plot, Rosehill Cem., 254
VON HOLST, HERMANN V.
  Commonwealth Edison E. 16th St.
    Substation, 373–74
  Commonwealth Edison Electric Power
    Substation, 230

Metra (Metropolitan Rail) Substation,
    373–74
VON WEISE ASSOCS.
  N. Wacker Dr., No. 150 (renov.), 90
VOY MADEYSKI ARCHITECTS
  Aon Center (renov.), 32, 56, 111
  Standard Oil Bldg. (renov.), 32, 56, 111
Voysey, C. F. A., 229
Vue 20, 376–77

W| Wabash Ave. YMCA, 396, **396**
Wabash/Randolph Center Self Park, 51
Wacker, Charles H., 13, 14
Wacker, Frederick, 183
Wacker (Charles H.) House, 183
Wacker (Frederick) House, 183
Wacker's Manual of the Plan of Chicago,
    13
Wacker Tower, 51
WADDELL, J. A. L. (engineer)
  Amtrak Bridge, **370**–71
  Chicago Transit Authority—Armitage
    Ave. Station, 191
  Pennsylvania RR—South Branch
    Chicago River Bridge, **370**–71
WADSKIER, THEODORE V.
  Luff (William M.) House, **338**–39
  Scottish Rite Cathedral, 136
  Unity Church, 136
WAESCHER, FREDERICK
  Blatchford (E. W.) & Co. Bldgs., 95–96
  Clinton St. Lofts, 95–96
  Grant's Seminary for Young Ladies,
    134–**35**
  Newberry House, 134–**35**
WAGNER, JOHN H.
  North Branch Center (add.), 139
Wagner, Otto, 84, 86
Waid (Dan Everett) House, 481
WALCOTT, CHESTER H.
  St. Chrysostom's Episcopal Church
    (add. & rem.), 174
  Walker (George C.) Museum, Univ. of
    Chicago, 443
WALLACE, DWIGHT G.
  DePaul Univ., Commons Bldg., 194
  DePaul Univ., Gymnasium, 194
  DePaul Univ., Lincoln Park Campus
    (East Portion), 194
Wallace Computer Services—Factory, 140
Wallach (David) Fountain, 463
WALLBAUM, AUGUST
  St. Michael's R.C. Church (rebuilt), 185
Waller (Edward C.) Apts., 307
Waller (William) House, 132
Walser (Joseph J.) House, 319
Walt Disney Magnet School, 228
Walter Burley Griffin Pl., 477–78
Walter Dyett M.S., 428
Walter Payton College Preparatory H.S.,
    139
Ward, Aaron Montgomery, 14, 34–36,
    378
Ward Bldg., 38–39
Warehouse & Offices, 141
Warming House, Lincoln Park, 210
WARNER, BREJCHA, EVANS & ASSOCS.
  Casa Bonita Apts. (renov.), 249, **250**
Warner Bros. Film Exchange, 150
Warner (Augustus) House, 175